PSALMS

Larry Thompson

Also by James Montgomery Boice

Witness and Revelation in the Gospel of John
Philippians: An Expositional Commentary
The Minor Prophets: An Expositional Commentary (2 volumes)
How to Live the Christian Life (originally, *How to Really Live It Up*)
Ordinary Men Called by God (originally, *How God Can Use Nobodies*)
The Last and Future World
The Gospel of John: An Expositional Commentary (5 volumes)
The Epistles of John: An Expositional Commentary
"Galatians," in the *Expositor's Bible Commentary*
Can You Run Away from God?
Our Sovereign God, editor
Our Savior God: Studies on Man, Christ and the Atonement, editor
Does Inerrancy Matter?
The Foundation of Biblical Authority, editor
Making God's Word Plain, editor
The Sermon on the Mount
Genesis: An Expositional Commentary (3 volumes)
The Parables of Jesus
The Christ of Christmas
The Gospel of Matthew: An Expositional Commentary (2 volumes)
Standing on the Rock
The Christ of the Empty Tomb
Foundations of the Christian Faith (4 volumes in one)
Christ's Call to Discipleship
Transforming Our World: A Call to Action, editor
Ephesians: An Expositional Commentary
Daniel: An Expositional Commentary
Joshua: An Expositional Commentary
Nehemiah: An Expositional Commentary
The King Has Come
Romans: An Expositional Commentary (4 volumes)
Mind Renewal in a Mindless Age
The Glory of God's Grace (originally, *Amazing Grace*)
Psalms: An Expositional Commentary (3 volumes)
Sure I Believe, So What?
Hearing God When You Hurt
Foundations of God's City (originally, *Two Cities, Two Loves: Christian Responsibility
    in a Crumbling Culture*)
Here We Stand!: A Call from Confessing Evangelicals, editor
    with Benjamin E. Sasse
Living by the Book: The Joy of Loving and Trusting God's Word
Acts: An Expositional Commentary
The Heart of the Cross, with Philip G. Ryken
What Makes a Church Evangelical?
The Doctrines of Grace, with Philip G. Ryken

PSALMS

Volume 3
Psalms 107–150

JAMES
MONTGOMERY
BOICE

BakerBooks

Grand Rapids, Michigan

1998

© 1998 by James Montgomery Boice

Published by Baker Books
a division of Baker Publishing Group
P.O. Box 6287, Grand Rapids, MI 49516-6287
www.bakerbooks.com

Paperback edition published 2005
ISBN 0-8010-6586-0

Printed in the United States of America

The Library of Congress has cataloged the hardcover edition as follows:
  Boice, James Montgomery, 1938–
      Psalms : an expositional commentary / James Montgomery Boice.
              p.   cm.
      Includes bibliographical references and indexes.
      Contents: v. 1. Psalms 1–41. v. 2. Psalms 42–106. v. 3. Psalms 107–150
      ISBN 0-8010-1077-2 (v. 1)
      ISBN 0-8010-1118-3 (v. 2)
      ISBN 0-8010-1164-7 (v. 3)
      1. Bible. O.T. Psalms—Commentaries. 2. Bible. O.T. Psalms—Homiletical
  use. I. Title.
  BS1430.3.B64   1994
  223′.2077—dc20   93-36246

To
Jesus Christ,
a priest forever
in the order of Melchizedek

Contents

Preface

How time flies! I have often heard this adage and believed it too, but it seems to be increasingly true as one grows older. It seems only yesterday that I began the writing of *Psalms* that comes to completion with the appearance of this volume, yet I find on checking my records that I began this work in the winter of 1989. Since I finished preaching my last sermon on the psalms in the summer of 1997, I realize that my study and writing on these great hymns of the Jewish and Christian church have occupied my time for the better part of eight and a half years.

What a time it has been! How worthwhile! I have been blessed in the work myself, discovering truths that I had not even begun to appreciate previously. I have also discovered that these studies have blessed many other people as they were preached first to the congregation of Tenth Presbyterian Church in Philadelphia, which I have served as senior minister for thirty years, and later to people across the country as they were aired over the weekend edition of the *Bible Study Hour,* one of the radio programs now sponsored by the Alliance of Confessing Evangelicals. I am sure these sermons have been helpful because the psalms themselves speak so powerfully to the hurts, fears, disappointments, faith, hope, and spiritual aspirations of God's people.

This third volume of *Psalms* contains expositions of the fifth and final book of the Psalter (Psalms 107–50). Volume 1 contained my studies of book one (Psalms 1–41), and volume 2 contained my studies of books two, three, and four (Psalms 42–106).

Two parts of this last section of the Psalter have been particularly important in the development of my own life and thinking, the first being Psalm 119, the massive psalm about the Bible. Psalm 119 is the longest chapter in the Bible, containing 176 verses, and nearly every verse, with few exceptions, mentions Scripture by one word or another. The psalmist refers to the Bible as God's law, statutes, ways, precepts, promises, decrees, commands, and words. He reflects on its importance to him in all circumstances and all moments of his life: The Bible was important in his youth, keeping him on track through life's many trials and disappointments. It was his textbook in God's school of discipleship. It gave great comfort, bore him up in times of affliction, taught him how to obey God, pray well, and walk by faith. Above all, it taught him to love the author of the Book.

All of us need all of these blessings also. In fact, so important are these fundamental lessons of how to live the Christian life through the study of the Bible that Baker Book House, which publishes most of my writing these days, offered the fourteen studies of Psalm 119 (from this book) in a special paperback volume entitled *Living by the Book: The Joy of Loving and Trusting God's Word. Living by the Book* appeared a year in advance of this volume, in 1997.

The second portion of this last book of the Psalter that has meant a great deal to me is the collection that follows the Songs of Ascents and closes the Psalter, Psalms 135–50. This section includes the final psalms of David (Psalms 138–45). What is particularly striking about these last psalms is that in one way or another they all deal with worship. All the psalms are intended for worship and have been used in worship throughout the ages, but these final psalms in particular teach us what true worship is, who should worship, and when and how we should praise God. I can think of few points of Bible teaching that are of greater importance for today's church, when worship of God in so many of our churches is at a low ebb.

As in all my books, I want to thank the session and congregation of Tenth Presbyterian Church for allowing me to spend so much of my time in Bible study and the writing of expository sermons. I also want to thank the staff of Tenth Church, particularly the ministerial staff, who attend to many of the demands of a thriving church that I do not have time for personally. These friends free me up for much of my writing and speaking. I owe special thanks to Miss Joan Borgard, my executive assistant, who handled my schedule and carried out much of my work, until her death last year. She is greatly missed.

May these studies be a source of spiritual nurture, grace, comfort, and instruction as you read them, and may he who gave them to us for those ends bless you in your own study of the Bible. The last verse of the Psalter says, "Let everything that has breath praise the LORD. Praise the LORD" (Ps. 150:6). It is what I have done as I have come to the end of these studies. May it be true of all who know the Lord Jesus Christ as Savior.

Soli Deo gloria! May God alone be glorified.

Book Five of the Psalter

Psalm 107

The Pilgrims' Psalm: Part 1

Through Many Dangers, Toils, and Snares

Give thanks to the Lord, for he is good;
his love endures forever.
Let the redeemed of the Lord say this—
those he redeemed from the hand of the foe,
those he gathered from the lands,
from east and west, from north and south.

Some wandered in desert wastelands,
finding no way to a city where they could settle. . . .

Some sat in darkness and the deepest gloom,
prisoners suffering in iron chains. . . .

Some became fools through their rebellious ways
and suffered affliction because of their iniquities. . . .

Others went out on the sea in ships;
they were merchants on the mighty waters. . . .
verses 1–23

 It may seem strange to anyone who knows anything about the English Puritans to speak of Psalm 107 as "The Pilgrims'

Psalm," not because they did not know, frequently read, and greatly cherish it, but because being people of the Book they loved and cherished the other psalms too. In fact, they cherished the entire Bible.

But that is not the whole story. As anyone who knows anything about the Pilgrims is aware, Psalm 107, more than any other portion of the Bible, aptly describes the many dangers, toils, and snares they experienced prior to, during, and after their courageous crossing of the Atlantic Ocean to found America's Plymouth Colony. Did they recognize this description themselves? There is reason to think they did, since Governor William Bradford in his account of the founding of the Plymouth Plantation explicitly referred to Psalm 107 in his well-known summation of their achievement:

> May not and ought not the children of these fathers rightly say: "Our fathers were Englishmen which came over this great ocean, and were ready to perish in this wilderness; but they cried unto the Lord, and he heard their voice and looked on their adversity," . . . "Let them therefore praise the Lord, because he is good: and his mercies endure forever." "Yes, let them which have been redeemed of the Lord, shew how he hath delivered them from the hand of the oppressor. When they wandered in the desert wilderness out of the way, and found no city to dwell in, both hungry and thirsty, their soul was overwhelmed in them. Let them confess before the Lord his loving kindness and his wonderful works before the sons of men."[1]

Those words are based on Psalm 107, which suggests that the psalm was often in the Pilgrims' minds. Since the Pilgrims came ashore on Monday, December 11, 1620, after having spent the prior day worshiping God, it is even likely that Psalm 107 was the basis for that Sabbath's meditation.

In its own setting Psalm 107 is a praise song of the regathered people of Israel after their Babylonian bondage. Thus Psalms 105, 106, and 107 form a trilogy. Psalm 105 recounts Israel's experience from the time of God's covenant with Abraham to the people's entrance into the promised land; Psalm 106 tracks their unfaithfulness during that same time period and reflects the years of their exile to Babylon; and Psalm 107 thanks God for their deliverance from that exile. Still, the psalm was aptly used by the Pilgrims and may be loved by us as well, since the examples it gives of the perils from which the people of God are delivered are at once common, varied, and suggestive. We can see ourselves in each of these situations.

The psalm has three parts: an opening (vv. 1–3), the main body (vv. 4–32), and a closing grateful reflection on God's sovereignty in human affairs (vv. 33–43, the subject of our next chapter).

A Call to Praise God

Charles Spurgeon wrote that the theme of the psalm is "thanksgiving and the motives for it."[2] Thanksgiving is the note struck in the opening verses as well as in the refrain of verses 8–9, 15–16, 21–22, and 31–32. The opening says,

> Give thanks to the LORD, for he is good;
>> his love endures forever.
> Let the redeemed of the LORD say this—
>> those he redeemed from the hand of the foe,
> those he gathered from the lands,
>> from east and west, from north and south.

This call should cause us to ask a probing, personal question, namely, Am I among the redeemed? meaning, Am I one who has been delivered from sin and so been gathered from my aimless secular wanderings to be a part of God's well-loved, well-grounded, and well-established covenant people? If you have been redeemed from your sin by the death of Jesus Christ, you should thank God for your deliverance and tell others that God is indeed "good" and that "his love endures forever," as the psalm says. This is its first lesson. According to the first chapter of Romans, it is a mark of the unregenerate that "they neither [glorify God] as God nor [give] thanks to him" (v. 21).

Pictures of Peril

The main body of Psalm 107 is comprised of verses 4–32, which fall into four clearly marked sections. Each is a poetic picture of some deadly peril common to mankind but from which God regularly delivers his people. These pictures may be images of the Babylonian captivity or possibly even literal descriptions of the conditions from which the Jews of that time were rescued, but they also picture our own spiritual condition apart from Jesus Christ. In each of these sections, after describing our peril and God's deliverance, the psalmist reminds us how much we should be thankful.

1. *Homes for the homeless.* Homelessness or perhaps just being lost in the wilderness is the first picture of peril (vv. 4–9). It is described in touching tones:

> Some wandered in desert wastelands,
>> finding no way to a city where they could settle.
> They were hungry and thirsty,
>> and their lives ebbed away.
> Then they cried out to the LORD in their trouble,
>> and he delivered them from their distress (vv. 4–6).

It is easy to understand why these words would have appealed to our Pilgrim fathers as describing their experiences. These poor people had been driven from their homes and were virtually hounded from place to place, at one time escaping England for Holland, until at last they set sail for the

American continent. According to William Bradford, they "were hunted and persecuted on every side. . . . Some were taken and clapped up in prison, others had their houses beset and watched night and day, and hardly escaped their [enemies'] hands; and the most were fain [constrained] to flee and leave their houses and habitations, and the means of their livelihood."[3]

These were the problems they faced in the early 1600s. So when they finally came to America and were settled in their own homes from 1620 on, however rustic these rude shelters may have been, the Pilgrims felt enormous gratitude to God. As the psalmist says,

> Then they cried out to the LORD in their trouble,
>   and he delivered them from their distress.
> He led them by a straight way
>   to a city where they could settle (vv. 6–7).

In our congregation at Tenth Presbyterian Church we have many people who have been homeless but who have cried out to the Lord and been given homes to live in. They are thankful for their homes. Even if you have never been homeless and have always had a home, should you not be even more grateful than those who have only been given homes recently? One of the greatest blessings of my life was the Christian home in which I was raised, where I was taught that Jesus is my Savior from sin, learned my first Bible verses, and was trained in such sound habits of Christian piety as prayer, regular church attendance, and joyful fellowship with God's people. If you had a good home or have one now, then do what the psalm says:

> Give thanks to the LORD for his unfailing love
>   and his wonderful deeds for men,
> for he satisfies the thirsty
>   and fills the hungry with good things (vv. 8–9).

I have looked at this image as part of the Pilgrim's experience and as our having literal homes today, but we are all homeless without God, who is our only true home. Apart from God we are like the prodigal son, who left his father's home to squander his substance in a far country. Salvation began when he came to his senses, confessed his sin, and returned to his father. Have you returned to God, crying, "Father, I have sinned against you!"?

2. *Freedom for captives.* The second image of this central section of the psalm (vv. 10–16) describes the distress of prisoners. The Pilgrims' leaders were often put in prison for dissenting from the established religion of the time, and when small groups tried to escape the persecution by sailing across the English Channel to Holland or elsewhere, they were frequently arrested on that account too.

Bradford tells of several such incidents. In one, the men were separated from their wives and children. "Pitiful it was to see the heavy case of these poor women in this distress; what weeping and crying on every side, some for their husbands that were carried away, . . . others not knowing what should become of them and their little ones; others again melting in tears, seeing their poor little ones hanging about them, crying for fear and quaking with cold. Being thus apprehended, they were hurried from one place to another and from one justice to another, till in the end they knew not what to do with them."[4] Bradford recounts how eventually they all nevertheless did manage to get to Holland, where they thanked God.

There are not many among us who can speak of being delivered from prison literally—though there are some—but all who are Christians can speak of being delivered from the prison house of sin. This prison is what Jesus seems to have had in mind in the synagogue at Nazareth when he spoke of having come "to proclaim freedom for the prisoners" (Luke 4:18; cf. Isa. 61:1–2). Jesus did not free anyone from a literal prison, as far as we know, but he has freed everyone who has ever believed on him from sin's shackles. We have been slaves to sin, but by his atoning death we have been forever liberated.

Each of us can say that we have "rebelled against the words of God and despised the counsel of the Most High," as the psalmist does in verse 11, and that God "brought [us] out of the darkness and the deepest gloom and broke away [our] chains," as he does in verse 14. Shouldn't we thank God for that deliverance? The refrain says (with appropriate variation from verses 8–9),

> Let them give thanks to the LORD for his unfailing love
> and his wonderful deeds for men,
> for he breaks down gates of bronze
> and cuts through bars of iron (vv. 15–16).

John Bunyan, the author of *Pilgrim's Progress* and a Puritan, saw verse 16 as a description of Christ's breaking through the bronze gates and iron bars of Bunyan's tightly closed-up heart to save him. He resisted Jesus, but Jesus proved all-powerful.[5] Has Jesus shown himself to be all-powerful for you? Shouldn't you be thankful he is?

3. *Healing for the sick.* The third image (vv. 17–22) pictures people who "suffered affliction because of their iniquities" (v. 17). It describes illness so severe that it brought those afflicted "near the gates of death" (v. 18). This section describes the Pilgrim experience too. Four of the original small band of 102 passengers died before they even reached America, one just before the ship landed. Most terrible of all, half of the remainder died in that first cruel winter, which Bradford called "the starving time." Only twelve of the original twenty-six heads of families and four of the original twelve unattached men or boys survived, and all but a few of the women perished.[6] As for the rest, there was much sickness.

You may have experienced God's deliverance from a serious illness, just as the psalmist describes and the Pilgrims experienced. The psalm is also depicting deliverance from spiritual sickness, since it refers to "affliction" caused by "their iniquities" and God's "word" as the agent of our healing (v. 20).

God's Word is the only thing that heals our spiritual sicknesses, for it is the only thing that has life. As the Bible pictures it, our condition apart from Christ is far worse than merely being sick. We are actually dead, so far as any ability to respond or come to God is concerned: "dead in [our] transgressions and sins" (Eph. 2:1). When God speaks his Word from the mouth of the preacher to our hearts, we experience a spiritual resurrection, just as Lazarus did when Jesus called him from the tomb (John 11:43–44). Using another image, Peter spoke of our being born again "not of perishable seed, but of imperishable, through the living and enduring word of God" (1 Peter 1:23).

If you are a Christian, God has saved you "from the grave" (v. 20) by that same life-giving Word. The psalm says you should be thankful for that salvation.

> Let them give thanks to the LORD for his unfailing love
> and his wonderful deeds for men.
> Let them sacrifice thank offerings
> and tell of his works with songs of joy (vv. 21–22).

4. *Safety for those at sea.* In the opinion of many commentators the most beautiful, most poetic, and certainly the most stirring section of Psalm 107 is the part that describes the peril of God's people while at sea (vv. 23–32). Although it was not, it might have been written as a description of that difficult sixty-five-day, late-fall crossing of the turbulent North Atlantic by the Pilgrim fathers and their families.

> Others went out on the sea in ships;
> they were merchants on the mighty waters.
> They saw the works of the LORD,
> his wonderful deeds in the deep.
> For he spoke and stirred up a tempest
> that lifted high the waves.
> They mounted up to the heavens and went down to the depths;
> in their peril their courage melted away.
> They reeled and staggered like drunken men;
> they were at their wits' end.
> Then they cried out to the LORD in their trouble,
> and he brought them out of their distress.
> He stilled the storm to a whisper;
> the waves of the sea were hushed.
> They were glad when it grew calm,
> and he guided them to their desired haven (vv. 23–30).

A person needs to have been on the ocean in a violent storm to appreciate how accurate those frightening words are.

Forget the ocean. Perhaps you have been in a situation of an entirely different nature but in which you have also been at your wits' end and cried to the Lord and were delivered. Perhaps you were facing a serious financial problem, a personality conflict at work, or a battle within your family. If you were delivered, listen to what the psalm says.

> Let them give thanks to the LORD for his unfailing love
>   and his wonderful deeds for men.
> Let them exalt him in the assembly of the people
>   and praise him in the council of the elders (vv. 31–32).

There is nothing so becoming the children of God as public acknowledgment of his unmerited favors and unfathomable goodness to them.

Thanks, Exaltation, and True Praise

In the next chapter we are going to look at this psalm's last section, in which the psalmist makes observations about God's acts. Before we do so, let us consider the refrain ending each of the preceding sections as they deal with God's rescue of the homeless, his deliverance of the prisoners, his healing of the sick, and his preservation of those who go to sea.

The refrain occurs four times. In each of these occurrences the first two lines are the same—"let them give thanks to the LORD for his unfailing love and his wonderful deeds for men"—but the next two lines vary. In the first two cases there are reasons for giving thanks to God: because God "satisfies the thirsty and fills the hungry with good things" (v. 9), and because "he breaks down gates of bronze and cuts through bars of iron" (v. 16)—that is, because of God's salvation. The last two cases suggest ways we can give God thanks: by offering him "thank offerings" (v. 22), and by exalting "him in the assembly of the people and prais[ing] him in the council of the elders" (v. 32).

How can we sacrifice thank offerings to God today? The only possible answer is by offering God ourselves. The apostle Paul wrote, "Therefore, I urge you, brothers, in view of God's mercy, to offer your bodies as living sacrifices, holy and pleasing to God—this is your spiritual act of worship" (Rom. 12:1). Nothing less than the offer of our complete selves is adequate. Nothing else is demanded. Having done that, we must then also speak about God's mercies to other people, as the psalm commands.

Psalm 107

The Pilgrims' Psalm: Part 2

Grace Has Led Us Home

He turned the rivers into a desert,
   flowing springs into thirsty ground,
and fruitful land into a salt waste,
   because of the wickedness of those who lived there.
He turned the desert into pools of water
   and the parched ground into flowing springs;
there he brought the hungry to live,
   and they founded a city where they could settle.
They sowed fields and planted vineyards
   that yielded a fruitful harvest;
he blessed them, and their numbers greatly increased,
   and he did not let their herds diminish.

Then their numbers decreased, and they were humbled
   by oppression, calamity and sorrow;
he who pours contempt on nobles
   made them wander in a trackless waste.

But he lifted the needy out of their affliction
and increased their families like flocks.
The upright see and rejoice,
but all the wicked shut their mouths.

Whoever is wise, let him heed these things
and consider the great love of the LORD.
verses 33–43

John Newton was a Puritan. He was also a pilgrim in one sense, though he lived a hundred years after the Pilgrims we have been talking about (in the previous chapter). In the third stanza of his best-known hymn, "Amazing Grace," he has given a summary of the Pilgrims' experience as well as an outline of the Pilgrims' psalm.

Through many dangers, toils, and snares,
    I have already come;
'tis grace has brought me safe thus far,
    and grace will lead me home.

In the first two parts of Psalm 107, the introduction (vv. 1–3) and the overview of the diverse deliverances of God's people (vv. 4–32), we have seen how God delivers his people from the many dangers, toils, and snares of this life. Now we will see how he also brings us home, anchoring our souls in a safe harbor at last.

Swiss psychiatrist Paul Tournier wrote a book entitled *A Place to Be*, which claims that a place to belong, a home, is what we all most deeply desire. Tournier says we long for it all our lives and are restless until we find it. Psalm 107 tells us that God provides just such a home for his people. We have a home in God here and now, a home enriched by our having Christian brothers and sisters. Even more important, we have the assurance of a happy, eternal heavenly home hereafter.

The Experience of the Pilgrims

The Pilgrims were dispossessed of their homes in England. They left their temporary homes in Holland. While making their perilous three-month crossing of the Atlantic Ocean they were without a home; even the Mayflower did not belong to them. When they reached the shores of Massachusetts Bay at what came to be called Plymouth Colony, they had a home of their own at last. During that first desperate winter they constructed rustic shelters for themselves and thus established the first permanent English settlement in North America.

They suffered terribly that winter, but in the spring the few healthy men planted crops, the sick recovered, and in the fall they gathered in their first harvest. What American does not know the story of that harvest and the first Thanksgiving? William Bradford tells of an abundance of fish and wild game that were added to the harvest celebration that November. It is not from Bradford that we learn the details of that thanksgiving celebration; they are found in a letter written by Edward Winslow to a friend in England in December 1621. Winslow tells of a three-day feast attended not only by the Pilgrims but also by the local Indians, the great chief Massasoit himself arriving for the feast with ninety men.[1]

Well might these hearty survivors have said, "Let them give thanks to the LORD for his unfailing love and his wonderful deeds for men" (vv. 8, 15, 21, 31), for "there he brought the hungry to live, and they founded a city where they could settle" (v. 36). We also should always thank the Lord for similar blessings.

The Other Side of the Story

There is another side to this story: The good times were succeeded by hard times again. The Pilgrims suffered anxiety over divisions caused by new colonists from other places, distress at being cheated by ship captains, and fear of war with distant Indian tribes. Then the crops sometimes failed or did poorly, and sicknesses returned.

Have you noticed how Psalm 107 acknowledges this pattern? It is not talking about the Pilgrims, of course, but it tells how in other cases God gave a fruitful harvest and increased the numbers of the people and their livestock but then also allowed the harvests of these same people to fail and their numbers to decrease. In fact, it repeats this cycle twice in the last section: hard times (vv. 33–34), blessing (vv. 35–38), hard times again (vv. 39–40), and blessing again (vv. 41–42).

At verse 33 there is such an abrupt change in tone and even (to some extent) in subject matter that some of the more liberal writers imagine the psalm was put together from two otherwise unrelated poems. The first half of the psalm rejoices in the deliverances accomplished by God and calls on the people who were delivered to praise and thank God for it. The final section reflects in a distant, settled way on God's sovereign workings by which his people are sometimes lifted up and sometimes brought low. The first few verses use images, noting how God "turned rivers into a desert" (v. 33) and "the desert into pools of water" (v. 35), "fruitful land into a salt waste" and "parched ground into flowing springs" (vv. 34–35). As far as the people were concerned, the psalm says God "blessed them, and their numbers greatly increased" but also that "their numbers decreased, and they were humbled by oppression, calamity and sorrow" (vv. 38–39).

The difference in tone and content is only a case of the psalmist's honesty, depth, and spiritual sensitivity being greater than our own. He is acknowledging that not everything the people of God experience can be described as a deliverance and be received with utter joy. Life has its pain and tragedies, even for Christians. Yet in spite of them, we can and should praise God for his wisdom and goodness, as the Pilgrims did.

We can do this by seeing God's wise, loving, and sovereign hand even in hardships. The psalm ends with a humble acknowledgment of God's sovereignty over all things and all circumstances, reminding us that even the bad things of life are in God's hands. The late Lutheran commentator H. C. Leupold calls this the psalm's important *general* truth: "The up's and down's, the success and the failure, the prosperity and calamity in the lives of individuals and nations are entirely in the control of and brought about by the will of the Almighty. None are brought low or raised on high unless he wills it."[2]

Here are two biblical confessions of that truth.

King Nebuchadnezzar had been struggling against the claims of the sovereign God, refusing to recognize that even his own destiny was in God's hands. When he took the glory of God to himself, claiming, as he looked out over the magnificent city of Babylon, "Is not this the great Babylon I have built as the royal residence, by my mighty power and for the glory of my majesty?" (Dan. 4:30), God punished him with insanity. He was driven from human company and lived among animals for seven years.

Later, when he acknowledged God to be "the Most High" God and had his sanity restored, Nebuchadnezzar praised God:

> His dominion is an eternal dominion;
>> his kingdom endures from generation to generation.
> All the peoples of the earth
>> are regarded as nothing.
> He does as he pleases
>> with the powers of heaven
>> and the peoples of the earth.
> No one can hold back his hand
>> or say to him: "What have you done?"

"Everything he does is right and all his ways are just. And those who walk in pride he is able to humble" (Dan. 4:34–35, 37). As I am fond of saying, not only is God able to humble people, he does humble them. In fact, Psalm 107 says this even of the righteous: "Then their numbers decreased, and they were humbled by oppression, calamity and sorrow" (v. 39).

The second biblical confession that none are brought low or raised on high unless God wills it is in the New Testament, in the psalm of the Virgin Mary that we know as the Magnificat.

> He has brought down rulers from their thrones
>> but has lifted up the humble.

> He has filled the hungry with good things
> but has sent the rich away empty (Luke 1:52–53).

Probably Mary was thinking only of the lifting up of the righteous and the debasing of the wicked, but we learn from Psalm 107, as well as from other passages of Scripture, that the righteous are sometimes brought low also.

Uses of This Doctrine

Since we are talking about the Pilgrims, who were Puritans, I want to do what the Puritan preachers often did. If you read their sermons, you will find that often, after having stated what they call "the doctrine," they give what they call "uses" of it. I suggest four uses of the doctrine that *even for the righteous God sends sorrow as well as joy, hardship as well as material blessing—yet is not arbitrary.*

1. *Reverence for God.* Since God's ways are not our ways and his ultimate purposes in life are usually beyond our finding out, we must revere him and be humble.

The apostle Paul ended the third section of Romans by explaining God's choice to bypass the majority of Jewish people in order to bring the gospel to the Gentiles but one day to work among the Jews again so that "all Israel will be saved" (Rom. 11:26). This is one of the most profound passages in the Bible, one that has proved difficult even for the most astute commentators. Paul seems to be probing the mind of God as only an inspired apostle could. Yet when he has finished his explanation of God's sovereign purposes in history, he does not boast in his understanding, as if he were saying, "Look what I have figured out." Instead he breaks into a doxology, writing,

> Oh, the depth of the riches of the wisdom and knowledge of God!
>   How unsearchable his judgments,
>   and his paths beyond tracing out!
> "Who has known the mind of the Lord?
>   Or who has been his counselor?"
> "Who has ever given to God,
>   that God should repay him?"
> For from him and through him and to him are all things.
>   To him be the glory forever! Amen (Rom. 11:33–36).

There is nothing wrong with trying to understand the judgments, paths, and mind of God. We are encouraged to do so. But we should never forget that God's ways will always be beyond our full understanding and that many times we will simply have to clap our hands over our mouths and wait to see what God will himself do or say, if anything.

Habakkuk tried to understand why God was raising up the Babylonians to overthrow his people, but he could not. So he concluded,

> I will stand at my watch
>> and station myself on the ramparts;
> I will look to see what he will say to me,
>> and what answer I am to give to this complaint (Hab. 2:1).

When God did speak he gave Habakkuk one of the greatest revelations in the Bible—"the just shall live by his faith" (Hab. 2:4 KJV)—the words that meant so much to Martin Luther.

2. *Looking for things that are eternal.* Looking beyond the seen to the unseen and eternal is faith. Abraham is one example of those with faith. He was called out of his home city of Ur to go to a land that God would give him. He never actually owned that land, except for the small part he purchased as a burial plot for his wife, Sarah, and his life was not easy even when he was living where God had told him to go. There were famines, disagreements with his nephew Lot, danger from marauding desert tribes. Difficulty was all right with Abraham because he knew that the best blessings he was promised were not to be enjoyed in this life but in the life to come. Hence the author of Hebrews sums up Abraham's lifetime walk of faith by saying, "He was looking forward to the city with foundations, whose architect and builder is God" (Heb. 11:10).

Although there are ups and downs in this life, the end of all things for God's people is not down but up. We can know this and look for it because we know that God is both good and sovereign. God loves us, and because he does he comforts us, preserves us, and brings us through even the hardest experiences of life. Psalm 107 ends on this note, for it calls us to "heed these things and consider *the great love* of the LORD" (v. 43, italics added).

3. *Calling sinners to repentance.* Although the ways of God in this life are not always within our understanding, nevertheless we do discern some important patterns, and one of them is that arrogance, strife, self-love, greed, and other forms of wickedness are generally punished, while virtue is frequently rewarded. This fact enables us to argue that we inhabit a moral universe governed by a moral God and to warn sinners against persisting in behavior that will eventually result in their eternal condemnation by God. The psalm's last verse is telling not only the righteous but also everyone to wise up and consider how things actually are.

4. *Thanksgiving.* Believers should thank God for being what he is and acting as he does—and not only when things are going our way or we have it easy.

The apostle Paul suffered enormous hardships in his efforts to take the gospel throughout the known Roman world, including an imprisonment at the end of which he was beheaded. But it was this very apostle who wrote, "I have learned the secret of being content in any and every situation, whether well fed or hungry, whether living in plenty or in want" (Phil. 4:12) and who told the Philippians, "Do not be anxious about anything, but in everything, by prayer and petition, *with thanksgiving*, present your requests to God. And the peace of God, which transcends all understanding, will guard your hearts and your minds in Christ Jesus" (vv. 6–7, italics added).

Heeding and Considering

Alexander Duff was an eloquent pastor and missionary pioneer, the first sent to India by the Presbyterian Church of Scotland. On October 14, 1829, he and his wife set out for the Indian subcontinent on a ship called the Lady Holland, and four months later, at midnight on the 13th of February 1830, the ship ran aground while attempting to navigate the Cape of Good Hope. The pounding surf soon destroyed the ship, washing everything it held away, but miraculously all the passengers and crew made it safely to land.

Nothing remained of their belongings, but as one sailor walked along the shore looking for food and fuel, he came upon two books, a Bible and the Scottish Psalm Book. He found the name of Alexander Duff in both of them, so he brought them to the missionary. Duff had been transporting eight hundred books to India, where he hoped to (and later did) establish a college, but of those eight hundred books only these two remained. In spite of this loss, Duff at once opened the Bible to Psalm 107 and read it to the other survivors, concluding with the words,

> Whoever is wise, let him heed these things
> and consider the great love of the LORD (v. 43).[3]

Can you do that? What matters most in life is not the number or severity of the perils from which we are delivered, but whether we are actually in the hands of that greatly loving God. If we are in his hands, we can "heed these things," "consider the great love of the LORD," and then praise him as Psalm 107 does. By this praise it has been a blessing to God's people throughout the ages.

Psalm 108

A Warrior's Morning Song

My heart is steadfast, O God;
   I will sing and make music with all my soul.
Awake, harp and lyre!
   I will awaken the dawn.
I will praise you, O LORD, among the nations;
   I will sing of you among the peoples.
For great is your love, higher than the heavens;
   your faithfulness reaches to the skies.
Be exalted, O God, above the heavens,
   and let your glory be over all the earth.

Save us and help us with your right hand,
   that those you love may be delivered.
God has spoken from his sanctuary:
   "In triumph I will parcel out Shechem
   and measure off the Valley of Succoth.
Gilead is mine, Manasseh is mine;
   Ephraim is my helmet,
   Judah my scepter.
Moab is my washbasin,
   upon Edom I toss my sandal;
   over Philistia I shout in triumph."

Who will bring me to the fortified city?
   Who will lead me to Edom?
Is it not you, O God, you who have rejected us
   and no longer go out with our armies?

> *Give us aid against the enemy,*
> *for the help of man is worthless.*
> *With God we will gain the victory,*
> *and he will trample down our enemies.*
>
> *verses 1–13*

O ne of the interesting things about studying the psalms is discovering that sometimes parts of them are drawn from other portions of the Old Testament, even from other psalms. For example, Psalm 96 was borrowed from 1 Chronicles 16:23–33, the middle portion of a historical psalm composed by David. Psalm 53 is an almost word-for-word repetition of Psalm 14.

Psalm 108 is made up of the endings of Psalms 57 and 60. In the earlier psalms David was writing under stress. According to the title of Psalm 57, David was hiding in a cave in order to escape from Saul, who was trying to kill him. The title of Psalm 60 refers to a time of war between David's armies and the Edomites. The earlier psalms each begin by describing the perils David faced, then they end on a positive note of praise and hope for the future. It is these two endings that are combined in Psalm 108 to produce what I have called "a warrior's morning psalm." In this psalm the king begins his day by praising God. He is awake even before the dawn, asking God for help in his battles and trusting that God will soon give him victory over his enemies, particularly those in the fortified cities of the secure mountain stronghold of Edom, which is where the psalm ends.

The title of Psalm 108 says that the psalm is "of David" but only because the psalms from which it is taken both identify David as their author. David is the author of the words, but this does not mean that David fused the two pieces together to form Psalm 108. On the contrary, the psalm is better explained as the work of a later author who, faced by a similar challenge from the surrounding nations, particularly Edom, looked to God for a new deliverance and victory, as had David before him. The new situation could be the abuse of the people by Edom that took place at the time of Jerusalem's fall, as prophesied by Obadiah.

Alexander Maclaren thought that the return from Babylon would be an appropriate occasion for the psalm. "The hopes of conquest in the second part, the consciousness that while much has been achieved by God's help, much still remains to be won before Israel can sit secure, the bar or two in the minor key in verse 11, which heighten the exultation of the rest of the song, and the cry for help against adversaries too strong for Israel's unassisted might, are all appropriate to the early stages of the return."[1]

This new use of older psalms points clearly to the continuing relevancy and power of the Scriptures in later Jewish life.

A Morning Praise Song

The first thing the author has to say is that his "heart is steadfast," or fixed. A few verses later we learn the secret of his stability. It is because God is a steadfast, or faithful, God, and the psalmist's confidence is in him. Indeed, God is more than just steadfast. He is also a God whose love and faithfulness reach as high as the sky or heavens, which is a way of saying that they are infinite and thus beyond our full comprehension.

> I will praise you, O LORD, among the nations;
>   I will sing of you among the peoples.
> For great is your love, higher than the heavens;
>   your faithfulness reaches to the skies (vv. 3–4).

It is because God is faithful that the psalmist can also be faithful. Are we faithful in this sense? Are our hearts steadfast? I am afraid that often they are not, not even in evangelical churches. People who attend evangelical churches have generally heard the Word of God preached faithfully, but they are like the people represented in Jesus' parable of the farmer who went out to sow seed. In the story some of the seed "fell along the path, and the birds came and ate it up. Some fell on . . . soil [that] was shallow. But when the sun came up, the plants were scorched, and they withered because they had no root. Other seed fell among thorns, which grew up and choked the plants." Only a fourth portion of the seed "fell on good soil, where it produced a crop—a hundred, sixty or thirty times what was sown" (Matt. 13:4–9).

Sometimes Jesus' stories are unexplained, which makes them hard for us to understand, but Jesus himself explained this one. The seed that fell on the path represents the way the Word of God is heard by people who do not understand it. It never sinks into their minds or hearts, and it is not long before the devil, like a scavenger bird, snatches the seed up and the person forgets entirely what he or she has heard. The shallow, rocky soil represents people who receive God's Word and seem to believe it; but faith withers as soon as the going gets hard. The thorns represent the cares of this world that deceive and ruin many who might have counted for something otherwise (cf. Matt. 13:18–23).

None of these types of people are steadfast, because the Word of God has not taken deep root in their minds and hearts. They are not grounded in God or the Word of God, and so they quickly fade away. Are you a hard, shallow, or worldly "believer"? If you are, you will never be able to go on to the confident dependence on God that marked the life of the psalmist and that he is earnestly commending to us.

Since the writer's confidence is in God, rather than in himself, we are not surprised to find the opening stanza of the psalm calling for God to be exalted: "Be exalted, O God, above the heavens, and let your glory be over all the earth" (v. 5). God *is* exalted above the heavens. His glory *does* fill the earth. The goal of history is that God might be known as God and be honored for it. Nothing will frustrate this worthy purpose of the Almighty. This verse is not a statement that God has or will be exalted. It is a prayer that he might be exalted, obviously in the king's own circumstances. The world thrills when human beings are exalted, but those who know God rejoice when God is exalted, especially when they have the privilege of exalting him in circumstances that may be disappointing or hard.

A Prayer for Deliverance and Victory

The second section of the psalm contains a prayer to God to save, help, and deliver those who have been attacked, probably by the Edomites (v. 6), followed by God's answer in the form of an oracle (vv. 7–9). The oracle follows so closely upon the appeal that we know faith has already won a victory, just as in Psalm 60, from which these words are taken.

When we were studying Psalm 60 (in vol. 2 of *Psalms*), I pointed out that there are two ways verses 7–9 (in Psalm 60, verses 6–8) may be understood. They are introduced as a word "God has spoken from his sanctuary." *Sanctuary* refers to the tabernacle precincts in Jerusalem. It is possible that this was a special revelation from God brought to David by Nathan or one of the other priests or prophets in order to be incorporated into Psalm 60 long before Psalm 108 was written. If that is the case, the oracle is a statement verifying that God gave the land of Israel to the Jewish people and a promise assuring that he would give victory over the enemies trying to take it from them.

The other way of looking at these verses is suggested by the fact that the place names are not what we might expect at any point in David's career—we would expect the names of the tribal territories perhaps—but seem to trace the occupation of the land from the time of the patriarch Jacob. Shechem was the place Jacob settled after his return to Canaan from Paddan Aram, where he had lived for twenty years with his uncle and later father-in-law Laban (Gen. 33:18). Succoth was the last place he had been previously (Gen. 33:17). These two places represent the eastern and western sides of the Jordan River. Gilead and Manasseh represent larger areas of the eastern side of the Jordan occupied by Israel at the time of the conquest under Joshua. Ephraim and Judah represent the most prominent tribes to the west.[2] If these place names are meant to remind us of this early history and of the fact that God had given the land to the people from the time of the patriarchs, then verses 6–9 are not necessarily an oracle from David's own time but rather a new phrasing of these important older promises.

As I pointed out in our study of Psalm 60 earlier, in either case the Word of God is the basis of the psalmist's faith. It is because God has spoken that the writer can have hope for the future and pray confidently for God's help and deliverance. Faith must always be grounded in the Word of God.[3]

A Prayer for Victory over Edom

The final stanza is a prayer for victory over Edom, which is what has probably been in the psalmist's mind from the first verse and is the occasion for this new composition. David had defeated Edom and made it a part of his kingdom years before. The account of David's conquest is in 2 Samuel 8:1–14 (a parallel account is in 1 Chronicles 18:1–13), which says, "David became famous after he returned from striking down eighteen thousand Edomites in the Valley of Salt. He put garrisons throughout Edom, and all the Edomites became subject to David. The LORD gave David victory wherever he went." By the time of our psalm the Edomites had apparently regained power, and a new battle was pending. The psalmist asks in verse 10:

> Who will bring me to the fortified city?
> Who will lead me to Edom?

It is a good question. There were a number of well-fortified cities in Edom, the source of the country's strength and great pride, but when the psalm speaks of *the* fortified city it can only mean Petra, the legendary, inaccessible, and apparently impregnable mountain stronghold of Edom. I have had the privilege of visiting Petra on two occasions. It is approached through a narrow cut in the limestone cliffs that winds inward for about a mile and is called a *siq*. The cliffs rise for thousands of feet on both sides, and in places the passage is so narrow that no more than two horses can pass abreast. A handful of brave men could defend this passage against an army, and even if the entrance to Petra could be breached, the defenders could retreat into the mountains surrounding the hidden inner valley and defend themselves from there. Only God could give victory over a fortress like that, and the writer knows it. So he cries to God, answering his own question:

> Is it not you, O God, you who have rejected us
> and no longer go out with our armies? (v. 11).

The only one who could bring the king into Petra and give him victory is God, so the writer acknowledges this fact and asks God, "Give us aid against the enemy, for the help of man is worthless" (v. 12). Will God do it? Being assured by the oracle recorded in verses 7–9, the psalmist is sure he will:

> With God we will gain the victory,
> and he will trample down our enemies (v. 12).

Two Conflicts, Two Victories

How can we take this psalm from its ancient setting and carry its value into our own time and beyond? There are two ways.

882 Book Five of the Psalter

1. *By gaining strength for our conflicts.* You and I are not kings. We do not have military battles to fight. We have never seen an Edomite. However, we as Christians have spiritual battles. We are members of the kingdom of the Lord Jesus Christ, and our task is to advance his kingdom in this spiritually hostile world. The apostle Paul spoke of this battle in Ephesians, explaining that "our struggle is not against flesh and blood, but against the rulers, against the authorities, against the powers of this dark world and against the spiritual forces of evil in the heavenly realms" (Eph. 6:12). Compared to the conquest of these hostile spiritual forces, the victory over Edom and the overthrow of its mountain stronghold Petra was easy. How can we gain this greater victory? Not by ourselves, or even with the help of other Christians. In this battle "the help of man is [truly] worthless." We need God to fight with us and for us.

Therefore, we need to ask God for help, as the psalmist does. James says, "You do not have, because you do not ask God" (James 4:2), and Jesus, expressing James's words positively, said, "Ask and it will be given to you; seek and you will find; knock and the door will be opened to you" (Matt. 7:7).

One thing we can ask for is victory for the gospel.

Nebuchadnezzar's vision, the one he could not remember but troubled him so much, was a vision of an enormous statue representing in sequence several of the powerful ancient kingdoms of this world: the kingdom of Babylon, those of the Medes and Persians and Greece, and finally the great empire of Rome. At the conclusion of the vision a rock "not cut by human hands" struck the statue and destroyed it and then grew up to become "a huge mountain" that "filled the whole earth" (Dan. 2:34–35). That rock is the Lord Jesus Christ, and the mountain is his kingdom, destined to triumph. If you are a Christian, you are part of that kingdom, and Christ's kingdom is something you can labor and pray for confidently.

2. *By trusting the warrior from Edom.* In Isaiah 63 there is a dramatic scene in which a bloodstained divine warrior comes marching up the valley of the Kidron from the west toward Jerusalem. The cry rings out,

> Who is this coming from Edom,
>> from Bozrah, with his garments stained crimson?
> Who is this, robed in splendor,
>> striding forward in the greatness of his strength?

The warrior answers,

> "It is I, speaking in righteousness,
>> mighty to save."

The prophet, looking down from the walls of the city of Jerusalem, then has another question, which he throws out to the warrior:

> Why are your garments red,
>> like those of one treading the winepress?

The traveler answers,

> "I have trodden the winepress alone;
>> from the nations no one was with me.
> I trampled them in my anger
>> and trod them down in my wrath;
> their blood spattered my garments,
>> and I stained all my clothing.
> For the day of vengeance was in my heart,
>> and the year of my redemption has come" (Isa. 63:1–4).

Who is this warrior? He is none other than the Lord Jesus Christ, return-ing to Jerusalem after having subdued the hostile peoples of this evil world. This is a vision of the end of time, a vision that takes us to the kind of descriptions we find in the very last book of the Bible, Revelation. Here we see the sure punishment of the wicked and the certain vindication of those who trust God and look to him for their deliverance.

That day has not yet come. For the time being there are still hard times and defeats for God's people. If the day of the vengeance of our God has not yet come, it is in order that God might show grace now to more people. In Peter's day there were skeptics who were saying that because things seemed to continue as they have been from the beginning, there will not be a judgment. It will never come. "Where is this 'coming' he promised? Ever since our fathers died, everything goes on as it has since the beginning of creation," they mocked (2 Peter 3:4).

Peter answered, "The Lord is not slow in keeping his promise, as some understand slowness. He is patient with you, not wanting anyone to perish, but everyone to come to repentance" (v. 9). God is delaying the ultimate working out of judgment until those whom he will call to faith in Jesus Christ come to him. Judgment is not yet; this is the day of God's grace. But judgment will come. If you are not a believer in Jesus, God warns you to believe on Jesus now, while there is still time.

Psalm 109

An Evil End for Evil Men

O God, whom I praise,
  do not remain silent,
for wicked and deceitful men
    have opened their mouths against me;
    they have spoken against me with lying tongues.
With words of hatred they surround me;
    they attack me without cause.
In return for my friendship they accuse me,
    but I am a man of prayer.
They repay me evil for good,
    and hatred for my friendship.

Appoint an evil man to oppose him;
    let an accuser stand at his right hand.
When he is tried, let him be found guilty,
    and may his prayers condemn him. . . .

With my mouth I will greatly extol the LORD;
    in the great throng I will praise him.
For he stands at the right hand of the needy one,
    to save his life from those who condemn him.

verses 1–31

$\mathbf{P}$salm 109 is the last of the imprecatory psalms.[1] Imprecation has to do with praying for or calling down curses on one's enemies, which followers of Christ are not supposed to do. For that reason the imprecatory psalms are among the most troubling parts of Scripture for Christians and Christian sensibilities.

Psalm 109 is not only the last of the imprecatory psalms, but it is also the strongest, most intense or worst. In his excellent and very fresh study of the psalms C. S. Lewis speaks of those in which a spirit of hatred "strikes us in the face . . . like the heat from a furnace mouth" and calls Psalm 109 "perhaps the worse" example.[2] Lewis is not the only writer to claim so. J. J. Stewart Perowne, an English commentator of the last century (1823–1904), wrote, "In the awfulness of its anathemas, the psalm surpasses everything of the kind in the Old Testament."[3] Many psalms have an occasional prayer for God's judgment on enemies, but by my count there are twenty-four curses in the imprecatory section of this psalm, and this is the main section (vv. 6–20). The imprecations are bracketed by prayers for God to hear and save the psalmist from his enemies (vv. 1–5, 21–31).

Imprecations of King David

Since this is the last of the imprecatory psalms and I have been going through the psalms in order from the beginning, I have already written a good bit about how these curses should be understood,[4] and I do not need to repeat all that I have written earlier. Let me briefly review, just to put Psalm 109 in perspective.

1. *All the imprecatory psalms are by David, and in these psalms David is writing as a king and not merely as a private citizen.* It is true that prayers for judgment on the incorrigibly wicked occur in psalms by writers other than David, but the specific and most intense of these curses are by a king whose responsibility as king was to see justice dispensed to evil persons. Moreover, David was God's "anointed" ruler in a way rulers of other kingdoms are not. So attacks on David were also attacks on God, God's kingdom, and God's righteousness. The curses do not flow from a feeling of resentment for personal hurts or wrongs.

2. *David leaves vindication and judgment in the hands of God; he does not take vengeance into his own hands.* David was well known, even praised, for being a nonvindictive, long-suffering, and merciful man. We have only to think of the two occasions when David could have killed his archenemy King Saul if he had wanted to (1 Sam. 24, 26). David did not even think of killing Saul. He said instead, "I will not lift my hand against my master, because he is the LORD's anointed" (1 Sam. 24:10). All the imprecatory psalms have the flavor of Romans 12:19: "'It is mine to avenge; I will repay,' says the Lord." They leave the execution of justice in God's hands.

3. *It is right to desire the punishment of evil and the triumph and reward of good people.* True, as Christians we desire first that those who are doing wrong might repent of their sin and find forgiveness through the work of Jesus Christ. But if they fail to do so, if they persist in doing harm to others, the only right thing is to desire their punishment—that they might be stopped

and their victims be protected. We could hardly ask God to reward evil people, could we? Besides, we want evil to be judged, though in our hypocritically sentimental age we are usually careful about saying so openly.

4. Finally, although we live in an age in which the wicked still have time to repent of their sin and come to Christ, *the judgments described in these psalms—and worse—are nevertheless exactly what will come to the wicked eventually.* They will come at the final judgment when Jesus himself will be the judge. One use of the imprecatory psalms, therefore, is to warn people how seriously God takes sin, urging them to seek grace while grace is available.

A Man of Prayer

Although Psalm 109 is filled with terrible curses, David begins mildly enough, merely asking God not to remain silent, which means to act against his foes (vv. 1–5). Why should God act? David's enemies' words are troubling David. These men speak against him "with lying tongues" and with "words of hatred" (vv. 2–3). It is by what they say that they repay "evil for good" and "hatred" for "friendship" (v. 5). These opening verses caused Martin Luther to see the psalm as being directed almost entirely "against those who disparage another's reputation."[5]

None of this enemy problem should be new or surprising for those who have studied David's other psalms. As I have pointed out several times earlier, there is hardly a psalm by David that does not refer to his enemies. He had many of them. Many of these psalms indicate that what David feared most was how his enemies were using words against him. We do not usually take words with great seriousness. "Sticks and stones . . ." we say, but people can hurt other people by words. In fact, words have probably done more serious and lasting damage to other people than any amount of specifically evil acts or violence. David knew this danger and so asked God for protection from lies, innuendo, slander, and false accusations.

What is David's reaction to such verbal assault? The key to his attitude is verse 4, which says, "But I am a man of prayer." The Hebrew is more abrupt and therefore even stronger. It says literally, "But I prayer." That is, "I am all prayer or characterized by prayer. While my enemies are uttering false words about me to other people, trying to do me harm, I am speaking to God. I am praying to God always."

Is that how you and I respond when people say something bad about us? Are we women and men of prayer? Do we see everything that happens in light of God's sovereignty over life and thus bring everything to God and leave it there as the apostle Paul describes in Philippians 4:6–7 and 12?

Curses Spoken and Received

When we pass from the opening stanza to the second, central portion of the psalm (vv. 6–20), we find an interesting change—quite apart from the curses. The references to David's enemies change from being plural (they) to being singular (he, him, and his). At verse 20 the references become plural once again ("accusers"). Use of the singular may be a Hebrew idiom meaning "each and every one of them," which verse 20 seems to suggest, since the plural there seems to be a summary. It is more likely that David is speaking of a specific individual. The apostle Peter took verse 8 specifically when he interpreted it as a prophetic reference to Judas Iscariot (in Acts 1:20).

The only reason why this change is important is that some commentators have used it to argue that the imprecations are not something David is saying about his enemies, but rather are what these evil men are saying about David, as if these verses began with the words, "They say . . ." That is, "They say, 'Appoint an evil man to oppose him. . . . When he is tried, let him be found guilty. . . . May his days be few; may another take his place of leadership'" and so on. Leslie C. Allen handles the psalm this way in the *Word Biblical Commentary*. He places verses 6–19 in quotation marks followed by verse 20, reading, "May this be the way Yahweh punishes my accusers."[6] In other words, "May the curses they speak against me fall on them." Another who interprets the verses this way is G. Campbell Morgan: "The passage . . . contains the singer's quotation of what his enemies say about him, rather than what he says about them."[7]

This approach removes the force of the curses being from David and makes them more acceptable to our sensibilities, which is why these writers like it. But it is not a good explanation. For one thing, it runs against Peter's use of the words in Acts 1:15–20. Peter said these are words "which the Holy Spirit spoke long ago through the mouth of David concerning Judas" (v. 16), and he quoted Psalm 109:8 specifically, as we have seen: "May another take his place of leadership" (v. 20). For another thing, if we accept this approach and verse 20 would say, in effect, "May the curses they have pronounced on me fall on them," David would still be wishing his enemies great harm.

Although we might like to get out of difficulty by using this method, it is best to take the curses as David's and accept them as being spoken against one or more of his foes. We will divide them into three sections for study.

1. *An accuser's accuser.* The setting of verses 6 and 7 is a court of law, giving the entire passage a legal or judicial tone. The curses that follow are not to be seen as David's striking out in a personal way against a person who has harmed him. On the contrary, they should be seen as his appeal to God to give justice to a person who has been extremely harmful, making sure that the one who has damaged others might himself be harmed.

The word "accuser" (v. 6) occurs throughout the psalm (vv. 20, 29, and "accuse" is the corresponding verb in v. 4). The one who ought to be standing at the right hand of the defendant is his advocate or lawyer, not an accuser. Here the psalmist imagines a scene in which his enemy is hauled into court by an evil man and while there discovers that his lawyer is also an evil man who accuses him rather than defends him. He has no defenders at all, in fact—because his actions are defenseless.

The word that is translated "accuser" is the Hebrew noun *satan,* which is also the name and title of the devil, Satan, the accuser of the brethren. (This is going to be important when we get to the end of the psalm.) I do not know whether David was thinking of Satan explicitly when he wrote, "Let an accuser stand at his right hand," but he may have. In any case, although evil persons may imagine in their evil course that the devil is somehow with them to protect them and prosper them, they will find that he is actually their accuser at the last. I think of the Faust legend and of those terrible final words in Christopher Marlowe's drama:

> O lente, lente, curite noctis equi!
> The stars move still, time runs, the clock will strike,
> The Devil will come, and Faustus must be damn'd.[8]

2. *Sin's solidarity.* The hardest part of the imprecatory section of the psalm is what comes next (vv. 9–15). Here the curses pronounced on the man who has been doing evil are extended in the future as maledictions on his children, in the present as curses on his wife, and in the past as judgments on his parents, his mother in particular. The best we can do with these curses is to see them as a reminder of the solidarity of humanity, whereby the sin of one person always harms others, especially those closest to him or her.

Why is this solidarity spelled out so clearly other than to warn us against doing wrong? It is not just in the imprecatory psalms that we find curses extending to family members. In the Ten Commandments, for example, after warning us against worshiping idols, the second commandment continues, "For I, the LORD your God, am a jealous God, punishing the children for the sin of the fathers to the third and fourth generation of those who hate me, but showing love to a thousand generations of those who love me and keep my commandments" (Exod. 20:5–6). Even Jesus recognized the principle of sin's solidarity when he wept over Jerusalem, having foreseen the day when the city would be destroyed and its children dashed to the ground because of their fathers' sins (cf. Luke 19:41–44).

3. *No repentance.* The last section of the imprecations makes clear that the person being spoken about is an incorrigible evildoer who shows no sign of repentance or remorse. In other words, this is not the case of a person who simply sins, as we all do. It is one who sins against God and others knowingly, deliberately, and gleefully and who fully intends to keep on doing so. This person "never thought of doing a kindness" (v. 16). "He loved to pronounce a curse" and "found no pleasure in blessing" (v. 17). Alexander Maclaren acknowledges that Jesus' prayer "'Father, forgive them' is the strongest conceivable contrast to these awful prayers," but he also notes that David's curses

imply that the sins in question were "unrepented sins" and should rightly be punished by "the 'cutting off the memory' of such a brood of evil-doers 'from the earth.'"[9]

The punishment asked for is with strict correspondence to the sins. Verses 16–20 explain the curses of verses 6–15, showing that the evil person will get exactly what he gave others. He cursed them, so he will be accursed.

A Passionate Appeal

With verse 21 the mood changes radically, the thought shifting from the evil person or persons of verses 6–20 to God: "But you, O Sovereign LORD . . ." In this last section David makes an appeal for God to act on his behalf and save him. David has three grounds for his appeal.

1. *God's name and honor.* The words "deal well with me for your name's sake" mean, Save me so that you may be known as a God who is on the side of the righteous and against evildoers. When we remember that the problem in this psalm is David's enemies' slander, their use of words to attack and destroy his reputation, it is remarkable that he is concerned here not so much with his own reputation as with God's. He wants God's name to be vindicated most of all. Do we, or do we actually care most about ourselves?

2. *The psalmist's weak condition.* Scholars who do not want to assign the psalm to David argue that a king such as David could hardly refer to himself as "poor and needy," but he could, and did. All of us feel this way at times and rightly, for we are all weak creatures at best, even the strongest of us. Furthermore, the righteous *are* despised (v. 25). In appealing to God for help, it is a powerful point to confess our weak and helpless condition.

3. *God's steadfast love.* The final grounds for appeal (vv. 26–29) is God's love and what God is both willing and able to do to help the psalmist. David's enemies may curse, but God, who loves to bless his people, will be sure to bless them and put their accusers to shame (vv. 28–29).

God at My Right Hand

The last two verses (vv. 30–31) are a powerful and effective ending to this admittedly difficult psalm. They anticipate the deliverance David has been asking for and promise that David will use his mouth to praise God for his deliverance. His accusers use their mouths to accuse and curse him. He will use his to extol and bless God because God has defended and saved him.

> With my mouth I will greatly extol the LORD;
>   in the great throng I will praise him.
> For he stands at the right hand of the needy one,
>   to save his life from those who condemn him.

Notice the deliberate contrast between this last sentence and the words that introduced the imprecatory section in verse 6. Verse 6 asked that an accuser might stand at the right hand of the one who is doing evil to accuse him and secure his condemnation. Here, in the case of the righteous, the accuser is replaced by God, who stands at the right hand of his own beloved people to defend and save them.

How do we become righteous when we are not? In the third chapter of Zechariah there is a vision that shows us how. In his vision the prophet saw Joshua, Israel's high priest, standing before the angel of the Lord, presumably representing the people before God in the temple. Satan, the accuser of the brethren, was there to accuse him. Since we are told later that Joshua was clothed in filthy clothes, representing his and the people's sin, Satan must have been pointing to these and declaring forcefully that Joshua was unfit to stand before God in this service. Joshua said nothing, perhaps because he had nothing to say. He *was* sinful. He *was* unworthy. He is a picture of ourselves in our sin.

But God spoke though his angel, and his words were a sharp rebuke to Satan: "The LORD rebuke you, Satan! The LORD, who has chosen Jerusalem, rebuke you! Is not this man a burning stick snatched from the fire?" (Zech. 3:2). Then Joshua's filthy clothes were taken from him and rich garments and a clean turban were put on him, while the angel of the Lord stood nearby.

If you see David's psalm in light of Zechariah's vision, you understand that in the divine scheme of things you and I are not righteous people being unjustly accused by the wicked, but rather the wicked who are being rightly accused for our sins and who need to be saved by God. That is exactly what has been done for us by Jesus Christ, for by his death Jesus has become "our righteousness, holiness and redemption" (1 Cor. 1:30).

Psalm 110

The Psalm Most Quoted in the New Testament: Part 1

David and David's Lord

The LORD says to my Lord:
    "Sit at my right hand
until I make your enemies
    a footstool for your feet."

The LORD will extend your mighty scepter from Zion;
    you will rule in the midst of your enemies.
Your troops will be willing
    on your day of battle.
Arrayed in holy majesty,
    from the womb of the dawn
    you will receive the dew of your youth.

verses 1–3

Near the end of Christ's earthly ministry, not long before his arrest and crucifixion, there was a time when the leaders of Israel were trying to trap him with trick questions and he turned the tables on them by asking a question beyond their ability to answer. "What do you think about the Christ? Whose son is he?" Jesus queried.

They thought the answer was easy. "The son of David," they replied.

Jesus continued, "How is it then that David, speaking by the Spirit, calls him 'Lord'? For he says,

> The Lord said to my Lord:
> "Sit at my right hand
>   until I make your enemies
> a footstool for your feet."

"If then David calls him 'Lord,' how can he be his son?" (Matt. 22:41–45; see Mark 12:35–37; Luke 20:41–44). Thus an apparently easy question suddenly became a profound and searching question. For if David called his natural physical descendant (the Messiah) his Lord, it could only be because the One to come would somehow be greater than David was, and the only way that could happen is if the Messiah were more than a mere man. He would have to be a divine Messiah, that is, God.

The answer to the question, "What do you think about the Christ? Whose son is he?" must therefore be, "He is *both* the son of David *and* the Son of God." In other words, it must be the exact teaching Paul develops in the early verses of Romans, where he writes that Jesus "as to his human nature was a descendant of David, and . . . through the Spirit of holiness was declared with power to be the Son of God by his resurrection from the dead" (Rom. 1:3–4).

The Greatest Messianic Psalm

When Jesus asked the Pharisees his question, he was referring to Psalm 110:1. He was also establishing a pattern for interpreting the Old Testament that his disciples picked up on enthusiastically. They loved to quote this psalm. In fact, they referred to it so often that it became the psalm most quoted in the New Testament, and verse 1 the most quoted verse. By my count, Psalm 110:1 is quoted directly or alluded to indirectly at least twenty-seven times, the chief passages being Matthew 22:44 (parallels in Mark 12:36; Luke 20:42–43); Acts 2:34–35; 7:56; 1 Corinthians 15:25; Ephesians 1:20; Colossians 3:1; Hebrews 1:3, 13; 12:2; and 1 Peter 3:22. Verse 4 is referred to in Hebrews 5:6; 7:17, 21; 8:1; 10:11–13 and is the dominating idea of those key chapters.

Why should Psalm 110 have been so important to the early church and to the New Testament writers? The answer is that Psalm 110 is the greatest of the messianic psalms. It alone is about the Messiah and his work exclusively, without any primary reference to an earthly king. There are not a large number of messianic psalms. They include Psalms 2, 22, 45, 72, and 110, plus a few others, but these mostly only contain messianic elements while other parts of them are apparently about the earthly king who was reigning at that time. By contrast, Psalm 110 is entirely about a divine king who has been installed at the right hand of God in heaven and who is presently engaged in extending his spiritual rule throughout the whole earth. It tells us that this divine Messiah is also a priest, performing priestly functions, and that additionally he is a judge who at the end of time will execute a final judgment on the nations and rulers of this earth.

Edward Reynolds (1599–1676) was one of the best expositors of Psalm 110, though he lived long ago, and he wrote that "this psalm is one of the fullest and most compendious prophecies of the person and offices of Christ in the whole Old Testament." He felt that "there are few, if any, of the articles of that creed which we all generally profess, which are not plainly expressed, or by most evident implication couched in this little model." Reynolds saw this psalm as teaching the doctrines of the divine Trinity; the incarnation, sufferings, resurrection, ascension, and intercession of Jesus Christ; the communion of saints; the last judgment; the remission of sins; and the life everlasting.[1]

Charles Haddon Spurgeon, the famous Baptist preacher of the nineteenth century, taught that Psalm 110 is exclusively about Jesus Christ. David "is not the subject of it even in the smallest degree," he wrote.[2] Walter Chantry, a contemporary Baptist preacher, also sees Psalm 110 as being exclusively about Christ. He divides it into four parts, namely, the powerful reign of Christ (v. 1), the spiritual reign of Christ (vv. 2–3), the priestly reign of Christ (v. 4), and the judicial reign of Christ (vv. 5–7). This is a good way of looking at the structure suggested by the stanzas of the New International Version.[3] The final two parts we will discuss in the next chapter. We will study the powerful reign of Christ by dividing verse 1 into two sections.

The Powerful Reign of Christ

1. *"The Lord says to my Lord."* It is easy to see why this first and most often quoted verse is so important. In Hebrew the first word for "Lord" in verse 1 is *Jehovah,* or *Yahweh,* which is indicated by its being printed in capital letters. It refers to the God of Israel. The second word for "Lord" is *Adonai. Adonai* refers to an individual greater than the speaker. Here is a case of David's citing God's words in which God tells another personage, who is greater than David, to sit at God's right hand until God makes the person's enemies a footstool for the person's feet. This person can only be a divine Messiah, who is Jesus Christ.

This argument depends on two assumptions. The first is that the psalm is by David. Otherwise, it could be construed only as an inferior member of the court flattering David by calling David "Lord" and suggesting that he was to rule with God's special blessing. The second is that David wrote by inspiration so that what he said about this divine figure really is true and is a prophecy of Jesus Christ. Jesus made both these assumptions when he said, "David, speaking by the Spirit . . ."

Jesus' words make it astonishing that so many commentators, including even some so-called evangelicals, credit Psalm 110 to another human writer.

They see it as flattery of a merely human king (though with messianic overtones) and explain Jesus' words as a concession to the widespread but mistaken opinions of his age regarding David's authorship of the psalms.[4] This is a terrible error, and it misses the point of the psalm completely.

Derek Kidner expresses the issue well.

> Nowhere in the Psalter does so much hang on the familiar title *A Psalm of David* as it does here; nor is the authorship of any other psalm quite so emphatically endorsed in other parts of Scripture. To amputate this opening phrase, or to allow it no reference to the authorship of the psalm, is to be at odds with the New Testament, which finds King David's acknowledgment of his "Lord" highly significant. For while other psalms share with this one the exalted language which points beyond the reigning king to the Messiah, here alone the king himself does homage to this personage—thereby settling two important questions: whether the perfect king was someone to come, or simply the present ruler idealized; and whether the one to come would be merely man at his best, or more than this.
>
> Our Lord gave full weight to David's authorship and David's words, stressing the former twice by the expression "David himself" and the latter by the comment that he was speaking "in the Holy Spirit" (Mark 12:36f.), and by insisting that his terms presented a challenge to accepted ideas of the Messiah, which must be taken seriously. Peter, too, on the Day of Pentecost, stressed the contrast in the psalm between David "himself" and his "Lord," who "ascended into the heavens" to be "exalted at the right hand of God" (Acts 2:33–35).[5]

Peter's conclusion from this verse is as valid today as it was when he quoted it as part of his sermon on the Day of Pentecost two thousand years ago: "Therefore . . . be assured of this: God has made this Jesus, whom you crucified, both Lord and Christ." When the people were convicted by his preaching to the point of crying out, "Brothers, what shall we do?" Peter answered, "Repent and be baptized, every one of you, in the name of Jesus Christ for the forgiveness of your sins" (Acts 2:36–38).

2. *"Sit at my right hand."* The first verse of Psalm 110 also speaks of Jesus' present position at the right hand of the Father in heaven and of his lordship over all things in heaven and on earth. It is cast in the form of an oracle from God: "Sit at my right hand until I make your enemies a footstool for your feet." We are familiar with this idea from the Apostles' Creed, for many Christians recite together each week, "He ascended into heaven, and sitteth on the right hand of God the Father Almighty."

What does it mean to sit at God's right hand? In the ancient world, to sit at a person's right hand was to occupy a place of honor; a seat at the right hand of the host would be a place of honor at a dinner. To sit at a king's right hand was more than mere honor; it was to share in his rule. It signified participation in the royal dignity and power.[6] This participation belongs to Jesus since, as Paul wrote to the Philippians,

> God exalted him to the highest place
>> and gave him the name that is above every name,
> that at the name of Jesus every knee should bow,
>> in heaven and on earth and under the earth,
> and every tongue confess that Jesus Christ is Lord,
>> to the glory of God the Father (Phil. 2:9–11).

What a tremendous gulf there is between God's evaluation of his beloved Son and the scorn people had for him when he was on earth. When he was here Jesus was despised and rejected. He was harassed and hated. At last he was unjustly arrested, tried, and cruelly executed. God reversed all that, for God raised him from the dead, received him into heaven, and then said, "Sit at my right hand until I make your enemies a footstool for your feet."

Today Jesus is at God's right hand, ruling over all things in heaven and on earth. Jesus' rule is God's doing. It is not up to us whether Jesus Christ will be Lord. Jesus *is* Lord, and God has made him such. We can fight that lordship and be broken by it—the verse says that Christ's enemies will be made his footstool—or we can submit to it in humble obedience with praise.

More of us need to begin to think of Jesus as he is today, exalted to a position of honor at God's right hand. Most people's image of Jesus is that of a baby in a manger. It is a sentimental picture best reserved for Christmas and other sentimental times. Others picture him hanging on a cross. That too is sentimental, though it is sentimentality of a different pious sort. Jesus is not in a manger today. That is past. No more is he hanging on a cross. That is past too, since Jesus came once to die for sin and after that to ascend to heaven to share in the fullness of God's power and great glory. When Stephen, the first martyr, had his dying vision of the exalted Christ it was of Jesus "standing at the right hand of God" to receive him into heaven (Acts 7:55). When John on the Isle of Patmos had his vision of Jesus it was of one who was as God himself. The apostle was so overcome by Jesus' heavenly splendor that he "fell at his feet as though dead" (Rev. 1:17).

We would do well to recover this understanding of who Jesus is and where he is now, for if we did, we would worship him better and with greater reverence. Walter Chantry says,

> Anyone who has caught a glimpse of the heavenly splendor and sovereign might of Christ would do well to imitate the saints of ages past. It is only appropriate to worship him with deep reverence. You may pour out great love in recognition of your personal relationship with him. He is your Lord. You are his and he is yours. However, you are not pals. He is Lord and Master. You are servant and disciple. He is infinitely above you in the scale of being. His throne holds sway over you for your present life and for assigning your eternal reward. A king is to be honored, confessed, obeyed and worshiped.[7]

Indeed, adds Chantry, "Such humble gestures of adoration are the response required in the gospel. 'If you confess with your mouth, "Jesus is Lord," and believe in your heart that God raised him from the dead, you will be saved' (Rom. 10:9)."[8]

The Spiritual Reign of Christ

Sitting signifies rest from Jesus' atoning work, as we will see in the next chapter, but it does not mean complete inactivity. A king rules from his throne, sitting upon it, and that is what Jesus is doing now. He is ruling from his throne in order to extend his kingdom throughout the whole world through the witness of his followers. The second section of this psalm (vv. 2–3) tells how Jesus directs his witnesses "from Zion." Two phrases in this stanza particularly show us what Jesus' reign is like.

1. *"In the midst of your enemies."* If this psalm were about a mere earthly king, it would never speak of ruling "in the midst of" enemies. That is not how earthly kings rule. They make boundaries; defend and extend their frontiers; and confront, fight, and overpower enemies. Here is a king who rules in the midst of his enemies. This can only mean that his is a spiritual rule that infiltrates the hostile powers of this world in a nearly invisible fashion. Moreover, it is a rule that he exerts indirectly, as it were, not by coming in power himself (though he will also do that in judgment at the end of time) but through his people, the church.

This verse meant a great deal to Martin Luther because of the nature of his battles at the time of the Reformation. At one point, when he was sick, he praised the psalm, saying, "If I were well, I would endeavor to make a commentary on it." Luther did get well and in time did write a commentary on Psalm 110 that ran to 120 pages. In it he said, "We must live in the midst of Christ's enemies. . . . However, it is not the meaning of this verse that we physically resist our enemies, which is part of the thinking of the anabaptists and other rebels. In his kingdom Christ has nothing to do with secular power and government. Nor are we Christians able to defeat and subdue the devil and the world by means of physical power or weapons."[9] No, said Luther. We are to fight for Christ by suffering, by faith, and by the preaching of God's Word.

The church has always gotten into deep trouble when it has tried to Christianize society, as if the secular world could be made Christian. From time to time believers suppose they can impose their idea of a just society on other people by enacting laws and proscribing civil penalties for those who break them. This is not our calling. Paul pointed out the right way when he wrote to the Corinthians, "Though we live in the world, we do not wage war as the world does. The weapons we fight with are not the weapons of the world. On the contrary, they have divine power to demolish strongholds" (2 Cor. 10:3–4).

What are our weapons? First, *participation*. Christians need to participate in secular life rather than merely shoot at secular people and what secular people are doing from the sidelines. Participation is implied in Paul's words "though we live in the world" and in the psalm's equivalent expression "in the midst of your enemies." Second, *persuasion*. Persuasion is opposed to coercion. Informed by God's Word, Christians must endeavor to persuade others of the truth. The verses from 2 Corinthians 10 that I cited earlier teach this by going on to say, "We demolish arguments and every pretension that sets itself up against the knowledge of God, and we take captive every thought to make it obedient to Christ" (v. 5). Third, *prayer*. We pray because we know that even with the best of scripturally informed arguments, without God's specific supernatural intervention the world will neither understand nor heed what we are saying.

Walter Chantry says rightly that the world is "in desperate need of a spiritual church using spiritual weapons to fight a spiritual war, under the spiritual reign of Christ."[10]

2. *"Your troops will be willing."* Those who are enlisted in Christ's service have enlisted willingly. The text says, "Your troops will be willing on your day of battle." There are no mercenaries in this battle, no slaves pressed into the ranks of Jesus' soldiers. This army is composed entirely of volunteers. True, these soldiers were not always willing—they were once as hostile to Christ and his kingdom as others still are—but they were made willing by that gentle working of Jesus' grace in their lives. Perceiving his sacrifice of himself for them and loving him for it, they have now made themselves willing sacrifices for him.

Are you willing? Have you presented yourself to Jesus as a living sacrifice? I hope you have. If not, perhaps what you need is a new vision of the exalted Lord Jesus Christ. When Isaiah saw the Lord seated on a throne, high and exalted, he heard the voice of the Lord saying, "Whom shall I send? And who will go for us?" Isaiah could only answer, "Here am I. Send me!" (Isa. 6:1–8).

Psalm 110

The Psalm Most Quoted in the New Testament: Part 2

The Order of Melchizedek

The LORD has sworn
   and will not change his mind:
"You are a priest forever,
   in the order of Melchizedek."

The Lord is at your right hand;
   he will crush kings on the day of his wrath.
He will judge the nations, heaping up the dead
   and crushing the rulers of the whole earth.
He will drink from a brook beside the way;
   therefore he will lift up his head.

verses 4–7

In the last chapter we saw how Psalm 110:1, the most quoted verse in the New Testament, defines the Messiah as the son both of David and God, a divine Messiah. Verse 1 also quotes God as giving him dominion over his enemies. That Messiah is Jesus.

Yet verse 1 is only the first of two oracles (special revelations) from God in these important seven verses, the psalm most quoted in the New Testament. The second is in verse 4, and to judge from the way it is handled, it is to be taken as being even more important than the first. It is introduced by two points of emphasis. First, we are told that the oracle is something "the LORD has sworn." God himself has given it special weight and significance. Second, we are told that "he will not change his mind." The words the Lord has sworn and about which he will not change his mind are these:

> "You are a priest forever,
>   in the order of Melchizedek."

What a strange thing to emphasize so strongly, and how neglected! Not many people in an average church would be able to explain why Melchizedek is important or even who he is.

Melchizedek appears at only three places in the Bible. He is introduced in Genesis 14, as part of the story of Abraham. After one thousand years and without any additional references, he suddenly appears again as a cryptic reference in the psalm we are studying. Then again, after another thousand years, he emerges as a major personage in Hebrews. The author of Hebrews mentions Melchizedek eight times (Heb. 5:6, 10; 6:20; 7:1, 10–11, 15, 17), uses the phrase "the order of Melchizedek" four times (Heb. 5:6, 10; 6:20; 7:17), and points us back both to the psalm and Genesis when he admonishes, "Just think how great he was" (Heb. 7:4). Let's try to discover why Melchizedek is so important, beginning with the original mention of him in Genesis.

Melchizedek, King of Salem

In Genesis 14 Abraham has succeeded in rescuing his nephew Lot, Lot's family, and Lot's possessions from a coalition of four kings who had attacked and overcome five other kings, including the king of Sodom, which is where Lot had been living. On his way back from the battle, Abraham is met by Melchizedek, who is identified as a "priest of God Most High." Melchizedek blesses Abraham, and Abraham gives him a tithe of the spoils of the battle. The entire story is told in just three verses.

> Then Melchizedek king of Salem brought out bread and wine. He was priest of God Most High, and he blessed Abram, saying,
>
>> "Blessed be Abram by God Most High,
>>   Creator of heaven and earth.
>> And blessed be God most High,
>>   who delivered your enemies into your hand."
>
> Then Abram gave him a tenth of everything (Gen. 14:18–20).

One of the problems with Melchizedek is that we have no idea who he was other than what is told us here. There is an ancient Jewish view, adopted by Martin Luther, that he was Shem, one of Noah's three sons and an ancestor of Abraham. According to the lifetime figures given in Genesis 11 he would have lived thirty-five years beyond the death of Abraham. Origin thought Melchizedek was an angel. Ambrose and some other commentators, both ancient and modern, suggest that he may have been a preincarnate appearance of Jesus Christ. There is no textual warrant for any of these ideas, and it is best to take him precisely as the author of Hebrews does, that is, simply as an important man who comes on the scene suddenly without any prior explanation. John Calvin described Melchizedek simply but respectfully as a man who, although we know nothing else about him, "alone in that land was an upright and sincere cultivator and guardian of religion."[1]

Melchizedek is not Jesus Christ, but although he is not, he is nevertheless an important Old Testament type of Christ. In that respect, two important things are told about him. First, there is his name. It is not necessarily a proper name, though it could have been. It is more of a title, meaning "king of righteousness." It means that Melchizedek stood for righteousness in an age when most other people did not. Melchizedek (king of righteousness) is a significant title for Jesus, who has become "our righteousness, holiness and redemption" (1 Cor. 1:30). Second, Melchizedek is said to have been a "king of Salem," which means "king of peace," another apt title for Jesus Christ. By becoming our righteousness and by his death on the cross Jesus has made peace between ourselves and God.

King and Priest in One Person

The second time Melchizedek appears in the Bible is in the psalm we are studying, and here he is clearly used as a type of the Messiah. The first verse described David's Lord as a divine Messiah to whom God has given dominion over enemies. The next two verses describe the extension of his rule through those who are his willing servants, that is, the church. Verse 4 adds that the Messiah will also be a priest, a priest according to "the order of Melchizedek."

The Messiah's being a priest would have been a novel and probably shocking idea to the Jews who read David's psalm initially, because kingly and priestly functions were never united in a single person in Israel. On the contrary, they were carefully kept apart. There seems to have been something like a system of checks and balances in Israel, much like we have it in the United States, where we separate the executive, legislative, and judicial branches of our government. We keep these branches apart, and we give each powers the others do not have. So also in Israel. No king could be a priest. No priest could be a king. In fact, when Uzziah, the king of Judah, attempted to offer incense to the Lord by entering the temple, where only priests were allowed to go, God judged him by afflicting him with leprosy (see 2 Chron. 26:16–23).

The reason for having a balance of governmental power is obvious: Human beings cannot be trusted with excessive or uncheckable power. As Lord Acton put it, "Power corrupts, and absolute power corrupts absolutely." Lord Acton's dictum does not apply to Jesus Christ, since he is no mere human being. Jesus is the God-man, as perfect in his divine as in his human attributes. Therefore, he (but he alone) is qualified to be both a priest and a king forever.

Melchizedek, being a type of Christ, was both; he is called "king of Salem" and "priest of God Most High" in Genesis. Psalm 110 rightly gives both titles to the Messiah, David's greater son; the first oracle noting his appointment as a king, the second as a priest (vv. 1, 4). Significantly, we find the same combination in Zechariah 6:9–15, where the Messiah is called "the Branch." It is said of him, "He will branch out from his place and build the temple of the LORD. It is he who will build the temple of the LORD, and he will be clothed with majesty and will sit and rule on his throne. And he will be a priest on his throne. And there will be harmony between the two" (vv. 12–13).

The Priestly Reign of Christ

We have looked at the first mention of Melchizedek in Genesis and the follow-up reference to Melchizedek in Psalm 110, where the oracle "you are a priest forever, in the order of Melchizedek" is cited. We must now turn to Hebrews, because the treatment of Melchizedek in Hebrews is an inspired New Testament exposition of each of the ideas in Psalm 110:4: "the LORD has sworn," "a priest forever," and "the order of Melchizedek."

1. *"The LORD has sworn."* Hebrews introduces Melchizedek as early as the fifth chapter, quoting Psalm 110:4 in verse 6 and referring to "the order of Melchizedek" again in verse 10. Then it breaks off, explaining, "We have much to say about this, but it is hard to explain because you are slow to learn" (v. 11). What the writer wants to explain is the significance of Psalm 110:4. So as soon as he gets back on track again he begins to explain the importance of God's swearing to some truth, as he does in Psalm 110, saying that an oath stresses the certainty of what is said.

> Men swear by someone greater than themselves, and the oath confirms what is said and puts an end to all argument. Because God wanted to make the unchanging nature of his purpose very clear to the heirs of what was promised, he confirmed it with an oath. God did this so that, by two unchangeable things in which it is impossible for God to lie, we who have fled to take hold of the hope offered to us may be greatly encouraged (Heb. 6:16–18).

One example is God's oath to Abraham: "I will surely bless you and give you many descendants" (Heb. 5:14). Another example, the author's main point, is God's oath in regard to Melchizedek. "Jesus . . . has become a high priest forever, in the order of Melchizedek," he says (Heb. 5:20).

This was not the case in the inauguration of Israel's priests. They were not confirmed by an oath. Because the priesthood of Jesus has been sworn to by God, his work as priest has become "an anchor for the soul, firm and secure" (Heb. 5:19). Another way of talking about this anchor is to speak of the eternal security of the believer or the perseverance of the saints. The reason the saints will persevere is that Jesus has done everything necessary for their salvation. Since he has made a perfect atonement for their sin and since God has sworn to accept Jesus' work, the believer can be as certain that he or she will be in heaven as that Jesus himself will be there.

2. *"A priest forever."* In chapter 7 the author continues his exposition of Psalm 110:4, focusing on the word "forever." He makes two points. First, because no genealogy of Melchizedek is given, this ancient king becomes an apt symbol of an eternal priesthood, that is, one without beginning or end. "Without father or mother, without genealogy, without beginning of days or end of life, like the Son of God he remains a priest forever" (Heb. 7:3).

The second point is the inverse of the first. Unlike the priesthood of Jesus, symbolized by that of Melchizedek, the ancient Jewish priesthood was not forever, since the priests followed one another in long succession and each died. Moreover, their deaths signified the transience of what they represented. "There have been many of those priests, since death prevented them from continuing in office; but because Jesus lives forever, he has a permanent priesthood. Therefore he is able to save completely those who come to God through him, because he always lives to intercede for them" (Heb. 7:23–25). The last verse of the chapter combines the idea of God's oath with the idea of forever, saying, "For the law appoints as high priests men who are weak; but the oath, which came after the law, appointed the Son, who has been made perfect forever" (Heb. 7:28).

3. *"The order of Melchizedek."* The last time the author of Hebrews mentions "the order of Melchizedek" is in 7:11, explaining that the words mean "the former regulation [order] is set aside because it was weak and useless (for the law made nothing perfect), and a better hope is introduced, by which we draw near to God" (Heb. 7:18–19). The new priesthood of Jesus is distinct from and superior to that of Aaron—it is "in the order of Melchizedek," not according to the order of Aaron—the basic point of the exposition in chapters 8 through 10. These chapters tell us three ways in which the priesthood of Jesus is superior to the priesthood of Aaron.

First, *it established a better covenant.* When the old covenant was established it was on the principle that if the people would remain faithful to God and obey God, he would protect and bless them. This was the covenant established at Mount Sinai. It was a good covenant, just as the law on which it was based was good, but the people were not able to live up to it. Therefore God pointed to a new and better covenant to come.

> The time is coming, declares the Lord,
>   when I will make a new covenant
> with the house of Israel
>   and with the house of Judah.
> It will not be like the covenant
>   I made with their forefathers
> when I took them by the hand
>   to lead them out of Egypt,
> because they did not remain faithful to my covenant,
>   and I turned away from them,
>   declares the Lord.
> This is the covenant I will make with the house of Israel
>   after that time, declares the Lord.
> I will put my laws in their minds
>   and write them on their hearts.
> I will be their God,
>   and they will be my people.
> No longer will a man teach his neighbor,
>   or a man his brother, saying, "Know the Lord,"
> because they will all know me,
>   from the least of them to the greatest.
> For I will forgive their wickedness
>   and will remember their sins no more
>
> Heb. 8:8–13; cf. Jer. 31:31–34

The covenant brought by Jesus does what the ancient covenant could not. It changes the heart, so that those who are affected by it both know and are able to obey God.

The second way Jesus' priesthood is superior to Aaron's is that *Jesus made a real atonement.* In the ninth chapter of Hebrews the author makes a contrast between the ceremonies carried out by the ancient Jewish priests and the true sacrifice for sin made by Jesus Christ. The old sacrifices were useful in teaching the way of salvation, pointing to the coming of Jesus and suggesting the nature of his work, but they did not actually remove sin and therefore did not truly clear the burdened conscience of the worshiper. "The gifts and sacrifices being offered were not able to clear the conscience of the worshiper. They are only a matter of food and drink and various ceremonial washings—external regulations applying until the time of the new order" (Heb. 9:9–10).

How different in Jesus' case! He actually made an atonement for sins. He did it by dying himself, offering his own blood in the place of those who had broken God's law. The writer argues that Jesus

> did not enter [the Most Holy Place of the tabernacle] by means of the blood of goats and calves; but he entered the Most Holy Place once for all by his own blood, having obtained eternal redemption. The blood of goats and

bulls and the ashes of a heifer sprinkled on those who are ceremonially unclean sanctify them so that they are outwardly clean. How much more, then, will the blood of Christ, who through the eternal Spirit offered himself unblemished to God, cleanse our consciences from acts that lead to death, so that we may serve the living God! (Heb. 9:12–14).

Third, Jesus' priesthood is superior because *it did not need to be repeated.* Jesus' priestly work was done once for all. Jesus made a true atonement for sins, and when he had completed his work he showed he had done it by sitting down at the Father's right hand.

Day after day every priest stands and performs his religious duties; again and again he offers the same sacrifices, which can never take away sins. But when this priest had offered for all time one sacrifice for sins, he sat down at the right hand of God. Since that time he waits for his enemies to be made his footstool, because by one sacrifice he has made perfect forever those who are being made holy (Heb. 10:11–14).

What is the conclusion? It is to leave the lesser ceremonies (or no ceremonies at all) and place one's full faith in Jesus Christ.

Therefore, brothers, since we have confidence to enter the Most Holy Place by the blood of Jesus, by a new and living way opened for us through the curtain, that is, his body, and since we have a great priest over the house of God, let us draw near to God with a sincere heart in full assurance of faith, having our hearts sprinkled to cleanse us from a guilty conscience and having our bodies washed with pure water. Let us hold unswervingly to the hope we profess, for he who promised is faithful. And let us consider how we may spur one another on toward love and good deeds. Let us not give up meeting together, as some are in the habit of doing, but let us encourage one another—and all the more as you see the Day approaching" (Heb. 10:19–25).

Have you trusted Jesus as God's appointed priest who has made atonement for your sins? If not, you have nothing to look forward to but condemnation, when he who now is offered as your Savior will appear again at the end of history as your Judge. The author of Hebrews reminds us that "the Lord will judge his people," adding, "It is a dreadful thing to fall into the hands of the living God" (Heb. 10:30–31; cf. Deut. 32:36).

The Judicial Reign of Christ

This is where Psalm 110 also ends. Psalm 110 is about the person and work of the Lord Jesus Christ, God's Messiah, in terms of (1) his enthronement; (2) his governmental rule through his people, the church; (3) his priestly work of atonement and intercession; and (4) the final judgment.

The last three verses of the psalm introduce this work of judgment, thereby moving from the Book of Hebrews to the themes of the last book of the Bible, Revelation.

In verses 5–7 God the Father and his Messiah are seen working together. The army of verses 2 and 3 has dropped out of the picture, and it is God himself, the Father and the Son, who judge and destroy all who have taken up arms against the deity. We remember that Melchizedek was a king of Salem, which means "king of peace." But here this King of Peace is engaged in a terrible war. These last verses recall Psalm 2, which say about Jesus and his enemies, "You will rule them with an iron scepter; you will dash them to pieces like pottery" (v. 9).

Alexander Maclaren says, "The choice for every man is, being crushed beneath his foot, or being exalted to sit with him on his throne. 'He that overcometh, to him will I give to sit with me on my throne, even as I also overcame, and am set down with my Father on his throne.' It is better to sit on his throne than to be his footstool."[2]

Psalm 111

An Acrostic Poem about God

Praise the LORD.

I will extol the LORD with all my heart
in the council of the upright and in the assembly.

Great are the works of the LORD;
they are pondered by all who delight in them.
Glorious and majestic are his deeds,
and his righteousness endures forever.
He has caused his wonders to be remembered;
the LORD is gracious and compassionate.
He provides food for those who fear him;
he remembers his covenant forever.
He has shown his people the power of his works,
giving them the lands of other nations.
The works of his hands are faithful and just;
all his precepts are trustworthy.
They are steadfast for ever and ever,
done in faithfulness and uprightness.
He provided redemption for his people;
he ordained his covenant forever—
holy and awesome is his name.

The fear of the LORD is the beginning of wisdom;
all who follow his precepts have good understanding.
To him belongs eternal praise.

verses 1–10

At the end of the last book of the Psalter (book four) we came across several psalms that were chiefly praise songs, each beginning and ending with the Hebrew word *hallelujah*, translated "Praise the LORD."[1] Psalm 111 is another psalm that begins with hallelujah, the first of three—Psalms 111, 112, and 113. After a break for Psalm 114 there is another grouping, Psalms 115, 116, and 117, each *ending* with hallelujah. There is also the well-known set of five psalms that close the Psalter, each of which both begins and ends with hallelujah.

Psalm 111 is an acrostic poem in which the first words of each of its twenty-two lines (minus the hallelujah of verse 1) begin with the successive letters of the Hebrew alphabet. Psalm 112 is also an acrostic poem, following a pattern identical to Psalm 111; in fact, the two psalms are an obviously matched pair.[2] The first is an acrostic poem about God; the second is an acrostic poem about the godly man. The specific verbal contents of the two psalms match even more than the patterns, for what is said about God in the first of these psalms is affirmed of the godly man in the second, which is a way of saying, "You will become like the god you worship. If you worship a false god or idol, you will become like your false god. But if you worship the true God of the Bible, you will become strong, gracious, compassionate, righteous, generous, just, and steadfast, as he is."

The theme of Psalm 111 is the goodness of God displayed in his works. The word "works" occurs in verses 2, 6, and 7; the equivalent word "deeds" in verse 3; "wonders" in verse 4.

Praise the Lord

After the initial hallelujah in verse 1, Psalms 111 and 112 each begin with a two-line sentence introducing the psalm's theme. In Psalm 112 this is a beatitude picking up on the last verse of Psalm 111 and telling us that the poem is about "the man who fears the LORD." In Psalm 111 the theme is praising God:

> I will extol the LORD with all my heart
> in the council of the upright and in the assembly.

In this verse the psalmist announces that he is going to praise God himself. He wants other people to do so too, and the bulk of the psalm gives them specific reasons and instructions for doing so. He is not asking others to do something he himself is not doing. If we want other people to praise God, we must praise God first. If we want them to love God, we must love him too. If we want others to serve God, we must serve him. We must set an example.

The writer next declares that he is going to praise God with all his heart. Some people do not praise God at all; they do not know him, so they cannot praise him. What is truly surprising is that among those who do know God, who have been introduced to him through Jesus Christ, there is so much halfhearted praise and casual devotion. It is surprising because if God is known at all, he must be known as One who is utterly worthy of our very highest praise. So let's do away with halfhearted worship. Instead, let's determine to praise God with all our heart, as the psalmist does.

Finally in this introduction the writer promises to praise God "in the council of the upright and in the assembly." "Council" probably refers to a small group of the genuinely upright. The assembly is the larger congregation. In either case the praise involved is public. That is, it is not merely the praise of private devotion but of open public testimony. In his praise of God the writer of the psalm wants to identify openly with the visible church, the assembly of believers.

The way the psalmist praises God has important bearing on how we worship God. It tells us that we should set an example by doing it, that we should worship intensely and with our whole heart, and that we should worship God publicly and identify publicly with the Christian assembly. You do the latter if you gather with the people of God to worship on the Lord's Day, but do you set an example at other times too? Do you worship wholeheartedly? The best way to worship is to prepare for worship, starting on Saturday night. You should think about Sunday and the worship that is coming, getting in a worshipful frame of mind. You should get enough rest; you would if you had an important business presentation the next morning or if you were going to compete in some important athletic contest. Should you do less for God? Is he less important?

The Works of the Lord

There is a science laboratory in Cambridge, England, called the Cavendish Laboratory, named after the eighteenth-century English chemist and physicist Sir Henry Cavendish (1731–1810). It is distinguished by having the words of Psalm 111:2 inscribed over the entrance to its building as a charter for every believing scientist:

> Great are the works of the LORD;
>   they are pondered by all who delight in them.

Sometimes Bible verses are taken out of context for such inscriptions, but here the choice is accurate since the psalmist really is thinking about the works of God in the broadest way, beginning with creation.

Later the psalmist focuses on the specific history of Israel (vv. 5–9), just as we rightly focus on God's specific works in our own lives; and after that he writes about God's even more specific acts of redemption (v. 9). Here in verses 1–3 he speaks about God's deeds generally: the greatness of his "works," the glory and majesty of his "deeds," and the unforgettable nature of his "wonders." It is a way of saying that wherever a person looks, if the person knows God and has eyes to see his wonders, the wonders of God are brilliantly displayed.

There is wonder in the heavens, in the multitude and majesty of stars, in the mysteries of quasars and black holes, in the varied distribution and composition of the planets. There is wonder in the microcosm, in quarks and neutrinos, in the cells of the body, in the mind and in matter. There is a mystery to all living things.

The unbeliever can look at these things and ponder them; many do. The Christian not only looks at them and ponders them but also delights in them, for he or she sees them as the works of an almighty and ever-glorious God. Recognizing their source leads the Christian to a delight in God himself. We can hardly miss this delight, for the adjectives that sprinkle these three verses are not just descriptive of the universe and its wonders, however much the psalmist may delight in what he sees and ponders, but of God himself. He tells us that the works of God are "great," "glorious," and "majestic" (vv. 2–3), adjectives referring also to God since he alone is truly great, glorious, and majestic. The section ends with adjectives that refer explicitly and exclusively to God, namely, "gracious" and "compassionate" (v. 4). If nothing else, God is gracious to place us in an environment of such beauty.

"Strange it is that with such evidences of a supernatural intelligence revealed in all creation that so many scientists are atheists," writes Arno C. Gaebelein. "It proves the truth of the Bible that man by nature has a darkened mind and does not know God."[3]

God's Provisions for His People

The psalmist's remembrance of God's works continues in verses 5–8, but there is a change, as the Lutheran commentator H. C. Leupold points out.[4] He notes that the verbs in this section are plain past tenses, not present tenses as the New International Version renders them, which means that they refer to specific incidents from Israel's history. Praise of God for his general works in creation has turned into praise of God for his specific saving works on behalf of the Jewish people.

In this context "food" in verse 5 is the manna God provided during the years of Israel's desert wandering. "Covenant" is the covenant established at Mount Sinai. The "works" of verse 6 are those of the exodus from Egypt. "Giving them the lands of other nations" refers to the conquest of Canaan. Verses 7 and 8 highlight the giving of God's law.

These are past events, but they continue, which is why the New International Version and others use the present tense. It is not entirely wrong to do so. God provides our food on a daily basis; Jesus taught us to pray, "Give us today our daily bread" (Matt. 6:11). As Christians we enjoy a better and more enduring covenant than the one the psalmist is referring to; the author of Hebrews says, "Jesus has become the guarantee of a better covenant" (Heb. 7:22), adding, "Christ is the mediator of a new covenant, that those who are called may receive the promised eternal inheritance—now that he has died as a ransom to set them free from the sins committed under the first covenant" (Heb. 9:15). Our exodus is the deliverance from sin (see next section); the conquest of Canaan is our promised eternal inheritance (referred to above). Lastly, the law is a permanent possession with present promises, demands, and implications; verses 7–8 say, "His precepts . . . are steadfast for ever and ever."

When we consider how good God has been to us and continues to be, can we not say with the psalmist, "I will extol the LORD with all my heart in the council of the upright and in the assembly"?

The Lord's Salvation

We have a similar parallel between God's past and present saving work in verse 9, which refers specifically to redemption, from Egypt and perhaps also from the Babylonian captivity if the psalm was written late, as most commentators believe. But how can we read verse 9—

> He provided redemption for his people;
> he ordained his covenant forever—
> holy and awesome is his name—

without thinking of the redemption from sin and its power that Jesus has achieved for us by his death on the cross? We cannot, for he is the one who has become for us "righteousness, holiness and redemption" (1 Cor. 1:30).

Redemption is a term borrowed from the ancient world of business, just as *propitiation* is borrowed from the language of religion and *justification* from the ancient world of law. Redemption refers to buying something in the marketplace and also to buying it *out* of the marketplace so it will not have to be sold there again. This means little if we think of it in regard to mere objects, but it means a great deal if we think of it in regard to people, especially slaves. To redeem a slave was to buy the slave out of the slave market so that he or she might be set free. This is what Jesus did for us. Paul touches on it in Romans 8 when he says that "through Christ Jesus the law of the Spirit of life set me free from the law of sin and death" (v. 2). He means that he was a slave to sin and death once, but Jesus had freed him from that slavery, as he has all who have been saved by him.

We have a splendid illustration of redemption in the Old Testament in the life story of Hosea, one of the minor prophets. Hosea's wife had been unfaithful to him, had fallen into slavery, and was eventually sold as a slave in the city of Samaria. God sent Hosea to buy her out of slavery, which he did for "fifteen shekels of silver and about a homer and a lethek of barley" (Hosea 3:2). For our emancipation from sin's slavery, the cost of redemption was Jesus' life.

When we were looking at the section of Psalm 111 dealing with God's general works in nature (vv. 2–4), I pointed out that the adjectives begin by describing the works but soon pass over into describing God himself. We have exactly the same thing in verses 5–9. Here the works of God are called "faithful," "just," and "trustworthy" (v. 7); "steadfast," "faithful," and "upright" (v. 8). These words even more aptly describe God himself, and the section ends with "holy and awesome is his [God's] name" (v. 9).

A Practical Conclusion

Psalm 111 has been a practical psalm exhorting us to praise God for his general and specific works: those seen in nature, in the salvation history of his people, and in redemption. So we are not surprised to find that this practical psalm also has a practical conclusion (v. 10).

> The fear of the LORD is the beginning of wisdom;
>   all who follow his precepts have good understanding.

This first part of this verse is the theme of the Bible's wisdom literature, found in various places: Job 28:28; Proverbs 1:7; 9:10; Ecclesiastes 12:13. Derek Kidner says it is "the key to what life is about," namely, that "from him, to him and through him are all things."[5]

It is probably a safe bet to say that most people today are not much interested in wisdom. They are interested in making money and in having a good time. Some are interested in knowing something, in getting an education. Almost everyone wants to be well liked. But wisdom? The pursuit of wisdom is not a popular ideal. Yet we need wisdom to run our lives, and lacking it we make shipwreck not only of our own lives but also of the lives of others. Examples are all about us.

Where does wisdom come from? How may it be found? The answer is in this verse. It says we must begin with reverence for God ("The fear of the LORD is the beginning of wisdom"), and it adds we must know God's Word, the Bible, since it is only those "who follow his precepts [who] have good understanding."

1. *Reverence for God.* The word translated "beginning" is *reshith,* which means "the starting point" or "the first principle." In other words, reverence for God is the bedrock requirement if a man or woman would be wise. This is where we go astray. Rather than bowing before God so that we might acknowledge him and thus begin our reflections on life and its purpose from this foundation and vantage point, we turn our backs on God and pursue our own "wisdom" instead. True wisdom begins with acknowledging or reverently bowing before God as God, and it progresses by getting to know God well, which includes not only our coming to know who he is but also learning that his thoughts and ways are infinitely above and beyond ours.

2. *Knowing the Bible.* It is only in the Bible and by a careful study of the Bible that God can be known and wisdom acquired. How foolish, then, that we do not take time to study the Bible carefully. Martin Luther once said,

"We are accustomed to admit freely that God is more powerful than we are, but not that he is wiser than we are. To be sure, we say that he is; but when it comes to a showdown, we do not want to act on what we say."[6]

When he was only twenty years old, Charles Spurgeon began his half-century-long career in London with a sermon on knowing God in which he argued that "the proper study of God's elect is God." Spurgeon said, "The highest science, the loftiest speculation, the mightiest philosophy, which can ever engage the attention of a child of God, is the name, the nature, the person, the work, the doings, and the existence of the great God whom he calls his Father." He argued that thinking about God improves the mind and expands it.[7]

Spurgeon was right. No people ever rise higher than their idea of God, and conversely, a loss of the sense of God's high and awesome character always involves a loss of a people's moral values and even what we commonly call humanity. We are startled by the disregard for human life that has overtaken large segments of the western world, but what do we expect when countries like ours openly turn their back upon God? We deplore the breakdown of moral standards, but what do we expect when we have focused our worship services on ourselves and our own often trivial needs rather than on God? Our view of God affects what we are and do, which is why this last verse prepares us for the teaching in the next psalm.

Psalm 112

An Acrostic Poem about Godliness

Praise the LORD.

Blessed is the man who fears the LORD,
who finds great delight in his commands.

His children will be mighty in the land;
each generation of the upright will be blessed.
Wealth and riches are in his house,
and his righteousness endures forever.
Even in darkness light dawns for the upright,
for the gracious and compassionate and righteous man.
Good will come to him who is generous and lends freely,
who conducts his affairs with justice.
Surely he will never be shaken;
a righteous man will be remembered forever.
He will have no fear of bad news;
his heart is steadfast, trusting in the LORD.
His heart is secure, he will have no fear;
in the end he will look in triumph on his foes.
He has scattered abroad his gifts to the poor,
his righteousness endures forever;
his horn will be lifted high in honor.

The wicked man will see and be vexed,
he will gnash his teeth and waste away;
the longings of the wicked will come to nothing.

verses 1–10

The last verse of Psalm 111 is the theme of Psalm 112. To put it another way, Psalm 112 picks up where Psalm 111 left

913

off. Psalm 111 ended with that classic description of true, godly wisdom found several places in the wisdom literature:

> The fear of the LORD is the beginning of wisdom;
>   all who follow his precepts have good understanding.
> To him belongs eternal praise (v. 10).

Psalm 112 describes the character of the person who fears the Lord and honestly obeys his precepts. In doing so the psalm makes the point that the person who truly loves and worships God will be like him. Anyone will be like the god he or she worships.

In the last chapter I pointed out that Psalms 111 and 112 are a matched pair in every way. They are the same length, fall into identical stanzas, and even have identical or similar phrases occurring at the same places in each. Both are precise acrostics; that is, they have twenty-two lines each of which begins with a successive letter of the Hebrew alphabet. J. J. Stewart Perowne summarizes the comparison:

> The same significant phrases occur in both, and occur in such a way as to mark the mutual relation of the two poems. In the 111th the mighty deeds, the glory, the righteousness of Jehovah are celebrated in the assembly of the upright. In the 112th the righteousness, the goodness, the blessedness of the upright themselves are described and enlarged upon. The one sets forth God, his work and his attributes; the other tells us what are the work and character of those who fear and honour God.[1]

The relationship of God to the godly person is like the relationship of the sun to the moon. The sun shines by its own glorious light. The moon does not, but still it shines, and the way it shines is by reflecting the light coming to it from the sun. If you are devoutly looking to God as you live your life, something of the glory of God will be seen in you and will be reflected from you to others. If nothing of God is reflected in you, it is a proof that you do not know him. It is because you are not truly a Christian.

A Great Beatitude

The psalm begins with a beatitude. A beatitude is a blessing that is also usually a promise. That is, it is a promise of blessing to a person who lives in a certain way. Most of us are familiar with the beatitudes with which Jesus began the Sermon on the Mount: The meek will inherit the earth, those who hunger and thirst for righteousness will be filled, and the pure in heart will see God—to give just three examples. Similarly Psalm 112:1 says,

> Blessed is the man who fears the LORD,
>   who finds great delight in his commands.

The specific blessings of the godly man or woman are described in the main part of this psalm, which follows (vv. 2–9), but this first verse has to be appropriated by itself before we get to the blessings, since it defines who the godly man is. His godliness consists of three things.[2]

1. *He fears God.* Most Christians know that when the Bible tells us to fear God it is not telling us to shake in terror before him. The fear the Bible is talking about is best described as a profound reverence; that is, we are to revere God, or stand in awe of him. On the other hand, we should not dismiss the idea of fear too easily, for in many respects God is truly terrifying. God is holy, majestic, forceful, and frighteningly opposed to everything that is unholy or would seek to diminish his glory. We cannot take God lightly. God cannot be inconsequential to us or weightless in our thinking or acting.

The person who is blessed according to this psalm is, first of all, the person who takes God seriously. Indeed, he or she takes him with full seriousness—as the starting point of everything, the critical factor in every calculation, and the end to which everything is moving and to whom we are all accountable.

2. *He obeys God.* If the great, majestic God of the Bible really is the most important thing to the godly person in every situation, he or she will obey God in every situation. In this text it is not God himself the godly person delights in, though that delight also is important. Minneapolis pastor and writer John Piper has written several books about the godly person's delight in God.[3] Here the emphasis is on conforming to God's "commands," that the godly woman or man is obedient.

3. *He delights in God's commands.* The godly person does not merely do what God says, though obedience is necessary; but he or she also delights in God's commands and obviously also in obeying them. There is a deliberate echo of the previous psalm here. Psalm 111:2 spoke of delight in God's *works.* In Psalm 112:1 we are told that God's people also delight in God's *words* (commands). Derek Kidner says rightly that "to this man God's word is as fascinating as are his works to the naturalist."[4]

We need to examine ourselves by this probing definition of the godly person. We all want and should want to be blessed by God, desiring to be in his good graces and be prospered by him. God wants to bless us too. He enjoys blessing his people, but there are conditions to blessing: We must fear or reverence him, obey him, and delight in his commandments. Putting these thoughts together with the earlier psalm, we understand that we will do these things if we truly and deeply appreciate the greatness of God in his works and to us personally.

The Blessedness of the Godly

The middle and chief section of this psalm (vv. 2–9) describes the specific blessings of the person who fears and joyfully obeys God. It does so in a remarkable way, combining two ideas. When you think of God's blessing, do you think of outward things such as wealth, health, security, or a good reputation or inward things such as godly character traits? Either one is right since both are blessings. In this section the two ideas are developed side by side: on the one hand, the visible blessings of the godly, and on the other hand, their inner godly character.

1. *Might with uprightness* (v. 2). The first blessing is on the children of the godly, saying that they will be mighty in the land. "Mighty" here means being of recognized stature or standing rather than being physically strong, and the character trait paired with this visible blessing is uprightness, a trait also mentioned again later (v. 4). Clearly there is a link between these blessings, for the verse is saying that the person who lives an upright life will see such character passed to his or her children, and they in turn will be regarded as people of high moral standing.

This generational similarity is a general observation. It applies in most cases, but it does not promise that the children of the godly will always turn out to be model citizens or suggest that disobedience in children is always their parents' fault.

2. *Riches with righteousness* (v. 3). We do not normally think of wealth being a promised blessing from God, and it is true that not all who live godly lives are prospered financially. There are many righteous persons among the poor. On the other hand, riches are said to be a gift to those who love wisdom (Prov. 3:16; 8:18; 22:4). Lest we dismiss this as being only an Old Testament idea, we should remember that Jesus said nearly the same thing in Mark 10:29–30: "I tell you the truth, . . . no one who has left home or brothers or sisters or mother or father or children or fields for me and the gospel will fail to receive a hundred times as much in this present age (homes, brothers, sisters, mothers, children, and fields—and with them, persecutions) and in the age to come, eternal life." Jesus balanced this statement by saying, "But many who are first will be last, and the last first" (Mark 10:31), as if to say that it is only a general principle and does not hold true in every case.

The second line of verse 3 is the same as the second line of verse 3 in the previous psalm but Psalm 111:3 referred to the righteousness of God and Psalm 112:3 refers to the righteousness of the godly man. This must have been an extremely important idea for the psalmist, because the same line occurs again in verse 9.

The psalmist probably had a different emphasis than we do when we consider righteousness and wealth today. We look at verse 3 and say, "If I am righteous, the chances are that I will do well in life; honesty does pay; God will probably bless me." The psalmist's point is probably something like this: "If I fear God and obey his commands, I will grow in righteousness, just as God is righteous. And, oh yes, incidentally, I will probably do well in business too." Wealth is a blessing, though it is no proof of godliness. There are many wealthy people who are scoundrels. But if we must choose between the two, from the godly person's point of view it is far more important to be godly than rich. We are told in the New Testament that "godliness with contentment is great gain" (1 Tim. 6:6).

3. *Light with compassion* (v. 4). Verse 4 is another place where Psalm 112 picks up on an idea from Psalm 111, and in precisely the same place. It is said in the preceding psalm that "the LORD is gracious and compassionate" (Ps. 111:4), an important revelation drawn from God's disclosure of his deepest character when he described himself to Moses on Mount Sinai as "the LORD, the LORD, the compassionate and gracious God, slow to anger, abounding in love and faithfulness" (Exod. 34:6).[5] Here the same terms are applied to the righteous person.

There is some difficulty determining who is the source of the light mentioned in this verse. Some have taken it as belonging to the godly man so that he becomes a light for other upright people, encouraging them. It is probably better to see it as God or God's light. Delitzsch says, "God himself is the light which arises in darkness for those who are sincere in their dealings with him."[6]

4. *Good with generosity and justice* (v. 5). "Good" is a very broad term, meaning "good things." Verse 5 is saying that good things come to the person who is generous with other people, willing to lend to those who are in need, and just in his or her affairs. Again these are characteristics affirmed of God in Psalm 111. God shows his generosity when he "provides food for those who fear him" (Ps. 111:5) and gives "the lands of other nations" for them to dwell in (Ps. 111:6). His justice is seen in both his "works" and "precepts" (Ps. 111:7).

5. *Stability with faith* (vv. 6–8). There are several temptations apt to beset a rich man: greed, abuse of the power wealth brings, indulgent vacillations, and fear that power and wealth might be lost. The latter half of this section, beginning with verse 5, shows how the godly man overcomes these temptations. Instead of being greedy, he is generous (vv. 5, 9). Instead of abusing the power wealth brings, he is just (v. 5). Instead of indulgent vacillations, he is steadfast in his way of life (v. 6). Instead of fear that his power and wealth might be lost, he is fearless because he trusts God (vv. 7–8).

Verses 6–8 emphasize the godly person's steady trust in God even when he or she receives bad news or deals with enemies. The very mention of bad news is an indication of how the earlier promises should be taken, for we are not to think that the godly person never has any trouble. He does have enemies, and he does get bad news from time to time. Nevertheless, he is not shaken either by his enemies or bad news, because his trust is in God and not in his material possessions.

It is hard not to think of Job at this point. Job had an enemy who is also our great enemy, Satan. Satan slandered Job to God, claiming that the only reason Job loved and served God was because God had made him a rich man. This was not true. So God allowed Satan to take away Job's rich store of livestock and even his family to prove it was a lie. In one day Job lost five hundred yoke of oxen and five hundred donkeys to the Sabeans, seven thousand sheep to lightning, three thousand camels to the Chaldeans; the servants who were caring for the livestock were all killed; and to top it off, all Job's children—seven sons and three daughters—were destroyed in a single evening when a tornado struck the house where they were feasting and it collapsed on them.

Here was both an enemy and bad news—bad news of the worst imaginable kind. Yet Job was a model of steadfast trust in God. When he was told of these disasters, he tore his robe and shaved his head, two ancient signs of mourning. Then stunningly, he fell to his knees and worshiped God, saying,

> Naked I came from my mother's womb,
>   and naked I will depart.
> The Lord gave and the Lord has taken away;
>   may the name of the Lord be praised (Job 1:21).

The chapter ends by saying, "In all this, Job did not sin by charging God with wrongdoing" (Job 1:22).

It takes strong character and steadfast faith in God to praise God in the midst of disaster, but it is exactly this character and trust that the person who fears God and obeys and delights in his commands acquires. The psalm says,

> He will have no fear of bad news;
>   his heart is steadfast, trusting in the Lord.
> His heart is secure, he will have no fear;
>   in the end he will look in triumph on his foes (vv. 7–8).

6. *Honor with compassion* (v. 9). The last verse of this section returns to three of the psalm's earlier themes: the godly man's generosity; his righteousness; and his well-deserved might, power, or reputation. The apostle Paul quotes this verse in 2 Corinthians 9:9 to encourage generosity in Christians.

> Remember this: Whoever sows sparingly will also reap sparingly, and whoever sows generously will also reap generously. Each man should give what he has decided in his heart to give, not reluctantly or under compulsion, for God loves a cheerful giver. And God is able to make all grace abound to you, so that in all things at all times, having all that you need, you will abound in every good work. As it is written:
>
> > "He has scattered abroad his gifts to the poor;
> >   his righteousness endures forever."
>
> Now he who supplies seed to the sower and bread for food will also supply and increase your store of seed and will enlarge the harvest of your righ-

teousness. You will be made rich in every way so that you can be generous on every occasion, and through us your generosity will result in thanksgiving to God (2 Cor. 9:6–11).

The reference to God supplying "bread for food" shows that Paul also saw the connection between Psalms 111:5 and 112:5, which I pointed out earlier.

The Life of the Wicked

I have handled verse 9 as a summary of what was written about the godly in the body of this psalm, but it would be equally right to link it to verse 10 so that these last verses together make a contrast, like Psalm 1, between two ways of life, the way of the godly and way of the wicked. Furthermore, these last two verses each have three lines and therefore fall together as opposed to the other verses of the psalm, which only have two lines. Derek Kidner says, "The companion psalm [Psalm 111], whose subject was the Lord, finished with a verse that invited man's response. The present psalm, having expounded that response, clinches the matter by showing how bitter, transient and futile is the only alternative way of life."[7]

Verse 10 says the wicked man "will gnash his teeth" when he looks on the prosperity of the righteous. I do not think that always happens in this life. The wicked often remain quite content with themselves and despise the righteous. But it will happen one day, when life is done. The Bible describes hell as a place where there is an eternal "weeping and gnashing of teeth" (Matt. 8:12). If you are not yet a Christian, don't wait until then to discover what life is actually about.

Psalm 113

Who Is Like God?

Praise the LORD.

Praise, O servants of the LORD,
praise the name of the LORD.
Let the name of the LORD be praised,
both now and forevermore.
From the rising of the sun to the place where it sets
the name of the LORD is to be praised.

The LORD is exalted over all the nations,
his glory above the heavens.
Who is like the LORD our God,
the One who sits enthroned on high,
who stoops down to look on the heavens and the earth?

He raises the poor from the dust
and lifts the needy from the ash heap;
he seats them with princes,
with the princes of their people.
He settles the barren woman in her home
as a happy mother of children.

Praise the LORD.

verses 1–9

What is God like? Have you ever asked yourself that question? It is a good question. The trouble is it is unanswerable, because there is nothing God can be compared to. He is in a category of his own, unique. Therefore, the only way we have to talk about him—and it is always inadequate—is by analogy. We can say, He is *like* a loving father. He is *like* a great king. Or less directly, we can report what he has done. We can say, God is the Creator of the heavens and the earth. Or, God is our Savior through the work of Jesus Christ.

Psalm 113 both describes God by analogy and tells what he has done, yet all the while it knows that God can never be adequately described. It asks, "Who is like the LORD our God, the One who sits enthroned on high, who stoops down to look on the heavens and the earth?" (vv. 5–6). The answer clearly is no one. No one and no thing is really like God.

Psalm 113 is the first of six psalms commonly sung by Jews at the time of the Passover, called the Egyptian Hallel. *Hallel* means "praise." These psalms were sung at the three great feasts—the feast of dedication and the feasts of the new moons—and by families at the yearly observance of the Passover. At the Passover two were sung before the meal and four afterward. Since this custom goes back a long way, we can assume that these were the psalms sung by Jesus and his disciples in the upper room before our Lord's arrest and crucifixion (Matt. 26:30; Mark 14:26).

They are called the Egyptian Hallel because the second in the series begins with the exodus from Egypt. True, it is the only psalm of the six that does; but, as Derek Kidner remarks, although "only the second . . . (114) speaks directly of the Exodus, . . . the theme of raising the downtrodden (113) and the note of corporate praise (115), personal thanksgiving (116), world vision (117) and festal procession (118) make it an appropriate series to mark the salvation which began in Egypt and will spread to the nations."[1]

A number of hymns have been based on Psalm 113 or parts of it. The best known is by Frederick W. Faber (1848), beginning,

> My God, how wonderful thou art,
> Thy majesty how bright!
> How beautiful thy mercy seat,
> In depths of burning light.

This psalm has been a blessing to the true people of God, both Jew and Gentile, through the centuries from the time of its composition.

A Summons to Praise God

Psalm 113 is a strong praise psalm. In fact, it is a superb example of what our praise of God should be. The psalm begins and ends with the words "Praise the LORD," and the first of its three stanzas repeatedly calls on all the servants of God to extol God, which is what the remainder of the psalm (stanzas two and three) does.

There is an important emphasis on the name of God in this first stanza, where the word *name* occurs three times, once in each verse. We do not think much about names today. For us they are usually just convenient tags for identifying people or things. They do not have much significance. It was quite different in Bible times, when names meant a great deal. They were thought to disclose something of the characters of the persons bearing them, and in some cases they were considered a portent bringing about the destiny the name implied. To give a person a bad name was the same thing as to curse him. To be told a person's name meant being brought into his confidence and friendship.

In the case of God "the name of the LORD" is all important, for it has to do with the revelation of who God is. In other words, it is not just any God we are to worship. We are to praise the one true "LORD," who has revealed himself in creation, on Sinai, and more recently in the person of his only Son, Jesus of Nazareth.

We must give special attention to the revelation given on Mount Sinai, because it was there that the name Jehovah was revealed to Moses, and Psalm 113 is emphasizing this important name. It is found four times in the first stanza, five if we count the opening "Praise the LORD." It is also found in verses 4 and 5 and in the closing "Praise the LORD."

There has been much debate about the meaning of this name. It is called the tetragrammaton, meaning "four letters" (the consonants *yod, hay, waw, hay*), written YHWH, and the problems come from the fact that the Jews considered this name too holy to pronounce. Therefore, the normal Hebrew vowel pointings that indicate how a word should be understood and pronounced were omitted, and as a result, no one today knows how it was pronounced.

The problem is not just in the area of pronunciation, however. That is a relatively insignificant matter. The far greater problem is how YHWH is to be understood. The consonants seem to be a form of the Hebrew verb "to be" *(hwh),* but depending on what vowels are supplied to the consonants, the verb can be understood either as a Hiphil form, indicating causality, or as a Qal form, meaning either "I am" or "I will be." If the verb is a Hiphil, indicating causality, the meaning would be "He who causes to be" or "He who brings into existence." The Jewish scholar David N. Freedman is insistent on this meaning, and there is certainly nothing wrong with it theologically since God is indeed the one who brings all things into being.

However, the only place in the Bible where YHWH is explained is Exodus 3:14, and this verse, reinforced by several New Testament passages (Matt. 22:32; Mark 12:26; John 8:58; and the important "I am" sayings in John's Gospel), seems to show that the simple meaning is preferable: "I am who I am" or "I will be what I will be." Though derived from the most basic of all verbs and expressed in the simplest verbal form, YHWH expresses a wealth of God's attributes.

1. *God is a person.* It is God who makes known his name to Moses and he does so by speaking to him. We are not dealing with the abstract God of the

Greek philosophers, with Plato's "divine reason" behind the observable particulars of life, nor with what the English scientist Sir James Jeans called "a great mathematical something." God is a divine person who has created and communicates with persons made in his image. It is because God is a person (actually three persons in one, as the doctrine of the Trinity affirms) that we can know him and fellowship with him. You cannot have fellowship with a mathematical equation or a mere cosmic force.

2. *God is self-existent.* God is self-existent, having no origins and therefore answerable to no one. In order to know something we have to determine its origins, how it came into being, what caused it. But God has no origins; nothing caused him or explains him. Hence, we cannot know God except as he reveals himself to us, and even then we do not know God in himself. We only know him anthropomorphically, that is, only to the extent that he compares himself to us and to the finite things we know.

A. W. Tozer says that the unknowability of God is one reason why philosophy and science have not always been friendly toward the idea of God. They are impatient with anything that refuses to give an accounting of itself.[2] Perhaps this is why even believing people seem to spend little time thinking about God's person and character.

3. *God is self-sufficient.* Self-sufficiency means that God has no needs, just as self-existence means that God has no origins. God does not need human beings. He did not need to create us, and having created us, he does not need us for anything we can do for him. Graciously he uses us to carry out his plans, just as he used Moses as his chosen servant to deliver Israel. But he did not need Moses any more than he needs us. God does not need helpers or defenders or worshipers. We contribute nothing to God.

John the Baptist said, "Do not . . . say to yourselves, 'We have Abraham as our father.' I tell you that out of these stones God can raise up children for Abraham" (Matt. 3:9).

When we realize that God is the only self-sufficient one, we begin to understand why the Bible has so much to say about the need for faith in God alone and why unbelief in God is such sin. If we refuse to trust God, what we are really saying is that some other thing or person is more trustworthy, which is both folly and a slander against God's character.

4. *God is eternal.* If God is the eternal "I am," as his name states, then he is everlasting, perpetual, or eternal. This quality is difficult to put into one word, hence the three words given. What they mean is that God is, has always been, and always will be, and that he is always the same in his eternal being. This attribute is beyond our full comprehension because we live in time and cannot think apart from space/time categories. Nevertheless, it is a comfort because God has set eternity in our hearts—we long to be immortal—and because we know that we shall enter into eternity if we are in him. Moses himself was aware of this comfort and wrote about it in Psalm 90.

5. *God is unchangeable.* God is immutable, meaning that God never differs from himself. What he is today he will be tomorrow. The one who "is what he is" does not evolve.

God's immutability has two important consequences for us. First, God can be trusted to remain as he reveals himself to be. The God who revealed himself to Moses is the same now as he was then. The God who revealed himself in Jesus Christ is and will always be like Jesus. God will never change in any of his attributes. God will always be sovereign, holy, wise, gracious, just, compassionate, and everything else he has revealed himself to be. Nothing will ever change God. Second, God is inescapable. He will not go away. We may try to ignore him now; but if we reject him now, we will have to reckon with him in the life to come.

God Looking Down

Having called upon the "servants of the LORD" to praise him "from the rising of the sun to the place where it sets," the psalm next turns to the praise of God directly, extolling him as the one who is "exalted over all the nations" and whose "glory [is] above the heavens" (v. 4). Verses 3 and 4 are paralleled almost exactly in Malachi 1:11, near the end of the Old Testament: "'My name will be great among the nations, from the rising to the setting of the sun. In every place incense and pure offerings will be brought to my name, because my name will be great among the nations,' says the LORD Almighty."

Verse 5 is in the middle of the psalm and is its theme, as I suggested by the way I began this study: "Who is like the LORD our God?" This is an important and often-asked question in the Old Testament. For example, it is the meaning of the name of the prophet Micah and the question he himself asks in Micah 7:18. What amazes Micah is that this great incomparable God forgives sin.

> Who is a God like you,
>   who pardons sin and forgives the transgression
>   of the remnant of his inheritance?
> You do not stay angry forever
>   but delight to show mercy.

(A more elaborate treatment of this question is in Isaiah 40:12–41:4.)

What amazes the psalmist is that God is exalted so high that he has to stoop low to see not only the earth but also the heavens, and yet at the same time he cares for the lowly. H. C. Leupold says, "He has done two things, each of which seems to make the other impossible. He has taken his seat so high that no one can match him, yet he has regard for the lowliest of the low in that he 'looks down so far.'"[3]

When we read of God stooping down to look on the heavens and the earth it is hard not to think of the Tower of Babel. In that story the people of the day decided they would build "a tower that reaches to the heavens" (Gen. 11:4). When God took notice of what they were doing, he had to "come down" from far above to see it (Gen. 11:5, 7). Anything human is infinitely beneath the infinitely exalted God. Yet the psalm goes beyond even that comparison when it says that God has to stoop to see not only the earth but also the heavens. Even the most exalted, wonderful, and glorious parts of creation are far, far beneath the Creator.

The New Testament goes beyond even the psalm when it describes how Jesus not only looked down on us to see us in our misery, sin, and sorrows but also actually came down to us to lift us up. Philippians 2:5–8 describes it.

> [He], being in very nature God,
>> did not consider equality with God something to be grasped,
> but made himself nothing,
>> taking the very nature of a servant,
>> being made in human likeness.
> And being found in appearance as a man,
>> he humbled himself
>> and became obedient to death—
>>> even death on a cross!

There is nothing more marvelous or more incomprehensible than Jesus' humiliation for our sakes. So we may well say, "Who is like the Lord our God?" and answer, "No one." No one is like our great Savior and Lord Jesus Christ.

The Downtrodden Looking Up

The last stanza of Psalm 113 tells us that God stoops down in order to lift up the downtrodden. Even better, he lifts them to be as he is. Can you see the parallel between verses 4–6 and 7–8? God is exalted over the nations, so he exalts the poor, raising them from the dust. God is enthroned on high, so he raises the poor to sit with princes.

> He raises the poor from the dust
>> and lifts the needy from the ash heap;
> he seats them with princes,
>> with the princes of their people (vv. 7–8).

These two verses are picked up almost exactly from the song of Hannah in 1 Samuel 2:8. Hannah had been childless, had prayed for a son, and was given one by God. He became the prophet Samuel, and her song is a psalm of praise to God for his goodness in giving her the child. The verses are also echoed later at a higher level in Mary's Magnificat in anticipation of the birth of her son, who was Jesus Christ (Luke 1:46–55).

Some modern, more pedantic scholars suggest that Psalm 113:9 is a weak ending. They fail to see how a psalm calling for praise of the exalted God can properly end on a reference to God's provision for "the barren woman."

> He settles the barren woman in her home
> as a happy mother of children (v. 9).

But that is exactly the point of the psalm. What is most praiseworthy about God, according to the psalmist, is that although he is infinitely exalted above everything, even the heavens, he nevertheless stoops to raise the poor from the dust, the needy from the ash heap, and even the barren woman from the disgrace her barrenness brought her in those days.

This psalm ends by saying that the great exalted God of the Bible is not only concerned about needy people in general but also with the individual. He cares about you. He cares for you and me personally. He cares for us specifically in two ways.

1. *He saves us from our sin one by one.* Not everyone has the experience in this life of being raised from the dust to a throne or from an ash heap to sit with princes, but all who are saved by Christ are lifted from the pigsty of this decadent world to sit with Jesus in his glory and rule with him. It happens one by one! In our sin you and I have been the lowest of the low, but God has raised us up through faith in Jesus Christ. Has that been your experience? Do you know Jesus not as some great Savior in general, but as your own personal Savior and Lord?

2. *He rescues us when we are cast down.* Downtrodden individuals are not a collective mass, though this is how society generally regards them. They are individual people who have suffered specific defeats or setbacks. They are not discouraged in some general way. God knows each of these persons individually. He knows you. If even the very hairs or your head are numbered (Luke 12:7), God clearly cares for you and knows exactly what you are suffering. Moreover, he is able to do something about it. He is able to lift you up and seat you with princes.

Charles Spurgeon said, "Such verses as these should give great encouragement to those who are lowest in their own esteem."[4] Has life cast you down? Turn to God who is able to lift you up, and trust him to do it. Then do as the psalm finally does: Praise the Lord!

Psalm 114

Make Way before God

When Israel came out of Egypt,
*   the house of Jacob from a people of foreign tongue,*
Judah became God's sanctuary,
*   Israel his dominion.*

The sea looked and fled,
*   the Jordan turned back;*
the mountains skipped like rams,
*   the hills like lambs.*

Why was it, O sea, that you fled,
*   O Jordan, that you turned back,*
you mountains, that you skipped like rams,
*   you hills, like lambs?*

Tremble, O earth, at the presence of the LORD,
*   at the presence of the God of Jacob,*
who turned the rock into a pool,
*   the hard rock into springs of water.*

*   verses 1–8*

A person who is not familiar with the psalms might suppose that they are very much alike. But as I have worked my

927

way through a careful study of them, one thing that has impressed me greatly is that each psalm is unique. Some are sad, some are happy. Some deal with national defeats or victories, some are entirely personal. Some deal with sin, others with praise, still others with trying to find the right way in confusing situations. Their structures vary too. Some are lengthy rehearsals of past historical events. Some are short. Some are acrostics. Some are lyrics.

Psalm 114 is a little masterpiece. Charles Spurgeon said it is "sublime."[1] Derek Kidner focuses on the fresh, exuberant tone of this psalm, noting how different it is from the actual struggles, doubt, and sin of the exodus. "Here is the Exodus not as a familiar item in Israel's creed but as an astonishing event: as startling as a clap of thunder, as shattering as an earthquake."[2] Isaac Watts, the English poet and hymn writer, called it "an admirable ode."[3] He loved this little lyric so much that he rendered it into a six-verse poem of his own, beginning,

> When Israel, freed from Pharaoh's hand,
> Left the proud tyrant and his land,
> The tribes with cheerful homage own
> Their King, and Judah was his throne.

Psalm 114 is the second of the six praise songs known as the Egyptian Hallel (Psalms 113–18; cf. p. 921). It falls into four matched stanzas, like verses of a hymn. As far as the tone goes, it is a bit like our hymn "Onward Christian Soldiers." However, here the triumph is not that of God's people but of God himself. God is going before his people, and it is before him that the seas draw back and the mountains skip like rams.

A Kingdom of Priests

Each stanza of this psalm is extraordinary in its own way, and the extraordinary thing about the first stanza is its description of Judah as God's sanctuary and Israel as his dominion. The names Judah and Israel are not being used in this psalm to denote the two separated parts of the nation as it existed after the split into the northern and southern kingdoms in the time of Rehoboam; they are two names for the one people that came out of Egypt at the exodus. This one people is declared to be both God's sanctuary and God's kingdom.

When God came down at Sinai and then took up a symbolic residence in the form of the Shekinah glory that filled the wilderness tabernacle and later the temple of Solomon in Jerusalem, Israel was literally God's sanctuary, or holy place, a place set apart by God's presence. Since God came not merely to be among but also to rule his people, the nation also became his unique dominion, or kingdom. No nation but Israel was ever a theocracy, that is, a nation ruled directly by God. No other nation was ever his sanctuary. Israel's experience was a fulfillment of the promise of God spoken at

Sinai, recorded in Exodus 19:6, "Although the whole earth is mine, you will be for me a kingdom of priests and a holy nation."

Yet although it is true that no other *nation* has ever been constituted a kingdom of priests and a holy nation, there is a *people* that has been, and that people is the church, the people of God. We are made God's sanctuary and kingdom by the presence of God in our midst. Do you remember how Peter referred to God's people in his first letter? Thinking of Exodus 19:6 and possibly Psalm 114:2, Peter wrote of the church, "But you are a chosen people, a royal priesthood, a holy nation, a people belonging to God, that you may declare the praises of him who called you out of darkness into his wonderful light" (1 Peter 2:9). How do we, the church, become God's sanctuary and dominion? We become a royal priesthood because of the presence of the Holy Spirit in the heart and life of every Christian. We become a dominion because of Jesus' rule over us as King.

1. *A royal priesthood.* Jesus Christ is the great priest, our high priest. By the sacrifice of himself for us he became both the sacrifice and the priest who offered the sacrifice, and he continues as our great high priest in heaven by interceding for us before the throne of God the Father.

We have an example of Jesus' work in his intercession for Peter. Peter had boasted that although the other disciples might forsake Jesus, he, Peter, would stand by him and be faithful; but Jesus told Peter, "Simon, Simon, Satan has asked to sift you as wheat. But I have prayed for you, Simon, that your faith may not fail. And when you have turned back strengthen your brothers" (Luke 22:31–32). Later that same evening Peter was frightened by Jesus' arrest and denied him three times when challenged in the courtyard of the high priest. However, his faith did not fail. When what he had done became clear to him, Peter was mortified and wept bitterly. He was humbled. It was a much stronger Peter who bowed before the Lord in Galilee and was recommissioned by him to his service (cf. John 21:15–19).

It is in this area of intercession that you and I, the members of the church, are priests. We cannot offer our lives on behalf of other people for their salvation, as Jesus did—only he is the Savior—but we can pray for others and be heard, as Jesus was. We can also offer ourselves to God as living sacrifices, which is what Paul urges in Romans 12:1–2. In this way it is not only Israel that was God's sanctuary; we are too.

2. *A holy nation.* We are also a nation of those in whom Jesus Christ rules. The Book of Revelation says,

> You have made them to be a kingdom of priests to serve our God,
>   and they will reign on the earth (Rev. 5:10).

How shall we reign? By serving others, for that is how Jesus rules in our midst. He does not lord it over us as a tyrant. Rather, he works for our good. Our rule is found not in privilege but in responsibility.

Out of Egypt

If it is the essence of poetry to capture a great deal of substance in a small space and in memorable language, then the second stanza of Psalm 114 (like the other stanzas) is wonderfully poetic. In four lines it captures the whole of the desert experience after the people had been called out of Egypt by God.

The first line refers to the parting of the Red Sea at the beginning of the journey, when the people were still being pursued by the Egyptians. As Moses stretched out his hand over the sea a strong east wind began to blow that drove the sea back, turning the sea bottom into dry land. The people crossed over in the morning, after which the wind ceased, the sea returned, and the pursuing armies of the king of Egypt were drowned. The second line of the stanza refers to driving back the waters of the Jordan River so the people could pass into Canaan at the end of their desert years. The last two lines (v. 4) refer to the trembling of the earth when God came down on Mount Sinai to give the people his law. Exodus says, "Mount Sinai was covered with smoke, because the LORD descended on it in fire. The smoke billowed up from it like smoke from a furnace, the whole mountain trembled violently, and the sound of the trumpet grew louder and louder" (Exod. 19:18–19). The Book of Hebrews reports, "The sight was so terrifying that [even] Moses said, 'I am trembling with fear'" (Heb. 12:21).

What Possible Cause?

What could possibly have caused such disturbances in the natural course of nature—the sea to part, the river to reverse its flow, the majestic peaks of Sinai to tremble? This is what the third stanza of the psalm asks rhetorically:

> Why was it, O sea, that you fled,
> O Jordan, that you turned back,
> you mountains, that you skipped like rams,
> you hills, like lambs?

In our text these lines are joined into one long interrogatory sentence, but in the Hebrew they are actually four teasing questions (teasing because the author already knows the answer and is asking them only for effect). At no place in the psalm has God yet been mentioned by name. The English translators have added the possessive form of the word "God" in verse 2, rendering "Judah became God's sanctuary," judging that in English it is improper to have a pronoun without a clear antecedent. But the word "God" is absent from the Hebrew text. The original merely has "his." So God has not been mentioned, and most certainly there has been no mention of God's name, Yahweh or Jehovah. The author must have been having fun as he wrote, knowing the answer and knowing we know the answer too, but holding it off. What could have caused the sea to part, the river to turn back, and the hills to tremble? he asks. For twelve lines he has allowed our interest to build for dramatic effect.

God, the God of Jacob

At last in the final stanza, the expected answer comes. It was "the presence of the LORD, . . . the presence of the God of Jacob" (v. 7). Seas, rivers, and mountains move only in the presence of their Maker. Hence, it was God alone who brought his people "out of Egypt" (v. 1) and "turned the rock into a pool, the hard rock into springs of water" (v. 8).

This is the climax of the psalm. In the New Testament Christians have an excellent equivalent of Psalm 114 in the apostle Paul's equally poetic statement in Romans 8 of the believers' security in Christ. The psalmist had asked the question, If God is for his people, what can possibly stand in their way to oppose them? The answer is, Nothing at all, neither seas nor rivers nor mountains. Similarly, the apostle completes his classic unfolding of the gospel message by asking,

If God is for us, who can be against us? He who did not spare his own Son, but gave him up for us all—how will he not also, along with him, graciously give us all things? Who will bring any charge against those whom God has chosen? It is God who justifies. Who is he that condemns? Christ Jesus, who died—more than that, who was raised to life—is at the right hand of God and is also interceding for us. Who shall separate us from the love of Christ? Shall trouble or hardship or persecution or famine or nakedness or danger or sword? As it is written:

"For your sake we face death all day long;
we are considered as sheep to be slaughtered."

No, in all these things we are more than conquerors through him who loved us. For I am convinced that neither death nor life, neither angels nor demons, neither the present nor the future, nor any powers, neither height nor depth, nor anything else in all creation will be able to separate us from the love of God that is in Christ Jesus our Lord (Rom. 8:31–39).

Sometimes Christians are accused of being unrealistic about life, as if it were nothing but a bowl of cherries for them, but that was not true of Paul. When Paul wrote that nothing "will be able to separate us from the love of God that is in Christ Jesus our Lord," he was not closing his eyes to reality or shutting his ears to the hostile and destructive forces that surround us. On the contrary, he opens his arms to these forces and invites them to come forward, saying nevertheless that they will never defeat God or succeed in detaching us from his love in Jesus Christ.

What are the forces arrayed against us? Paul lists seven. Although they are formidable, all will bow before the presence of our God.

1. *Trouble.* "Trouble," or as the older King James Version has it, "tribulation," means being pressed down by life so that we feel crushed by it. You may have experienced trouble. You may have been abused as a child, lost your job, been deprived of a husband or wife, or undergone severe illness. Paul says that no tribulation, however severe it may be, will separate you from Christ's love.

2. *Hardship.* "Hardship" is slightly different from "trouble." The Greek word is composed of two separate words that mean a "narrow space or territory." So the idea is not so much being pressed down by life as being confined.

Take the example of a man who is in a dead-end job. He entered his company with hopes for advancement, but he is in his late forties and has been passed over for promotions several times. It is getting to where he cannot make a good lateral move. Meanwhile, he has a wife and children to support. There is a mortgage to pay. He would like to be free of these confining circumstances, but he knows that he cannot break free and still honor his commitments. Or imagine a woman in her thirties with two or three children making tremendous demands on her, who has to survive on a rather meager budget and who knows there is no immediate future for her apart from the present circle of school, supermarket, baby-sitters, and the other marks of a confined domestic life.

How are you to triumph in such tight circumstances? It is to realize that God has fixed his love upon you and that nothing is ever going to separate you from his love. You may be in narrow straits now, but you are an heir to heaven, and one day your horizons will be as vast as the universe and as soaring as the stars. Nothing will deprive you of this destiny.

3. *Persecution.* The Greek word for "persecution" denotes relentless attempts to do harm. Very few of us suffer much outright persecution today, though Christians in other parts of the world endure it; but there are often subtle persecutions, and these will probably become stronger and more open if the present secularizing trends of western life continue.

Two things we can be sure of regarding persecutions: First, they are a normal response to any forthright Christian witness or stand, and second, we will experience them to the extent that we confront the world with Christ's claims. Jesus said, "In this world you will have trouble," but he added, "Take heart! I have overcome the world" (John 16:33). Persecutions may separate us from a more lucrative worldly future or a more attractive image before the world, but persecutions will never separate us from Christ's love.

4. *Famine.* The ancient world knew famine in a way very few today do, though there are places that experience chronic famine, such as areas of North Africa. Hunger is a terrible thing for those who experience it, but even hunger cannot detach us from Christ.

5. *Nakedness.* Today this word means a state of undress normally associated with sex or pornographic magazines, but in Paul's day it had to do with

poverty so severe that a person was unable to buy the clothes he or she needed. It is a corresponding term to famine and, like it, may refer to economic hard times deriving from natural disasters or war.

6. *Danger.* Dangers are of various types, though the focus here is on dangers to which Christians are exposed simply because they are Christians. In some places Christians are arrested, tried, and imprisoned. In others they are attacked, beaten, and even killed.

7. *Sword.* This last term pushes the violence implied in the earlier ones to its furthest extremity, meaning circumstances in which Christians are executed or even murdered for their faith. Organizations dealing with international violations of human rights say that even today as many as 600,000 Christians are killed every year for their faith. Even if we are not literally being put to death for our religion, Christians nevertheless are often considered sheep fit only to be slaughtered, as Paul says. If God were not our protector, even in modern enlightened western lands like the United States of America, we would soon be cut off. It is the Lord's providence that averts such injuries, or overrules events for the protection of his people.

In view of the many dangers, toils, and snares that come into the lives of Christians, how can Paul say that there is nothing that can separate us from Christ's love? It is because of the power of the God before whom no evil can stand and because of the nature of God's covenant love. In view of that power and steadfast love, we may well look at the troubles of this life and cry out boldly, "Make way before God!"

Tremble, O Earth, before God

Here is one last thought for those who have not yet believed in Christ. Notice how the last stanza speaks of the earth trembling before the approach of God. The startling and utterly inexplicable thing is that human beings, who are in far greater danger than the earth, which is actually in no danger at all, fail to do what the earth does. Human beings face judgment apart from Jesus Christ. Yet they go on as if all is well with them and as if they do not need a Savior.

If that has been true of you, I encourage you to learn from nature even if you will learn nowhere else. An earlier psalm says, "Kiss the Son, lest he be angry and you be destroyed in your way, for his wrath can flare up in a moment. Blessed are all who take refuge in him" (Ps. 2:12).

Psalm 115

The Victors' Psalm at Agincourt

Not to us, O L<small>ORD</small>, not to us
but to your name be the glory,
because of your love and faithfulness.

Why do the nations say,
"Where is their God?"
Our God is in heaven;
he does whatever pleases him.
But their idols are silver and gold,
made by the hands of men.
They have mouths, but cannot speak,
eyes, but they cannot see;
they have ears, but cannot hear,
noses, but they cannot smell;
they have hands, but cannot feel,
feet, but they cannot walk;
nor can they utter a sound with their throats.
Those who make them will be like them,
and so will all who trust in them. . . .
It is not the dead who praise the L<small>ORD</small>,
those who go down to silence;
it is we who extol the L<small>ORD</small>,
both now and evermore.

Praise the L<small>ORD</small>.

verses 1–8, 17–18

Henry V of England was a remarkable king who might have become emperor of Europe if he had not died of a fever in France at the age of thirty-five. He had been wild and frolicsome in his younger days, a lifestyle effectively dramatized by Shakespeare in *Henry IV, Parts 1 and 2,* but he changed when he assumed the throne, becoming "honest, grave and modest," as one contemporary historian has recorded.[1]

Henry dedicated himself to uniting Christendom against the advancing Turks, conquering France, the hereditary enemy of England, on the way. So on August 11, 1415, he left England with 1,300 ships and 11,000 men, landed at Harfleur near the mouth of the Seine, and after capturing that city advanced toward Calais. The French met him at Agincourt on October 25, St. Crispin's Day. The opposing army relied on its mounted cavalry, but its knights were no match for the English bowmen. Their horses were mired in mud caused by the heavy fall rains, and they were unable to advance against the sharp stakes the English had planted at an angle to protect their bowmen. When the horses turned back they pressed against their own army, and the English fell upon the chaotic mass of retreating soldiers with maces, hatchets, and swords. King Hal fought in the thick of the battle, too excited for fear, and the triumph was overwhelming. French historians put the English losses at 1,600 men against the French losses of 10,000.[2] In his patriotic play *Henry V* Shakespeare puts the English losses at just four commanders and twenty-five common soldiers!

Several years before Agincourt, when he had been called to share in the government by his father, Prince Hal had been given Psalm 115:1 as a guide. Now as Henry V, the king commanded the victorious English armies to kneel in the mud of Agincourt and sing the hymn together: *Non nobis, Domine, sed tibi sit gloria* ("Not to us, O Lord, but to thyself be glory"). In Shakespeare's version the king declares, "O God, thy arm was here; and not to us, but to thy arm alone, ascribe we all."[3]

Most of the commentators on this psalm do not see it as a victory hymn but, to the contrary, as a plea for God's help emerging from a time of distress and discouragement in Israel. Their reasons are largely based on verse 2, where the heathen are reported as taunting Israel with the query, "Where is their God?" It is a reasonable position, but I confess that I do not see it this way. I think the tone of the psalm is anything but distress and discouragement. Its dominant note is trust in God (vv. 9–11). I think it is saying, God has helped us in the past; he will help us in the future; therefore trust him, and tell others how great our God is.

The opinion of the majority of scholars is that the psalm is liturgical, intended to be sung by alternating groups of worshipers: the priests, the high priest, the people, and so on. It reads that way, but it is useless to spend time trying to decide who said what part. The scholars themselves differ widely.

This is the third psalm in the Egyptian Hallel (Pss. 113–18).

The Gods of the Heathen

The first major section of the psalm, after the thematic statement of verse 1, is the polemic found in verses 2–8 against idols. It is the first polemic against idols in the Psalter, though there was one brief reference to idols in Psalm 96:5. This infrequency is somewhat surprising but may indicate that Psalm 115 was written after the Jews' return from the Babylonian captivity, where they would have witnessed the Babylonians' idol worship firsthand.[4] These verses are highly sarcastic and profoundly mocking, much like several passages in Isaiah (Isa. 44:6–20; 46:5–7; similarly Deut. 4:28; 28:36; Jer. 2:8; 16:19; Hab. 2:18; Isa. 41:21–24).

Idols are only objects made by human hands; hence, they are less significant than those who made them, even if they are made of precious metals such as gold and silver. They are certainly not gods. The psalmist cries,

> They have mouths, but cannot speak,
>   eyes, but they cannot see;
> they have ears, but cannot hear,
>   noses, but they cannot smell;
> they have hands, but cannot feel,
>   feet, but they cannot walk;
>   nor can they utter a sound with their throats (vv. 5–7).

I have not found Saint Augustine's massive commentary on the psalms to be very helpful for studying the psalms today, since he sees almost all that is in the psalms as prophecies of Christ; but Augustine, like the Israelites, had witnessed the futility of pagan idol worship firsthand, and his comments about verses 5–7 are both wise and witty. "Even their artist surpasses them, since he had the faculty of molding them by the motion and functions of his limbs. . . . Even you surpass them, though you have not made these things, since you do what they cannot do. Even beasts excel them. . . . For they see and hear and smell and walk, and some apes, for instance, handle with hands." He observes that mice, snakes, and birds have sometimes made their home in the larger idols or settled on them. "A man then moves himself that he may frighten away a living beast from his own god; and yet worships that god who cannot move himself, as if he were powerful, from whom he drove away one better than the object of his worship." At the end of this sharp paragraph Augustine adds the greatest indignity of all: "Even the dead surpass a deity who neither lives nor has lived."[5]

Worshiping an invisible God was incomprehensible to Israel's pagan neighbors. Even the great Roman general Pompey was surprised to find nothing in the Most Holy Place of the temple when he looked into it. But there was a profound and important reason for God's forbidding the use of images in his worship: namely, God cannot be represented by idols without being grossly misrepresented. God is not less real than the material idol but infinitely more real, infinitely greater, infinitely higher. Thus any representation of God by anything material merely debases God and misleads the worshiper.

This debasement of God by idol worship is why the second commandment is so strong.

You shall not make for yourself an idol in the form of anything in heaven above or on the earth beneath or in the waters below. You shall not bow down to them or worship them; for I, the LORD your God, am a jealous God, punishing the children for the sin of the fathers to the third and fourth generation of those who hate me, but showing love to thousands who love me and keep my commandments (Exod. 20:4–6).

Idols not only mislead their worshipers, but they also debase them, which is why this section closes by saying, "Those who make them will be like them, and so will all who trust in them" (v. 8). It means that human beings are drawn downward, not upward, by false gods.

Trust in the Lord

What should the people of God, those who know the true God of Israel, do? They should worship God, of course, but the next stanza of Psalm 115 (vv. 9–11) says something equally significant. It tells us that the people of God should trust God. Why? Because he is our true "help and shield." The idols offer nothing; they are utterly impotent, as has just been described. By contrast, God lifts the downtrodden, helps us in our weakness, and shields us from our foes.

There is a lot of repetition in this psalm, and these three verses are almost entirely repetition. They repeat three times the idea of trusting God, calling on Israel, the house of Aaron (the priests), and all who fear God to trust him.

> O house of Israel, *trust in the LORD*—
> he is their help and shield.
> O house of Aaron, *trust in the LORD*—
> he is their help and shield.
> You who fear him, *trust in the LORD*—
> he is their help and shield (italics added).

I sometimes say that if God tells us something once we should listen very carefully, because he is God. If he says something twice we should pay the most strict attention. How then if he repeats something three times? In that case we should drop everything else we are doing, give our full attention to, study, ponder, memorize, meditate on, and joyfully obey what God has said. In this case, we should "trust in the Lord" and not the other things that so easily take God's proper place in our lives.

Do you trust him? We say we do, but do we trust him really? I think of the famous acrobat of the last century, Jean Francois Gravalet, known as Blondin because of his blond hair. His most acclaimed feat was crossing Niagara Falls on a tightrope 160 feet above the water. On one occasion he went halfway across, stopped to cook an omelette, ate it, then went on to the other side. On another occasion he carried his manager across the falls on his back. Afterward he turned to a man in the crowd and asked him, "Do you think I could do that with you?"

"Of course," the man said. "I just saw you do it."

"Well, then," said Blondin, "hop on and I'll carry you across."

"Not on your life," said the bystander.

So it is with us. We say we trust God, but when it comes to an actual test we fail to believe him.

The Lord's Blessing

If we do trust the Lord, will we be disappointed? Those who trust in their idols or false gods will be disappointed, because the idols are nothing and can do nothing. The worshiper will get nothing from them. But those who trust God will never be disappointed, because he is the living, true, compassionate God who delights to do good to those who seek, trust in, and obey him.

Stanza four (vv. 12–13) contains more repetition, corresponding to the repetitive sentences already found in stanza three (vv. 9–11). In stanza three the "house of Israel," the "house of Aaron," and "all who fear him" were challenged to trust God. In stanza four these same people are addressed and are declared to be recipients of God's blessing. Plus there is an initial general statement that God "will bless us."

> The LORD remembers us and *will bless* us:
>   He *will bless* the house of Israel,
>   he *will bless* the house of Aaron,
> he *will bless* those who fear the LORD—
>   small and great alike (italics added).

What is new in this stanza is its emphasis on the blessing of God—for "small and great alike." Lest we miss this point, the next stanza elaborates on it by pronouncing a blessing on both the adult people of God and their children. God's blessing is for you, whoever you may be, if you will only stop trusting in yourself and your own devices and instead begin to trust God.

God blesses small and great alike with salvation. Not all are being saved. No one who expects God to recognize his or her own good works or merit will enter heaven. Salvation is by the grace of God through the work of Christ alone. If you will come that way, trusting him rather than yourself, then you will be saved, even if you are poor or uneducated or of low esteem either in your own or others' eyes. Children may be saved. The despised may be saved. Those who are overlooked or abused may be saved. The text says, "he will bless those who fear the LORD—small and great alike" (v. 13).

God blesses small and great alike in matters of the Christian life. You do not have to be a highly favored individual to grow in grace and in the knowledge of our Lord Jesus Christ. In fact, it is often the disfavored and disadvantaged who grow most and deepest, because they are not trusting their own wisdom or strength but in the Lord. The Bible says, "If any of you lacks wisdom, he should ask God, who gives generously to all without finding fault, and it will be given to him" (James 1:5). Proverbs says,

> Trust in the LORD with all your heart
>> and lean not on your own understanding;
> in all your ways acknowledge him,
>> and he will make your paths straight (Prov. 3:5–6).

God blesses small and great alike in the hour of death. If you are trusting him, how could it be that the one who has been faithful to bless you throughout your life should abandon you in death's hour? Rather the opposite is the case: God will be even closer to you then. The very next psalm says, "Precious in the sight of the LORD is the death of his saints" (Ps. 116:15).

Praise the Lord

So what should our response to God be? Since God is all-powerful, unlike the idols who can do nothing, we should trust him. But further, what should our response be to his goodness to us and faithfulness to bless us—small and great alike? The last stanza of Psalm 115 suggests two additional answers.

1. *Be faithful stewards.* Verse 16 says, "The highest heavens belong to the LORD, but the earth he has given to man." This verse does not mean that God has abandoned all interest in the earth or merely, following up on verse 15, that God has decided to keep heaven for himself but give the earth to man. It means that the God who is "the Maker of heaven and earth" (v. 15), and therefore possesses both, has made men and women stewards of the material world so that they are responsible to him for what they do with it. They can use it to enrich themselves, often at the expense of others or even of the world itself, as many do. They can abuse creation. Or they can use their share of this world's goods and resources to honor God.

Lord Burghley was the greatest statesman in England during the reign of Queen Elizabeth, and he was a diligent student of the psalms all his life. When he came to die, his will, dated October 20, 1579, disposed of his lands and wealth in a manner that he hoped, he said, "shall not offend God, the giver of them all to [him]; considering, as it is in the psalm, 'Coelum coeli Domino, terram dedit filiis hominum ("The whole heavens are the Lord's; the earth he has given to the children of men," Ps. 115:16).'"[6] During his lifetime Burghley had used his wealth to honor God. He wanted to do the same thing when he died.

2. *Praise God constantly.* We must praise God as the wonderful, reliable, and benevolent God he is, letting others know about it. We should do this as long as we live, so that God's people extol him before others "evermore," as the psalm says. The last words are a challenge.

> It is not the dead who praise the LORD,
>> those who go down to silence;
> it is we who extol the LORD,
>> both now and evermore.

> Praise the LORD.

These verses do not argue against belief in the afterlife, as some tunnel-vision scholars have suggested. They merely state the obvious, that no praises are given to God on earth by dead people. The dead are silent. Therefore if we are going to praise God, as we should and must do if we are Christians, it is going to have to be now while we are living. Like the English at Agincourt who survived the battle, we Christians have been given tremendous spiritual victories. We could describe them as victories over sin, death, and the devil. The question is, Do we acknowledge these victories, remember them, and praise God for them?

Spurgeon wrote, "Though the dead cannot, the wicked will not and the careless do not praise God, yet we will shout 'Hallelujah' for ever and ever."[7]

Psalm 116

Help of the Helpless

I love the LORD, for he heard my voice;
*   he heard my cry for mercy.*
Because he turned his ear to me,
*   I will call on him as long as I live. . . .*

How can I repay the LORD
*   for all his goodness to me?*
I will lift up the cup of salvation
*   and call on the name of the LORD.*
I will fulfill my vows to the LORD
*   in the presence of all his people.*

Precious in the sight of the LORD
*   is the death of his saints.*
O LORD, truly I am your servant;
*   I am your servant, the son of your maidservant;*
*   you have freed me from my chains.*

I will sacrifice a thank offering to you
*   and call on the name of the LORD.*
I will fulfill my vows to the LORD
*   in the presence of all his people,*
in the courts of the house of the LORD—
*   in your midst, O Jerusalem.*

Praise the LORD.

verses 1–19

Psalm 116 is a hymn by an individual celebrating God's deliverance from a sickness so severe he thought he was going to die. More than that, it is a poem about prayer and thanksgiving. It begins by stating the writer's love for God *because* God heard his cry for mercy. This means that he prayed or "called" on God and God heard him. Because of this, he says, "I will call on him as long as I live" (v. 2). The two statements "I called" and "I will call" are repeated throughout the psalm, in verses 2, 4, 13, and 17. They teach that God cares for those who are helpless, that he hears their prayers and saves them when they cannot save themselves. Henry F. Lyte prays to the God of the helpless in the hymn "Abide with Me," written in 1847.

> When other helpers fail, and comforts flee,
> Help of the helpless, O abide with me.

The fact that this individualistic psalm is part of the Egyptian Hallel (Pss. 113–18) is a bit puzzling at first, but the deliverance of the nation has parallels in God's deliverance of individuals, and therefore individuals as well as the people as a whole should praise God. You should praise him, and so should I. "I," "me," or "my" occurs in every verse of the psalm but two (vv. 5, 19). "I" occurs eighteen times, "my" nine times, and "me" seven times in the New International Version.

The Septuagint and Vulgate treat Psalm 116 as two separate psalms, the first being verses 1–9, the second, verses 10–19.[1] The verses belong together, but the fact that they have been divided indicates an easy two-part division of the psalm. In the first part the writer tells what God has done for him. In the second part he tells what he will do as a response. This grouping may be a bit too simplistic; themes found in either part one or two are also found in the other part, and there are conclusions about the character and ways of God that are scattered throughout and draw the psalm together.

Part One: What God Did for the Psalmist

In general the first eleven (or nine) verses of the psalm tell what God did for the psalmist: God delivered him from the threshold of the grave.

> The cords of death entangled me,
>   the anguish of the grave came upon me;
>   I was overcome by trouble and sorrow (v. 3).

> I was in great need (v. 6).

> For you, O Lord, have delivered my soul from death,
>   my eyes from tears,
>   my feet from stumbling (v. 8).

> I believed; therefore, I said,
>> "I am greatly afflicted" (v. 10).

The theme of deliverance dominates part one, but it also appears as an echo in part two: "You have freed me from my chains" (v. 16). What was this affliction? It could be nearly anything, but it is probably best to take the words at face value. The psalmist was sick to the point of death, and God delivered him.

There is an important link here between the past, the present, and the future. God heard the psalmist's prayer; therefore, he hears and will hear. God delivered him; therefore, he delivers and will deliver. In his helpful exposition of the psalms Alexander Maclaren rightly reminds us that this link is possible only because God is unchanging. Everything connected with mere human beings changes. Even the supposed "fixed" laws of nature are not permanent. One day the sun will cease to rise, for the heavens and the earth will pass away. Only God is unchanging. Because he is, we can count on him to do in the present and future what he has in the past. Maclaren says, "His past is the guarantee and the revelation of his future, and every person that grasps him in faith has the right to pray with assurance."[2]

The last two verses of this section, verses 10 and 11, are hard to understand, and the result has been somewhat different translations in the versions. The problem is that the connecting Hebrew particle translated "therefore" in the New International Version ("I believed; therefore, I said . . .") can mean different things. Roy Clements spells out four possible translations before settling finally on the New International Version rendering.

1. *"I believed even when I said . . ."* "Even when" would mean that the writer had said some wrong things when he was sick but had been trusting God even then. This is a true picture of what we all sometimes do. We believe even when we speak or act badly. The problem with this translation, as Clements writes, is that it "seems to strike a rather smug note which does not fit easily with [the] mood of total helplessness the psalmist is confessing. It is as if he was rather congratulating himself on how tenacious his faith had really been in spite of all his pessimistic comments."[3] We can probably lay this translation aside.

2. *"I believed even though I said . . ."* If "even though" is the meaning, the sense of these verses would be one of clarification. The psalmist had said something in his sickness that might be misconstrued as if he had abandoned his faith. Now he is trying to set the record straight. H. C. Leupold takes this approach and suggests this paraphrase: "I did not cast away my faith at the time when I said what could be misconstrued; true, I was greatly afflicted and spoke under the stress of strong emotion; but what I said at the time was: 'All men are utterly unreliable.'" He continues, "That was, however, not so much a pessimistic reflection upon how evil other men are

but rather a statement to the effect that, in the last analysis, help must be sought from" God alone.[4] Again, this is possible, but it is a bit too elaborate an explanation to be convincing.

3. *"I believed **because** I said . . ."* "Because" would mean that faith was something the writer came to simply because he had nowhere to turn but to God. He believed, but it was out of sheer desperation. J. J. Stewart Perowne explains, "He *stays himself* upon God ('I believe'), for he had looked to himself, and there had been nothing but weakness; he had looked to other men and found them all deceitful."[5]

4. *"I believed; **therefore** I said . . ."* The final view is the one reflected in the New International Version, and it is probably the best in many ways. For one thing, it greatly changes the force of the remembered words "I am greatly afflicted" and "All men are liars." Instead of being sullen, cynical comments, they become keen insights into the psalmist's own desperate condition and the complete unreliability of human beings. It was because he had come to believe in God that he could see his own condition and human unreliability.

Clements thinks the psalmist is saying, "In my moment of crisis, I discovered I was a believer, a real believer, not just a nominal churchgoer and that faith I discovered enabled me to verbalize my distraught emotions, not just to myself, but to God. I told him exactly how I felt. . . . In that situation, there was only one thing I could be with God, and that is honest, brutally honest. Maybe that's why he listened, for listen he did. I tell you that I never realized it was possible to feel so much devotion to God until the day I realized he paid attention to me, deliberately turning his ear to my prayer. I love the Lord for he heard my voice."[6]

The Conclusions

The experience of having been sick, having prayed, and having God answer him so clearly and powerfully left such an impression on the psalmist that he spent some time reflecting, and these reflections are scattered throughout not only the first part of the psalm but the second part too. They are not arranged in any logical order, but they jump out at us unmistakably.

1. *"The Lord is gracious and righteous . . . full of compassion"* (v. 5). At this point some writers work hard at explaining why the word "righteous" is in verse 5. Some argue that it points to the cross since God is able to be compassionate only because of the death of Jesus Christ for sin, which satisfied the demands of his righteous justice. That is a true observation, but it is not what the writer is thinking of here. He is thinking of God's righteousness in remembering his covenant and therefore of being gracious even to such an insignificant person as himself.

Have you experienced anything of the grace and compassion of God? It is hard for me to imagine you have not, if you are a Christian. Well, then, don't you ever reflect on that fact and marvel at how good God is? Almost every one of the psalms in this last book of the Psalter does so. If you are a Christian, you should too.

2. *"The Lord protects the simplehearted"* (v. 6). Not only is God gracious, he is also gracious to the little people, to the plain, to commoners, to the everyday person on the bus or in the shop—to people like the psalmist. That is one of the great glories of our God. When Jesus called his disciples, he called fishermen and tax collectors. When the angels announced the birth of Jesus, they appeared to shepherds.

Isn't the most wonderful thing about the gospel that God made it known to you, the simplehearted? If you think you are too important to fit into that category, I question whether you know anything about the gospel. You certainly know very little about the meaning of God's grace.

3. *"Be at rest once more, O my soul"* (v. 7). The psalmist concluded that he could rest in God once more, more securely and with greater trust than he had possessed before. He was truly a believer before but his trouble had thrown his soul into turmoil. As a believer he turned to God, God answered him in a marvelous way, and now he is able to settle down and rest in him again. Shouldn't your answers to prayer enable you to do the same? Every touch of God upon your life should make you stronger. Learn that you can continue to put all your trust in him.

4. *"You . . . have delivered my soul from death . . . that I may walk before the* LORD *in the land of the living"* (vv. 8–9). God delivers his people not only so they appreciate his grace and rest in him but also so they live for him, walk with him, follow after him. In other words, there is work to do; if his people have been spared from death, it is so they might be useful to God by doing his work. One commentator said that resting in God is a matter of our *confidence* in God; walking before him has to do with our *obedience*.

Farther on in the psalm the writer explains what walking before the Lord means.

> O LORD, truly I am your servant;
> I am your servant, the son of your maidservant (v. 16).

These words remind us of Jesus' teaching about discipleship. Jesus called us to be servants who would follow him as his disciples even to death. He said, "If anyone would come after me, he must deny himself and take up his cross daily and follow me" (Luke 9:23). Walking obediently before God really does mean being a servant. As Paul wrote to the believers at Corinth, "You are not your own; you were bought at a price. Therefore honor God with your body" (1 Cor. 6:19–20).

Yet while he called us to be servants, Jesus also said, "I no longer call you servants, because a servant does not know his master's business. Instead, I have called you friends, for everything that I learned from my Father I have made known to you" (John 15:15). Our service is to be an informed service, so that we serve not blindly but with understanding and love. Paul told the Ephesians, "Do not be foolish, but understand what the Lord's will is" (Eph. 5:17).

If we are to make sense of Paul's teaching and of the psalmist's conclusion in verse 9, we are going to have to study the Bible, since there is nowhere else the will of God is disclosed. Above all else the Bible is an unfolding of the mind of God. It is where we find what God demands of us, how far short of those demands we have fallen, and what God has done in Christ to restore us to himself. What God demands of us now is that we "believe in the one he has sent" (John 6:29).

5. *"Precious in the sight of the Lord is the death of his saints"* (v. 15). God is particularly close to his people when they stand at death's door. God watches over his people when they are sick or dying, coming close to them and making his presence known so that they have comfort in death's hour. He also frequently intervenes and does not allow them to perish. In either case, the Lord does what is best.

Paul spoke of death as a blessing. "If I am to go on living in the body, this will mean fruitful labor for me. Yet what shall I choose? I do not know! I am torn between the two: I desire to depart and be with Christ, which is better by far; but it is more necessary for you that I remain in the body" (Phil. 1:22–24). One thing is certain: The people of God are immortal until their work on earth is done.

Part Two: What the Writer Will Do

The last half of Psalm 116 (vv. 12–19) asks, "How can I repay the LORD for all his goodness to me?" How *can* we repay the Lord for his goodness? He needs nothing. In Romans 11 Paul asks this very question rhetorically. "Who has ever given to God, that God should repay him?" (Rom. 11:35). No one can give God anything, "for from him and through him and to him are all things" (v. 36). Every good gift comes from God.

Without suggesting that there is any intrinsically valuable thing we have to give God, the psalmist does suggest ways we can respond to God's goodness. First, we need to tell others about God's mercy to us. In the very last verses the psalmist speaks of thanking God and calling on him "in the presence of all his people, in the courts of the house of the LORD" (vv. 18–19). He means that we should give public testimony to God's redeeming grace.

Second, we need to "lift up the cup of salvation and call on the name of the LORD" (v. 13). This metaphor is based on the libation or drink offering prescribed in Numbers 28:7. In the postbiblical period the rabbis said there were to be no sacrificial gifts without libations, noting that the two are joined in Joel 1:9. They also said that the words of Judges 9:13 ("wine, which cheers both gods and men") were to be pronounced as a blessing over the cup. But there is a big difference between the drink offering of Numbers 28 and what the psalmist says here. In Psalm 116 the writer is not talking about *giving* God anything, though that might be expected from his question ("How can I repay the LORD?"). Instead he talks about *taking* something, that is, the cup of salvation. It is a profound insight: The only way we can repay God from whom everything comes is by taking even more from him. Spurgeon noted that this is the wisest of all possible replies. He then quoted this verse:

> The best return for one like me,
> So wretched and so poor,
> Is from his gifts to draw a plea
> And ask him still for more.[7]

"I will lift up the cup of salvation" is immediately joined to "and call on the name of the LORD" because we receive God's gift and then go on in the same relationship, forever asking and receiving from him.

Jesus and the Twelve must have sung Psalm 116 at the Last Supper after Jesus had instituted the communion service with its "cup of salvation." That cup represented the blood of Jesus, which was poured out as an atonement for our sins. It speaks of giving all the way, 100 percent. "Salvation comes from the LORD" (Jonah 2:9), but it is also a cup that needs to be taken by us, which is what we symbolize by taking it at the Lord's Supper. It is a spiritual cup, and the way it is taken is by faith, by believing that Jesus is truly the Son of God and our Savior.

Psalm 117

The Shortest Psalm of All

Praise the LORD, all you nations;
extol him, all you peoples.
For great is his love toward us,
and the faithfulness of the LORD endures forever.

Praise the LORD.

verses 1–2

T his is the shortest psalm in the Psalter, but, as Derek Kidner rightly notes, its faith is "great" and "its reach is enormous."[1]

Over the years I have been impressed with how much teaching the Holy Spirit is able to pack into a small space, and sometimes I have been able to demonstrate it by my expositions. I remember teaching John 11:35, the shortest verse in the Bible. It contains only two words: "Jesus wept," but I explained it on four separate Sundays.

Psalm 117 is not so short—it has two verses instead of two words—but it is the shortest chapter in the Bible as well as the shortest psalm. It contains an impressive amount of teaching. In his massive *Treasury of David,* Charles Spurgeon cites a writer who found five profound doctrines in this chapter: the calling of the Gentiles, a summary of the gospel, the end and goal of such blessing, the duties of God's people, and their privileges.[2]

Martin Luther devoted thirty-six pages to this psalm, expounding it in four important categories: (1) *prophecy* (the Gentiles will participate in gospel blessings), (2) *revelation* (the kingdom of Christ is not earthly and temporal but rather heavenly and eternal), (3) *instruction* (we are saved by faith alone and not by works, wisdom, or holiness), and (4) *admonition* (we should praise God for such a great salvation).[3] Luther's treatment of Psalm 117 is a masterpiece of exposition and well worth a very careful reading.

There is so much in this short psalm that Derek Kidner is quite right when he says by way of summary, "The shortest psalm proves, in fact, to be one of the most potent and most seminal."[4] It is the fifth psalm of the Egyptian Hallel (Pss. 113–18).

All the Nations

The first striking feature of this psalm is that it calls upon all nations and all peoples to praise God. "Nations" is the Hebrew word *goyim*, often translated "Gentiles," though it does mean Gentiles strictly speaking. It is sometimes used even for Israel itself. "Peoples" is a rare plural form of the word *am*. It refers to the wide diversity found in national and ethnic groupings. Together the words embrace all peoples everywhere, precisely the sense present in Revelation 7:9, where John speaks of "a great multitude that no one could count, from every nation, tribe, people and language, standing before the throne and in front of the Lamb."

Here then is a true Christian universalism, not that all people will be saved regardless of the god they believe in, but rather that all people may be saved through Jesus Christ. To put it in other words, this is a profound missionary psalm, for it is calling on people everywhere to praise God.

We are always in danger of rejecting or restricting this universalism and forgetting our calling to be a missionary people, because we tend to be self-satisfied and look down on others. This was true of the Jews at the time of the early Christian mission. At the very beginning of the Bible God taught that the gospel was to be for all people, since he told Abraham, "All peoples on earth will be blessed through you" (Gen. 12:3). The Jews forgot that, just as we do. They were willing for Gentiles to become Jews, if they did not do it in too great numbers and if they respected the Jewish traditions and customs, but they were not willing to have the Gentiles remain Gentiles and become the people of God too. This was the battle Paul had to fight at the first church council, when he argued that Gentile believers had been accepted by God even though they were not circumcised and did not keep the traditional Jewish laws.

Christians have been guilty of exactly the same thing. They have been so in love with their own ways of being Christians that they have rejected or been suspicious of believers who are different, and sometimes they have been so resistant to having anyone else become part of their own precious inner circle that they have neglected their missionary responsibility entirely, even to people in their own cities or neighborhoods. We should be ashamed of any such narrow exclusivism.

Jews and Gentiles

Here is the place to notice how Paul cites Psalm 117:1 near the end of a significant section of Romans (Rom. 14:1–15:13). This long section deals with how Christians who consider themselves strong should treat their weaker brothers and sisters and how the weak should regard the strong. As usual, Paul ends the section by citing proofs from the Old Testament, in this case Psalm 18:49 (Rom. 15:9), Deuteronomy 32:43 (Rom. 15:10), Psalm 117:1 (Rom. 15:11), and Isaiah 11:10 (Rom. 15:12). The surprising thing is that the texts he cites do not deal with the relationship between weaker and stronger people specifically but rather are prophecies that the gospel would one day be extended to the Gentiles.

> Therefore I will praise you among the Gentiles;
>   I will sing hymns to your name.

> Rejoice, O Gentiles, with his people.

> Praise the LORD, all you Gentiles,
>   and sing praises to him, all you peoples.

> The root of Jesse will spring up,
>   one who will arise to rule over the nations;
> the Gentiles will hope in him.

It is wonderful and amazing that the gospel should be extended to the Gentiles, for the Old Testament taught the exclusive privileges of the Jews as God's unique people and no hope for the Gentiles apart from their becoming Jews. Earlier in Romans Paul had asked whether there was any advantage in being a Jew, and he answered, "Much in every way! First of all, they have been entrusted with the very words of God" (Rom. 3:2). He meant that the Jews had the Bible, while the Gentiles did not. Paul interrupted his listing of the Jewish advantages at that point but picked it up again in chapter 9, adding, "Theirs is the adoption as sons; theirs the divine glory, the covenants, the receiving of the law, the temple worship and the promises. Theirs are the patriarchs, and from them is traced the human ancestry of Christ" (vv. 4–5). The Gentiles had none of these advantages. Therefore, Paul was able to tell the Ephesians that before they had heard about Christ and had believed on him, they were "excluded from citizenship in Israel and foreigners to the covenants of the promise, without hope and without God in the world" (Eph. 2:12).

That is a very grim assessment. But if "salvation is from the Jews," as Jesus himself told the woman of Samaria (John 4:22), meaning that God had been working with Jews almost exclusively from the time of Abraham to the time of Jesus Christ, then it is accurate. For many centuries God was working with Israel specifically and there was literally no hope of salvation for the masses of the world who were not Jewish.

Fortunately, this former absence of hope is not the final word for Gentiles, since Gentile salvation was promised in the Old Testament, though in the future. Gentile salvation is the great insight of Psalm 117. When we notice how many verses Paul cites to hammer home his point, we get a glimpse of how carefully and persistently he must have had to argue the truth about Gentile salvation when teaching Jews.

The Greatness of God's Love

The second thing we need to notice about Psalm 117 is that the reason the Gentiles (along with Jews) are called upon to praise God is God's love, for it is a love that "endures forever" (v. 2).

Verse 2 is based on the favorite text of the postexilic Jewish community, namely Exodus 34:6, which is picked up as early as David's psalm of praise on the occasion of his bringing the ark of God to Jerusalem (1 Chron. 16:34) and is repeated at length in the very next psalm (vv. 1–4, 29). Exodus 34:6 says, "And he [that is, God] passed in front of Moses, proclaiming, 'The LORD, the LORD, the compassionate and gracious God, slow to anger, abounding in love and faithfulness, maintaining love to thousands, and forgiving wickedness, rebellion and sin." It would be false to say that teaching about God's love is absent from the earlier psalms, but it is emphasized only as we come to the end of the Psalter, probably because it was the attribute of God uppermost in the minds of the chastened remnant as they returned to Israel from their seventy-year-long Babylonian captivity. The Egyptian Hallel would have focused their thoughts on the greatness of the love of God that had preserved them as a nation in spite of their great sin.

Yet if the Jews who returned from Babylon were aware of the greatness of God's love, how much more should we be aware of it—we who have come to know it through the atoning death of God's Son, Jesus Christ!

I think here of John 3:16, undoubtedly the best loved and most memorized and quoted verse in the entire Bible: "For God so loved the world that he gave his one and only Son, that whoever believes in him shall not perish but have eternal life." God's gift to us of Jesus is alone the full measure of the magnitude of God's love.

John 3:16 was the verse by which D. L. Moody, the famous evangelist, learned the greatness of God's love. Moody traveled to England early in his ministry and met a young English preacher named Henry Moorhouse, who later pioneered Christian social service work in London's poorer areas. One day Moorhouse told Moody, "I'm thinking of going to America."

Moody said, "Well, if you should ever get to Chicago, come to my church and I'll give you a chance to preach."

Moody was only being polite when he said this, because he had not heard Moorhouse and didn't know what he might say. He put the matter out of his mind, thinking that Moorhouse would probably never get as far west as Chicago. Sometime after Moody had gone back to America, he received a telegram that said, "Have arrived in New York. Will be in Chicago Sunday." Moody didn't know what to do, especially since he was scheduled to be away that weekend. Finally he told the leaders of the church, "I think we should let him preach once. Put him on; then, if the people enjoy him, let him preach again."

Moody was gone for a week following that Sunday, and when he got back he asked his wife, "How did the young preacher do?"

"He's a better preacher than you are," she said. "He's telling sinners that God loves them."

"That's not right," Moody replied. "God doesn't love sinners." He had not yet learned very much about the love of God.

"Well, if you don't think so, go and hear him."

"What?" said Moody. "Do you mean to tell me he is still here, that he is still preaching?"

"Yes, he has been preaching all week, and he has only had one verse for a text. It is John 3:16."

Moody went to the meeting. Moorhouse began by saying, "I have been hunting for a text all day, and I have not been able to find a better one than John 3:16. So I think I will just talk about it once more." He began to preach, and afterward Moody testified that on that night he received his first clear understanding of the gospel of grace and the greatness of God's love.

Not only is God's love great, but also there is nothing greater in all the world. I think here of the often-told story about Karl Barth, the Swiss theologian. He was an old man at the time and was in this country for a series of lectures. At a discussion period following one of his addresses an American asked a typically American question: "Dr. Barth, what is the greatest thought that has ever gone through your mind?" Barth paused for a long time as he thought about his answer. Then he raised his head and said with great simplicity,

> Jesus loves me! This I know,
> For the Bible tells me so.

There is no greater truth than the fact that God has loved us in Jesus Christ with a love that endures forever.

The Prevailing Power of God's Love

I have taken the "great" in verse 2 in our normal English sense, as something that is large, remarkable, distinguished, or superior. While this meaning is accurate, many commentators also note that in Hebrew the word has the sense of someone or something having prevailed over something else because of his or its superior qualities. For example, it is used of the stronger side in battle, as in Exodus 17:11. "As long as Moses held up his hands, the Israelites were *winning* ('prevailing,' italics added)" over their

enemies the Amalekites. Genesis 7:18 says that the waters of the flood "rose
. . . *greatly* on the earth" (that is, "prevailed" over it, italics added). The same
word is used in Psalm 65:3 to describe our sins: "When we were *overwhelmed*
by sins, you atoned for our transgressions (italics added)."[5] The point is that
when this word is used of the love of God for his people, it also has the
thought of God's love prevailing over any obstacles or enemies.

Martin Luther's handling of this word is particularly fine. Luther had
enemies, as we know, chiefly among the churchmen of his day. They were
trying to get him killed. But when he writes about this verse he thinks not of
these earthly or physical enemies, which we might have expected him to do,
but of sin and temptation.

> Although sin makes itself felt, death bares its teeth, and the devil frightens
> us, still there is far more grace to prevail over all sin, far more life to prevail
> over death, and far more God to prevail over all devils. In this kingdom sin,
> death and the devil are nothing more than the black clouds of the material
> heaven. For a time they may well conceal heaven, but they cannot prevail.
> They must stay beneath the heavens and suffer it to remain, prevail, and
> rule over them; and at last they must pass away. Therefore although sin bites
> us, death frightens us, and the devil throws his weight around with tempta-
> tion, these are still only clouds. The heaven of grace prevails and rules; in
> the end they must remain below and surrender.[6]

Isn't this exactly what Paul says in Romans 8, which we looked at in connection with Psalm 114? He closes that chapter by saying, "I am convinced
that neither death nor life, neither angels nor demons, neither the present
nor the future, nor any powers, neither height nor depth, nor anything else
in all creation, will be able to separate us from the love of God that is in
Christ Jesus our Lord" (Rom. 8:38–39).

The Enduring Power of God's Truth

The word rendered "faithfulness" in verse 2 actually is the word *amen*,
and it can equally well be translated "truth," "steadfastness," or "reliability."
In the New Testament, in the words of Jesus, it is often rendered, "Truly,
truly."

Amen is found in nearly every language of the world, one of the few words
in that category, but it originates from a Hebrew verb meaning "to support
with the arm" or "carry." In its intransitive form the verb meant "that which
is supported" or "that which is held up." Thus it came to mean "firm" or
"unshakable." The word occurs in this original sense in Isaiah 22:23 in reference to a firm place in a wall, where a nail can be driven: "I will drive him
like a peg into a *firm* place." Isaiah is speaking about the unshakable character of Christ's kingdom.

Over the years this old Hebrew word took on two important uses that at last became dominant ones. First, the word was used of God, as one of his attributes, which is what we have in Psalm 117. This usage was perfectly natural, for if the word meant "unshakable," then it is rightly applied to God, who alone is utterly unshakable. Heaven and earth will pass away, but God will never pass away, nor will his words. Therefore we find God spoken of as the Amen or, as some versions have it, as the God of truth. It is in this sense that Isaiah speaks of God, saying,

> Whoever invokes a blessing in the land
>> will do so by the God of truth;
> he who takes an oath in the land
>> will swear by the God of truth (Isa. 65:16).

The Hebrew says literally, "by the God of the amen."

Being faithful is one of God's characteristics, and it is his faithfulness that is mentioned in our psalm. Strictly speaking, in this verse it is the faithfulness of God that endures forever and the love of God that prevails. Verse 2 is an example of the psalms' characteristically parallel constructions so that what is said in one line is repeated in the second line with only the slightest alteration in meaning. Since the terms are parallel we can as easily say that the love of God endures forever and the faithfulness of God prevails. In fact, it is because God is the faithful God, who does not lie in his words or vary in his commitments, that his love prevails; and it is because his love does not vary that he can be trusted.

The second use of amen is familiar. It is used by human beings to express agreement with what God says. God says something, and we say, "Amen," meaning that we are setting our seal to the fact that God is truthful. Can you say, "I have found that God's love is indeed great and prevails and that his truth endures forever. Amen."? If so, you will say as the psalm does, "Praise the Lord."

Psalm 118

Thanks to Our Good God: Part 1

"His Love Endures Forever"

Give thanks to the LORD, for he is good;
his love endures forever.

Let Israel say:
"His love endures forever."
Let the house of Aaron say:
"His love endures forever."
Let those who fear the LORD say:
"His love endures forever." . . .

The stone the builders rejected
has become the capstone;
the LORD has done this,
and it is marvelous in our eyes.
This is the day the LORD has made;
let us rejoice and be glad in it.

O LORD, save us;
O LORD, grant us success.
Blessed is he who comes in the name of the LORD.
From the house of the LORD we bless you.

verses 1–4, 22–26

Psalm 117 is a fit introduction to Psalm 118, for its major message—"great is his [God's] love toward us, and the faithfulness of the LORD endures forever" (Ps. 117:2)—is what Psalm 118 elaborates at length.

As I mentioned, Psalm 117:2 is based on the favorite text of the postexilic Jewish community, Exodus 34:6, and was given prominence in Israel as early as David (see p. 951). Psalm 118:1 repeats it exactly:

> Give thanks to the LORD, for he is good;
>   his love endures forever.

This theme is echoed in verses 2–4 and then is repeated at the psalm's close, in verse 29.

Processions from the Past

There are good reasons for thinking that this psalm was used for praise by the congregation of Israel on festive processional occasions. The repetitive language alone suggests this, as well as the progression of ideas from anguish (v. 5) to worship at God's altar (v. 27). The psalm even contains the words "festal procession" (v. 27).

Jeremiah describes such a scene, quoting Psalm 118:1 and perhaps implying a singing of the entire hymn:

> This is what the LORD says: "You say about this place, 'It is a desolate waste, without men or animals.' Yet in the towns of Judah and the streets of Jerusalem that are deserted, inhabited by neither men nor animals, there will be heard once more the sounds of joy and gladness, the voices of bride and bridegroom, and the voices of those who bring thank offerings to the house of the LORD, saying,
>
> > 'Give thanks to the LORD Almighty,
> >   for the LORD is good;
> >   his love endures forever.'
>
> For I will restore the fortunes of the land as they were before," says the LORD (Jer. 33:10–11).

In writing down this prophecy, Jeremiah must have been remembering such festal processions and singing.

This psalm may have been used when the foundation of the temple was laid in the days of Ezra. Verse 22 mentions the foundation stone of the temple, and Ezra 3:10–11 reads:

> When the builders laid the foundation of the temple of the LORD, the priests in their vestments and with trumpets, and the Levites (the sons of Asaph) with cymbals, took their places to praise the LORD, as prescribed by David king of Israel. With praise and thanksgiving they sang to the LORD:

> "He is good;
> his love to Israel endures forever."

And all the people gave a great shout of praise to the LORD, because the foundation of the house of the LORD was laid.

From Egypt to Mount Zion

Psalm 118 is long, consisting of ten stanzas plus an opening theme verse and two closing ones (according to the NIV). It begins with a summons to Israel to praise God, repeating the second line of verse 1 ("His love endures forever," vv. 2–4). Next it describes the anguish of one who was enslaved ("In my anguish I cried to the LORD, and he answered by setting me free," v. 5) and the danger he faced from the nearby hostile nations ("All the nations surrounded me," v. 10; "I was pushed back and about to fall," v. 13). This is followed by remembrance of victories given to Israel by God ("Shouts of joy and victory resound in the tents of the righteous," v. 15). There is a call for opening the temple gates for the righteous to enter ("Open for me the gates of righteousness," v. 19), a grateful recognition that those who had been rejected have been heard and delivered from their foreign oppression ("The stone the builders rejected has become the capstone," v. 22), then a final festive procession ("With boughs in hand, join in the festal procession up to the horns of the altar," v. 27).

When we trace this progression we understand why Psalm 118 is the last and climactic psalm in the Egyptian Hallel. Its parts suggest the passage of Israel from slavery in Egypt to the security and joy of Mount Zion. Parts of the psalm echo the Exodus narrative. For example, verse 14 is a direct quote of Exodus 15:2, from Moses's victory song after the deliverance of the people from Pharaoh and his armies at the Red Sea.

> The LORD is my strength and my song;
> he has become my salvation.

We can appreciate how the Jews used this psalm to remember their deliverance from bondage and their birth as a nation.

A Christian Psalm

It is not only Jews who can use this psalm to recall God's grace to them. Christians can use it (and have used it) to remember the work of Jesus Christ. In fact, what strikes us most about this psalm are the verses quoted in the Gospel accounts of Palm Sunday and Passion Week referring to Jesus Christ. The psalm is not strictly Messianic; it is about God's deliverance of Israel. Even "the stone the builders rejected" is about Israel primarily. Still, several key verses are used about Jesus in the New Testament, and in this sense the psalm is Messianic, the last of such Messianic psalms.

1. *"O LORD, save us"* (v. 25) and *"Blessed is he who comes in the name of the LORD"* (v. 26). Verses 25–26 were used by the people who were entering Jerusalem on what we call Palm Sunday to honor Jesus. All four evangelists quote one or both of these verses in their account of the triumphal entry (see Matt. 21:9; Mark 11:9–10; Luke 19:39; John 12:13). The words "Blessed is he who comes in the name of the Lord" are found exactly as we have them in our English versions. Verse 25 is quoted differently, but we can see the connection if we know that the words "save us" (from "O LORD, save us" in the first half of the verse) are literally "save us now," which is the Hebrew word *hosanna*. The people exclaimed, "Hosanna to the Son of David!" and "Hosanna in the highest!" (Matt. 21:9).

When we remember that Psalm 118 is part of the Egyptian Hallel, that the Hallel was sung by Jews at the time of the Passover, and that it was Passover when Jesus entered Jerusalem and later died on Calvary, it is understandable that these words would have been in the minds of the people who greeted him as he entered the city. Jesus entered Jerusalem on the day the lambs were being taken into the Jewish homes in preparation for the sacrifice.

Did the people understand that Jesus was the Son of God and that he was coming to give his life as a ransom to save his people from their sins? No, though some, like Mary of Bethany, seem to have known that he was about to die (see John 12:7). Whether the masses understood it or not, these verses describe what Jesus was doing and was about to do. He had indeed come "in the name of the Lord" to do the will of his Father in heaven, and what he had been sent to do was "save" his people from their sins. He would do it by dying.

2. *"The stone the builders rejected has become the capstone"* (v. 22) and *"This is the day the LORD has made; let us rejoice and be glad in it"* (v. 24). In the context of the psalm verses 22 and 24 refer to Israel primarily. As a nation, Israel was rejected by the great empire builders of her day as something insignificant, but God was going to make her the focal point of his work of building a new people of God. He would do this by sending Jesus to be born as a Jew, a descendant of King David. These words have also rightly been applied to Jesus himself, since he was rejected by the Jews and their leaders, yet God made him both the Savior of his people and the focus of their devotion.

> Therefore God exalted him to the highest place
> and gave him the name that is above every name,
> that at the name of Jesus every knee should bow,
> in heaven and on earth and under the earth,
> and every tongue confess that Jesus Christ is Lord,
> to the glory of God the Father (Phil. 2:9–11).

Specifically, Psalm 118:22 pictures Jesus' death and resurrection. Jesus himself used these words. In the same chapter of Matthew in which we read about the people of Jerusalem hailing Jesus with verses 25 and 26 of Psalm

118, we also find Jesus quoting verses 22 and 23 in reference to himself (Matthew 21). He had just told a parable about farmers to whom the owner of a vineyard had leased a field. They were to care for it, harvest the grapes, and then give the owner his share of the profit when the time came. When the harvest was drawn in the owner sent servants to collect his profit, but the tenants beat, stoned, and killed the servants. Finally, the owner sent his son, thinking they would respect him. Instead they killed the son, hoping to gain the land for themselves. Jesus then asked the chief priests and elders to whom he was telling the story, "When the owner of the vineyard comes, what will he do to those tenants?" (Matt. 21:40).

They answered, "He will bring those wretches to a wretched end, . . . and he will rent the vineyard to other tenants, who will give him his share of the crop at harvest time" (Matt. 21:41).

This was the right answer, of course, but Jesus then applied it by quoting Psalm 118:22–23: "Have you never read in the Scriptures:

> 'The stone the builders rejected
>   has become the capstone;
> the Lord has done this,
>   and it is marvelous in our eyes'" (Matt. 21:42).

The chapter ends by noting, "When the chief priests and the Pharisees heard Jesus' parables, they knew he was talking about them" (Matt. 21:45).

There can be no question about how Jesus understood these verses. God was the owner of the vineyard. The leaders of Israel were the evil tenant farmers. The servants were the prophets, and the son who was killed was Jesus himself, the Son of God. Therefore, he is also the stone rejected by the builders who was to become the capstone of all true religion. Those who receive the vineyard are the members of the church, composed of all believing Jews and Gentiles. We are members of that church today if we believe on Jesus.

Psalm 118:22 meant a lot to the apostle Peter. The first time he used it was in one of his defenses before the Sanhedrin after Jesus' death and resurrection. Peter and John had healed a crippled beggar and been arrested. When they were brought before the Jews' high court they were asked, "By what power or name did you do this?" (Acts 4:7).

Peter responded with a short but mighty sermon.

> Rulers and elders of the people! If we are being called to account today for an act of kindness shown to a cripple and are asked how he was healed, then know this, you and everyone else in Israel: It is by the name of Jesus Christ of Nazareth, whom you crucified but whom God raised from the dead, that this man stands before you completely healed. He is
>
> > "the stone you builders rejected,
> >   which has become the capstone."

Salvation is found in no one else, for there is no other name under heaven given to men by which we must be saved (Acts 4:8–12).

Peter quoted Psalm 118:22 in this sermon (Acts 4:11) but with one significant change. When Luke, the author of Acts, quotes verses from the Old Testament, as he does here, he almost invariably quotes from the Septuagint, the translation of the Old Testament used among Greek-speaking people. Luke was writing to Greek-speaking people, so he used the Septuagint. In quoting from the Septuagint at this point Luke varied the quotation slightly, adding the word "you." The Septuagint says, "The stone the builders rejected has become the capstone." Luke changes it to say, "The stone *you* builders rejected . . ." (italics added), undoubtedly because that is what Peter said. Peter used the text to reinforce what he had been teaching about the guilt of Israel's leaders. He took this impersonal Old Testament text and made it pointed.

Pastor Frederick W. Evans Jr. has a sermon on this verse in which he speaks of Jesus being rejected by the "experts." That is what these teachers of religion considered themselves to be.[1] They had examined Jesus, and they had decided that he would have to die. Why?

In the first place, they did not approve of his origin. He came from Galilee, and they said, "Look into it, and you will find that a prophet does not come out of Galilee" (John 7:52). They did not like his lack of formal education, meaning that he had not been trained in their schools. They said, "How did this man get such learning without having studied?" (John 7:15). They did not approve of his disregard of their religious rules, particularly their rules for the Sabbath. They asked, "Why are you doing what is unlawful on the Sabbath?" (Luke 6:2). They did not like his choice of friends. They demanded of the disciples, "Why does your teacher eat with tax collectors and 'sinners'?" (Matt. 9:11).

Above all they did not like his teaching. He knew their hidden sins, self-righteousness and hypocrisy, and he exposed them. Moreover, he taught that salvation was of God and that neither these leaders nor anyone else could be justified before God by his or her own actions. He said, "No one can come to me unless the Father has enabled him" (John 6:65). He taught that certain people belonged to him because they had been given to him by God and that he had come to save them by dying for them (John 10:14–15). He called the leaders thieves who only wanted to enrich themselves.

So they rejected him. Frederick Evans says, "He wasn't two years into his ministry when they decided he had to go. They were the builders, and they were going to build in their own way, without him. Yes, they would build over his dead body. They would put him to death. If they could not stone him according to Jewish law, they would see to it that he was nailed to a cross according to Roman law."[2] That is exactly what they did.

Yes, but God made him "the capstone" by raising him from the dead. The psalm says, "the LORD has done this, and it is marvelous in our eyes" (v. 23).

There are lots of things about the gospel that the world does not like. It does not like to hear about human guilt—nobody likes to feel guilty. It does not like to hear about the resurrection. Of all the things the world does not like, probably the most hated is that God always accomplishes what he wants in spite of our opposition. He is going to accomplish what he wants with you. You may fight him to the end, but in the end it will be his will rather than yours that will be done. What is his will? God wants Jesus Christ, his Son, to be honored and exalted, even by you. He will be, one way or another, since "at the name of Jesus every knee [will] bow" (Phil. 2:10). It would be far better for Jesus to be exalted by your praise of his great grace and mercy in saving you than to be exalted in his power as he judges you justly for your sin.

Building on That Stone

If Jesus is the stone that has been made the foundation of God's building or temple, then the only wise thing for us to do is build on it.

I wrote that Peter loved and often quoted Psalm 118:22. He quoted it before the Sanhedrin and also used it in his first letter, combined with Isaiah 8:14 and 28:16 (see 1 Peter 2:4–8). In introducing these quotations Peter says, "As you come to him, the living stone—rejected by men but chosen by God and precious to him—you also, like living stones, are being built into a spiritual house to be a holy priesthood, offering spiritual sacrifices acceptable to God through Jesus Christ" (1 Peter 2:4–5). What a privilege and joy but also responsibility. You must not stumble at God's grace in Jesus Christ, as many have, tripping over that stone. You should come to Jesus instead and build your life on that secure foundation.

Psalm 118

Thanks to Our Good God: Part 2

Ours to Live and Testify

The LORD is with me; I will not be afraid.
What can man do to me? . . .

It is better to take refuge in the LORD
than to trust in man.
It is better to take refuge in the LORD
than to trust in princes. . . .

I will not die but live,
and will proclaim what the LORD has done. . . .

The LORD is God,
and he has made his light shine upon us.
With boughs in hand, join in the festal procession
up to the horns of the altar.

You are my God, and I will give you thanks;
you are my God, and I will exalt you.

Give thanks to the LORD, for he is good;
his love endures forever.
                              verses 6–17, 27–29

P salm 118 tells us not only about Jesus Christ and his work of redemption but also about ourselves and of our need to trust God and praise him in all circumstances.

This was the favorite psalm of Martin Luther. In the preface to his sixty-page exposition of the psalm, dedicating the work to Fredrich, Abbot of Saint Giles of Nuremberg, Luther wrote:

> This is my own beloved psalm. Although the entire Psalter and all of Holy Scripture are dear to me as my only comfort and source of life, I fell in love with this psalm especially. Therefore I call it my own. When emperors and kings, the wise and the learned, and even saints could not aid me, this psalm proved a friend and helped me out of many great troubles. As a result, it is dearer to me than all the wealth, honor, and power of the pope, the Turk, and the emperor. I would be most unwilling to trade this psalm for all of it.[1]

Strength for the Martyrs

One way of appreciating Psalm 118 is to realize how much it meant to the Protestant martyrs. Rowland E. Prothero tells about some of them in his study of *The Psalms in Human Life*. One was Louis Rank, a Huguenot pastor who was captured and condemned to die in Grenoble in 1745. He was offered life if he would renounce his faith, but he rejected the offer and was led to the scaffold singing a French versification of verse 24, which might be roughly translated,

> Here now is the happy day
> For which we have been waiting.
> Sing praise to God who gives us joy
> And pleasures unabating.[2]

A few weeks after the martyrdom of Louis Rang, another Huguenot pastor, Jacque Roger, likewise strengthened himself with this verse. He was seventy years old and had escaped his enemies for nearly forty years, often by only a hairsbreadth. When the king's soldiers finally tracked him down and asked who he was, Roger replied, "I am he whom you have sought for thirty-nine years. It is time you should find me." Roger spent his last days in prison encouraging other Protestant prisoners to remain true to the faith, and when the officers came to escort him to his place of execution, Roger quoted the same verse Louis Rang had sung just weeks before.[3]

The last of the Huguenot martyrs in France was Francois Rochette, who died seventeen years after Rang and Roger, in 1762. He was seized in a time of civil turmoil in Toulouse. As with the others, Rochette too was offered life if he would renounce his Protestant faith. He also refused. As he was led through the crowded streets, thronged with spectators, he encouraged the faithful to the very end and mounted the scaffold chanting, "Here now is the happy day for which we have been waiting." Prothero says, "It was fitting that the last words of the last Protestant martyr should be taken from that

Book of Psalms which, through two centuries of conflict and persecution, had meant so much to the Huguenots."[4]

Psalm 118 is a psalm in which individual verses leap out at us. In the last chapter I looked at verses that strike us in regard to Jesus Christ and his Passion. In this chapter I want to look at four more verses that strike us for different reasons.

"What Can Man Do to Me?"

The first verse that strikes us forcefully is verse 6. It is quoted in the New Testament in Hebrews 13:6 and is also found in a quite similar form in Psalm 56:4 and 11. It is that psalm's theme. Psalm 118:6 reads,

> The LORD is with me; I will not be afraid.
> What can man do to me?

When we were studying Psalm 56 I replied to that question by answering, "A lot!" Men can oppress, slander, hurt, hate, maim, and murder me, for starters, just as they did the martyrs. But the point is not what harm humans are capable of inflicting on others. Psalms 56 and 118 are saying that although evil people can do very evil things, in the end they cannot really harm us because our lives are preserved by God.

When David wrote Psalm 56 he was nearly a prisoner of the Philistines in Gath. He had been forced to escape from King Saul because Saul was trying to kill him; had gone to Nob, one of the towns of the priests, where Ahimelech, the head priest, assisted him by giving him food and a weapon; and because he was not safe there he had gone on to Gath.

Gath was the hometown of Goliath, whom David had killed not long before. David entered Gath with Goliath's great sword, which is the weapon Ahimelech had given him. The story of David and Goliath in 1 Samuel 17 does not describe the sword but says that Goliath was over nine feet tall and his body armor and bronze javelin were unusually large and heavy. His sword must have been large too. It would have been remembered by the people of Gath and have been recognized by them, and not with kind thoughts toward the one who carried it. There are only two ways any sane man would walk into Gath under those conditions: in arrogance or desperation. Since we know from the psalm that David was afraid rather than arrogant, he must have gone to Gath in near despair.

Moreover, when David arrived in Gath his presence was reported at once to Achish, the king of Gath. The people told Achish, "Isn't this David, the king of the land? Isn't he the one they sing about in their dances:

> 'Saul has slain his thousands,
> and David his tens of thousands'?" (1 Sam. 21:11).

Those "tens of thousands" were Philistines, and some of the former residents of Gath (as well as Goliath) were among them. Thus we are not surprised to read that David "was very much afraid" (v. 12).

Yes, but he was trusting God too. The psalms say, "*In God I trust;* I will not be afraid" (Ps. 56:4, 11, italics added) and "*the LORD is with me;* I will not be afraid" (Ps. 118:6, italics added). God outweighs the dangers. Therefore, although we may be as alone or even in as immediate danger as David was, yet we can still say, "I will not be afraid, because I trust in God." In Romans 8 Paul wrote, "We face death all day long; we are considered as sheep to be slaughtered," quoting from Psalm 44:22 (Rom. 8:36). But he added, "I am convinced that neither death nor life, . . . nor anything else in all creation, will be able to separate us from the love of God that is in Christ Jesus our Lord" (Rom. 8:38–39).

The Middle Verses of the Bible

The second passage I call to your attention consists of verses 8 and 9. It is reported by people who count such things that there are 31,174 verses in the Bible, and if that is so, then these verses, the 15,587th and the 15,588th, are the middle verses. That position should be reason enough to give them prominence.

What do you suppose a middle verse should say? Shouldn't the middle verse of the Bible be John 3:16, or its equivalent? Or something from Psalm 23? At least it should be about God's love, perhaps "God is love" (1 John 4:8). Actually, the middle verses of the Bible are none of these or anything else we might naturally expect, though in their simplicity they are of vast importance. Significantly, they are about putting our trust in God rather than in mere human beings.

> It is better to take refuge in the LORD
>   than to trust in man.
> It is better to take refuge in the LORD
>   than to trust in princes (Ps. 118:8–9).

Why it is better to trust in God rather than man? In his massive study of the psalms Spurgeon gives five answers. First, it is wiser. God can be trusted; man cannot. Second, it is morally better. God tells us to trust him, teaching at the same time that mere human beings are corrupt, selfish, and untrustworthy. Third, it is safer. It is dangerous to trust those who are disposed to let us down, for they will certainly do it. Fourth, it is better in its effect upon ourselves. We grow in faith and character when we trust God, not when we place that same kind of trust in other people. Fifth, it is better as far as its results are concerned. God honors our trust by blessing it broadly.[5]

The world does not understand trusting God, which is not surprising since the world is blind in spiritual matters. Martin Luther said that when his friend and protector Duke Frederick of Saxony was alive (1486–1525) his enemies taunted him, saying, "Luther's heresy is dependent on two eyes; when those are closed, his heresy will die." They meant that it was only the power and protection of Frederick that preserved the Reformation. But Frederick died, Luther lived, and the doctrines that Luther recovered and taught are powerful today. "The work continues and, please God, will continue even better until the end," wrote Luther.[6]

It Is the Living Who Praise the Lord

When we were studying Psalm 115, I noted that the last two verses of that psalm say rightly that it is not the dead who praise the Lord but the living.

> It is not the dead who praise the LORD,
>   those who go down to silence;
> It is we who extol the LORD,
>   both now and forevermore (Ps. 115:17–18).

That is a fairly obvious observation. Dead people do not speak. Only the living can praise God. But it raises an important question, namely, do we praise God? Or are we as silent as those who have died and been buried? If we have been saved from our sin and kept alive by God, rather than being taken to heaven, it is in order to praise him. We live to be God's witnesses.

Psalm 118:17, the next verse that particularly strikes me, says, "I will not die but live, and will proclaim what the LORD has done." This verse may have been in the mind of Jesus as he meditated on his pending death and resurrection, but it is also a verse for us since Jesus calls us to live and be his witnesses. Jesus said, "He who believes in me will live, even though he dies; and whoever lives and believes in me will never die" (John 11:25–26), and "You are witnesses of these things" (Luke 24:48).

This verse meant a great deal to William Cowper, the hymn writer and poet who was a personal friend of John Newton. Cowper was a fragile soul who had a delicate mental and physical constitution. He was taunted and abused as a young student at a school in Hertfordshire, and later in his life he was committed to an asylum for the mentally ill at St. Albans. Yet Cowper recovered, and when he did he expressed in the language of our psalm his joy over his recovery. "The Lord is my strength and my song, and is become my salvation—I shall not die but live," he said (vv. 14, 17). It was this man who gave us such beloved hymns as "God Moves in a Mysterious Way His Wonders to Perform," "There is a Fountain Filled with Blood, Drawn from Immanuel's Veins" and "O for a Closer Walk with God."[7]

Martin Luther had Psalm 118:17 written on his study wall. He called it "a masterpiece," adding, "He [the psalmist] so immerses himself in life that death is swallowed up by life (1 Cor. 15:55) and disappears completely, because he clings with a firm faith to the right hand of God. Thus all the saints have sung this verse and will continue to sing it to the end. . . . So far as the world is concerned, they die. Yet their hearts say with a firm faith: 'I shall not die, but live.'"[8]

During World War I Donald Grey Barnhouse, one of my predecessors as senior pastor of Tenth Presbyterian Church, served in the American Army and spent some time flying open-cockpit biplanes that the army was using at the time. Someone asked Barnhouse if he was not afraid to fly in those planes, especially since they might be used in combat. He answered that God had reassured him with a verse from the psalms, Psalm 118:17. He rephrased it in rhyme:

> Ours is not to fly and die.
> Ours to live and testify.

Testify he did, for many long years after that destructive, fierce, but eventually passing world conflict.

Sometimes too our witness to Christ must expose and denounce evil as well as proclaim good news. To be truth, truth must reveal error, and to be good, good must expose evil. John Wycliffe, the Protestant Reformer, fell sick at one point as the result of his incessant labors for the gospel. The friars heard that their enemy was dying and hastened to his bedside. Surely Wycliffe would be overcome with remorse for his Protestant heresies. Surely he would renounce his views and ask for God's forgiveness and the friars' blessing. A crowd of monks representing four major orders of the friars gathered around him. They began by wishing him health, then quickly changed their tune and urged him to make a full confession since he would soon have to give an accounting of himself to God. Wycliffe waited patiently until they had ended. Then, asking his servant to raise him a little so he could speak better, Wycliffe fixed his keen eyes on them and said in a commanding voice, "I shall not die but live and proclaim . . . *the evil deeds of the friars.*"[9]

Light for the Gentiles

The last three verses are a powerful summary and application of the psalm.

> The LORD is God,
>   and he has made his light shine upon us.
> With boughs in hand, join in the festal procession
>   up to the horns of the altar.
>
> You are my God, and I will give you thanks;
>   you are my God, and I will exalt you.
>
> Give thanks to the LORD, for he is good;
>   his love endures forever (vv. 27–29).

These verses make three powerful statements about God and about our right relationship to him.

1. *"The LORD is God"* (v. 27). In verse 27 the word "LORD" is the proper name Jehovah, or Yahweh. The verse is saying that it is Jehovah, the God of the Old Testament, who is truly God, not one of the other competing gods of this rebellious, evil world. This is the great issue of religion, not, Is there a god? (the Bible says it is only the fool who questions this—Psalm 14:1), but rather, Who is the true God? In this verse the psalmist says that Jehovah is the true God and that he has revealed this to us by making his light shine on us. This is the God who is being worshiped at the altar in Jerusalem, he and none other.

2. *"You are my God"* (v. 28). This God is the psalmist's own personal God, not merely the God of Israel, even less a God who is the result of some abstract philosophical speculation. Jehovah is his God, one in whom he has placed his own personal trust and to whom he has made a personal commitment. Is this God your God?

3. *"The Lord . . . is good"* (v. 29). In verse 29 the psalmist calls on the people among whom he is bearing witness to thank God because this true God "is good." The psalm began and now also ends with these words, drawing us back to consider the experience of the psalmist (and ourselves) once again.

The writer found that God is good because God had been good to him. He had been oppressed, but God had freed him from his oppression. He had been attacked, but God had delivered him from his enemies. He had been about to fall, but God had raised him up and given him important work to do, testifying to God's goodness. Is it any different for those who have been saved by Jesus Christ? We too have been freed from sin, delivered, and given work to do. If that is your case, thank God and get to work.

Psalm 119

Delight in God's Decrees: Part 1

First Things First

Blessed are they whose ways are blameless,
who walk according to the law of the LORD.
Blessed are they who keep his statutes
and seek him with all their heart.
They do nothing wrong;
they walk in his ways.
You have laid down precepts
that are to be fully obeyed.
Oh, that my ways were steadfast
in obeying your decrees!
Then I would not be put to shame
when I consider all your commands.
I will praise you with an upright heart
as I learn your righteous laws.
I will obey your decrees;
do not utterly forsake me.

verses 1–8

Not long ago we were studying the shortest psalm in the Psalter, which is also the shortest chapter in the Bible. Here, two psalms later, we are dealing with the longest psalm and the longest chapter. Psalm 117 contained two verses and five lines. Psalm 119 contains 176 verses and 315 lines. The first tells us to praise God. This psalm praises God for his Word, the Bible, because God has given us the Bible and it is only through the Bible that we can come to know who God is and how to praise him.

The German commentator Franz Delitzsch wrote, "Here we have set forth in inexhaustible fullness what the word of God is to a man and how a man is to behave himself in relation to it."[1] Derek Kidner, a more modern writer, says, "This giant among the psalms shows the full flowering of that 'delight . . . in the law of the Lord' which is described in Psalm 1, and gives its personal witness to the many-sided qualities of Scripture praised in Psalm 19:7ff."[2]

So much has been written on Psalm 119 that it is impossible to do full justice to it. In his *Treasury of David* Charles Spurgeon devotes 349 pages to it, which is virtually a book in itself. Charles Bridges, a Church of England evangelical of the last century, wrote 481 pages about it (Banner of Truth Trust edition). His book contains a sermon for each of the psalm's twenty-two stanzas and was issued in 1827, when Bridges was only thirty-three years old. Most impressive of all is the three-volume work on Psalm 119 by Thomas Manton, one of the most prolific of the Puritans. Each volume is from 500 to 600 pages in length, for a total of 1,677 pages (Banner of Truth Trust edition). The work has 190 long chapters, more than one for each verse.

There are many fascinating stories connected with this psalm. One of the most amusing concerns George Wishart, a Bishop of Edinburgh in the seventeenth century.[3] Wishart was condemned to death along with his famous patron, the Marquis of Montrose, and he would have been executed, except for this incident. When he was on the scaffold, he made use of a custom of the times that permitted the condemned to choose a psalm to be sung. He chose Psalm 119. Before two-thirds of the psalm was sung a pardon arrived, and Wishart's life was spared. The story has been told as an illustration of God's intervention to save a saintly person. The truth is different. Wishart was more renowned for shrewdness than for sanctity. He was expecting a pardon, requested the psalm to gain time, and, happily for him, succeeded in delaying the execution until his pardon came.[4]

Psalm 119 is an acrostic psalm, the most elaborate in the Psalter.[5] It is divided into twenty-two stanzas, one for each letter of the Hebrew alphabet, and each verse of each stanza begins with one of these letters in sequence. Thus each of the first eight verses begins with the letter *aleph,* each of the next eight verses begins with the letter *beth,* and so on. The acrostic pattern is marked by subheads in some English versions. The closest parallel to this pattern is chapter 3 of Lamentations. It is divided into twenty-two sections also, like Psalm 119, but each of its sections only has three verses.

The most striking feature of Psalm 119—one that every commentator mentions because it is so important to the psalm's theme—is that each verse of the psalm refers to the Word of God, the Bible, with only a small handful of exceptions. The Masoretes said that the Word of God is referred to in every verse but verse 122. Derek Kidner claims that there are three exceptions, verses 84, 121, and 122. Kidner seems to be right about verse 84, but verse 121 may not be an exception, if "righteous and just" can be understood as an oblique reference to God's Word. On the other hand, verses 90 and 132 also fail to mention the Bible, unless "faithfulness" in verse 90 and "name" in verse 132 mean God's Word. Whatever the case, at least 171 of the Psalm's 176 verses refer to the precepts, word, laws, commandments, or decrees of God explicitly.

There are at least eight synonyms for Scripture that dominate this psalm: "law" *(torah)*, which occurs twenty-five times; "word" *(dabar)*, twenty-four times; "rulings" or "ordinances" *(mispatim)*, twenty-three times; "testimonies" *(hedot)*, twenty-three times; "commandments" *(miswoth)*, twenty-two times; "decrees" or "statutes" *(huqqim)*, twenty-one times; "precepts" or "charges" *(piqqudim)*, twenty-one times; and "sayings," "promise," or "word" *('imra)*, nineteen times. However, there are other terms that are close to being synonyms, such as "way" *(derek)* three times, and "path" *(natiyb)* three times, and I have already mentioned the possibility that "righteous and just" and "name" mean the Bible. The rabbis said that there are ten synonyms for the Scriptures in this psalm, one for each of the Ten Commandments.

How to Be Blessed

When I started this chapter I quoted Derek Kidner, who referred to Psalm 119 as "the full flowering of that 'delight . . . in the law of the Lord' which is described in Psalm 1." Psalm 119 also begins like Psalm 1 by pronouncing a blessing on the one who forms his or her life according to the Word of God. Psalm 1 begins with a beatitude.

> Blessed is the man [whose] . . .
>   delight is in the law of the LORD (Ps. 1:1–2).

In a sense, Psalm 119 is the Bible's most thorough exposition of the beatitude of Psalm 1, which it indicates from the start by its opening lines:

> Blessed are they whose ways are blameless,
>   who walk according to the law of the LORD.
> Blessed are they who keep his statutes
>   and seek him with all their heart (vv. 1–2).

Many writers acknowledge that to be happy is a universal goal of men and women. The only people who do not want to be happy are abnormal. Apart from being instructed by God, human beings do not know how to achieve happiness. They think they will be happy if they can earn enough money, be respected by those with whom they work, acquire enough power to do whatever they like or to be free from all restraints, or discover someone who will love them without conditions. But these pursuits do not ensure happiness, and sin always warps and destroys even the best achievements.

How can a person find happiness? The Bible tells us that the path to a happy life—the Bible's word for it is "blessedness"—is conforming to the law of God.

When we hear the word "law" we think of the kind of laws that are made by local, state, and federal legislatures, things like tax laws, environmental laws, traffic laws, and scores of other kinds of laws. These laws are intended for our good, but they are essentially restrictive and for the most part we have a negative reaction to them. There are laws like that in the Bible too, of course: "You shall not murder," "You shall not commit adultery," "You shall not steal," and so on; but generally when the Bible speaks of the "law" *(torah)* of God, it has something much bigger in mind. It is referring to the whole of God's spoken and written revelation, containing all the various elements that the other words for law in this psalm suggest, including "words," "testimonies," "charges," "promises," and "ways."

We will look at each of those terms in detail as we go along. Here it is enough to say that what is being commended to us at the start of Psalm 119 is getting to know and live by the whole of God's revelation, which is what we call the Bible.

I stress living by the Bible, because that is what these opening verses emphasize. The blessedness they speak of is for those who "walk" according to God's Law and "keep" his statutes. In other words, from the beginning we are to understand that this keeping of the law is a practical matter, a way of life and not merely a course of academic study. On the other hand, it is also clear that we cannot live by the Bible unless we know it well. As the first psalm says, it must be our "meditat[ion] day and night" (Ps. 1:2).

May I suggest that if we are to meditate on the Bible day and night, we must have at least some if it committed to memory, which is what Christians in past ages of the church did. When I preached the sermon that is printed in this volume as the chapter on Psalm 117 ("The Shortest Psalm"), I suggested that because it is such a short psalm it might easily be memorized, which would be a good thing to do. Afterward at least one person said he intended to do it. What if I told you that in past days it was not uncommon for people to memorize Psalm 119?

John Ruskin was not a minister or even a theologian. He lived in the nineteenth century and was a British writer who specialized in works of art criticism. He had been raised by a Calvinistic mother who was unsparing both of herself and others and who, in his youth, had made him memorize large portions of the Bible. He memorized Psalms 23, 32, 90, 91, 103, 112, 119, and 139, to give just some examples. Later in his life Ruskin wrote of Psalm 119, "It is strange that of all the pieces of the Bible which my mother taught me, that which cost me most to learn, and which was, to my childish mind, chiefly repulsive—the 119th Psalm—has now become of all the most precious to me in its overflowing and glorious passion of love for the Law of God."[6]

William Wilberforce, the British statesman who was largely responsible for the abolition of the slave trade throughout the empire, wrote in his diary in the year 1819, "Walked today from Hyde Park Corner, repeating the 119th Psalm in great comfort."[7] Does it seem strange that busy Wilberforce should know this psalm by heart? Henry Martyn, pioneer missionary to India, memorized Psalm 119 as an adult in 1804. He had an extremely arduous life, but he confessed that it was the Bible alone that gave him strength to keep going. He died of exhaustion in 1812. David Livingstone, pioneer missionary to Africa, won a Bible from his Sunday school teacher by repeating Psalm 119 by heart—when he was only nine years old.

Each of these persons achieved a great deal for God. Who is to say that it was not their personal, word-for-word knowledge of the Bible that enabled them not only to live a godly life but also to accomplish what they did?

Derrick Bingham, a powerful Irish lay preacher whom I had the privilege of meeting in the summer of 1986 when I was in England taking part in the Keswick convention, told how he was called to the ministry through his mother. Every Irishman has a deathbed story about his mother, it seems, and Derrick is no exception. As his mother was dying, she said to him, "Derrick, my boy, you have the gift of gab. But you don't know the Word. If you'd learn the Word, the Lord might be able to use you." Derrick took that to heart, determined to study the Bible, and within three weeks of his mother's death was preaching.

We are not all called to be preachers, of course, but I am sure we could accomplish a great deal more of spiritual value than we do if we would only determine to get to know the Bible as John Ruskin, William Wilberforce, Henry Martyn, David Livingstone, and Derrick Bingham did. But we allow ourselves to be taken captive by the patterns of this world and fill our heads with its passing idle pleasures and fantasies instead.

Knowing and Obeying God's Word

Maybe I have said too much about *knowing* the Bible. That is where we must start, but the point of the opening verses of Psalm 119 is not merely that we must know the Bible but that we must determine to live by it—to keep, or obey, it. Verses 3 and 4 reiterate the point.

> They do nothing wrong;
> they walk in his ways.
> You have laid down precepts
> that are to be fully obeyed.

The reason we are not happy is that we sin, and the main reason we sin as much as we do is that we do not know the Bible well enough. These verses tell us that the happy people are those who "do nothing wrong." However, if we ask how they have learned not to do wrong, the answer surely is that they have learned to "walk in [God's] ways" and "obey" his precepts.

H. C. Leupold asks us to "note throughout [the psalm] how the law is sought for the very purpose of being kept, not for the sake of attaining a theoretical knowledge of it."[8] This is a truth taught elsewhere in the Bible, but it is very apparent in Psalm 119. Notice the words referring to human response and responsibility in just this one stanza: "walk," "keep," "obey," and "learn."

An Honest Wish

Sometimes when we read the Bible we get the idea that its characters were special people very unlike ourselves, and we are likely to do that here unless we are careful. We are only beginning our study of this psalm, but already we are reading about those happy people who are so because they live blamelessly according to the Law of the Lord, keep his statutes, and seek him with their whole heart. The psalmist must be one of these very blessed people, we think, otherwise he would not be writing as he does. However, we do not get very far into the psalm before we discover that he is very much like ourselves, at least in the respect that he has not yet gotten to be like the happy, blessed ones he is describing. He wants to be, but he is not yet. Therefore, he cries,

> Oh, that my ways were steadfast
> in obeying your decrees! (v. 5).

There is something that rings true and is commendably honest about this heartfelt cry of the psalmist. He is a very godly man, but he is acutely aware of how ungodly he still is.

I think he is saying in this verse almost exactly what the apostle Paul wrote at much greater length in Romans 7:

> I do not understand what I do. For what I want to do I do not do, but what I hate I do. . . . I have the desire to do what is good, but I cannot carry it out. For what I do is not the good I want to do; no, the evil I do not want to do—this I keep on doing. . . . So I find this law at work: When I want to do good, evil is right there with me. For in my inner being I delight in God's law; but I see another law at work in the members of my body, waging war against the law of my mind and making me a prisoner of the law of sin at work within my members" (Rom. 7:15–23).

Some people who have written about Romans 7 have supposed that in these verses Paul is writing about himself as an unbeliever, that is, before he came to know Jesus Christ as his Savior. That is not the case at all. Paul is writing as a Christian, saying that life even for an apostle is a struggle. Although we want to keep the Law of God, we do not keep it and, in fact, cannot keep it, at least not in our own power. It is a case of what J. I. Packer calls "spiritual realism."[9] It is a case of sheer honesty before the living God.

Honesty is not the whole story. The psalmist is like us in that he has not yet attained the obedience for which he yearns. He admits this openly. But it is possible to admit many things honestly and never go beyond the honesty, never making any progress toward a better or more obedient way of life. By contrast, the psalmist does want to make progress. So the question for us now is not so much, Is the psalmist like us? as, Are we like him? Are we like him in his desire to seek God, know the Bible, and actually obey God's commands?

A Strong Resolution

How determined was he? The final verse of the stanza is determined resolution.

> I will obey your decrees;
>   do not utterly forsake me.

This verse is a strong resolution, a sincere confession, and an urgent plea. The resolution: "I am resolved to obey God's decrees." The confession: "I cannot obey God's decrees unless God enables me do it." The plea: "Therefore, do not forsake me, O my God." The psalmist does not think God might somehow abandon him in the matter of his salvation. He was as aware as we should be that God's calling is unalterable. God has said, "Never will I leave you; never will I forsake you" (Heb. 13:5; cf. Deut. 31:6). What he is asking is for God to stick by him in his determination to live according to God's Law.

This first stanza has moved from statements about the Bible as a source of blessing for all persons to a very personal resolution. If the psalm is to be helpful to us, it must become personal in our lives too.

Psalm 119

Delight in God's Decrees: Part 2

Starting Young

How can a young man keep his way pure?
  By living according to your word.
I seek you with all my heart;
  do not let me stray from your commands.
I have hidden your word in my heart
  that I might not sin against you.
Praise be to you, O LORD;
  teach me your decrees.
With my lips I recount
  all the laws that come from your mouth.
I rejoice in following your statutes
  as one rejoices in great riches.
I meditate on your precepts
  and consider your ways.
I delight in your decrees;
  I will not neglect your word.
                                    verses 9–16

In the last chapter I pointed out that Psalm 119 is an acrostic poem in which the first words of each eight-verse stanza begin with one of the letters of the Hebrew alphabet, each stanza in succession. The second stanza's verses, verses 9–16, start with *beth*. The interesting thing about *beth* is that the word also means "a house," and as Herbert Lockyer notes, the underlying thought of the stanza is "making our heart a home for the Word of God."[1]

What is the condition of your heart, your home? Apart from the grace of God in your life it will always be occupied by such filthy evil spirits as lust, greed, pride, and self-love. If you try to drive these demons out by yourself, they will only return in greater numbers and your latter state will be worse than at the first (see Luke 11:24–26). God alone can cleanse the heart, and he does so through the agency of his Word, the Bible.

When Should We Begin?

In order to live a holy life we must give ourselves to God's Word, learning it and living by it. When should we start? The world has its answer. It says, Have your fling when you are young and settle down to being religious when you get old, if then. God's answer is quite different. God says, If you are going to live for me, you must begin at the earliest possible moment, without delay, preferably when you are very young (v. 9). If you do not live for me when you are young, you will probably not live for me when you are older either, and the end of your life will be ruinous.[2]

It does not require a great deal of wisdom to see why this is such good advice and so necessary. It is because the decisions of youth form habits that guide us from that point on and are hard to break. If we form good habits when we are young—reading the Bible, spending time in prayer, enjoying the company of God's people, going to church, rejecting sin, and practicing to be honest and do good—these habits will go with us through life and make good choices later in life easier. If on the contrary we make bad choices, later we will find good choices harder to make and the bad habits nearly impossible to break.

This point is so important that the Bible gives us numerous examples of young men who decided for God early and were blessed for it. Daniel and his three young friends are one example. When they were taken from their home in Jerusalem and brought to Babylon to serve the court of King Nebuchadnezzar, they were given the best of the food of Babylon, as favored civil servants. But we read early in the first chapter, "Daniel resolved not to defile himself with the royal food and wine" (Dan. 1:8).

This was the first of many tests that came into Daniel's life during his lengthy career in Babylon, but it established a pattern that enabled him to stand against the traps laid by his enemies later. To us, whether he would eat the king's food or drink his wine seems a small matter, hardly something to be fussed over. We have nothing to do with kosher rules and very little to do with diet. Yet it is the small things that form habits, and it is our habits that determine the course and outcome of our lives.

Years ago when I was studying Daniel I wrote,

Are you a young person? Then you should pay particularly close attention to this point. Most young people want their lives to count, and most Christian young people want their lives to count for God. Youth dreams big. That is right. You should dream big. But youth is also often impatient and undisciplined, and young people are tempted to let the little things slide. You must not do that if you are God's young man or God's young woman. God will make your life count, but this will not happen unless you determine to live for him in the little things now.[3]

This section of Psalm 119 is telling us that the best possible way to live for God and establish and maintain a pure life is by starting young.

In his last will and testament the Protestant Reformer Theodore Beza thanked God for the mercy of having been called to the knowledge of the truth when he was a youth of sixteen and thus, during a course of more than seventy years' walk with God, of having escaped "the pollutions of the world through lust."[4]

What Should We Do?

Psalm 119:9–11 also tells us what we should do to live for God: Hide God's Word in our hearts. Hiding his Word in our hearts means not just to read it but also to study it and even memorize it. In fact, memorizing is precisely what is called for, since it is only when the Word of God is readily available in our minds that we are able to recall it in moments of need and profit by it.

This point is closely tied to starting young, for it is far easier to memorize and retain material when a person is young than when he or she is older. Here is one of the sad failures of the contemporary church. If children and other young people can memorize easily, memorization should be stressed by churches for those in the early years. Instead of doing this, many churches, along with the general culture, have been "dumbing down" Christian education so that today children are barely taught anything in these vital early years. Instead of solid biblical theology, Bible memorization, and historic hymns, they are offered trivial stories, pointless games, and banal songs.

Years ago we determined to resist this trend at Tenth Presbyterian Church. Shortly after I began my pastorate in the late 1960s, a number of interested people put together a Sunday school curriculum in which the emphasis is on the great truths of the Bible, taught in three-year cycles. The first year teaches them as a sequence of important doctrines. The second year approaches the same truths in terms of a person's relationships to God and other people. The third year looks at these same teachings from the standpoint of history, asking, What is God doing in history? and, How do I fit in? The curriculum repeats this cycle every three years, so there is a constant reinforcement of these truths among the young people.

With this curriculum we outlined a thorough Bible memorization program in which parts of verses are learned by the youngest students, the whole of these verses and short passages by older children, and eventually several long chapters by those who are coming to the end of their Sunday school years. We also have the children memorize a simplified catechism, based on the Westminster Shorter Catechism, and we teach them some of the tried and true hymns of the church instead of choruses.

Does it work? It is impossible to produce the regenerating work of the Spirit of God in their hearts by any amount of good teaching, of course. Regeneration and growth are the work of God, not the work of people, but if what we are seeking is going to happen in any way, it is going to be by such teaching, since it is only through the saving revelation of God in Scripture that God himself may be found. We should notice that in Psalm 119:9–11 the poet links pursuit of God's Word to the pursuit of God himself. "I seek you with all my heart" (v. 10). Therefore, I live "according to your word" (v. 9).

Why Should We Do It?

Now we ask why we should engage in such study. We have already seen one answer: to know God. But what the poet is particularly interested in here is for us to live holy lives, that we "might not sin against [God]" (v. 11).

We live in a corrupt and sinful world, and there is nothing in the world that in itself will help us live a pure life. More than one hundred years ago the Bible teacher Alexander Maclaren wrote that the world is "a great deal fuller of inducements to do wrong than of inducements to do right, . . . a great many bad things that have a deceptive appearance of pleasure, a great many circumstances in which it seems far easier to follow the worse than to follow the better course. And so unless a man has learned the great art of saying, 'No!' 'So did not I because of the fear of the Lord,' he will come to rack and ruin without a doubt."[5]

What can preserve us from ruin? What can empower us to say no to temptation? What can enable us to live a holy life in the midst of our most wicked surroundings? Only the Word of God, the Bible, which we must study and hide away in our hearts. Jesus told his disciples, "You are already clean *because of the word* I have spoken to you" (John 15:3, italics added). He also prayed to the Father on their behalf, saying, "Sanctify them *by the truth*," and adding, *"your word is truth"* (John 17:17, italics added).

Here is an outline for verse 11 that may help you to remember what we have noticed in the psalm so far.

The best thing—"thy Word"

Hidden in the best place—"my heart"

For the best purpose—"that I might not sin against thee"[6]

Remember that the Bible is God's cleansing agent for sin and that without it we will never live a holy life.

How Can We Do It?

There is a fourth important teaching in this stanza: We cannot understand God's Word by ourselves, and therefore we need God himself for our teacher. Verse 12 notes this need by coupling a line of praise with a line of petition.

> Praise be to you, O LORD;
> teach me your decrees.

The Protestant Reformers talked about this truth by stressing the necessary link between God's Word and God's Spirit. These men—Martin Luther, John Calvin, and others—had a strong trust in the Bible. They recognized that although God has revealed himself in a general way in creation so that people are without excuse if they fail to seek him out and thank him for life and its blessings, and although he has also revealed himself preeminently in Jesus Christ, the only place we have saving revelation and the only way we can know about Jesus is in the Bible. They understood that the only way we can get to know God is through God's self-revelation in his written Word.

At the same time they were also aware of our need of the Holy Spirit to teach us if we are to understand and rightly apply the Bible. They thought of such verses as 1 John 5:6: "The Spirit . . . testifies, because the Spirit is the truth" and 1 Corinthians 2:12–14: "We have not received the spirit of the world but the Spirit who is from God, that we may understand what God has freely given us. This is what we speak, not in words taught us by human wisdom but in words taught by the Spirit, expressing spiritual truths in spiritual words. The man without the Spirit does not accept the things that come from the Spirit of God, for they are foolishness to him, and he cannot understand them, because they are spiritually discerned."

When they thought of these verses and others concerning the work of the Holy Spirit, Luther, Calvin, and the others understood that although we have the Bible to study we must also have the Holy Spirit to teach us what is taught in it. They said that without the Spirit the Bible is a dead book. Therefore, the person "without the Spirit" cannot understand it. On the other hand, without the Word as an objective guide from God, claims to a special leading by the Holy Spirit lead to error, excess, or foolishness.

When we study the Bible we must also pray, asking God to be our teacher. It is God himself we are seeking, after all, and his thoughts are not our thoughts, neither are his ways our ways (Isa. 55:8). Besides, we have sinful and deceitful hearts that will keep us from hearing and obeying God unless God himself breaks through to teach us.

Four Helpful Exercises

The psalmist seems to be writing primarily to the young in this stanza, so it is not surprising to find him ending with four points of very simple, practical advice, expressed in terms of his own experience. We might call them four exercises designed to help us master Scripture.

1. *"With my lips I recount all the laws that come from your mouth"* (v. 13). One of the best ways to learn anything is to verbalize it or teach it to others. I have a far easier time learning some truth and I retain it longer if I work it into a sermon or make it part of one of our Bible study seminars.

Not long ago I attended a meeting of the Board of Directors of Bible Study Fellowship and learned about an African woman who attends one of the large classes in Nairobi. Each week, after attending the Nairobi class, she goes back to her village and teaches what she has learned in the city to about forty women who gather to hear her in the village. Who do you think learns most from the Nairobi class? Who will retain it longer? If we are alive for God, our lives will be like the muscle of the heart, which is constantly expanding to take in a fresh supply of blood—the life—and then contracting to push it on and give it out.

Martin Luther observed that some people speak God's truth but do not have it in their hearts, while others have it in their hearts but are afraid to proclaim it vigorously for fear of losing friends and making enemies and persecutors. He said, "It is not enough to believe with the heart unto righteousness, unless confession unto salvation is also made with the mouth (Rom. 10:10)."[7]

2. *"I rejoice in following your statutes"* (v. 14). It is a natural tendency of a healthy mind to remember the pleasant and forget the unpleasant. A person who does the opposite is psychologically unstable. It follows that one good way to learn and retain God's Word is to rejoice in it, which is what the psalmist says he has been doing. Rejoicing in God's Word can be done in a lot of ways, privately in our personal devotions and publicly in witnessing situations. One very excellent way is by joyful worship in regular church services. I am seldom more joyful than when I am singing the great hymns of the faith in church with other Christians.

3. *"I meditate on your precepts"* (v. 15). Meditation is recalling what we have committed to memory and then turning it over and over in our minds to see the fullest implications and applications of the truth. The Virgin Mary meditated after the birth of her son, the Lord Jesus Christ, for we are told in Luke 2:19, "Mary treasured up all these things and pondered them in her heart."

4. *"I delight in your decrees; I will not neglect your word"* (v. 16). "Delight" in this last verse is not the same word as in verse 14 ("rejoice"). The former is an exuberant, festive joyfulness; the second a settled pleasure. But the two are parts of the same emotion, so what is new in the last line is the determination not to neglect Bible study. It is easy to do, but we must determine not to allow other pressing matters to crowd out the study of God's Word.

The future tense ("I will") in the last line (in some translations the future tense occurs earlier) shows how the author passes from declaring what he has done or is in the habit of doing to what he will do. What he says he will do is "not neglect" the Bible. He is determined to study it. Are you?

Psalm 119

Delight in God's Decrees: Part 3

Trials on the Way

Do good to your servant, and I will live;
  I will obey your word.
Open my eyes that I may see
  wonderful things in your law.
I am a stranger on earth;
  do not hide your commands from me.
My soul is consumed with longing
  for your laws at all times.
You rebuke the arrogant, who are cursed
  and who stray from your commands.
Remove from me scorn and contempt,
  for I keep your statutes.
Though princes sit together and slander me,
  your servant will meditate on your decrees.
Your statutes are my delight;
  they are my counselors.

I am laid low in the dust;
  renew my life according to your word.
I recounted my ways and you answered me;
  teach me your decrees.
Let me understand the teaching of your precepts;
  then I will meditate on your wonders.
My soul is weary with sorrow;
  strengthen me according to your word.

verses 17–28

E. M. Blaiklock is a Bible scholar from
Australia and a former professor of classics at the University of Auckland,
New Zealand. He has written a book called *The Bible & I* about the influence of the Bible on his life.[1] At one point in this book he thinks back
over the weeks he once spent lecturing on Psalm 119 and how, as he studied and lectured, he came to appreciate the suffering the writer seems to
have gone through.

> He had known persecution, that most hideous of man's sins (22, 23); he had
> suffered under the heavy or the ruthless hand of authority, as Christians (and
> Jews) still do in the lands where the blanket of the dark has fallen (61, 69).
> His faith had staggered under the load of it all (6, 22, 31). He had known
> pressure to give in and conform. . . . The third section [which we are to study
> now, along with the fourth] seems to be particularly autobiographical. The
> writer had known deprivation and fear for his life (17), the dryness of soul of
> which Cowper wrote ("where is the blessedness I knew . . .") when the word
> itself seems to lose its savor (18) under the stress of life. He had known loneli-
> ness and rejection (19) [and] the agony of seeming abandonment (20).[2]

As Blaiklock worked through these prayers and expressions, a man seemed
to emerge through the mist of words whom he seemed both to know and
understand. The psalmist is a person we too should know and understand,
simply because he is so much like us—at least in these experiences.

For Righteousness' Sake

There are many references throughout the psalm to trials the writer had
gone through, as Blaiklock's overview indicates. We will see more of them
in the three sections comprising verses 65–88 (*teth, yodh,* and *kaph*), but
there are also many examples in verses 17–32, the stanzas marked *gimel* and
daleth. What is unique about these specific trials is that they seem to have
come to the psalmist because of his determination to adhere to God's
Word. There are not just trials and tribulations but rather persecutions for
righteousness' sake (see Matt. 5:10).

The psalmist writes, in the first stanza, of the blessedness that comes to
the person who determines to live according to the Law of God. In the second stanza he suggests that the time to start living by God's law is when a
person is young. Now, in stanzas three and four, he speaks of four trials that
will come to one who is walking in that way.

1. *Alienation* (v. 19). The psalmist calls himself "a stranger on earth."
There are two ideas in this expression. First, it suggests that we are only pass-
ing through this world for a short while, with little time to know and live by
God's Word. Therefore, we should devote ourselves to getting to know the
Bible well. The verses around this phrase seem to support this idea: "I am a

stranger on earth"; therefore, "do not hide your commands from me" (v. 19) and "My soul is consumed with longing for your laws at all times" (v. 20). The meaning is similar to that bit of doggerel we sometimes hear:

> Only one life, it will soon be past,
> Only what's done for Christ will last.

In this case the concern of the psalmist is with getting to know and then actually living by God's Word.

Second, there is the idea of being out of place in this world. Believers are alienated from the world by belonging to God, whom the world does not know or honor. This idea seems supported by the larger context, for after speaking of his own desire to know God's commands, the poet writes of the "arrogant, who are cursed and who stray from your commands" (v. 21) and the "princes" who "sit together and slander [him]" (v. 23).

This is an important truth to know and come to terms with: If you are trying to follow God, the world is going to treat you as an alien, for that is what you will be. You cannot expect to be at home in it, and if you are, well, it is an indication that you really do not belong to Christ or at least are living far from him. Do you think that is too harsh? Jesus expressed it in even stronger terms.

> If you belonged to the world, it would love you as its own. As it is, you do not belong to the world, but I have chosen you out of the world. That is why the world hates you. Remember the words I spoke to you: "No servant is greater than his master." If they persecuted me, they will persecute you also (John 15:19–20).

We may not be at home in a world that does not know God, but we have a home in God and can rejoice in him because he alone is fully satisfying. Saint Augustine said it well: "Thou hast formed us for thyself, and our hearts are restless till they find rest in thee."[3]

2. *Slander* (vv. 22–23). One form of the poet's alienation was the slander directed against him by the rulers. Yet slander is a step beyond mere alienation. Believers feel like "strangers on earth" because they really are strangers—they do not fit in. "Stranger" is an accurate description of their condition. Slander, however, deals with accusations that are untrue. It assigns false motives to the good we may be trying to do and even charges us with evil that we do not do. Not to fit in seems bad enough, but to be falsely accused when we are actually trying to live for God and do good is worse.

Alexander Maclaren wrote how slander follows the writer's determination to live by God's Law.

> In verse 22 he prays that reproach and shame, which wrapped him like a covering, may be lifted from him; and his plea in verse 22b declares that he lay under these because he was true to God's statutes. In verse 23 we see the

source of the reproach and shame, in the conclave of men in authority, whether foreign princes or Jewish rulers, who were busy slandering him, and plotting his ruin; while, with wonderful beauty, the contrasted picture in [verse 23]b shows the object of that busy talk, sitting silently absorbed in meditation on the higher things of God's statutes.[4]

When we are falsely accused, all we can do is take our cause to God, who will vindicate us in his own time. Meanwhile we must continue to study the Bible and try to live for God as well as we can.

3. *Abasement, or humiliation* (v. 25). In the next stanza *(daleth)* the writer says he is "laid low in the dust" (v. 25) because he had determined to live according to God's Word. The Hebrew actually speaks of "cleaving" to the dust, of being so low that one actually seems to be bonded to humiliation.

4. *Sorrow* (v. 28). The writer says that his soul has been made "weary with sorrow." There are different things one can feel sorrow for: the unregenerate world that is perishing, one's own sins, the loss—either through death or misunderstanding—of a person who has been close to us. Here the psalmist seems to be expressing sorrow at his abased condition, because he has been rejected, slandered, and humiliated by other people.

Have you ever felt that way? I am sure you have. Most of us have at times. We just feel terribly down, as we say. There is nothing wrong with feeling down in itself. It is a natural response to the kind of trials the psalmist has been describing. What is wrong is allowing such feelings to turn us inward, or even worse, away from God. Instead of looking inward, the writer renews his determination to hold fast to the promises of God.

Living by God's Word

The psalmist's trials added up to the threat of death, but he wants to live. That is the point from which each of these two stanzas sets out.

> Do good to your servant, and I will live . . .
> renew my life according to your word (vv. 17, 25).

It is not mere physical life that he is wanting; he wants the fullness of spiritual life. Hence, his concern is to live by the Word of God. He says that he is "consumed with longing" for it (v. 20), that it is his "delight" (v. 24), that he has "chosen the way of truth" (v. 30), and that he wants to "hold fast to [God's] statutes" (v. 31).

The writer of this psalm lived hundreds of years before Jesus Christ, but if he had been living in Christ's day, he would have understood readily Jesus' reply to the first of the devil's temptations. Jesus had been led into the wilderness by God's Spirit, and after having fasted for forty days he was hungry. The devil came to him suggesting, "If you are the Son of God, tell these stones to become bread" (Matt. 4:3).

Jesus replied, "It is written: 'Man does not live on bread alone, but on every word that comes from the mouth of God'" (Matt. 4:4), quoting from Deuteronomy 8:3. He meant that it is more important to feed spiritually on God's Word than to feed physically on food. Likewise, the psalmist knew that it was more important for him to meditate on God's decrees and obey them than to escape the world's contempt and hatred if escaping that hatred meant turning his back on God's Word.

Wonderful Things in God's Law

In each of the stanzas we have studied we found the writer's confession that although he was determined to study God's Word and live by it, he could not do so by himself. In the first stanza he cried out, "I will obey your decrees; do not utterly forsake me" (v. 8). In the second stanza he prayed, "teach me your decrees" (v. 12). It is the same in stanzas three and four. Here he is reflecting on his many trials because of wanting to live by God's Law. But if he is to live by it, God will have to open it up to him, teach him, give him understanding, and keep him from false ways. He prays four things.

1. *"Open my eyes"* (vv. 18–19). The verb "open" in verse 18 is used in the Balaam story where the Lord opened Balaam's eyes so he could see the angel of the Lord standing in the road with his sword drawn (Num. 22:31). It has to do with removing a veil, or covering. Here it does not mean that the Word itself is covered, as if it were somehow unclear. The Bible is perfectly clear. That is what we mean when we speak of the clarity or perspicuity of Scripture. There is nothing dull about it; rather, the dullness is in us. Therefore, what we need is the removing of the veil from our eyes so we can see those "wonderful things" that are in the Bible.

Howard Carter was the world-renowned Egyptologist who discovered the marvelous gold artifacts of the tomb of King Tutankhamen in 1922. When he exposed the steps leading down to the burial chamber, Carter summoned Lord Carnarvon, the expedition's sponsor, to be present when the tomb was opened. The two men made their way to the tomb and had the workmen push back the last covering to the door of the entrance chamber.

Lord Carnarvon asked impatiently, "Do you see anything?"

"Yes, wonderful things," was Carter's memorable answer.

And wonderful they were! The most lavish, most beautiful objects ever found in any ancient tomb. Still they were pale compared to the far more wonderful things to be found in Scripture by anyone when God opens his or her spiritually blind eyes to perceive them. These treasures are wonderful in themselves, wonderful because their source is in God, wonderful because of what they do in us and for us, and wonderful because they are everlasting when everything else we know is rapidly passing away.

Jesus opened the eyes of the two Emmaus disciples to see how he had to suffer and then enter into his glory. Afterward they testified, "Were not our hearts burning within us while he talked with us on the road and opened the Scriptures to us?" (Luke 24:32).

It is important that God open our eyes, but that is not the whole story. While he was praying, the psalmist was also doing his part, which he describes in verse 20 and following as "longing for [God's] laws" (v. 20), "meditat[ing] on [God's] decrees" (v. 23), and "delight[ing]" in [God's] statutes (v. 24).

In the *Treasury of David* Charles Spurgeon cites John Kerr as writing, "A man will never grow into the knowledge of God's word by idly waiting for some new gift of discernment, but by diligently using that which God has already bestowed upon him, and using at the same time all other helps that lie within his reach."[5] In other words, if we want to see wonderful things in the Scriptures, it is not enough for us merely to ask God to open our eyes that we might see them. We must also study the Bible carefully. The Holy Spirit is given not to make our study unnecessary but to make it effective.

2. *"Teach me your decrees"* (v. 26). This is the same request he made in stanza two, verse 12. When we were looking at that verse, I called attention to the way the Protestant Reformers always stressed how the written Word of God and the activity of the Spirit of God go together. The Spirit speaks through the Word. So if we desire to grow in grace, we need both to study the Bible and also ask God through his Holy Spirit to be our teacher.

3. *"Let me understand the teaching"* (v. 27). This addition to the request of verse 26 could simply be one more case of the parallelism that is so major a feature of Hebrew poetry, but it is probably more, since verse 27 goes on to speak of meditating on the Bible's wonders. In other words, it is concerned with a deep understanding, one that goes beyond a mere understanding of the words to a profound understanding of what they reveal about the nature of God, the gospel, and God's ways.

4. *"Keep me from deceitful ways"* (v. 29). The last of the psalmist's four requests is to be kept from sin, which is what he has been thinking about all along. How? It is by the grace of God, but more specifically, it is by the grace of God exercising itself through the written word. Verse 29 makes this point more strongly in the Hebrew text than in English, since the verb translated "be gracious" in our text actually has the sense of "graciously teach," a single word. The full thought is, If we are to be kept from sin, it must be by the grace of God exercised through the teaching of his Word. "How can a young man keep his way pure? By living according to your word" (v. 9).

Running the Race

We have already seen in the third stanza that although God must be our teacher, there are nevertheless things we need to do: "long for" God's laws (v. 20), "meditate" on his decrees (v. 23), and "delight" in his statutes (v. 24). It is the same as we come to the end of stanza four. Here, in the last three verses, the psalmist indicates by three powerful verbs what else is required if we are to live a godly life.

1. *We must choose the right way* (v. 30). Nobody ever just stumbles onto the right path. If we are going to live for God by learning and obeying his Word, the Bible, we must choose to do so and apply ourselves firmly to the task. The psalmist indicates the nature of his choice when he says,

> I have chosen the way of truth;
> I have set my heart on your laws.

2. *We must hold God's statutes fast* (v. 31). "Hold" is the same word as "laid low" in verse 25. Literally it means to "cleave." In verse 25 the psalmist said he was cleaving to the dust so great was his humiliation; here he is found cleaving to God's Word. Would this were the case with each of us, that the result of our being greatly abased is that we would likewise be greatly committed to God's Word! We may be struck down, but in our abasement we need to hold the Word high. Indeed, what else is there to do? In times of acute distress there is nothing to cleave to but God and his testimonies. It was said of Moses that he spent forty years in the wilderness learning to be nothing so that he might spend the next forty years proving God to be everything.

3. *We must run the course set before us* (v. 32). This fourth stanza began with the psalmist being "laid low." Here it ends with him running vigorously and freely in God's way. Do you see your Christian life as a race to be won, or do you regard it merely as a casual stroll and follow your Lord apathetically and at a distance? Hebrews 12:1 urges, "Let us throw off everything that hinders and the sin that so easily entangles, and let us run with perseverance the race marked out for us." Likewise, the apostle Paul declared, "I have fought the good fight, I have finished the race, I have kept the faith. Now there is in store for me the crown of righteousness, which the Lord, the righteous Judge, will award to me on that day—and not only to me, but also to all who have longed for his appearing" (2 Tim. 4:7–8).

Psalm 119

Delight in God's Decrees: Part 4

In God's School

Teach me, O LORD, to follow your decrees;
  then I will keep them to the end.
Give me understanding, and I will keep your law
  and obey it with all my heart.
Direct me in the path of your commands,
  for there I find delight.
Turn my head toward your statutes
  and not toward selfish gain.
Turn my eyes away from worthless things;
  renew my life according to your word.
Fulfill your promise to your servant,
  so that you may be feared.
Take away the disgrace I dread,
  for your laws are good.
How I long for your precepts!
  Renew my life in your righteousness.
                              verses 33–40

Christianity and learning have always gone hand in hand. Wherever the gospel of Jesus Christ has gone in this world, grammar schools, literacy classes, and schools of higher learning have inevitably followed. The gospel opens the mind not only to matters of the soul but also to the mind itself, to nature, humanity, history, and the marvels of the world God created. In the fifth stanza of Psalm 119 we have the important combination of learning and religion, but the kind of learning the psalmist has in mind is learning God's Word. He wants to learn God's Word so he might walk in it, or obey it. In order to make progress in this school he asks God to be his teacher, as he did in verses 12, 26, and 27.

This stanza is filled with prayers, nine in all. There is a linguistic reason for all the prayers. As Leslie Allen points out, this is the fifth, or *he*, stanza of the psalm, *he* being the fifth letter of the Hebrew alphabet, and in Hebrew *he* is used at the beginning of verbs to make them causative.[1] In English we would translate such verbs as "Cause me to learn," "Cause me to have understanding," "Cause me to walk," and so on, which sound awkward. The verbs are better rendered as petitions, which is what the Hebrew sentences actually are. As a result, we have: "Teach me, O Lord, to follow your decrees" (v. 33), "Give me understanding" (v. 34), "Direct me in the path of your commands" (v. 35), "Turn my heart toward your statutes" (v. 36), and so on throughout the stanza. The fifth stanza of Psalm 119 is a series of prayers for acceptance, progress, assistance, and perseverance in God's school of spiritual learning.

Matriculating in God's School

Often when a person is applying to a school in this country one of the questions on the application form will be, Why do you want to come to this university? A clever student will usually commend himself by the way he or she answers. A good answer could be, "I hope to become the well-rounded, intelligent contributing person I know I can be and that I believe only your school can make me." In the first two verses of this stanza the author is applying for matriculation in God's school, only he is applying not because of what he has and wants to develop, but because of what he does not have but needs to have to live a holy life.

Verses 33–34 ask God to "teach" the psalmist to follow God's decrees and "give . . . understanding" to keep God's Law, both of which are virtually the same thing. The reason he is asking for this instruction is so he might be able to keep God's decrees "to the end" and be able to obey God's Law "with all [his] heart." "To the end" means without time limit, and "with all my heart" means without reservation. What the writer says he is lacking is understanding and the ability to do even what he is brought to understand. Charles Bridges wrote wisely, "We are equally ignorant of the path of God's commandments, and impotent to go in it. We need therefore double assistance. Our minds must be enlightened; our hearts constrained."[2] We too must start with this confession, if we would learn God's ways.

Advancing in God's School

One of the things a superior student should care about once he or she is admitted to a good school is achieving a well-rounded education. Much of today's education is essentially only learning a trade so a person can earn a decent living, but years ago in many places and still today in some places there was and is concern for students to develop in many areas of knowledge. Such schools require a prescribed number of courses covering the humanities, social sciences, and physical sciences. There should be a concern for the arts, opportunities to participate in music groups and perhaps also in drama, and also athletic programs of various kinds.

It is useful to think in terms of a balanced education to understand what is going on next in Psalm 119. A well-rounded education is education for the whole person, and this is what the psalmist wants for himself. What is the best way to achieve a well-rounded education in God's school? Verses 34–37 teach that it is by keeping God's Word before one's mind, feet, heart, and eyes—four important parts of the body.

1. *The mind: "Give me understanding"* (v. 34). The wisdom the writer seeks is practical. It is walking according to God's law as well as knowing it. It is necessary to know it; in fact, it is necessary to have an intellectual understanding of God's ways before the application, simply because we cannot apply what we are ignorant of. That is why the apostle Paul began the application section of Romans with words about the renewal of the mind (Rom. 12:1–2). Likewise, the psalmist begins with the mind, asking God to help him understand the Bible.

Does your mind matter? Years ago John R. W. Stott, the former rector of All Soul's Church in London, wrote a little book insisting that it does. It is titled, significantly enough, *Your Mind Matters.*[3] It deals with six areas of Christian living, arguing that each is impossible without a proper and energetic use of our minds: Christian worship, Christian faith, Christian holiness, Christian guidance, Christian evangelism, and Christian ministry.

Our minds matter in worship, because worship is honoring God for who he is, and in order to do that we must understand something about his wonderful attributes. We must praise him for being sovereign, holy, merciful, wise, omniscient, and so on. Without a mental understanding of God's attributes worship becomes only an emotional binge in which we indulge our feelings.

Our minds matter for faith, because faith is believing and acting on the promises of God, and in order to believe God's promises we must understand what they are. Apart from a right use of the mind, faith becomes only a feeling or, worse yet, wishful thinking.

Our minds matter for growth in holiness, which is what we are chiefly concerned about in this psalm, because growth in holiness (sanctification) is not a matter of emotions or simply following a formula for living—the two most popular approaches to sanctification today—but rather knowing what God has done in us when he joined us to Christ, and then acting on it because there is really no other way for us to act. As I said in my studies of Romans 6, it is knowing that we cannot go back to being what we were and therefore that there is no direction for us to go but forward.[4]

Our minds matter in seeking personal guidance as to how we should live and what decisions we must make, because the principles by which we must be guided are in the Bible. God does not guide us by mystical revelations, and we cannot count on God's providential ordering of events alone, though he does indeed order all things. The chief and usually the only way God guides is by the Bible. To be guided by God we need to study to understand God's Word and then apply its principles. That cannot be done without thinking.

Our minds matter in evangelism, because if a person must have faith to be saved and if faith is responding to the Word of God and acting on it, then we must present the teaching of the Bible and the claims of Jesus Christ so others can understand them. They must know what they are believing. If they do not understand what they are believing and therefore are only able to respond emotionally, theirs is not a true faith nor a true conversion.

Finally, our minds matter in ministry, first, in seeking out a sphere of service (What am I good at? Where do my spiritual gifts lie? What is God leading me to do for him?) and second, to serve in that sphere well (How should I go about the work I have been given?).

Stott argues that anti-intellectualism is "part of the fashion of the world and therefore a form of worldliness. To denigrate the mind is to undermine foundational Christian doctrines." He asks pointedly, "Has God created us rational beings, and shall we deny our humanity which he has given us? Has God spoken to us, and shall we not listen to his words? Has God renewed our mind through Christ, and shall we not think with it? Is God going to judge us by his Word, and shall we not be wise and build our house upon this rock?"[5]

2. *The feet: "Direct me in the path of your commands"* (v. 35). If we are going to make progress in God's school, we need God's Word before our feet, to guide our paths. The great Puritan commentator on Psalm 119, Thomas Manton, wrote, "David, in the former verses, had begged for light, now for strength to walk according to this light."[6]

What is this way in which we should walk? The Hebrew word translated "path" is from a root verb meaning "to tread" and therefore means "the trodden way," not a new direction. In other words, it is a path because of the many who have gone before us. Herbert Lockyer speaks of "an accustomed trail, plain with the track of all the pious pilgrim's feet of past times."[7]

It is hard not to think here of Jeremiah 6:16, a verse that meant so much to the Puritans and others who have followed in their paths.

> Stand at the crossroads and look;
>   ask for the ancient paths,
> ask where the good way is, and walk in it.

We live in an age of constant innovations. Everything old is thought to be bad, and what is good is new. Even old products are sold by giving them a new twist or look: "The New Ford Taurus" or "New Improved Efferdent." We tend to think this way too, because of our cultural environment. The psalm reminds us that the Lord's way is not a new or novel way but rather that old established way in which the people of God have walked from the very beginning of his dealings with the race.

In terms of the Christian life we are not innovators; we are imitators. We want to be like those who have gone before us and walk as they walked. We want to be like Abraham and Moses and David and the apostle Paul and the Reformers and the Puritans and the giants of our own time. But we also remember that this is a narrow path and there are only a few who walk it (Matt. 7:13–14).

3. *The heart: "Turn my heart toward your statutes"* (v. 36). In order to make progress in God's school we have to want to walk it, which is what the author prays for next when he implores, "Turn my heart toward your statutes and not toward selfish gain."

This is the first time in this stanza that the writer has mentioned a negative alternative to what he is asking God to help him do. He is asking God to turn his heart toward the Bible *rather than* allowing him to pursue selfish gain. For the first time he is confessing to a potentially divided mind. He wants to pursue God's Law, but he knows his heart and is aware that he could very well also decline into covetousness, which is the ruin of the soul. Jesus said, "You cannot serve both God and money" (Matt. 6:24). The psalmist knew that fact. Moreover, he knew the appeal riches have and his inclination to pursue them. So he asks God to incline his heart away from riches toward God and his Law instead.

4. *The eyes: "Turn my eyes away from worthless things"* (v. 37). Eyes are needed for study of God's Word. Here the author does not even speak of what the eyes should be turned toward, only what he wants them to be turned from. He wants to be delivered from "worthless things," or "vanities."

This verse follows naturally from the one before it, for once the writer has begun to consider what might keep him from a profitable study of the Bible, he realizes that he is tempted by more than mere riches. There are many worthless things, and they are all alluring. If we are to advance in God's school, we must fix our eyes on the things of God, which are lasting, rather than the things of this world, which are passing away.

Verse 37 occurs in *Pilgrim's Progress* at a familiar point in the narrative, when Christian and Faithful come to Vanity Fair on their way to the Celestial City. Here all the merchandise of the world is for sale, but those who are on their way to the Celestial City do not fit in with these people, and when they are asked to stop and buy, they put their hands to their ears and run away, crying, "Turn away mine eyes from beholding Vanity," and look toward heaven to show where the business of their lives is.[8] That sentence—"Turn away mine eyes from beholding Vanity"—is Psalm 119:37 in the version available to Bunyan. It is the Christian's only wise response to the allurements of this world.[9]

Encouragement in God's School

Faced by temptations and the dangers of life, the psalmist is aware that he needs help. Where is help to be found? The only help is from God, and the only reason he can hope for God's help is that God has promised to help him, as he indicates in verse 38: "Fulfill your promise to your servant, so that you may be feared."

What promise is this? There is no reason to think he is singling out any one promise. Rather he is thinking of the entire Word of God, as he has been doing all along. The noun translated "promise" here is actually one of the Hebrew terms for "word" (*'mra*), sometimes translated "a saying" since it comes from the verb "to say." The King James Version and the Revised Version translate it as "word" throughout. The Jerusalem and New English Bibles use "promise." The Revised Standard Version has a combination of the two. The reason for the choice of *'mra* here is that the psalmist knows if he is to complete his course of study, he will have to live by God's Word at all times and in all its parts, not picking and choosing, as it were. This verse is a perfect Old Testament expression of what Jesus said to Satan when he was tempted by him to turn stones into bread. He told him, "Man does not live on bread alone, but on every word that comes from the mouth of God" (Matt. 4:4; cf. Deut. 8:3).

In a sense, all God's Word is promise—a promise of life to those who repent of sin and determine to go in God's way, and a promise of death and judgment for those who reject the gospel message. The psalmist is clinging to the promise of life because he fears, or stands in awe of, God. If we are to profit from his example, we must do the same. Do you fear God? Do you live by every word from his mouth?

Not Dropping Out of God's School

The last two verses of this section bring in a new idea that in terms of attending God's school compares to the mistake of dropping out. When young people drop out of high school, as many do today, especially from city schools, there is very little future for them. They can labor at unskilled, low-paying jobs. Or they can sell drugs. It was because of the acute nature of this problem in Philadelphia that Tenth Presbyterian Church began City Center Academy.

The problem the psalmist says might cause him to drop out is "disgrace" ("reproach," as some of the versions have it). "Take away the disgrace I dread, for your laws are good," he implores.

Disgrace in verse 39 can be thought of in either of two ways. On the one hand, it could be the disgrace brought on by God because of the writer's sin. That is, he could disgrace himself by his disobedience. On the other hand, it could be disgrace heaped on him by sinners because of his faithful adherence to God's Law. Franz Delitzsch argues that "the reproach which the poet fears in verse 39 is not the reproach of confessing, but of denying God."[10] Alexander Maclaren interprets the verse as describing reproach before God too, because it gives a better meaning to the words "for your laws are good."[11] However, H. C. Leupold chooses the second interpretation, that it is referring to reproach heaped on the psalmist by sinful men, for the same reason, that it gives a better sense to the second half of verse 39. He writes, "God's ordinances should be confessed and upheld, and whatever reproach we may suffer in upholding them God is readily able to turn away from us."[12] Thomas Manton thinks it is the reproach of enemies too: "the reproach which was like to be his lot and portion in the world, through the malice of his enemies."[13]

This disagreement probably cannot be resolved with certainty, at least at this stage of our scholarship. In either case, the danger is the same: the danger of dropping out of God's school either because of personal failure or because of other people's scorn. Are you tempted to drop out because of your own failures or because of other people's scorn? Do not do it. Keep on! Remember Jesus' words: "All men will hate you because of me, but he who stands firm to the end will be saved" (Matt. 10:22).

Psalm 119

Delight in God's Decrees: Part 5

Finding God in His Word

May your unfailing love come to me, O LORD,
your salvation according to your promise;
then I will answer the one who taunts me,
for I trust in your word.
Do not snatch the word of truth from my mouth,
for I have put my hope in your laws.
I will always obey your law,
for ever and ever.
I will walk about in freedom,
for I have sought out your precepts.
I will speak of your statutes before kings
and will not be put to shame,
for I delight in your commandments
because I love them.
I reach out my hands for your commandments, which I love,
and I meditate on your decrees.

Remember your word to your servant,
for you have given me hope.
My comfort in my suffering is this:
Your promise renews my life. . . .

You are my portion, O LORD.
I have promised to obey your words.
I have sought your face with all my heart;
be gracious to me according to your promise. . . .
The earth is filled with your love, O LORD;
teach me your decrees.

verses 41–64

Bruce Waltke is professor of Old Testament studies at Regent College, Vancouver, British Columbia, and a former teacher at a number of evangelical schools, including Westminster and Dallas seminaries. He is an outstanding scholar, and he has written a book in which he testifies to the importance of prayer in getting to know God through Bible study.

He explains that early in his life he used to read the Bible for its academic merit and that he got nothing out of it. Then one day he heard a preacher say it is necessary to ask God for enlightenment. So he began praying, "Lord, speak to me through your Word." At first his reading seemed much the same, but soon it changed. He writes, "Within three weeks of praying that prayer as I read, my heart began to burn within me. I started to see new things in Scripture. God began revealing to me how his Word should change my life. I developed a love for his teaching. God heard my prayer and began to speak to me through his Word."[1]

What Waltke found is what the writer of Psalm 119 tells us in the next three sections of his psalm, namely, that the purpose of Bible study is not to get to know the Bible in some abstract or academic sense, but actually to get to know God. The key is prayerful Bible study.

The psalmist has been expressing his desire to know God all along. He has used the first-person pronoun more than is the case in other psalms, and he has addressed God directly again and again. It is always "I" and "you." But in these three stanzas (*waw, zayin,* and *heth*) he rises to new heights in expressing his desire to know the God of love and all comfort. The climax comes in verse 57, when he declares, "You are my portion, O LORD."

Finding God's Love

The first of these three stanzas concentrates on God's love, which is the most wonderful of his attributes and certainly a fitting place for the psalmist to begin. Surprisingly, it is the first stanza in which he speaks of God's love. Not only that, but it is also the first stanza in which he speaks of God's salvation. The two words occur together in verse 41.

> May your unfailing love come to me, O LORD,
>   your salvation according to your promise.

It may seem surprising that this is the first time the writer has mentioned God's love, but it is not the least bit surprising that the first time he mentions love he also mentions salvation. The proof of God's love is his provision of salvation for sinners. It is out of the great love of God that salvation comes.

When the Old Testament saints wrote about salvation they could only have had a rudimentary idea of all that was involved. We live on the far side of the cross and know how the love of God and the death of Christ came together. The apostle Paul linked the two ideas in Romans 5: "Very rarely will anyone die for a righteous man, though for a good man someone might possibly dare to die. But God demonstrates his own love for us in this: While we were still sinners, Christ died for us" (Rom. 5:7–8). Nor can we forget John 3:16, the best-known verse in the Bible. "For God so loved the world that he gave his one and only Son, that whoever believes in him shall not perish but have eternal life."

We have already discovered that the author of this psalm is a practical man in the matter of his religion. At this point he does not dwell at length on God's love itself but instead mentions two important results of getting to know God's love personally.

1. *Obedience.* "I will always obey your law, for ever and ever" (v. 44). Does it seem surprising that one of the first results of coming to know God as a God of love is obedience? It does to many people, but the reason it does is that they have an inadequate and even warped idea of what love means. We think of love as mere sentimentality, a feeling to be enjoyed and wallowed in. In the Bible, love is a relationship resulting in moral actions. Jesus taught his disciples, "If you love me, you will obey what I command" (John 14:15).

The words translated "always," "for ever," and "ever" (NIV) render three different Hebrew words that come at the very end of verse 44, like this: always, eternally, and forever. It is an effective way of saying that the psalmist's obedience is going to go on and on. There will never be a time when the godly stop obeying God.

2. *Speaking about God's love to others.* A compulsion to speak about God and his love to others, particularly to those who are opposed to him and ridicule righteous persons like himself, is emphasized strongly in this stanza. "Then I will answer the one who taunts me," says the psalmist (v. 42). "Do not snatch the word of truth from my mouth," he adds (v. 43). And still again,

> I will speak of your statutes before kings
> and will not be put to shame (v. 46).

This last verse has often been used by historians to describe Martin Luther's heroic stand before the Diet of Worms. Luther had been summoned to Worms to appear before the newly elected emperor Charles V and the assembled champions of the church to answer for heresies that were believed to be in his writings. It was a moment ominous with danger, because others who had been similarly summoned had been arrested and then cruelly executed for their supposed offenses against both church and state. Everyone remembered Jan Hus, who had been burnt at Constance on the Rhine about a hundred years before. Like Hus, Luther could have been martyred.

When Luther arrived on that fateful day, after a night of prayer and serious self-examination, the moderator of the assembly pointed to a table containing Luther's books. "Will you retract these writings?" he asked.

Earlier, Luther had attempted to draw the council into a discussion of the teachings themselves, but nobody wanted to debate with Luther. Instead he was confronted with a yes or no decision. The demand was insistent.

Luther replied:

> Since your most serene majesty and your high mightiness require from me a clear, simple, and precise answer, I will give you one, and it is this: I cannot submit my faith either to the pope or to the councils, because it is clear to me as the day that they have frequently erred and contradicted each other. Unless therefore I am convinced by the testimony of Scripture, or by the clearest reasoning—unless I am persuaded by means of the passages I have quoted—and unless they thus render my conscience bound by the Word of God, I cannot and I will not retract, for it is unsafe for a Christian to speak against his conscience. Here I stand. I can do no other. May God help me. Amen.[2]

In this way Martin Luther did exactly what Psalm 119:46 is describing. He spoke of God's statutes before kings, and he was not put to shame.[3]

We can summarize this stanza of the psalm by noting that it deals with three kinds of love: God's love for us disclosed in his provision of salvation, which the writer speaks of finding; our love for God, which is implied in obedience; and love of God's commandments, which results in our wanting to tell others about them (vv. 47–48). Do you tell others about God's commands and God's love? It is a measure of your love for God whether you tell others. If you love God and thus also love the Word, how can you not tell others about him?[4]

Finding God's Comfort

The theme of this small grouping of stanzas—getting to know God by means of a prayerful study of the Scriptures—continues in stanza seven, the *zayin* stanza. Each stanza has its own emphasis, and here the emphasis is on finding God to be a comfort in life's sufferings. Comfort is mentioned twice, in verses 50 and 52.

> My comfort in my suffering is this:
> Your promise renews my life.
>
> I remember your ancient laws, O LORD,
> and I find comfort in them.

Although this stanza deals with suffering, there is only one direct prayer to God for help ("Remember your word to your servant, for you have given me hope," v. 49), and even in it the psalmist does not specifically ask to be delivered from suffering. All the other verses of the stanza are statements by the writer that he trusts what God has written in his law and will continue to love it and obey its teachings. It is a way of acknowledging that suffering is common to human beings. We are not always able to avoid it. What is important is not escaping the suffering, even with God's help, but continuing to trust God and prove him a genuine source of comfort even while we are going through the trial.

One prominent word in this stanza is "remember." It occurs three times, in verses 49, 52, and 55. In the first case it is an appeal to God to remember his words of promise, which the author is sure he will do and which is his source of comfort. In the next two uses of "remember" he asserts that he will not forget but rather will remember God's "ancient laws" (v. 52) and "name" (v. 55). In other words, he will use his times of suffering to meditate on God's Word and character, knowing that one purpose of his suffering must be to give him time to get to know God better.

Verse 54 also speaks of singing in the midst of suffering, so wonderful is God's comfort in such times. Is that really possible? Paul and Silas sang in prison at Philippi, after having been severely beaten. They were doing it in the middle of the night, which is another thing the psalmist mentions ("In the night I remember your name, O LORD," v. 55). The story in Acts says, "About midnight Paul and Silas were praying and singing hymns to God, and the other prisoners were listening to them" (Acts 16:25). After witnessing such faith it is no wonder the Philippian jailer and many others believed on the Jesus Paul and Silas proclaimed and no wonder God established a strong, enduring church in Philippi. It was this church that backed Paul's missionary work, time and again helping with his expenses (Phil. 4:15–16).

It has always been natural for Christians to sing of what is lodged joyfully in their hearts, and their worship services have always been characterized by joyous hymn singing. Our contemporaries do not sing much today, though they listen to other people perform songs for them, and many of these songs are ugly. It is because life for our contemporaries is ugly. How beautiful are the hymns of Christians by contrast!

Henry Wadsworth Longfellow (died 1882), the American poet who gave us "Evangeline" and "The Song of Hiawatha," wrote this about musical renderings of God's Word:

> Such songs have power to quiet
>   The restless pulse of care,
> And come like the benediction
>   That follows after prayer.
> And the night shall be filled with music,
>   And the cares that infest the day
> Shall fold their tents like the Arabs,
>   And as silently steal away.

The singing of Christians does not make the causes of their sorrows go away—though the Lord sometimes does that himself—but it does lift their spirits and testifies to the goodness of God, who provides comfort even in bad times.

Finding God Himself

Everything we have looked at so far leads up to stanza eight (the *heth* stanza, the last of this little grouping of three) and to its key verse: "You are my portion, O LORD" (v. 57). What is really involved in a prayerful study of God's Word is not finding comfort only or even getting to know one aspect of God's character, even one as important as love, but rather getting to know and possess God himself. Spurgeon wrote wisely of this stanza, "In this section the psalmist seems to take firm hold upon God himself: appropriating him (v. 57), crying out for him (v. 58), returning to him (v. 59), solacing himself in him (vv. 61, 62), associating with his people (v. 63), and sighing for personal experience of his goodness (v. 64)."[5]

When the psalmist wrote that God was his "portion," he was using a word that had rich meaning in Jewish religious history. When the Israelite tribes came out of the desert and made their conquest of the land of Canaan and every tribe received its appointed portion, the priestly tribe of Levi did not receive land. Instead they were given forty-eight priestly cities scattered throughout the land and were to live there so that their priestly service would always be widely available. They had no land, but they were given something better. It was said of them that they had "no inheritance [portion]" in the land because "their inheritance [portion] was the LORD" (Josh. 13:33).[6]

The psalmist is saying that, like the Levites, he wants his portion of divine blessing to be God himself since nothing is better and nothing will ever fully satisfy his or anyone else's heart but God himself. To possess God is truly to have everything.

It requires effort to acquire this treasure, however, because God is discovered in his Word—this is the most important teaching of the psalm—and it requires effort to get to know the Bible. Therefore, in the remaining verses of this stanza we are encouraged in our study of the Bible by being reminded of what the psalmist did.

1. *He sought God's face* (v. 58). To seek God's face means to seek God himself, to labor at getting to know him on a personal basis. Will those who seek God earnestly find him? Of course! Jesus said of prayer in general, "Ask and it will be given to you; seek and you will find; knock and the door will be opened to you" (Matt. 7:7). If that promise applies to such common things as food and clothing and a place to live, can we suppose that it will apply less to the pursuit of God? Those who seek God will surely find him.

2. *He followed God's statutes* (v. 59). The psalmist followed after, or lived by, God's Word as a way of life. Blaise Pascal, the brilliant French philosopher and devout Christian, loved Psalm 119. He is another person who had

memorized it, and he called verse 59 "the turning point of man's character and destiny."[7] He meant that it is vital for every person to consider his or her ways, understand that our ways are destructive and will lead us to destruction, and then make an about-face and determine to go in God's ways instead.

3. *He obeyed God's commands* (v. 60). To find God is to find him who is the king of the universe and our Lord. Therefore, it is necessary and inevitable that we obey him. Jesus asked pointedly, "Why do you call me 'Lord, Lord' and do not do what I say?" (Luke 6:46).

4. *He remembered God's Law* (v. 61). One of the big problems with trying to live as a Christian is that we forget God's Law, indeed even his many mercies to us. The psalmist determined not to forget. He wanted to remember God's Law whatever the circumstances, so he might be encouraged by it and do it.

5. *He thanked God for his laws* (v. 62). The writer of this psalm is no grim pedant, merely plodding after God's Law with a dour determination to conform to it. He recognized that God's Law is good, the greatest of all treasures. Therefore he thanked God for it. Indeed, he made God's decrees the theme of his midnight melodies (vv. 54–55).

6. *He identified with others who also follow God's precepts* (v. 63). The psalmist recognized that he was not in this devoutly chosen way of life alone. There were others moving along the same path, other believers, and he was one of them. He wanted to be their friend, to encourage them and be encouraged by them. H. C. Leupold wrote that the last words of this stanza put the writer into "that select company of men who both fear the Lord and keep his precepts," adding that "in the last analysis this is the procedure followed by all true children of God."[8] It is a great blessing to belong to the company of such saints.

Psalm 119

Delight in God's Decrees: Part 6

Affliction

Do good to your servant
    according to your word, O LORD;
Teach me knowledge and good judgment,
    for I believe in your commands.
Before I was afflicted I went astray,
    but now I obey your word.
You are good, and what you do is good;
    teach me your decrees.
Though the arrogant have smeared me with lies,
    I keep your precepts with all my heart.
Their hearts are callous and unfeeling,
    but I delight in your law.
It was good for me to be afflicted
    so that I might learn your decrees.
The law from your mouth is more precious to me
    than thousands of pieces of silver and gold.

Your hands made me and formed me;
    give me understanding to learn your commands.
May they who fear you rejoice when they see me,
    for I have put my hope in your word.

I know, O LORD, that your laws are righteous,
  and in faithfulness you have afflicted me. . . .

All your commands are trustworthy;
  help me, for men persecute me without cause.
They almost wiped me from the earth,
  but I have not forsaken your precepts.
Preserve my life according to your love,
  and I will obey the statutes of your mouth.

                                                    verses 65–88

Most people have heard the tired atheistic rebuttal to Christianity based on the presence of suffering in the world. It has been expressed in different ways depending on the viewpoint of the unbeliever who uttered it. One common form of the rebuttal goes like this: If God were good he would wish to make his creatures happy, and if God were almighty he would be able to do what he wished; but his creatures are not happy, therefore God lacks either goodness or power or both.[1] That objection is insulting in its superficiality, for it assumes that the ultimate good in this world is our lack of suffering and that the only possible factors in our quandary are the alleged benevolence and alleged omnipotence of God.

Any serious thinker and all Christians know that there is more to the problem of suffering than this. Nevertheless, the problem of pain is a big one. What is more, it is also personal and inescapable, because there is no one on earth who does not go through some suffering at some time.

Our psalmist endured a lot of it. We have already looked at some of this man's trials in an earlier study, focusing on those that came to him because of his determination to live faithfully by God's Word. In the sections of the psalm to which we come now *(teth, yodh,* and *kaph)* we see trials of a much broader nature, trials that the writer refers to as afflictions. "Afflicted" is a new word in these stanzas, occurring three times in verses 65–88. It is found twice in stanza nine (vv. 67, 71) and once in stanza ten (v. 75). Although it does not actually occur in stanza eleven, that stanza describes the poet's afflictions in the saddest and most pitiful language of all.

Taking these stanzas together and in sequence, they teach us about the purpose, source, and result of suffering for the Christian.

Affliction: Its Purpose

Why do the righteous suffer? When we look for the answer to this question in the Bible as a whole we find that there are various explanations, which is not surprising since this is not a simple problem.

First, some suffering is simply the common lot of man. We live in an imperfect world. We get hurt; we get sick; we die. It is not always the case that we are to read cosmic meaning into such afflictions. That supreme sufferer Job said, "Man is born to trouble as surely as sparks fly upward" (Job 5:7).

Second, there is suffering that is corrective. This is the most obvious category of suffering for most Christians, and it is what the psalmist is chiefly speaking of in this psalm when he says, "Before I was afflicted I went astray, but now I obey your word" (v. 67). He is confessing that the afflictions he endured were sent by God to get him back onto the path of obeying God's Word.

Third, some suffering is constructive. That is, it is used by God to sharpen our skills and develop our character. Paul wrote in Romans 5, "Suffering produces perseverance; perseverance, character; and character, hope" (Rom. 5:3–4).

Fourth, some suffering is given only to glorify God in it and by it. The afflictions of the man born blind were of this nature, for Jesus explained that he had been suffering neither for his own sin nor that of his parents, but only "that the work of God might be displayed in his life" (John 9:3). He meant that he had been allowed to endure blindness his whole life in order for Jesus to heal him at this point in history and so bring glory to God as the one who gives physical and spiritual sight.

The fifth purpose of suffering is cosmic, and Job is the Bible's most profound and detailed example of cosmic suffering. Cosmic suffering demonstrates before Satan and the angels that a person can love and trust God for who he is in himself and not merely for what he gets out of him.

Psalm 119:65–88 explores the second of these five uses of affliction in the believer's life. The writer says God sent affliction into his life as a divine corrective to teach him to obey and understand God's Word.

1. *To obey God's Word* (v. 67). The Hebrew in verse 67, "Before I was afflicted I went astray, but now I obey your word," does not suggest that the writer had plunged into deliberate and willful sin and was then reproved by God and returned to the path of righteousness. Going astray has to do mostly with ignorance. It means that before God brought affliction into his life he trusted his own judgment and wandered into vain and harmful paths. When things did not go well for him, he turned to God's Word and discovered the right way to live. He began to obey the Bible's teachings.

We can gain solace here by remembering that the Bible says even of Jesus, "Although he was a son, he learned obedience from what he suffered" (Heb. 5:8).

2. *To understand God's Word* (v. 71). We might think that the order of these two verses is reversed, since knowing God's decrees should precede obeying them. That is true, but it is not what the psalmist means when he says, "It was good for me to be afflicted so that I might learn from your decrees." When he read God's law he knew it well enough to obey it then,

and did. As he was continually driven to the study of the Word by continuing afflictions, however, he came to understand the Bible more fully and at increasingly deeper levels.

This is what Martin Luther meant when he confessed, "I never knew the meaning of God's word, until I came into affliction. I have always found it one of my best schoolmasters."[2] Luther already understood God's Word; he had been teaching it. But he came to understand it more deeply when God led him through the deep waters of affliction.

"What You Do Is Good"

Affliction is not the most frequently mentioned matter in stanza nine. The most prominent word in these verses is "good." This is the *teth* stanza. *Teth* is the first letter of the Hebrew word "good" *(tov)*, so it was a natural thought for the composer of the psalm to use "good" at the beginning of these verses. The word occurs at the beginning of five of them (vv. 65, 66, 68, 71, 72).

It is not just because the word for "good" begins with the letter *teth* that the psalmist reflects so often on what is good. It is because he had discovered that suffering is good when it flows from God's unvarying goodness toward us. Affliction is not good in itself and does not usually seem good to us when we are enduring it, but it has a good purpose when God sends it, as he frequently does in the case of his cherished children.

Here are the verses that begin with the word "good."

Verse 65: "Do good to your servant according to your word, O LORD." This verse is a general statement, asking God to do good to the psalmist, which God has done and is certain to continue doing. Some writers call this the text for which the rest of the stanza is the sermon. One way God does good is by sending afflictions.

Verse 66: "Teach me knowledge and good judgment, for I believe in your commands." This verse is an elaboration of the general statement, explaining that the good the psalmist wants is not merely the affliction itself, but rather knowledge of God's ways leading to good judgment, which he was able to learn because of his suffering. Every believer needs such knowledge and the good judgment related to it.

Verse 68: "You are good, and what you do is good; teach me your decrees." Verse 68 is the middle verse of the five, and it is pivotal, anchoring goodness in the very nature of God: God is good and he is always doing good.

Verse 71: "It was good for me to be afflicted so that I might learn your decrees." This verse applies the general goodness of God's character to the specific matter of the psalmist's affliction. Since God is good and since he sends suffering, the suffering itself must have a good purpose. This verse is an equivalent of Romans 8:28, which we probably know better: "And we know that in all things God works for the good of those who love him, who have been called according to his purpose."

Verse 72: "The law from your mouth is more precious [good] to me than thousands of pieces of silver and gold." This verse returns to the theme of God's Word, which the writer says is better (the NIV has "more precious") even than many thousands of pieces of gold and silver.

Herbert Lockyer recounts a story concerning the largest Bible in the world, a Hebrew manuscript weighing 320 pounds in the Vatican library. Long ago a group of Italian Jews asked to see this Bible and when they had seen it they told their friends in Venice about it. As a result a syndicate of Russian Jews tried to buy it, offering the church the weight of the book in gold. Julius the Second was Pope at that time, and he refused the offer, even though the value of such a large amount of gold was enormous. Wrote Lockyer, "Thousands of gold and silver pieces are nothing in comparison with the inestimably precious Word of God."[3]

Today we pay little to possess multiple copies of God's Word. But do we value it? In many cases, I am afraid not.

Affliction: Its Source

The tenth stanza of Psalm 119 is the *yodh* stanza, the Hebrew letter Jesus referred to when he said, "Until heaven and earth disappear, not the smallest letter, not the least stroke of a pen, will by any means disappear from the Law until everything is accomplished" (Matt. 5:18). The *yodh* is a mere dash of a letter, but in Psalm 119 the *yodh* section does not deal with trifles. On the contrary, like the stanzas before and following, it deals with the afflictions that come into the life of the trusting child of God.

This second stanza states explicitly what was only assumed earlier, namely, that God is the ultimate source of the affliction.

> I know, O LORD, that your laws are righteous,
> and in faithfulness you have afflicted me (v. 75).

The stanza begins not by mentioning the psalmist's suffering but by confessing that he was "made" and "formed" by God (v. 73). The reference to God's forming him is a deliberate echo of Genesis 2, which says God "formed man from the dust of the ground and breathed into his nostrils the breath of life" (Gen. 2:7). God did not make man as the beasts, which have no understanding; he made man to know and understand the ways of God. Hence, the psalmist in the second half of verse 73 prays for the gift of understanding God's commands. He comes to understand quite a few things.

1. *God is faithful even in the affliction* (v. 75). God is faithful, but to what or whom? If the affliction were occasioned by the poet's sin, "faithfulness" refers to God's faithfulness to his own righteousness and justice. The judge of all the earth must punish sin. Yet we have no reason to think of the writer's afflictions in this light, therefore the faithfulness mentioned here probably refers to God's faithfulness to the psalmist, a proof that God continues to love him and is working to have him grow and mature by means of the affliction. We need to see that ourselves when things are not going exactly as we would wish.

2. *God's unfailing love is a comfort* (v. 76). God's unfailing love caused God to send afflictions to the psalmist. Therefore, the psalmist can be comforted even while going through them. He had asked God for understanding concerning his afflictions, and God gave it to him; these stanzas are proof. Even so, suffering is bitter and the afflicted one needs comfort. The psalmist needed to remember that God loved him in spite of and even through what he was suffering.

3. *God is compassionate* (v. 77). God does not need to be compassionate. The word signifies "mercy," and mercy is grace shown to those who are undeserving, those who deserve the opposite. God *is* merciful. His very name is mercy (see Exod. 33:6–7). Thus, regardless of what we are going through and whether it is the result of our sin and whether we have brought it on ourselves, we can appeal to God's mercy and be assured that we will find it.

4. *One's handling of suffering can be an encouragement to other believers* (v. 79; also v. 74). For the most part the poet has been thinking about and praying for himself, but he realizes that what happens to him and how he reacts to it can be a source either of discouragement or encouragement to others. He wants to be an encouragement, hence his two prayers: "May they who fear you rejoice when they see me" (v. 74) and "May those who fear you turn to me, those who understand your statutes" (v. 79). Are other believers happy when they see you?

In the latter half of this stanza the writer voices three prayers: for the arrogant, that they will be put to shame (v. 78); for other believers, that they will be encouraged by his example (v. 79); and for himself, that he will be enabled to live blamelessly (v. 80). The heathen used to wish for "a sound mind in a sound body." The psalmist wants more. He wants "a sound heart," blameless because it is grounded in the Word of God.

Affliction: Its Result

The last of these three stanzas brings us to the lowest point in the psalm, placed here just before the halfway mark. Spurgeon wrote, "This octave is the midnight of the psalm, and very dark and black it is." He also noted, however, that even in the blackness, "stars . . . shine out, and the last verse gives promise of the dawn."[4] It may be significant in this respect that verse

84 is the first in the psalm to fail to mention the Word of God by one of the ten or so synonyms for it. When the psalmist was most down, did he lose sight of God's Word temporarily?

This stanza has a great deal to say about the psalmist's enemies, as if at this point his thoughts were nearly monopolized by them. He has spoken of them before and will again, though they assume a far less threatening role from stanza twelve to the end. Here he reports that these enemies have been persecuting him (v. 84), digging pitfalls for him (v. 85), and trying to wipe him from the earth (v. 87). The last phrase is literally "in the earth," which seems odd until we remember verse 85, which reports that his enemies were digging pits for him. They wanted to kill him and see him buried. No wonder he has been so depressed.

Depressed, but not defeated! For at the very end of this discussion of affliction and this anxious reflection on his enemies, he turns his attention once again to God's Word (v. 88). The ancients had a saying, *dum spiro spero* ("while I breathe I hope"). Here the child of God does better. He exclaims, *dum expiro spero* ("even while I expire I hope"). He expected to be blessed.

Some writers, among them Saint Jerome and the excellent Ambrose, pointed out that for the ancients there was often significance in the shape of the Hebrew letters. Such is the case here. This is the *kaph* stanza. *Kaph* is a curved letter, similar to a half circle, and it was often thought of as a hand held out to receive some gift or blessing.[5] Here the author is in need, and he knows that the only one who can answer his need is God. Hence, he holds out his hand toward him as a suppliant.

That is all any of us can do. We can hold out empty hands. If we hold out hands filled with our own good works, there is no way God can fill them. But if we hold out empty hands, God will fill them, to the praise of the glory of his great grace.

Psalm 119

Delight in God's Decrees: Part 7

The Eternal Word

> *Your word, O LORD, is eternal;*
>   *it stands firm in the heavens.*
> *Your faithfulness continues through all generations;*
>   *you established the earth, and it endures.*
> *Your laws endure to this day,*
>   *for all things serve you.*
> *If your law had not been my delight,*
>   *I would have perished in my affliction.*
> *I will never forget your precepts,*
>   *for by them you have renewed my life.*
> *Save me, for I am yours;*
>   *I have sought out your precepts.*
> *The wicked are waiting to destroy me,*
>   *but I will ponder your statutes.*
> *To all perfection I see a limit;*
>   *but your commands are boundless.*
>   *verses 89–96*

Psalm 119 is not offered to us as the personal life experiences of the psalmist. It is a collection of inspired reflections on the nature of God's Word and of the righteous person's proper response to it. Nevertheless, it is hard to escape feeling that at least in some places the writer is speaking personally. He seems to be doing so in the stanzas we looked at in the last chapter and in the stanza we come to now.

In moving from a study of the *kaph* to the *lamedh* stanzas (from stanza eleven to stanza twelve), we are passing the midpoint of the psalm and are moving beyond its lowest level. Stanzas nine through eleven described the psalmist's afflictions, and they did so in such a powerful and poignant way that we can hardly doubt that these were sufferings the writer actually did experience. In stanza eleven he says his soul had fainted with longing for God's salvation (v. 81), his eyes had failed (v. 82), he was "like a wineskin in the smoke" (v. 83), and he had almost perished (v. 87). The stanza ends with a gasping cry to God: "Preserve my life according to your love, and I will obey the statutes of your mouth" (v. 88).

Now we come to stanza twelve and find that God had indeed preserved his life and there is an entirely different tone as a result. From this point on, the writer begins to move forward and upward again, building his life on the only foundation that is truly steadfast and eternal. It is as if he had been struggling in a pounding ocean surf, trying desperately to reach land, and had at last drawn himself up on a big rock standing by the shore; or as if he had been sinking in quicksand and had suddenly found solid ground beneath his feet. That rock, that solid foundation, is the Word of God. If the psalmist had known this hymn from the *Selection of Hymns* by Rippon, he might well have sung:

> How firm a foundation, you saints of the Lord,
> Is laid for your faith in his excellent Word!
> What more can he say than to you he has said,
> To you who for refuge to Jesus have fled?

Actually, he has sung it (the content, if not the very words) in the stanza we come to now.

God's Everlasting Word

Martin Luther once wrote of God's Word, "The Bible is alive, it speaks to me; it has feet, it runs after me; it has hands, it lays hold of me. The Bible is not antique or modern. It is eternal."[1] The everlasting nature of the Bible is the theme of this stanza, particularly of verses 89–91.

Each of these verses is more or less parallel to the others; each says that God's Word is everlasting and therefore something a person can build on not only for this life but also for eternity. Verse 89 says, "Your word, O LORD, is eternal; it stands firm in the heavens." Verse 90 says, "Your faithfulness continues through all generations; you established the earth, and it endures." Verse 91 observes, "Your laws endure to this day, for all things serve you."[2]

If "faithfulness" in verse 90 refers to God's Word, then these verses are saying that because God's Word is eternal in heaven, it can also clearly be depended upon on earth. If it refers to a separate attribute of God, then they are saying that three things are eternal: God's Word in heaven; God's faithfulness on earth; and the laws of God that, like the heavens and the earth, endure "to this day." The laws of God will endure even longer, of course, since, as the last and summarizing verse of this section states, they are "boundless" (v. 96).

Jesus clearly taught the everlasting nature of God's Word. For example, in the Sermon on the Mount, in what is some of his most extensive teaching on the Scriptures, Jesus said, "Do not think that I have come to abolish the Law or the Prophets; I have not come to abolish them but to fulfill them. I tell you the truth, until heaven and earth disappear, not the smallest letter, not the least stroke of a pen, will by any means disappear from the Law until everything is accomplished" (Matt. 5:17–18).

The older versions spoke of "a jot or a tittle," which was accurate but unclear to most people, which is why the New International Version expands the phrase to read "not the smallest letter, not the least stroke of a pen." The "jot" or "smallest letter" is the *yodh*, the tiny mark of a letter that begins each verse of the tenth stanza of Psalm 119. You may have it in the heading to that section. It is like an apostrophe. The "tittle" is not a letter. It is part of a letter, a small protrusion called a serif. You can see what a "tittle" is by comparing the letter found before verse 9 of Psalm 119 (a *beth*) with the letter before verse 81 (a *kaph*). The letters are similar, but the first has a small protrusion (a "tittle") at the bottom. The same "stroke of a pen" distinguishes *daleth* from *resh* and *waw* from *zayin*.

Jesus was teaching that not even the smallest mark of the sacred text will be lost from Scripture until every single portion of it is fulfilled. And not even then! For as he said elsewhere, "Heaven and earth will pass away, but my words will never pass away" (Matt. 24:35). The psalmist wrote, "Your word, O Lord, is eternal" (Ps. 119:89).

Neither you nor I can see things from the perspective of eternity—only God can—but we can testify to the enduring qualities of Scripture throughout observable history. Indeed, one reason among many for believing the Bible to be God's Word and not the word of mere human beings is its extraordinary preservation through the centuries. Today, after the Bible has been translated, in part or whole, into many hundreds of languages, many with multiple versions, and after millions of copies have been printed and distributed, it would be nearly impossible to destroy the Bible. However, such conditions did not always prevail. Until the time of the Reformation, when Gutenberg's remarkable discovery of moveable type enabled the Bible as well as other literature to be mass-produced and distributed easily throughout civilized lands, the text of the Bible was preserved by the laborious and time-consuming process of copying it over and over again by hand, at first onto papyrus sheets and then onto parchments. Throughout much of this time, the Bible was an object of extreme hatred by many in authority. They tried to stamp it out, but the text survived. In the early days of the church, Celsus, Prophyry, and Lucien tried to destroy it by arguments. Later the emperors Diocletian and Julian tried to destroy it by force. In some periods of history it was a capital offense to possess a copy of the Bible. Yet the text survived.

If the Bible had been only the thoughts or work of mere men, it would have been eliminated long ago, as other books have been. We know from passing references in other ancient books that we have lost masterpieces by many of the greatest writers of the past. But the Bible has endured and has endured intact. Isaiah wrote,

> The grass withers and the flowers fall,
>> but the word of our God stands forever (Isa. 40:8).

God's Liberating Word

I have noted several times how practical the writer of Psalm 119 is, and this is a quality we see again here. His theme is the eternal or enduring character of God's Word. Starting with that truth, he then reflects on three things this eternal, or indestructible, Word has done for him.

1. *God's Word rescued him* (v. 92). Verse 92 picks up on the theme of the last three stanzas: affliction. It tells us that God heard and answered the prayer with which those stanzas end. What was it that got the psalmist through those extremely hard times? God, of course, but that is not the way the writer states the answer. He says, *"If your law had not been my delight,* I would have perished in my affliction" (italics added). In other words, what got him through his afflictions was his lifelong habit of reading, marking, learning, meditating upon, spiritually digesting, and above all obeying God's Law. Thus, even in stanza eleven, the lowest point of all in this long psalm, he maintains:

> I have put my hope in your word (v. 81).
> I do not forget your decrees (v. 83).
> I have not forsaken your precepts (v. 87).
> I will obey the statutes of your mouth (v. 88).

When we get in trouble we usually go to God for help, which the writer did too. But we often stop at that point, expecting God to intervene all by himself, miraculously, without any work on our part. The psalmist was wiser than we are, for while he prayed for help, he also did what he was able and obliged to do: He studied and meditated on the Bible. He knew that although it is God who must work, God nevertheless works through means, and in the matter of lifting us out of our trouble and setting our feet on a sure foundation, the only indispensable means of deliverance and growth is Bible study.[3]

The four synonyms for Scripture occurring in verses 81, 83, 87, and 88 have slight distinctions. "Word" (*dabar,* v. 81) is the most general of these terms. It embraces everything that God has said in the Bible, whether it be law or gospel, commands or promises. "Decrees" (*huqqim*, sometimes rendered "statutes," v. 83) refers to binding rules or laws, such as those inscribed on a stone tablet—the Ten Commandments, for instance. "Precepts" (*piqqudim*, v. 87) is like our word "regulations." It is what a government official might issue after he has looked into a problem and figured out what detailed rules might resolve it. "Statutes" (*hedot*, sometimes rendered "testimonies," v. 88) pictures the Bible as God's faithful witness to his people, containing warnings of distress and judgment if the Word is disobeyed and promises of blessing and joy if it is heeded.

In his affliction the psalmist took the whole of the Bible as his and clung to it tenaciously. He knew, as the apostle Paul also knew, that *"all Scripture* is God-breathed and is useful for teaching, rebuking, correcting and training in righteousness, so that the man of God may be thoroughly equipped for every good work" (2 Tim. 3:16–17, italics added). We never know what portion of the Bible God will use to bless us and keep us steady in hard times.

2. *God's Word renewed him* (v. 93). The psalmist found renewal as he studied the Bible in his afflictions, which makes verse 93 synonymous with verse 92. In fact, verses 94 and 95 are synonymous too, making three parallel statements of deliverance that correspond to the three parallel and nearly synonymous statements about the eternal qualities of God's Law in verses 89–91. Still, each of these ideas has its own particular flavor.

Prayers for renewal are a recurring motif in this psalm. The psalmist prayed for renewal as early as verse 25, saying, "Renew my life according to your word," a sentence he repeated word for word in verse 37. In verse 40 he wrote, "Renew my life in your righteousness." Verse 50 declared, "Your promise renews my life." The same thought occurs in the latter half of the psalm: verse 107 says, "Renew my life, O LORD, according to your word" and is repeated in verse 149; verse 154 says, "Renew my life according to your promise"; and verse 156 says, "Renew my life according to your laws." In the stanza we are studying now, the psalmist is not praying for renewal, he is declaring that God *has* renewed him. The renewal came about as he remembered God's Word, which is what the other verses also affirm.

> I will never forget your precepts,
> for by them you have renewed my life (v. 93).

How do we think of renewal? We think of it as something God does by his Holy Spirit, which is right, but we tend to forget the link between the Holy Spirit and God's Word. We must remember that the Word and the Spirit always go together, as I pointed out in an earlier chapter. God *speaks to us* through the Word, and only through the Word does the Spirit *renew us* inwardly.

Although affliction was the theme of the preceding three stanzas—where it was developed at great length—and although it has reoccurred in this

stanza (v. 92), it appears here only briefly and as something in the past. God
has indeed renewed the psalmist so he is no longer under that depression
of spirit that his afflictions caused.

3. *God's Word saved him* (vv. 94–95). Verses 94 and 95 belong together
because they deal with salvation from the psalmist's enemies. These enemies were part of his afflictions (cf. vv. 84, 87). God delivered him from
those wicked people who were against him, renewing his life and spirits.
This truly was salvation. Now we discover from verse 95 ("the wicked are
waiting to destroy me") that these wicked people were still around; therefore, the third of these statements of what God has done is in the form of
an ongoing prayer ("Save me") and not a statement of something in the
past, as was the case with the others ("I would have perished" and "You have
renewed my life"). The writer needed God's salvation constantly.

So do we. If God were not with us every moment of every single day, sustaining our lives and preserving us from constant dangers, perceived and
unperceived, we would certainly perish in an instant. Even more, we need
God's constant salvation from our sins. We sometimes speak of three tenses
of salvation: salvation in the past, meaning Jesus' death and atonement for
our sin and God's forgiveness on the basis of that utterly sufficient atonement; salvation in the present, by which we grow in grace and holiness by
the power of God's Spirit working through his written Word, attaining to
higher and higher levels of obedience and understanding; and salvation in
the future, when we shall be taken to heaven and delivered from the presence of sin and of all desires to yield to it.

Our assurance of salvation comes because "he who began a good work in
[us] will carry it on to completion until the day of Christ Jesus" (Phil. 1:6).
That is a promise. In other words, to go back to the theme of this stanza,
stated in verses 89–91, because the Word of God "is eternal" and "stands
firm in the heavens," because it "continues through all generations" and
endures "to this day," we can rest assured in God's salvation.

Look at the words "for I am yours" in verse 94. Each word has only one
syllable; they are simplicity itself, but what an amazing truth, that we should
belong to God! If we belong to him, we can count on him to save us—now
and to the very end. Charles Spurgeon called verse 94 "a comprehensive
prayer with a prevailing argument," noting that "if we are confident that we
are the Lord's, we may be confident that he will save us."[4]

Standing on the Rock

The last verse of this section stands alone as a summary statement linking
the truth that God's Law is eternal (vv. 89–91) with the salvation that is ours
through believing and acting on God's commands (vv. 92–95):

> To all perfection I see a limit;
>> but your commands are boundless (v. 96).

Earlier in the stanza the psalmist wrote that God "established the earth, and it endures" (v. 90), earthly physical laws corresponding to the Word of God in heaven. Here he seems to acknowledge that even this apparently stable earth will disappear at last. "Heaven and earth will pass away . . ." (Matt. 24:35), Jesus affirmed years later. "To all perfection I see a limit . . ." (v. 96), the psalmist says. Like Jesus, the psalmist also knew that there is one thing that will remain forever, and that is God's Word. Jesus added, ". . . but my words will never pass away" (Matt. 24:35). The psalmist adds, ". . . but your commands are boundless."

Derek Kidner wrote, "This verse could well be a summary of Ecclesiastes, where every earthly enterprise has its day and comes to nothing, and where only in God and his commandments do we get beyond these frustrating limits."[5]

So why don't we stand on this foundation and build on it? If you wanted to build a house and had a choice between a solid rock and sand for your foundation, wouldn't you choose the solid rock? If you were investing for your retirement years and had a choice between a proven blue-chip firm and a fly-by-night, over-the-counter adventure, wouldn't you choose the blue-chip firm? Why, then, should you do differently with your life, which is of far greater value than a house or a bank account? Why should you not build on a foundation that will stand firm when the tempests of life come (see Matt. 7:24–27)?

I like what Anglican bishop John Charles Ryle said on one occasion when it was pointed out to him that the Bible was under attack by the higher critics. Ryle said, "Give me the plenary, verbal theory of biblical inspiration with all its difficulties, rather than the doubt. I accept the difficulties and I humbly wait for their solution. But while I wait, I am standing on rock."

Psalm 119

Delight in God's Decrees: Part 8

Loving God's Word

O, how I love your law!
    I meditate on it all day long.
Your commands make me wiser than my enemies,
    for they are ever with me.
I have more insight than all my teachers,
    for I meditate on your statutes.
I have more understanding than the elders,
    for I obey your precepts.
I have kept my feet from every evil path
    so that I might obey your word.
I have not departed from your laws,
    for you yourself have taught me.
How sweet are your promises to my taste,
    sweeter than honey to my mouth!
I gain understanding from your precepts;
    therefore I hate every wrong path.
                                    verses 97–104

W hat an uplifting stanza this is, the
mem stanza! It is filled with joy and with love for God's Law, so much so

that there is not even a single petition in it. Can this be the same poet who was sunk in near despair just two stanzas earlier? It is the same person exactly, and the reason for the change is precisely what the poet is now praising God for, namely, the Bible.

Love for God's Law

Verse 1 sets the theme of the stanza, which is the writer's love for the Bible. He has mentioned loving God's Law before (vv. 47–48), but not as often as we might have expected. Here it is his chief emphasis.

In his short study of the psalms, *Reflections on the Psalms,* C. S. Lewis has a chapter on the love of God's Law that the various psalm writers express. He confesses how strange this seemed to him when he was starting to study the psalms. He understood how a writer could respect a good law and try to obey it, but to love it or delight in it seemed to him a bit like loving the instruments with which a dentist pulls out teeth or loving the front line of a battlefield. Part of the answer to this problem is that "law" means more than "laws." It means the whole of God's written revelation, including promises as well as warnings, blessings as well as judgments. Yet this distinction cannot be the whole answer, because the psalmists seem to rejoice in—perhaps even emphasize—those specific commandments of the Bible that keep them from every evil path. In other words, it is not just the promises that delight them but the laws as well.

Lewis discovered that what the psalmists love about God's Law is what Lewis calls the engaging moral order of the divine mind. We think of love primarily as an emotion, but Psalm 119 is not a particularly emotional psalm. It is an ordered, carefully constructed psalm, reflecting in its very pattern something of what the psalmist saw in the mind of God and not only respected but also loved deeply.

Lewis wrote:

> The Order of the Divine mind, embodied in the Divine Law, is beautiful. [Therefore] what should a man do but try to reproduce it, so far as possible, in his daily life? His "delight" is in those statutes (16); to study them is like finding treasure (14); they affect him like music, are his "songs" (54); they taste like honey (103); they are better than silver and gold (72). As one's eyes are more and more opened, one sees more and more in them, and it excites wonder (18). This is not priggery nor even scrupulosity; it is the language of a man ravished by a moral beauty. If we cannot at all share his experience, we shall be the losers.[1]

Lewis concludes by suggesting that a Chinese Christian might be able to appreciate Psalm 119 better than most westerners, because of the value Chinese culture places on a life that is arranged according to a cosmic order.

In this stanza the writer gives five reasons why he has learned to love God's Law and thus why we should love it too: It is the source of true wisdom; it keeps us on the right path and off wrong ones; when we study it we have God himself as our teacher; it is sweet to our spiritual taste, like honey; and it not only keeps us from evil, but it also causes us to hate every wrong path.

Wisdom from on High

The first of the psalmist's reasons why he learned to love God's Law is the one most emphasized, being repeated in parallel fashion three times in verses 98–100. It is that God's Word is the source of true wisdom. This idea is repeated so often that many scholars regard wisdom, rather than love of God's Law, as the stanza's actual theme.

These verses have several sets of parallel ideas. As far as God's Word is concerned, the writer refers to it as "your commands" (v. 98), "your statutes" (v. 99), and "your precepts" (v. 100). As far as wisdom is concerned, he reflects on being "wiser" (v. 98), having "more insight" (v. 99), and possessing "more understanding" than other wise people (v. 100). As far as others who might claim to be wise are concerned, he says that the Bible has made him wiser than his "enemies" (v. 98), his "teachers" (v. 99), and "the elders" of the people (v. 100).

How can the writer claim to be wiser than these others, particularly his teachers and the elders? Is this only the boast of some smart young student who thinks he has all the answers when he actually hardly even knows the right questions? No, in each of these comparisons the psalmist is thinking of those who appear wise by the world's standards but who lack the deeper wisdom that comes from the Law of God.

This comparison is clearest in regard to his enemies. He has a lot to say about enemies in this psalm (as other psalm writers, especially David, also do), but he is not thinking here of the particular threat his enemies may be to him personally. He is thinking of their skill in manipulating truth and circumstances to their own worldly advantage. In this skill they are indeed shrewd. Even Jesus said, "The people of this world are more shrewd [KJV, 'wiser'] in dealing with their own kind than are the people of the light" (Luke 16:8). Yet to "look out for number one" in this way is not genuine wisdom, since at its best it is for this life only, and at its worst it is perverted and destructive. We remember how Jesus also asked, "What good will it be for a man if he gains the whole world, yet forfeits his soul?" (Matt. 16:26). It is that better, spiritual wisdom—the salvation of his soul—that the psalmist gains by love for and obeying God's Word. The point is not that the psalmist is made wise enough to outsmart these worldly enemies on their own terms; it is rather that these people have set themselves against God's Law, considering themselves to be superior to it, and the psalmist finds he is made wiser than they are by his submission to God's commands.

How about his teachers and the elders? Again, the point is not that there is nothing to be learned from one's teachers; they have accumulated knowledge. Elders have accumulated experience. The psalmist is not saying he has out-stripped those who have studied longer or lived longer than he has. There is always much to learn from other wise people. Rather he is comparing spiritual learning with mere worldly wisdom and experience and is saying that the wisdom of God goes beyond anything he can learn from mere secular instructors.

Furthermore, worldly wisdom is transient. "Where there is knowledge, it will pass away," wrote Paul (1 Cor. 13:8). The knowledge of one generation is constantly being outmoded, especially by the fast pace of modern life, but the knowledge gained from the Bible is eternal. It will be as true on the day of our deaths as when we first learned it.

The Paths of Righteousness

The second reason why the psalmist loves God's Law is that it keeps him in the path of righteousness, on the right path and off the wrong one. Earlier in the psalm the writer asked pointedly, "How can a young man keep his way pure?" (v. 9). He answered, "By living according to your word." He is saying the same thing now (v. 101), only the other way around: "I have kept my feet from every evil path so that I might obey your word." The idea is what one of the older evangelists wrote on the flyleaf of his Bible: "This book will keep you from sin, or sin will keep you from this book."

These verses are not saying that the best of many valuable ways to keep one's way pure is by studying God's Word; they are saying that this is the only way. A pure, or right, way is the opposite of a sinful way, and knowledge of sin requires a knowledge of God's Law. What is sin? "Sin is any want of conformity unto, or transgression of, the law of God," says the *Westminster Shorter Catechism* (answer to question 14). Apart from the Law of God there may still be wrong behavior, but it can only be defined as a violation of the laws of the state, which is crime, or offenses against humanity, which is to break the law of nature. Only the Law of God can tell us what offends God, hence, what sin is. Then only the Law of God can show us the right path in which to walk.

Moreover, only the Word of God can empower us to walk in the right path. To be sure, the Law as law does not do it. The law exposes sin and condemns the sinner. But it is also true that the Spirit works through the whole of Scripture for our good, reviving, illumining, and empowering the child of God first to believe the gospel of salvation by the work of Jesus Christ and then to live by his teachings.

God Is My Teacher

The third reason why the psalmist says he has learned to love God's Law is that when he studies it, he finds God to be his teacher: "I have not departed from your laws, for you yourself have taught me," he says (v. 102).

In Hebrew, as in many languages, it is not necessary to have a pronoun before a verb, because the ending of the verb indicates whether the subject is I, you (singular), he, she, it, we, you (plural), or they. In this verse the ending is "you," meaning God: "you taught me." However, the verse also contains the additional separate pronoun "you," which can only be in the verse for emphasis. This is why the New International Version adds the word "yourself," saying, "for you *yourself* have taught me" (italics added). When the writer studied the Bible, what he heard in it was not the words of other people, even though they had been used of God to record the revelation, but the voice of God himself. It is God who spoke to him. God speaks to us in Scripture making the Bible unlike any merely human book.

It is hard to read this verse without thinking of Genesis 3:8 and its reference to God "walking in the garden in the cool of the day." The verse suggests that this was God's regular pattern, that Adam and Eve used to meet God in Eden in the cool evening hours, after the work of the day was done, and that they used to converse with God and be taught by him. The reason they hid from him in Genesis 3 is not that God's coming was unusual but that they had sinned by eating of the tree of the knowledge of good and evil and were now afraid of him.

Christians sometimes think back on those halcyon days before the fall nostalgically, musing on how wonderful it would be to have God walk with us and talk to us in such an intimate way. We sometimes sing about it in the words of C. Austin Miles's hymn (1912), not really believing what we say:

> I come to the garden alone,
> While the dew is still on the roses;
> And the voice I hear, falling on my ear,
> The Son of God discloses.
> And he walks with me, and he talks with me,
> And he tells me I am his own,
> And the joy we share as we tarry there
> None other has ever known.

That is a pretty sentimental piece of bad poetry, and it probably says the wrong thing to most people who sing it. Just me and Jesus! Nobody else, no Bible! No mediated revelation! Yet there is a sense in which the psalmist says this is exactly what he finds when he studies Scripture. It takes him back to Eden, not in an unfallen state to be sure but to a place where he is personally taught by God. What this means for us is that, although we have forfeited Eden, we have a taste of Eden or—better yet—of heaven, when we come to the Bible and find that God himself speaks to us.

It is this quality of Scripture that the Reformers had in mind when they said that Scripture is "self-authenticating." They meant that a true Christian does not need a church, a church council, or the pope to tell him what

Scripture is, since the Bible bears on its very surface the stamp of the divine mind and of God speaking.

Sweeter than Honey and the Honeycomb

The fourth thing the psalmist says about God's Law and why he loves it so much is that it is sweet to his taste:

> How sweet are your promises to my taste,
> sweeter than honey to my mouth! (v. 103).

This is almost exactly what David wrote in Psalm 19:10, which shows that the writer of our later psalm must have been acquainted with the earlier one. David had written that God's ordinances "are sweeter than honey, than honey from the comb."

We hardly think of anything being sweet except certain kinds of food, like sugar donuts, Godiva chocolates, or honey. Even if we did think of other things as being sweet, it is hard to think of God's Word or laws in this way. Do we ever think of the Scriptures being sweet? Do we even know what that means?

We might gain insight by noting that what the psalmist says is sweet are the "promises" or "sayings" of God (plural). He might be thinking about not the whole of God's Book, considered as a gigantic block of revelation, but of individual verses he had learned and is turning around in his head. No one is able to take it all in, to master the Bible as a whole, but what the writer was able to do, and commends to us, is to take the specific sayings of God and learn to love them one by one. Doing so may be difficult, first, because most of us do not love the words of God like the psalmist did and therefore cannot relate to the experience, and second, because different verses affect different people differently. But let me try to give you the idea of it.

Many people love the Twenty-Third Psalm. The picture it paints of God as our loving, caring, and ever faithful Shepherd is truly a beautiful one. I love all kinds of poetry, but I confess that there is something exceptional about the shepherd image in this psalm. Is anything more exquisite than this? More sweet to the taste?

> The LORD is my shepherd, I shall lack nothing.
> He makes me lie down in green pastures,
> he leads me beside quiet waters,
> he restores my soul (Ps. 23:1–3).

I am sure the psalmist himself knew Psalm 23 and turned it over and over again both in his mind and on his tongue. So should we. If you can't find anything beautiful or sweet in these verses, your taste buds are terribly dulled and your eyes horribly glazed over by the tawdry glitz of our culture.

Or how about this?

O LORD, our LORD,
> how majestic is your name in all the earth! (Ps. 8:1, 9).

I think every syllable of that psalm is a treasure.

There is John 3:16 or Romans 8:28 or 11:32–36. There is the very last promise of the Bible, Revelation 22:20: "He who testifies to these things says, 'Yes, I am coming soon,'" and our response to it: "Amen. Come, Lord Jesus." We live in a garish, loud, mean, harsh, strident, ugly, and abusive age. Can't you find it sweet to turn aside from all that, at least from time to time, and fill your heart with something really beautiful? If you have never done it, why don't you try? Try memorizing some particularly delightful parts of Scripture. You will find that it will make you a bit more delightful too. It will soothe the bitter experiences of life with God's sweetness, the ugly things with God's beauty, and the sad times with a genuine joy.

Hating Every Wrong Path

Yes, but the Christian life is not all sweetness. To say it is would be to wrongly sentimentalize it. It has its sweet moments, and there is incomparable beauty in God. But we still live in a sour, ugly world, and it is equally important to learn to hate evil as well as love the good. The fifth thing the psalmist says God did for him through his study of the Bible and why he came to love God's Law is this:

> I gain understanding from your precepts;
> > therefore I hate every wrong path (v. 104).

The psalmist ends exactly opposite of how he began. He began with love: "Oh, how I love your law." He ends with hate: "therefore I hate every wrong path." We never learn that anything is really good unless we also learn that its opposite is not good and turn from it. For us "attraction to the true and revulsion against the false are . . . acquired tastes," says Derek Kidner.[2] Discrimination is the only real test of wisdom, and hatred of evil is the only ultimate proof that we love God.

Are you indifferent to the Bible? Do you find it boring, unattractive? If so, you will not be kept from sin or from what is ugly and offensive in this world. You will make your home in it. Don't do that! Instead, read, study, learn, and meditate on God's Word, and you will find that it grows sweeter and sweeter to your taste. Equally important, you will learn that sin is to be avoided at all costs.

Psalm 119

Delight in God's Decrees: Part 9

The Clarity of God's Word

Your word is a lamp to my feet
and a light for my path.
I have taken an oath and confirmed it,
that I will follow your righteous laws.
I have suffered much;
renew my life, O LORD, according to your word.
Accept, O LORD, the willing praise of my mouth,
and teach me your laws.
Though I constantly take my life in my hands,
I will not forget your law.
The wicked have set a snare for me,
but I have not strayed from your precepts.
Your statutes are my heritage forever;
they are the joy of my heart.
My heart is set on keeping your decrees
to the very end.

verses 105–12

The nighttime journeys of Israel through the wilderness were illumined by a pillar of fire that moved before them on their march. Most of the time the pillar stood in the center of their camp over the Most Holy Place of the tabernacle, where during the day it was a pillar of cloud; but when they marched, it went before them to lead the way, and at night it also illumined their path by becoming a flaming pillar of light (see Exod. 40:36–38).[1] In a similar way our nighttime passage through the dark and dangerous journey of this life is illumined by God's Word, the Bible, as stanza fourteen of Psalm 119 (the *nun* stanza) says when it begins,

> Your word is a lamp to my feet
> and a light for my path (v. 105).

Alexander Maclaren comments on the fact that God's Word is pictured both as a lamp and a light. "A lamp is for night; light shines in the day," he says. "The Word is both to the psalmist." His antithesis may mean that the Law gives "light of every sort" or in all "the varying phases of experience." It is a light for our darkness and for our brighter times as well.[2]

The Clarity of God's Word

This stanza emphasizes the clarity of Scripture, the attribute of the Bible that meant so much to the Protestant Reformers, who also called it perspicuity.

What they meant by clarity or perspicuity is that the Bible is basically comprehensible to any open-minded person who reads it. Therefore it does not require an ordained clergyman or official church magisterium to tell the normal believer in the church what it means. That is not to say that all parts of the Bible are equally clear or that there are no difficult passages. It does not mean that there is no value in an educated clergy or in acquiring some knowledge of the accumulated wisdom of the church. The creeds, catechisms, confessions, and theologies of the church are valuable for digesting and remembering what the Bible teaches. A serious student of the Bible is foolish to neglect them.

Even more, the clarity of the Bible is not an excuse for releasing an undisciplined tide of merely private opinion—what the Bible "means to me"—as if any harebrained notion of the Bible's teaching is to be thought as valid as any other. In fact, perspicuity means exactly the opposite. It means that the Bible is sufficiently clear so that any normal individual can read it and discover what it, the Bible, is saying.

Why then are there so many differing theologies in the church? For one thing, we are sinners who have a built-in tendency to misread and misinterpret the Bible to our personal advantage, seeing its teaching through our own distorted grids. This tendency is not unique to our reading the Bible. We have a tendency to rework the simplest facts to put ourselves in a good light and other people in the wrong. This tendency is why cultures develop elaborate legal systems to try to get to the heart of disputed matters. It is why we must pray when we study the Bible, asking God to keep our sinful, self-serving biases from getting in the way. It is also why we use the work of believers from the past, drawing on the wisdom others had before us.

For another thing, in spite of our sinful distortions of God's Word there is far more agreement among Christians on what the Bible teaches than the objection assumes. In spite of our many divisions, some of them hardened by centuries of ecclesiastical disputes and warfare, there is still agreement among true Christians on most essentials of the Bible's teaching. We believe in a Triune God, the full deity and full humanity of Jesus Christ, our sin, Jesus' vicarious death in our place for sin so that we might be saved from it, the work of the Holy Spirit in leading us to faith, the church, the moral law of God, the return of Christ, the resurrection of the dead, and the final judgment. That is only a quick overview of Christian theology, but it is a lot. It is basically what is expressed well in the ecumenical creeds: the Apostles' Creed, the Nicene Creed, and others.

Our problem with the Bible's teaching on these matters is not that they are hard to understand, but that we do not want to understand them or do not take time to. Recently I read a candid article, by a theology professor from a major seminary, arguing that to say the Bible is true is a complex, nearly impossible matter. The professor did not want to dispel the complexity. "Complexity," he said, "is what keeps us in our jobs."

Light on Our Dark Path

The Bible is not only clear itself, but it is also clarifying, which means that we see other things clearly by its light. The writer lists seven things clarified by the light of the Word.

1. *The way we should go* (v. 105). The way we should live our lives is what the psalmist means when he calls God's Word a lamp to his feet and a light to his path. We do not know how to live our lives, but the Bible shines on the path before us to expose the wrong, dangerous ways we might take and light up the right ones.

Many Christians suppose the Bible exists to give them detailed instructions concerning what job they should take, whom they should marry, where they should live, how they should spend their vacations, and other such details of daily living. This is not how the Word of God functions. It does not offer special or mystical leadings. It unfolds the kind of character a Christian should have and shows the priorities that should govern his or her thinking. This is true light on our path, and it is only the Bible that provides it. Nothing in the world gives the same illumination. On the contrary, the world always sets the wrong priorities and extols perverted character.

2. *Righteous behavior* (v. 106). Verse 106 is not talking about the righteousness of God imputed to us through faith in Jesus Christ; it is concerned with righteous actions, which is why it speaks of following God's "righteous laws." Why do we need the Bible to know what is right and

wrong? Doesn't the world have an intrinsic sense of right and wrong that enables it to enact good laws and convicts it by supplying a bad conscience? Yes, to a point. There is such a thing as natural law, which provides a moral foundation common to human beings almost everywhere. Generally people know that it is wrong to kill, steal, lie, and dishonor one's parents, for instance.

But these are not the areas in which we have our greatest problems. If a choice is black and white, we know what to do. Unfortunately the problems we face are usually not black and white but gray. We suspect we should do one thing, but there is another side to it. If the situation does not seem gray to us immediately, if we talk to our friends it becomes gray soon enough, since everyone sees it from a different point of view. Only by studying, meditating upon, and seeking to apply the Bible can we find our way through the gray landscape of life. The Bible is not gray. There are things in it we may not fully understand, but when we do understand them, which is often enough, they are very clear. Thus the Bible is a light on our moral path. The path is dark because the world is dark, but the Bible clarifies the issues and shows us how to walk through the darkness.

3. *Suffering* (v. 107). "I have suffered much," says the psalmist. The Bible can help by explaining the various reasons for suffering, which we studied earlier when looking at verses 65–88. Nothing but God's Word can show us that some suffering is merely common to man, some corrective, still other suffering constructive, Christ-glorifying, or even cosmic.

Yet reasons are not what the psalmist is talking about in this particular verse, for what follows is the prayer, "Renew my life . . . according to your word." In his suffering the writer turned to the Bible and found God present in its pages as well as finding promises for renewal of his life and spirit when he goes through hard times. It was God's presence and God's promises that kept him going. If ever there was a light on his dark path, it was then. If ever there was a light at the end of his dark tunnel, it was when he opened the Bible's pages.

4. *Right worship* (v. 108). The next verse speaks of praising God with our mouth and being taught God's laws. These two things belong together because they are what right worship and the practice of true religion are all about.

Praise and teaching ought to go on in church. When we come to church, first and foremost we should be taught the Bible. God has spoken in the Bible, and it is in the Bible that he continues to speak. There is nothing more important for Christian growth and the health of the church than sound Bible teaching. Yet sadly, serious Bible teaching is being widely neglected in our day, even in so-called evangelical churches. Instead of Bible teaching, people are being fed a diet of superficial pop-psychology, self-help therapy, feel-good stimulants, and entertainment, and the ignorance of the Bible in the churches is appalling. George Gallup has followed the rise of biblical illiteracy for decades, and he reports that although Americans revere the Bible highly—almost every home in America has a Bible, and most people say they believe it—only small percentages know who preached the Sermon on the Mount, are able to name the four Gospels, or recall even one of the Ten Commandments.

Not long ago the staff of CURE (Christians United for Reformation) was at the National Christian Booksellers Convention and conducted an informal survey to determine if people there could name the Ten Commandments. Shane Rosenthal, the producer of their radio program, *The White Horse Inn,* asked 256 people if they could name the Ten Commandments just off the top of their heads. In that huge assembly, not of secular people but of evangelical staffpersons and leaders, only a very few people could do it. These are people who are lobbying to get the Ten Commandments restored to the walls of our courtrooms and the public schools!

The other element of worship mentioned in this verse is the "willing praise" of God with our mouths. We praise God whenever we speak of him gratefully, but it is natural in this context to think of how we are praising God in our singing. There is much emotional music and frequently repeated words and slogans in churches nowadays, but as I travel around the country speaking in evangelical churches, I have noticed the loss of the great hymns of Christianity. This might be all right if the church's hymns were being replaced by better ones, but who can suppose that this is really the case? The new hymns are not better. They are usually trite, theologically vacuous, man-centered, and often simply misleading.

The downfall of our musical praise is related to our sad, pitiful ignorance of the Bible, and it will not be corrected until we recover some biblical depth. If we knew the Bible, it would expose our bad practices, enable us to correct them quickly, and draw us to a true biblical worship of God again. We cannot even know what might please God in our worship unless we find it in Scripture.

5. *The dangers of this life* (v. 109). The Hebrew of verse 109 says literally, "My soul in my hands constantly." The idea is the same as the English idiom, "I am taking my life in my hands." It means that the writer is in constant danger.

Whenever we find the psalms talking about danger, we usually think of physical danger, and it is true that the psalmists, particularly David, did face physical danger. David's enemies were always out to get him. But the psalms also speak of spiritual dangers like falling into sin or forgetting God. Verse 109 combines these two ideas. When the writer speaks of taking his life in his hands, he is expressing the idea of actually losing it. When he adds, nevertheless, "I will not forget your law," he is confessing that the far greater danger would be for him to abandon God's Word and begin to live a purely secular life. In other words, the Bible clarifies the nature of the danger and shows where his true peril lies.

Do we understand the danger of abandoning God's Word? I do not think so, and the fact I would put into evidence is the nature of our prayers. The prayers I hear have to do almost exclusively with having good health (or getting better when we or someone else is sick), succeeding at our jobs, passing a test, or perhaps someone else's salvation. Where are the prayers that we might be kept from sin, that we or those close to us might become more godly, that we might be able to live better for God or get to know God better? We need the Bible to clarify our true danger. We will never be aware of our danger without it.

6. *Enemies* (v. 110). Verse 110 teaches the same lessons as the one before it, making clear that the writer really was in danger of being killed by his enemies. They are "the wicked" who had set snares for him. If we are trying to live for Christ, we will have similar experiences. Ungodly people will also set snares for us, because they hate us and the Lord we are serving. They will try to make us look bad before our friends or fail at our jobs. If we are going to see our way through this problem and remain on the right path spiritually, we are going to have to study God's Word to get our priorities straight and be reminded that it is far more important to be approved by God than by other people.

When we read of the wicked fixing snares for us we think also of our even greater enemy, the devil, who we are told is "crafty" (Gen. 3:1), "the father of lies" (John 8:44), and "like a roaring lion looking for someone to devour" (1 Peter 5:8). If we are going to triumph over this most terrible enemy, we will need to know everything the Bible says about him and his tactics. We will need to know that he is powerful, but also that he is a defeated foe. Most important of all, we will need to know that the greatest battles we face are "not against flesh and blood [that is, what other people might do], but against . . . the spiritual forces of evil in the heavenly realms" (Eph. 6:12). The Bible clarifies the nature of these struggles, showing that it is our spiritual battles, rather than mere material or physical success, that really matter.

7. *The believer's true heritage* (v. 111). What is the psalmist's spiritual heritage, that is, what is he looking toward and working for? Some heavenly reward? A word of praise from God? Surprisingly, he says that his heritage is what he has been speaking about all along: God's Word itself.

> Your statutes are my heritage forever;
> they are the joy of my heart.

What a remarkable statement! Why does he say that all he desires for his inheritance is what he already possesses? Why should we say it?

First, of all the many seemingly weighty and important things we know on this earth, the only thing that will last forever is God's Word. Jesus was not exaggerating when he said, "Heaven and earth will pass away, but my words will never pass away" (Matt. 24:35). Our houses will pass away. Our bank accounts will pass away. Our earthly achievements and reputations will pass away. Everything. Only the Word of God will not pass away. It makes sense that the psalmist would fix his mind on God's Word and cherish it.

Second, because the law of God is the very Word of God, it is actually part of God himself, just as our words are part of what we are. In fact, it is what we possess of God here. So when the writer says that God's statutes are his heritage forever, what he is actually saying is that God himself is his heritage. He said it explicitly earlier: "You are my portion, O LORD" (v. 57). There is nothing better than God, so he does not look for anything better.

Third, the psalmist has found God's statutes to be "the joy of [his] heart." He is fully satisfied with God's Law. Therefore, he wants nothing more than to go on enjoying God's words forever. Isn't it true that the reason so many of us are dissatisfied with life is that we have not found the satisfaction in God and his Word that the psalmist has? He was spiritually rich. By contrast, we are rich in things but poor in soul.

Persevering to the Very End

I have pointed out several times already that the psalmist was a practical person. We see this quality again in the way the *nun* stanza ends (vv. 105–12), with a statement of fierce determination: "My heart is set on keeping your decrees to the very end" (v. 112). He wants to keep God's decrees because he will be able to live a God-pleasing life, he will understand the nature of true righteousness, he will possess a divine perspective on suffering and triumph in it, he will be able to worship God rightly, he will not be turned aside from obedience to God's Law by any physical danger, nor be distracted by the snares of evil men, and he will have a heritage that will last forever.

Sometimes we talk about having a biblical world-and-life-view, as opposed to having a secular worldview. A secular worldview is bound by what we can see and by the here-and-now. A biblical worldview sees all things in the light of God and from the perspective of God's revelation. This worldview can be expressed many ways, but there is probably no better statement of what is involved in it than these eight verses as they deal with God, life, righteousness, suffering, worship, danger, enemies, and our heritage in the light of the Word. They are what life is about. The only way the psalmist attained this perspective is because the Word of God articulates it clearly.

The evangelical church needs to turn from its sad worldliness and once again begin to live by the truths of God's Word. We are where this radical reorientation must begin.

Psalm 119

Delight in God's Decrees: Part 10

Walking by God's Word

I hate double-minded men,
though a vacillating man, in his inmost

I hate double-minded men,
  but I love your law.
You are my refuge and my shield;
  I have put my hope in your word.
Away from me, you evildoers,
  that I may keep the commands of my God!
Sustain me according to your promise, and I will live;
  do not let my hopes be dashed.
Uphold me, and I will be delivered;
  I will always have regard for your decrees.
You reject all who stray from your decrees,
  for their deceitfulness is in vain.
All the wicked of the earth you discard like dross;
  therefore I love your statutes.
My flesh trembles in fear of you;
  I stand in awe of your laws. . . .

Because I love your commands
  more than gold, more than pure gold,
and because I consider all your precepts right,
  I hate every wrong path.

verses 113–28

H
ave you ever noticed how novelists
make use of the way a person walks to highlight his or her character?
Proud men walk erect, their heads held high. Beautiful women glide or
float. Villains slouch, sneak, creep, or swagger. The need to describe different ways of walking has enriched our language. *The Oxford Thesaurus*
lists dozens of synonyms for walking: trek, shuffle, ramble, march, roam,
wander, and others. According to Eugene A. Nida of the American Bible
Society, the Zulu language has at least 120 words for walking: to walk
pompously, to walk with a swagger, to walk crouched down as when hunting a wild animal, to walk in tight clothes, and so on.

How should Christians walk? The Bible tells us "to walk worthy" of our
calling (Eph. 4:1 KJV), "uprightly" (Isa. 57:2), and "in the light" (1 John 1:7).
Micah 6:8 says, "What does the LORD require of you? To act justly and to
love mercy and to walk humbly with your God." In the section of Psalm 119
we come to now (the *samekh* and *ayin* stanzas, vv. 113–28) the writer is concerned with his walk, and the burden of his concern is that it be according
to God's Word. Walking according to God's Word was introduced as a
theme in the previous stanza (*nun,* vv. 105–12), beginning with the words,
"Your word is a lamp to my feet and a light for my path" (v. 105). In the last
chapter we looked at those words in terms of the Bible's clarity. Yet they also
have to do with walking along a right path, the theme that continues
through verse 128, concluding, "I hate every wrong path."

Seeing the Right Path Clearly

In regard to the believer's walk, stanza fourteen (*nun,* vv. 105–12) says
that *if we are to walk as God wants us to walk, we must be able to see the right way
clearly.* We will never be able to see it by ourselves since this is a dark world,
we have no natural light in ourselves, and there are deviating paths. We can
only see the right path if the Word of God shines on it and lights it up for
us. The Bible teaches us the way we should go and actually enables us to
walk in it.

This stanza has two ideas in regard to walking, one positive and the other
negative. Positively, the psalmist says he has taken an oath to "follow [God's]
righteous laws" (v. 106). He has determined to obey the Bible's teaching.
The Bible shows him the right path to follow. Negatively, the psalmist says
he has "not strayed from [God's] precepts" (v. 110).

I think here of the apostle Paul's instruction in his second letter to Timothy.
In chapter three he warns Timothy of "terrible times in the last days," noting
that the world will be filled with vices: "People will be lovers of themselves,
lovers of money, boastful, proud, abusive, disobedient to their parents,
ungrateful, unholy, without love, unforgiving, slanderous, without self-control,
brutal, not lovers of the good, treacherous, rash, conceited, lovers of pleasure

rather than lovers of God" (2 Tim. 3:2–4). This is an apt description of today's world. Worse, these vices will be in the church, for they will exist in those who have "a form of godliness" but deny "its power" (2 Tim. 3:5).

How can Timothy keep to the right path and avoid falling into the snares set for him by the wicked? It is by continuing in what he has learned from the Bible, Paul says (2 Tim. 3:14). The Bible is not like other books. It is God's Book, and it alone will make his way plain. "All Scripture is God-breathed and is useful for teaching, rebuking, correcting and training in righteousness, so that the man of God may be thoroughly equipped for every good work" (2 Tim. 3:16–17).

There are those positive and negative points again. Teaching and training are the positive terms. Rebuking and correcting are the negatives. We need both if we are to walk in the right path and avoid the wrong ones.

Choosing Right and Rejecting Wrong

The point of the previous stanza was that the Bible alone enables us to see the right way clearly. The point of this stanza (vv. 113–20) is that *if we are to walk as God wants us to walk, we must determine to do it, since there are many contrary paths and much opposition.*

Alexander Maclaren wrote that "this section is mainly the expression of firm resolve to cleave to the Law." He said that verses 113–15 "breathe love and determination." Verses 116 and 117 pass into "prayer in view of the psalmist's weakness and the strength of temptation." Finally, in verses 118–20 "the fate of the despisers of the Law intensifies the psalmist's clinging grasp of awe-struck love."[1]

1. *Determination to obey God's Law* (vv. 113–15). How are you and I ever going to keep on obeying God's Law in a sinfully enticing world like ours? There are several answers to that question. The psalm itself elaborates on quite a few of them. One thing is certain: We are never going to obey God's Law unless from the very beginning we determine to do it. That is our starting point. If we are to live for God, we must determine to obey him regardless of any enticing Siren calls to sin.

The biggest problem we face is suggested in verse 113, where the writer declares, "I hate double-minded men." The adjective "double-minded" is from the same root as the word that is translated "two opinions" in 1 Kings 18:21. In that chapter Elijah is on Mount Carmel challenging the people of Israel to follow Jehovah rather than the false god Baal. "How long will you waver between two opinions? If the LORD is God, follow him; but if Baal is God, follow him," he says. Double-minded people are people who know about God but are not fully determined to worship and serve him only. They are those who want both God and the world. They want the benefits of true religion, but they want their sin too.

The psalmist says that he hates people who are like this. He hates them as much as he loves God's Law. I believe he is also saying he hates the same double-mindedness in himself. Otherwise, why does he continue by asking God to sustain him, according to his promise, and uphold him so that he might be kept from sin? These verses breathe out love of God's Law and determination to avoid double-mindedness, as Maclaren says, but it is only against the dark background of his tendency to be lukewarm that the strong fixing of his mind and will to obey God's Law makes sense.

If the psalmist needed to fix his mind on obeying God, don't we too? James thought so. He urged his readers to pray in faith, not wavering through any kind of weak indecision and doubt. The one who does waver "should not think he will receive anything from the Lord; he is a double-minded man, unstable in all he does" (James 1:7–8). Unfortunately, we often do not pray in faith. We waver, and the love of the world and its pleasures draws us away from God's Word.

Yet the situation is not hopeless. In fact, there is great ground for confidence because of God, who is not double-minded and who is on the believer's side. The writer calls God his "refuge and . . . shield" (v. 114). God is our refuge from those who would harm us and our shield against temptations. He also calls God "my God" in verse 115, the only place in the psalm where these words occur. They highlight a double gripping: on the one hand, the writer's grip on God, and on the other, God's grip on him. It is what we might call the perseverance of the saints, which also has to do with a double persevering. The saints must persevere, and will, but the reason they do is that God first of all perseveres with them.

2. *Prayer for God's grace* (vv. 116–17). If we persevere because God first of all perseveres with us, then we need to look to him for sustaining grace to walk on the path he has set before us. This means that we must ask God for help. It is what the psalmist does next (vv. 116–17).

In the Middle Ages, under the monastic order of the Benedictines, when a novice's period of preparation was ended and he was ready to become attached to the monastery for life, there was an induction ceremony in which, with outstretched arms, the novice recited Psalm 119:116 three times:

> Sustain me according to your promise, and I will live;
> do not let my hopes be dashed.

The community repeated the words and then sang the Gloria Patri, which was a way of acknowledging that the commitments of the monastic life could only be sustained by God, to whom all glory belongs.[2] So too with the Christian life as a whole. If we are to read, study, understand, and actually obey God's Word, it will only be by God's grace, helping us to do it. We must get into the habit of asking him for that help often.

3. *Standing in awe of God* (vv. 118–20). The last three verses of this stanza reflect a reordered outlook on the world and God, doubtless resulting from the psalmist's times of prayer. He has understood his inability to obey God's

Law. He has sought God's help. Now having been with God, he sees afresh the deceitful vanity of the world and the greatness of God before whom he now trembles in reverential awe.

It is only as we tremble before the exalted and holy God that we will ever see the world and its distorted values to be the empty things they are. If we do not tremble before God, the world's system will seem wonderful to us and consume us pleasantly.

Verse 120 should be read carefully, prayerfully, and with repentance by every Christian, particularly the evangelical Christians of our day. It is speaking of a reverent awe of God, an important element of walking uprightly before him. There is precious little of this spirit today. Instead of being in awe before God, many in our day seem to regard him more as a buddy, which only shows that we do not know much about God at all. And isn't that why there is so little truly godly conduct and why we are so much like the world? In his classic treatment of the weaknesses of the contemporary evangelical church, *No Place for Truth,*[3] David F. Wells speaks of the weightlessness of God, meaning that God seems to have very little bearing on the actual life of today's Christians. They do not disbelieve in him; they are Christians, after all, but he is remote from their thinking. He just doesn't enter in.

In a fascinating essay the English writer William Hazlitt (1778–1830) described an evening in which various literary figures of his day discussed people from the past they wished they had seen. They suggested almost everyone you might think of: Homer, Dante, Shakespeare, Columbus, Caesar, Napoleon, even Jonathan Edwards. But Charles Lamb had the last word: "There is only one other person I can ever think of after this," he said. "If Shakespeare was to come into the room, we should all rise up to meet him; but if that person [Jesus] was to come into it, we should all fall down and try to kiss the hem of his garment!"[4]

That is not nearly reverence enough, but it gets at the idea. Today many would merely cry out, "Hey, Jesus, come on over here and tell us how it's goin'." The psalmist says that he trembled before God and stood in awe of his laws, which is why he was a godly person and why he has been able to give us the profound teaching we have from him in this psalm.

Looking for God's Deliverance

In the last of these three stanzas (*ayin,* vv. 121–28) that have to do with walking by God's Word, familiar contrasts recur: clear direction versus a sin-dark world, the threat of enemies versus the sustaining grace of God, the hatred of sin versus the love of God's Word. Based on the writer's awe of God introduced at the end of the last stanza, what this stanza emphasizes is that *if we are to walk as God wants us to walk, we must keep looking to him intently, at all times.* As far as sin is concerned, we must look to God's commandments. As far as dangers go, we must look to God for deliverance.

The words that seems to tie the stanza together are "your servant," found in verses 122, 124, and 125. These words present the psalmist as God's servant in contrast to those who are God's enemies and who are therefore oppressing him. The writer has spoken of these enemies earlier. They are the wicked of stanza fourteen, who have set snares for him (v. 110), the double-minded persons, evildoers, and wicked of the earth of stanza fifteen, whom he has turned his back on in order to follow after God (vv. 113, 115, 119). Now in stanza sixteen they are oppressing him, so much so and for so long that his eyes have failed, looking for God's salvation. He needs deliverance. Therefore, he is going to keep on looking to God until help comes.

According to the Masoretes, verse 122 is the only verse in the psalm that does not mention the Word of God. We have seen that verse 84 also seems not to mention it; verses 90, 121, and 132 may be examples too. The fact that the Bible is not mentioned here, in verse 122, may be an indication of the depth of mental anguish to which the psalmist fell as a result of the oppression he had endured from wicked men. For a moment his eyes seem to be off the Bible and on his fierce oppressors instead.

Not for long! He is God's servant, and "as the eyes of slaves look to the hand of their master" and "as the eyes of a maid look to the hand of her mistress" (Ps. 123:2), so does he look up anxiously to God, expecting God to act. This stanza gives three arguments for why God should save him:

1. *Because God is a loving God* (v. 124). The psalmist has learned that God is not an indifferent, unconcerned deity. He is a loving God; that is why he has given us the Bible. Since he is a loving God, should he not care for those he loves and deliver them?

2. *Because the writer is God's servant* (v. 125). Masters normally value those who are part of their households. If that is true on earth, shouldn't it also be true in heaven? Can God be any less caring than a good master on earth?

3. *Because it is time for God to act* (v. 126). We might expect the writer to have said that God should act now because if he delays it will be too late; he will be crushed by his oppressors. We have seen this argument in other psalms.[5] Here, instead of pleading his own desperate condition, he calls on God to act because God's "law is being broken." How interesting! Because he is God's servant, he is more concerned for God's name and Law than he is for his own condition.

The last two verses of this section repeat a contrast we saw in verse 113, namely, hatred of what is wrong and love of what is good.

> Because I love your commands
>   more than gold, more than pure gold,
> and because I consider all your precepts right,
>   I hate every wrong path (vv. 127–28).

We live in days when it is hard for people, even alleged Christians, to accept such a statement. Our age is being described as postmodernity, a time in history when truth is regarded in the Hegelian sense, that is, that something may be true for you or me or for now, but it does not have any binding validity for others or for all times. Since there are no absolutes, there is nothing we can call false. To call something false is an inexcusable power play. All ways of life must be equally valid and the only thing that is absolutely wrong is to say that the path taken by someone else is wrong. It is inexcusable to hate it. The time is probably coming when Christians holding to absolute standards will be considered criminals.

But Christians do hold to absolutes, and must hold them. We cannot love God and Satan too. We cannot hold to God's standards without separating from the contrary standards of the world. We cannot love the right path without hating the wrong ones. Jesus put it this way: "No one can serve two masters. Either he will hate the one and love the other, or he will be devoted to the one and despise the other. You cannot serve both God and Money" (Matt. 6:24).

Are you willing to hate what God hates? If not, you will never learn to love God truly, and you will certainly never walk in the way that brings true blessing. If you are hesitating, I encourage you to read Psalm 1 once again. It contrasts the way of the wicked to the way of the godly. The former "*walk* in the counsel of the wicked," "*stand* in the way of sinners," and "*sit* in the seat of mockers" (v. 1, italics added). By contrast, the godly "delight . . . in the law of the LORD" and meditate on it "day and night" (v. 2). As a result, they are like well-nourished trees that yield good fruit in their season (v. 3). The psalm ends by observing,

> The LORD watches over the way of the righteous,
> but the way of the wicked will perish (Ps. 1:6).

Psalm 119

Delight in God's Decrees: Part 11

God's Wonderful Words

Your statutes are wonderful;
*   therefore I obey them.*
The entrance of your words gives light;
*   it gives understanding to the simple.*
I open my mouth and pant,
*   longing for your commands.*
Turn to me and have mercy on me,
*   as you always do to those who love your name.*
Direct my footsteps according to your word;
*   let no sin rule over me.*
Redeem me from the oppression of men,
*   That I may obey your precepts.*
Make your face shine upon your servant
*   and teach me your decrees.*
Streams of tears flow from my eyes,
*   for your law is not obeyed. . . .*
Your righteousness is everlasting
*   and your law is true.*

Trouble and distress have come upon me,
but your commands are my delight.
Your statues are forever right;
give me understanding that I may live.

                                        verses 129–44

Many good things from the past are disappearing in today's modern and postmodern society, and one of them is wonder. People used to have their sense of awe incited by some new or unexpected thing. They had expressions like "wonder-worker," "seven-day-wonder," and "wonders never cease." They read books like *Alice's Adventures in Wonderland* or watched movies like *It's a Wonderful Life*. Nothing seems wonderful anymore. There is no mystery in anything. Everything seems commonplace, predictable, dull.

One reason is technology, which gives the impression that all reality is explicable and everything we can imagine can be done. Another reason is television, whose insatiable appetite for material means that everything that can possibly be analyzed, discussed, or exploited is—and at every hour of the day or night. About fifteen years ago Neil Postman wrote a book titled *The Disappearance of Childhood,* which argued that television more than anything else robs childhood of its lovely and appealing qualities, including a sense of wonder at the unexpected, unexplained, and surprising beauties of life.[1]

Yet the real reason is not technology or television. It is loss of an awareness of God, who alone is truly wonderful and the source of every other "wonder." If God goes, what is genuinely wonderful goes with him.

For example, when I was preparing for this chapter by looking in dictionaries of quotations for what people over time have said about wonder, wonders, or things wonderful, I noticed that a large percentage of the quotations came from the Bible, the Book of Common Prayer, or from writers who were intentionally echoing the Bible's language. The Bible speaks of "signs" and "wonders" (2 Cor. 12:12). It says that one of the great names for Jesus is "Wonderful Counselor" (Isa. 9:6). It notes that we are "fearfully and wonderfully made" and that all God's "works are wonderful" (Ps. 139:14). The Psalms contain this idea especially. In the New International Version "wonder," "wonderful," and their derivatives occur thirty-two times in the Psalter.

Many English writers use "wonder" in reference to God, the Bible, and God's works. Here is a favorite example of mine by Richard Crashaw (1612–1648), from "Hymn to the Nativity":

> Welcome, all wonders in one sight!
> Eternity shut in a span,
> Summer in winter, day in night,
> Heaven in earth, and God in man.
> Blest little one, whose all embracing birth
> Lifts earth to heaven, stoops heaven to earth.

"Your Statutes Are Wonderful"

The author of Psalm 119 had not lost his sense of wonder, because he had found the Bible to be wonderful. Early in the psalm he prayed, "Open my eyes that I may see wonderful things in your law" (v. 18). Farther along he spoke of "meditat[ing] on your wonders" (v. 27). Now he asserts, "Your statutes are wonderful; therefore I obey them" (v. 129). This verse represents the theme of the *pe* and *tsadhe* stanzas (vv. 129–44): the wonder of God's Law tied to the obedience that follows from a proper appreciation of it. Wonder and obedience are linked throughout the stanzas, the word "obey" being repeated three times, in verses 129, 134, and 136.

Nineteenth-century Baptist preacher Charles Haddon Spurgeon says how wonderful God's Word is. It is

> full of wonderful revelations, commands and promises. Wonderful in their nature, as being free from all error, and bearing within themselves overwhelming self-evidence of their truth; wonderful in their effects as instructing, elevating, strengthening, and comforting the soul. Jesus the eternal Word is called Wonderful, and all the uttered words of God are wonderful in their degree. Those who know them best wonder at them most. It is wonderful that God should have borne testimony at all to sinful men, and more wonderful still that his testimony should be of such a character, so clear, so full, so gracious, so mighty.[2]

Spurgeon remarks about the connection between the wonder of God's Law and the psalmist's obedience: "Their wonderful character so impressed itself upon his mind that he kept them in his memory; their wonderful excellence so charmed his heart that he kept them in his life."[3]

Because They Give Understanding

These stanzas offer seven reasons why God's words are wonderful, and the first is that they give "understanding to the simple."

> The entrance of your words gives light;
>   it gives understanding to the simple.
> I open my mouth and pant,
>   longing for your commands (130–31).

The Hebrew word for "entrance" is *pethach*. Depending on whether it is pronounced with a short or long *e* it can mean either "door" (with a short *e*) or "revelation" (with a long "e"). The New International Version, following the King James, takes it the first way, saying, "The entrance of your words gives light." Martin Luther thought it had to do with revelation; so his translation read, *"Wenn dein Wort offenbar wird"* ("When your word is revealed"). The explanation for this double meaning is that in the early days of the formation of the Hebrew language the Jews were bedouins, who lived in tents. The only opening in a tent was the flap of skin that was the door. So when the door was opened, light came into the tent, illuminating everything inside. The writer captures this image exactly when he speaks of the entrance of God's words giving light.

Reading the Bible throws light on life, on all its problems and trials, on the confusing behavior of other people, on what is important and what is not, on right behavior, right goals, and right priorities. If you have not found this to be true, it is because either you are not really studying the Bible or you are approaching it in a superior or vain frame of mind, judging it by your own limited views rather than allowing it to judge you.

Martin Luther made a strong point of the Word's giving understanding "to the simple," which is what the verse says. He argued that the wisdom of the Bible is hidden from those who are wise in their own eyes but disclosed to those who are "ready, prepared, eager always to be taught, judged, and to hear, rather than to teach, judge and be heard."[4]

How this works is illustrated by the way Jesus dealt with the Emmaus disciples in the story recorded in Luke 24. These two people, probably Cleopas and his wife, Mary, were returning home after the crucifixion when Jesus drew near them on the road. They did not recognize him. When he asked why they were downcast they replied by telling him what had happened in Jerusalem at the time of the Passover.

They told him about Jesus: "He was a prophet, powerful in word and deed before God and all the people." They told him how the chief priests and rulers "handed him over to be sentenced to death, and . . . crucified him." As they related their experience it came out that they had been in Jerusalem that very morning and heard tales from the women who had been to the tomb, who reported the body was no longer there and angels had appeared proclaiming Jesus was alive. This had not interested them. They did not believe in resurrections. They had not even bothered to go to the tomb to see it for themselves, although they were within a short walk of the burial garden. They had no understanding about Jesus' death and resurrection.

Jesus began to teach them from the Scriptures. "How foolish you are, and how slow to believe all that the prophets have spoken! Did not the Christ have to suffer these things and then enter his glory?" Then beginning with Moses and going through all the prophets "he explained to them what was said in the Scriptures concerning himself" (see Luke 24:13–27).

This story (and its sequel) contains three profound revelations that were openings, just like the word "entrance" in our psalm. The first is the opening of the Scriptures. After Jesus had disappeared from their sight, these two disciples said to each other, "Were not our hearts burning within us while he talked with us on the road and *opened the Scriptures* to us?" (Luke 24:32, italics added). Second, *"their eyes were opened* and they recognized him" (Luke 24:31, italics added). Third, "*he opened their minds* so they could understand the Scriptures" (Luke 24:45, italics added).

That is how it works. First, there is the opening of God's Word, then, the opening of the eyes to see Jesus, and finally, the opening of the mind, or understanding.

Yet the result is not understanding alone, but obedience to what is understood. That is why verse 131 follows verse 130. Because the entrance of God's words gives light, the psalmist says that he opens his mouth, panting after those words, longing for God's commands. The verse reminds us of Psalm 81:10, where God makes the promise, "Open wide your mouth and I will fill it."

Because We Find Mercy in These Pages

The second reason why God's words are wonderful is that we find the mercy of God in them, and mercy is what we need. Not justice, not pity, not recognition of tarnished "good" deeds, but a mercy that reaches out to save those who are truly wretched and helpless because of sin. The psalmist expresses this idea as a prayer:

> Turn to me and have mercy on me,
> as you always do to those who love your name (v. 132).

This is the last of the verses in Psalm 119 that do not mention the Word of God specifically, though it is possible that "your name" refers to the words of God indirectly. Whatever the case, it is in the Bible that the psalmist finds mercy, and the mercy of God to sinners is the most wonderful of all wonders. Charles Wesley captured it a bit in his greatest hymn, "And Can It Be," particularly in the third verse:

> He left his Father's throne above,
> (So free, so infinite his grace!)
> Emptied himself of all but love,
> And bled for Adam's helpless race.
> 'Tis mercy all, immense and free;
> For, O my God, it found out me.

Have you found the mercy of God in the Word of God? Until you have, you will never think of the Bible as being wonderful. What you need is to pray the prayer of the publican, the tax collector who stood at the edge of the crowd and cried, "God be merciful to me a sinner" (Luke 18:13 KJV). He found mercy through the shed blood of Jesus Christ and went home justified, according to Jesus. You will too if you allow the Bible to point you to Christ, the Savior of sinners, and put your faith in him.

Because They Give Direction for Life

The third reason the psalmist finds the words of God to be wonderful is something we have noticed many times already. It is because they give right guidance for his life. They give direction for his footsteps, victory over sin, and salvation from those who have been trying to destroy him (vv. 133–34). What is new in these verses is the emphasis on obedience, which occurs throughout the *pe* stanza. It is by obeying God's Word that the writer finds direction, victory, and deliverance. Yet the reverse is also true. It is because he has found direction, victory, and deliverance from God's Word that he determines to obey it.

Because God Is in Them

The fourth reason the psalmist finds the Scriptures to be wonderful is because God himself is in them and because he reveals himself to the one who studies them. "Make your face shine upon your servant," he says (v. 135). This verse is a conscious echo of the Old Testament benediction known as the Aaronic blessing:

> The LORD bless you and keep you;
> the LORD make his face shine upon you
>   and be gracious to you;
> the LORD turn his face toward you
>   and give you peace (Num. 6:24–26).

What was the deep longing and aspiration of the Old Testament saints, the best blessing they could possibly conceive? It was to see the face of God. Moses asked to see the face of God. God told him that he could not grant this request, saying, "No one may see me and live" (Exod. 33:20). Nevertheless, God placed Moses in a cleft of the mountains, covered him with his hand, and passed by, saying his covenant name (see Exod. 34:6–7). In that way Moses did indeed "see" him.

That is how we see God too, not in some imaginary, direct, unmediated revelation of God to souls, but in the Bible. It is there alone that we see God. Jesus told the disciples, "Anyone who has seen me has seen the Father" (John 14:9), but it is in the Bible that we see Jesus.

Verse 136 is the third of the verses in this stanza that contain the idea of obedience, but here the writer's concern is that God's Law is "not obeyed." This brings tears to his eyes because of the dishonor it brings to God, but also because of the misery and harm it brings to those who are guilty of disobedience.

Instead of weeping over people who disobey and even flaunt God's laws, many Christians in our time get angry with such persons and fight them verbally. Matthew Henry said, "The sins of sinners are the sorrows of saints."

Jesus wept over Jerusalem (see Luke 19:41). Paul said that he had "great sorrow and unceasing anguish" in his heart because of the widespread unbelief of Israel (see Rom. 9:1–4). Tears show compassion, and compassion wins others far more effectively than belligerent arguments and certainly more effectively than anger. Do we weep for others, sorrowing over the pain we know their unbelief and disobedience bring?

Because They Are Altogether Righteous

The theme of the next stanza of Psalm 119 is righteousness, doubtless because the Hebrew word for "righteous" *(tzedek)* begins with the letter starting each verse in this section *(tsadhe)* and was the obvious word to begin with. Furthermore, it is close to the word for the letter in form and pronunciation. It is found in verses 137, 138, 142, and 144.

Another reason why the psalmist knew that God's words are wonderful is because they are altogether righteous. The source of righteousness is the character of God ("Righteous are you, O LORD," v. 137; "Your righteousness is everlasting," v. 142), and the Law of God gives expression to that righteousness ("Your laws are right," v. 137; "The statutes you have laid down are righteous," v. 138; "Your statutes are forever right," v. 144). The Bible mirrors the character of God. Anyone who cares about knowing what is righteous and wants to act righteously should study the Bible. Statesmen should study it; so should judges, policemen, teachers, parents, ministers—indeed, everyone who believes that morality matters.

Because They Have Been Tested and Proved

In the middle of this discussion of the righteousness of God's laws a new, sixth reason why God's Word is wonderful occurs. It is that God's words have been tested and proved to be reliable (vv. 140–41). In other words, they really do give understanding; disclose God to be a God of great mercy; provide direction for life, victory over sin, and deliverance from man's oppression; reveal God himself; and teach what true righteousness is. Moreover, they show that God, who has given the Scriptures, can be trusted, since all his promises are "amen and amen." They never fail of fulfillment.

Have you found God's Word to be fully trustworthy? Years ago there were Christians who used to put the promises of God to the test and when they received what was promised would write "T and P" in their Bible next to the promise. The letters stood for "tried and proven," exactly what the psalmist says he found to be true in his experience.

Because They Are True

The last of these seven reasons why the Word of God is wonderful in the view of the psalmist is because God's words are true. "Your law is true," he says

(v. 142). So much of what we hear from other sources, even those considered to be reputable and reliable, is false. Who trusts anyone's words today? A number of years ago two researchers named James Patterson and Peter Kim wrote a book called *The Day America Told the Truth* in which they claimed that Americans lie all the time and often for no apparent reason.[5] Politicians lie. Directors of large corporations lie. Employees lie. Husbands and wives lie.

Is there anyone who does not lie? God does not lie. Every word he has spoken can be trusted. Every word! That is something truly wonderful!

Psalm 119

Delight in God's Decrees: Part 12

Using God's Word in Prayer

I call with all my heart; answer me, O LORD,
*   and I will obey your decrees.*
I call out to you; save me
*   and I will keep your statutes.*
I rise before dawn and cry for help;
*   I have put my hope in your word.*
My eyes stay open through the watches of the night,
*   that I may meditate on your promises.*
Hear my voice in accordance with your love;
*   renew my life, O LORD, according to your laws.*
Those who devise wicked schemes are near,
*   but they are far from your law.*
Yet you are near, O LORD,
*   and all your commands are true.*
Long ago I learned from your statutes
*   that you established them to last forever.*

verses 145–52

W e are coming near the end of Psalm
119, so it is not surprising that the danger threatening the psalmist all along

should emerge again strongly, though not for the final time. It has to do with his relentless enemies. The presence of these enemies has been alluded to earlier.[1] Verses 145–52 (the *qoph* stanza) seem to concentrate on this reality: "I call out to you; save me" (v. 146); "I rise before dawn and cry for help" (v. 147); "Those who devise wicked schemes are near" (v. 150).

What is to be done in the face of their cruel threats and machinations? The writer turns to God in prayer, praying with an open Bible before him, as it were. His Bible reminds him that although "those who devise wicked schemes are near" (v. 150), God is also "near" (v. 151). That makes all the difference! Derek Kidner writes, "The threat is not glossed over; it is put in perspective by a bigger fact."[2]

Yet these verses are not really about the psalmist's enemies, as bad as they were. They are about the writer's prayer life and how he had learned to use God's Word when praying.[3]

Praying Earnestly

The first thing we can learn from this stanza is that prayer should be earnest. The psalmist's prayers were, and it is this earnestness that drove him to God's Word. The fact that he was driven to the Bible again and again is expressed in almost every verse of this section, but his fervency in prayer emerges most clearly in the first two verses, which say that he is calling on God to answer him and save him, and that he is doing so "with all [his] heart."

In the Hebrew text, as well as in English, the petitions "answer me" and "save me" are short, staccato utterances, which are appropriate for one who is in trouble and earnestly seeking help. In different circumstances a person might pray leisurely with carefully thought-out petitions. He might even compose a prayer. Most of the psalms are carefully composed petitions, but not when one is in trouble! When one is in trouble one prays earnestly, seriously, desperately. Even if one is not in trouble, earnestness in prayer is an important prayer element.

Two instructive examples from the New Testament come to mind. First, we think of Peter when he was sinking into the Sea of Galilee. His prayer to Jesus to save him then was identical to that of the psalmist. Jesus had been teaching on the Gentile side of the lake, and when he had finished and fed the crowds, he sent his disciples in a boat ahead of him to the other side while he remained behind in the hills overlooking the lake to pray. On the lake the boat ran into stormy weather, and while the disciples were working hard to bring it to safety Jesus came to them walking on the water. They were afraid. They thought they were seeing a ghost. When Jesus called out, "Take courage! It is I! Don't be afraid," Peter realized that it was Jesus and asked Jesus if he could come to him on the water.

"Come," Jesus said.

The story continues, "Then Peter got down out of the boat and walked on the water to Jesus. But when he saw the wind, he was afraid and, beginning to sink, cried out, 'Lord, save me!'" (Matt. 14:29–30). Jesus reached out his hand immediately, caught Peter, and brought him back to the boat and safety.

When we cry to Jesus to save us, we find that he is not far away and that he is ready to answer us and save us immediately. It is when our prayers are most earnest and we are most desperate that we are most immediately heard.

The second New Testament example of earnest prayer is from the Book of James. James has a lot to say about prayer, and toward the end of the book he says that "the prayer of a righteous man is powerful and effective" (James 5:16). The King James Version says, "The effectual fervent prayer of a righteous man avails much." Then James offers the example of Elijah. "Elijah was a man just like us. He prayed earnestly that it would not rain, and it did not rain on the land for three and a half years. Again he prayed, and the heavens gave rain, and the earth produced its crops" (James 5:17–18).

James is reminding us that Elijah had the same weaknesses we have. After his victory on Mount Carmel when the fire of God consumed Jehovah's sacrifice and the prophets of Baal were all taken away and killed, Jezebel warned Elijah, "May the gods deal with me, be it ever so severely, if by this time tomorrow I do not make your life like that of one of them" (1 Kings 19:2). Elijah was terrified and hid. So obviously he was sometimes weak and fearful. Nevertheless, says James, Elijah was a man who was used by God to speak spiritual words and bring judgment on Ahab's kingdom.

God told Elijah to tell the king that it would not rain, and it did not. The grass dried up; the crops withered; the animals began to die. The kingdom was devastated. Then, after three years, God sent Elijah to tell Ahab that it would rain again.

Elijah went up to Mount Carmel. He put his head between his knees in an attitude of prayer and sent a servant to the edge of the hill to look for some indication of rain. The boy returned, saying, "All I see is a broad expanse of the blue sky over the Mediterranean."

Elijah said, "Go look again." The boy went back, and Elijah continued to pray earnestly. When the boy returned, Elijah asked again, "Did you see anything?" Nothing. The sky was absolutely clear. Elijah sent the young man back seven times.

The seventh time the servant reported, "A cloud as small as a man's hand is rising from the sea." Elijah knew that was it. So he said, "Go and tell Ahab, 'Hitch up your chariot and go down before the rain stops you'" (1 Kings 18:44). Then he gathered his robes around himself and ran ahead, outdistancing the chariot. The rains came down, and the drought was broken.

James is reminding us how God worked through Elijah when he prayed earnestly. He is encouraging us to be people of earnest prayer too—not men and women of presumption, who get an idea in their heads and baptize it by prayer, saying, "This is what God is going to do," when God has promised nothing of the sort, but those who earnestly seek God's will and pray for it and thus become agents of the blessing God brings. At the end of the book he even gives us a place to start, suggesting that we pray for sinners. For "whoever turns a sinner away from the error of his way will save him from death and cover a multitude of sins" (James 5:20).

Praying Always

When Paul was writing to the Thessalonians in his first letter and was coming to the closing section in which he was accustomed to giving some practical applications of the earlier teaching, one thing he told these believers was to "pray continually," that is, at all times (1 Thess. 5:17). The author of Psalm 119 seems to have learned this lesson too, since the next pair of verses speak of his daily prayer pattern. He began his prayers before sunrise, and he continued even into the watches of the night.

> I rise before dawn and cry for help;
> I have put my hope in your word.
> My eyes stay open through the watches of the night,
> that I may meditate on your promises (vv. 147–48).

When Paul told the Thessalonians to "pray continually," he did not mean that they were to do nothing but pray. They would never get anything else done. He meant instead that prayer is to be a natural and constant part of our lives. It is not to be restricted only to special prayer seasons or special prayer days. We are to be people whose lives are marked by an attitude of prayer consistently.

Yet there is something to be said for specific prayer times too, since these fix our minds on God's words and determine how we will be thinking and acting in the remaining hours. The psalmist seems to have prayed early in the morning—"before dawn"—and "through the watches of the night." In other words, he was a person committed to strong spiritual disciplines, and regular morning and evening prayer times, together with Bible study, were important parts of his discipline.

One very important word that we have not yet adequately considered is "meditate." It occurs in verse 148 as an explanation for why the writer remained awake during the watches of the night. It was to "meditate on [God's] promises." Christians today need to learn about and develop the habit of biblical meditation.

Biblical meditation is more than merely reading the Bible and perhaps praying afterwards. It is more even than memorizing certain portions of it. It is internalizing the Bible's teaching to such an extent that the truths discovered in the Bible become part of how we think, so that we think differently and then also function differently as a result. It is what God demanded of Joshua when he was about to lead the people of Israel in the conquest of Canaan:

> Be strong and very courageous. Be careful to obey all the law my servant Moses gave you; do not turn from it to the right or to the left, that you may be successful wherever you go. Do not let this Book of the Law depart from your mouth; *meditate on it day and night,* so that you may be careful to do everything written in it. Then you will be prosperous and successful" (Josh. 1:7–8, italics added).

One person who knows a great deal about biblical meditation is Ronald A. Jenson, former president of the School of Theology of the International Christian Graduate University. In a booklet published by the International Council of Biblical Inerrancy he tells how he had developed a successful pornography business when he was still in elementary school, buying sexually explicit literature and pictures and selling them to friends at a profit. He ran it out of his basement. When he became a Christian, what he was and what he had been doing changed dramatically. Nevertheless, although he abandoned his pornography business and got active in church work, he still had trouble with his thought life because the strong sexual material he had been feeding on had become part of what he was. He described it by saying, "When you sow a thought, you reap an action. When you sow that action, you reap a habit. When you sow that habit, you reap a character. When you sow that character, you reap a destiny."[4] He had been sowing lustful thoughts, and a lustful character had been formed.

What delivered him from a pornographic pattern of life was discovering how to meditate on the Bible's teaching. He learned how to be transformed "by the renewing of [his] mind" (Rom. 12:2). Meditation involved thinking what the passage he was studying was about and internalizing it, imagining what it would mean for him in specific acts of conduct. He even worked on singing specific verses to whatever tune seemed to fit them, because singing helped fix the biblical truths in his mind. He was changed. His conclusion was this: "Biblical meditation is hard work, but the reward is worth it—a consistent, victorious Christian life."[5]

Praying Biblically

The third thing the psalmist teaches about prayer in these verses is that prayer is best when it is biblical, that is, when it accompanies and flows from serious Bible study and when it is, in a sense, repeating God's very words, teaching, decrees, and promises back to him. It is when our own prayer words become biblical. The psalmist expresses this when he talks about God's hearing him "in accordance with [God's] love" and renewing his life "according to [God's] laws" (v. 149). What distressed him about the wicked is that "they are far from [God's] law" (v. 150).

In his homiletical commentary on Ephesians, Harry Ironside tells about meeting an older, very godly man early in his ministry. The man was dying of tuberculosis, and Ironside went to visit him. His name was Andrew Fraser. He could barely speak above a whisper because his lungs were almost consumed by the disease, but he said, "Young man, you are trying to preach Christ, are you not?"

"Yes, I am," replied Ironside.

"Well," he said, "sit down a little, and let us talk together about the Word of God." He opened his Bible, and until his strength was gone he unfolded one passage after another, teaching truths that Ironside at that time had not appreciated or even perceived. Before long, tears were running down Ironside's cheeks, and he asked, "Where did you get these things? Can you tell me where I can find a book that will open them up to me? Did you get them in a seminary or college?"

Fraser replied, "My dear young man, I learned these things on my knees on the mud floor of a little sod cottage in the north of Ireland. There with my open Bible before me, I used to kneel for hours at a time and ask the Spirit of God to reveal Christ to my soul and to open the Word to my heart. He taught me more on my knees on that mud floor than I ever could have learned in all the seminaries or colleges in the world."[6]

I am not disparaging education, of course. I have received a great deal of it myself and have profited from it, but it is possible to have a theological education and still know very little about God, if that learning is only intellectual or academic. What counts is time spent prayerfully in the Bible.

Praying in Faith

The fourth truth to be learned about prayer in these verses is that prayer must be in faith, believing. It must be earnest, a constant way of life, and biblical, but it must also be in faith. I referred earlier to the Book of James because James has so much to say about prayer, looking at the close of chapter 5. James also writes about prayer in chapter 1. In that chapter he is urging us to pray for wisdom, promising that if a man asks for wisdom, God will give it. Then he adds wisely, "But when he asks, he must believe and not doubt, because he who doubts is like a wave of the sea, blown and tossed by the wind. That man should not think he will receive anything from the Lord; he is a double-minded man, unstable in all he does" (James 1:6–8).

But suppose we do doubt—and we do—what then? Clearly we must ask God even for the faith we need to pray in faith. We must be like the man who asked Jesus to heal his demon-possessed son. He begged Jesus, "If you can do anything, take pity on us and help us."

"If you can?" said Jesus in mild surprise. "Everything is possible for him who believes."

The man exclaimed, "I do believe; help me overcome my unbelief!" (Mark 9:24). Jesus healed his son.

Like that desperate father, our faith is not strong. It is always mixed with unbelief and doubt, but God gives faith and strengthens faith. Moreover, we do not need an overwhelming amount of faith for God to hear us, since the believer's strength is not in his faith but in God, who is faith's object. We remember how Jesus also said, "If you have faith as small as a mustard seed, you can say to this mountain, 'Move from here to there' and it will move. Nothing will be impossible for you" (Matt. 17:20).

How is this faith cultivated? It is cultivated by studying the Bible, by learning what God is like. As we study the Bible we get to know God, and our faith is made strong because it is in him.

The psalmist studied the Bible prayerfully day and night, and what he learned specifically was that although his enemies were "near" (v. 150), God was also "near" (v. 150), the truth we saw at the beginning of this chapter. It is the presence of God perceived in Bible study that frees us from our fears and makes us strong in faith. The last line says about God's statutes, "You established them to last forever." The person who builds on them will also stand firm and forever. We sing about it in that great hymn from Rippon's "Selection of Hymns" (1787):

> How firm a foundation, you saints of the Lord,
> Is laid for your faith in his excellent Word!
> What more can he say than to you he has said,
> To you who for refuge to Jesus have fled?
>
> "Fear not, I am with you, O be not dismayed;
> For I am your God, and will still give you aid;
> I'll strengthen you, help you, and cause you to stand,
> Upheld by my righteous, omnipotent hand.
>
> "The soul that on Jesus has leaned for repose,
> I will not, I will not desert to his foes;
> That soul, though all hell should endeavor to shake,
> I'll never, no never, no never forsake."

Nothing is more certain than our security in Jesus Christ. Jesus was ordained to be our Savior from sin before the foundation of the world. He achieved that salvation by his perfect atonement for us in time. God has promised that nothing will ever separate us from him. We need to have this fact firmly fixed in our minds and live it with confidence. The only way we can do so is by prayerful Bible study. The only way God's people will ever be strong and be unshaken by enemies and life's many trials is by being people of the Book.

Do we value God's Book? Spurgeon wrote, "Bubbles please boys, but men prize those things which are solid and substantial, with a foundation and a bottom to them which will bear the test of ages."[7]

Psalm 119

Delight in God's Decrees: Part 13

Obedience while Waiting

Look upon my suffering and deliver me,
    for I have not forgotten your law.
Defend my cause and redeem me;
    renew my life according to your promise.
Salvation is far from the wicked,
    for they do not seek out your decrees.
Your compassion is great, O LORD;
    renew my life according to your laws.
Many are the foes who persecute me,
    but I have not turned from your statutes.
I look on the faithless with loathing,
    for they do not obey your word.
See how I love your precepts;
    preserve my life, O LORD, according to your love.
All your words are true;
    all your righteous laws are eternal. . . .

I wait for your salvation, O LORD,
    and I follow your commands.
I obey your statutes,
    for I love them greatly.
I obey your precepts and your statutes,
    for all my ways are known to you.

verses 153–68

There is a link between the previous stanza (*qoph*, vv. 145–52) and these two stanzas (*resh* and *sin/shin*, vv. 153–68). The enemies of the psalmist are still present, and he is still praying for deliverance. Derek Kidner says there even seems to be "a mounting urgency" in the psalmist's repeated pleas for salvation.[1] At the same time there is also a significant change. The *qoph* stanza was almost entirely a prayer. In these stanzas the petitions tend to drop away—stanza twenty-one (the *sin/shin* stanza) has no explicit prayers at all—and in their place comes a quiet, obedient waiting for God.

Obedience is the new element. It is introduced in a negative way in verse 158, "The faithless . . . do *not obey* your word" (italics added), and it reappears twice positively at the end:

> I *obey* your statutes,
>   for I love them greatly.
> I *obey* your precepts and your statutes,
>   for all my ways are known to you (vv. 167–68, italics added).

This writer knows that obedience is not optional. He knows that it is essential to genuine discipleship and is the only basis on which he can have any claim on God for God's swift intervention and deliverance.

Profession without Practice

How little obedience there is, even in strong Christian circles! I suppose that is why Jesus spoke about obedience so directly toward the end of the Sermon on the Mount (Luke's version). Jesus had been followed by many people who made a verbal profession of discipleship. They called him "Lord," which meant that they were calling him their master and themselves his servants. But they were also disregarding his teaching. Jesus showed the contradiction by asking pointedly, "Why do you call me, 'Lord, Lord,' and do not do what I say?" (Luke 6:46). He was teaching that he is not our Lord if we do not obey him; and if he is not our Lord, then we do not even belong to him.

Disobedience—profession without practice—has been a problem throughout history. It was true of Israel. On the day before Ezekiel learned of the fall of the city of Jerusalem to the Babylonians the Lord appeared to him to explain why this was happening:

> Your countrymen are talking together about you by the walls and at the doors of the houses, saying to each other, "Come and hear the message that has come from the LORD." My people come to you, as they usually do, and sit before you to listen to your words, but they do not put them into practice. With their mouths they express devotion, but their hearts are greedy for

unjust gain. Indeed, to them you are nothing more than one who sings love songs with a beautiful voice and plays an instrument as well, for they hear your words but do not put them into practice (Ezek. 33:30–32).

Jerusalem was destroyed because the people were wanting only to be entertained by God's words and not obey the instructions.

Isaiah said the same thing in words Jesus later referred to when he was teaching his disciples: "The Lord says: 'These people come near to me with their mouth and honor me with their lips, but their hearts are far from me'" (Isa. 29:13). Jesus also used this text to reprove teachers of the law who made a profession of adhering to God's words when actually they were obeying only man-made regulations. He called them "hypocrites" and "blind guides" (see Matt. 15:1–14; cf. Mark 7:1–16).

Apparently, the problem of profession without practice was also present in the early Christian community, as indicated in the Epistle of James:

> Do not merely listen to the word, and so deceive yourselves. Do what it says. Anyone who listens to the word but does not do what it says is like a man who looks at his face in a mirror and, after looking at himself, goes away and imme-diately forgets what he looks like. But the man who looks intently into the per-fect law that gives freedom, and continues to do this, not forgetting what he has heard, but doing it—he will be blessed in what he does (James 1:22–25).

"Faith" without obedience is worthless, even contemptible, yet it is com-mon. One writer says, "Open sin, and avowed unbelief, no doubt slay their thousands. But profession without practice slays its tens of thousands."[2]

What the Psalmist Knew

The psalmist knew that if he was serious about his discipleship, he would have to immerse himself in the Bible; and he knew that if he did immerse himself in the Bible, he would have to obey it. We sometimes think of obedi-ence as something we just have to grit our teeth and do, but the psalmist thought of it as a joyous, natural response to what he learned about God when he studied his Word. These stanzas show four things he had learned.

1. *God is merciful* (v. 156). Our translation of this verse says, "Your com-passion is great," but the same Hebrew words might equally well be ren-dered, "Many are your mercies." Whatever the translation, the fact that God is rich in mercy is the most wonderful thing we can know about him. We have already seen that this is what God revealed to Moses when he placed him in a cleft of mountain rock, covered him with his hand, and passed by, saying, "The LORD, the LORD, the compassionate and gracious God, slow to anger, abounding in love and faithfulness, maintaining love to thousands, and forgiving wickedness, rebellion and sin" (Exod. 34:6–7). In the Old Testament these are the most frequently cited of all verses (cf.

Num. 14:18; Deut. 5:9–10; Ps. 86:15; Joel 2:13; Jonah 4:1; Jer. 34:18; and Neh. 9:17), and with good reason since mercy is what we all desperately need. As New Testament believers, we know that we have this mercy through the Lord Jesus Christ.

2. *God's Word is true* (v. 160). The truth of God's Word is a vital lesson for the psalmist to have learned, or for anyone to learn, so it is not surprising that it figures strongly in these last stanzas. We find it in verse 142 ("your law is true"), verse 151 ("all your commands are true"), and verse 160 ("all your words are true").

Have you learned how true, how utterly trustworthy God's Word is, even when everything and everyone around you proves false and untrustworthy? Spurgeon wrote,

> The ungodly are false, but God's word is true. . . . God's word has been true from the first moment in which it was spoken, true throughout the whole of history, true to us from the instant in which we believed it, true to us before we were true to it. . . . The Scriptures are as true in Genesis as in Revelation, and the five books of Moses are as inspired as the four Gospels. Neither in the book of revelation nor of providence will there be any need to put a single note of *errata*. The Lord has nothing to regret or to retract, nothing to amend or to reverse."[3]

The Bible was as true for your grandmother and grandfather as it is for you. The same Word that speaks truthfully to you spoke truthfully to poor tillers of the soil in England two hundred years ago and to martyrs standing against the cruel persecutions of imperial Rome or the church's own terrible Inquisition in the Middle Ages.

3. *Personal peace comes from personal obedience* (v. 165). In the Hebrew "peace" is the word *shalom*. Like "salvation" to which it is closely linked,[4] *shalom* is a large, embracing word for the good that comes to one God favors. It has to do with personal well-being in all respects. On the spiritual level it embraces "peace with God" through the work of Jesus Christ. On the material level it can mean prosperity. On the personal level it has to do with a tranquil state of mind that comes from placing one's entire hope in God's Word. Alexander Maclaren speaks of it as encompassing "a restful heart, . . . a submitted will, . . . an obedient life . . . [and] freedom from temptations."[5]

The verse does not promise peace to those who perfectly keep God's Law, for who can keep it? It promises peace to those who "love" God's Law, which means, I suppose, those who love it because they have found God to be merciful by reading it.

4. *The obedient are secure* (v. 165). Where else can we find security in this life? Our only true security is in God. I think here of a wonderful section of Saint Augustine's *City of God* in which that father of the church reflects on the uncertainties of this life.

What numberless casualties threaten our bodies . . . extremes of heat and cold, storms, floods, inundations, lightning, thunder, hail, earthquakes, houses falling; or from the stumbling, or shying, or vice of horses; from countless poisons in fruits, water, air, animals; from the painful or even deadly bites of wild animals; from the madness which a mad dog communicates, so that even the animal which of all others is most gentle and friendly to its own master, becomes an object of intenser fear than a lion or dragon, and the man whom it has by chance infected with this pestilential contagion becomes so rabid, that his parents, wife, children, dread him more than any wild beast!

What disasters are suffered by those who travel by land or sea! What man can go out of his own house without being exposed on all hands to unforeseen accidents? Returning home sound in limb, he slips on his own doorstep, breaks his leg, and never recovers. What can seem safer than a man sitting in his chair? Eli the priest fell from his, and broke his neck.[6]

Surely there is no security for any of us in this life except in loving and living by the unshakable and eternal Word of God.

Obedience and the Word of God

If trusting God involves obeying God's Word, as it certainly does, then there can be no real discipleship apart from Bible study. Indeed, study of the Bible cannot even be an occasional, minor, or "vacation time" pursuit. It must be the consuming passion of a believer's life. This is because it is only by the study of the Word of God that we learn what it is to obey God and follow Jesus. If you want to know God as he speaks to you through the Bible, you should do the following:

1. *Study the Bible daily.* We can study the Bible more than once each day, of course. The psalmist has already spoken of rising early for his devotional time and of meditating on God's Word through the watches of the night. In the *shin* stanza he speaks of praising God "seven times a day," presumably in the context of serious Bible study.[7] The psalmist probably means only that he worshiped God continuously. What is important is that we discipline our lives to include regular periods of Bible study, just as we discipline ourselves to have regular periods for sleep, eating our meals, and so on. These things are necessary if the body is to be healthy and if good work is to be done. On occasion we may miss a meal, but normally we should not. In the same way, we must feed regularly on God's Word if we are to become and remain spiritually strong.

What happens if we neglect regular Bible reading? We grow indifferent to God and lax in spiritual things. We throw ourselves open to temptation and the sin that easily follows.

2. *Study the Bible systematically.* Some people read the Bible at random, dipping here or there. This may be characteristic of the way they do most things in life, but it is a mistake in Bible study. It leads to a lack of proportion and depth that is often characteristic of American Christians. A far bet-

ter system is a regular, disciplined study of certain books of the Bible as a whole. The psalmist did this. The proof is the great variety of terms he uses for the Scriptures. As he saw it, the Bible embraces the law, statutes, ways, precepts, decrees, commands, words, and promises of God. He did not want to neglect even one of them.

3. *Study the Bible comprehensively.* Alongside study of one book or section of the Bible, there should be an attempt to become acquainted with the Bible as a whole. This means reading it comprehensively. True, many parts of the Bible will not appeal to us at first, but if we never make an attempt to become acquainted with them, we limit our growth and may even warp our understanding. Paul told Timothy, "*All* Scripture is God-breathed and is useful for teaching, rebuking, correcting and training in righteousness" (2 Tim. 3:16, italics added). Jesus will speak to you and tell you what to do, not only in the red-ink portions of those Bibles that indicate Jesus' own words in that fashion but in many portions of Scripture.

4. *Study the Bible devotionally.* Nothing is clearer in this psalm than the close, indissoluble link between knowledge of God and study of the Word of God, between loving God and loving the Bible. There is a danger when we speak of daily, systematic, and comprehensive Bible study of implying that such study is mechanical and can be pursued in much the same manner as one would study a secular text in a university. That is not the case. In other books, we study to become informed. In reading the Bible, we study to know God, hear his voice, and be changed by him as we grow in holiness.

Furthermore, if we really want the Bible to become a part of us so that by this means the mind of Christ, which is expressed in the Bible, becomes our mind at least in part, then we must memorize important sections of Scripture. Our educational system does little to stress memorization today, but those who were educated a generation ago will testify that what they memorized then, whether simple verses or more complex passages from Shakespeare or other distinguished writers, have remained with them and have thereby become a part of who they are. As Christians we need to allow the Word of God to become a part of us. To have that happen we must memorize it.

Pat Williams, the general manager of the Orlando Magic, is a very busy man. He is always under pressure. Nevertheless, he spends twenty minutes a day in uninterrupted Bible study and in addition to that spends whatever time is necessary to memorize one verse of the Bible every day. He has memorized a verse a day for years, and he testifies that this is the single most important factor in his spiritual growth.

5. *Study the Bible prayerfully.* It is impossible to study the Bible devotionally without praying, since we are coming to God in Scripture and must communicate with him verbally if we do. But although prayer is part of a devotional study of Scripture, prayer is worth stressing for its own sake, if only because we so often neglect it. The best way to study the Bible is to encompass the

study in prayer. (The previous chapter discusses prayer in the section "Using God's Word in Prayer.")

Before we begin to read we should say, "Lord God, I am turning to your Word. I cannot understand it as I should. I need your Holy Spirit to instruct me and draw a proper response from me. What I understand I want to obey. Help me to do that for Jesus' sake." Then we must study the passage, and when we find something that pertains to our lives, we must stop and acknowledge it prayerfully. Without regular, personal Bible study and prayer, we are not really walking with Christ as his followers, and we are certainly not obeying him in specific areas.

Deliverance from Sin and Self

Suppose we do pursue regular, personal Bible study? Suppose we do earnestly seek to know the mind of our Savior and obediently follow where he leads? What do we find then? Some would say that we plunge into a dull monotony of life or at best have a list of dull rules to follow, but those who actually follow Christ find something different. They find adventure with God and a deliverance from self that is an amazing form of liberty.

Once when Jesus had been expounding on the source of his teachings and many who listened had believed on him, he told them, "If you hold to my teaching, you are really my disciples. Then you will know the truth, and the truth will set you free" (John 8:31–32). This angered some of his listeners. They replied, "We are Abraham's descendants and have never been slaves of anyone. How can you say that we shall be set free?" (John 8:33). Jesus did not reply that they had actually been slaves to many foreign governments, though he could have. Instead, he spoke of bondage to sin and showed that true freedom consists of deliverance from sin through obedience. "I tell you the truth, everyone who sins is a slave to sin. . . . If the Son sets you free, you will be free indeed" (vv. 34, 36). Freedom comes as we determine to obey Jesus.

Psalm 119

Delight in God's Decrees: Part 14

This Poor Sheep

May my cry come before you, O LORD;
    give me understanding according to your word.
May my supplication come before you;
    deliver me according to your promise.
May my lips overflow with praise,
    for you teach me your decrees.
May my tongue sing of your word,
    for all your commands are righteous.
May your hand be ready to help me,
    for I have chosen your precepts.
I long for your salvation, O LORD,
    and your law is my delight.
Let me live that I may praise you,
    and may your laws sustain me.
I have strayed like a lost sheep.
    Seek your servant,
    for I have not forgotten your commandments.
                     verses 169–76

There is a tremendous difference between this stanza (*taw*, vv. 169–76) and the previous—in fact, between this stanza and the entire preceding psalm. The previous stanza was all assertion, chiefly about the poet's obedience to God's Word and his rejoicing in it. This stanza is all petition, and there is little confidence. Instead, there is humble recognition of the writer's lost condition and his constant need of God's grace.

The author had not become self-righteous by his devotions, despite his reiterated claims to have obeyed the Bible's teachings. Derek Kidner writes, "The note of urgent need on which the psalm ends . . . is proof enough that the love of Scripture . . . need not harden into academic pride. This man would have taken his stance not with the self-congratulating Pharisee of the parable, but with the publican who stood afar off, but went home justified."[1]

Verse 175, the next to the last verse, is a good biblical statement of what the Westminster Shorter Catechism calls "the chief end of man," namely, to glorify God and enjoy him forever: "Let me live that I may praise you." But verse 176, the last verse, reminds us that this praise comes from poor, weak, lost, and straying sinners like ourselves.

Simul Justus et Peccator

I have to take issue with some of the writers on this psalm who argue that the psalmist cannot be thinking of himself as a lost sheep in the same sense as the sheep in Jesus' parable, since he is "one who does not forget God's commandments."[2] They think that the issues here are not spiritual, that the psalmist is not writing about sin and salvation. They argue that he is thinking of himself as a lost sheep only in the sense of being exposed to enemies and thus being always in need of God's care.

If that is the case, why does he speak of himself as having "strayed," rather than as merely being weak? Or ask God to "seek" him, rather than to strengthen or protect him? This is not the language of mere temporal distress; it is spiritual language, the language of Isaiah, who wrote,

> We all, like sheep, have gone astray,
> each of us has turned to his own way (Isa. 53:6).

What the writer of Psalm 119 is saying is that this is the only right description of himself as he is apart from the grace of God. He is a poor, lost sheep. So what is needed—what he needed and what we need too—is what Isaiah wrote about in the second half of the above verse. He needed that One upon whom "the Lord has laid . . . the iniquity of us all."

Martin Luther spoke of believers in Christ being *simul justus et peccator,* that is, at once "both justified and a sinner." Luther wrote of verse 176, "This verse is extremely emotional and full of tears, for truly we are all thus going astray, so that we must pray to be visited, sought, and carried over by the most godly Shepherd, the Lord Jesus Christ, who is God blessed forever. Amen."[3]

Luther began the Ninety-five Theses that he posted on the door of the Castle church in Wittenberg at the commencement of the Protestant

Reformation by writing, "When our Lord and Master, Jesus Christ, said 'repent,' he meant that the entire life of believers should be one of repentance." In other words, there is never a moment, even after we are saved, when we can stop thinking of ourselves as lost sheep. Therefore, as another writer says, "The highest flights of human devotion must end in confession of sin. . . . The sincerest professions of human fidelity must give place to the acknowledgment of helplessness. . . . The loftiest human declarations of love to God's law must come down to the mournful acknowledgment that we have only not forgotten it."[4]

In this last verse the psalmist is speaking of himself as he really is. It might be useful to go back and study Psalm 119 all over again with these last prayers and this most humble self-description in mind.

The Psalmist's Sad Condition

In Psalm 23, the Shepherd's Psalm, David wrote of the many things he did not lack with God as his good shepherd. "I shall lack nothing," he says at the beginning (Ps. 23:1). Then he spells it out, saying, as it were, "I shall not lack rest; I shall not lack life; I shall not lack guidance; I shall not lack safety; I shall not lack comfort; I shall not lack provision; I shall not lack heaven."[5] In these last verses of this psalm, in helpful contrast, the writer lists what he *does* lack, unless God is his shepherd. He is lacking in five areas.

1. *Understanding* (v. 169). We might think that the person who wrote this psalm, or any psalm, a man obviously blessed and inspired by the Holy Spirit, would be conscious of how much he knew of God and God's ways, or at least of how much he was learning. Instead, he is conscious of how little he knows and that if he is to understand anything at all about God and God's ways, God must open his eyes and give him understanding as he studies the Bible. So understanding is what he asks of God as he begins this final stanza:

> May my cry come before you, O LORD;
>   give me understanding according to your word.

Do we think we are wise? If we do, we are the most foolish of all people. On the other hand, if we recognize our foolishness and come to God for his instruction, we can begin to gain wisdom.

The Christians at Corinth thought they were wise but were allowing their pseudo-wisdom and prejudices to divide the church. Paul wrote them,

> Where is the wise man? Where is the scholar? Where is the philosopher of this age? Has not God made foolish the wisdom of the world? For since in the wisdom of God the world through its wisdom did not know him, God was pleased through the foolishness of what was preached to save those who believe. Jews demand miraculous signs and Greeks look for wisdom, but we

preach Christ crucified: a stumbling block to Jews and foolishness to Gentiles, but to those whom God has called both Jews and Greeks, Christ the power of God and the wisdom of God. For the foolishness of God is wiser than man's wisdom, and the weakness of God is stronger than man's strength (1 Cor. 1:20–25).

The psalmist was writing before the birth of Jesus, of course. He did not know what we know about the life, death, and resurrection of Jesus, or even a whole lot about the gospel, though he probably looked for a Redeemer, the Messiah, to come. Nevertheless, he knew that all genuine understanding comes from God and that he needed to ask God for it. So he does.

2. *Salvation, or deliverance* (v. 170). "Deliver me according to your promise," says the psalmist. "Deliver" is a rich word, with many meanings, just like "save," which is a close equivalent and even a possible translation of the Hebrew word in this sentence. Deliverance could mean deliverance from the power of death or enemies, which is how it has frequently been used in this psalm. Commentators who think that the poet is referring to himself as a lost sheep only in the sense of being weak and in danger from those who hate him take it this way. They think that when he says "deliver me," he must mean "deliver me from my enemies."

Perhaps. But if he is thinking of spiritual things, as I believe he is, then "deliver" really does mean "salvation." It means deliverance from sin—from its penalty, power, and presence—from the evil influences and outlook of the world, and perhaps even from the power of the devil. Whatever the case, it is clear that we are lacking salvation in that sense. We can do nothing to deliver ourselves. We need to ask God for salvation, which is what the psalmist does.

Charles Bridges believed the psalmist was thinking of deliverance spiritually, particularly because of verse 174: "I long for your salvation." Toward the end of his five-hundred-page commentary on Psalm 119 Bridges considered four things about our salvation: its "fullness," which includes all the mercy of God's covenant of grace; its "ground," the work of Christ on the cross; its "simplicity," not keeping the sinner away from God in useless moral striving or bewilderment, but opening the way through faith in Christ's atonement; and its "unchangeableness," which is above and beyond and superior to all our weak feelings and failures. He concluded, "Is not this an object for the longing of the soul, that feels its own pressing wants and sees in this salvation an instant and full supply?"[6]

Are you longing for the salvation that only God can supply? If you are not, it can only be because you do not have a true sense of need. You think you can handle things yourself. Learn from this psalm. These first petitions reflect the two great needs of fallen men and women, namely, to know God and to be saved from sin.

3. *The ability to worship God rightly* (vv. 171–72). If God is his Savior, the psalmist ought also to praise God for his salvation. How is he to do that? If

he is to worship God rightly, he needs two things: He needs to know what pleases God in worship, that is, the elements of worship that God has himself determined; and he needs to have a heart so filled with love for God that his worship is genuine and not merely the repetition of empty words or the practice of vain exercises. He prays,

> May my lips overflow with praise,
> > for you teach me your decrees.
> May my tongue sing of your word,
> > for all your commands are righteous.

It comes as a surprise to many people to learn that God has fixed the ways we should worship him and that not all currently passing for worship is acceptable. In the Old Testament period God was to be worshiped at the tabernacle (later the temple), and he was to be worshiped according to the Levitical priestly system. In fact, if people tried to approach him in any way other than by what he had determined, God's judgment was swift and terrible. We have examples in Nadab and Abihu, who offered unauthorized fire and were consumed (see Lev. 10:1–2); Korah, who abrogated priestly functions to himself and was swallowed by the earth (see Num. 16:1–35); or Uzziah, who offered incense that only the priests could offer and was judged by leprosy (see 2 Chron. 26:16–21).

God has prescribed acceptable forms of worship for people in the New Testament age too. We no longer worship in Jerusalem at the temple. It has been destroyed, and Jesus has said, "God is a spirit, and his worshipers must worship in spirit and in truth" (John 4:24). This verse does not mean that just anything goes. "In truth" must mean according to the revelation of God in the Bible.

What does the Bible teach about how we should worship God today? Bible students differ about some elements: for example, whether it is right for ministers to wear clerical vestments, whether drama or liturgical dance are permitted; whether organs or other musical instruments can be used. There are churches, like Spurgeon's church in London, that only permit *a capella* singing. Other things are quite clear. We are not to offer animal sacrifices, since Jesus' sacrifice of himself fulfilled the Old Testament system and abolished it forever. We are not to be raucous or immoral, as some had been in Corinth (see 1 Corinthians 11, 14). Paul told the Corinthians, "Everything should be done in a fitting and orderly way" (1 Cor. 14:40). On the positive side, we are instructed to pray, sing hymns, and listen to the teaching of the Bible—especially to listen to the Bible.

When the Protestant Reformation took place in the sixteenth century and the principles of the Word of God, which had long been covered over by the ceremonies of the medieval church, again became prominent, there was an immediate elevation of the Word of God in Protestant services. John Calvin particularly carried this out with thoroughness, ordering that the altars (long the center of the Latin mass) be removed from the churches and that a pulpit with a Bible on it be placed in the center of the building. The pulpit was not to be on one side of the room, but at the center, where every line of the architecture would carry the gaze of the worshiper to that Book. This was a good thing, something we do not want to lose today, though it is being lost in many churches.

How do we know how to worship? How do we develop a sincere, devout, and worshipful heart in ourselves? The psalmist realizes we cannot do either by ourselves. We lack what we need to worship God. Therefore, we need to ask God how to worship him and for the ability to worship him, which is what the psalmist does.

4. *Power to live an upright life* (vv. 173–74). The next two verses might be seen as asking God's help in dealing with enemies, but if the writer is thinking along spiritual lines, as I have been suggesting, then when he prays, "May your hand be ready to help me" (v. 173), what he is probably thinking of is power to obey the "precepts" and "law" of God that he mentions next (vv. 173–74).

We cannot live an upright life by our own power or determination. The apostle Paul knew the futility of such an attempt, which is why he wrote, "I am unspiritual, sold as a slave to sin. . . . For what I want to do I do not do, but what I hate to do. . . . I know that nothing good lives in me, that is, in my sinful nature. . . . What a wretched man I am! Who will rescue me from this body of death?" (Rom. 7:14–15, 18, 24). Thankfully, Paul knew the answer to his own question: "Thanks be to God—through Jesus Christ our Lord!" (v. 25). Clearly, if we really believe we are unable to live for God by ourselves and yet really want to, we will come to God for help, as Paul does. We will pray, "Lord, help me to live an upright life."

5. *Strength to persevere* (v. 175). If we want to live an upright life not just for the present moment but to our life's end, we will keep on praying. We will pray as the psalmist, "Let me live that I may praise you, and may your laws sustain me" (v. 175).

Salvation Is of the Lord

We have been looking at what the psalmist means when he ends this extraordinary psalm by calling himself a lost sheep. In a sense, he has been anticipating the teaching of Jesus, who said, "Apart from me you can do nothing" (John 15:5). Nothing does not mean a little something. It means nothing, nothing at all. Yet all is not hopeless, since although in ourselves we can do nothing it is also true, as Paul said, that "[We] can do everything through Christ who gives [us] strength" (Phil. 4:13).

Although the psalmist has described himself as lost, a lost sheep; and although he has confessed his need for understanding, deliverance, right worship, an upright way of life, and perseverance; and although he even needs God to seek him since he will never find the way to God himself; nevertheless, he remains God's "servant" (v. 176). A poor, lost, weak, sinful—yes, even an unprofitable—servant (see Luke 17:10), but still a servant of God. Even though he has not been able to keep God's commandments well, he has not forgotten them and knows that he will yet keep them—by the grace and power of his Master.

What a blessing for us if we, like the psalmist, are also God's servants! Charles Bridges wrote, "I cannot forbear to plead, that although a rebellious prodigal, I am still thy servant, thy child. I still bear the child's mark of an interest in thy covenant. . . . Let me then lie humbled and self-abased. But let me not forget my claim—what he has done for me."[7]

The meaning of these last two verses has been captured in a stanza by Richard Mant.

> Though like a sheep estranged I stray,
> Yet have I not renounced thy way.
> Thine hand extend; thine own reclaim;
> Grant me to live, and praise thy name.[8]

When Jonah was praying from inside the great fish he summarized what he had learned of God by saying, "Salvation comes from the LORD" (Jonah 2:9). This is the last important teaching of this psalm. What does the shepherd do with such weak, sinful, and helpless people as ourselves? Jesus said that when the sheep are lost the shepherd hunts until he finds them (see Luke 15:3–7). He said of his own mission, "The Son of Man came to seek and to save what was lost" (Luke 19:10).

Psalm 120

Marching to Zion

I call on the Lord in my distress,
  and he answers me.
Save me, O Lord, from lying lips
  and from deceitful tongues.

What will he do to you,
  and what more besides, O deceitful tongue?
He will punish you with a warrior's sharp arrows,
  with burning coals of the broom tree.

Woe to me that I dwell in Meshech,
  that I live among the tents of Kedar!
Too long have I lived
  among those who hate peace.
I am a man of peace;
  but when I speak, they are for war.

verses 1–7

A number of years ago when I was in a Christian bookstore I saw a book I knew absolutely nothing about but purchased anyway. I do not normally do that. Books cost too much money to buy without knowing something about them, but I bought this book because of its title. It was called *A Long Obedience in the Same Direction.* That sounded like an apt description of the Christian life to me, and I thought there must be something good in it.

The title came from the atheistic German philosopher Friedrich Nietzsche, who once wrote, "The essential thing 'in heaven and earth' is . . . that there should be long obedience in the same direction; there thereby results, and has always resulted in the long run, something which has made life worth living."[1] I never thought I would be attracted by the words of a pagan philosopher, but I had been. I had been snared by them.

The book was about the Songs of Ascents, a fifteen-psalm "Psalter within the Psalter"[2] to which we have now come in our study of these ancient Hebrew poems. The author is Eugene H. Peterson, currently a professor of spiritual theology at Regent College, Vancouver, B.C.

Discipleship in an Instant Society

The subtitle of Peterson's book is "Discipleship in an Instant Society," and it is a clue to what he sees as the importance of these songs for today. They are discipleship songs—I will explain more about that in a minute—and the reason they are important today is that Christians in our time know very little about discipleship.

We live in an "instant society," and one way that has impacted the way we think is the nearly universal assumption that anything worthwhile can be acquired quickly. Peterson wrote,

> It is not difficult in such a world to get a person interested in the message of the gospel; it is terrifically difficult to sustain the interest. Millions of people in our culture make decisions for Christ, but there is a dreadful attrition rate. Many claim to have been born again, but the evidence for mature Christian discipleship is slim. In our kind of culture anything, even news about God, can be sold if it is packaged freshly; but when it loses its novelty, it goes on the garbage heap. There is a great market for religious experience in our world; there is little enthusiasm for the patient acquisition of virtue, little inclination to sign up for a long apprenticeship in what earlier generations of Christians called holiness.[3]

I do not think Peterson is exaggerating this judgment in the slightest. And I also think he is right when he challenges us to look at these psalms for their teaching about discipleship or a pilgrim mentality. Christianity is a long-obedience religion, and if we do not know that about it, we know very little about Christianity. In fact, if we are not in it for the long haul, we are not even Christians.

Songs of Ascents

There has been a great deal of debate about what the title Song of Ascents means. The Hebrew phrase, *shir hama'aloth*, allows for several interpretations. The first word, *shir*, means a hymn or song, but the second word, *ma'alah* (the singular of *ma'aloth*) means both a step or stair and a "going up." "Going up" where? Or how? Or when? To complicate matters, the Latin (Vulgate) translation is *canticum graduum,* that is, "the gradual (or graded) songs." What does that mean? Scholars have come up with four explanations.

1. *Ascents are steps (or gradations) within the psalms.* This view was advanced nearly two hundred years ago (in 1812) by Gesenius, the author of the Hebrew dictionary and grammar (with Kautsch and Cowley), and it has been argued since by Franz Delitzsch.[4] Gesenius said that *ma'aloth* comes from a pattern within the psalms in which an idea introduced in one verse is picked up and developed in the next verse, and so on, so that there is a steplike, constantly upward moving progression of ideas. A good example is Psalm 121. In that psalm "help" in verse 1 is picked up and developed in verse 2; "watches over" in verse 3 is picked up in verses 4–5; and "harm" in verse 5 recurs in verse 7.

There are two problems with this interpretation. First, although this feature is noticeable in some of the psalms, like Psalm 121, it is absent in others. Second, this steplike feature is also found in psalms not in the collection. Thus, as H. C. Leupold writes, "What is regarded as the chief requirement of this interpretation is a bit more conspicuous by its absence than by its presence."[5]

2. *Ascents are steps leading up to the sanctuary.* This explanation is based on the same interpretation of the Hebrew word but regards it as referring to the fifteen steps leading from the courtyard of the women to the courtyard of the men outside the Jerusalem temple. The Talmud says that the fifteen songs correspond to the fifteen steps between these courtyards (*Middoth* ii. 5; *Succa* 51b). Some have even supposed that the songs were sung by the Levites from these steps, though this is pure speculation. There is no evidence that this was ever done, and even the Talmud does not say it was. The Talmud only notes a correspondence in the number fifteen—fifteen songs and fifteen steps—which is a typical way of thinking among the rabbis.

3. *Ascents are the "going up" from Babylon to Israel at the end of the exile.* The strength of this position is that the singular form of *ma'aloth* was used of the return of the people from Babylon to Israel at the restoration in the days of Ezra and Nehemiah. This meaning appears in Ezra 7:9 (translated "journey," NIV). It is a reasonable way to describe a trip from the lowlands of Babylon to the highlands of Israel, and the Songs of Ascents could well have been sung on such a journey. Psalm 126 even refers to the return. The problem with this view is that the word is plural in these titles, "goings up" not "going up," which seems to mean that it is referring to repeated trips to Jerusalem and not just to the return from exile.

4. *Ascents are the "goings up" of pilgrims at the annual feasts.* These various considerations have led most writers today to think of these psalms as songs sung by Jewish pilgrims as they made their way to Jerusalem for the three annual festivals—Passover, Pentecost, and the Day of Atonement—and to

think of the Songs of Ascents as pilgrim songs. Support for this view comes from the fact that "going up" is often used for going up to Jerusalem (see 1 Sam. 1:3) and that a number of these psalms reflect the experiences of such pilgrims, for example: "I rejoiced with those who said to me, 'Let us go to the house of the LORD'" (Ps. 122:1); "Our feet are standing in your gates, O Jerusalem" (Ps. 122:2); and "Let us go to his dwelling place; let us worship at his footstool" (Ps. 132:7).[6]

These fifteen psalms (Psalms 120–34) seem to have been used by pilgrims who were making their way to Jerusalem for the three major annual feasts. Joseph and Mary would have sung these psalms as they made their way to the city with the young Jesus (see Luke 2:41), and Jesus would have sung them himself when he went up to Jerusalem with his disciples.

It has been said that these psalms do not reflect the high level of faith and spirituality found in other psalms. "They are marked by a kind of plaintive note, by a mild sadness."[7] If so, it is appropriate for those who were on their way to God's city but had not reached it yet. It is this note of sadness that makes these songs so descriptive of the Christian's similarly hard and upward pilgrimage through this dark world toward heaven.

Strangers in This World

At first glance, Psalm 120 seems a strange psalm with which to begin this series, or even have in it, since it does not mention Jerusalem or even contain the thought of going there. Still, it is appropriate in this context, for it begins with the feelings of homesick people settled in a strange land and thus sets the tone for the joyful upward journey reflected in the psalms that follow. Derek Kidner says, "It appropriately begins the series in a distant land, so that we join the pilgrims as they set out on a journey which, in broad outline, will bring us to Jerusalem in Psalm 122, and, in the last psalms of the group, to the ark, the priests and the Temple servants who minister, by turns, day and night at the house of the Lord."[8] There are two things that seem to have bothered the author of this psalm and those who would have sung it on their travels.

1. *Lying neighbors* (vv. 1–4). In verse 3 the singers of this psalm seem to be speaking of a single individual, since they use the singular terms "you" and "O deceitful tongue," but the circumstances have to be understood more broadly since the prayer of verse 2 is for God to save the singers from "lying lips" and "deceitful tongues" (plural). The prayer reminds us what the world we live in is like. It is a world filled with lies. Thus, the starting place for our spiritual pilgrimage is seeing the world for what it is in order to turn from it.

A pilgrim is a person who has grown dissatisfied with where he or she has been and is on the way to something better. Peterson says that a Christian pilgrim is one who repented of the lies that surround him (and are in him) and who is now going to God, and whose path for getting there is Jesus Christ.

Peterson writes at some length about the lies the world tells us. The world says that human beings are basically nice and good, that everyone is born equal and innocent and self-sufficient, that we are born free, and that if we are in chains now, it is someone's fault, and we can correct it with just a little more intelligence or effort or time.[9] When people discover the real world, most get angry and fret like spoiled children, rather than recognizing the lie and turning from the lie to God's truth.

If we want to be Christians, we need to ask God to deliver us from these lies, as the psalmist does in verse 2.

> Save me, O LORD, from lying lips
> and from deceitful tongues.

Peterson elaborates on what this verse should mean in our culture:

> Rescue me from the lies of advertisers who claim to know what I need and what I desire, from the lies of entertainers who promise a cheap way to joy, from the lies of politicians who pretend to instruct me in power and morality, from the lies of psychologists who offer to shape my behavior and my morals so that I will live long, happily and successfully, from the lies of religionists who "heal the wounds of this people lightly," from the lips of moralists who pretend to promote me to the office of captain of my fate, from the lies of pastors who "leave the commandment of God, and hold fast the tradition of men" (Mark. 7:8). Rescue me from the person who tells me of life and omits Christ, who is wise in the ways of the world and ignores the movement of the Spirit.[10]

Peterson admits that many of these lies are factual. They contain right data, but they are lies all the same because they leave out God. They do not tell us that we come from God and have our destiny in God and that we are here to know and serve God. "They tell us about the world without telling us that God made it. They tell us about our bodies without telling us that they are temples of the Holy Spirit. They instruct us in love without telling us about the God who loves us and gave himself for us."[11]

2. *Hostile neighbors* (vv. 5–7). Most people today want to think of themselves as peaceful and peace loving, but they are not. None of us are. On the contrary, we are warlike people, and the proof of it is in our fierce competition and fights with other people, and in our anger and grief when others are more successful than we are or are preferred over us.

Nothing has more characterized the human race in history than war. One scholar observed that war is "man's chief legacy," meaning that it is the chief thing one generation passes to the next. Each of the treaties of history has been hailed by someone at some time as the road to a just and lasting disarmament—politicians are doing it today—but the ink had scarcely dried on most of these treaties when the guns began to sound for the next encounter.

Gunpowder, tanks, airplanes, missiles, and nuclear weapons have been said to make war far too horrible to contemplate, but there is never a horror so great that someone will not use it to try to impose his will on other people.

One of the earliest of all historical records, a Sumerian bas-relief sculpture from Babylon (c. 3000 B.C.), shows soldiers fighting in close order, wearing helmets and carrying shields. Wars fill the history of every ancient culture—Babylon, Syria, Assyria, Egypt, Phoenicia. The twenty-seven-year-long Peloponesian War destroyed Greece even at the height of the great civilization she had created as the fruit of Athens's Golden Age. Rome made war a way of life, but even she was eventually defeated and overrun by the barbarians.

In the Middle Ages war ravaged Europe, culminating in the horrors of the Thirty Years War, which ended in 1648. The *Encyclopedia Britannica* lists 278 wars in the centuries between 1480 and the end of World War II. One hundred and thirty-five of these were international. Speaking of World War II, the *Britannica* says,

> Wars showed a slight tendency to decrease in length during the modern period, but in all other aspects they tended to increase in magnitude. There were more battles, more participants, larger forces, larger numbers of casualties, more extensive areas of occupation and mechanization resulting in much heavier economic costs. The costs of the Thirty Years War of the 17th century were very great. World War II, however, was greater in all these respects than any other war in history.[12]

Approximately thirty million people perished in World War I. People were horrified. But within a quarter of a century World War II was fought in the same amphitheater by the same parties and for much the same reasons. It resulted in the loss of sixty million lives while the costs quadrupled from an estimated $340 billion to an estimated $1 trillion.

Since World War II there have been "at least 12 limited wars in the world, 39 political assassinations, 48 personal revolts, 74 rebellions for independence, 1162 social revolutions, either political, economic, racial, or religious," wrote *U.S. News and World Report* in the December 25, 1967, issue. By now the totals obviously need to be increased in every category.

Meshech and Kedar, which the psalmist mentions in verse 5, are names of peoples. Meshech is mentioned by the historian Herodotus, who says that in his day the people of this name lived in the province of Pontus in northern Turkey.[13] Later they pushed north and east of the Black Sea into the Caucasus, Kasakastan, and the Ukraine. Kedar was a son of Ishmael (Gen. 25:13) and refers to a wild Arab tribe of the desert (Isa. 21:16–17; Jer. 49:28–29).[14] These two peoples were located so far apart geographically that they can only be taken here as "a general term for the heathen."[15] No one person could have lived among both. They are examples of warlike tribes, among whom the singers of Psalm 120 had no true home.

Strangers in the World Today

Do you have no lasting or real home here and is your real home in heaven? If not, you are not a Christian. If so but you just do not know it, then although you may be a Christian, you are not a pilgrim. The apostle Peter is speaking to you when he writes, "Dear friends, I urge you, as aliens and strangers in the world, to abstain from sinful desires, which war against your soul. Live such godly lives among the pagans that, though they accuse you of doing wrong, they may see your good deeds and glorify God on the day he visits us" (1 Peter 2:11–12).

The old camp song says,

> This world is not my home; I'm just a passin' through.
> My treasures are laid up somewhere beyond the blue.
> The angels beckon me from heaven's open door,
> And I can't feel at home in this world anymore.

It is not very good poetry, but those old hymns often contained strong truths, and this is one of them. The song reminds us that if we are Christians, this world is not our real home. We cannot settle down in Meshech or be at home in Kedar. So if you are, stop trying to conform to this world's lies and ways of life. Put on your hiking shoes. Strap your pack to your back. Say good-bye to your sins, and start marching to Zion. The King of Glory is waiting for you.

Psalm 121

Unto the Hills

I lift up my eyes to the hills—
    where does my help come from?
My help comes from the LORD,
    the Maker of heaven and earth.

He will not let your foot slip—
    he who watches over you will not slumber;
indeed, he who watches over Israel
    will neither slumber nor sleep.

The LORD watches over you—
    the LORD is your shade at your right hand;
the sun will not harm you by day,
    nor the moon by night.

The LORD will keep you from all harm—
    he will watch over your life;
the LORD will watch over your coming and going
    both now and forevermore.

verses 1–8

All of us have scenes from childhood that we remember gratefully, even if our childhood days were not particularly happy. Mine were. I think back on them with growing thanksgiving as the years go by. Some of the scenes I remember thankfully are when my mother would gather our family together to read Psalm 121 and pray with us before one of the children left home or the family started on a trip.

He will not let your foot slip—
    he who watches over you will not slumber. . . .

The LORD will keep you from all harm—
    he will watch over your life;

> the LORD will watch over your coming and going
> both now and forevermore.

I can close my eyes and see our family seated in a circle in our living room and hear those words now. This was my mother's psalm for her family. Because so many of those "goings out" and "comings in" were my own, there is a sense in which Psalm 121 became my travel psalm.

The Traveler's Psalm

It has been for other Christians too. David Livingstone, the famous missionary and explorer of the continent of Africa, read Psalm 121 and Psalm 135, which praises God for his sovereign rule over all things, as he worshiped with his father and sister before setting out for Africa in 1840. His mother-in-law, Mrs. Moffat, wrote him at Linyardi that Psalm 121 was always in her mind as she thought about and prayed for him.

J. S. Watson, a Rear Admiral in the United States Navy and the successor to Admiral Dewey, who commanded the U.S. fleet in the Philippines during the Spanish American War, wrote, "My favorite chapter is the Traveller's Psalm, Psalm 121. The seventh and eighth verses mean more to me than any other."

William Edwards was a British magistrate caught in the Indian Mutiny of 1857. His escape after hiding out for months is a thrilling story. He wrote at one point, "Nothing new has been settled about our plans, and we are much harassed. Heavy guns were firing at Turruckabad today. We know not for what cause, but they reminded us painfully of our fearful proximity to that place where so many are thirsting for our lives. Amidst it all, the psalms are most consoling and wonderfully suited to our cause, especially the 121st: 'I will lift up mine eyes unto the hills, from whence cometh our help' [KJV]."[1]

These are only a few of what must be many thousands of instances when, in danger, God's people have turned to Psalm 121 and found comfort.

Faith of a Trusting Pilgrim

Psalm 121 is the second of the pilgrim psalms, the Songs of Ascents devout Jews must have sung as they made their way to the highlands of Judah, where Jerusalem was located, for the annual feasts. When we remember that there were no real roads in those days, only well-trodden paths across the valleys, along the rivers, and over mountain passes, it is easy to imagine how this psalm might have been sung by a hopeful but very weary pilgrim. He has been traveling for days. His feet are sore. His muscles ache. Jerusalem, the end of his pilgrimage, seems very distant. Suddenly he sees the hills of Judah in the distance, and he breaks into song:

> I lift up my eyes to the hills—
> where does my help come from?

> My help comes from the LORD,
> the Maker of heaven and earth (vv. 1–2).

Some writers have suggested that this was the traditional evening song for the last encampment of those who would arrive in Jerusalem the next day, noting that the next psalm speaks of the travelers actually standing within the city's walls.

All this is pure speculation, however. Other scholars have suggested that this was a song for those living in Babylon who could only see the far-off hills of Judah in their imaginations. That is speculation too. What is not speculation is the marvelous spirit of tranquil trust in God that the psalm breathes from beginning to end. It is this trust that makes Psalm 121 such a strong discipleship song for pilgrims of all times and all countries. In the first of these songs the disciple was starting out from Meshech and Kedar, two symbols for the unbelieving world. In this psalm we find him turning his eyes toward heaven, expressing trust in God.

Charles Spurgeon wrote that Psalm 121 "is several steps in advance of its predecessor, for it tells of the peace of God's house, and the guardian care of the Lord, while Psalm 120 bemoans the departure of peace from the good man's abode, and his exposure to the venomous assaults of slanderous tongues. In the first instance his eyes looked around with anguish, but here they look up with hope."[2]

Protection by God, under the watchful eye of God, is the dominant idea in the psalm. In the Hebrew text only one word is used for what our versions translate variously as "watches over," "preserves," and "keeps." That word *(shamar)* is used six times. It is found twice in the second stanza (vv. 3–4), once in the third stanza (v. 5), and three times in stanza four (once as "keep" and twice as "watch over," vv. 7–8).

Who are the "I" and "my" of verses 1 and 2 versus the "you" and "your" of verses 3–8? As we might expect, quite a few commentators argue over various interpretations in which an individual Israelite is answered by a priest, or travelers answer one another in antiphonal fashion, or even a father addresses a son who is starting out on a journey.[3] It is probably best to think of this as an internal dialogue of the psalmist with himself. We have a good example of internal dialogue in Psalms 42 and 43: "Why are *you* downcast, O my soul? . . . Put your hope in God, for *I* will yet praise him" (Pss. 42:5, 11; 43:5, italics added).

"Maker of Heaven and Earth"

The original King James translation of verse 1 suggested a wrong thought to many people, namely, that the psalmist was looking to the mountains for his help. This is not the idea at all. The first stanza can mean either of two things. First, for a pilgrim approaching Jerusalem the mountains around the city suggested Jerusalem itself, and Jerusalem was God's city, the place

God had chosen for his earthly dwelling. Therefore, to look "to the hills" really meant looking to God as one's true help. The King James Version translators no doubt intended this by their translation.

Second, the stanza can be a rejection of the hills for God himself. The mountains, with their high places, had been centers for Canaanite religion. Their gods were identified with the mountains, and they were worshiped there with cultic prostitution. These "high places" are mentioned seventy-eight times in the Old Testament, where we are told that the Jews did not destroy them when they occupied Canaan and that they often worshiped there themselves. If this is what the psalmist is thinking of, what he is telling us is that his gaze did not stop when he looked upward to the hills but that he looked beyond them to God, who made the mountains.

In any case, the God the psalmist worships and to whom he looks for help is the "Maker of heaven and earth" (v. 2). This phrase reoccurs several times in the Songs of Ascents (see Pss. 124:8; 134:3). To worship the gods of the mountains or any other gods or even the mountains themselves is idolatry, and it is as useless as it is wicked. What we need is not the gods of nature, but nature's God. We need the Creator. Derek Kidner captures this idea when he writes of verse 2, "The thought of this verse leaps beyond the hills to the universe; beyond the universe to its Maker. Here is living help: primary, personal, wise, immeasurable."[4]

Likewise, Charles Spurgeon wrote, "The purposes of God; the divine attributes; the immutable promises; the covenant, ordered in all things and sure; the providence, predestination, and proved faithfulness of the Lord—these are the hills to which we must lift up our eyes, and from these our help must come."[5]

God, Our Protector

If the first stanza asks where the help of the devout pilgrim comes from and answers that it is from the God who made heaven and earth, the next stanzas explore various ways in which that Creator God helps his weak disciple. Stanzas two and three explore by images, suggesting that God is like a watchman, who does not sleep, or like shade from the harmful effects of the sun or moon. The last stanza abandons imagery and says directly that God is our protector at all times and in all circumstances.

1. *A vigilant watchman* (vv. 2, 4). When a person asked the Greek general Alexander the Great how he could sleep soundly when he was surrounded by so much personal danger, he replied that Parmenio, his faithful guard, was watching. How much more soundly should we sleep when God, who never slumbers nor sleeps, is guarding us!

2. *The shade at our right hand* (vv. 5–6). There is genuine danger of sunstroke in such hot regions as the Near East, but there is no reason for thinking of the moon as threatening, in spite of the fact that the word "lunatic" (from the Latin word *luna* for "moon") reflects the ancient belief that expo-

sure to the moon's rays can disorder the mind. What the psalmist really means, though in figurative language, is that nothing either of the day or night can harm us if God is keeping guard. God is our covering against every calamity. He is our shade against the visible perils of the day as well as the hidden perils of the night.

3. *Our protector always* (vv. 7–8). The powerful fourth stanza sums up the preceding verses in a series of intensifying statements:

God will keep us from *all harm,*

God will watch over our *lives,*

God will watch over our *comings and goings,* and

God will do all of that both *now and forever.*

These verses remind a New Testament believer of that great corresponding passage at the close of Romans 8, or the doxology that ends the Book of Jude. To the Romans Paul wrote,

Who shall separate us from the love of Christ? Shall trouble or hardship or persecution or famine or nakedness or danger or sword? . . . No, in all these things we are more than conquerors through him who loved us. For I am convinced that neither death nor life, neither angels nor demons, neither the present nor the future, nor any powers, neither height nor depth, nor anything else in all creation, will be able to separate us from the love of God that is in Christ Jesus our Lord (Rom. 8:35–39).

Jude wrote,

To him who is able to keep you from falling and to present you before his glorious presence without fault and with great joy—to the only God our Savior be glory, majesty, power and authority, through Jesus Christ our Lord, before all ages, now and forevermore! Amen (Jude 24–25).

When Troubles Assail Us

Is it actually true that we will be protected from all harm if God is with us? Will we never have troubles? Sometimes Christians are accused of being unrealistic, and this accusation is probably accurate in many instances. But the Bible is not unrealistic—neither in Psalm 121, nor in Romans, nor in Jude.

When Psalm 121 says, "My help comes from the LORD," it is acknowledging that we are going to need help on our journey. When it speaks of the Lord watching over us day and night, it implies that we need watching.

Similarly, when Jude writes that God "is able to keep us from falling," he is admitting that there is much that would cause us to fall and even that we sometimes do fall but that God can and does bring us through to his glorious presence in heaven in spite of it.

As for Paul, when he says that nothing "will be able to separate us from the love of God that is in Christ Jesus our Lord" he is not closing his eyes or shutting his ears to the hostile and destructive forces that surround the Christian. On the contrary, he actually opens his arms to these forces and invites them to come forward, saying that they will never succeed in detaching us from Jesus Christ.

What are the forces arrayed against us? Paul lists seven of them (Rom. 8:38–39), maybe choosing this number to suggest completeness: trouble, hardship, persecution, famine, nakedness, danger, and the sword. These are terrible dangers, yet not one of them will be able to separate the Christian from God.

Some will comment, "Well, that is all right for Paul to say, since he was an apostle and undoubtedly enjoyed special privileges. I am only a normal Christian. Can this really apply to me?" Let me remind you of Paul's experience. True, he was an apostle, but his apostleship meant that he had to endure greater, rather than lesser, hardships than ourselves.

He writes about them in 2 Corinthians.

> I have worked much harder, been in prisons more frequently, been flogged more severely, and been exposed to death again and again. Five times I received from the Jews the forty lashes minus one. Three times I was beaten with rods, once I was stoned, three times I was shipwrecked, I spent a night and a day in the open sea, I have been constantly on the move. I have been in danger from rivers, in danger from bandits, in danger from my own countrymen, in danger from Gentiles; in danger in the city, in danger in the country, in danger at sea; and in danger from false brothers. I have labored and toiled and have often gone without sleep; I have known hunger and thirst and have often gone without food; I have been cold and naked. Besides everything else, I face daily the pressure of my concern for all the churches. Who is weak, and I do not feel weak? Who is led into sin, and I do not inwardly burn? (2 Cor. 11:23–29).

Every danger Paul wrote about in Romans 8 is in these verses as something Paul had experienced himself or was in danger of experiencing. Eventually he was even put to death for his convictions.

Paul is not writing from some ivory tower or speaking "off the wall," as we might say. He experienced great difficulties. Yet none of these things separated him from Christ's love, and today he is in the presence of the Lord Jesus Christ in heaven, and he will be forever.

Kept from All Evil

The point of Psalm 121 is not that we will not have problems, but that God will keep us safe as we go through them. In the previous chapter (on

Psalm 120) I mentioned Eugene H. Peterson and his book on the Songs of Ascents. He deals with the reality of the disciple's ills frankly, noting that the promise of this psalm is not that we shall never stumble or stub our toes, but that "no injury, no illness, no accident, no distress will have evil power over us, that is, will be able to separate us from God's purposes in us."[6]

So what is the disciple of Jesus to expect? Peterson answers,

> The Christian life is not a quiet escape to a garden where we can walk and talk uninterruptedly with our Lord; nor a fantasy trip to a heavenly city where we can compare blue ribbons and gold medals with others who have made it to the winners' circle. . . . The Christian life is going to God. In going to God Christians travel the same ground that everyone else walks on, breathe the same air, drink the same water, shop in the same stores, read the same newspapers, are citizens under the same governments, pay the same prices for groceries and gasoline, fear the same dangers, are subject to the same pressures, get the same distresses, are buried in the same ground.
>
> The difference is that each step we walk, each breath we breathe, we know we are preserved by God, we know we are accompanied by God, we know we are ruled by God; and therefore no matter what doubts we endure or what accidents we experience, the Lord will preserve us from evil, he will keep our life.[7]

The mature Christian is neither blind to trouble nor in fear of it, for he is following after Jesus Christ, who said, "In this world you will have trouble. But take heart! I have overcome the world" (John 16:33).

Psalm 122

Pray for the Peace of Jerusalem

I rejoiced with those who said to me,
"Let us go to the house of the LORD."
Our feet are standing
in your gates, O Jerusalem.

Jerusalem is built like a city
that is closely compacted together.
That is where the tribes go up,
the tribes of the LORD,
to praise the name of the LORD
according to the statute given to Israel.
There the thrones for judgment stand,
the thrones of the house of David.

Pray for the peace of Jerusalem:
"May those who love you be secure.
May there be peace within your walls
and security within your citadels."
For the sake of my brothers and friends,
I will say, "Peace be within you."
For the sake of the house of the LORD our God,
I will seek your prosperity.

verses 1–9

A short time ago I was talking with a Jewish man who had just returned from Jerusalem. He had been there three times, and he told me that whenever he went to Jerusalem he felt he was standing at the very center of the world. He was always profoundly moved by the experience. I told him it is not only Jews who feel this way; many Christians who have visited Jerusalem have been profoundly moved too.

I have been to Jerusalem twice, the first time more than thirty years ago, passing through the famous Mendelbaum gate from the Jordanian occupied sector of the city to the part then under Jewish control, while guards from both nations directed their automatic weapons at those who were entering.

The second time was in 1995. The city was unified then, and I had an opportunity to explore it for several days on foot, as I had not done before. One of my most moving experiences was passing along the base of the great eastern wall and actually reaching out and touching stones that Nehemiah had caused to be raised from the Kidron Valley, where they had been thrown at the time of the Babylonian conquest in 586 B.C., and to be reassembled to form the new walls of the reconstituted city. That was four and a half centuries before the birth of Christ and twenty-four hundred years before I stood there, but I could have said with the psalmist,

> I rejoiced with those who said to me,
> "Let us go to the house of the LORD" (Ps. 122:1).

On Entering Jerusalem

Psalm 122 is the third of the Songs of Ascents. In the first of this small group of fifteen psalms, Psalm 120, the singers are in a foreign land, beginning to turn their faces toward God's city. In the second, Psalm 121, they seem to have sighted the city or are at least very near it at the end of their journey. In this psalm the travelers reflect on their joy when they were asked to join the pilgrim party and thrill that their feet are now actually standing within Jerusalem's gates (v. 2).

Many of us may have a love for the towns or cities in which we were born or brought up, and there may even be some affection for Washington, D.C., our nation's capital. But none of our towns, cities, or even our capital can mean for us what Jerusalem has meant for Jews throughout history, or for that matter, what it means to devout pilgrims of varied faiths today.

In the biblical record, Jerusalem is first mentioned as the city of which Melchizedek was king ("king of Salem," Gen. 14:18). We know nothing about the city then, but we do know that the site was inhabited by people known as Jebusites from about 3500 B.C. on, judging from the pottery remains that have been found there. Jerusalem became a Jewish city and achieved biblical prominence under King David, who wrested it from the Jebusites and made it both his political and religious capital. He made it a political center by constructing his palace and other governmental buildings there (see 2 Sam. 5:6–12). He made it the Jews' religious center by bringing the ark of the covenant to Jerusalem, a story told at length in

2 Samuel 6 and 1 Chronicles 15 and 16. It was placed within the relocated tabernacle. Later Solomon built the glorious golden temple, which David had wanted to build, and the ark was placed in its Most Holy Place. The temple thus became the center of the city, which was the center of the nation.

In many of the psalms Jerusalem is lauded as a truly holy city, the city of God; for example, in the "Psalms of Zion" (Psalms 46, 48, 76, 84, 87), or the Songs of Ascents, which we are studying. Alas, Jerusalem was still only an earthly city, and the people themselves were far from holy, which is why in the end the city was overthrown by God's determined judgment and the people were deported to Babylon.

Could Psalm 122 have been written by David, as the title claims?[1] Most contemporary scholars deny David's authorship and date the psalm after the exile, as they do the other psalms in this collection, but it is quite possible that David did write it. In fact, it is reasonable to suppose that he wrote it both to express joy in his new capital city and to encourage love for and loyalty toward it as the focal point of the nation's political life and worship. (Jeroboam later tried to undermine that unity by establishing his capital at Shechem and by building alternate worship centers at Dan and Beersheba [see 1 Kings 12:25–33].)

The psalm may be looked at in three very different ways, all with good biblical warrant. Literally, it is about earthly Jerusalem, growing out of David's hopes or a later poet's remembrance. Symbolically, it can be applied to the church, as the author of Hebrews applies it, specifically in chapter 12. Prophetically, Psalm 122 can direct our thinking to the new Jerusalem, of which the earthly city is but an incomplete type.

The Earthly City

At its best, Jerusalem was only a weak type of the heavenly city to come, but it still caused joy in the heart of the arriving pilgrim, which is what the opening verses describe. We can imagine the writer standing inside the gates of the city after his long journey, looking around at the stately government buildings, the homes of the wealthy Jerusalem residents, and the city's massive walls, and marveling. He has come from the country and has never seen a real city before, let alone Jerusalem. We catch a sense of this wonder from the disciples' comments to Jesus when they were leaving the temple to go to the Mount of Olives: "Look, teacher! What massive stones! What magnificent buildings!" (Mark 13:1). Sadly, Jesus warned of a time not far off when "not one stone here will be left on another; every one will be thrown down" (Mark 13:2). There were three things that impressed the psalmist as he stood joyfully inside the city's gates and walls.

1. *Its unity* (vv. 3–4). When the psalmist refers to Jerusalem as "a city that is closely compacted together" (v. 3), there are a couple of things he could be writing about, depending on who wrote the psalm and when it was writ-

ten. If it was written by David and was therefore written rather early in the history of the monarchy, the writer could be referring to the physical setting of the city. During David's reign and for some time thereafter, Jerusalem was a small city located on the crest of Mount Zion and Mount Moriah, bounded on two sides by steep descents to the Kidron and Tyropaeon valleys, and thus no more than half a mile in breadth. It had a dramatic setting for one approaching it from a distance, and its tight structure would have impressed anyone observing it.

On the other hand, if the psalm was written later, perhaps even after the return of the Jews from exile, the city would have been larger and the reference to its being "compacted together" would refer to the orderly rows of fine houses bordering its narrow, twisting streets. If it was written even later than this, it might refer to the way new homes had now replaced the rubble-filled lots left behind after the Babylonian desolation.

Yet the psalmist is not thinking in merely physical terms, as we might be inclined to do. He notices the physical compactness of the city, but it is merely an appropriate way of noting the role Jerusalem had played in the compacting or unifying of the nation. At one time the people had thought more in terms of their tribal identities than of their national identity. In fact, even after David had become king there was intense rivalry between the tribe of Judah, from which David came, and Benjamin, which was the tribe of his enemy and predecessor Saul. Jebusite Jerusalem was a border town that belonged to none of the existing tribes. So by choosing it as his capital, David chose a city that would belong to the entire nation. Here people from each of the tribes could go up and know that he or she belonged to one united people—people from Judah and Benjamin, from Dan, Ephraim, and Manassah, from Reuben and Naphtali, and from all the tribes.

More important, the reason for their going up was to worship the one true God of the nation, Jehovah, who had called them into existence by his blessing on Abraham, by his deliverance of the people from Egypt, and by giving the people his laws at Mount Sinai. The unity of the nation was not merely political. In fact, the outward political unity fractured early on, in the days of Rehoboam, Solomon's successor. The real unity was spiritual, for regardless of the tribal or political divisions, every Jew came to Jerusalem to worship one true and the same God.

2. *Its justice* (v. 5). The reference to God's "statute," or law, in verse 4 also leads the writer to think of how Jerusalem was the center for dispensing legal justice to the people.

> There the thrones for judgment stand,
> the thrones of the house of David (v. 5).

"Thrones" may be a reference to the king's courts, located in the palace of the monarch or in other government buildings, but they may be something more, something the pilgrim actually saw as he or she passed through the gates of the capital city. We remember that when Absalom was trying to win the allegiance of the people, to turn them from obeying and serving his father David, he stood in the gates of the city to offer judgment to those who came to it with their legal suits. Judgment was often rendered at a city's gates (see Ruth 4:1–12; Job 29:7), and "thrones for judgment" may be something pilgrims actually noticed when they entered the city.

Derek Kidner says that dispensing justice is "a ruler's first duty and best gift" (referring to Psalm 72:1–4 and Isaiah 2:4 and 42:3).[2] Dispensing justice is one of the two God-given functions of right government. The other is defending its citizens against violence either from within or from without (see Rom. 13:1–7). When the kings of Israel took this responsibility seriously and gave just judgments, the city and nation were blessed by God and prospered. When they neglected this duty, the nation was troubled, and the result was often civil war, as in the days of David and his rebellious son Absalom.

3. *The need for peace* (vv. 6–8). It may be a sober realization of how difficult it is to provide genuine justice in this world that leads the psalmist to compose the prayer and write the vow of the psalm's last stanza. There can be no true or lasting peace without justice. Justice is hard to achieve. Therefore, "Pray for the peace of Jerusalem," he intones. Then, lest we should suppose that he is urging on others what he is unwilling or too lax to do himself, he leads the prayers:

> "May those who love you be secure.
> May there be peace within your walls
>   and security within your citadels."
> For the sake of my brothers and friends,
>   I will say, "Peace be within you" (vv. 6–8).

This is not a onetime prayer or idle words unmatched by deeds. The psalmist wants to work for the peace and prosperity of Jerusalem too. Hence, he ends his composition with a vow: "For the sake of the house of the LORD our God, I will seek your prosperity" (v. 9). It is a firm resolve.

"Pray for the peace of Jerusalem!" And well we might. No city has ever been a center for such fierce military battles, destruction, and loss of life as Jerusalem has been. Its very name incorporates the rich Hebrew word for *peace (shalom),* meaning "habitation of peace," but no habitation has ever been less peaceful. It has been attacked and destroyed many times, as I was reminded when I stood at the eastern wall and laid my hands on the stones that had been restored by Nehemiah. It is in turmoil today.

Our Jerusalem, the Church

The church of Jesus Christ is for us what Jerusalem was for ancient Israel, and it is a tremendous step beyond it, as the author of Hebrews points out to the Jewish believers of his day. The ancient city with its temple and temple worship was a wonderful gift of God to be highly valued and loved, but something much better has come by the work of Jesus Christ. Jesus has established a new, spiritual temple by the sacrifice of himself on the cross, and he has brought us not to Mount Sinai or to the old Mount Zion, but to a new Mount Zion and a new Jerusalem.

> You have come to Mount Zion, to the heavenly Jerusalem, the city of the living God. You have come to thousands upon thousands of angels in joyful assembly, to the church of the firstborn, whose names are written in heaven. You have come to God, the judge of all men, to the spirits of righteous men made perfect, to Jesus the mediator of a new covenant, and to the sprinkled blood that speaks a better word than the blood of Abel.
>
> Therefore, since we are receiving a kingdom that cannot be shaken, let us be thankful, and so worship God acceptably with reverence and awe, for our God is a consuming fire (Heb. 12:22–24, 28–29).

This Jerusalem, the church, has important parallels to the Jerusalem that was the destiny of the pilgrims and the subject matter of the psalm. It too is a compacted, unifying place where people from various human tribes can come together and be one people. Here we are neither "Jew nor Greek, slave nor free, male nor female, for [we] are all one in Christ Jesus" (Gal. 3:28). Our Jerusalem is also a place where justice has been provided and should be worked for still. God has justified us through the atoning death of the Lord Jesus Christ, our Savior, and we are to be concerned for justice too—in the church above all, but also, where possible, in society too.

Should we not pray for the peace of our Jerusalem? Wars erupt in the church, just as they do in other places. We think of the troubles that disturbed the church at Philippi, of Paul's plea to Euodia and Syntyche "to agree with each other in the Lord" (Phil. 4:2).

Murdoch Campbell says of our discipleship, "One great evidence of our being in the way to that glorious city is that there is nothing in this world that commands our concern or interest more than the prosperity of God's Zion and of all those who seek its good in every part of the world."[3]

The New Jerusalem

And yet, we also look for the heavenly Jerusalem still to come, for we are still pilgrims. We have not yet fully arrived, and our eyes are fixed not even on the church, as wonderful as it can be, but on the heavenly "city with foundations, whose architect and builder is God" (Heb. 11:10).

We catch a glimpse of that city in Revelation, where the Holy City, the new Jerusalem, descends from heaven. It is no mere copy of the earthly city that had been destroyed for its sins. It is a glorious new city described in what we would call surrealistic terms.

It shone with the glory of God, and its brilliance was like that of a very precious jewel, like a jasper, clear as crystal. It had a great, high wall with twelve gates, and with twelve angels at the gates. On the gates were written the names of the twelve tribes of Israel. . . . The wall of the city had twelve foundations, and on them were the names of the twelve apostles of the Lamb (Rev. 21:11–14).

When John looked for the city's temple he did not see one because "the Lord God Almighty and the Lamb are its temple." Moreover,

the city does not need the sun or the moon to shine on it, for the glory of God gives it light, and the Lamb is its lamp. The nations will walk by its light, and the kings of the earth will bring their splendor into it. On no day will its gates ever be shut, for there will be no night there. . . . Nothing impure will ever enter it, nor will anyone who does what is shameful or deceitful, but only those whose names are written in the Lamb's book of life (Rev. 21:22–27).

A river of life is in the city, flowing down from the throne of God. It causes trees to bear fruit, and their leaves are for "the healing of the nations" (Rev. 22:2). John's description ends by glancing at God's servants, those who see God's face and bear his name on their foreheads. They dwell in perpetual light and reign with him "forever and ever" (Rev. 22:5).

These descriptions bear ties to reality, for heaven is a real place, not merely an idea; yet they are also clearly symbols, all with a rich biblical history, pointing to the glories, joys, and eternal security of those who are truly God's people. What really matters is that we are going there. Christians are pilgrims who know that God is able to keep them from falling and at last to present them before his glorious presence with great joy (see Jude 24).

Psalm 123

Looking Up

I lift up my eyes to you,
*   to you whose throne is in heaven.*
As the eyes of slaves look to the hand of their master,
*   as the eyes of a maid look to the hand of her mistress,*
so our eyes look to the LORD our God,
*   till he shows us his mercy.*

Have mercy on us, O LORD, have mercy on us,
*   for we have endured much contempt.*
We have endured much ridicule from the proud,
*   much contempt from the arrogant.*

*   verses 1–4*

Psalm 121 began with the same words as this psalm: "I will lift up my eyes to . . ." But while the former poet lifted up his eyes to "the hills," asking as a secondary thought, "Where does my help come from?" this poet goes straight to the one whose throne is in heaven. The goal of the pilgrim is not Jerusalem, as important as that city was, or even the temple in Jerusalem, as important as it was, but God himself, whose true throne is not anywhere on earth but in heaven. In the pilgrimage of this life it is always to God and to God alone we go and to whom we look for help and guidance here.

A Psalm for Weary Eyes

This is a beautiful psalm, and one way of getting into it is to observe that it is a psalm for the eyes. "Eyes" occurs four times (in vv. 1–2). Then, in reference to eyes, "lift up" occurs once (v. 1) and "look to" occurs three times more (v. 2).

If we want a New Testament equivalent, we can think of Hebrews 12:2–3, which says, "Let us fix our eyes on Jesus, the author and perfecter of our faith, who for the joy set before him endured the cross, scorning its shame, and sat down on the right hand of the throne of God. Consider him who endured such opposition from sinful men, so that you will not grow weary and lose heart." As we read this psalm we discover that the people are in circumstances in which they could lose heart, but they are not cast down or defeated by their circumstances, because they are looking beyond them to God.

What beautiful images the psalmist employs! He begins the psalm in the first person, saying, "I lift up my eyes. . . ." Immediately following he draws in those who are about him, noting that they are together like slaves who stand in eager expectation of the least sign from their master. He thinks of male slaves first, then adds the image of a female slave who likewise looks to the hand of her mistress. Since there were many slaves in the ancient world, everyone would understand this picture immediately. This is not an endorsement of slavery, of course. It is a way of saying that the disciple's dependence on God and submission to God should be no less total than the most obedient servant of an earthly master.

How should God's servants look to their heavenly Master? Alexander Maclaren says, "They should stand where they can see him; they should have their gaze fixed upon him; they should look with patient trust, as well as with eager willingness to start into activity when he indicates his commands."[1] Spurgeon writes, "We must use our eyes with resolution, for they will not go upward to the Lord of themselves, but they incline to look downward, or inward, or anywhere but to the Lord."[2]

He continues:

> True saints, like obedient servants, look to the Lord their God *reverentially;* they have a holy awe and inward fear of the great and glorious One. They watch *obediently,* doing his commandments, guided by his eye. Their constant gaze is fixed *attentively* on all that comes from the Most High; they give earnest heed, and fear lest they should let anything slip through inadvertence or drowsiness. They look *continuously,* for there is never a time when they are off duty; at all times they delight to serve in all things. Upon the Lord they fix their eyes *expectantly,* looking for supply, succor and safety from his hands, waiting that he may have mercy upon them. To him they look *singly;* they have no other confidence, and they learn to look *submissively,* waiting patiently for the Lord, seeking both in activity and suffering to glorify his name. When they are smitten with the rod they turn their eyes *imploringly* to the hand which chastens, hoping that mercy will soon abate the rigor of the affliction.[3]

Do we look to God like that—reverently, obediently, attentively, continuously, expectantly, singly, submissively, imploringly? Probably not, but we should.

Opposition by Ridicule

None of these psalms gives much detail for helping us fix the time when they were written. Most scholars think of the majority as having been written in the early days after the Jews' return from exile in Babylon, when the tiny group of people who came back to Jerusalem with high hopes found themselves scorned by their settled, more comfortable, malicious neighbors. That is certainly the note struck in the second of this psalm's two stanzas. It is why they are looking so hopefully to God.

If the return from exile is the true background for the psalm, then Nehemiah 4 can tell us what was going on. The rebuilding of the walls of Jerusalem had begun, and the leaders of the surrounding people had begun to oppose it.

The easiest way to oppose something you do not like is to ridicule the effort, and this is the first thing these hostile leaders did. Their names were Sanballat and Tobiah. They got the army of Samaria together and made fun of the Jews in what must have been a large public forum, saying, "What are those feeble Jews doing? Will they restore their wall? Will they offer sacrifices? Will they finish in a day? Can they bring the stones back to life from those heaps of rubble—burned as they are?"

Tobiah added, "What they are building—if even a fox climbed up on it, he would break down their wall of stones!" (Neh. 4:2–3).

The reason people ridicule what they oppose, aside from it being so easy, is that it is demoralizing and frequently effective. It is effective because it strikes at the hidden insecurities or weaknesses that almost everybody has. Each of Sanballat's five rhetorical questions and Tobiah's taunt triggered a legitimate sense of weakness that Nehemiah and the others must have had.

"What are those feeble Jews doing?" The Jews were feeble, and they knew it. How could anyone as weak as they were hope to rebuild their city's walls?

"Will they restore their wall?" Indeed! How could they restore a wall one-and-one-half to two-and-one-half miles in circumference? It had been built by people much more numerous and stronger than they were. How could they even hope to reassemble those huge stones?

"Will they offer sacrifices?" Most commentators take this question as referring to sacrifices of thanksgiving to be offered after the walls were finished. I think Derek Kidner is correct when he regards it as meaning, "Are these fanatics going to *pray* the wall up? It's their only hope!"[4] The taunt was an attack on the Jews' faith, which was not that strong anyway at this period. Don't you find it difficult when someone ridicules your faith? "Maybe you think God's going to help you!" or "Why don't you go home and pray about it (chuckle)?" they say. It is hard not to be unsettled by such ridicule.

"Will they finish in a day?" This means, "Don't they realize what an enormous task they are taking on?" The Jews knew exactly how large the task was.

"Can they bring the stones back to life from those heaps of rubble—burned as they are?" This was an exaggeration. The gates had been burnt but not the walls. They were not limestone, which might well have been calcined by the intense heat of the fire used to destroy Jerusalem at the time of Nebuchadnezzar's conquest. The walls were not crumbled, only tumbled, but the question was nevertheless effective in reminding the Jews of the overwhelming dimensions of the task.

Tobiah's taunt, "What they are building—if even a fox climbed up on it, he would break down their wall of stones," had bite because, as archeological studies of these walls have shown, they did not turn out to be of the same quality as those that stood before them.

Despite the taunts, something important was going on and was perceived by these two governors as being likely to succeed. Their anger revealed that what they were ridiculing threatened them.

An Important Lesson from Nehemiah

Nehemiah dealt with these attacks the way the psalmist does in Psalm 123, though the psalm's account is briefer. There is one thing Nehemiah did not do, and two he did.

Nehemiah did not retaliate. The first thing most of us do when we are ridiculed is snap back. We would say, "So they think we're feeble, do they? Well, they're not so strong themselves. Sanballat, you're just a petty governor of a petty province of a remote area of the empire. Tobiah, you're only governor of that hot little desert area of Ammon. Who would want to live there?" If Nehemiah had retaliated, he would merely have lowered himself to the level of his critics, and he would have come out second best since they were stronger and more important in the world's eyes than he was. This attitude is characteristic of the writer of Psalm 123. He is talking to God, not talking back to those who scorned his people.

Nehemiah did pray, just as the psalmist does. He laid the problem before God and asked God to intervene. The alternative, bottling up our feelings or trying to suppress them, solves nothing. Nehemiah admitted that he was hurt and angry. "We are despised," he said (Neh. 4:4). Nevertheless, the work was God's, and he was able to leave it in God's hands. "Turn their insults back on their own heads," Nehemiah asked. "Give them over as plunder in a land of captivity. Do not cover up their guilt or blot out their sins from your sight, for they have thrown insults in the face of the builders" (Neh. 4:4–5).

Nehemiah also went on with the work. Since he had left the taunts of his enemies with God, he no longer needed to be concerned about them and could get on with the task God had given him. What he says is nice: "So we rebuilt the wall till all of it reached half its height, for the people worked with all their heart" (Neh. 4:6). In the same way, the psalmist is intent on pursuing his pilgrimage to Jerusalem.[5]

Have Mercy on Us

Earlier in this chapter I pointed out that Psalm 123 might be called a psalm for the eyes because the word "eyes" occurs four times. It is the dominant word in the first of the psalm's two stanzas. We can equally well call attention to the word "mercy." It occurs three times (once in verse 2 and twice in verse 3) but is the dominant word in the second stanza. In fact, mercy is the most important word in the psalm, because it is what the psalmist is praying for.

Mercy ends the first stanza in verse 2, explaining that the psalmist is looking to God as a slave looks to his master or a maid to her mistress until God shows him mercy. It is picked up in the first line of the last stanza, as a prayer: "Have mercy on us, O LORD, have mercy on us" (v. 3).

Mercy is one of three words often found together in the Bible, with goodness and grace. Goodness is the most general term, involving all that emanates from God: his decrees, his creation, his laws, his providences. It extends to the elect and to the nonelect, though not in the same way. God is good, and everything he does is good. Grace denotes favor, particularly toward the undeserving. There is "common grace," the kind of favor God shows to all persons in sending rain on the just and unjust alike. There is also "special" or "saving grace," which is what he shows to those he is saving from their sins. Mercy is an aspect of grace, but the unique quality of mercy is that it is given to the pitiful, in this case to those who have endured "much ridicule from the proud, much contempt from the arrogant." Arthur W. Pink says, "Mercy . . . denotes the ready inclination of God to relieve the misery of fallen creatures. Thus 'mercy' presupposes sin."[6]

Eugene Peterson writes about verse 3, saying,

> The prayer is not an attempt to get God to do what he is unwilling, otherwise, to do, but a reaching out to what we know that he does do, an expressed longing to receive what God is doing in and for us in Jesus Christ. In obedience we pray *have mercy upon us* instead of "give us what we want." We pray *have mercy upon us,* and not "reward us for our goodness so our neighbors will acknowledge our superiority." We pray *have mercy upon us* and

not "punish us for our badness so we will feel better." We pray *have mercy upon us* and not "be nice to us because we have been such good people."[7]

I suppose that most people think exactly what Peterson is denying, that is, that God should be merciful to them because they deserve it or are nice people. There is no confidence in this thinking. The confidence we have when we approach God, asking for mercy, is in God's own merciful character, not in our character. The Jews knew about God's merciful character because of how God had declared his name to Moses, saying, "The LORD, the LORD, the compassionate and gracious God, slow to anger, abounding in love and faithfulness, maintaining love to thousands, and forgiving wickedness, rebellion and sin" (Exod. 34:6–7). We know God's mercy in Jesus Christ. Therefore, "Let us approach the throne of grace with confidence, so that we may receive mercy and find grace to help in time of need" (Heb. 4:16).

A Slave of Slaves

The only thing that will ever lift you out of your sin and complacency, put you on the pilgrim trail, and keep you there throughout life is a profound awareness of the mercy and grace of God.

Consider the example of John Newton, the hymn writer. When Newton was a young boy he ran away to sea and eventually went to Africa to participate in the slave trade. His reason for going, as he wrote in his autobiography years later, was that he might "sin his fill." Sin he did! But the path of sin is downhill, and Newton's path descended so far that he was eventually reduced to the position of a slave in his master's African compound. This man dealt in slaves, and when he went off on slaving expeditions Newton fell into the hands of the slave trader's African wife, who hated Europeans and vented her venom on Newton. Newton was forced to eat his food off the dusty floor like a dog, and at one point he was actually placed in chains. Sick and emaciated, he nearly died.

Newton escaped from this form of his slavery eventually, but he was still chained to sin and again went to sea transporting slaves from Africa to the New World. It was on his return from one of these slave voyages that Newton was wondrously converted.

The ship was overtaken by a fierce storm in the North Atlantic and was nearly sinking. The rigging was destroyed, water was pouring in. Newton was sent down into the hold to pump water. He pumped for days, certain that the ship would sink and he would be drowned. As Newton pumped water in the hold of that ship, God caused him to remember Bible verses he had learned from his mother as a child, half a lifetime earlier, and these verses led to his repentance, faith, and conversion. Right there in the ship! While the storm was raging!

The ship survived the storm. The sailors were saved. Sometime later, after Newton had left the slave trade, this former slave of slaves studied for the

Christian ministry and eventually became a popular preacher in England. He even preached before the queen.

What was Newton's motivation? It was a profound awareness of the grace and mercy of God toward him. It was this John Newton who wrote,

> Amazing grace!—how sweet the sound—
> That saved a wretch like me!
> I once was lost, but now am found,
> Was blind, but now I see.

Newton never forgot God's mercy to him. Once, a friend was complaining about someone who was resistant to the gospel and living a life of great sin. "Sometimes I almost despair of that man," the friend remarked.

"I never did despair of any man since God saved me," said Newton.

In his most advanced years Newton's mind began to fail and he had to stop preaching. When friends came to visit him he frequently remarked, "I am an old man. My mind is almost gone. But I can remember two things: I am a great sinner, and Jesus is a great Savior." Certainly the mercy of God moved Newton to offer his body as a living sacrifice to God and to seek to please him.

Love So Amazing

You and I often waver in our discipleship and stumble on the pilgrim pathway. We get discouraged and are sometimes inclined to quit. One thing that will keep us going is knowledge of the mercy of our God.

Ephesians 2 describes our experience. It says that before God revealed his mercy to us, we were "dead in . . . transgressions and sins" (Eph. 2:1). We "followed the ways of this world and of the ruler of the kingdom of the air" (Eph. 2:2) and were "by nature objects of [God's] wrath" (Eph. 2:3). Now listen to what God did.

> Because of his great love for us, God, who is rich in mercy, made us alive with Christ even when we were dead in transgressions—it is by grace you have been saved. And God raised us up with Christ and seated us with him in the heavenly realms in Christ Jesus, in order that in the coming ages he might show the incomparable riches of his grace, expressed in his kindness to us in Christ Jesus (Eph. 2:4–7).

Shouldn't God's mercy motivate you to the most complete offer of yourself to God and to the highest level of obedience? How can it do otherwise?

Psalm 124

─── ───

"If"

─── ───

If the LORD had not been on our side—
    let Israel say—
if the LORD had not been on our side
    when men attacked us,
when their anger flared against us,
    they would have swallowed us alive;
the flood would have engulfed us,
    the torrent would have swept over us,
    the raging waters would have swept us away.

Praise be to the LORD,
    who has not let us be torn by their teeth.
We have escaped like a bird
    out of the fowler's snare;
the snare has been broken,
    and we have escaped.
Our help is in the name of the LORD,
    the Maker of heaven and earth.
                                    verses 1–8

I am one of those people who love English poetry, and over the years I have tried to memorize a good bit of it. One of the poems I have tried to memorize but have not succeeded in memorizing completely is "If" by Rudyard Kipling.

> If you can keep your head when all about you
>   Are losing theirs and blaming it on you,
> If you can trust yourself when all men doubt you,
>   But make allowance for their doubting too;
> If you can wait and not be tired by waiting,
>   Or being lied about, don't deal in lies,
> Or being hated don't give way to hating,
>   And yet don't look too good, nor talk too wise . . .

The poem continues similarly for four stanzas and then ends with the well-known lines,

> If you can fill the unforgiving minute
>   With sixty seconds' worth of distance run,
> Yours is the Earth and everything that's in it,
>   And—which is more—you'll be a Man, my son!

I think of that poem now because of Psalm 124, which begins with the same word, "if." In fact, "if" leads off verses 1 and 2. Yet the psalmist is not thinking of what it means to be a man, as Kipling was. He is thinking of God and his people and the enormous difference it has made for them that God is on their side.

This psalm is a wonderful praise statement of the Lord's protecting care of Israel when the people were faced by some grave national calamity. It is also for us. It is what we would call theologically a statement of God's wonderful perseverance with his saints.

When Did This Happen?

When did this deliverance take place? One possibility is that the psalm is referring to Israel's deliverance from Babylonian captivity. H. C. Leupold holds this view though he suggests other possibilities too.[1] So does J. J. Stewart Perowne, whose major argument is the position of Psalm 124 among the other Songs of Ascents: "The last psalm was the sigh of an exile in Babylon, waiting in absolute trust and dependence upon God for the deliverance of himself and his people from captivity. This psalm is the joyful acknowledgment that the deliverance has been vouchsafed. The next psalm (the 125th) describes the safety of the new colony, restored to its native land and girt round by the protection of Jehovah."[2] Alexander Maclaren holds the same opinion. "It [Psalm 124] is most naturally taken as the expression of the feelings of the exiles on their restoration from Babylon."[3]

There are two problems with this view. First, the expressions of the psalm ("when men attacked us," "swept us away," "escaped like a bird") sound more like a military attack and deliverance from it than captivity. Second, we are not even sure that the Songs of Ascents were linked to the return from Babylon. They were not if they were composed for pilgrims making their way to Jerusalem for one of the three annual feasts, as I have argued (see pp. 1069–70).

Some see these words as a psalm sung by David's armies as they returned to Jerusalem after their victory over the armies of Absalom. Others see them as a song of thanksgiving composed after the deliverance of the Jews from Haman in the days of Queen Esther.

Yet the title line identifies the psalm as a song "of David." This ascription is somewhat uncertain because it is omitted by the Septuagint and even by some Hebrew manuscripts. However, if the psalm is by David, then we know something about the threat from these enemies. They were the Philistines, and they came very close to swallowing the young Jewish state alive, engulfing it, and sweeping it away, which is what the psalm describes (vv. 3–5). The Philistines had defeated Saul and his armies. Saul and his son Jonathan had been killed. Now the Philistines set out to capture David, spreading out in large numbers in the Valley of Rephaim (see 2 Sam. 5:17–25). Derek Kidner thinks Psalm 124 is a psalm of David and reflects on how serious a danger this attack by the Philistines was.[4]

It is easy to see how a psalm praising God's protection from the early days of Israel's national history might be incorporated into the songs pilgrims sang on their way to Jerusalem, which David had made his capital. It would be a way of saying, "The God we are going to Jerusalem to worship is a very great God indeed."

What If?

Psalm 124 is a beautiful and moving psalm, and the chief reason is the power of the six images that occur here one upon another.

1. *An animal swallowing its prey* (v. 3). The enemy was fierce. If God had not intervened, we would have been devoured by that fierce foe, the psalmist says. The foe could have been any of a number of nations, including the Philistines that were such a threat to David—or even the Babylonians—but can we read this psalm without thinking of our great enemy the devil, who "prowls around like a roaring lion looking for someone to devour" (1 Peter 5:8)? Surely, we say, if the Lord had not been on our side, the devil would have swallowed us up.

2. *A flood submerging its victims* (v. 4). The flood is a frequent figure in the Old Testament for sudden life-threatening dangers (see Pss. 32:6; 66:12; 69:1–2; 144:7; Isa. 8:7–8; 28:17; 43:2; Lam. 3:54), and with good reason. In the dry, rugged mountains of central Palestine the cracks and gullies of the hills are all connected so that any rain falling on the hard-baked soil quickly runs off and collects into wadis, where it can rise to dangerous heights in just a few minutes. Jesus was thinking of such a situation when he warned his hearers against building their spiritual life-houses on sand. "The rain came down, the streams rose, and the winds blew and beat against that house, and it fell with a great crash" (Matt. 7:27).

Surely, if the Lord had not been on our side to provide us with a solid foundation for the building of our lives, we would have been engulfed many times before this by life's quick and unexpected tragedies. Are you building on Jesus, who is himself the rock? Will you survive when troubles come?

3. *A torrent rushing over everything* (v. 4). In the first line of verse 4 the image was of being engulfed by quickly rising floodwaters. Here the idea is of a torrent sweeping over helpless people, leaving them destitute and devastated, and then rushing on.

Sometimes our troubles are like that. It is not so much a question of being submerged by troubles—buried by them, as we might say. It is more like being hit by a truck, which crushes us by its great weight, leaving us mangled by the roadside while it disappears on down the highway. The Greek word for "trouble" or "tribulation" (used by Paul in Rom. 8:35) is *thlipsis,* and it has to do with pressure and being pressed down by something. The Latin word, which is used to translate *thlipsis* in the Vulgate version, is *tribulum,* from which we get our word "tribulation." It is even stronger. It means a threshing sled, which was drawn over grain on a threshing floor to break the heads and thus to separate the whole grain from the chaff. Sometimes our problems are like threshing. They press on us so fiercely that we feel we are being broken up like stalks of grain. We can say, If the Lord had not been on our side to lift us up, bind up our wounds, and heal us, we would have perished utterly.

4. *Waters sweeping everything before them* (v. 5). The next line takes this image a final step, imagining a flood that not only engulfs and destroys, but also sweeps away everything before it. Some people experience everything in their lives suddenly being swept away—everything they had been counting on as sure and necessary for their well-being. Can we not say, If the Lord had not been on our side, we would have been swept away ourselves? The only reason we have survived is that the Lord has set our feet on a rock and established our goings out and our goings in forever.

5. *An animal grinding its prey* (v. 6). The last two of these images are from the poem's second half, which is thanking God for his deliverance rather than reflecting on what would have happened "if the Lord had not been on our side." The first is the image of an animal actually grinding away on a carcass. This is what King Darius expected to see when he rushed to the lion's den early in the morning following the day he had reluctantly caused Daniel to be lowered into it. "Daniel, servant of the living God, has your God, whom you serve continually, been able to rescue you from the lions?" he cried out (Dan. 6:20). Daniel might have replied, "If the Lord had not been on my side, I would have been ground to pieces by their teeth." What he did say was, "My God sent his angel, and he shut the mouths of the lions. They have not hurt me" (Dan. 6:22). Many of us can also say quite accurately, If the Lord had not been on our side, our enemies would have ground us into little pieces, swallowed us up, and spit out the bones.

6. *A bird entangled in a trap* (v. 7). Rowland E. Prothero records in his valuable volume *The Psalms in Human Life* that there is an old seal, still in existence, that was "once the property of a Huguenot refugee, which bears as its device a net below, and above, a bird soaring upwards." It has as its text the words of verse 7, "My soul is escaped even as a bird out of the snare of the fowler."[5] This Huguenot refugee, who came in time to America, knew that he had been delivered from the snare of his fierce enemies by God alone.

Should we not say the same thing? If the Lord had not been on our side, we should never have escaped the snares our enemies set for us.

What If, Indeed?

Those images only represent external, physical trouble! What about sin and its punishment? If Jesus had not died in our place, taking our punishment upon himself, we would be under God's just wrath and judgment and would surely suffer for our sins forever. Instead, we can say, "There is now no condemnation for those who are in Christ Jesus" (Rom. 8:1).

What if God did not intervene to keep us on the path of discipleship? We are like Peter, who would have fallen away and been lost if Jesus had not interceded for him. Jesus told Peter, "Simon, Simon, Satan has desired to sift you as wheat. But I have prayed for you, Simon, that your faith may not fail. And when you have turned back, strengthen your brothers" (Luke 22:31–32). It is hard to miss seeing that in these words Jesus does not call Peter by the name he gave him: Peter, meaning "stone." He uses his former name to call attention to his weakness. Peter thought he was strong enough to stand by Jesus no matter what might happen, but when the time of testing came he denied Jesus three times. Peter would have fallen away completely as a result of his failure and humiliation were it not for Jesus' prayers for him. But Jesus did pray, and later he also came to Peter to recommission him for service.

What if God did not preserve our work for Christ? It would all be for nothing. Our lives would be without any meaning. We remember that even Moses, after all his labors, prayed,

> Establish the work of our hands for us—
> yes, establish the work of our hands (Ps. 90:17).

What if God did not preserve us from death? Death too is sometimes pictured as a flood that rises up to engulf the living and perhaps carry them away. The Bible views death as a mighty enemy, but God promises to walk with us through death's waters. More than that, he promises a resurrection beyond:

> "Where, O death, is your victory?
> Where, O death, is your sting?"

The sting of death is sin, and the power of sin is the law. But thanks be to God! He gives us the victory through our Lord Jesus Christ" (1 Cor. 15:55–56). King David wrote, "Even though I walk through the valley of the shadow of death, I will fear no evil, for you are with me" (Ps. 23:4).

Praise the Lord

Those cries of deliverance lead to the second half of Psalm 124, which is a declaration of thanks to God for his deliverance. The words "Praise be to the LORD," which begin the second stanza, mean "Thank you." We praise God because we are thankful to him for his many spiritual and material deliverances.

The sequence of thought between the two stanzas can be summed up by the short English connecting words if, then, but, and therefore: *If* the Lord had not been on our side . . . *then* we would have perished . . . *but* the Lord has been on our side . . . *therefore* we will praise him. It bothers me that there is so little genuine thanksgiving to God expressed by Christian people. It is not heard in our everyday speech very often, and it is not even a major element in our worship services. Why is this? I think the explanation is in this sequence. God has been so faithful to us that we take his protection and deliverances for granted. However, if we were aware of what would happen if God were not protecting us, that we would perish instantly, then we would be thankful and would praise God wholeheartedly and often.

We should develop this biblical way of thinking. *If* the Lord had not been on my side, *then* I would have perished utterly; *but* God is on my side and will continue to be, *therefore,* I will praise him. "Praise be to the LORD, who has not let us be torn by their teeth" (v. 6).

The People's Testimony

The final verse of Psalm 124 is an echo of Psalm 121:2. Similar verses occur throughout the psalms, and many worship services have begun with these words or others like them. Job Orton (1717–1783) reported in the late eighteenth century that the French Protestants always used this verse to begin their public worship.[6] Rightly so, for these words direct our thoughts to God, who is the only sure help of his people and the only rightful object of our true devotion. There are three important emphases in this verse.

1. *"Our help is in the name of the Lord."* Others may offer to help us, but we dare not turn to them since they do not have what we need. Only the Lord, the Maker of heaven and earth, is adequate for us in our weakness. He is omniscient; he always knows what we need and knows it perfectly. He is omnipresent; he is always there when we need him. He is omnipotent; he can do what needs to be done. He is loving and gracious; he always has our spiritual best interest at heart. With a God like this why should we ever trust other gods or lean so much on other people?

2. *"Our **help** is in the name of the Lord."* Everything we need or can possibly need is in God, but particularly we rejoice that our *help* is in God, since we are so helpless. Spurgeon observed that in God we have help "as troubled sinners," being delivered from the punishment and guilt of our sin. We have help "as dull scholars," being taught to know and understand God's Word. We have help "as trembling professors," being witnesses to his gospel, God giving us words to speak and blessing our testimony in the lives of others. We have help "as inexperienced travellers" on life's journey, being guided on the right paths and kept from perilous pitfalls and wasteful detours. We have help "as feeble workers," being unprofitable servants at best, but God is blessing the work of our hands and making it of lasting value.[7]

3. *"**Our** help is in the name of the Lord."* The help that is to be found in God is *our* help—not someone else's, but our very own help. We have tested God's Word and have found God to be everything he has described himself as being. We look to the past and testify, "The Lord has helped me." We look to the present and assert, "The Lord is my help even this very day." We look to the future and affirm, "The Lord will be my help forever."

> Our help is in the name of the LORD,
> the Maker of heaven and earth.

Psalm 125

Like Mount Zion

Those who trust in the LORD are like Mount Zion,
which cannot be shaken but endures forever.
As the mountains surround Jerusalem,
so the LORD surrounds his people
both now and forevermore.

The scepter of the wicked will not remain
over the land allotted to the righteous,
for then the righteous might use
their hands to do evil.

Do good, O LORD, to those who are good,
to those who are upright in heart.
But those who turn to crooked ways
the LORD will banish with the evildoers.

Peace be upon Israel.

verses 1–5

There have not been many epochs in history when people believed their lives and fortunes were secure. Life has always been uncertain. Still ours seem like particularly insecure times. Our culture is in a state of decline, so that things we used to take for granted are disappearing—things like honesty, courage, concern for other people, self-discipline, responsibility, and hard work—and in their place we are producing a generation of cultural barbarians whose only thought is for their own immediate self-gratification. These are the new Dark Ages.[1]

Thomas Cahill, the director of religious publishing at Doubleday in New York, has written a book about the role of the Irish in preserving classical learning in the Middle Ages. Early in that book he has a chapter on the breakdown of Roman civilization. The elements of that breakdown are almost exactly what we are dealing with today:

> The changing character of the native population, brought about through unremarked pressures on porous borders; the creation of an increasingly unwieldy and rigid bureaucracy, whose own survival becomes its overriding goal; the despising of the military and the avoidance of its service by established families, while its offices present unprecedented opportunity for marginal men to whom its ranks had once been closed; the lip service paid to values long dead; the pretense that we still are what we once were; the increasing concentration of the populace into richer and poorer by way of a corrupt tax system, and the desperation that inevitably follows; the aggrandizement of executive power at the expense of the legislature; ineffectual legislation promulgated with great show; the moral vocation of the man at the top to maintain order at all costs, while growing blind to the cruel dilemmas of ordinary life.[2]

These problems are all very familiar, and they unsettle us, just as they unsettled the Romans before the collapse of their civilization in the early 400s. No wonder we feel unsettled in these times. We have much to be unsettled about. Even Christians should be worried.[3]

Unshaken like Mount Zion

This is where Psalm 125 comes in. It is the sixth of the Songs of Ascents, and it is speaking of the security believers have in God, even in bad times. It compares them to Mount Zion, on which Jerusalem is built. It is bedrock, high and secure. Moreover, it is surrounded by other mountains, which the writer compares to God, who likewise surrounds his people. The civilization of these people had collapsed and they were trying to rebuild it. As they did, they were to know that God was beneath them as their firm foundation and about them as their defense against danger.

There is a false trust in Zion, a trust that does not go beyond the mere city or presumes on the commitment of God to preserve the city. The people so presumed in the decades before the fall of the city and were warned about their presumption by the prophets. The psalmist is not advocating such false trust. He is actually looking beyond Jerusalem to the Lord, who alone truly endures forever. He is teaching that our security can never be in ourselves or in circumstances. It must always be in God.

Founded on the Rock

I think of the apostle Peter as an illustration. At one point in his life, Peter took his eyes off Jesus, looked at the water on which he was walking, and began to sink. He was an insecure man. But there was a later incident in his life in which Jesus taught him what it was to be rock solid. Jesus had asked who the disciples thought he was, and Peter had answered, "You are the Christ, the Son of the living God."

Jesus replied, "This was not revealed to you by man, but by my Father in heaven. And I tell you that you are Peter, and on this rock I will build my church" (Matt. 16:16–18).

Many people have understood these words to mean that Jesus was going to build his church on Peter. The Roman Catholic Church has interpreted Jesus' words as a promise that Peter would become the first pope and that the church would be built on Peter and his successors. Most Protestants take the words as referring not to Peter himself but to Peter's confession of Jesus as the Messiah, the Son of God, and argue that the church is to be built on this confessional foundation.

How did Peter understand Jesus' words? He answers that question in 1 Peter 2:4–8, where he insists that the rock upon which the church or any individual Christian is to build is Jesus Christ. He does not suggest even for a moment that he is himself the rock. Peter must have understood Jesus' words to him as a contrast, meaning, You are Peter (Peter means "a little stone"), *but* on this rock (that is, Jesus Christ himself) I will build my church. Peter learned that Jesus is the only possible foundation for a sure and stable life, and Peter wanted to be built on him.

Peter had biblical grounds for understanding Jesus' teaching this way. He indicates it by three Old Testament quotations.

1. *Isaiah 28:16.* Isaiah speaks of God's laying "a stone in Zion, a chosen and precious cornerstone." Peter added, "The one who trusts in him will never be put to shame" (1 Peter 2:6). We build on Jesus by faith. We are to "trust in him." By believing on Jesus we become stones worked into the great spiritual temple God is constructing.

2. *Psalm 118:22.* Jesus applied Psalm 118:22 to himself during his earthly ministry, so Peter probably learned to interpret the verse this way from Jesus. Jesus told a parable about farmers to whom the owner of a vineyard had leased a field. They tried to appropriate the field for themselves, eventually killing the owner's son, who had been sent to collect his profits. "When the owner of the vineyard comes, what will he do to those tenants?" Jesus asked.

They answered, "He will bring those wretches to a wretched end, and he will rent the vineyard to other tenants, who will give him his share of the crop at harvest time." That was the right answer. Jesus then applied it to himself by quoting from Psalm 118: "Have you never read in the Scriptures:

'The stone the builders rejected
    has become the capstone'?" (Matt. 21:33–42).

God is the owner of the vineyard. The leaders of Israel were the evil tenant farmers. The servants were the prophets, and the son who was killed was

Jesus himself. Therefore, he is also the stone rejected by the builders who was to become the capstone of religion and the only sure foundation for his people. Psalm 118:22 must have meant a lot to Peter because he cited it not only here but also in his speech before the Sanhedrin (Acts 4:11).

3. *Isaiah 8:14.* Peter used Isaiah 8:14 to add the thought of stumbling to the prior thought of rejecting Jesus.

> A stone that causes men to stumble
> and a rock that makes them fall (1 Peter 2:8).

Peter meant that rejecting God's anointed Messiah is no small matter. It has a fatal consequence, which is to fall down spiritually, or be lost forever.

As the Mountains

Not only has God become the foundation for his people's faith, which is what the mountain location of Jerusalem suggested to the author of Psalm 125, but he also surrounds his people, as the mountains surround Jerusalem.

There is a story in the Old Testament that teaches this truth clearly. In the days of Elisha the prophet, Ben Hadad, the king of Syria, had been fighting the king of Israel. But every time he made plans to attack Israel, God revealed his plans to Elisha, Elisha told the king of Israel, and the Jewish armies escaped. Ben Hadad thought there was a traitor among his officers. Someone told him the truth, and he decided to capture Elisha. Elisha was at Dothan with a young man who was his servant, so Ben Hadad marched his armies to Dothan by night and placed them around the city. At daybreak, when the young man went out from the gates of the city to draw water, he saw the soldiers and was terrified.

"Oh, my lord, what shall we do?" he asked Elisha.

"Don't be afraid," Elisha told him. "Those who are with us are more than those who are with them" (2 Kings 6:16). Then Elisha prayed, asking God to open the eyes of the servant, and when God did, the young man saw that the hills were "full of horses and chariots of fire all around Elisha" (2 Kings 6:17). David was probably prophesying these events when he wrote in Psalm 27,

> The angel of the LORD encamps around those who fear him,
> and he delivers them (Ps. 27:7).

God afflicted the enemy soldiers with blindness so that Elisha was able to lead them into Israel's own capital city of Samaria, where they were captured but then treated kindly and sent home. After this the Syrian bands stopped raiding Israel's territory.

"Those who are with us are more than those who are with them." It is not that Christians have no enemies. We do. Nor that we have no reasons to feel insecure. There are many things to make us feel insecure. Still God is for

us—under us as a sure foundation and about us to defend us from our enemies and all other causes for anxiety.

The Presence of the Wicked

The person who wrote this psalm knew that it is not under perfect conditions that we have to trust God, but in an evil and wicked world. Therefore
the next two stanzas acknowledge the presence of the wicked in Israel and
their threat to righteous persons.

What is the situation here? H. C. Leupold and J. J. Stewart Perowne think
the psalm fits the age of Ezra and Nehemiah best,[4] and perhaps it does. It
reflects a time when the Jews were in their land but the land was ruled by or
at least dominated by a foreign power, called "the scepter of the wicked"
(v. 3). This verse could refer to Persia, the dominant world power at that
time, or to the small surrounding kingdoms of Samaria, Ammon, Arabia, or
Philistia, which did everything they could think of to hinder Nehemiah's
work.

This is very like the condition of God's people at any time in history. We
live in the world by God's decree. We are to be an influence for good, but
we do not rule the world. The world is ruled by largely secular people operating through secular governments. This rule is by God's decree, for God
has given secular power to the state, not to the church. Our duties to the
state are to submit to it and pray for our rulers (see Rom. 13:1–7).

The state does not always perform well, of course. The psalmist knows
this and is concerned about something that should concern us too, namely,
the influence for evil that the surrounding secular environment can have
on God's people. There is a danger that secular power can be used to do
evil—even by God's people, who can be deceived by it—and a danger that
God's people could be corrupted by the secular powers. He has four significant responses to these dangers.

1. *A promise* (v. 3). The wicked will not rule over the people of God forever but there will be a deliverance from God eventually. Our problems now
will not last forever, and there will be deliverance in time. Knowing the outcome is a great help for staying on the right path now.

This promise can be taken in several ways. If the psalm is from the days
of Nehemiah, it would be a prophecy of the deliverance of Israel from foreign domination. For most of us it can be a promise that the problems we
face will not last; that God has not forgotten us; and that he will soon intervene to help us in our personal lives, in our relationships with other people,
in our work, or whatever it may be. In the largest scheme of things it is a
reminder of Christ's return, when the wicked will be judged, their works
destroyed, and the people of God be established in the heavenly city of
God, which will endure forever.

2. *A prayer* (v. 4). In the meantime, those who are trying to serve God live
in this world and need help. So the psalmist has a prayer for them, a prayer

for God to be gracious to them here, where they need it: "Do good, LORD, to those who are good, to those who are upright in heart."

It is important to notice the difference between the writer's *prediction* of God's sure judgment on the wicked and his *petition* for blessing on the righteous. He does not need to ask that the wicked will be judged, because their judgment is certain, sometimes sooner than either we or they expect! The church father Athanasius said of Julian the Apostate, the last major persecutor of the church, when he heard that he had died, "That little cloud has quickly passed away."[5] The wicked are devoted to destruction.

By contrast with his prediction of judgment on the wicked, the psalmist asks for God's blessing on the righteous, because none actually are righteous and any goodness they have or receive must be due to God's goodness to them. None of the righteous have any claim on God. God owes us nothing. At the same time, there is no end to the good things God has prepared for those who have been made righteous by the work of Christ, and it is proper for us to pray for an abundance of good things, as the psalmist does. We have a good God, and we can ask him to be good to us and to others who know and love him too. The apostle Paul expressed this boldly when he wrote, "We know that in all things God works for the good of those who love him, who have been called according to his purpose" (Rom. 8:28).

3. *A warning* (v. 5). Those who suppose themselves to be righteous because they are living among God's people but are not actually his—those "who turn to crooked ways"—the writer warns are not really among the regenerate and says "the LORD will banish with the evildoers." Remember, mere formal membership with the people of God counts for nothing. We must actually be trusting and obeying God. We must belong to Jesus Christ.

4. *A blessing* (v. 5). "Peace be upon Israel," concludes the psalmist. This is a blessing Paul seems to echo in Galatians 6:16, where he refers to Christians as the "Israel of God." This is an accurate use of the Old Testament, for this is the way "Israel" is used in the psalm, not of ethnic Israel but of God's true people. We remember that Jerusalem means "peace" *(shalom)*. Thus, we are told, we shall not only be like Salem but shall have salem too.

Trusting God in Uncertain Times

Early in this chapter I mentioned Thomas Cahill and his study of the role of the Irish in preserving learning during the Dark Ages. I return to him here because of what he has to say about St. Patrick, the young Roman who brought Christianity to Ireland. Patrick had been captured in England by Irish pirates when he was only sixteen years old and had been put to work as a slave for an Irish chieftain. He escaped after six years, returned to his family, but was then called by God to return to Ireland as a missionary.

What a task Patrick faced! Behind him lay the collapsed wreck of Roman civilization. Before him were the fierce, wild natives of Ireland. Patrick had no outward security, but he persevered at his calling, dying at last at the age of seventy-six. In thirty years of ministry Patrick changed Ireland so thoroughly that, as Thomas Cahill reports in his study, "As the Roman lands went from peace to chaos, the land of Ireland was rushing even more rapidly from chaos to peace."[6] Instead of viewing the collapse of his culture as an unmitigated tragedy, Patrick seized it as an unprecedented opportunity to propagate Christ's gospel.

Where did Patrick find strength in such times? He gives his answer in a surviving prayer known as "St. Patrick's Breastplate."

> I arise today through God's strength to pilot me: God's might to uphold me, God's wisdom to guide me, God's eye to look before me, God's ear to hear me, God's word to speak for me, God's hand to guard me, God's way to lie before me, God's shield to protect me, God's host to save me from snares of devils, from temptations of vices, from everyone who shall wish me ill. . . .
>
> Christ to shield me today against poison, against burning, against drowning, against wounding, so that there may come to be abundance of reward. Christ with me, Christ before me, Christ behind me, Christ in me, Christ beneath me, Christ above me, Christ on my right, Christ on my left, Christ when I lie down, Christ when I sit down, Christ when I arise. . . .
>
> I arise today through a mighty strength. . . .[7]

That is true security, a security we need. It is the same security given to the people of God throughout the ages so that they could be "like Mount Zion which cannot be shaken but endures forever" (v. 1).

Psalm 126

Those Were the Days

When the LORD brought back the captives to Zion,
  we were like men who dreamed.
Our mouths were filled with laughter,
  our tongues with songs of joy.
Then it was said among the nations,
  "The LORD has done great things for them."
The LORD has done great things for us,
  and we are filled with joy.

Restore our fortunes, O LORD,
  like streams in the Negev.
Those who sow in tears
  will reap songs of joy.
He who goes out weeping,
  carrying seeds to sow,
will return with songs of joy,
  carrying sheaves with him.

  verses 1–6

O ne of the literary techniques that
contributes to effective poetry is the use of sharp contrasts, like John Milton's description of blind Samson in *Samson Agonistes:*

O dark, dark, dark, amid the blaze of noon,
Irrecoverably dark, total eclipse
Without all hope of day!

Or the opening lines of William Shakespeare's *Richard the Third:*

1109

> Now is the winter of our discontent
> Made glorious summer by this sun of York.

The psalmists use this device too, and one example is the psalm to which we come now: Psalm 126, the seventh of the fifteen Songs of Ascents. It begins with a scene of nearly delirious joy, a scene from Israel's past when the people were released from their Babylonian captivity and returned to Zion. The second half jumps to the age in which the psalm was written, a time of difficult, unrewarding labor and even weeping. This stanza describes these hard times, but it also contains a prayer for and a prophecy of better days to come.

The Joy of Men Set Free

It is hard for us to appreciate the opening stanza, because not many of us have experienced anything quite like this homecoming. These ecstatic people had been released from a dreary, seventy-year-long captivity and returned to their native land, and they were so overwhelmed with this sudden turn of fortune that they almost imagined they were dreaming.

Their deliverance was such a remarkable occurrence that even the Gentiles who were looking on recognized that it had been accomplished by God. "The LORD has done great things for them," they said. And it was true! "The LORD *has* done great things for us, and we are filled with joy," they respond (italics added).

A few experiences in life might be close to that of the returning exiles. For some people falling in love is a bit like this "almost dreaming" joy, but in most cases it lacks the release from something terrible beforehand. Recovery from a serious illness might be an example of deliverance, but such recoveries usually lack the element of suddenness. Besides, after a prolonged illness recovery is most likely to be a sober, cautious thing, like the reaction of Boniface in Byron's "Prisoner of Chillon," who, the poet tells us, regained his freedom "with a sigh."

Perhaps the closest approach to what Psalm 126 describes is some persons' experiences of conversion to Jesus Christ, for that really is a deliverance, a great deliverance, and rare is the sudden conversion that is not accompanied by great joy and genuine thanksgiving to God.

Exceptional joy usually doesn't last a long time. It can't, really, because life is always a combination of ecstasy and agony, good times and bad times, joy and suffering. Joy is wonderful. Eugene Peterson calls it "a product of abundance . . . the overflow of vitality . . . life working together harmoniously." It is God's gift to his greatly loved children. But Peterson also adds honestly, "Inadequate sinners as we are, none of us can manage that for very long."[1]

It didn't last forever for the psalmist and his generation. If this psalm is about the return of the Jews from Babylon, as it seems to be, we know that those first years in the land were filled with the hard tasks of trying to get established, rebuild the temple, and reconstitute a lost society. The books of Ezra, Nehemiah, Haggai, and Zechariah tell how difficult those years were. The work on the temple was begun (the foundations were laid), then stopped, then begun again. This second temple was so inferior to the first temple—destroyed by Nebuchadnezzar and his armies—that the older Jews, who recalled the former days, wept at the disappointing contrast.

The first days of the exiles' return were certainly wonderful, but they had been succeeded by many days of dark discouragement and hard work.

The Present

We may have trouble thinking of joyful times to match those of stanza one of Psalm 126, but we do not have much difficulty thinking of times in which we have lost some former joy, however great or, more likely, weak or moderate it may have been. I leave aside here the loss of merely worldly joys—like teenage slumber parties or football weekends in college, or even memorable vacations at the shore. I think rather of the loss of spiritual good times. There are four joys that are commonly lost by Christians.

1. *The joy of salvation.* The loss of the first joy of our salvation is nearly universal for those who have been believers for any length of time. For many believers, especially those who became Christians later in life, and especially those who became Christians after living far from God for a time—perhaps in bondage to some sin—conversion to Christ was thrilling. It was the most wonderful thing imaginable. It was impossible to stop talking about Jesus, exactly like a lover who finds it impossible to stop talking about his or her beloved. But that initial joy passes. It should be succeeded by the more settled and equally valuable attitudes of quiet trust, but the songs and laughter are gone. It may even be the case—it certainly is for some—that the discouragement of defeats and even doubts slip in, so that the Christian begins to wonder if he or she is a Christian after all. Even John Wesley once wrote a hymn containing the lines, "Where is the joy I knew when once I saw the Lord?"

The loss of this initial joy does not mean that the person is no longer a true Christian, but it is still a difficult experience to live through and one from which some believers never quite seem to recover.

2. *The joy of spiritual victory.* The joy of spiritual victory comes later in the Christian life, when we have begun to be conscious of some sin and are struggling against it. Before we were Christians there would have been no hope of victory; in fact, not even a desire for it. We would have been happy as we were. But God pointed out the sin, we struggled, and suddenly there was a real breakthrough. That unforgiven grudge against the person who wounded us is gone; we have forgiven him or her. The addiction to alcohol or drugs that was destroying us physically, mentally, and spiritually has been removed. Ruptured family relationships have been healed. We have repented of a theft and have restored what we took from another person.

What joy we have when we realize that God has operated powerfully in our lives in such ways, making us more like Jesus Christ than before. Yes, but it is not long before we come up against another besetting sin and become conscious of other perhaps even more significant failures. Soon the former joy is only a faded memory. Will these struggles never end? we wonder. Will we ever really be happy again?

3. *The joy of Christian fellowship.* The joy of Christian fellowship is a wonderful thing, probably the closest thing we can know of the joys of heaven in this life. It can be lost in a variety of ways. The person we are closest to may die. Sin on the part of one or the other party may destroy the relationship. Whole churches may be destroyed by the sins of some. Or again, the fellowship we value may be lost by such a simple but unavoidable thing as the physical relocation of our friend because of a change of schools, a job, or retirement. True, there is a communion of saints that transcends physical barriers on earth, even death, but who would deny feeling some deep loss when people who are close to us and have meant much to us in our Christian walk are removed?

4. *The joy of a new work for God.* If you are at all like I am, you know the joy of taking on a new challenge or launching a new project. I also know that the excitement of a new beginning soon settles down to the tiring mechanics of hard work, and it is difficult to be as excited about slugging along in the trenches as planning the campaign.

What are we to do when the slugging times come? Are we to give up and settle down to merely humdrum Christian living?

A Prophecy of Better Times

For the psalmist, as for us, memory of the past could have become mere nostalgia. Those were the days! we say; wonderful, but gone forever. In Psalm 126, the memory of those singing, laughter-filled days of the past becomes, not nostalgia, but the ground of a strong hope for even better days to come. This is not just wishful thinking, pie-in-the-sky Christianity. It is a strong, realistic Christianity, because it is based on the character of God. God is good. He is unchanging in his goodness. He has granted us wonderful joys in the past. Therefore, he can be counted on to give us wonderful days again. That is the psalm's message and thought sequence.

So what does the psalmist do after he has remembered those earlier days in which their "mouths were filled with laughter" and "tongues with songs of joy"? He does two things.

1. *He asks God for the good times again.* Instead of simply settling down to the dreary tasks of the present, without any thought of better times except as a memory, the psalmist asks God to restore the good times again. In other words, he prays. In his prayer he asks for what is good, desirable, and glorifying to God. "Restore our fortunes, O LORD, like streams in the Negev" (v. 4).

The Negev is a desert, which the psalmist felt his life to be at the time he wrote this psalm. It has gullies that are the remains of former streams. They are parched, barren, hot, and comfortless. At those rare times when rain descends on the highlands to the north, the rivulets of water come together in streams descending from the hills and then rush down to fill the barren wadis with abundant sparkling and refreshing water.

The essence of this image is how suddenly these gullies fill up, which is how the people's freedom from Babylon came. One moment they were in exile. The next they were on their way home. Their deliverance was entirely of God, for only God could bring about the sudden return of a formerly exiled people. No nation carried into exile has ever returned to reconstitute itself, as Israel did. This event was so evidently of God that even the Gentiles knew it (v. 2). And if God did it once, he could do it again. He could restore the former fortunes and joys.

2. *He prophecies a time of joy to follow sorrow.* While prophecy is a prediction of something to come, and this is a prediction, we usually think of prophecy as a prediction given to a chosen spokesman by God, and I am not sure that is the best description of these last verses. They are more like a proverb than a prophecy in the classic sense. They have been taken as a proverb by countless generations of God's people as they have looked up from the difficulties of their present work expecting blessings from God.

> Those who sow in tears
>   will reap songs of joy.
> He who goes out weeping,
>   carrying seeds to sow,
> will return with songs of joy,
>   carrying sheaves with him (vv. 5–6).

In the first image (the sudden filling of the desert streams, v. 4) the results are sudden and unearned. In the second image (the harvest after the difficult work of plowing and sowing seed, vv. 5–6) the results come only after a long period of hard work and waiting. This is a good dose of spiritual reality. At times God does work suddenly and without any labor on our part. He did it in our conversion. We contributed nothing. But how many returns from captivity are there, after all? In most situations in life, the rewards only come after much hard work, even when we know that God is the source of the blessing, like the blessing of the harvest. So remember the past and be encouraged by it, keep praying, and keep working, because the Lord who gives us work to do also sends the harvests.

Application and Encouragement

The psalm speaks of sowing seed in order to reap in God's time, reminding us of Jesus' parable of the farmer who went out to sow seed. Some seed fell on the path, where the birds came and ate it up. Some fell on rocky places, where it sprang up quickly but was soon scorched by the sun because the soil was shallow. Some landed among thorns, where it seemed to do well at first but was later choked out by the weeds that sprang up with it. Only a portion of the seed, a fourth part, fell on good soil, where it eventually produced a good crop—a hundred, sixty, or thirty times what was sown (see Matt. 13:1–9).

When the disciples asked the meaning of the parable, Jesus explained that it had to do with teaching God's Word, which is what sowing seed refers to. The seed is the Word of God, he said. Some teaching is snatched away by Satan before it sinks into the listeners' hearts and is able to do them good. Some gains an immediate reception, but it does not last; troubles come and soon scorch it out. Still other teaching is choked by the deceitfulness of wealth and other earthly entanglements. Only a portion of the teaching takes root and produces a good crop.

A portion of what is sown *does* take root and *does* produce a harvest. So don't despair if the labor is long, the days are hot, and much that we do for God seems unprofitable. It is God who is Lord of the harvest, not ourselves. As Paul said when writing to the Christians at Corinth, "I planted the seed, Apollos watered it, but God made it grow" (1 Cor. 3:6). No work that is done for God will ever be entirely fruitless. No word spoken on behalf of the gospel, no kindness practiced out of love for Christ, no righteous stand taken because of God's righteousness will ever go unnoticed or unrewarded.

So don't give up. Of course, the labor is hard; this is a hard and sinful world. But the one who sows in tears "*will* reap with songs of joy." The one "who goes out weeping, carrying seeds to sow, *will* return with songs of joy, carrying sheaves with him" (vv. 5–6, italics added). Is there anything comparable to our joy in heaven when we stand before the Lord with those who have been saved through our own faithful sharing and teaching of God's Word?

Paul told the Corinthians, "Therefore, my dear brothers, stand firm. Let nothing move you. Always give yourselves fully to the work of the Lord, because you know that your labor in the Lord is not in vain" (1 Cor. 15:58).

Finally, your difficult labor and tears, particularly the tears, are noticed by God himself. The Greeks had the idea that God could not be touched by any human passions on the grounds that if he could, then we would have power over God, manipulating him by our distress. They called this unmovable quality in God *apatheia,* from which we get the word "apathy." That may be acceptable philosophy, but it is not good theology. We cannot manipulate God; God is entirely sovereign over all his thoughts and actions. But God is not untouched by the feelings of our infirmities. Jesus himself wept at the tomb of Lazarus when confronted by the ultimate consequence of sin, which is death (see John 11:35), and as he looked out over the glorious city of Jerusalem, soon to be destroyed because it "did not recognize the time of God's coming" (see Luke 19:41–44).

Neither the Father nor the Son is unmoved by your sorrows. God knows what it is to weep. He knows your suffering. He also knows that one day those tears will be wiped away, and they will be replaced by indescribable joy that will last forever.

We learn about this joy in one of the very last scenes of the Bible, from Revelation. John writes,

> Then I saw a new heaven and a new earth, for the first heaven and the first earth had passed away, and there was no longer any sea. I saw the Holy City, the new Jerusalem, coming down out of heaven from God, prepared as a bride beautifully dressed for her husband. And I heard a loud voice from the throne saying, "Now the dwelling of God is with men, and he will live with them. They will be his people, and God himself will be with them and be their God. He will wipe every tear from their eyes. There will be no more death or mourning or crying or pain, for the old order of things has passed away" (Rev. 21:1–4).

Eugene Peterson summarizes Psalm 126, saying,

> The psalm does not give us . . . joy as a package or as a formula, but there are some things it does do. It shows up the tinniness of the world's joy and affirms the solidity of God's joy. It reminds us of the accelerating costs and diminishing returns of those who pursue pleasure as a path toward joy. It introduces us to the way of discipleship which has consequences in joy. It encourages us in the way of faith to both experience and share in joy. It tells the story of God's acts which put laughter into people's mouths and shouts on their tongues. It repeats the promises of a God who accompanies his wandering, weeping children until they arrive home, exuberant, "bringing in the sheaves." It announces the existence of a people . . . who along with whatever else is happening are able to say, at the center, "We are glad."[2]

Psalm 127

God's Blessing on the City

Unless the LORD builds the house,
   its builders labor in vain.
Unless the LORD watches over the city,
   the watchmen stand guard in vain.
In vain you rise early
   and stay up late,
toiling for food to eat—
   for he grants sleep to those he loves.

Sons are a heritage from the LORD,
   children a reward from him.
Like arrows in the hands of a warrior
   are sons born in one's youth.
Blessed is the man
   whose quiver is full of them.
They will not be put to shame
   when they contend with their enemies in the gate.

verses 1–5

Useless!" That was the first word of a sermon I heard some years ago, and it was arresting. The speaker was R. C. Sproul, and in the introduction to that sermon he said that of all the words in the English language *useless* was the word he hated most, at least if it was applied to him. He was willing to work hard, to start early and labor late. He was willing to forego present pleasures or benefits. But not if it was useless!

"Because," he explained, "if you say that what I do is useless, you are saying that I am useless. And what that means is that somehow I don't count."

Most of us would agree wholeheartedly, but what strikes me strongly and sadly is that much of what we pour our lives and energies into is just that: useless—at least in the light of eternity.

A television commercial for Infinity, the Japanese luxury car import, that aired some time ago began with provocative questions: "Why do you work so hard? Why do you start early and stay late? Why do you care?" Good questions. Why indeed? Unfortunately the answer seemed to be, "In order to own a luxury car," since the commercial ended with a woman's voice saying, "Infinity. Thinking of you." It was not clear whether this comment referred to the company thinking of its customers or the customers thinking of the car. In either case, it was hard to listen to that commercial without thinking how meaningless it all was. For, in spite of the sophistication of the ad, the bottom line is surely that our extremely hard work and caring is vain if all we get out of it at the end of life's rat race is a car.

Then there's the tee shirt with this statement on the front: "The one who dies with the most toys wins." On the back it says, "But he dies nevertheless."

Well, that is half of the message of Psalm 127, the eighth of the Songs of Ascents.

Psalm of the Vanities

Psalm 127 is said to have been written by Solomon, the son of David, which makes it one of only two in the Psalter with his name (the other is Psalm 72). Most modern scholars do not like the idea that Psalm 127 might have been written by Solomon since they want to date all the Songs of Ascents from the time of the Jews' return from the Babylonian exile or later, but there is no compelling reason for refusing Solomon authorship of this psalm any more than for refusing David authorship of those Songs of Ascents appearing under his name (Psalms 122, 124, 131, 133). It would only be a case of an earlier psalm being added to a later collection because of its appropriate subject matter. Who can deny that the theme of Psalm 127 is directly out of Solomon's other writings? Solomon's best-known words are, "Meaningless! Meaningless! . . . Utterly meaningless! Everything is meaningless" (Eccles. 1:2). The more familiar King James Version said, "Vanity of vanities . . . All is vanity!" In Psalm 127 the words "in vain" or "vanity" occur three times, two times in verse 1 and a third time in verse 2.

Besides, there may be a cryptic reference to himself by Solomon in the words "those he loves" (v. 2). In Hebrew the words are actually "his beloved" (as in the KJV), the name God gave Solomon according to 2 Samuel 12:25: Jedidiah, meaning "Beloved of Jehovah."

"Useless!" "Meaningless!" "In vain!" Is everything meaningless? Yes—*if we leave God out of the picture.* Building is useless—*unless* the Lord builds the house. Precautions are useless—*unless* the Lord watches over the city. *Unless* the Lord blesses our work, *unless* the Lord blesses our family, our Herculean labors are in vain. They are not in vain if God is in what we are doing.

A Latin motto says, *Nisi Dominus Frusta*. It comes from the first words of this psalm and means "Without the Lord, Frustration." It is the motto of the city of Edinburgh, Scotland, appearing on its crest, and is affixed to the city's official documents. It could be attached to the lives of many who are trying to live their lives without the Almighty.

The American statesman Benjamin Franklin was not a Christian; he was a deist, though he appreciated Christians. He thought well of George Whitefield, the Calvinistic evangelist, for example. Franklin understood the futility of work without God and expressed it well in his "Speech to the Convention for Forming a Constitution for the United States," delivered in Philadelphia in 1787.

> In the beginning of the contest with Britain when we were sensible of danger, we had daily prayers in this room for the Divine protection. Our prayers, Sir, were heard, and they were graciously answered. All of us who were engaged in the struggle must have observed frequent instances of a superintending Providence. To that kind Providence we owe this opportunity of consulting in peace on the means of establishing our future national felicity. And have we now forgotten this powerful Friend? Or do we imagine that we no longer need his assistance? I have lived for a long time (81 years), and the longer I live the more convincing proof I see of this truth, that God governs in the affairs of men. And if a sparrow cannot fall to the ground without his notice, is it possible that an empire can rise without his aid? We have been assured, Sir, in the sacred writings, that "Except the Lord build the house, they labour in vain that build it." I firmly believe this, and I also believe that without his concurring aid we shall proceed in this political building no better than the builders of Babel.[1]

Three Encouraging Truths

There are people who understand the futility of life, even without knowing God, and despair is the result. People who commit suicide have confessed the futility of a godless life in the most extreme way imaginable. Others who are less extreme simply drop out of the race. Timothy Leary expressed this philosophy for the drug culture of the 1960s by the slogan "Tune in, turn on, drop out." The Bible shows a better way.

1. *God works.* God himself works, so there must be some kind of work that is meaningful. God worked on each of the six days of creation to bring light out of darkness; separate dry land from water; cause the land to produce an amazing variety of trees, shrubs, and plants; create animals, birds, and fish; and eventually make man and give him meaningful work to do. Adam and Eve were to manage the garden, name the animals, and "rule over the fish of the sea and the birds of the air and over every living creature that moves on the ground" (Gen. 1:28).

In Psalm 127 we are reminded that if we are willing, "*the Lord* builds the house" and "*the Lord* watches over the city" (v. 1, italics added). In other words, the work of God did not stop on the seventh day of creation when God "rested from all his work" (Gen. 2:2). God continues to work and works constantly. Part of what God does is work in, with, and through those who are working for him and in his name. Eugene Peterson says that one of the reasons Christians read the Bible repeatedly and carefully is to find out how God works in us and in the world "so that we can work in the name of Jesus Christ."[2]

2. *God makes our work meaningful.* If the architects, carpenters, roofers, bricklayers, electricians, and carpenters labor without any thought of God and apart from him, the buildings they erect will be meaningless. But if they work with God and for his glory, the structures they build will not be in vain. God's blessing will be on the workers, and, like God himself, they will be able to look at their work and say, "That is good." If the watchmen stand guard without any consideration of God, their protective oversight will be useless and the city will be overthrown. But if they watch with God in mind and for him, then God will protect the city himself, and they will reflect on their security and say, "That is good." It is the same with whatever we are doing. Without the Lord, frustration. With the Lord, satisfaction. The important thing is to look to God for the blessing.

3. *God rewards our work for him.* The first stanza of the psalm tells us that work without God is useless. The second stanza lists blessings for those who work for and with God. The change from the negative to the positive occurs in the last line of the stanza, which cites a reward: "He grants sleep to those he loves" (v. 2). This statement suggests that having worked for God and at God's direction, the psalmist now rightly lies down to sleep and sleeps well since he is able to leave the results of his work in God's hands. God, who was building the house, watching over the city, and doing whatever this writer may have been working at personally, also works now to give his worker rest.

Paul told the Colossians, "Whatever you do, work at it with all your heart, as working for the Lord, not for men, since you know that you will receive an inheritance from the Lord as a reward" (Col. 3:23–24). We often receive rewards here, too, of course, though not always. If we serve God, we can be certain of rewards in heaven.

This valuable boon comes after the toil. God works, and we must work. After we have worked, we can lie down to rest and leave the outcome in God's hands.

The Quiet Blessings God Gives

In contrast to the frantic, self-absorbed, and self-sufficient work ethic described in the first stanza (vv. 1–2), the second stanza (vv. 3–5) unfolds the quiet blessing of God on a family through the gift of children. This stanza seems so different from the first, both in its subject matter and its tone, that quite a few scholars believe that it must have been an entirely different psalm originally. They are far from thinking like an ancient Jewish person for whom the well-being of his family was never far removed from every other concern or endeavor. Most of us think of work and our families in nearly separate categories. We live highly compartmentalized lives. But the Jew would ask, Why is the house being built if it is not for the family? and why are the watchmen protecting the city if not for the families that live in it? Then as now, the family was the basic unit and most important element of society. The only difference is that the ancient Jew knew it, and we generally do not. There are a number of truths from these verses and from their position that we need to recognize and appropriate personally.

1. *The growth of a family is God's work.* The second stanza begins by confessing that children are a gift of God, a heritage, and a reward.

> Sons are a heritage from the LORD,
>   children a reward from him (v. 3).

God builds the house and the family to live in it; he guards the city and raises up the families protected by its walls. The psalmist makes this connection by writing as he does. Families are God's idea. It was God who gave the first woman to the first man in Eden and told them, "Be fruitful and increase in number; fill the earth and subdue it" (Gen. 1:28). It follows from this that we must thank God for our families and look to him for wisdom to raise them rightly.

2. *God's blessing on the city begins with his blessing on the family.* Since the family is the basic unit of society, if the family prospers, the nation will prosper too. If families are neglected and decline, the entire society will decline with them. In the United States of America at the present time families are disintegrating, children are neglected, and the frequency and magnitude of violent crimes are soaring. This theme is so important to the psalmist that he carries it over into the next psalm and with the same relationships. Psalm 127 begins with the city and moves to a consideration of the family. Psalm 128 begins with the family but moves to the city.

Psalm 127 speaks of many children and of sons especially, saying that a large number of sons is a blessing since they will be able to stand by their father and defend him when "they contend with their enemies in the gate" (v. 5). We may perceive the numbers a bit differently today, when large numbers of children are not necessarily an asset to a family. On a farm perhaps they would be, where they could work the fields, but not necessarily in an urban environment, and not when the cost of a college education for just one child is approaching $100,000 and is supposed to be $200,000 by the time today's toddlers become teens. Nor are sons a greater blessing than daughters in today's world.

But those are contemporary matters. Details aside, the point of Psalm 127 stands: Children are a blessing from God, and they with their parents are among the vital foundation blocks of a healthy, thriving society. God's blessing on the city begins with his blessing on the family, and where our families stand, our cities will stand too.

3. *The growth of families is slow and unpretentious.* Friends may take notice and celebrate the birth of a baby, a new addition to a family. They may help to celebrate a child's birthday or observe a special event like a high school graduation, but mostly the growth of a family goes unnoticed by other people, sometimes even by the father and mother, because it is slow and unspectacular. It is a blessing that builds over time. That is the way God usually works, isn't it? God works slowly but surely, like the German proverb says: *langsam aber sicher.* Yet this slow and unspectacular blessing is a true blessing and a biblical pattern.

There is an excellent example in God's gift of children to Abraham, the father of the Old Testament covenant people. God told Abraham that he would have descendants "as numerous as the stars in the sky and as the sand on the seashore" (Gen. 22:17) and that he would be the "father of many nations" (Gen. 17:5), but it was many years before Abraham and Sarah had Isaac, the son of God's promise. In fact, they were both past the age of having children, Abraham one hundred years old and Sarah ninety, when they had Isaac. It required a miracle. Even after Isaac the growth of the family was slow. Isaac had only two children, Esau and Jacob. In Jacob's generation, the third, there were twelve sons, the patriarchs of the Jewish tribes. Even then it was not until after four hundred years of terrible slavery in Egypt and under the most oppressive circumstances that the nation grew to the million or more persons who eventually came out of Egypt under the leadership of Moses.

The same is true of the people of the new covenant. Jesus called twelve disciples. They carried the gospel to others, but it was only after several generations and as a result of much difficult and unpretentious effort that the church took firm root and spread throughout the Roman world.

4. *We cannot raise our families without God.* If it is a vain act to build a house without God or watch over a city without depending on God to preserve it, then it is even greater folly to try to raise a family without God. A house is at least an inanimate object that will benefit from sound workmanship, and threats to an ancient city were mostly only from enemies outside the city. But what about ourselves and our children? We carry the seeds of our destruction within us. We are sinful people, with rebellious spirits and an inborn tendency to turn our backs on God. Like ourselves, our children are also rebellious, obstinate, self-centered, and wayward.

We must seek God's help and do everything we are told to do in order to raise our children well. We need to pray for our children, teach them the Bible, bring them to church, and above all set an example by living for God ourselves. If we do this, the work expended on our families will not be worthless. On the contrary, God will bless us and our children too.

The City of God

Thus far we have been thinking of houses, cities, and families literally, as we should, since this is the way the psalmist obviously intends his words to be taken; but these are pilgrim psalms, and we can hardly apply them to ourselves without thinking of our own Christian lives. For us the house that is being built is God's spiritual temple, composed not of earthly materials but of "living stones" (1 Peter 2:5). The city is not Jerusalem, important as it has been as a symbol of God's presence in this world, but the heavenly "city with foundations, whose architect and builder is God" (Heb. 11:10). The family involved is not our mere physical family but the whole spiritual family of those who belong to Jesus Christ (John 1:12–13).

It is spiritual work in which we are engaged as Christian people. We are engaged in important projects, but our effort will be useless if we are not guided and blessed by God. I relate two of our contemporary works to verse 1: first, building a ministry, which often becomes merely a money-making business; and second, defending the faith against false teaching, which often becomes a self-serving and self-promoting crusade. These efforts are useless unless God builds our spiritual house and defends our spiritual city.

As for families, well, the engendering and birth of new spiritual children is God's work, and we must look to him to do it. In our society it is possible, I suppose, to have too many physical children, but it is never possible to have too many spiritual children. Therefore, blessed is the man or woman—or church or nation—whose quiver is full of them.

Psalm 128

God's Blessing on the Home

Blessed are all who fear the LORD,
*   who walk in his ways.*
You will eat the fruit of your labor;
*   blessings and prosperity will be yours.*
Your wife will be like a fruitful vine
*   within your house;*
your sons will be like olive shoots
*   around your table.*
Thus is the man blessed
*   who fears the LORD.*

May the LORD bless you from Zion
*   all the days of your life;*
may you see the prosperity of Jerusalem,
*   and may you live to see your children's children.*

Peace be upon Israel.

verses 1–6

*B*lessing is a wonderful word. In spiritual matters it has to do with God's particular favors to his people. Because God is generous and great, his blessings are generous and great as well. Once we have begun to experience them they seem to be without limit. God's blessings go on and on, both here and in the life to come.

Book Five of the Psalter

Blessing is the unifying word of Psalm 128, where in most of our English translations the related words "blessed," "blessings," and "bless" occur four times (vv. 1, 2, 4, 5). Only verses 3 and 6 are without it. In Hebrew two rich words are used, *asher* in the first part of the psalm (vv. 1–2) and *barak* in the second part (vv. 4–5). The last verses are a specific blessing pronounced on the man who walks in God's ways.

Psalm 127 talked about God's blessing on the family, saying that sons are "like arrows in the hands of a warrior" and that the man who has many sons is blessed: "Blessed is the man whose quiver is full of them" (Ps. 127:5). In this psalm the words about God's blessing begun in Psalm 127 continue, which is why the psalms come together as they do. In the former, God's blessing was on a man and his sons. Here we also have mention of the man's wife and children, and even of his children's children. So the earlier blessing is extended throughout the whole family and to several generations, even to the whole people of God.

Kidner says, "The quiet blessings of an ordered life are traced from the center outwards in this psalm, as the eye travels from the godly man to his family and finally to Israel. Here is simple piety with its proper fruit of stability and peace."[1] This psalm deals first with the God-fearing man or woman, second with the God-fearing family, and last of all with the God-fearing city or nation.

The God-Fearing Man or Woman

Since this psalm has so much to say about God's blessings, we are not surprised to find that it begins with a blessing, like the Psalter itself, which starts with Psalm 1 ("Blessed is the man . . ."), or like Christ's beatitudes at the beginning of the Sermon on the Mount. Psalm 1 pronounces a blessing on the man who does not follow in the way of wicked persons but delights in the Law of the Lord instead (vv. 1–2). In the Sermon on the Mount Jesus pronounces a blessing on the poor in spirit, those who mourn, the meek, those who hunger and thirst for righteousness, the merciful, the pure in heart, the peacemakers, and those who are persecuted because of righteousness (see Matt. 5:3–10). In the first verse of Psalm 128 the blessings of adequate material prosperity and family happiness are promised to the man who does two things: (1) fear, or reverence, God (Solomon said, "The fear of the LORD is the beginning of wisdom," Prov. 9:10); and (2) walk in God's ways.

The fear of the Lord is hammered home again in verse 4: "Thus is the man blessed who fears the LORD."

There is an important balance between this psalm and the earlier one. In Psalm 127 the psalmist wanted to show that all blessings are attributable to God alone. Unless God is working in us and with us, every human endeavor is in vain. In Psalm 128 the poet reminds us that there are nevertheless several important responsibilities that rest on the person who would partake of God's blessings. In short, he must fear God and obey him.

1. *The fear of the Lord.* Later on in this psalm it is clear that it is addressed primarily to the godly man, the head of his household. It speaks of his work, his wife, his sons, and his children's children. Even though the psalm is addressed to a husband and father primarily, it is important to see that the blessing promised in verse 1 is for "all." That is, it is for anyone who will reverence God. A family is a true gift of God, but if God does not give a person a family, there will be other blessings.

What does it mean to fear the Lord? It is customary to say, when Bible teachers are talking about the fear of the Lord, that fear does not mean being afraid. The intent of the word is reverence or respect. Yet *Webster's Ninth Collegiate Dictionary* calls respect "a *profound* reverence or awe, especially toward God" (italics added), therefore fear, at least in the sense of holy awe, is not far from what we are talking about as a proper God-directed attitude.

God must be taken seriously. He must not be trifled with. He must be, as he actually is, the center of everything we are, think, or aspire to do. He must be our starting point for every project, the strength we seek for every valuable endeavor, the one we earnestly desire to please and honor as our goal.

There is no point at which the profound difference between the world and those who are truly God's people is more radical than here. For those who think as the world does, God is a plaything of the mind and spiritual realities are mere "God-talk." For the world the only meaningful reality is what can be seen, felt, and measured by the senses. In other words, rather than being spiritual in their thinking, the people of the world are secularists, particularly in our day.

"Secular" comes from the Latin word *saeculum,* meaning "this age." So people who are secular, as opposed to being spiritual, are people whose mental boundaries are limited by this place and time. I often say that the clearest expression of pure secularism that I have ever come across is Carl Sagan's line in *Cosmos,* the television series, when he looked out at the splendors of God's starry nighttime heavens and declared, "The cosmos is all that is or was or ever will be." That statement is the exact opposite of what the psalmist said: "The heavens declare the glory of God; the skies proclaim the work of his hands" (Ps. 19:1). Francis Schaeffer called secularism operating in a closed universe, a universe containing nothing spiritual, nothing beyond itself.

Christian thinking is altogether different. Harry Blamires is an Englishman who was a student and then a friend of C. S. Lewis. He wrote a book called *The Christian Mind* in which he said, "To think secularly is to think within a frame of reference bounded by the limits of our life on earth; it is to keep one's calculations rooted in this-worldly criteria. To think Christianly is to accept all things with the mind as related, directly or indirectly, to man's eternal destiny as the redeemed and chosen child of God." The psalmist is directing us to begin with God, continue with God, and end with God, and to do so in all our thoughts and actions.

2. *Walking in God's ways.* Merely thinking about God is not enough in itself. Right thinking leads to right acting, which is why the psalm goes on to say that those who are blessed are not merely those "who fear the Lord" but also those "who walk in his ways." On *The Bible Study Hour,* my radio program, I describe our purpose as "preparing people to think and act biblically."

Enoch was a man who walked with God. In fact, in Genesis 5, the place in the Bible where we meet him for the first time, we are told twice in the space of just four verses that Enoch "walked with God": "When Enoch had lived 65 years, he became the father of Methuselah. And after he became the father of Methuselah, Enoch walked with God 300 years and had other sons and daughters. Altogether, Enoch lived 365 years. Enoch walked with God; then he was no more, because God took him away" (Gen. 5:21–24). Three hundred years is a long time to walk with God. It is no casual stroll. But that is what Enoch did and is remembered for.

What did he do during those three centuries? Jude says that Enoch was a preacher and that he obeyed God by prophesying judgment to those who lived on earth before the flood of Noah's day. His message was, "See, the Lord is coming with thousands upon thousands of his holy ones to judge everyone, and to convict all the ungodly of all the ungodly acts they have done in the ungodly way, and of all the harsh words ungodly sinners have spoken against him" (Jude 14–15). This could hardly have been a popular sermon, especially at a time when people were banding together to build cities and develop other tangible forms of civilization, as Genesis 4 indicates they were. Nevertheless, this is what walking with God meant for Enoch. It is a reminder that a Christian walk, while at heart chiefly a matter of the individual and God, is never a purely private matter and always involves how we act with and what we say to other people. It concerns how faithful we are to the truths God has made known to us in Scripture.

A faithful walk is what pleases God, for the bottom line of this story, as it is recorded in Hebrews 11:5, is that Enoch "was commended as one who pleased God." He feared God, walked in his ways, and was commended by him. It should be God's verdict on the life and walk of every Christian.

God's Blessing on Our Work

Having explained what the God-fearing person will do in order to share in God's blessings, the psalmist next explains in broad categories what some of those blessings are. The first is a blessing on our work. If you will fear God and walk in his ways, he says, then "you will eat the fruit of your labor" and "blessings and prosperity will be yours" (v. 2).

The previous psalm says that everything we do will be in vain unless the Lord is in it. The builders will build in vain; the watchmen will watch in vain; the family will be established in vain. Starting from the other side of this truth, Psalm 128 declares that if we fear and obey God, then nothing we do will be in vain. Our labors will bear fruit; our projects will prosper; even our families will thrive. We may not see all the blessing, and there will always be difficulties, but we will thrive.

The words "eat the fruit of your labor" are referring to what Jesus was thinking of when he taught us to pray, saying, "Give us today our daily bread" (Matt. 6:11), that is, that God's provision of what we need to live day by day is linked to our labors. In Genesis 3:19 man was condemned to eat bread by the sweat of his brow, that is, by the curse of difficult labor. In Psalm 128, while work is still necessary, the curse is turned into a blessing by God's promise that if the God-fearing man or woman does work, that person will eat bread as God provides it.

Our spiritual work will thrive too! Paul encouraged us to believe so when he wrote, "Therefore, my dear brothers, stand firm. Let nothing move you. Always give yourselves fully to the work of the Lord, because you know that your labor in the Lord is not in vain" (1 Cor. 15:58).

The God-Fearing Family

I imagine that anyone who has ever tried to raise a family comes to the Bible's pictures of domestic joy with a certain amount of skepticism. There is good reason for it. Families are made up of people; people are sinners; and sin disrupts even the best of relationships. Psalm 128 is not promising utopia. When it speaks of the God-fearing, fruitful family, as it does in verse 3, it is not implying that there will never be difficulties any more than it is promising material blessing, as it does in verse 2, without the frustrations and even failures of physical work. Of course there will be problems, but if a man truly fears and obeys God, God will bless him with a fruitful wife and prospering children.

Are there exceptions? Yes, otherwise every child who disobeys his or her parents and dishonors the family could be excused on the grounds that the failure was that of the child's father or mother. Nor is every loud, ignorant, crude, or disagreeable wife the husband's failure. This is wisdom literature, after all. It is in the same category as Proverbs 22:6, which says,

> Train a child in the way he should go,
> and when he is old he will not turn from it.

This verse does not mean that no properly raised child will ever rebel against his or her background. The children of godly parents can and often do rebel. What it does mean is that *as a rule* godly training issues in godly lives. As the twig is bent, so grows the tree. That is the kind of thing being said in this psalm: *As a rule* the person who is God-fearing and tries to obey God will be blessed with a God-fearing and obedient family. The psalmist uses two colorful images to describe this fruitful family.

1. *The wife: "like a fruitful vine."* This image does not mean simply that the wife will produce lots of children, though children are described as blessings and a wife who had many children usually reckoned herself as greatly blessed by God. We see how important bearing children was in the ancient world by the dismay of Sarah (the mother of Isaac), Rachel (the mother of Joseph and Benjamin), and Hannah (the mother of Samuel) before they had these sons and were childless. Bearing many children is part of the picture, but it is not the whole.

Actually, in the Bible the vine with its grapes and the wine that is made from them is a symbol of refreshment and lavish enjoyment, including sexual enjoyment (see Song of Songs 7:8–9; Judg. 9:13), and it is linked to times of national and family celebration (see Joel 3:18; Amos 9:13–14; John 2:1–10). Wine stands for harvest abundance at the end of a long, dry summer. It "gladdens the heart of man" (Ps. 104:15). The psalm is promising that however hard the day-to-day work in the fields may be for a laboring man, to come home to a good wife is somewhat like coming home to harvest. It is a time to forget the hard summer work and enjoy God's bounty.

2. *The children: "like olive shoots around your table."* Olive trees take a long time to mature and become profitable. Patiently cultivated, they become quite valuable and continue to produce a profitable crop for centuries, longer perhaps than any other fruit-producing tree or plant. The interesting thing about these two images, vines and olive plants, is that they are biblical symbols of the abundant life. They are not food staples like wheat or corn. They symbolize rich blessing.

Blessing on the Two Cities

In the last stanza of this psalm the family focus broadens out to embrace the larger people of God and even the city in which they live. This stanza is a reminder that however blessed we or our families may be personally, that blessing is always incomplete unless it embraces other people too. It must include those living around us, as well as generation after generation down the long road of life.

Here the psalmist seems to step back from addressing the individual man and his family to speak from the perspective of the whole. He asks God to bless them as part of his overall blessing on all his people.

> May the LORD bless you from Zion
>> all the days of your life;
> may you see the prosperity of Jerusalem,
>> and may you live to see your children's children (vv. 5–6).

When the Jews were carried into exile in Babylon, Jeremiah had a word for them from God concerning their new situation:

Build houses and settle down; plant gardens and eat what they produce. Marry and have sons and daughters; find wives for your sons and give your daughters in marriage, so that they too may have sons and daughters. Increase in numbers there; do not decrease. Also, seek the peace and prosperity of the city to which I have carried you into exile. Pray to the LORD for it, because if it prospers, you too will prosper (Jer. 29:5–7).

In Psalm 128 the writer has advanced from the well-being of the individual to his environment as the only way, in the long run, that the family can be blessed. If it was a necessary emphasis in Babylon, which was a notoriously pagan city, how much more should it be true of Jerusalem, which was the capital and spiritual homeland of the newly reconstituted people?

For the Jews, Jerusalem was both a secular and spiritual capital. We likewise are members both of a secular and spiritual city, what Saint Augustine called the City of God and the city of man. Some Christians have withdrawn from man's city, that is, from their secular responsibilities, because they think they should have nothing to do with anything that is godless. Those who have done so need to hear the prophet's advice: "Build houses and settle down; plant gardens. . . . Seek the peace and prosperity of the city. . . . Pray to the LORD for it, because if it prospers, you too will prosper." Christians should reside in our cities and work for their good. Just as our families are a blessing to the city—the city needs sound, wholesome, productive families more than any other single thing—so will the city bless us, if it prospers. If it does not, then we will suffer too even if we attempt to escape its influence by going someplace far away and more attractive.

Who will help if we do not? Ronald J. Sider put it in stark terms, "Tens of thousands of evangelicals ought to move back into the city. . . . If one percent of evangelicals living outside the inner city had the faith and courage to move in town, evangelicals would fundamentally alter the history of urban America."[2]

If what was needed in Babylon was necessary for Jerusalem too, and for our cities, then what is required is even more necessary for the spiritual city of which we are a part. The church is that city. It is the channel of God's grace, essential for our spiritual health. So we can never be merely individualistic believers; we need each other. Therefore, let us pray for our church, and let us work for its good too. If it prospers, we will prosper. If God is blessing there, we will be blessed.

Psalm 129

Struck Down, but Not Destroyed

> *They have greatly oppressed me from my youth—*
> *let Israel say—*
> *they have greatly oppressed me from my youth,*
> *but they have not gained the victory over me.*
> *Plowmen have plowed my back*
> *and made their furrows long.*
> *But the LORD is righteous;*
> *he has cut me free from the cords of the wicked.*
>
> *May all who hate Zion*
> *be turned back in shame.*
> *May they be like grass on the housetops,*
> *which withers before it can grow;*
> *with it the reaper cannot fill his hands,*
> *nor the one who gathers fill his arms.*
> *May those who pass by not say,*
> *"The blessing of the LORD be upon you;*
> *we bless you in the name of the LORD."*
>
> *verses 1–8*

Whereas most nations tend to look back on what they have achieved, Israel reflects here on what she has survived," says Derek Kidner as he begins his study of this psalm.[1] It seems a strange thing to say or do, bordering even on paranoia, but it is not strange when you think of Israel's history. The Jews are the longest-enduring distinct ethnic people on the planet. They have been slandered, hated, persecuted, expelled, pursued, and murdered throughout their long existence, but they have survived intact. In fact, many are now back in their own traditional homeland of Israel. They are a brilliant, talented people, but survival has been their chief achievement.

Suffering and Survival

Near the end of the last century Frederick the Great, the king of Prussia, was having a discussion with his chaplain about the truthfulness of the Bible. The king had become skeptical and unbelieving, largely due to Voltaire, the famous French rationalist skeptic. He said to his chaplain, "If your Bible is really true, it ought to be capable of very brief proof. So often when I have asked for proof of the inspiration of the Bible I have been given some enormous volume that I have neither the time nor disposition to read. If your Bible is really from God, you should be able to demonstrate the fact simply. Forget long arguments. Give me the proof of the Bible's inspiration in a word."

The chaplain replied, "Your Majesty, it is possible for me to answer your request quite literally. I can give you the proof you ask for in a single word."

Frederick looked at the chaplain skeptically and asked, "What is this magic word that carries such a weight of proof?"

The chaplain answered, "'Israel,' your Majesty." Frederick, the story goes, was silent.

The intent of the chaplain's argument is what Psalm 129 describes, the survival of the Jews in spite of centuries—even millennia—of persecutions, thanks solely to the sovereign will and protecting presence of God. Nothing else can explain the Jews' survival.

This psalm is a lot like Psalm 124 in its theme and form, especially in its call for repetition of the opening line by someone like a cantor: "If the LORD had not been on our side—let Israel say—if the LORD had not been on our side when men attacked us . . ." At this point the people are presumably with him, repeating or singing the psalm, which describes their deliverance and survival by God.

In Psalm 129 the cantor calls, "They have greatly oppressed me from my youth—let Israel say—" And the people begin, "They have greatly oppressed me from my youth, but they have not gained the victory over me" (vv. 1–2).

Israel's "youth" was the time when the nation was first coming into existence in Egypt. Hosea quotes God as referring to the Egyptian years this way: "When Israel was a child, I loved him, and out of Egypt I called my son" (Hosea 11:1). These were years of persecution and oppression, as the Pharaoh first extracted hard slave labor from the people and then, when he perceived that they were growing in numbers anyway, began to kill the newly born male children. Moses, the emancipator, was born and survived in these latter days of this excessively cruel oppression.

It was not only *in* her youth that Israel was oppressed and suffered, but it was also *from* her youth, as the psalmist writes. That is, it was from the earliest days of Israel's existence until the time the psalm was written and beyond. In the days of the judges, Israel was oppressed by the many hostile nations that surrounded the small but thriving state: the Philistines, Syrians, Moabites, Ammonites, Edomites, and others. We capture a sense of the scope and intensity of this oppression from the early chapters of Amos, which mention in succession the surrounding peoples of Damascus, Gaza, Tyre, Edom, Ammon, and Moab and list the offenses for which they were judged, namely, cruelty, treachery, and wanton destruction.

What about the period of the monarchy, especially that of the later kings? Josiah was killed in an Egyptian invasion led by Pharaoh Necco (see 2 Kings 23:29–30). The northern kingdom of Israel was invaded and harassed by Syrian forces and later destroyed by Assyria's armies under Shalmaneser III (858–824 B.C.), Tiglath-pileser III (745–727 B.C.), Shalmaneser V (727–721 B.C.), and Sargon II (721–705 B.C.). When Samaria fell to Sargon, as it did in 721 B.C., the first year of his reign, the people were deported and the history of the northern kingdom ended.

In 701 B.C. Sennacherib (705–681 B.C.), Sargon's son, invaded Judah (see 2 Kings 18–19; Isaiah 36–37). He was turned back by God's angel, who killed 185,000 Syrian soldiers in one night. Not long after this, after Assyria was replaced by Babylon as the dominant power in the Near East, the armies of Babylon attacked and eventually destroyed Jerusalem and the southern Jewish kingdom. Jerusalem fell in 586 B.C., and the people were carried to Babylon to begin the seventy-year-long exile from which they had only recently returned when this psalm was written.

That is only the history of the Jews up to the time the psalm was written! They have suffered since at the hands of the Greeks and Romans; in the Middle Ages by virtually all the European powers, which expelled them from their territories repeatedly or else confined them to Jewish ghettos; most recently—this is still fresh in our memories—by the Nazi regime with its dreadful extermination policy.

Well may Israel say—"They have greatly oppressed me from my youth, but they have not gained the victory over me."

Why have they not gained the victory? Why has Israel survived? The psalmist seems to hold the answer in poetical suspense until the end of the first stanza, though it has been understood all along. It is not because Israel herself is so strong. It is because of God, who is "righteous" and "has cut [the psalmist] free from the cords of the wicked" (v. 4). "Righteous" means that God is faithful to his covenant with Israel. Cutting "free from the cords" means deliverance from slavery and is a parallel statement to "We have escaped like a bird out of the fowler's snare" in Psalm 124:7.

Judgment on Those Who Hate Zion

The second stanza of this psalm is imprecatory. That is, it asks God to judge those who "hate Zion" and oppress her people.

It always amuses me how some commentators on these passages wriggle and squirm to try to get out from under appeals for judgment that they think are unworthy of a biblical writer. They consider them vindictive and contrary to the spirit of Jesus, who told us to pray for our enemies and those who use us badly (see Matt. 5:44–45). It is true that we are to pray for our enemies. Jesus justifies these prayers on the ground that "God causes his sun to rise on the evil and the good, and sends rain on the righteous and the unrighteous" (v. 45), meaning that we are to pray for our enemies because of common grace. This does not mean that God is not going to judge the wicked in due time or that we should not wish that justice might be meted out eventually, especially when those we are praying against are seen to be God's enemies—here, "all who hate Zion"—and not merely our own.

What should we pray for in regard to those who persist in evil? That they should repent and be converted, of course. But if they do not? Surely we are not to pray that they might prosper!

Charles Spurgeon says:

> If this be an imprecation, let it stand; for our heart says "Amen" to it. It is but justice that those who hate, harass, and hurt the good should be brought to nought. Those who confound right and wrong ought to be confounded, and those who turn back from God ought to be turned back. . . . How can we wish prosperity to those who would destroy that which is dearest to our hearts? This present age is so flippant that if a man loves the Savior he is styled a fanatic, and if he hates the powers of evil he is named a bigot. As for ourselves, despite all objectors, we . . . would revive in our heart the old practice of Ebal and Gerizim, where those were blessed who bless God, and those were cursed who make themselves a curse to the righteous. . . . Study a chapter from the "Book of Martyrs," and see if you do not feel inclined to read an imprecatory psalm over Bishop Bonner and Bloody Mary. It may be that some wretched nine-teenth-century sentimentalist will blame you; if so, read another *over him.*[2]

Yet for all this controversy over the imprecatory portions of the psalms, it is striking in this case at least how mild these imprecations are. The psalmist is not asking that those who have harmed Israel be sent to hell, or even that they experience the same sufferings they have inflicted on others. He asks only that they and their designs might not prosper. There are three negative things he wants them to experience:

1. *No honor* (v. 5). The honor Israel's enemies seek is what would come from a military victory, especially if Israel were crushed completely. The psalmist asks that her enemies might be turned back, knowing the shame of defeat instead. Shouldn't we seek defeat for any who are dishonorable or seek the ruin or overthrow of righteous persons? We should pray that they might be defeated and that their failure might be known. We should ask that their shameful characters might be exposed for what they are.

2. *No success* (vv. 6–7). The psalmist uses a quaint but effective image at this point, asking that Zion's enemies might be like grass on the rooftop "which withers before it can grow." In Israel's day the houses had dirt roofs where

seeds might take root, but the soil was shallow, and there was no provision for watering the roof. Any grass that grew on a roof would wither quickly.

Even dried grass can be of some use, however. The stubble of a field that has been harvested of grain can be collected and used for fuel. The psalmist does not want the wicked to have even that small measure of success. He wants their plans to shrivel so completely that the reaper will not find enough of their effort even to fill his hands or gather in his arms to carry home. Can it be wrong for us to pray that the efforts of evil persons might be so unsuccessful that in the end there is nothing at all left of their schemes? Rather, it is the case that we err by being too tolerant and accepting of evil, rather than too firm in our opposition to it.

3. *No blessing* (v. 8). This request is connected to the harvest image of verse 7, for it was common practice to bless those who worked in the fields at harvest time. We have an example in Ruth 2:4, where Boaz arrives in his field and blesses the harvesters, saying, "The LORD be with you." "The LORD bless you," they call back. Is it wrong to withhold prayers for blessings from evil persons? The opposite, to bless evil, would be a betrayal of righteousness and an offense to God.

What has been the end of those who have set themselves against the Lord and his Anointed, those who are, as Derek Kidner writes, "not only choosing the way of hate, which is soul-destroying, but setting themselves against God, which is suicide"?[3] The answer is just that: self-destruction and suicide. We think of Pharaoh, and especially in our days of Adolf Hitler, who committed suicide in his Berlin bunker at the end of World War II.

The Suffering Servant

Whenever we think of anti-Semitism, we cannot miss saying that the ultimate cause of it is not just hatred of a people who have been set apart by God to be different—there are many unique peoples on earth, after all—but rather Satan's hatred of Israel as the people through whom God promised to send the Messiah to destroy both the devil and his works. We have a picture of this connection in Revelation, where the devil is pictured as a terrible dragon, standing before a woman who is about to give birth "so that he might devour her child the moment it was born" (Rev. 12:4). Clearly, the woman stands for Israel, and her child is Jesus Christ.

In this prophetic picture the child is saved by being "snatched up to God and to his throne" (Rev. 12:5), which is where Jesus is now. When we look at this picture in the light of the entire Bible, we understand that although Jesus has defeated the devil and is victorious, Satan nevertheless "got his licks in" on Jesus. It was prophesied that he would, as early as God's words to Satan recorded in Genesis 3: "He will crush your head, and you will strike his heel" (Gen. 3:15). Satan struck at Jesus throughout his entire life, even when Jesus was a child in Bethlehem and Satan goaded Herod to murder the infants of that city in an attempt to exterminate this alleged pretender to his throne. At last Satan succeeded in having Jesus beaten and killed at the time of his arrest, trial, and crucifixion.

This brings us back to the third verse of Psalm 129, which I passed over earlier, the verse in which Israel describes its former mistreatment, saying, "Plowmen have plowed my back and made their furrows long." This is a powerful metaphor, combining the idea of a vicious, painful scourging with the painstaking and thorough effort a farmer would make to plow a field.

This verse describes Jesus, the Messiah, as well as the Jews from whom he came. Jesus was beaten literally. The prophet Isaiah, who anticipated Jesus' harsh treatment, wrote, "With his stripes we are healed" (Isa. 53:5 KJV). He continues,

> He was pierced for our transgressions,
>   he was crushed for our iniquities;
> the punishment that brought us peace was upon him. . . .
>
> We all, like sheep, have gone astray,
>   each of us has turned to his own way,
> and the LORD has laid on him
>   the iniquity of us all (Isa. 53:5–6).

This attack on Jesus was a real oppression, to use our psalm's word (vv. 1–2). Like Israel, Jesus might well have said, "They have greatly oppressed me from my youth." Jesus would certainly have added also, as the psalm does, "but they have not gained the victory over me."

How could they? Jesus is God, the only sovereign ruler of the universe. Therefore, although Satan and the united kings of the earth should gather together "against the LORD and against his Anointed One" (Ps. 2:2), God the heavenly King only laughs at them, for he has rescued us from sin by Christ's death, raised Jesus from his dark tomb, and lifted him to glory, therefore announcing triumphantly, "I have installed my King on Zion, my holy hill" (Ps. 2:6).

The victory we are speaking of here will never go to Satan. It goes to Jesus. In fact, it is his already, for he has triumphed, and we now shout,

> The kingdom of the world has become the kingdom of our
>   Lord and of his Christ,
>   and he will reign for ever and ever (Rev. 11:15).

Treasure in Jars of Clay

Because Jesus lives we also live, and because he has been victorious we shall be victorious too. Victory is not gained by avoiding our share of this world's oppression. Jesus said, "In this world you will have trouble," but added, "Take heart! I have overcome the world" (John 16:33). We must triumph as he did, enduring oppression and ultimately passing through the portal of death to resurrection.

Often in the long course of history Christians have been forced to cry, as Israel did, "They have greatly oppressed me from my youth!" It is the echoing cry of God's people down the long corridors of human history. However, underneath that cry and sometimes even over it we also hear the confession, "But they have not gained the victory over me."

Why is this pattern of oppression and suffering so necessary, a pattern observed in Israel, in the life of Christ, and in the lives of Christ's followers? The answer is, So the world might know that our power is not from ourselves, but from God.

The apostle Paul suffered many things as the first missionary to the Gentiles. He was repeatedly imprisoned, beaten, stoned, shipwrecked, starved, and threatened, but here is what he wrote to the young believers at Corinth to encourage them:

> We have this treasure [the gospel] in jars of clay to show that this all-surpassing power is from God and not from us. We are hard pressed on every side, but not crushed; perplexed, but not in despair; persecuted, but not abandoned; struck down, but not destroyed. We always carry around in our body the death of Jesus, so that the life of Jesus may also be revealed in our body. For we who are alive are always being given over to death for Jesus' sake, so that his life may be revealed in our mortal body (2 Cor. 4:7–11).

There is a forceful Christian battle cry, composed in Latin and placed next to the burning bush: *Nec tamen consumebatur!* It means "Yet not consumed." God's people may be oppressed, but they are never consumed and so can cry, "Thanks be to God! He gives us the victory through our Lord Jesus Christ" (1 Cor. 15:57).

Psalm 130

Luther's "Pauline Psalm"

Out of the depths I cry to you, O LORD;
O Lord, hear my voice.
Let your ears be attentive
to my cry for mercy.

If you, O LORD, kept a record of sins,
O Lord, who could stand?
But with you there is forgiveness;
therefore you are feared.

I wait for the LORD, my soul waits,
and in his word I put my hope.
My soul waits for the Lord
more than watchmen wait for the morning,
more than watchmen wait for the morning.

O Israel, put your hope in the LORD,
for with the LORD is unfailing love
and with him is full redemption.
He himself will redeem Israel
from all their sins.

verses 1–8

People who have read extensively on the psalms notice that writers tend to get shorter in their treatments as they get toward the end of the Psalter. They write many pages on the earlier psalms, less for those in the middle, and few for those at the end. I do not know why this should be, perhaps because they get tired of writing or run out of things to say, but I have noticed it. Ever since leaving Psalm 119, the longest in the Psalter, I have found that other writers' treatments of the psalms have been shorter.

Until Psalm 130! Psalm 130 is a profound psalm, and because it is a profound psalm, it has been profoundly treated.[1]

A Psalm Greatly Loved

The reason for these extensive treatments is that many of God's people down through history have considered this psalm blessed and have loved it as a result. It is blessed because it contains a penetrating statement of the gospel.

Most of us know the story of John Wesley's conversion on the evening of May 24, 1738, when he attended a meeting in a little nonconformist chapel on Aldersgate Street in London and heard someone reading from the Introduction to Martin Luther's work on Romans. It was the occasion when he described his heart as being "strangely warmed." What is not so well known is that on the afternoon of that same day Wesley attended a vesper service at St. Paul's Cathedral, in the course of which Psalm 130 was sung as an anthem. Wesley was greatly moved by the anthem, and it became one of the means God used to open his heart to the gospel of salvation.[2]

Martin Luther loved Psalm 130. He called it one of the "Pauline Psalms" (with Psalms 32, 51, 143) because of its offer of forgiveness by grace apart from human works. In fact, it is one of the best expositions in the Old Testament of the way of salvation by grace on the basis of Christ's atonement. Luther wrote a fine exposition of this psalm as well as a hymn based on it. The hymn begins,

> From depths of woe I raise to thee
>   The voice of lamentation;
> Lord, turn a gracious ear to me
>   And hear my supplication:
> If thou iniquities dost mark,
> Our secret sins and misdeeds dark,
>   O who shall stand before thee?

Psalm 130 is a penitential psalm, the sixth of seven.[3] It starts in the lowest depths of despair, but it progresses steadily upward until, as Derek Kidner writes, "at the end there is encouragement for the many from the experience of the one."[4] In this sense Psalm 130 is itself a literal Song of Ascents, for it climbs from the abyss of depression to the high ground of steadfast hope. We see this progression mirrored in each of the psalm's four stanzas as they deal in turn with sorrow over sin, forgiveness, faith in God, and testimony.

In the Depths

The psalm begins with the writer in "the depths" or, as the Latin says, *de profundis*. In Hebrew being in "the depths" refers specifically to being caught in dangerous and deep waters, a powerful image for a people who were largely land-based and not at all seafaring. This image occurs many places in the Old Testament (e.g., Isa. 51:10; Ezek. 27:34), but nowhere more powerfully than in Psalm 69:1–2.

> Save me, O God,
>   for the waters have come up to my neck.
> I sink in the miry depths,
>   where there is no foothold.
> I have come into the deep waters;
>   the floods engulf me.

What is it that has brought the writer of Psalm 130 into this dangerous condition? Eugene Peterson thinks the problem being discussed is suffering and understands the psalm to be offering dignity by immersing suffering in God. The answer to suffering, as he sees it, is hope through learning to wait on the Lord.[5]

I think Peterson misses the point here. It is not suffering that is troubling the psalmist in this psalm; it is sin. The psalmist writes about "a record of sins" in verse 3, forgiveness in verse 4, and redemption in verses 7–8. John Owen writes,

> He cries out under the weight and waves of his sins. This the ensuing psalm makes evident. Desiring to be delivered from these depths out of which he cried, he deals with God wholly about mercy and forgiveness; and it is sin alone from which forgiveness is a deliverance. The doctrine also that he preached upon his delivery is that of mercy, grace and redemption, as is manifest from the close of the psalm. . . . Sin is the disease, affliction only a symptom of it.[6]

Our problem today, especially in appreciating a psalm like this, is that most of us do not have much awareness of sin. We live most of our lives with very little awareness of God, and where God has been abolished an awareness of sin is inevitably abolished also, because sin is defined only in relationship to God. It is "any want of conformity unto, or transgression of, the law of God" (*Westminster Shorter Catechism,* answer to question 14).

We need to recover a sense of sin. We need to discover how desperate our condition is apart from God. We need to know that God's wrath is not an outmoded theological construct but a terrible and impending reality. We need to come out of our sad fantasy world and begin to tremble before the awesome holiness of our almighty Judge.

Suppose you *are* aware of your sin. Suppose you are one of those apparently rare people in our day who truly *are* troubled by their many great wrongs and transgressions. Suppose you *are* in "the depths." Where can you turn for help? You will not find it in yourself certainly, any more than the

writer of this psalm found it in himself. The only source of help for you is
God, and in his mercy, at that. You need to prostrate yourself before him
and ask for help. In other words, your stance must be the exact opposite of
that defiant cry of William Henley (1849–1903), who wrote,

> Out of the night that covers me,
> Black as the Pit from pole to pole,
> I thank whatever gods may be
> For my unconquerable soul.[7]

God pity any man or woman who thinks like that. If you are looking
inward, you are only going to sink deeper and deeper into the black abyss
until you are lost forever. What you need is God, who alone is able to pull
you out, set your feet on a rock, and establish your goings (see Ps. 40:2 KJV).
The psalmist knew he needed God, which is why he called out: "O Lord,
hear my voice. Let your ears be attentive to my cry for mercy" (v. 2).

Forgiveness

Sin is the problem, then, and what the psalmist seeks is forgiveness,
which God gives freely. How terrible it would be if all we could expect of
God is a record of our sins. No one could stand before God then, as Paul
wrote in Romans 3, citing Psalms 14 and 53,

> There is no one righteous, not even one;
>   there is no one who understands,
>   no one who seeks God.
> All have turned away,
>   they have together become worthless;
> there is no one who does good,
>   not even one (Rom. 3:10–12; cf. Pss. 14:1–3; 53:1–3).

Ah, but there is good news. That good news, that gospel, is that there is
forgiveness in God. *"But with you there is forgiveness"* (v. 4). Let that be said
again: *"But with you there is forgiveness."* What a wonderful word it is, this
"but"! You may not find forgiveness with other people. Your husband or
your wife may not forgive you, if you have wronged him or her. Your children may not forgive you. Your coworkers may not forgive you. You may not
even be able to forgive yourself. There is one who will, and that one is God.
Write down where you can see and reflect on it often: Our God is a forgiving God. He will not remember our transgressions against us. He will
remove them as far as the east is from the west—if we ask him for mercy.

Moses asked to see God and received this defining revelation of what
God is like: "The LORD, the LORD, the compassionate and gracious God,
slow to anger, abounding in love and faithfulness, maintaining love to thou-

sands, and forgiving wickedness, rebellion and sin" (Exod. 34:6–7). What a wonderful word for Moses! What wonderful, joyful, comforting good news for anybody!

This is such important good news that I am tempted to spend the rest of this chapter on it. I won't, but let me mention four things about God's forgiveness.

1. *God's forgiveness is inclusive.* Verse 4 does not say, "There is forgiveness for this sin or that," while leaving out some other sin, perhaps the one you have committed. It sets no limits at all. It says, "There is forgiveness," forgiveness for any sin by anybody. Murder, adultery, lying, stealing, coveting, failing to keep the Lord's Day, taking the name of God in vain, whatever it may be. There is forgiveness with God. You may be utterly ignorant of the Bible. You may not know a single item of theology. Know this at least: "There is forgiveness" with God.

2. *God's forgiveness is for now.* The translators have rightly used the verb "is," putting "But with you there is forgiveness" in the present tense, but the force of the sentence is even stronger in the Hebrew, where there is no verb at all. The Hebrew simply says, "With you forgiveness." You do not have to hope that somehow you might have forgiveness at the last day, at the final judgment, but need to stand in trembling uncertainty until then. You do not have to work for it or earn it; you could never earn it anyway. There is forgiveness now, at this very moment; and it is for you, whoever you may be, wherever you are, or whatever you have done. At this very moment you can pass from death to life and know that your sins have been forgiven forever.

3. *God's forgiveness is for those who want it.* It is there, but you must ask God for it and trust him to give it to you. The writer of the psalm is confessing his sin, not covering it up, which would be a way of pretending that he does not need forgiveness (v. 1). He is asking God for mercy, for he has no claim on God (v. 2). He is believing, or trusting, God, for he says, "With you there is forgiveness" (v. 4). Thousands of people confess that each week in the words of the Apostles' Creed: "I believe . . . in the forgiveness of sins." Have they actually asked God for forgiveness? Many do not even know what the words mean. Do not be among those unbelieving masses. Come to God, and ask him for the forgiveness you need and he provides.

4. *God's forgiveness leads to godly living.* Some have objected to the Bible's teaching about salvation on the grounds that free forgiveness must lead to wickedness. "If God forgives us for anything we do, why shouldn't we just go on sinning?" they argue. It doesn't work that way. The forgiveness we are talking about does not lead to license, as some suppose, but to a heightened reverence for God. It is what verse 4 teaches when it adds to forgiveness the words "therefore you are feared."

Feared? Shouldn't the verse have said "loved"? Well, I would think so until I remember that in the Bible fear has to do with a holy reverence of God that is the essence of true religion. It is what is drawn from us when we know that we have been loved and saved by God in spite of our sin and former disregard of him. Spurgeon, who has a wonderful sermon on this text, translates this verse as, "There is forgiveness with thee, that thou mayest be loved and worshipped and served."[8]

The true and inevitable effects of forgiveness are love and worship and service. By these effects you can measure whether you have actually confessed your sin, believed on God, and been forgiven or are merely presuming on forgiveness without any genuine repentance or faith. Those who have been forgiven are softened and humbled and overwhelmed by God's mercy, and they determine never to sin against such a great and fearful goodness. They do sin, but in their deepest hearts they do not want to, and when they do they hurry back to God for deliverance.

Waiting on God

In the beautiful, poetic third stanza the psalmist says that he is trusting (hoping) in God's Word and waiting for the Lord, indeed, "more than watchmen wait for the morning, more than watchmen wait for the morning" (v. 6).

What specifically is he waiting for? He is not waiting for deliverance from his trouble, which is what Peterson believes the psalm is teaching, for the psalm is not about his troubles; it is about his sin. He is not waiting for forgiveness either, which we might suppose next, for the earlier stanza says he has already found forgiveness; in fact, we see the first result of this discovery in a reverential fear of God. He is waiting for God himself. It is God whom he has offended by his sin, and it is fellowship with God that has been broken and needs to be restored. Notice that the forgiveness does not depend on his feeling forgiven. He is forgiven whether he feels it or not, because he has asked God for it and God has promised to forgive. Now he also wants the intimacy with God that should and will follow, and he is waiting for it. He is waiting in faith.

Trust God Also

The last stanza of this remarkable psalm is extraordinary. Up to this point all the psalmist's sorrow for sin, all his repentance, prayer, faith, and hope in God were centered around himself. In this last stanza, having found forgiveness, he turns to those about him, to Israel, and encourages them to put their "hope in God" too, because of God's nature, because with the Lord is unfailing love and full redemption. (Coverdale wrote "plenteous redemption," a felicitous translation that has been preserved by the King James and Revised Standard Versions.)

In other words, what the psalmist found when he confessed his sin and sought forgiveness from God was not a once-in-a-blue-moon experience. It is something anyone can discover, for it is based on God's nature, which does not change. God is as forgiving now as he has ever been, and he will always be this same forgiving God. Therefore, says the writer, "Put your hope in the LORD" (v. 7).

The psalm ends with a profound promise: "He himself will redeem Israel from all their sins." At this stage in the historical unfolding of God's progressing revelation, the psalmist may not have understood exactly how forgiveness could be provided by a God who is nevertheless also just and must act justly in regard to sin. A just God must punish sin, not forgive it. Paul says this fact about God was not made entirely clear until the death of Jesus, which came centuries later (see Rom. 3:25–26). Even if the psalmist did not understand the specific details of what was involved, he understood a lot, for he is looking ahead to the promised day when God would accomplish an effective redemption from sin's penalty that would justify the forgiveness he had already been giving to all who had trusted him and asked him for it.

We can understand this redemption because it has been accomplished by Jesus Christ and because its meaning has been explained in the Bible. The wages of sin are death (Rom. 6:23), but Jesus took that death in our place, bearing sin's full punishment so that God can forgive us freely and we can be freed from sin's power.

Do you understand how great that gospel is? It is the greatest truth you can ever know. It is the greatest fact of history. Believe it! Turn from your sin, ask God for forgiveness, and know that you will have it through the death of Christ.

Psalm 131

Like a Satisfied Child

My heart is not proud, O LORD,
my eyes are not haughty;
I do not concern myself with great matters
or things too wonderful for me.
But I have stilled and quieted my soul;
like a weaned child with its mother,
like a weaned child is my soul within me.

O Israel, put your hope in the LORD
both now and forevermore.

verses 1–3

It is hard to imagine anyone spending three years with Jesus Christ and still wanting to be important himself, instead of just letting Jesus be important. But the disciples did, and we do too, even after years of exposure to Jesus' teachings.

Matthew tells us something along these lines that happened soon after Jesus' transfiguration. The Lord was healing the sick and teaching, attracting so much attention that the disciples were impressed with themselves just for hanging around with him. They were sure Jesus was going to set up his kingdom very quickly, so they began to wonder which of them would have the most important position in it. They asked him, "Who is greatest in the kingdom of heaven?" (Matt. 18:1). I do not know what kind of answer they expected, but I know that the answer they got was not what they expected. Jesus called a little child and had him stand among them. Then he said, "I tell you the truth, unless you change and become like little children, you will never enter the kingdom of heaven. Therefore, whoever humbles himself like this child is the greatest in the kingdom of heaven" (vv. 3–4).

1144

It was a serious answer. In order to be saved from sin and enter God's kingdom, they had to become like little children, and in order to become like children they had to change, humbling themselves instead of jockeying for "top dog" position.

An Easy Psalm with a Hard Lesson

The person who wrote Psalm 131 had learned that lesson and had changed. In fact, his psalm is a record of what happened and a testimony of the point to which he came when he wrote it. It is a short psalm, only nine lines in three verses, one of the easiest of all psalms to read, but its lesson is one of the hardest to learn. Spurgeon said that it is "a short ladder" yet one that "rises to a great height."[1]

The heading identifies this as another psalm of David. There are four of David's psalms among the Songs of Ascents (Psalms 122, 124, 131, 133), and this is the third. Many scholars, including a large majority of modern ones, do not want to acknowledge David as the author because they consider this specific collection (Psalms 120–34) to have been written after the exile. Yet it is like David in its content and tone, being a humble composition and using humble metaphors. The same writer who compared himself to a sheep under the care of its divine shepherd earlier (Psalms 23) here easily compares himself to a child in its mother's arms.

Franz Delitzsch is one of the best older conservative commentators on the psalms. He thought a later author, not David, wrote Psalm 131 as an intended echo of David's reply to his wife Michal in the incident described in 2 Samuel 6:16–23. When the ark of God was brought to Jerusalem David was so joyful that he danced in the procession dressed only in a common priestly ephod, rather than proceeding in a stately manner clad in his royal robes. Michal despised him for it and called him "a vulgar fellow." But David replied, "I will become even more undignified than this, and I will be humiliated in my own eyes" (2 Sam. 6:22). David was not a person to stand on his honor. He was willing to humble himself (and did humble himself), because he knew that at best he was merely an unprofitable servant of the only true and ever-to-be-exalted Most High God.

If this psalm is by David, why should it appear here among the Songs of Ascents, especially since it does not have any obvious connection with Jerusalem or with those who were on a pilgrimage to it? The best answer seems to be because it follows the previous psalm so naturally. Psalm 130 was about the grace of God in salvation, a grace manifested apart from any human works. This psalm is about humble trust in God, which should follow for those who have been saved. In this sense, it is a pilgrim psalm after all, but the pilgrimage involved is now a spiritual journey in grace.

There are two other links between Psalms 131 and 130. First, both end the same way, telling Israel, "Put your hope in the LORD" (Pss. 130:7; 131:3). Second, the words of personal testimony at the emotional center of each psalm are alike in substance and in form. In each case the line that embodies the psalm's most powerful image is repeated for emphasis and effect. Thus in Psalm 130:6 we read:

> My soul waits for the Lord
>> more than watchmen wait for the morning,
>> more than watchmen wait for the morning.

And in Psalm 131:2 we read:

> But I have stilled and quieted my soul;
>> like a weaned child with its mother,
>> like a weaned child is my soul within me.

This beautiful portrait of the child with its mother also fits in nicely with the pictures of family blessing developed in Psalms 127 and 128.

The Self-Sufficient Self

Psalm 131 is a personal testimony, as I said earlier, and one part of it is its acknowledgment of what David was or was inclined to be before God changed him and he learned to be satisfied with God alone. He speaks of these things negatively in verse 1, saying what he is *not* like now because of God's grace. He must have been inclined to these things once, which is why he is rejecting them.

1. *Pride: "My heart is not proud."* We do not normally think of David as being prideful, and if he was, he certainly mastered this vice early since he was known for his humility later on. Yet David's success in life must have tempted him to be prideful, and it may be that he was inclined to be just a bit conceited in his youth.

There is a suggestion of this possibility in something that happened when his father, Jesse, sent him to his brothers, who were in the Jewish army being threatened by Goliath, the Philistine giant and champion. David was appalled that Goliath should be allowed to defy the armies of the living God, and he expressed his indignation to the soldiers. Eliab, his oldest brother, heard what he was saying and grew angry. "Why did you come down here?" he demanded. "And with whom did you leave those few sheep in the desert? I know how conceited you are and how wicked your heart is; you came down only to watch the battle" (1 Sam. 17:28).

Eliab's accusation was not entirely true. David had been sent to the army by his father; he had not come just to watch the battle. Moreover, we detect a note of jealousy in Eliab's words; he was afraid of Goliath after all, while David was not. Yet family members usually know us and have a way of putting their finger on our deepest flaws, and it may be the case that Eliab also had it right when he accused David of conceit. David was an extraordinary man. It would be a miracle if he were not somewhat impressed with his own unusual abilities—at least when he was a young man.

But David had learned to subdue pride, which is what he claims in verse 1. What is remarkable here is that he is able to claim this with humility, there being no hint of the Pharisee in what he says.[2]

Learning to subdue pride is the most important of all lessons in Christian character, since pride is the most serious and pervasive of all vices. Therefore, the Bible has much to say about humility. Just a few psalms later we read,

> Though the LORD is on high, he looks upon the lowly,
> but the proud he knows from afar (Ps. 138:6).

Proverbs 3:34 is a key text: "He mocks proud mockers but gives grace to the humble." James quotes it in James 4:6: "That is why Scripture says: 'God opposes the proud but gives grace to the humble,'" and so does Peter in 1 Peter 5:5: "All of you, clothe yourselves with humility toward one another, because, 'God opposes the proud but gives grace to the humble.'" James also writes, "Humble yourselves before the Lord, and he will lift you up" (James 4:10). James must have learned the importance of humility from Jesus, for he would have heard Jesus say, "Come to me, all you who are weary and burdened, and I will give you rest. Take my yoke upon you and learn from me, for I am gentle and humble in heart, and you will find rest for your souls" (Matt. 11:28–29).

Some years ago when the American film star John Wayne had his first operation for cancer, I remember seeing a film clip in which he emerged from the hospital claiming soberly but hopefully, "I licked the big *C*," meaning cancer. He hadn't and later died from it, but I want to suggest that each of us need to "lick the big *P*," which is pride. We can do it by doing exactly what Jesus challenged us to do, namely, taking up his yoke and learning from him. Indeed, the closer we get to Jesus the less pride we will have since all true greatness is in him.

2. *Arrogance: "my eyes are not haughty."* Arrogance is an expression of pride. It is the proud who are arrogant, but arrogance goes beyond pride in that it is pride looking down on other people. *Haughty* comes from the word *high*. David is saying, My eyes are not high (or lifted up). This is a quite different way of lifting up one's eyes than in Psalm 121:1, which says, "I lift up my eyes to the hills," meaning that the psalmist is standing below and looking up beyond the hills to God. In Psalm 131 the picture is of a proud person who has moved up to take God's place, from which he is then able to look down on other people.

There is nothing in the record of David's life that would lead us to think he was ever really arrogant, but if God delivered him from pride, which he claims, then God must have delivered him from arrogance too. The important thing is that we should not be arrogant, which we will not be only if we learn to humble ourselves under the hand of God. Peter wrote, "Humble yourselves, therefore, under God's mighty hand, that he may lift you up in due time" (1 Peter 5:6).

3. *Ambition: "I do not concern myself with great matters or things too wonderful for me."* Overcoming ambition does not mean that David did not want to achieve anything or that we should be passive, doing nothing. David is rejecting an ambition that goes beyond what God has for him at any time. For example, David allowed God to give him the kingdom of Israel in God's own time and way, even though the crown had been promised to him years before. David was content to be pursued by Saul for ten years and then to rule over the tiny principality of Hebron for seven more years before eventually becoming ruler of the united kingdom.

In the last chapter I disagreed with Eugene Peterson's treatment of Psalm 130, but here what Peterson says about ambition, particularly about its being the distinct stumbling block to Christian maturity and growth thrown up by our materialistic western culture, is exactly on target. He calls ambition "aspiration gone crazy."[3] He doesn't mean that trying to be your best or working to achieve the most for God and his glory is wrong. It is not wrong; it is right. What is wrong is the ambition to get everything we can get for ourselves, at whatever cost, for our own glory, which is what our civilization fervently teaches us to do.

Peterson says,

> It is . . . difficult to recognize unruly ambition as a sin because it has a kind of superficial relationship to the virtue of aspiration—an impatience with mediocrity, and a dissatisfaction with all things created until we are at home with the Creator, the hopeful striving for the best God has for us—the kind of thing Paul expressed: "I press on toward the goal for the prize of the upward call of God in Christ Jesus" (Phil. 3:14). But if we take the energies that make for aspiration and remove God from the picture, replacing him with our own crudely sketched self-portrait, we end up with arrogance. Robert Browning's fine line on aspiration, "A man's reach should exceed his grasp, or what's a heaven for?" has been distorted to "Reach for the skies and grab everything that isn't nailed down." Ambition is aspiration gone crazy. Aspiration is the channeled, creative energy that moves us to grow in Christ, shaping goals in the Spirit. Ambition takes these same energies for growth and development and uses them to make something tawdry and cheap, sweatily knocking together a Babel when we could be vacationing in Eden.[4]

If we are to be true Christians in this area, we must learn to stand against the distorted values of our culture, knowing that character is more important than career, godliness more important than success, and helping others more important than amassing great wealth.

What David seems to be concerned about in this verse is not so much the *accomplishment of great deeds,* the kind of achievements that usually bring one worldly fame, but rather peering into the hidden purposes of God, which is what the words "great matters" and "things too wonderful for me" usually refer to in the Bible. He is saying he had learned that he did not have to understand everything God was doing in his life or know when he would do it. All he really had to do was trust God.

We also do not have to understand all God is doing in our lives, but we do need to trust him completely. As Deuteronomy 29:29 says, "The secret things belong to the LORD our God, but the things revealed belong to us and to our children forever, that we may follow all the words of this law." Although we need to learn what God has revealed in the Bible for our instruction and obey it, beyond that what we need is to trust God completely for the wise ordering of our lives.

Anselm, the English monk who lived in the eleventh century, prayed, "I do not seek, O Lord, to penetrate thy depths. I by no means think my intellect equal to them: but I long to understand in some degree thy truth, which my heart believes and loves. For I do not seek to understand that I may believe, but I believe, that I may understand."[5] Those words "I believe that I may understand" *(fides quarens intellectum)* were the passion of Anselm's life. They are the opposite of "aspiration gone crazy." They are the expression of a Christian in his right mind.

The Trusting, Born-Again Self

Having spoken of the negatives that once frowned on his life in verse 1 (pride, arrogance, and ambition), David turns next to the right, positive attitude, saying in verse 2 that he had learned to trust God completely like a weaned child who has learned to trust his or her mother. It is not unusual in the Bible to find God pictured as a father (see Deut. 1:31; Hosea 11:1–4; Matt. 6:9), but as far as I know, the only other passages that picture God as a mother are toward the end of Isaiah, where God asks,

> Can a mother forget the baby at her breast
>   and have no compassion on the child she has borne?
> Though she may forget,
>   I will not forget you! (Isa. 49:15).

A few chapters later God says,

> As a mother comforts her child,
>   so will I comfort you (Isa. 66:13).

In these passages the emphasis is on God's determination to remember, care for, and comfort his spiritual children like a mother cares for and comforts the children God has given her. In Psalm 131 the emphasis is on the child, to whom David compares himself. He says that he is "like a weaned child with its mother" (v. 2).

The key word here is "weaned." This word is one reason I have been writing about the *change* to which David is testifying and not merely about the virtues of humility and trust, the opposites of pride and ambition. When David says that his soul is "like a weaned child," he is not saying that he has always been content with God or even merely that he is content with God now. He is reflecting on the difficult weaning process in which a child is broken of its dependence on its mother's milk and is taught to take other foods instead. Weaning is usually accompanied by resistance and struggle on the child's part, even by hot tears, angry accusing glances, and fierce temper tantrums, and it is difficult for the mother. But weaning is necessary if the child is to mature. David is saying that he has come through the weaning process and has learned to trust God to care for him and provide for him, not on David's own terms but on God's terms.

Before he was weaned, David wanted God only for what he could get from God. After he was weaned, having learned that God loved him and would care for him even if it was not exactly the way he anticipated or most wanted, he came to love God for God himself. That was a better and much more mature relationship. Have you learned to love God for himself and not merely for what you can get from him?

The Lesson to Be Drawn

There are few psalms in the Psalter that are more personal than this. Yet even though David is writing about himself and his own experience of learning to trust and love God, he does not leave the psalm there but instead, at the end of the psalm, looks to those about him, to Israel, and challenges them to learn what he learned and "put [their] hope in God."

> O Israel, put your hope in the LORD
> both now and forevermore (v. 3).

Only God is utterly worthy of our hope and will never disappoint us. To know that truth is to be spiritually mature. Sadly many Christians are still infants.

Psalm 132

The Ascent of God's Ark to Zion

O LORD, remember David
  and all the hardships he endured.

He swore an oath to the LORD
  and made a vow to the Mighty One of Jacob:
"I will not enter my house
  or go to my bed—
I will allow no sleep to my eyes,
  no slumber to my eyelids,
till I find a place for the LORD,
  a dwelling for the Mighty One of Jacob."

We heard it in Ephrathah,
  we came upon it in the fields of Jaar:
"Let us go to his dwelling place;
  let us worship at his footstool—
arise, O LORD, and come to your resting place,
  you and the ark of your might.
May your priests be clothed with righteousness;
  may your saints sing for joy."

  verses 1–9

Psalm 132 is about the ascent of the ark of God to Jerusalem in the days of David. It is the longest of the fifteen Songs of Ascents, roughly twice as long as any other, yet it is an appropri-

1151

ate psalm for this collection for two reasons. First, it was sung by pilgrims who were making their way up the steep mountain roads to Jerusalem, tracing the ark's journey. Second, the ark was deposited in the Most Holy Place of the temple, the spiritual focal point of these pilgrimages. Since the psalm deals with the climax of the pilgrimages, it is also appropriately placed toward the end of the collection, being followed only by Psalm 133 (which concerns the unity of God's people) and Psalm 134 (which is about the servants of God who minister continually in the temple).

Two other psalms also seem to mark the coming of the ark to Jerusalem, Psalms 24 and 68, but this is the only psalm that actually mentions the ark. In this case, the emphasis is on David, whose idea it was to bring the ark to Zion. The first half of the psalm (vv. 1–9) is about David's oath in which he promised to bring the ark to Jerusalem. The second half (vv. 11–18) records God's corresponding oath in regard to David, promising him an everlasting dynasty. In the second half the ideas of the first half are repeated, but they are heightened as God characteristically promises to do more than his people either ask or expect. In this way Psalm 132 is an anticipation of Ephesians 3:20–21, which says, "Now to him who is able to do immeasurably more than all we ask or imagine, according to his power that is at work within us, to him be glory in the church and in Christ Jesus throughout all generations, for ever and ever! Amen."

Verse 10 shows that the psalm was not by David—it is an appeal to God in David's name—but by another king who looks back to David and claims God's promise to him. Since verses 8–10 are quoted in 2 Chronicles 6:41–42 as part of Solomon's prayer at the dedication of the temple, the psalm probably dates from Solomon's reign even though the title does not identify it as Solomon's psalm. H. C. Leupold is typical of many commentators when he writes that the psalm is from Solomon's period and was composed, along with other psalms, for the temple's dedication.[1]

Stephen refers to verse 5 in the speech recorded in Acts 7 (Acts 7:46), and Peter refers to verse 11 in his Pentecost sermon recorded in Acts 2 (Acts 2:30).

David's Oath

A moment ago I wrote that the psalm focuses on David and his desire to bring the ark to Jerusalem. We see this focus from the beginning, for the psalm starts, "O Lord, remember *David* and all the hardships he endured" (v. 1, italics added). The next verses tell of David's vow and its result. Then verse 10 mentions David again in a prayer: "For the sake of *David* your servant, do not reject your anointed one" (italics added). The second half tells how "the Lord swore an oath to *David*" (v. 11, italics added), and the psalm ends with the promise, "Here I will make a horn grow for *David* and set up a lamp for my anointed one" (v. 17, italics added).

Was David wise in making this vow? Generally speaking, it is not wise to make vows because we vow unwisely and are usually unable to perform what we have promised. David may not have been wise in his vow. Of course, we do not need to take his words literally. When he said,

> I will not enter my house
>   or go to my bed—
> I will allow no sleep to my eyes,
>   no slumber to my eyelids,
> till I find a place for the LORD,
>   a dwelling for the Mighty One of Jacob

the words were only a figure of speech meaning, I will not rest until . . . Still, David vowed more than he could fulfill. He was promising to build "a dwelling for the Mighty One of Jacob,"[2] a temple to house the ark. However, it was not David who built the temple. Solomon, his son, built it, though David collected the costly materials for its construction.

The historical accounts in 2 Samuel 6 and 1 Chronicles 13–16 say nothing about David's oath. This is the only place in the Old Testament where it is mentioned. And David is not remembered here for his excessive zeal; he is remembered for his good intentions. He was motivated by a desire for God's honor. Are you equally intent on honoring God's house? Charles Spurgeon wrote ironically, "Alas, we have many around us who will never carry *their* care for the Lord's worship too far! No fear of *their* being indiscreet! They are housed and bedded, and as for the Lord, his people may meet in a barn, or never meet at all, it will be all the same to them. . . . [David] could not enjoy sleep till he had done his best to provide a place for the ark."[3]

We may not want to make vows of our dedication to God's honor and God's work, but we should be intent on seeing that the work of God is done and done well, and we should repent if we are not. In our day the majority of believers do not even give a tenth of their income for God's work let alone give abundantly and sacrificially to see that work progress.

The Accomplishment of David's Oath

The next section of the psalm (vv. 6–9) recounts how the ark was found "in the fields of Jaar" in David's time and how it was brought to Jerusalem. It is an accurate piece of historical remembrance.

The ark was a wooden box about a yard long and eighteen inches high and deep covered with gold. It contained the law of God written on tablets of stone, and it was closed by a solid gold covering called the mercy seat, which was where the high priest sprinkled the blood of a sacrifice for the sins of the nation once a year on the Day of Atonement. The ark was made in the wilderness during the years of the people's wandering and was kept within the Most Holy Place of the portable wilderness tabernacle. It symbolized God's presence. When the people traveled from place to place the ark was carefully covered by the priests, for no one was allowed to look at it, and carried by them before the advancing hosts of Israel.

When the people came to the Jordan River on the brink of their entry into the promised land, the ark carried by the priests led the way. When the ark reached the river the water parted, and the people passed over on dry ground. The ark was first deposited at Shiloh (Josh. 18:1). After that it was at Bethel (Judg. 20:27), then at Mizpah (Judg. 21:5), then for twenty years at a place called Keriath-jearim (1 Sam. 7:2).

In Psalm 132 Keriath-jearim is the place referred to when the psalm says, "We came upon it in the fields of Jaar." *Jaar* means "wood" or "thicket," and it is the singular form of the plural noun *jearim*. Jaar is only a shortened form of Keriath-jearim. The location of the ark seems to have been forgotten during the reign of Saul when it was at Keriath-jearim (1 Chron. 13:3), and it was only found there later (in David's day) after a time of serious searching.[4]

What happened then is described in detail in 2 Samuel 6 and 1 Chronicles 13–16. First, David attempted to transport the ark to Jerusalem on a cart drawn by oxen, which is not how God had said the ark was to be moved. It was to be carried by the priests. Besides, when the oxen stumbled, a man named Uzzah reached out his hand to steady the ark and was immediately struck down for his "irreverent act" (2 Sam. 6:7). This spoiled the party, of course. David was angry, and for three months the ark was left where it was. It was taken aside into the house of a man named Obed-Edom.

However, when David heard that God was blessing Obed-Edom because of the ark's presence, he tried again, this time making sure that the ark was moved in the way God had appointed. So the ark came to Jerusalem at last.

We have several remembrances of the details of that event in verses 8 and 9. Verse 9 remembers the role of the priests in that second successful attempt and asks that they might be "clothed with [an actual] righteousness," as they were symbolically clothed on that occasion. First Chronicles 15:12 says that the priests sanctified themselves before the ceremony. Verse 8 of Psalm 132 says that the people also uttered the traditional marching cry of Israel (see Num. 10:35–36), used when the ark was made ready to move before them on their journeys. When the people were to move, the Shekinah cloud, which symbolized God's presence, rose up from over the tabernacle and went before them, and when they reached their destination the cloud settled down once again.

A Brief Prayer

Verse 10 marks a break in the psalm, a transition between its first and second halves. In it the reigning king ("your anointed one"), or someone speaking on his behalf, seeks acceptance with God on the grounds of God's covenant promises to David, his predecessor. The specifics of this prayer are not given, but we remember that God had promised David an everlasting dynasty, swearing that David's descendants would sit on his throne forever. It is clear that the one speaking in verse 10 seeks the fulfillment of this covenant promise for the current king.

In the same way, we seek admission to God's presence on the basis of the work of our greater King Jesus Christ and of God's promises to him.

God's Oath to David

Having appealed to God on the basis of God's covenant with David, it is natural for the next verses of the psalm to rehearse the terms of that covenant in abbreviated form. This restatement marks the psalm's second half and is a conscious parallel to David's oath, which began part one. It is why verse 11 uses the word "oath" instead of "covenant" as in verse 12. First, we had David's oath and its fulfillment (vv. 2–9). Here, we have God's oath and its fulfillment (vv. 11–18).

The original account of God's promises to David are in 2 Samuel 7:4–17. Those verses promise that God will establish his people in their own land; that he will give David an heir who will succeed him; that he will bless this successor, though he will also discipline him when he does wrong; that the successor is the one who will actually build the temple; and that the throne of David will be established forever. The last and most important words of this covenant are "Your house and your kingdom will endure forever before me; your throne will be established forever" (v. 16).

There are two levels of promise here, the first being a promise to the heirs of David, that they would not cease to occupy the throne of David as long as they keep God's covenant and statutes. The second is a promise of the divine Messiah, who alone would perform all the requirements of the law and rule forever. The promise of a Messiah is always in the background when God's covenant with David is mentioned, but it becomes fairly explicit here when God speaks of Zion, saying,

> This is my resting place for ever and ever;
> here I will sit enthroned, for I have desired it.

The Accomplishment of God's Oath

What is most striking about verses 13–18 is that they correspond to the things the people prayed about in verses 8 and 9, for in each case the answer goes beyond the petitions. Alexander Maclaren observed, "The shape of the responses is determined by the form of the desires, and in each case the answer is larger than the prayer."[5]

The people had asked God to come to his resting place as the ark was brought to Jerusalem; God says that he will sit enthroned there "for ever and ever." They asked righteousness for the priests; God promises to clothe the priests with salvation, which is a greater concept. The people asked that the saints might sing for joy; God promises that they will sing for joy forever. This heightened fulfillment points beyond the present to the future Messianic age, which is how the rabbis understood this closing section of the psalm prior to the Christian era. Many Old Testament prophetic passages were understood to be about the Messiah until the claims of Christians that they had been fulfilled by Jesus caused the rabbis to view them differently.[6] This greater future fulfillment involves three things:

1. *The establishment of God's throne in Jerusalem* (vv. 13–14). Part of the promise involves the earthly throne of David, for God said that he would establish it as long as David's descendants kept God's covenant and obeyed his statutes (v. 12). But when God speaks of establishing Zion as his resting place "for ever and ever" (v. 14), it is clear that this must go beyond the endurance of a mere earthly kingdom. It is about the Messiah and his throne.

The earthly throne of David did not endure forever. It ended when the last of the Davidic kings, Jeconiah (also known as Jehoiachin), was carried off to Babylon at the time of the exile and died there. This man was so disobedient that it was prophesied in Jeremiah 22:30 that no descendants of his would prosper nor "sit on the throne of David or rule anymore in Judah." And they did not. On the other hand, the throne of Jesus really is eternal. Jesus reigns even now in heaven, and in the opinion of some he will also rule on earth literally in a future day. Revelation 11:15 speaks of this rule, saying,

> The kingdom of the world has become the kingdom of
> our Lord and of his Christ,
> and he will reign for ever and ever.

2. *God's blessing on the people, both physically and spiritually* (vv. 15–16). God's blessing on the people involves material prosperity, ample provisions for the poor, salvation for the priests, and joy for all the people—in other words, an idyllic future state. For centuries political leaders have dreamed of a Golden Age and have promised to establish it if only they are elected to or are retained in power. Plato wrote about a perfect age in his *Republic*. Virgil popularized the theme for the Romans in his Fourth Eclogue. In more recent history the dream of a utopia has been voiced by Thomas More, Samuel Butler, and Edward Ballamy, as well as by Henry David Thoreau, Robert Owen, and Leo Tolstoi, who actually tried to create one. In our time the same vision has been enlarged by communists, who saw it as a "classless society" and by western governments, who think of it as a system of infinitely expanding prosperity.

The difficulty is that no culture has ever achieved this ideal, and even the future, which has always been the bright hope of dreamers, does not look promising. One observer wrote,

The rule of man . . . has been characterized with irreconcilable ambitions and conflicts of interests. The brains of man have been dedicated to the production of military machines and accouterments for the scattering of death and desolation among the inhabitants of the earth. . . . Man has looked for peace and found war. He has talked of brotherhood and love and has seen hatred and persecution. He has boasted of his civilization, enlightenment, and progress, and the so-called heathen have upbraided him for his godless practices. . . . He has spent billions of dollars for war; millions for pleasure; and only a few paltry thousands for the spreading of the gospel of Christ. . . . It . . . gives no promise of improvement. As it was, so it is, and will be until the King comes back. There has not been a period since the fall of man in which the race has enjoyed or witnessed the condition which prophecy declares shall obtain in the Kingdom of the Lord Jesus Christ.[7]

Those words are not too harsh. In fact, they are truer now than they were when they were first written, in 1938. We dream of a Golden Age, but if there is ever to be such an age, certainly God himself and not man must establish it.

3. *The coming of the Messiah and the establishment of his kingdom* (vv. 17–18). The last two verses of Psalm 132 describe how God will cause "a horn" to grow for David, that is, a powerful ruler who will achieve all that God has promised. His crown and his alone will be resplendent (v. 18). He is the Messiah.

Nowadays people look to the government to solve their problems; but even a freely elected, benign government like ours will never solve our problems, and to trust that it will is statism, a worship of the government in place of God. At a meeting of the National Association of Evangelicals in the 1980s, after President Ronald Reagan had spoken and the audience was applauding wildly, Charles Colson stepped to the rostrum and reminded everyone that "the Kingdom of God does not arrive on Air Force One."

But it will arrive with Jesus, and because it will, we who are on the pilgrimage of the Christian life must keep our eyes on him. The author of Hebrews noted that although "God left nothing that is not subject" to Jesus, "at present we do not see everything subject to him." He added, "But we see Jesus" (Heb. 2:8–9). That is enough! For as we look to Jesus, we move on toward the goal that is set before us, "to win the prize for which God has called [us] heavenward in Christ Jesus" (Phil. 3:14).

Psalm 133

Unity and Community

> How good and pleasant it is
>   when brothers live together in unity!
> It is like precious oil poured on the head,
>   running down on the beard,
> running down on Aaron's beard,
>   down upon the collar of his robes.
> It is as if the dew of Hermon
>   were falling on Mount Zion.
> For there the LORD bestows his blessing,
>   even life forevermore.
>
> *verses 1–3*

E *Pluribus Unum!* One out of many! That used to be the American ideal, one people formed out of many diverse cultures, languages, and nations. One nation under God! The great melting pot! But we have discovered in our not-so-long history that unity is not that easy to attain, and today what unity we had is fracturing as self-conscious, competing, and even hostile groups selfishly pursue their own way. Nor is it always different in the church of Jesus Christ. We are supposed to be one. "We are not divided, all one body we," we sing, but sadly, the community of the saints is fractured too.

Psalm 133 is about unity, the unity of those who "live together" as "brothers" (v. 1). The title says it is by David, a leader who aspired to this blessing for his kingdom. Even David, great as he was, did not see his kingdom

1158

achieve this ideal, and the later years of his reign were marked by rancorous divisions and even civil war. Is unity possible? Yes. It is a fruit of community, but genuine community can only be established by Jesus through the power of his kingdom. This important fact makes Psalm 133 an appropriate psalm to follow the promise of blessing through the Messiah's reign, which came at the end of Psalm 132.

Psalm 133 is beautiful poetry, sometimes quoted by those who know almost nothing about the rest of the Psalter. J. J. Stewart Perowne, a Church of England bishop of the last century, wrote, "Nowhere has the nature of true unity—that unity which binds men together, not by artificial restraints, but as brethren of one heart—been more faithfully described, nowhere has it been so gracefully illustrated, as in this short ode."[1]

There is nothing in the psalm to help us date it. It could have come from nearly any period of Israel's history. However, if it was written by David—we have no real reason for rejecting the claim—it could date from the crowning of David at Hebron when the leaders of the nation were, for a time at least, of one heart and mind (see 2 Sam. 5:1; 1 Chron. 12:38–40). After the divisive years of Saul's reign, the ascension of David would have marked an exciting beginning, and it would have been appropriate to celebrate it with these hopeful words. The Hebrew text (though not the NIV) begins with "behold," drawing attention to what must have seemed an extraordinary reality at that time.

The Blessing of Unity

This short poem is so beautiful in its classic celebration of unity and community that it is almost a pity to analyze it. Some literary treasures die slow deaths by dissection. Still, it is worth the risk to look at a few of the more obvious points the psalm makes about unity.

1. *Unity is a gift from God.* The first of the psalm's two images is an anointing with oil—specifically the anointing of Aaron, the high priest.[2] Anointing was done at God's direction, in his way, with his authority, and any blessing it conferred was from God. In verse 2 the threefold repetition "running down," "running down," and "down"—the Hebrew uses the same verb each time—emphasizes that the blessing of Aaron's anointing was from above himself, that is, from God.

We are sinners, and one of the first sad marks of sin is that it separates, creating disharmony and hostility. It takes God to overcome sin and bring harmony again. All real unity—at least all lasting unity—is from him.

2. *Unity is for the small and great alike.* The second of the psalm's two images is of the dew of Mount Hermon falling on Mount Zion. Hermon was the highest mountain in Israel, located several hundred miles north of Jerusalem. It was proverbial for the dew that fell on its lofty reaches. Here that dew is also said to fall on Zion, which is not very high. Like the preceding metaphor, dew comes from above and illustrates that unity is from God,

but the chief point of this image is that the dew is for little Zion as well as great Hermon. J. J. Stewart Perowne says, "It is not the refreshing nature of the dew, nor its gentle, all-pervading influence, which is the prominent feature. That which renders it to the poet's eye so striking an image of brotherly concord, is the fact that it falls alike on both mountains."[3]

When a country, a church, or even a family is at peace, it benefits not only the most prominent or most important persons but also everyone. All are blessed, especially the small, the unimportant, and the weak. Likewise, disharmony hurts everyone.

3. *The blessing of unity flows from one person to another.* The anointing of Aaron was a blessing from God for him, but he was the high priest, which meant that he in turn blessed others. The description of the oil running down from his beard "upon the collar of his robes" also suggests the flow of the blessing. There is even the hint that, since the oil was "precious oil"—the best oil blended with myrrh, cinnamon, cane, and cassia (Exod. 30:22–24)—the anointing would have been wonderfully fragrant and would have filled the air wherever Aaron went. In Exodus 30:33 this special oil is called "perfume."

In the same way, a person who is at peace with himself or herself or a people who are united are a blessing wherever he, she, or they go. They tend to win people to their unity and spread it.

4. *Unity is a foretaste of heaven.* The final verse of the psalm speaks of "life forevermore." Some things are good for us but not pleasant. Other things are pleasant but not good. But the unity we have as God's people is both good and pleasant. It is even a bit of heaven now.

Loss of Unity Today

Unity is certainly more noticeable by its absence than by its presence today. Unity was an American ideal at one time. Our country was the great "melting pot" where diverse peoples willingly blended together with similar goals to form a common destiny. Today a competing pluralism is the ideal. People no longer work for harmony; instead, they struggle with each other for group advantages and individual rights.

This pluralism has roots in our current understanding of what it means to be an individual. In the last twenty or thirty years something terrible has happened to Americans in how they relate to other people. Prior to that time there was still something of a Christian ethos in this country, and people used to care about and help other people. They believed this was the right thing to do. Today the majority of people focus on themselves and deal with others only for what they can get out of them.

In 1981 a sociologist named Daniel Yankelovich published a study of the 1970s titled *New Rules: Searching for Self-Fulfillment in a World Turned Upside Down.* It documented a massive shift in values by which many and eventually most Americans began to seek personal self-fulfillment as the ultimate goal in life rather than operating on the principle that we are here to serve and even sacrifice for others, as Americans for the most part really had done previously.[4] He found that by the late 1970s, 72 percent of Americans spent much time thinking about themselves and their inner lives.[5] So pervasive was this change that as early as 1976 Tom Wolfe tagged the '70s as the "Me Decade" and compared it to a third religious awakening.[6]

Shouldn't thinking about ourselves make us happy? If we redirect our energy to gratifying even our tiniest desires, shouldn't we be satisfied with life? Self-absorption fails on the personal level, and it fails in the area of our relationships with other people too.

In 1978 Margaret Halsey, a columnist who frequently writes for *Newsweek*, referred to Wolfe's description of the '70s as the "me" generation, highlighting the belief then rampant that "inside every human being, however unprepossessing, there is a glorious, talented and overwhelmingly attractive personality [that] will be revealed in all its splendor if the individual just forgets about courtesy, cooperativeness and consideration for others and proceeds to do exactly what he or she feels like doing."[7]

The problem, as Halsey pointed out, is not that there are not attractive characteristics in most people, but that human nature consists even more basically of "a mess of unruly primitive elements" that spoil the self-discovery. These unruly elements need to be overcome, not indulged, which means that the attractive personalities we seek really are not there but rather are natures needing to be developed through choices, hard work, and lasting commitments to others. When we ask, What's wrong with me? it is the me, me, me that is the problem.

The pursuit of self affects our relationships to other people too, because, in spite of what humanism seems to promise, it makes our world inhuman. A failure to relate to other people hurts not only them, but also us.

Charles Reich in his best-selling book *The Greening of America* wrote,

> Modern living has obliterated place, locality and neighborhood, and given us the anonymous separateness of our existence. The family, the most basic social system, has been ruthlessly stripped to its functional essentials. Friendship has been coated over with a layer of impenetrable artificiality as men strive to live roles designed for them. Protocol, competition, hostility and fear have replaced the warmth of the circle of affection which might sustain man against a hostile environment. . . . America [has become] one vast, terrifying anti-community.[8]

Are our churches exempt? Sometimes perhaps, but not everywhere and not always. Michael Scott Horton has written,

> Our churches are one of the last bastions of community, and yet, they do not escape individualism. . . . Many of us drive to church, listen to the sermon, say "hello" to our circle of friends, and return home without ever having really experienced community. Earlier evangelicalism was so focused on cor-

porate spirituality that communion was taken with a common cup. . . . We hear endless sermons on spiritual gifts and how the body of Christ is supposed to operate in concert. And yet, our services often are made up of the professionals (particularly the choir) who entertain us and the individual, separate believers who are entertained.[9]

"I Will Build My Church"

We have already seen that unity comes from God. It can be rediscovered and reestablished in the church, but only as men and women get outside of themselves and submit their own selfish individualism to a higher and more worthy cause than self-indulgence.

The Bible shows the way. As far back as the Garden of Eden we find God looking at the world he had made and observing, "It is not good for the man to be alone" (Gen. 2:18). God wanted man to live with relationships and in harmony; so he created a woman with whom the man would be able to share God's bounty and the joys of the work God gave to our first parents. Adam and Eve shared in bounty and joy, until sin caused mutual accusations and disharmony.

In the New Testament when Jesus established the new people of God, he did not abandon to themselves and their own devices those who are saved from sin but brought them into a new fellowship: the Christian church (Matt. 16:18). Jesus prayed for the church, and one thing he prayed was for God to give his people unity.

> My prayer is not for them alone [the original disciples]. I pray also for those who will believe in me through their message, that all of them may be one, Father, just as you are in me and I am in you. May they also be in us so that the world may believe that you have sent me. I have given them the glory that you gave me, that they may be one as we are one: I in them and you in me. May they be brought to complete unity to let the world know that you sent me and have loved them even as you have loved me (John 17:20–23).

This is not an artificial or an enforced unity; it is a unity based on a common participation in Christ and his gospel. It is analogous to the unity that is in God.

A Model Church

When we pass beyond the Gospels to the Book of Acts, the history of the early church, we find that Jesus' prayer was answered in the community formed in Jerusalem after his resurrection and ascension. It is written of that church, "They devoted themselves to the apostles' teaching and to the *fellowship,* to the breaking of bread and to prayer" (Acts 2:42, italics added).

Let's think about that church, since it is the New Testament counterpart to the community pictured in Psalm 133. It was an inner-city church, for one thing. It was also a large church, and it had a multiple-staff ministry. It needed the latter because of the 3,000 people who were added to the church at Pentecost, making the total number of believers 3,120 (there were 120 in chapter 1). It began with the twelve apostles, but when the twelve found that there were not quite enough people to do the work, they asked the church to elect seven deacons. However, the church grew because all the people (not just the nineteen) shared in the ministry.

A church this large had its problems, of course. All churches do. It had hypocrites. It had doctrinal errors. It had sinful human beings of all types. Yet it was a model church in many respects.

One of the most striking things about this church was its commitment to fellowship, which means unity. Fellowship has to do with holding something in common. Christian fellowship means "common participation in God," and it is this that had drawn the early Christians together. Someone has said, "The stronger your vertical fellowship is, the stronger your horizontal fellowship will be." That is right, and this church is a good example of it. These believers had strong relationships with God. Therefore, they also had strong relationships with one another. There are four specific elements mentioned in the description of the church in Acts 2.

1. *The apostles' teaching.* Real unity or community can be established only around a common set of convictions and beliefs, and what drew these believers together in their fellowship was a common devotion to the teaching of the apostles. This is the first thing Luke, the author of Acts, mentions in this passage. He stresses that in these early days, in spite of an experience as moving as that of Pentecost, which might have caused them to focus on their experiences, the disciples devoted themselves first to the apostolic teaching.

It could have been a temptation for the early believers to look back to Pentecost and try thereafter always to focus on the past. They might have remembered the way the Holy Spirit came and how he used them to speak so that those in Jerusalem each heard them in his or her own language. They might have longed to experience something like that again. They might have been praying, "Please, Lord, do something miraculous again." This is not what we find. They are not revelling in their past experiences. Instead, they are revelling in the Word of God.

I suggest that this is always the first mark of a Spirit-filled church. A Spirit-filled church always devotes itself to the apostles' teaching. It is a learning church that grounds its experiences in Scripture and tests them by the Word of God.

2. *The fellowship.* Love of the Scriptures led these believers to love one another also, which meant that they had genuine unity as God's people. The most important thing about them, both individually and as a community, was their devotion to the teaching. Because of it, they cared for one another. They even shared their material possessions and gave generously to all who were in need.

3. *The worship of God.* In this early church there was "the breaking of bread" and "prayer." "Breaking of bread" stands for the communion service; and prayer, although it is something we can do individually and at different times, is in this passage actually the formal exercise of prayer in the assembly. In the Greek the definite article occurs before the word "prayer," so the verse actually says, "to the prayers." These Christians devoted themselves "to *the* breaking of bread and to *the* prayers" (italics added). They got together to observe the Lord's Supper, pray, and praise God.

Verse 46 says that they did this "in the temple courts." The Court of the Gentiles was a large place, holding perhaps 200,000 people. It was the only place in Jerusalem where you could get such a large crowd together. The Christians did not worship in this formal setting only. They worshiped informally as well, for the very next phrase adds that "they broke bread in their homes" (v. 46). It is a deliberate repetition. In verse 42 "they devoted themselves . . . to the breaking of bread." Then in verse 46 "they broke bread in their homes." They had formal worship, and they had informal worship too. The informal worship included, and perhaps was largely centered on, the communion service.

The Heavenly Ideal

We have followed the biblical ideal of unity and community from Genesis 2, through Psalm 133, to Jesus' prayer for his church and the example of the first, model church in Jerusalem in the days of the apostles. We should end by also looking to the end, that is, to the perfect unity that will exist in heaven. The psalm indicates heaven when it speaks of God bestowing the blessing of "life forevermore" from Mount Zion (v. 3).

Earthly Zion is a type of heavenly Zion. Hebrews speaks of it as a place of "joyful assembly" (Heb. 12:22) and "an enduring city" (Heb. 13:14). Revelation calls it "new Jerusalem," in which there will be no sin, no evil, no pain, and no death, and in which there will be no disharmony because the desire of every one of God's redeemed people will be for God's glory and for the glory of the Lamb, who is Jesus Christ (see Rev. 21:1–22:6). We sing,

> Blest be the tie that binds our hearts in Christian love:
> The fellowship of kindred minds is like to that above.

These words are an anticipation of that perfect future unity that will cause us to seek and to maintain our unity now.

Psalm 134

Praising God in Zion

Praise the LORD, all you servants of the LORD
  who minister by night in the house of the LORD.
Lift up your hands in the sanctuary
  and praise the LORD.

May the LORD, the Maker of heaven and earth,
  bless you from Zion.
                                                verses 1–3

What is the chief end of man? We know the answer to that question. It is the first response of the Westminster Shorter Catechism: "Man's chief end is to glorify God, and to enjoy him forever." Do we know what it means really to glorify, praise, or worship God?

John R. W. Stott, former rector of All Souls' Church, Langham Place, London, wrote, "Christians believe that true worship is the highest and noblest activity of which man, by the grace of God, is capable."[1] That is true. Yet Stott's statement highlights what is probably the greatest failure of the evangelical church in our day, namely, that for large segments of the church, perhaps the majority of churches, true worship is almost nonexistent. Millions of believers have forgotten what true worship is and many churches have abandoned it entirely.

The Highest Point of Ascent

Psalm 134, the last of the Songs of Ascents (Psalms 120–34), is about worship. It is also the highest point of ascent in this collection.

The pattern formed by these songs is not perfect, but generally speaking they have progressed from a distant land (Meshech and Kedar, Psalm 120), to the first sight of Jerusalem (Psalm 121), to standing within the city's gates (Psalm 122), to various reflections on the grace, presence, and blessings of God on his people (Psalms 123–32), to delight in the unity that prevails among God's people (Psalm 133), to the perpetual and joyful worship of God by those who are appointed to serve him day and night in his temple (Psalm 134). In one sense they are all about worship, but this concluding psalm is so exceptional. It is the climax.

Psalm 134 does not only cap the Songs of Ascents, but it introduces the psalms that follow too, for a call to worship is the chief emphasis of Psalms 135–50. We are alerted to this call from the start since verse 1 of Psalm 134 is immediately echoed in Psalm 135:1–2.

> Praise the LORD, all you servants of the LORD
> who minister by night in the house of the LORD (Ps. 134:1).

> Praise the name of the LORD;
> praise him, you servants of the LORD,
> you who minister in the house of the LORD (Ps. 135:1–2).

The opening words of Psalm 134, "Praise the LORD," are the closing theme of the Psalter. They are found seven times in Psalm 135, and the last five psalms both begin and end with "Praise the Lord."

Psalm 134 is a short psalm; only Psalm 117 is shorter. In the New International Version Psalm 134 has just forty-three words arranged in six lines (the Hebrew text has a mere twenty-three words). Yet although it is very short, it is also exceptionally powerful. Derek Kidner writes, "The Songs of Ascents, which began in the alien surroundings of Meshech and Kedar . . . , end fittingly on the note of serving God, 'day and night within his temple.'"[2] Eugene Peterson says, "The way of discipleship that begins in an act of repentance . . . concludes in a life of praise."[3]

Service of the Levites

We may wonder, Who are the servants ministering by night in God's temple? The answer is the priests, or Levites, not the people in general. There are scores of scholarly theories about who is speaking here: a single priest calling to the other priests to praise God, one half of the priestly choir calling to the other half, the people calling to the Levites, and the Levites blessing the people. The only thing that makes sense in the context of the Songs of Ascents is that those who have made their way to Jerusalem to worship and have completed their devotions are now returning home, singing this song. They will not be able to worship in the temple again until their next journey. As they leave the city, they are encouraged to know that the priests will be remaining behind to represent them at the temple and so they will be worshiping God there continually.

The duty of the Levites is explained in 1 Chronicles 9:26–33; 23:28–32; 25:1, 6 (see also Deut. 10:8). The Levites were in charge of the temple worship, specifically responsible for the work "day and night" (1 Chron. 9:33). The departing people rejoiced, knowing that the worship they had shared in during their pilgrim days in Jerusalem would be carried on by the Levites in their absence.

So it is, so it has been, and so it will continue to be! God has always had and will always continue to have his worshipers. There have been sad periods in the history of the church when worshipers have been few and true worship has almost been eclipsed, but true worship has never been blotted out entirely. Charles Spurgeon wrote, "When night settles down on a church the Lord has his watchers and holy ones still guarding his truth, and these must not be discouraged, but must bless the Lord even when the darkest hours draw on."[4]

Even when they were placed in a dungeon, bleeding from their beatings, Paul and Silas sang praise to God at night (Acts 16:25). It was while they were singing that the foundations of the prison were shaken and the prison doors flew open. During the Dark Ages monks worshiped God in their cloisters. It is the same in our time.

Today's "Mac-Worship"

Although God always has those who know him and bless his name in wise and thankful worship, there are times like ours when this kind of worship is scarce. John H. Armstrong is editor of a journal called *Reformation and Revival*. The 1993 winter issue of that journal was devoted to worship, and in it Armstrong called much of what passes for the worship of God today "Mac-Worship," meaning that worship has been made common, cheap, or trivial. Why is so little of the wise and thankful worship that characterized past ages of the church seen among us? I think there are several reasons.

1. *We are trivial.* Ours is a trivial age, and the church has been deeply affected by this pervasive triviality. Ours is not an age for great thoughts or even great actions. Our age has no heroes. It is a technological age, and the ultimate objective of our popular technological culture is entertainment.

In recent years I have been holding seminars in various parts of the country on developing a Christian mind, and I have written a book on the subject, based on Romans 12:1–2.[5] In it I argue that the chief cause of today's mindlessness is television, which is not a teaching or informing medium as most people suppose but rather a means of entertainment. Because it is so pervasive—the average American household has the televi-

sion on more than seven hours a day—it is programming us to think that
the chief end of man is to be amused. How can people whose minds are
filled with the brainless babble of the evening sitcoms have anything but
trivial thoughts when they come to God's house on Sunday morning if, in
fact, they have thoughts of God at all? How can they appreciate his holiness
if their heads are full of the moral muck of the talk shows?

2. *We are self-centered.* Ours is a self-absorbed, man-centered age, and the
church has become sadly, even treasonously, self-centered. Worship is being
concerned with God and his attributes. It is knowing, acknowledging, and
praising God for being who he is. We cannot do that if all we are thinking
about is ourselves.

We have seen something like a Copernican revolution in the evangelical
church's understanding of worship in our lifetimes. In the past, true worship may not have taken place always or even very often. It may have been
crowded out by the churches' "program," as A. W. Tozer maintained it was
in his day, fifty years ago. In 1948 Tozer wrote,

> Thanks to our splendid Bible societies and to other effective agencies for the
> dissemination of the Word, there are today many millions of people who hold
> "right opinions," probably more than ever before in the history of the church.
> Yet I wonder if there was ever a time when true spiritual worship was at a lower
> ebb. To great sections of the church the art of worship has been lost entirely,
> and in its place has come that strange and foreign thing called the "program."
> This word has been borrowed from the stage and applied with sad wisdom to
> the type of public service which now passes for worship among us.[6]

Yet in Tozer's day worship was at least understood to be the praise of God,
something worth aiming at. Today we do not even aim at it, at least not
much or in many places.

R. Kent Hughes, senior minister of the College Church in Wheaton,
Illinois, was exactly right when he wrote,

> The unspoken but increasingly common assumption of today's Christendom
> is that worship is primarily for *us*—to meet our needs. Such worship services
> are entertainment focused, and the worshipers are uncommitted spectators
> who are silently grading the performance. From this perspective preaching
> becomes a homiletics of consensus—preaching to felt needs—man's con-
> scious agenda instead of God's. Such preaching is always topical and never
> textual. Biblical information is minimized, and the sermons are short and full
> of stories. Anything and everything that is suspected of making the marginal
> attender uncomfortable is removed from the service. . . . Taken to the nth
> degree, this philosophy instills a tragic self-centeredness. That is, everything
> is judged by how it affects man. This terribly corrupts one's theology.[7]

It corrupts worship too, for we cannot focus on God and his attributes,
praising him for them, if we are really thinking about ourselves and if we

are coming to church mainly to have our needs attended to, whatever they may be.

3. *We are oblivious to God.* Our age is oblivious to God, and the church is barely better, judging from its so-called worship services. The tragedy is not that Christians in our time deny basic Bible doctrines, such as the nature and existence of God. They are not heretics. The problem is that although they acknowledge Bible truth, it fails to make a difference.

In the profoundly disturbing book *No Place for Truth: Or Whatever Happened to Evangelical Theology?* author David Wells points out that American evangelicalism is either dead or dying as a religious force.[8] It is not dying as a sociological presence, since it has money and numbers, but it is dying as a significant religious force, because it no longer cares about truth. Because it does not care about truth, it is drifting along with the surrounding secular culture and is mostly indistinguishable from it, which is what George Gallup has been telling us for years.

The symptoms are all there. The decline is everywhere apparent. What is the cause? The answer is the inconsequentiality of truth in our lives or, as Wells maintains, the weightlessness of God on our experience. We do not reject God; he just doesn't matter very much. We live as if God were nonexistent. The logical conclusion is that we really do not know God at all. If we do not know God, how can we possibly begin to worship him?

Toward a Biblical Solution

If we are to worship God, we must get to know God, and this means that we must begin to study God's own revelation of himself in the Bible. Every Christian must do this. If we are to praise and glorify God as we ought, we will have to watch television less and study God's Word more. We will have to become men and women of the Book.

But I do not think Bible study is the point of this psalm, important as Bible study is. What we glean from Psalm 134 is the responsibility of the appointed ministers of God to worship God themselves and by doing so to show God's people how to worship and to lead them in worship. There is no mistaking the fact that congregations learn from their ministers' examples and will either worship well or fail to worship based on the patterns they see. How will people learn to praise God if all they discover in church is a minister who is trying to be a stand-up comic or entertainer whose chief goal in the service is to make the people go home feeling good? Reference to the Levites in Psalm 134 leads to several conclusions regarding the responsibilities of ministers.

1. *Ministers must lead in prayer.* Verse 2 says to "lift up your hands in the sanctuary." In biblical times raising one's hands toward heaven was the normal posture of those who were praying. In 1 Timothy 2:8 Paul says, "I want men everywhere to lift up holy hands in prayer." It is a meaningful gesture, because lifting one's hands to heaven reminds us that we are looking to God

in our worship and that whatever gifts or blessings we may be seeking come from him.

This recognition is precisely what is vanishing in our contemporary evangelical assemblies. I attend scores of evangelical worship services in the course of a normal year, and one thing I have noticed is the striking absence of any serious prayer. Usually there is prayer at the beginning of the service, an invocation, though that is gradually being replaced with a chummy greeting. There is always a prayer when the offering is received. We seem to recognize our need for God's supernatural intervention there—to make normally stingy people generous. But the pastoral prayers are gone. There is no adoration of God, no confession of sin, no thanks for what God has already abundantly given. And if we need to make a supplication—if Mary Jones is having an operation and needs to be prayed for—that is often merely tacked on to the offering prayer because there is no other place to put it.

Many things rightly go on in church, but what is happening if we are not praying? We are not worshiping God, certainly. We are not even thinking about God. We are actually focusing on ourselves and our needs exclusively. Good ministers must lead the way in prayer and thus teach the people how to direct their deepest thoughts to the Almighty.

2. *Ministers must read and teach the Bible.* The reading and teaching of the Bible was one of the Levites' chief duties, even though Psalm 134 does not list this responsibility explicitly. We have an excellent example in Nehemiah. After reassembling the fallen walls of Jerusalem, Nehemiah brought Ezra, who was a priest and scribe, to the large open square before the water gate to read from the Book of the Law from daybreak until noon in the hearing of the people. We are told that "all the people listened attentively to the Book of the Law" (Neh. 8:3). The people "lifted their hands" in prayer, saying, "Amen! Amen!" and bowed with their faces to the ground, after which "the Levites . . . instructed the people in the Law while the people were standing there." The text says, "They read from the Book of the Law of God, making it clear and giving the meaning so that the people could understand what was being said" (Neh. 8:8). What a wonderful picture of the duties of ministers: to read the Law, make it clear, and give the meaning!

Sadly, serious Bible exposition is rapidly disappearing as preachers prepare little feel-good talks for people who do not know one end of the Bible from the other, let alone what it is teaching. Many services do not even contain the reading of the Bible anymore, at best just a few verses before the sermon as a pretext for it. Christians used to say that in prayer we speak to God, and in the Bible God speaks to us. What is happening in services where neither prayers nor serious Bible expositions occur? Whatever is happening, there is no communication between God and man, so it is not worship.

Today's ministers need to recover the priorities of the apostles, who said, "It would not be right for us to neglect the ministry of the word of God . . . We . . . will give ourselves to prayer and the ministry of the word" (Acts 6:2–4).

3. *Ministers must oversee the music.* Today in many churches music is turned over to a minister of music, who often has no biblical or theological training and who chooses the service music for its emotional impact on the people rather than for its value as an element in the genuine worship of God. The function of the Levites should instruct us here, for one of the responsibilities assigned to them was the direction and even the performance of the music. David gave them this task, as described in 1 Chronicles 25. They were to direct the music, employing such instruments as cymbals, lyres, and harps. There were 288 of these musicians.

We do not know anything about the music itself, but we know the content of their songs. They were the psalms, the very hymns we have been studying. What wonderful content! What edifying compositions! Often ministers cannot perform the music—at least I cannot—but they need to make sure that any music performed in the services is biblically correct and actually directs the thoughts and emotions of the people to God and his gospel, and that it is not merely self-centered, self-indulgent, or sentimental.

4. *Ministers must reverence God.* Ministers must make clear in every aspect of their lives and speech that they hold God in awesome regard and are never flippant where spiritual matters are concerned. The Levites modeled this reverence in the way they guarded God's house, prepared the flour and wine, oil, incense, and spices for the temple services, and oversaw the purification of these items (1 Chron. 23:28–29). We need to recapture something of their reverence for God and his holiness in our day. Many ministers act as if God were our buddy, one with whom we are to have a good time but who does not need to be taken seriously.

Blessing and Being Blessed

What will happen if you do take God seriously and worship him reverently, as he needs to be worshiped? The "Maker of heaven and earth" will "bless you from Zion" (v. 3).

This last blessing is not merely something tacked on, like a thoughtless benediction at the end of a morning service. In the Hebrew text the word "praise," as in "Praise the LORD" in verses 1 and 2, is the same word as "bless" in verse 3. So the thought is that if we bless God in our worship, as we must, then God will also bless us abundantly in our daily lives. This is the only ultimate goal of any Christian: to bless God and to be blessed by him—to glorify God and to enjoy him forever, which is where we began!

Psalm 135

Praise the Lord

Praise the LORD.

Praise the name of the LORD;
  praise him, you servants of the LORD,
you who minister in the house of the LORD,
  in the courts of the house of our God.

Praise the LORD, for the LORD is good;
  sing praise to his name, for that is pleasant.
For the LORD has chosen Jacob to be his own,
  Israel to be his treasured possession. . . .

O house of Israel, praise the LORD;
  O house of Aaron, praise the LORD;
O house of Levi, praise the LORD;
  you who fear him, praise the LORD.
Praise be to the LORD from Zion,
  to him who dwells in Jerusalem.

Praise the LORD.

verses 1–21

Not long ago I was invited to take part in a worship service that was an hour and a half long. Four congregations had combined for this service.

It was a lively morning. About half of the service was music led by a youthful worship team. There were overheads and choruses, some of them repeated several times. There was even one hymn. My part, the sermon, was about forty minutes long. What struck me about this service was its lack of traditional worship elements, especially since it was on a Sunday morning and had been promoted as a united *worship* service. There was no invocation, no confession of sin, no pastoral prayer, and although there was a Scripture reading, it was there only because I had chosen it as the passage I was to teach from later.

This was not a bad service, but it is part of a sad contemporary trend, and it shows how far many churches have moved from the older, better worship that was once genuinely God-centered, as all true worship must be.

Recently the *Los Angeles Times Magazine* reported on a church in southern California that advertises its service as "God's Country Goodtime Hour" and promises "line dancing following worship." Their band is called the Honkytonk Angels, and the pastor takes part.[1] The *Wall Street Journal* reports on a church located in America's Bible belt called "The Fellowship of Excitement." Not long ago the church ran an advertisement for a Sunday evening service that read:

Circus

See Barnum and Bailey bested as the magic of the big top circus comes to The Fellowship of Excitement! Clowns! Acrobats! Animals! Popcorn! What a great night!

This same church once had the pastoral staff put on a wrestling match during a Sunday service, having hired a professional wrestler to train them how to throw one another around the ring, pull hair, and kick shins without actually hurting one another.[2]

Whatever people may be doing in these services, they are not worshiping God. How can they if they have jettisoned the reading and exposition of the Bible, in which God speaks to us, and abandoned substantive prayer, in which we speak to God? True worship is thoughtful praise of God for who he truly is and for what he has done, and if that praise is not the very center and heart of what we are doing, our so-called worship is not true worship at all.

The Worship Psalms

For the last fifteen chapters we have been studying the Songs of Ascents (Psalms 120–34), those well-known psalms that seem to have been sung by Jewish pilgrims as they made their way to Jerusalem for the three annual feasts adult Jewish males were required to attend. With Psalm 135 we begin the final section of the Psalter (Psalms 135–50), which specifically emphasizes the worship or praise of God.

Psalm 135 signals the start of this new section by the words "Praise the LORD." These three words occur seven times in this psalm, twice at the beginning (vv. 1, 3) and five more times at the end (vv. 19–21). Besides these imperatives the single word "praise," either as a verb (vv. 1, 21) or noun (v. 3), occurs four times more. Since the psalm both begins and ends with these words it is a way of saying that all of life should be filled with praise to God.

In this psalm "every verse . . . either echoes, quotes or is quoted by some other part of Scripture."[3] This repetition probably points to how important its chief subject was considered by the other Bible writers.

The psalm falls into four clearly delineated parts: (1) an invocation (vv. 1–2); (2) the actual worship, explaining why God must be praised (vv. 3–14); (3) a contrast between the one true God and the impotent gods of the heathen (vv. 15–18); and (4) a final call on all who know God to praise him (vv. 19–21).

An Invocation

An invocation is a call to worship, which is what verses 1 and 2 are. Specifically, they call on those who serve God in his temple to lead the way in worship. These verses closely echo the words with which the previous psalm began (see also Ps. 113:1).

Many books dealing with worship say that worship is hard to define. I think it is easy to define. The problems—and there are many of them—are not problems of definition.

If we had been living in England in the days of the formation of modern English, between the period of Geoffrey Chaucer and William Shakespeare, we would not have used the word *worship* at all; instead we would have spoken of *worth-ship*. We could have used it of noteworthy people, like the king or members of the ruling class, acknowledging their worthiness (Your Worth-ship). Or, if we used it to describe what we now call worship, we would have meant that we were assigning to God his true worth. *Worth-ship* would refer to praising God as he has revealed himself to be by his creation and through the Scriptures. Since *worship* means "to attribute worth," to worship God rightly is to ascribe to him supreme worth, for he alone is supremely worthy. To worship is to honor God supremely.

Worship also has bearing on the worshiper, however, which means that it changes him or her. No one ever truly comes to know, honor, or worship God without being changed in the process. The best definition of worship I have come across is from the pen of former Archbishop of Canterbury William Temple: "To worship is to quicken the conscience by the holiness of God, to feed the mind with the truth of God, to purge the imagination by the beauty of God, to open the heart to the love of God, to devote the will to the purpose of God."[4]

In that definition the attributes of God are foremost: holiness, truth, beauty, love, and purpose. These, if rightly acknowledged and praised, impact the worshiper by quickening the conscience, feeding the mind, purging the imagination, opening the heart, and devoting (or winning) the will. According to Psalm 135 and the other specific worship psalms of this last section of the Psalter, if we are not quickened, fed, purged, opened to God, and deepened devotionally, we are not worshiping.

The Praise of God Proper

The heart of Psalm 135 is the four stanzas covering verses 3–14, for it is in these verses that God is actually praised. He is praised because he alone is praiseworthy. The verses give reasons why, introducing several of them (though not all) by the word "for": "Praise the LORD, *for* the LORD is good" (v. 3); *"For* the LORD has chosen Jacob to be his own" (v. 4); and *"For* the LORD will vindicate his people" (v. 14, italics added). The King James Version also used "for" to introduce verse 5. The psalm gives us at least five reasons why God is praiseworthy.

1. *God's inherent goodness* (v. 3). Verse 3 says, "Praise the LORD, for the LORD is good." Derek Kidner writes of this statement, "This is one of three related verses in the Psalter in which we are reminded that the Lord's name (the reputation he deserves) is good (52:9), that he himself is good (135:3) and that praising him is good (147:1); further, that both his name (here) and the act of worship (147:1) are delightful."[5]

What could be more basic than this, that God is good? Nothing at all, since this is God's essential nature. Even the word *God* is a shortened form of "the Good." God is good in all things and in all ways. He is good in himself; indeed, he is goodness itself. His wisdom is good. His knowledge is good. His judgments are good. His power is good. His works are all good. When God was creating the universe he said after each step of his creation, "It is good" (Gen. 1:4, 10, 12, 18, 21, 25, 31). And so it was! Nothing God did could have been done better.

It is the same in matters of salvation. God's thoughts toward us are good. It was good that he loved us and chose us in Christ before the foundation of the world. The way he chose to save us was good. It was good that he sent Jesus at the appointed time to be our Savior. It was good that he called us to faith in Jesus by the power of his Holy Spirit. It is good that he has called us to fellowship with himself and with one another in the church. God's ways with us are good. And at the end of all things, at the time of the final judgment and beyond, the glorified saints will confess that he who began a good work in them has indeed carried it on to a perfect completion (Phil. 1:6). The writer of Psalm 119 said of God, "You are good, and what you do is good" (Ps. 119:68). David cried,

> Taste and see that the LORD is good;
> blessed is the man who takes refuge in him (Ps. 34:8).

2. *God's electing love* (v. 4). The psalmist acknowledges God's electing love in the case of Israel, saying, "For the LORD has chosen Jacob to be his own, Israel to be his treasured possession" (v. 4).

The allusion to Israel as Jacob is significant, because Jacob is the best Old Testament example of how God elects people without any reference to any supposed good in those who are elected, as Paul shows in his definitive treatment of election in Romans 9. In that chapter Paul goes back to the very start of Israel's history and traces God's election through the first three generations of the nation: his choice of Abraham, his choice of Isaac, and his choice of Jacob. Abraham was called out of pagan Ur when he didn't even know the true God. Isaac was chosen rather than his half-brother Ishmael. Yet the chief example is Jacob. Paul writes,

> Not only that, but Rebekah's children had one and the same father, our father Isaac. Yet, before the twins were born or had done anything good or bad—in order that God's purpose in election might stand: not by works but by him who calls—she was told, "The older will serve the younger" (Rom. 9:10–12).

This is a remarkably effective example, since it proves everything that Paul needed to make his point.

First, Jacob and Esau were born of the same Jewish parents. That is, each was "a Hebrew of the Hebrews," the phrase Paul used to describe his own Jewish ancestry in Philippians 3:5. Each was a pure-blooded Jew, so there is no case of one having been chosen on the basis of a better ancestry and the other having been rejected on the basis of a lesser one. The supposed reason for the choice of Isaac over Ishmael is eliminated in this case.

Second, the choice of Jacob rather than Esau went against the normal standards of primogeniture, according to which the elder should have received the greater blessing. The boys were twins, but Esau actually emerged from Rebekah's womb first, though Jacob was chosen. There is nothing to explain this choice except God's sovereign right to dispose of the destinies of human beings as he pleases.

Third—and this is the most important point of all—the choice of Jacob instead of Esau was made before either child had an opportunity to do either good or evil. It was made while the children were still in the womb. This means—we cannot miss it—that election is not on the basis of anything done by the individual chosen. It is no wonder then that Psalm 135 looks back to this choice and sees in it nothing but the sovereign grace of God for which those who have been saved should and must praise him.

3. *God's sovereign power* (vv. 5–7). The third stanza of the psalm (vv. 5–7) refers to God's power in creation, echoing similar expressions of praise in Exodus 18:11, Psalm 115:3, and Jeremiah 10:13. Verse 7 occurs word-for-word in Jeremiah 10:13 and 51:16.

It is amazing to me that anyone can look at the wonders of creation and not be led to praise God as the source of these wonders, but so it is. In the popular television series *Cosmos* Carl Sagan looked at the starry heavens in all their nighttime splendor and said, "The cosmos is all that is or that ever was or that ever will be," missing entirely the most important thing that can be known about the cosmos. The psalmist had it right when he declared, "The heavens declare the glory of God; the skies proclaim the work of his hands" (Ps. 19:1). In Psalm 135 the writer sees the glory of God in the heavens and the earth, the seas and clouds, the lightning, rain, and wind. These declare that "the LORD is great" (v. 5) and that he should be acknowledged, praised, and worshiped by the creatures he has made.

4. *God's persevering grace* (vv. 8–12). Most of the phrases in verses 8–12 also appear in the next psalm (Ps. 136:10, 18–22), where they are followed in each case by the words "his love endures forever." In other words, each of God's acts shows his continuing grace toward those he has called by his electing love.

By calling Abraham, Isaac, and Jacob to know him, God called the Jews to be his chosen people. Yet that was not the end. Having chosen his people, God continued to bless them, first by setting them free from bondage at the time of the Exodus and then by bringing them into Canaan, their promised inheritance. The possession of Canaan was accomplished by many great victories, of which two are mentioned specifically: the victories over Sihon king of the Amorites and Og king of Bashan (see Num. 21:21–35; Deut. 2:24–3:11). In the same way, we praise God not only for our deliverance from sin but also for his persevering grace throughout the entirety of our lives and for many victories over spiritual opposition and oppression.

5. *God's everlasting renown* (vv. 13–14). The importance of verses 13 and 14 is that they look to the future as the previous verses looked to the past, concluding that the God who has been gracious in past days will continue to vindicate his people and have compassion on them in days yet to come (v. 14). God's love will indeed endure forever (Psalm 136, refrain). Therefore, his renown will also last forever (v. 13). God does not change. He is immutable, to use the proper theological word for his unchangeability. God is not only good; but he will also always be good. He is always the same in his eternal attributes. We will never find him to be less good than he has been to us in the past.

The Gods of the Heathen

Verses 15–18 contrast the true God with the impotent gods of the heathen. These verses are repeated from Psalm 115:4–6, 8.

The problem with other gods is that they are not gods at all, for there is only one holy and true God. In his *Treasury of David* Charles Spurgeon tells about a missionary to India named John Thomas who one day saw a large number of people waiting near an idol temple. As soon as the doors were opened the people streamed into it, and Thomas went in with them. An idol was there before the people. Thomas walked up to it and raised his hands for silence. When the people became quiet he touched the idol's eyes and said, "It has eyes, but it cannot see!" He touched its ears, saying, "It has ears, but it cannot hear!" He continued similarly, saying, "It has a nose, but it cannot smell! It has hands, but it cannot handle! It has a mouth, but it cannot speak! Neither is there any breath in it."

Thomas might have been killed for his boldness, but at the moment when the people might have rushed upon him to beat him and kill him, an old Brahmin, convicted of his folly by what had been said, cried out, "It has feet, but it cannot run away!" The people agreed, being ashamed of themselves, and left the temple.[6]

Would that people today might see the folly of worshiping what is nothing, things that cannot either help or save. Sadly,

> Those who make them will be like them,
> and so will all who trust in them (v. 18).

If we worship things that people produce, we will become as impotent and empty as those things, but if we worship God, by the grace of God we will become like God, and we will both "glorify God and enjoy him forever."

A Summons to Praise

In the last stanza the call to worship uttered at the start is extended to all "who fear" God, that is, to all who know him (vv. 19–21). John MacArthur, from whom I drew some of the material about nonworship at the beginning of this chapter, explains what happened in his church when people began to take the nature of true worship seriously. "They began to look at superficialities as an affront to a holy God. They saw worship as a participant's activity, not a spectator sport. Many realized for the first time that worship is the church's ultimate priority—not public relations, not recreation and social activities, not boosting attendance figures, but worshiping God." They were "drawn to the only reliable and sufficient worship manual," which is "Scripture."[7] This worship is exactly what God wants.

Psalm 136

His Love Endures Forever

> *Give thanks to the LORD, for he is good.*
>   *His love endures forever.*
> *Give thanks to the God of gods.*
>   *His love endures forever.*
> *Give thanks to the LORD of lords:*
>   *His love endures forever. . . .*
>
> *to the One who remembered us in our low estate*
>   *His love endures forever.*
> *and freed us from our enemies,*
>   *His love endures forever.*
> *and who gives food to every creature.*
>   *His love endures forever.*
>
> *Give thanks to the God of heaven.*
>   *His love endures forever.*
>   *verses 1–26*

A disaster such as the one that has overtaken the evangelical church in regard to its worship is not going to be cured overnight, but we ought to make a beginning, and one way to begin is by studying what the psalms teach about worship. After all, the psalms were the chief worship vehicle of both the Old Testament and New Testament church for most of its history. In fact, it is only recently that the psalms have been eclipsed by the popular hymns, songs, and choruses we are accustomed to sing today.

We will be studying how to praise God from this point to the end of the Psalter. Psalms 135–50 are almost all praise psalms, the greatest to be found anywhere in Scripture.

"Give Thanks to the LORD"

We began our study of these psalms with a look at Psalm 135, a psalm marked at both its beginning and ending with a call to "Praise the LORD." In Hebrew these are the words *hallelu jah,* which we contract into the single word "hallelujah." The words "Praise the LORD" occur often in these psalms and they both begin and end Psalms 146–50, just as they begin and end Psalm 135. Because of this summons these psalms have been called the Hallel (or Praise) Psalms.

In Jewish tradition Psalm 136 has been called the Great Hallel (or Great Psalm of Praise). It does not use the words *hallelu jah,* but it is called the Great Hallel for the way it rehearses God's goodness in regard to his people and encourages them to praise him for his merciful and steadfast love.

In Psalm 136 the words that take the place of *hallelu jah* ("Praise the LORD") are *hodu le yahweh,* which the New International Version translates as "Give thanks to the LORD."[1] They occur three times at the beginning, at the start of each of the first three verses, and once at the end at the start of verse 26. This demand is important—it indicates what the psalm is about—but the words themselves are more important, for they are probably to be understood as the beginning of most of the psalm's twenty-six verses, each verse containing a reason why God's people should thank God. It is not hard to imagine the psalm actually being written that way, which it might have been were it not that each of the verses ends with the repeating phrase "his love endures forever" instead, completing the pattern of two lines per verse.

Because they replace the summons to "praise the LORD" (in Psalms 135, 146–50, and others), the words "give thanks" are a reminder to us that thanksgiving should be an important and regular part of worship. If God is good, as he is, and if we praise him for being as he is, which is what worship is all about, clearly we must thank him too. If we do not, we are not actually worshiping God, whatever else we may be doing. In our worship of God are we consistently and joyfully thanking God for his many great and kind acts toward us?

Derek Kidner points out in his study of the psalm that the words "give thanks" do not express the full meaning of this critical imperative. Basically the original intent is "to confess," or "to acknowledge," but since the phrase also contains the thought of thanksgiving, it is probably best rendered "thankfully confess" or "acknowledge gratefully."[2] Our worship of God should also be a form of Christian confession. When we come to church, the confession of our faith should be a regular part of our worship. We are going to find that this psalm is very much like our common confession of faith: "I believe in God the Father Almighty, Maker of heaven and earth . . ."

Why Thank God?

The first verse of Psalm 136 sets the tone for everything that follows, for it gives an overall answer to the question, Why should we thank God? The answer is, We praise him because he is good; we thank him for his many good acts toward us and to all persons.

There is an echo in the first three verses of this psalm of Deuteronomy 10:17, which says, "The LORD your God is God of gods and Lord of lords, the great God, mighty and awesome." The names or titles for God in Psalm 136 are from that verse: the LORD (Jehovah), God of gods, and Lord of lords. This is the only true God, and he is mighty, as the following verses that deal with his power in creation remind us. He is also good, which means that his mighty acts are good acts and for our benefit. That is why the refrain "his love endures forever" is so appropriate as a response to each of the psalm's twenty-six assertions about God.

How good is God? Superlatively good, wonderfully good. Here is how Spurgeon writes of God's goodness: "He is good beyond all others; indeed, he alone is good in the highest sense; he is the source of good, the good of all good, the sustainer of good, the perfecter of good, and the rewarder of good. For this he deserves the constant gratitude of his people."[3] If you want to know what real goodness is and enjoy it, the place to find goodness is in God.

The Goodness of God in Creation

The first place God's goodness is seen is in his creation. This is the first thing the psalm mentions (vv. 4–9). It is also what we confess first in the Apostles' Creed when we begin, "I believe in God the Father Almighty, *Maker of heaven and earth*" (italics added). We confess that God has been good to us by making the world and by placing us in this very good world to enjoy his creation.

What a difference there is between the biblical approach to creation and the approach we see the world take. Because the unregenerate world does not acknowledge God as the creator of the universe, it does one of two bad things. Either it bows down to creation itself and worships it, making mere things into god or gods (idols), perhaps worshiping some impersonal "force" in nature; or it treats creation as something to be exploited, "ripping it off," as it were, for personal benefit.

In sharp contrast to these errors, the psalm takes us back to the first chapter of Genesis—verses 4–9 echo language from three of the six creation days—and invites us to look at the world as God looks at it and respond accordingly. What we find in Genesis is God's declaration that everything he made is "good" (vv. 4, 10, 12, 18, 21, 25, 31). So not only is God good (Ps. 136:1), but everything he makes is good also. That goodness has certain consequences for how we are to regard nature.

1. *We should be thankful for it.* In some expressions of Christian thought, only the soul or other invisible things have value. Although it is true that the invisible is more valuable than the visible—all things visible will pass away (see 2 Cor. 4:18)—this does not mean that the things we see have no value

now. The Christian understanding of creation is that God has made everything and that it therefore has value and should be valued by us because of its origin in God.

2. *We should delight in it.* Delight is related to being thankful, but it is a step beyond it. It is a step that many Christians do not seem to have taken. Frequently Christians have looked at nature only as one of the classic proofs of God's existence: there must be a God, because nothing but God can account for the universe we see. This is true, but the believer also needs to go beyond viewing creation as proof and really enjoy what he or she sees because God has been good in what he has created for us. We can delight in creation even more than the non-Christian, more even than so-called "nature worshipers," because we have knowledge of the God who stands behind everything.

3. *We should treat it responsibly.* Treating creation responsibly does not mean that it cannot still be used in a proper way. A tree can still be cut down to make wood for a home, but it should not be cut down simply for the pleasure of cutting it down or because it is the easiest way to increase the value of our land. In such matters there must be a careful thinking through of the value and purpose of the created object, and there must be a Christian rather than a purely utilitarian approach to it.

The Goodness of God in Salvation

The next section of Psalm 136 (vv. 10–24) thanks God for his specific good acts toward Israel: his deliverance of the people from bondage in Egypt (vv. 10–15); his leading them through the desert to the borders of the promised land (v. 17); his defeat of Israel's enemies, specifically Sihon king of the Amorites and Og king of Bashan, who opposed them (vv. 18–20); and his final settling of the people in their land (vv. 21–24). Our equivalent is thanks to God for delivering us from the bondage of sin through the work of Jesus Christ.

I said earlier that there is a parallel between the way this psalm is written and our confession of faith by the Apostles' Creed. Here the next words of the creed come in, for having praised God the Father as creator, the confession goes on to say:

> I believe in Jesus Christ, his only Son, our Lord,
>> who was conceived by the Holy Spirit,
>> and born of the virgin Mary.
>> He suffered under Pontius Pilate,
>> was crucified, died, and was buried;
>> he descended into hell.
>> The third day he rose again from the dead.
>> He ascended into heaven
>> and is seated at the right hand of God the Father Almighty.
>> From there he will come to judge the living and the dead.

The third and final section of the creed tells how we have benefited from Christ's work by the application of that work to us by the Holy Spirit, consisting of "the communion of saints, the forgiveness of sins, the resurrection of the body, and the life everlasting." This is our equivalent to the second major section of Psalm 136, in which the worshiping people praised God for their deliverance from Egypt, victory over their enemies, and those powerful acts of God that eventually saw them established in their own land.

This basic core of Christian teaching, this gospel, needs to be at the heart of our worship too. The very essence of the gospel is its focus on what God has done for his people, not necessarily on what we have experienced. True, what God has done affects us; we acknowledge his work with thanksgiving. But the gospel, the center of our worship, is not about what has happened to us but rather about what God accomplished by Jesus Christ two thousand years ago when Jesus died for our sin and then rose from the dead for our justification. Our worship must be God-centered rather than man-centered if it is to be worship that actually pleases God.

In recent years I have noticed in many evangelical churches a decline and in some cases the total absence of worship elements that focus our minds on God. With that absence is a loss of the importance of the gospel. Specifically, five things are in decline.

1. *Prayer.* It is almost inconceivable to me that something called a worship service can be held without any significant prayer, but that is precisely what is happening. There is usually a very short prayer at the beginning of the service and another prayer at the time the offering is received. Longer prayers, pastoral prayers, are vanishing. Whatever happened to the ACTS acrostic in which *A* stands for adoration, *C* for confession of sin, *T* for thanksgiving, and *S* for supplication? Now and then a few supplications are tacked onto the offering prayer, but there is no rehearsal of God's attributes or confession of sin over against a serious acknowledgment that God is holy. How can we say we are worshiping when we do not even pray?

2. *The reading of the Word.* In the Puritan age ministers regularly read one long chapter of the Old Testament and one chapter of the New Testament. Our Scripture readings are getting shorter and shorter, sometimes only two or three verses, if indeed the Bible is read at all. In many churches there is not even a text for the sermon.

3. *The exposition of the Word.* We have very little serious teaching of the Bible today. Instead, preachers try to be personable, to relate funny stories, to smile, above all to stay away from topics that might cause people to become unhappy with the church and leave it. One very popular television preacher will not talk about sin on the grounds that doing so makes people feel bad. Preachers are told to preach to felt needs, not real needs necessarily, and this generally means telling people only what they want to hear. This is all utterly man-centered, and there is no gospel.

4. *Confession of sin.* Who confesses sin today—anywhere, not to mention in church as God's humble, repentant people? It is not happening, because there is so little awareness of God. Instead of coming to church to confess our transgressions and seek forgiveness, we come to church to be told that we are really all right and do not need forgiveness.

5. *Hymns.* One of the saddest features of contemporary worship is that the great hymns of the church are on the way out. They are not gone entirely, but they are going. In their place have come trite jingles that have more in common with contemporary advertising ditties than the psalms. The problem here is not so much the style of the music, though trite words fit best with trite tunes and harmonies; rather it is with the content of the songs. The old hymns expressed the theology of the Bible in profound and perceptive ways and with winsome, memorable language. Today's songs are focused on ourselves. They reflect our shallow or nonexistent theology and do almost nothing to elevate our thoughts about God.

Worst of all are songs that merely repeat a trite idea, word, or phrase over and over again. Songs like this are not worship, though they may give the church-goer a religious feeling; they are mantras, which belong more in a gathering of New Agers than among the worshiping people of God.

The Goodness of God to Everyone

One striking feature of Psalm 136 is the way it works around to where it started out. It began with a call to thank God, and it ends the same way. In verse 25 it even moves back to thoughts of a general benevolence of God to all people, not just Israel.

All people benefit from creation, as the psalm acknowledged in verses 4–9. Here we are reminded that God also "gives food to every creature." Jesus spoke about this general benevolence of God when he reminded his Jewish listeners that God "causes his sun to rise on the evil and the good, and sends rain on the righteous and the unrighteous" (Matt. 5:45). Paul echoed the same truths in Lystra when he taught the Gentiles there that God "has shown kindness by giving you rain from heaven and crops in their seasons; he provides you with plenty of food and fills your hearts with joy" (Acts 14:17). In each case the goodness of God is given as a reason why those who have benefited from it should repent of their sin and seek God. But people do not do this. As Paul said writing to the Romans, "Although they knew God, they neither glorified him as God nor gave thanks to him" (Rom. 1:21).

"His Love Endures Forever"

What is most striking about this psalm is its chorus: "His love endures forever." I have held a discussion of it until last, because it is the believer's worshiping response to the acts and person of God. This sentence occurs twenty-six times in this psalm, as a response to each of its twenty-six affirmations about God. There is nothing like it anywhere else in the psalms or anywhere else in the Bible. The closest thing is the fourfold repetition of the same sentence at the start and ending of Psalm 118.

As a chorus, the words may seem a bit too repetitious in our English versions, but they do not come across this way in Hebrew. The right English effect was achieved by the seventeenth-century English poet John Milton, who used Psalm 136 as the basis for his hymn "Let Us with a Gladsome Mind." Milton wrote it while he was a student at Cambridge University when he was only fifteen years old.

> Let us with a gladsome mind, praise the Lord for he is kind:
> For his mercies aye endure, ever faithful, ever sure.
>
> Let us sound his name abroad, for of gods he is the God:
> For his mercies aye endure, ever faithful, ever sure.
>
> He with all consuming might filled the new-made world with light:
> For his mercies aye endure, ever faithful, ever sure.

And so on for all the hymn's twenty-four stanzas.[4]

The word that is used for "love" in this refrain is the powerful Hebrew term *hesed,* which means "covenant love" or the favor God shows to those with whom he has entered into a covenant relationship. Sometimes it is translated "steadfast (or 'enduring') love." It is enduring because God is a God of his word. He is forever good, and he does not break his covenant.

One night in February 358 A.D. the church father Athanasius held an all-night service at his church in Alexandria, Egypt. He had been leading the fight for the eternal sonship and deity of Jesus Christ, knowing that the survival of Christianity depended on it. He had many enemies—for political even more than theological reasons—and they moved the power of the Roman government against him. That night the church was surrounded by soldiers with drawn swords. People were frightened. With calm presence of mind Athanasius announced the singing of Psalm 136. The vast congregation responded, thundering forth twenty-six times, "His love endures forever." When the soldiers burst through the doors they were staggered by the singing. Athanasius kept his place until the congregation was dispersed. Then he too disappeared in the darkness and found refuge with his friends.[5]

Many citizens of Alexandria were killed that night, but the people of Athanasius's congregation never forgot that although man is evil, God is good. He is superlatively good, and "his love endures forever."

Psalm 137

By the Rivers of Babylon

By the rivers of Babylon we sat and wept
    when we remembered Zion.
There on the poplars
    we hung our harps,
for there our captors asked us for songs,
    our tormentors demanded songs of joy;
    they said, "Sing us one of the songs of Zion!"

How can we sing the songs of the LORD
    while in a foreign land?
If I forget you, O Jerusalem,
    may my right hand forget its skill.
May my tongue cling to the roof of my mouth
    if I do not remember you,
if I do not consider Jerusalem
    my highest joy.

Remember, O LORD, what the Edomites did
    on the day Jerusalem fell.
"Tear it down," they cried,
    "tear it down to its foundations!"

O Daughter of Babylon, doomed to destruction,
    happy is he who repays you
    for what you have done to us—
he who seizes your infants
    and dashes them against the rocks.

verses 1–9

The Bible is filled with contrasts that lend substance and life to its teaching, and one of these is between Babylon, which stands for the world and its culture, and Jerusalem, which stands for God's kingdom. This contrast is both literal and figurative, literal because there was an actual earthly Babylon matched by a literal earthly Jerusalem— earthly Babylon overthrew the earthly Jerusalem in 586 B.C.—but figurative, too, because the Bible also speaks of Mystery Babylon (see Revelation 18–19) and a new heavenly Jerusalem (see Revelation 21–22).

It was a recognition of this distinction and the extent to which it is found throughout Scripture that led Saint Augustine to compose that first Christian philosophy of history, *The City of God. The City of God* was probably the most influential of all books throughout the Middle Ages. In it Augustine wrote, "Two cities have been formed by two loves; the earthly by the love of self, even to the contempt of God; the heavenly by the love of God, even to the contempt of self."[1] He pursued that contrast carefully from Genesis to Revelation.

A Plaintive, Powerful Psalm

Because of the importance of the theme of Babylon versus Jerusalem, it is hard to understand why there is not more of it in the psalms, particularly those psalms that were composed after the fall of Jerusalem to Babylon, the resulting exile, and the restoration. In fact, there are only two psalms in the entire collection that even mention Babylon (though there are many that mention Jerusalem): Psalms 87 and 137. Psalm 87 is the one John Newton used for the basis of his strong, stirring hymn, beginning,

> Glorious things of thee are spoken,
> Zion, city of our God.

Psalm 137 is a powerful, plaintive psalm, but it is also a hard psalm to read and handle, as well as an unusual one for this specific place in the Psalter. We remember that in this final section of the Psalter (Psalms 135–50) we are dealing with psalms of praise. Here is a psalm that admits to a time and place when such praise was emotionally impossible. Moreover, along with the pathos of the opening stanza there is a harsh, angry outburst at the end against those who destroyed Jerusalem and its people and others who merely rejoiced in the city's fall.

But it is moving. Derek Kidner wrote, "Every line of it is alive with pain, whose intensity grows with each strophe to the appalling climax."[2] According to verses 1–3 the exile is past, but it is not in the very distant past. Therefore, the date of writing is shortly after the return.

Remembrance of Sad Days

We begin with the pathos, for that is what the opening stanza contains. Here the Jews who have returned from the exile recall those sad moments when they were sitting by the rivers and canals of far-off Babylon, far from their beloved mountain homeland, and were asked by their captors to sing one of the songs of Zion. Some writers suggest that this was demanded in a mocking tone: "Let's hear you sing about that land you will never see again," but there is no reason to imagine such cruelty, even though the psalm speaks of "tormentors" in verse 3. Speculation adds nothing to the pathos.

The request was sincere, but in answer the psalmist speaks for his people when he says, in effect, "We were asked to sing about Zion, but how could we sing about our homeland when we were so depressed because we were far from it? Singing should lift one's spirits and promote an atmosphere of joy. How could we sing when there was nothing to be joyful about? To be joyful in Babylon would have been treasonous for those who belong to God's city." The fourth verse summarizes their sadness in two wonderfully poetic lines.

> How can we sing the songs of the LORD
>   while in a foreign land?

The circumstances and words are sad enough without any commentary, but there are three details that might help us appreciate the pain better.

1. *The poem's sounds.* The English words are sad, even mournful, but the words have an even sadder sound in the Hebrew language. Verses 1–3, which lead up to and explain the pathetic question of verse 4, repeat nine times the pronoun ending *nu* (meaning "we" or "our"), which sounds mournful. It is like crying "ohhh" or "woe" repeatedly.

2. *The contrast with Psalms 135 and 136.* The two preceding psalms celebrated God's gift of the land to his people. Both speak of God's having "struck down the firstborn of Egypt" (Pss. 135:8; 136:10), having overthrown "Sihon king of the Amorites" and "Og king of Bashan" (Pss. 135:11; 136:19–20), and as having given the land of these kings as "an inheritance . . . to Israel" (Pss. 135:12; 136:22). Psalm 135 even ends by calling on all who fear God to "praise the LORD . . . *from Zion*" (Ps. 135:21, italics added). But in Psalm 137 the people are no longer in the land and mourn the loss of it.

3. *The "songs of Zion."* These are some of the loveliest compositions in the Psalter. I like Psalm 84 especially.

> How lovely is your dwelling place,
>   O LORD Almighty!
> My soul yearns, even faints,
>   for the courts of the LORD;
> my heart and my flesh cry out
>   for the living God. . . .
>
> Better is one day in your courts
>   than a thousand elsewhere;

> I would rather be a doorkeeper in the house of my God
> than dwell in the tents of the wicked (Ps. 84:1–2, 10).

Think how painful it would be to sing a song like that while in exile.

God's People in Man's City

We do not need to allegorize Psalm 137 to feel its relevance. We need only think how hard it is to sing the hymns of the church when we are immersed in this world's culture. It is why we escape to church to do it. Or we may think of how sad we become considering the state of the church itself when it is weak or plunged into apostasy or is in spiritual decline and when we seem unable to do anything about it.

The famous Baptist preacher Charles Spurgeon wrote of such times:

> Even thus do true believers mourn when they see the church despoiled and find themselves unable to succor her; we could bear anything better than this. In these our times the Babylon of error ravages the city of God, and the hearts of the faithful are grievously wounded as they see truth fallen in the streets and unbelief rampant among the professed servants of the Lord.[3]

Struck Down, but Not Destroyed

Distress is not despair, however. So even though we are struck by the pathos of the psalm's opening verses, and even identify with them, we also notice that the singer's faith in God is intact. Or to express it in terms of the psalm's unique imagery, we notice that although the exiles were unable to sings the songs of Zion in Babylon, they nevertheless did not break their harps in pieces or throw them in the stream. Instead they hung them on the poplars, presumably saving them for what would surely be a better day. This is faith that is determined never to forget Jerusalem, as we see in the next section:

> If I forget you, O Jerusalem,
>   may my right hand forget its skill.
> May my tongue cling to the roof of my mouth
>   if I do not remember you,
>   if I do not consider Jerusalem
>   my highest joy (vv. 5–6).

For a right-handed person the expression in verse 5 would be a way of referring to his greatest skill and strength. In the context of the opening verses the right hand is referred to probably because it was the hand used to play the harp. Likewise the writer refers to the tongue because it would have been used to sing the songs of Zion, which he will not do under these disloyal circumstances.

In this stanza the pronouns turn from the plural to the singular, from "we" to "I." Thus, in these verses each individual pledges his or her own personal loyalty to Jerusalem. Suffering may be shared; it often is. But determination to remember God and walk in his ways is something each of us must do individually. You must do it, and so must I!

If the psalmist is determined to forget neither God nor Jerusalem, is he expecting to be delivered from his present evil state and be able to sing the songs of Zion in Zion at some future date? We do not know what any individual Israelite thought while he or she was in Babylon, but we know that God eventually brought his people back to their own land through the decree of Cyrus in the days of Zerubbabel the governor and Joshua the high priest. In fact, it is in Jerusalem that the present psalm was written and from Zion that the words of the psalm were first sung.

Christians also endure bad times, but we do not despair, because we know that God will bring us through them, sometimes sooner than we expect. About four hundred years ago, in 1605, a French priest named Vincent de Paul was traveling from Toulouse to Marseille by sea. The ship he was in was seized by Barbary pirates, the passengers were carried to Tunis on the coast of Africa, and Vincent de Paul was sold as a slave to an apostate Christian from Nice, who took him inland to work on his farm. As he labored in this man's fields under a burning equatorial sun he attracted the interest of one of his master's Turkish wives, who asked him to sing some of the praises of his God. Vincent remembered the captive Israelites and their plaintive 137th psalm and began to sing it: "By the rivers of Babylon we sat and wept when we remembered Zion."

The song touched the woman's heart. She told her husband that he had done wrong to change his faith, and she praised the religion the priest had explained to her. Her words revived her husband's slumbering conscience. He left north Africa and returned to France, landing at Aigues Mortes, where he set Vincent de Paul free, two years after his capture by the pirates.[4]

A Terrible Imprecation

"Remember" occurs three times in the psalm. In verse 1 the poet says that he and the other captives remembered Zion while in Babylon. In verse 6 he pronounces a judgment against himself if he should not remember Jerusalem. Now in verse 7 he calls on God to remember as he remembered and apply an appropriate judgment to those who destroyed the holy city.

A problem comes with how the writer asks God to remember Jerusalem's destruction: It is so God might pour out a corresponding judgment on these enemies, specifically the people of Edom, who encouraged the destruction, and the Babylonians, who actually carried it out. In what is surely one of the fiercest imprecatory portions of the entire Psalter, the writer cries out,

> O Daughter of Babylon, doomed to destruction,
>   happy is he who repays you
>   for what you have done to us—
> he who seizes your infants
>   and dashes them against the rocks.[5]

Christians have been taught to forgive their enemies, and even for those living in our time who are not Christians those words seem unduly vindictive, vicious, and violent. But before we get too self-righteous in reading them we should remember that none of us has experienced anything like the cruelties that were inflicted on Jerusalem at the time of its fall or those that would have been inflicted on the inhabitants of any ancient city in such warfare.

Spurgeon wrote,

> Let those find fault with it who have never seen their temple burned, their city ruined, their wives ravished, and their children slain; they might not perhaps be so velvet-mouthed if they had suffered after this fashion. It is one thing to talk of the bitter feeling which moved captive Israelites in Babylon, and quite another thing to be captives ourselves under a strange and remorseless power, which knew not how to show mercy, but delighted in barbarities to the defenseless. . . . [Psalm 137] is a fruit of the Captivity in Babylon, and often has it furnished expression for sorrows which else had been unutterable.[6]

The fact that we might feel the same way under the same circumstances does not make our feelings right. So we should note that the psalmist is not just sinfully venting his feelings, as three particular facts about this imprecation point out.

1. *The words are an appeal to God for justice.* Here, as in each of the imprecatory psalms, the psalmist is not suggesting that he is about to take revenge on his enemies or even that he would if he could. On the contrary, he is appealing to God to do what is right and judge those who have been excessively wicked and cruel in their actions. Derek Kidner says that the first thing to notice about verses 7–9 is their "juridical background." The divine Judge is being presented with evidence against Edom and Babylon.[7]

2. *The judgments are only what God himself decrees in other places.* An entire book of the Bible was written to declare God's coming judgment on Edom. That book is Obadiah, and the reason given for the judgment is precisely what is alluded to in this psalm, namely, that when Jerusalem fell the people of Edom did not mourn for their brother nation's suffering, as they should have, but rejoiced in the destruction instead. The prophet adds that the Edomites "stood aloof," "rejoice[d]," "seize[d] their wealth," and even "hand[ed] over the survivors" when they caught them (Obadiah 11–14). Other judgments on Edom may be found in Isaiah 34:5–15; 63:1–4; Jeremiah

49:7–22; Lamentations 4:21–22; Ezekiel 25:12–14; 35:1–15; 36:5; Joel 3:19; and Amos 1:11–12.

There are extensive prophecies against Babylon in Isaiah 13:1–14:23; 21:1–17; 47:1–15; and Jeremiah 50:1–51:64. Most telling is the account of the destruction of Mystery Babylon in Revelation 18 and 19. In those chapters the kings, merchants, sea captains, and other peoples of the earth mourn for the city. An angel joins in, and even the redeemed rejoice in God's judgment, crying, "Hallelujah!" as they praise God for it.

3. *This is precisely what God has done.* Romans 2:6 says that God "will give to each person according to what he has done" (citing Ps. 62:12; Prov. 24:12). He has done it! Today the fortresses of ancient Edom are a desolate waste, and the site of ancient Babylon is a ruin. God cannot be mocked. "A man reaps what he sows" (Gal. 6:7), and "the one who sows to please his sinful nature, from that nature will reap destruction" (Gal. 6:8).

"Except We Repent"

Do we deserve heaven while the Edomites, Babylonians, and others like them deserve hell? Jesus answered that question when he was asked about the death of a few apparently innocent people in his day. Some Galileans had been murdered by Roman soldiers, and a tower had collapsed on some people who were standing beside it. The onlookers asked Jesus how it was possible that things like this could happen in a world ruled by a just, yet merciful, God. Was it because these people were worse sinners than others? Was it because God was either too weak to avert the tragedies, or didn't care?

Jesus replied,

> Do you think that these Galileans were worse sinners than all the other Galileans because they suffered this way? I tell you, no! But unless you repent, you too will all perish. Or those eighteen who died when the tower of Siloam fell on them—do you think they were more guilty than all the others living in Jerusalem? I tell you, no! But unless you repent, you too will all perish (Luke 13:2–5).

Jesus' point was that the question is not why God judges some, but rather why he has spared us, we being the sinners we are. If we knew how sinful we are, we would understand that we are the ones who should have perished. We should be judged. Knowing that, we should repent of our sin and turn to God for the salvation he makes available in Jesus Christ, before the day of salvation is past.

Psalm 138

A Bold Man's Praise

I will praise you, O LORD, with all my heart;
before the "gods" I will sing your praise.
I will bow down toward your holy temple
and will praise your name
for your love and your faithfulness,
for you have exalted above all things
your name and your word.
When I called, you answered me;
you made me bold and stouthearted.

May all the kings of the earth praise you, O LORD,
when they hear the words of your mouth.
May they sing of the ways of the LORD,
for the glory of the LORD is great.

Though the LORD is on high, he looks upon the lowly,
but the proud he knows from afar.
Though I walk in the midst of trouble,
you preserve my life;
you stretch out your hand against the anger of my foes,
with your right hand you save me.
The LORD will fulfill his purpose for me;
your love, O LORD, endures forever—
do not abandon the works of your hands.

verses 1–8

In Psalm 137 the captive Israelites were unable to sing praise to God in the presence of their heathen captors, but in Psalm 138 a time has come not only when such praises are sung but also when the writer anticipates the praises of God being sung by the heathen themselves, even by their kings (vv. 4–5). These psalms have been placed together to make this contrast and to teach that although there is a time for silence, lest we cast our pearls before swine (Matt. 7:6), there is also a time for bold confession. We must be bold to praise God when others will not praise him.

David's Last Songs

Psalm 138 is the first of a group of eight psalms ascribed to David, the last of David's psalms in the Psalter. Overall about half the psalms are ascribed to him.[1]

Recent studies of the psalms question these ascriptions, especially of these last psalms. There is no reason why they cannot have been written by David; in fact, there is much to suggest that David was the author. Psalm 138 sounds much like David's other compositions. For example, verse 1 echoes Psalm 9:1, verse 2 echoes Psalm 5:7, verse 7 echoes Psalm 23:4, and verse 8 echoes Psalm 57:3.[2] Psalm 138 is also aware of enemies, as virtually all David's psalms are, and it expresses both zeal for God and humility before him, which is almost a Davidic signature. Derek Kidner says, "There is a fine blend of boldness and humility from the outset: boldness to confess the Lord *before the gods,* humility to *bow down* before him."[3] Alexander Maclaren says of these compositions, "[They stand] where a 'find' of Davidic psalms at a late date would naturally be put," noting that Psalm 138 is "unlike those which precede it and has many affinities with the earlier psalms ascribed to David."[4]

If Psalm 138 is by David, it may be a grateful response to God's promise to him recorded in 2 Samuel 7. God promised David a kingdom that would endure forever through the reign of a future king. H. C. Leupold suggests that this promise is exactly what the psalm is about, pointing out that some great promise must be intended by the claim of verse 8: "The LORD will fulfill his purpose for me."[5] If this is the case, then the psalm is basically a psalm of thanks to God for this blessing, especially since the word translated "I will praise" in verses 1, 2, and 4 more precisely means "I will give thanks." The psalm is even somewhat messianic since it is before this coming Messiah that the kings of the earth will bow when they come to praise God (vv. 4–5).

A Bold Man's Bold Thanksgiving

Since this is a worship psalm and its dominant note is thanksgiving, we are reminded at the start that worship involves thanksgiving. Up to now in our study of these last psalms we have stressed that worship is acknowledging God as the great God he truly is and praising him for it. In other words, worship has to do with confessing God's attributes. We are reminded here that it also has to do with thanking God for what he has done. These two parts of worship must go together since, as is the case, the only way we can know what God is like is through his actions.

One beautiful hymn version of Psalm 138 recognizes it as a psalm of thanksgiving when it begins,

> With grateful heart my thanks I bring,
> Before the great thy praise I sing;
> I worship in thy holy place
> And praise thee for thy truth and grace.
> *The Psalter* 1912

The opening verses of this psalm (vv. 1–3) have two puzzling parts.

1. *"Before the 'gods.'"* The Hebrew word for "gods" in verse 1 is *elohim,* a plural word, which is nevertheless most often used for God himself, as in the very first verse of the Bible: "In the beginning God *(elohim)* created the heavens and the earth" (Gen. 1:1). Some writers think God himself is meant here, but it seems a bit strange to most readers to have the psalmist saying, in effect, "I will praise you, O God, before God." Thus most commentators on Psalm 138 look for other possibilities.

One idea is that "before God" means "before the ark of God," that is, in the sanctuary. That meaning is unusual and even a bit redundant since the next verse says, "I will bow down toward your holy temple."

Martin Luther and John Calvin thought the word refers to angels since it is used that way in a few other places, as in Job 1:6, where the "angels" ("sons of God") present themselves before God.

Some of the older versions of the Bible as well as some of the newer interpreters suggest that it refers to kings or judges. This is the probable meaning of the word in Psalm 82:6, which Jesus referred to, saying, "If he called them 'gods,' to whom the word of God came, . . ." (John 10:35). Jesus seems to mean the judges of Israel. An extension of this meaning would be "the great of the earth" before whom David, a king himself, would most naturally express his praise of God. This is the view of Franz Delitzsch.[6]

The final possibility is that *elohim* refers to the idols or false gods before whom David would be declaring the existence of the one and only true God. This was the view of some of the older commentators, such as J. J. Stewart Perowne, H. C. Leupold, and Alexander Maclaren.[7]

Any of these interpretations is possible, and there is not a great deal that hinges on the outcome, but two facts point in the direction of "gods" meaning kings, judges, or other powerful people of the earth. First, if the background of the psalm is God's promise of a lasting dynasty for David as recorded in 2 Samuel 7, then verse 9 of that chapter would explain the reference. God said, "I will make your name great, like the names of the greatest men of the earth." David would want to praise God before these other men, his peers. The verse would teach that we are to praise and exalt the Lord before those who are our peers also.

Second, David mentions these kings explicitly in verse 4: "May all the kings of the earth praise you." In other words, he wants to praise God before the powerful of this world so that they might learn to praise God also, following his example. To my mind, this interpretation makes the most sense, given the context.

2. *God's "word" exalted above God's "name."* Verse 2 says literally, "You have magnified your word above all your name." This seems a strange thing to say since God's name, which is a way of referring to all that God is, is above everything. How can God's word be exalted above that which is above everything else? Seeing this difficulty, some translators have guessed that the letter *waw* (meaning "and") has been erroneously omitted from the text. Then they reinstate it to get something like the meaning found in the New International Version: "You have exalted above all things your name *and* your word." Derek Kidner agrees with this emendation on the grounds that "Scripture does not encourage bibliolatry."[8] Other people render the verse: "You have magnified your name . . . *in* your word."

The problem is that the text does not say either of these things as it stands, and the actual reading may be best despite its initial difficulty. It would be as if God is saying, "I value my integrity above everything else. Above everything else I want to be believed." The verse does not have to mean that God's other qualities are moved to second place.[9]

If what is driving David in his thanksgiving is gratitude for the great blessing promised by God's establishing his throne forever, the verse becomes entirely appropriate. For David would be fixing his confidence on God's word. There is nothing in human life to suggest that an earthly dynasty or anything else is forever. All things human perish. Heaven and earth themselves will pass away (Matt. 24:35). But if God has promised David an everlasting dynasty, then God will surely perform what he has promised.

In fact, the reference to God's supremely exalted word may refer to something recorded explicitly in 2 Samuel 7, for in verses 20 and 21 of that chapter David responds to God's promise of an eternal kingdom noting, "What more can David say to you? For you know your servant, O Sovereign LORD. For the sake of your word and according to your will, you have done this great thing and made it known to your Servant."

A Bold Man's Gracious God

Enough of the problems. What is David praising God for in these verses? The answer is God's "covenant love" *(hesed)* and "faithfulness" (v. 2). Surely there are no greater qualities of God than these where the people of God are concerned.

Yet strikingly, these two attributes are under attack today. In fact, they have always been. People attack God's covenant love because they want to substitute a religion of their own sullied works. They do not want grace; they want recognition of their own nonexistent merit. They attack God's truth or faithfulness to his truth because they prefer their own perceptions or hunches instead. These were the same attacks Satan used in his temptation of Eve in the garden of Eden. His first temptation was an attack on God's goodness, for the question "Did God really say, 'You must not eat from any tree in the garden'?" means "If God has forbidden one tree, he might as well have forbidden you to eat from all the trees; clearly he does not have your best interests at heart." His second temptation was an attack on God's word: "You will not surely die." That means "God is lying."

David had learned that God does not lie and that all God's thoughts and actions toward us flow from love and persist in faithfulness. God is good, and he is always good. Therefore, David wanted to thank God for his goodness and praise him for his covenant love and faithfulness before everyone.

David also praises God for providing what he needed when he needed it, and that immediately. David records that he called on God and God answered him right away. Moreover, God made him bold and stouthearted, no doubt in the face of the attacks of his enemies that he mentions a little further on (v. 7).

A Bold Man's Bold Desire

Verses 4 and 5 are describing the coming day of messianic blessing when the promised king will come to rule from his throne forever. As I pointed out before, because David is himself a king he is concerned for kings and looks forward to a day when all the rulers of the earth will bow before him who is King of kings and Lord of lords.

That day will come. Philippians 2:9–11 tells us that God has given to Jesus

> . . . the name that is above every name,
> that at the name of Jesus every knee should bow,
> in heaven and on earth and under the earth,
> and every tongue confess that Jesus Christ is Lord,
> to the glory of God the Father.

In this psalm David similarly notes that the result of the Messiah's coming will be God's glory. In David's case these words are not so much a declaration of what God has done, as in Philippians, or even a prophecy of what he will yet do, but a prayer or desire that the kings of the earth might thank God and sing his praises.

Kings will bow by the power of God when Jesus Christ returns, that day when every knee will be forced to bow before him. David also says that the kings of the earth will praise God "when they hear the words of [his] mouth"

(v. 4). This might mean when they hear God himself on the day he thunders from Zion, but it probably means when those who know God declare his words to them. In other words, the psalm is acknowledging the need for the people of God to be missionaries.

This interpretation fits the context of the psalm, in which the writer is making a bold confession of God's love and faithfulness himself, but it is also what makes the psalm especially relevant to us and our time. Yes, God has exalted Jesus, having given him a name above every name, and everyone in heaven and on earth will acknowledge that one day; but in the meantime, our great commission is to make God and his gospel known. As Jesus himself said, we are to make disciples of all nations until "the very end of the age" (Matt. 28:19–20).

A Bold Man's Humility

In the last stanza of the psalm the writer comes back to his own needs. He knows that God is great, that he has compassion for the lowly and disdain for those who vainly exalt themselves (v. 6). He knows that God preserves his life, that he stretches out his hand in anger against his foes, that he saves him by the power of his strong right hand (v. 7). But still he walks "in the midst of trouble" and cannot survive unless God preserves his life and stands by him (v. 7). So he prays, "Do not abandon the works of your hands" (v. 8).

The most important line in this last stanza is one I mentioned earlier, the first line of verse 8, though it is most memorable in the King James Version: "The Lord will perfect that which concerneth me." This is an Old Testament version of Philippians 1:6, which assures us that "he who began a good work in you will carry it on to completion until the day of Jesus Christ."

In Psalm 138 David was probably thinking of God's purpose in sending the Messiah to reign on his throne, but we ought to think of this line in terms of God's avowed purpose concerning us. What is God's purpose for us? Paul states it nicely in Romans 8:28–30.

> We know that in all things God works for the good of those who love him, who have been called according to his purpose. For those God foreknew he also predestined to be conformed to the likeness of his Son, that he might be the firstborn among many brothers. And those he predestined, he also called; those he called, he also justified; those he justified he also glorified.

In other words, God's purpose is to make us like Jesus Christ and to bring us to glory.

Our assurance rests in God's eternal love. The next to last line of this psalm declares, echoing the repeated refrain of Psalm 136, "Your love, O Lord, endures forever." Those who know God do not have any confidence in themselves. We know that we are only weak, guilty sinners saved by grace.

Apart from the persevering grace of God we would all be certain to fall away into sin and perish. Our confidence is not in ourselves; it is in him who loved us and gave himself for us. So we say, "The LORD will fulfill his purpose for me" and "Your love, O LORD, endures forever." And we pray, "Do not abandon the works of your hands."

Herbert Lockyer wrote rightly, "Our hope of final perseverance is the final perseverance of the God we love and serve. Because his mercy endureth for ever, his work in and for us will continue until we are perfected when we see him in all his perfection."[10]

Martin Luther strongly held to the doctrine of perseverance, but he still prayed: "Confirm, O God, in us that thou hast wrought, and perfect the work that thou hast begun in us."[11] Augustus M. Toplady declared:

> The work which his goodness began,
> The arm of his strength will complete;
> His promise is Yea and Amen,
> And never was forfeited yet.

J. W. Burgon wrote wisely, "His creating hands formed our souls at the beginning; his nail-pierced hands redeemed them on Calvary; his glorified hands will hold our souls fast and not let them go for ever. Unto his hands let us commend our spirits, sure that even though the works our hands have made void the works of his hands, yet his hands will again make perfect all that our hands have unmade."[12]

Psalm 139

A Hymn to the All-Knowing God: Part 1

Safe in God's Thoughts

O LORD, you have searched me
  and you know me.
You know when I sit and when I rise;
  you perceive my thoughts from afar.
You discern my going out and my lying down;
  you are familiar with all my ways.
Before a word is on my tongue
  you know it completely, O LORD.

You hem me in—behind and before;
  you have laid your hand upon me.
Such knowledge is too wonderful for me,
  too lofty for me to attain.

Where can I go from your Spirit?
  Where can I flee from your presence?
If I go up to the heavens, you are there;
  if I make my bed in the depths, you are there.
If I rise on the wings of the dawn,

if I settle on the far side of the sea,
even there your hand will guide me,
your right hand will hold me fast.

If I say, "Surely the darkness will hide me
and the light become night around me,"
even the darkness will not be dark to you;
the night will shine like the day,
for darkness is as light to you.

verses 1–12

Somewhere in J. I. Packer's writings there is a reference to Puritan theology as theology of that "older, better, wiser and more practical sort." That applies to the Puritans, but it applies even more to Psalm 139. Here is theology that is even older, even better, even wiser, and even more practical. It is theology of the very best sort.

Sometimes we speak of "doing theology" today, and we often talk about the conflict between the head and the heart, saying that either one alone is inadequate. A theology that is all of the head is cold, dry, barren, and of little practical value. A theology that is all heart may be warm, comforting, and practical, but it will lack substance, and because it does it will be subject to every theological fad that comes along and will not hold up in hard times. Psalm 139 has both head and heart. It is strongly theological, dealing with such important doctrines as God's omniscience (it is probably the weightiest part of the Bible for discussing God's omniscience), omnipresence, and omnipotence; but it is also wonderfully personal, because it speaks of these attributes of God in ways that impact the psalmist and ourselves.

Theology for Worship

H. C. Leupold, the Lutheran scholar, observes that the thinking of the psalm "is not formulated in theological abstractions but in terms of personal religious experience."[1] Leslie C. Allen, a contributor to the *Word Biblical Commentary*, calls it "applied theology."[2] Alexander Maclaren, one of the best expositors of the nineteenth century, wrote, "Not mere omniscience, but a knowledge which knows *him* altogether, not mere omnipresence, but a presence which *he* can nowhere escape, not mere creative power, but a power which shaped *him*, fill and thrill the psalmist's soul."[3]

The personal theology of Psalm 139 is the very essence of worship, the matter we are dealing with especially in our study of these last psalms (Psalms 135–50). Psalm 139 is specifically dedicated to "the director of music," obviously for worship uses in the temple.

Although Psalm 139 deals with some of the highest and most important of all theological concepts, the omniscience, omnipresence, and omnipotence of God, it nevertheless has two practical aims that become clear at its close (vv. 19–24). First, the writer wants to separate himself from all who deliberately practice evil. Second, he wants God to search him out thoroughly and purge him of anything that might be offensive to God so that he might walk in the way everlasting. It is hard to think of any more practical reasons for theology than those.

The psalm's seven stanzas fall into four easily recognizable parts: praise of God for his omniscience (vv. 1–6); praise to God for his omnipresence (vv. 7–12); praise to God for his omnipotence, especially in the creation of the psalmist himself (vv. 13–18); and a response to what has been said, indicating the two ways a person can relate to the all-knowing God (vv. 19–24). Each of these sections has six verses that fall into two parts each. The first four verses are descriptive; they introduce the main idea of the section. They are followed by two more verses that are reflective. Each stanza of this brilliant composition anticipates and leads into the ideas to be developed in the following verses. We will look at the first two of these sections (vv. 1–12) in this chapter and the last two sections (vv. 13–24) in the following chapter.

Praise to God for His Omniscience

The theme of the first six verses is the omniscience of God, the proper term for the fact that God sees and knows everything. Omniscience is not expressed here as mere doctrine; it is confessed in wonder and adoration, as the other doctrines (omnipresence and omnipotence) will also be. Confession is one way in which we worship God.

The unique quality of the knowledge possessed by God is perfection. God knows all things, and he knows them exhaustively. We also know things, therefore we have some idea of God's omniscience, but our knowledge is only partial and imperfect. Arthur W. Pink wrote,

> God . . . knows everything; everything possible, everything actual; all events, all creatures, of the past, the present, and the future. He is perfectly acquainted with every detail in the life of every being in heaven, in earth, and in hell. . . . Nothing escapes his notice, nothing can be hidden from him, nothing is forgotten by him. . . . He never errs, never changes, never overlooks anything.[4]

A. W. Tozer expands this description by adding negatives.

> God has never learned from anyone. God cannot learn. Could God at any time or in any manner receive into his mind knowledge that he did not possess and had not possessed from eternity, he would be imperfect and less than himself. To think of a God who must sit at the feet of a teacher, even

though that teacher be an archangel or a seraph, is to think of someone other than the Most High God, maker of heaven and earth. . . .

God knows instantly and effortlessly all matter and all matters, all mind and every mind, all spirit and all spirits, all being and every being, all creaturehood and all creatures, every plurality and all pluralities, all law and every law, all relations, all causes, all thoughts, all mysteries, all enigmas, all feeling, all desires, every unuttered secret, all thrones and dominions, all personalities, all things visible and invisible in heaven and in earth, motion, space, time, life, death, good, evil, heaven, and hell. . . .

Because God knows all things perfectly, he knows no thing better than any other thing, but all things equally well. He never discovers anything, he is never surprised, never amazed. He never wonders about anything nor (except when drawing men out for their own good) does he seek information or ask questions.[5]

This knowledge is what the psalmist is writing about in the six opening verses of Psalm 139. Verse 1 states the psalm's theme, God's perfect knowledge of the psalmist: "O LORD, you have searched me and you know me." The next three verses develop three important aspects of that knowledge: the psalmist's thoughts ("you perceive my thoughts from afar," v. 2); his ways ("you are familiar with all my ways," v. 3); and his words ("Before a word is on my tongue you know it completely, O LORD," v. 4). After this, in verse 5, he begins to anticipate the theme of the psalm's next section, God's omnipresence, since the ideas overlap. But he breaks off the pursuit of that idea to wrap up his contemplation of God's knowledge in verse 6:

> Such knowledge is too wonderful for me,
> too lofty for me to attain.

This is the note the apostle Paul struck in his profound doxology concluding the eleventh chapter of Romans:

> Oh, the depth of the riches of the wisdom and knowledge of God!
> How unsearchable his judgments,
> and his paths beyond tracing out! (Rom. 11:33).

The Threat of Omniscience

The perfection of God's knowledge is also disturbing, however, which is one reason why people try so hard not to think about God. As long as we only think about God knowing things or other people, the idea of God's knowledge is only amusing, like our reaction to the report about schoolchildren who were asked whether they thought God understood computers, and the majority thought he did not. We are amused because we know that God does understand computers. The subject is not so amusing when we consider that God also knows about *us*. What are we to do with a God "before whom all hearts are open, all desires known"? An all-knowing God is immensely threatening, which is why we try to banish him from our minds.

Arthur W. Pink notes that the thought of divine omniscience "fills us with uneasiness."[6] A. W. Tozer is even stronger: "In the divine omniscience we see set forth against each other the terror and fascination of the Godhead. That God knows each person through and through can be a cause of shaking fear to the man that has something to hide—some unforsaken sin, some secret crime committed against man or God."[7] Roy Clements says that David's description of God is like some "master-detective who snoops . . . into every detail of his existence, armed with x-ray cameras and laser probes." He is like the oppressive, all-seeing eye of "Big Brother" in George Orwell's futuristic anti-utopian novel *1984*.[8]

For an unsaved person this powerful, pervasive knowledge seems intrusive and frightening, and with good reason. God is the end-time judge with whom we must reckon. Strikingly, the response of the psalmist is not fear. He is not trembling when he thinks of God's omniscience. On the contrary, he shelters himself in God's knowledge and marvels at it. For the psalmist, God's knowledge is not a threat; it is a refuge.

Praise to God for His Omnipresence

Isn't it a natural reaction to want to escape God's all-seeing, all-knowing presence, and actually try to? Yes, and that is probably why David's thoughts turned in verses 7–12 to God's omnipresence.

Some commentators see in these verses a desire of David to escape God's gaze. Although that might be a natural response to reflecting on God's omniscience, as I suggested, it is not at all what David is saying. In a sense, David is still meditating on God's omniscience, noting that the reason why God sees everything and knows everything is that he is everywhere to see and know it. In fact, since the psalmist is making these points of theology personal, what impresses him is that God will always be wherever he goes. Try as he might, he would never be able to escape him. But he is not fearing that or dreading it; he is comforted by the thought.

H. C. Leupold denies that the psalmist is actually trying to flee from God, and he is right. David is not wanting to flee from God at all. He is thinking about what would be the case if a person should attempt it. Leupold suggests that the right idea would be conveyed more effectively by translating verse 7 as, "Where *could* I go" from your presence.[9] The New International Version gets close to this meaning when it asks, "Where can I go?"

Well, where? In verses 8–12 David imagines three areas in which escape from God might be thought to be possible, but he dismisses each one.

1. *Up or down.* The first thought that might come to us is to climb higher than God so God can't reach us, or descend so low that we will lie beneath his grasp; but the highest point to which we can rise is heaven and God is obviously there, and the lowest point to which we can descend is hell (the

Hebrew word is *sheol*) and God is there too. He is there in his judicial aspect. In fact, the thing that makes hell so terrible is that it is run by God. It is not ruled by the devil in spite of such popular descriptions of hell as John Milton's in *Paradise Lost*.[10]

Amos uses this same language to describe the folly of people who think they can escape God's judgments.

> Though they dig down to the depths of the grave,
>   from there my hand will take them.
> Though they climb up to the heavens,
>   from there I will bring them down (Amos 9:2).

2. *East or west.* Well, if it is impossible to escape God by going up or down, perhaps we can do it by going east or west. This is what David considers next, in verses 9 and 10. Dawn rises in the east, and from David's perspective in Israel the far side of the sea was west. To "rise on the wings of the dawn" probably means to flash from east to west as fast as the dawn's early light streaks from horizon to horizon. Would that help? Even if it were possible, it would not enable us to escape God, for when we get to that far distant horizon, we find that God is already there before us.

> If I rise on the wings of the dawn,
>   if I settle on the far side of the sea,
> even there your hand will guide me,
>   your right hand will hold me fast.

Jonah tried to do it, fleeing from Joppa in the direction of Tarshish on the coast of Spain, but God was present even on the expansive Mediterranean Sea. God pursued him in the storm and brought him back, inside the great fish.

3. *The darkness.* People pursue evil in the dark, thinking, "Surely the darkness will hide me" (v. 11), but even the darkness is light to God. Light is God's own creation (Gen. 1:3), and he does not need it to know what is going on in the secret places of the earth. These verses, which describe the darkness, lead into the next stanza, which speaks of the formation of man in the womb.

These are the best-known verses of the psalm, and rightly so. They are magnificent verses. "Never has the pen of man more effectively described the omnipresence of God."[11] These verses are worth the most careful study. Indeed, we should memorize them and thereby hide them in our hearts.

No Escape from God

In the next chapter we will see how David responded to his meditation on God's omniscience and omnipresence. It is the response of one who learned what it is to be known by God and loved by him anyway, to be always with

God and not fear his presence. What about those who are still trying to get away from him? What about you if you have not yet come face-to-face with God in Jesus Christ and surrendered to him? Do you really think you can escape from the omnipresent God or hide from the Omniscient?

Verses 7–12 prompted Francis Thompson's classic poem "The Hound of Heaven," a poem in which the poet describes how he tried unsuccessfully to hide from God.

> I fled Him, down the nights, and down the days;
>   I fled Him, down the arches of the years;
> I fled Him, down the labyrinthine ways
>   Of my own mind, and in the mist of tears
> I hid from Him, and under running laughter.
> Up visaed hopes I sped;
> And shot, precipitated,
> Adown Titanic glooms of chasmed fears,
>   From those strong Feet that followed, followed after.

Thompson fled from God, but he could not escape the omnipresent One, because God always followed after him, "followed, followed after."

If you are not yet a Christian, let me remind you that you will have to stand before God one day. How do you suppose you will be able to escape his just judgment on you for your sins? The Bible says, "Nothing in all creation is hidden from God's sight. Everything is uncovered and laid bare before the eyes of him to whom we must give account" (Heb. 4:13). What will you do on the day when all your sins will be read out? On that day you will be abased, confounded, speechless, and overwhelmed as God unfolds the records of your sinful past life paragraph after paragraph and page after page. "Stop!" you will cry. But God will not stop until every sinful thought, every evil deed, every curse, every theft, every lie, every neglect of what you should have done is read out and justly punished.

Do not wait for that day. Jesus died so that sinners like you and me might be saved from judgment. He is pursuing you so you might be saved.

Psalm 139

A Hymn to the All-Knowing God: Part 2

Safe in God's Hands

For you created my inmost being;
*   you knit me together in my mother's womb.*
I praise you because I am fearfully and wonderfully made;
*   your works are wonderful,*
*   I know that full well.*
My frame was not hidden from you
*   when I was made in the secret place.*
When I was woven together in the depths of the earth,
*   your eyes saw my unformed body.*
All the days ordained for me
*   were written in your book*
*   before one of them came to be.*

How precious to me are your thoughts, O God!
*   How vast is the sum of them!*
Were I to count them,
*   they would outnumber the grains of sand.*
When I awake,
*   I am still with you.*

If only you would slay the wicked, O God!
  Away from me, you bloodthirsty men!
They speak of you with evil intent;
  your adversaries misuse your name.
Do I not hate those who hate you, O LORD,
  and abhor those who rise up against you?
I have nothing but hatred for them;
  I count them my enemies.

Search me, O God, and know my heart;
  test me and know my anxious thoughts.
See if there is any offensive way in me,
  and lead me in the way everlasting.

verses 13–24

$$W$$hen I introduced Psalm 139 in the
last chapter, one of the things I said about it is that it is made up of four
matched parts in which three of God's greatest attributes are discussed:
omniscience (God knows all things), omnipresence (God is everywhere at
all times), and omnipotence (God is supremely powerful). The fourth part
of the psalm is a response to these attributes.

I also observed that there is a sense in which the only attribute actually
being talked about is omniscience, for the only reason David adds a reflection on God's omnipresence to the psalm is to explain why it is that God
knows everything: God sees and knows everything because God is everywhere. Now we will see that the psalmist's discussion of omnipotence is also
linked to omniscience because, according to David, a further reason God
knows everything is that he has also made everything and controls it.

John Stott expressed this connection when he wrote, "God's omniscience, which in the previous section has been attributed to his omnipresence, is now attributed to his omnipotence. God can search man out not
only because he sees him, but because he made him."[1] Derek Kidner says,
"The third stanza brings together and carries forward the thought of the
first two: God not only sees the invisible and penetrates the inaccessible, but
is operative there, the author of every detail of my being."[2] Or as H. C.
Leupold says, "What is being demonstrated is the fact that in his very being
man [establishes] both the omniscience and the omnipresence of God."[3]

Praise to God for His Omnipotence

Since Psalm 139 is a worship psalm, we are not going to find abstract
reflections on God's power, though they occur in other places and are
proper in their place. These words are personal.

If we do not understand that God is all-powerful, we do not have a right understanding of God at all; we are thinking of some other being. If God is not all-powerful, there must be some power or powers greater than God. If that is the case, God's power must be thwarted and his proper sovereignty restricted by circumstances, human beings, or Satan. What kind of a God would that be? Arthur W. Pink wrote, "A 'god' whose will is resisted, whose designs are frustrated, whose purpose is checkmated, possesses no title to Deity, and so far from being a fit object of worship, merits nought but contempt."[4] If we want to know God, we need to think in the clearest possible way about God's might and what it means.

We have already seen that David is writing with his heart as well as with his head in this psalm, and this means that he is not thinking of God's omnipotence abstractly, but as it applies to him. More particularly, he is thinking of the power of God in forming him while he was still in the womb of his mother. No wonder God knows me, he says. God made me. He formed me from my very first moments, from my beginning.

> For you created my inmost being;
>> you knit me together in my mother's womb.
> I praise you because I am fearfully and wonderfully made;
>> your works are wonderful,
>> I know that full well.
> My frame was not hidden from you
>> when I was made in the secret place.
> When I was woven together in the depths of the earth,
>> your eyes saw my unformed body.
> All the days ordained for me
>> were written in your book
>> before one of them came to be (vv. 13–16).

A Person Even in the Womb

These verses plainly teach the individuality of a child while it is still in its mother's womb. David is not writing about abortion, of course. Nothing could be farther from his mind. But no one can read these verses thoughtfully today without considering their obvious bearing on this important contemporary problem.

The chief issue in discussions about abortion concerns the identity of the fetus. People who argue for the right of a woman to have an abortion—"It's my own body; I can do with it as I please"—usually argue that the fetus is not yet a person, but is only a part of the woman's body, like a gallbladder or appendix that she can elect to have removed. That is why language describing the unborn child has changed so radically. A generation ago everyone referred to the unborn child as a baby, and pregnant women knew they were carrying a baby. It is hard for anyone to think calmly about killing a baby. So today people talk about the fetus or the embryo or even mere "tissue" instead. To get rid of tissue doesn't seem so bad. But this is not the way the Bible speaks of the unborn child.

What is more, growing medical knowledge of unborn children undermines that comfortable delusion. The Greek philosopher Aristotle speculated that the fetus becomes human when it quickens in the womb, that is, when the mother feels it move. We know today that the movement of the fetus is only a matter of degree; the baby is moving all the time. Others have argued that the fetus becomes human only when it is old enough to survive outside the womb, but advances in the care of premature babies make it possible for even extremely small infants to survive, certainly infants that are younger and smaller than many being aborted. It is increasingly common today to identify life with brain activity, but we know there is brain activity in the unborn child even before the mother is aware that she is pregnant. For that matter, there is a beating heart and the circulation of the baby's own blood as well.

The problem with trying to determine a point before which the developing child is fully human is that there isn't one. There is an uninterrupted development of the child from the very moment in which the sperm of the father joins the ovum of the mother and the cell begins to divide. The father's seed cannot multiply by itself, nor can the mother's egg, but as soon as the two sets of chromosomes combine, not only does the development of life continue steadily unless interrupted, either accidentally or deliberately, but the life that is developing is a unique life. There is no other combination of chromosomes exactly like these new ones. The fetus is already a uniquely determined individual.

In the perceptive wording of this psalm David is speaking of his unique individuality from the first moments of his existence in the womb. From that very first moment, God knew him and had ordained what his life was to be.

> All the days ordained for me
> were written in your book
> before one of them came to be (v. 16).

If that is how God views the unborn child, dare we call it only tissue and destroy the unborn, as we are doing in this country at the rate of more than a million-and-a-half babies each year?

No Separation from God

In the next two verses David reflects on the abundance of God's thoughts toward him, ending with, "When I awake, I am still with you." These words are a bit puzzling and have been understood in various ways. Some people suppose the writer to have been drowsing, even when he was composing the psalm. They imagine that he woke up at this point. Others suggest that he may be referring to death followed by resurrection. If that is the case, then verses 13–18 would move nicely from the earliest moments of his existence, before his birth, to his continuous conscious existence after death. Womb to tomb, and beyond! Of course, it is more likely that David is only observing that waking or sleeping he is always with God, since God is everywhere. However we interpret the verse, its point is that nothing will be able to separate the child of God from God, the exact point made in the apostle Paul's powerful ending to Romans 8.

Reflections on All the Above

We can rebel against God's knowledge and pursue evil instead—David notes this response in verses 19–22 and repudiates it—or we can ask God to search us with the goal of being directed in his way. The writer describes this response as his own in verses 23–24. By repudiating the first and embracing the second option the psalmist articulates a personal twofold response to this teaching.

1. *He wants nothing to do with evil or evil persons.* This is another of those passages that seems imprecatory, the psalmist calling down judgment on the wicked, but judgment is not the actual thrust of these verses, though it is of similar passages elsewhere. In keeping with the personal tone of the psalm so far, what David is actually saying is that he wants no part of the evil that evil men devise. We say, "Hate the sin, but love the sinner!" It is nice advice, but it is also hard to do since love of the sinner, if we are not extremely careful, leads first to a love of the sinner's sinful ways and then to a participation in them. David was not at all sure that he could successfully love one and hate the other. So his decision was to separate from evil persons entirely. This separation does not mean that David never had anything to do with sinful people; he himself was one. It only means that he did not want to be with those who were openly marked by evil or were hatching evil actions. So taken was he with the greatness of God that he wanted nothing to endanger his relationship to God.

2. *He wants to continue walking and growing in God's way.* The last two verses of this psalm are extremely beautiful and are often memorized and quoted.

> Search me, O God, and know my heart;
>   test me and know my anxious thoughts.
> See if there is any offensive way in me,
>   and lead me in the way everlasting (vv. 23–24).

The problem David perceives is that although he wants to keep clear of evil people and their ways, he nevertheless has evil in himself. In fact, his avoidance of evil people is not because he is too good for such people, but because he cannot trust himself in evil company. He is too sinful; he is prone to the very same sins. So here he appeals to God to search him out in order to be led in a righteous way, a way everlasting. Actually, he prays for four things: for God to know him and expose his thoughts; for God to try, or perfect, his thoughts; for God to purge away whatever evil remains in him; and for God to lead him in the way everlasting.

Isn't it interesting that a psalm beginning with an unparalleled declaration that God knows all things should end with the request for God to search and know the psalmist? This is a practical psalm, embracing practical theology, and David is asking that God use this great, perfect, and pervasive knowledge to benefit David personally. He wants God to use the knowledge God has of him to lead him in the right way.

"Search me, O God, and know my heart!" It is a serious thing to pray, because it invites painful exposures and surgery, if we truly mean it. Still it is what every wise believer should desire. Arno Gaebelein wrote,

> Happy the Christian who prays thus every day! Who puts himself into the presence of the all-seeing God, who stands in his light, and is willing to have anything and everything which is not right brought to light and judged. This is the true walk "in the light." Even the thoughts must be so dealt with. In the New Testament it is expressed in this wise, "bringing into captivity every thought to the obedience of Christ" (2 Cor. 10:5). Then there is the willingness to put away anything which is grievous to God and to his Spirit and to be led in the way everlasting.[5]

A Practical Summing Up

In the course of this study we have been looking at God's omniscience, omnipresence, and omnipotence—that God knows everything, is everywhere, and is all-powerful. We have also seen that the overriding theme, the one for which the others are mentioned, is omniscience. Here is what appreciation of the omniscience of God should do for every Christian.

1. *It should humble us.* I think here of Job. God allowed Satan to attack Job to demonstrate that a believer is able to love God solely for who he is and not merely for the many blessings he gives. Job didn't know what God was doing. When his friends came to see him they argued that since God is a just God and this is a moral universe, bad things do not happen without good reasons. Therefore, Job must have sinned in some way and have brought his troubles on himself. Job did not consider himself to be innocent of sin, but he knew that he had done nothing to deserve what was happening to him. Who can explain it?

For thirty-seven chapters God is silent. At last, toward the very end of the book, he speaks. We might expect God to explain things to Job, to tell him about Satan's accusations and reveal how Job had been singled out as a righteous man who would trust God even in misery, but this is not what we find. Instead, we find God rebuking Job for presuming to think that he could understand God's ways, even if they were explained to him. This is in the form of a lengthy interrogation having to do with God's perfect knowledge contrasted with Job's ignorance. It goes on for four chapters—a total of 129 verses, less five verses that introduce and then sustain the narrative—and at the end Job is completely humbled. He replies to God,

> Surely I spoke of things I did not understand,
>   things too wonderful for me to know. . . .
> Therefore I despise myself
>   and repent in dust and ashes (Job 42:3, 6).

If we ever begin to appreciate the perfect knowledge of God and by contrast our own pathetic understanding, the first effect this will have on us will be humility, as in Job's case. We will be embarrassed to think that we ever supposed we could contend with God intellectually.

2. *It should comfort us.* God knows the worst about us and loves us anyway. He knows the best about us even when other people do not and blame us for things that are not our fault. Job expressed his comfort in God's knowledge, saying, "He knows the way that I take; when he has tested me, I will come forth as gold" (Job 23:10).

3. *It should encourage us to live for God.* In Psalm 139 David has been reflecting on the omniscience of God, and it has led him to ask God to help him lead an upright life. He knows that God will do it precisely because God knows him so well.

We know very little. We do not even know ourselves, but God knows us. He knows our weaknesses and our strengths. He knows our sins but also our aspirations toward a godly life. He knows when isolation will help us grow strong but also when we need companionship to stand in righteousness. He knows when we need rebuking and correcting but also when we need teaching and encouragement. If anyone can "lead me in the way everlasting," it is God. Moreover, since I know he knows me and wants to help me, I can be encouraged to get on with upright living.

4. *It should help us to pray.* In the Sermon on the Mount Jesus encouraged his followers to pray to God confidently, expecting answers. "When you pray, do not keep on babbling like pagans, for they think they will be heard because of their many words. Do not be like them, for your Father knows what you need before you ask him" (Matt. 6:7–8). This is then followed by what we call the Lord's Prayer, a model prayer consisting of just fifty-two words.

God's knowledge of what we need is so perfect that he often answers even before we pray to him. "Before they call I will answer; while they are still speaking I will hear," wrote Isaiah (Isa. 65:24). Who can be terrified by a God who knows and answers us like that?

Psalm 140

Evil for Evil's Sake

Rescue me, O LORD, from evil men;
    protect me from men of violence,
who devise evil plans in their hearts
    and stir up war every day.
They make their tongues as sharp as a serpent's;
    the poison of vipers is on their lips.

Selah

Keep me, O LORD, from the hands of the wicked;
    protect me from men of violence
    who plan to trip my feet.
Proud men have hidden a snare for me;
    they have spread out the cords of their net
    and have set traps for me along my path.

Selah

O LORD, I say to you, "You are my God."
    Hear, O LORD, my cry for mercy.
O Sovereign LORD, my strong deliverer,
    who shields my head in the day of battle—
do not grant the wicked their desires, O LORD;
    do not let their plans succeed,
    or they will become proud.

Selah

Let the heads of those who surround me
    be covered with the trouble their lips have caused.
Let burning coals fall upon them;
    may they be thrown into the fire,
    into miry pits, never to rise.
Let slanderers not be established in the land;
    may disaster hunt down men of violence.

*I know that the L*ORD* secures justice for the poor*
and upholds the cause of the needy.
Surely the righteous will praise your name
and the upright will live before you.

verses 1–13

Ihave been arguing for a number of
pages that the final psalms in the Psalter, beginning with Psalm 135, are
chiefly about worship. They tell us what worship is and how we are to worship God acceptably.

There are some psalms that do not seem to fit this category nicely, and
this is one of them. Psalm 140 is about people who are incorrigibly wicked,
who seem to practice evil for its own sake. Does a psalm about evil really
belong with others that are written chiefly to praise God? I think it does, for
two reasons. First, it is a reminder that even in our moments of most tran-
scendent praise we still praise God in the midst of a very wicked world.
Second, in spite of its somber theme, Psalm 140 nevertheless does deal with
praise, particularly in the last stanza.

I know that the LORD secures justice for the poor
and upholds the cause of the needy.
Surely the righteous will praise your name
and the upright will live before you.

Psalm 140 is used in Romans 3:13 as an inspired witness to human deprav-
ity. This psalm describes us as we truly are. If we have become something
other than those who love evil for evil's sake, it is only because of Christ's
work, and we should praise God for that.

A Psalm of David

The general opinion of scholars is that Psalm 140 is not by David even
though the heading claims it is. They believe that it is only in the style of
David's writing. J. J. Stewart Perowne is a conservative commentator, but he
wrote, "The impression left upon the mind in reading [Psalms 140–42] . . . is
that they are cast in David's vein and in imitation of his manner rather than
written by David himself."[1] Similarly, Alexander Maclaren, another conservative exegete and preacher, wrote, "The present writer receives the impression strongly from the psalm that it is cast in the Davidic manner by a later
singer, and is rather an echo than an original voice."[2]

That may be. "A psalm of David" might mean only "a psalm like David's."
But I do not know how to judge whether a psalm is by David other than by
its inscription and by whether it sounds like David, and this one certainly

sounds like David. Many of his undisputed psalms speak of enemies and ask God to deliver him from them. All of them sustain a steadfast confidence in God in spite of danger. Even the images are Davidic. Instead of disputing David's authorship, it seems better to think of Psalms 138–45 as a block of psalms by David discovered at some late date and added to this last book of psalms by its late compilers.

Besides, there may be a connection between this and the former psalm. In Psalm 139:19–22 David asks God to "slay the wicked." In this psalm he asks for the same thing (vv. 9–11), as well as to be delivered from such men (vv. 1–8). Herbert Lockyer highlights a number of such links, observing, "In Psalm 138, David sets forth God's promise as the anchor of hope; in Psalm 139, God's omniscience as our consolation in danger and motive for shunning evil; in Psalm 140, our danger from calumnious enemies, and our only safety in Jehovah our strength."[3]

People of the Lie

The first two stanzas of this psalm (vv. 1–3 and 4–5) are nearly perfect parallels, describing those who love evil. Such people, says the psalmist, "devise evil plans," "stir up war," "plan to trip [his] feet," "spread out the cords of their net," and "set traps . . . along [his] path." David has previously written about people who were his personal enemies. What is unique about these verses is their portrait of people who love evil for evil's sake.

The description reminds me of a book by M. Scott Peck, a New England psychiatrist who wrote about the reality of evil in *People of the Lie.*[4] It was on the *New York Times* best-seller list for many weeks. Peck has had a distinguished career: being a magna cum laude graduate of Harvard University in 1958, earning an M.D. degree from Case Western Reserve University School of Medicine in 1963, acting as assistant chief of psychiatry for the U.S. Army from 1963–1972. Peck now practices privately in Litchfield County, Connecticut. It was this clinical practice that led him to the conviction that some people really are evil, having passed over the line from mere bad behavior and given in to evil, and to the belief that psychiatry must take the reality of evil far more seriously than it has so far.

Sometimes the evil Peck saw was relatively limited and harmful only to the person involved, as in the case of a woman called Charlene, who merely wanted to toy with him. She lied to him "because it's fun," as she put it.[5] In other cases, the evil was terribly destructive, as in the case of narcissistic parents who had almost destroyed their children, or a couple who seemed to be destroying one another. Toward the end of the book Peck writes about several exorcisms in which he took part.

Peck defines this specific form of evil as absolute autism, that is, living for and thinking only of oneself. He describes it clearly in the case of Charlene. At one point, trying to get her to express what she thought life was about, he pressed her, saying, "You were raised in the Christian Church. . . . Surely you're not so dumb as to be unaware of what Christians say is the meaning of life, the purpose of human existence."

Thus goaded, Charlene replied in a flat, low monotone, "We exist for the glory of God."

"Well?" Peck asked.

There was a reflective silence. Then the woman burst out, "I cannot do it. There's no room for *me* in that. That would be my death." Peck thought for a moment she would cry. Then what had seemed to be her choked-back sobs burst into a roar. "I don't want to live for God. I will not. I want to live for me. My own sake!"[6]

After years of therapy and much careful analysis, Peck concluded that Charlene seemed most of all to want power. Yet it was power purely for its own sake. She did not want power to improve society, care for a family, make herself a more effective person, or in any way accomplish anything creative. "Her thirst for power was unsubordinated to anything higher than itself," Peck said.[7] It was this case more than any other that led him to the studies reflected in his book and to his role in exorcisms.

All Have Sinned

I find *People of the Lie* perceptive and stimulating, but I find David's psalm to be even more perceptive, particularly when I remember Paul's use of the psalm in Romans 3. It is true that in these verses David is describing evil persons, men who were seeking to destroy him. David would recognize in a moment the personality type the psychiatrist is describing. He is fully aware that such people advance themselves by evil stratagems and lies. But what is most disturbing is how the apostle Paul picks up verse 3 as part of a collage of verses to describe the human race collectively. He writes,

> ". . . there is no one who does good,
>   not even one."
> "Their throats are open graves;
>   their tongues practice deceit."
> "The poison of vipers is on their lips."
>   "Their mouths are full of cursing and bitterness."
> "Their feet are swift to shed blood;
>   ruin and misery mark their ways,
> and the way of peace they do not know."
>   "There is no fear of God before their eyes" (Rom. 3:12–18).[8]

Speaking of the psalm, Charles Spurgeon says, "David's enemies were as violent as they were evil, as crafty as they were violent, and as persistent as they were crafty."[9] That is true, but if Paul's use of the psalm is accurate, these judgments must also be made of us. We also are violent, evil, and crafty, either actually or potentially. If that is the case, then David's prayer for deliverance from those who love evil for its own sake must also be a prayer for deliverance from ourselves. We too need a Savior, and the only one who can save us from ourselves is God.

In Psalm 139 David prayed for two things: that God would keep him away from evil men, and that God would lead him in the way everlasting. I said when we were considering those two points of application that David did not want to be kept from evil persons because he was too good for them but because he recognized some of their evil nature in himself. He couldn't afford the exposure. This admission is exactly what we are seeing in Psalm 140, and it is probably why Psalm 140 is placed immediately after Psalm 139. The connection between the two psalms and the use of Psalm 140:3 in Romans 3 remind us that we can never make progress in the Christian life unless we begin with a recognition of our own wickedness before the holy God.

Seeing these verses in light of our personal sin does not negate our need for deliverance and protection from evil people, however. In fact, it is precisely when God is delivering us from ourselves that we most need protection from others. Evil people hate those who are being saved by God and often try to destroy them.

Prayer and Praise

So what do we do when we are surrounded by "people of the lie," above all when we find so much of their terrible evil in ourselves? The answer is to do what David did. We turn to God as the only one who can deliver us both from others and ourselves; we place our needs before him; and then we praise him for the deliverance he gives.

Spurgeon had a sermon on the second half of this psalm, beginning with verse 6, in which he traced a rising note of confidence in David as David did what I have described. His sermon had five points based on five important things David says.[10]

1. *Possession: "You are my God"* (v. 6). The ground for David's appeal to God is his relationship to God. God is his God, and this one true God, Jehovah, is his hope.

"You are my God!" Those are simple words, each of one syllable, but we should not take them for granted since nothing is more amazing than that God should be ours. It is not amazing for us to be his. Everything is his, even the cattle on a thousand hills. Everything is God's because God made it. But for God to belong to us, that truly is amazing. Even more, it is something we would not dare to claim were it not for God's solemn affirmation that he has given himself to his people. "I will be their God," God said to Abraham in regard to Abraham's descendants (Gen. 17:8). "I will be your God," God said to Moses on the brink of the Exodus from Egypt (Exod. 6:7) and afterwards, "I am the LORD your God, who brought you out of Egypt, out of the land of slavery" (Exod. 20:2). The words "I am the LORD your God" occur twenty-two times in Leviticus, and again and again throughout the Old Testament. In the New Testament we read of Thomas, who fell at Jesus' feet exclaiming, "My Lord and my God!" (John 20:28). It is the climax of John's Gospel.

Is Jehovah, the God of the Bible, your God through faith in Jesus Christ? Can you say, "You are my God" to God, as David does? It is one thing to say to the minister that God is your God; it may even be easy to say it to some friend as a pious profession; but can you say it to God? That is the acid test of your profession. God will know whether it is a true confession. Remember how in the preceding psalm David claimed that God knew him thoroughly—his thoughts, his ways, and his words. You cannot fool God. So the proof of your profession is whether you can address God directly and say, "You are my God." There is joy for those who can truly say it.

2. *Petition: "Hear, O LORD, my cry for mercy"* (v. 6). Whenever we turn our thoughts to God, the first thing that should strike us is God's holiness and, by contrast, our sin. We must never come to God claiming that we deserve something from him because of our good works, faithfulness, or even sincerity. We are at best unworthy servants, and the only way we can ever come to God is on the basis of his mercy, which he has given to us in Jesus Christ. It is because David asks for mercy, here as in many of his other psalms, that we know his words about evil men are not self-righteous. The difference between David and his enemies was not that they were evil and he was not, but that he had confessed his wickedness and had come to God for the forgiveness and cleansing God provides.

God is a merciful God. It is a good thing, too, because we need mercy! In fact, his mercy is the only possible ground on which we can come to him. You will never be received by God unless you come as the tax collector did when he prayed, "God, have mercy on me, a sinner" (Luke 18:13). Jesus said that it was this man, rather than the self-righteous Pharisee, who went home justified.

3. *Preservation: "O Sovereign LORD, my strong deliverer, who shields my head in the day of battle"* (v. 7). Verses 8–11 elaborate on the subject of preservation, for having reminded himself that God had preserved him in the past, David asks for protection in the present, specifically against those persons who have been perpetrating evil.

David asks God to confound his enemies. They have been setting traps to snare him (v. 5); therefore, he asks, "Do not let their plans succeed" (v. 8). They have been troubling others with their belligerent designs (v. 2); therefore, he asks, "Let the heads of those who surround me be covered with the trouble their lips have caused" (v. 9). They have been trying to destroy others (v. 1); therefore, he asks, "Let burning coals fall upon them; may they be thrown into the fire, into miry pits, never to rise" (v. 10). They have been wounding faithful citizens of Israel by their slanders (v. 3); therefore, he asks, "Let slanderers not be established in the land" (v. 11).

4. *Protection: "The LORD secures justice to the poor and upholds the cause of the needy"* (v. 12). David's confidence in God has been growing throughout the psalm. He reminded himself that God was his protection in the past. He asked God to protect him in the present. Now he looks to what is future and asserts confidently that God will act justly in coming days too. What is more, God will do it not merely for David but also for the poor and needy everywhere who are suffering.

The Judge of all the earth will do right. Therefore David is able to rest in that assurance. Those who practice evil will get what they have earned.

5. *Praise: "Surely the righteous will praise your name and the upright will live before you"* (v. 13). David's confidence reaches its climax in the final verse of the psalm. He has looked at those who are practicing evil and has identified their evil. He has looked to God, recalling God's protection of him in the past. He has expressed his confidence for the future. Now he concludes that because God is God and because he acts justly, the righteous will praise his name and the upright will live before him.

David's great psalm about evil persons ends by praising God.

Psalm 141

A Prayer before Retiring

O LORD, I call to you; come quickly to me.
    Hear my voice when I call to you.
May my prayer be set before you like incense;
    may the lifting up of my hands be like the evening sacrifice.

Set a guard over my mouth, O LORD;
    keep watch over the door of my lips.
Let not my heart be drawn to what is evil,
    to take part in wicked deeds
with men who are evildoers;
    let me not eat of their delicacies.

Let a righteous man strike me—it is a kindness;
    let him rebuke me—it is oil on my head.
    My head will not refuse it.

Yet my prayer is ever against the deeds of evildoers;
    their rulers will be thrown down from cliffs,
    and the wicked will learn that my words were well spoken.
They will say, "As one plows and breaks up the earth,
    so our bones have been scattered at the mouth of the grave."

But my eyes are fixed on you, O Sovereign LORD;
    in you I take refuge—do not give me over to death.
Keep me from the snares they have laid for me,
    from the traps set by evildoers.
Let the wicked fall into their own nets,
    while I pass by in safety.

verses 1–10

Several chapters ago, toward the beginning of these studies of the final worship psalms of the Psalter (Psalms 135–50), I listed some elements that belong in worship services: singing, prayer, confession of sin, reading the Bible, and the exposition of God's Word. These are practices for which we have biblical warrant, and they need to be recovered in our day when serious worship of God has almost disappeared in many churches. The psalms that end the Psalter help us make this recovery, for they instruct us not only in what we should praise God for—his goodness, holiness, omniscience, omnipresence, love, and mercy, for example—but also how we should do it.

Some of these psalms seem to focus on a specific worship element. Psalm 135 is about praise. Psalm 136 shows how to reflect on God's past acts in creation and salvation as a basis for our worship. Psalm 139 explores one of God's great attributes, omniscience, and shows the effect an awareness of God's omniscience should have on the worshiper. Later psalms deal with singing and even with the use of instruments in worship. This psalm deals with prayer.

A Psalm about Prayer

Psalm 141 is a psalm in which every word and sentence is a prayer. It has been called an evening psalm or a psalm to be sung before retiring because of verse 2, where David prays,

> May my prayer be set before you like incense;
>   may the lifting up of my hands be like the evening sacrifice.

There are other similar psalms, particularly toward the beginning of the Psalter. Psalm 4 and Psalm 63 have been called evening psalms. Psalm 5 is a morning psalm. In the liturgical tradition of the church Psalm 141 has been used for vespers.

It is common in scholarly writing about Psalm 141 to find it said that it is difficult, not because of the words themselves—they are clear enough—but because it is hard to find a meaningful sequence of ideas. The various verses, particularly in the middle of the psalm, seem to stand in isolation, though the New International Version does an adequate job of showing their relationship.

This is not the biggest problem in getting to know and profit from the psalm. The biggest problem is that the psalm is about prayer, and prayer is something most of us find difficult and sometimes even try to avoid. The proof of my theory, apart from a lack of serious prayer in our own devotional life, is the way prayer has been disappearing from evangelical worship services. The explanation for this removal, we are told, is that people today find prayer boring. There are a number of reasons why.

1. *God's thoughts are not our thoughts.* Prayer is talking to God and God is not like us. Isaiah quotes God as saying, "My thoughts are not your thoughts, neither are your ways my ways. . . . As the heavens are higher than the earth, so are my ways higher than your ways and my thoughts than your thoughts" (Isa. 55:8–9). Because we are not like God and do not know God well, we are usually unsure what we should pray for, and when we pray we sense often that we are somehow off the mark, that we should be praying for something else but hardly know what.

2. *We do not know the Bible.* Our ignorance of God is traceable to our ignorance of the Bible. While it is true that God's thoughts are not our thoughts and his ways different from our ways, it is nevertheless also true that God has revealed his thoughts and ways to us in the Bible, at least those we are able to understand. So our ignorance of God is not his fault; it is ours. If we want to pray well, we must get to know the Bible, for only then will we begin to be able to think God's thoughts after him. The best prayer always goes together with the best Bible study.

3. *We do not feel in need of God's help.* Having said all the above, however, I sense that the main reason why we have so much trouble praying and do not pray is that we do not feel we need God's help. We think we can manage very well without God. We are instinctively moved to pray when things go wrong, when we lose a job or find some important relationship going sour—we know we should pray then, and we do—but at other times we feel self-sufficient.

In spite of his power and authority as king, David did not feel self-sufficient. He knew he was in peril every single day. Therefore, he prayed every day, and he prayed powerfully. His prayer teaches us to do likewise.

The Invocation

The first two verses of this psalm are an invocation, a call to God to hear what the psalmist is about to pray for. Even more, they are the starting point for true worship. Worship is praising God, and in order to praise God we must address him.

May I suggest that the most important moments in our prayer or worship times are before we even start. This is because in those moments of preparation we settle our thoughts and remind ourselves that we are actually coming into the presence of almighty God. Our worship times are not like other times. They are not like the hours we spend with our friends or our families or our coworkers. Those are important and valuable times, but they are not the same. Our times of prayer are when we meet with God. So we must be conscious that we are actually meeting with him. We must focus our thoughts, ask God to hear our prayers, and be sure that we are actually praying to him and not merely going through some religious exercise.

Reuben A. Torrey, an influential Bible teacher of an earlier generation, used to say that "we should never utter one syllable of prayer, either in public or in private, until we are definitely conscious that we have come into the presence of God and are actually praying to him." Torrey testifies that this insight transformed his own prayer life.

> I was brought up to pray. I was taught to pray so early in life that I have not the slightest recollection of who taught me to pray. . . . Nevertheless, prayer was largely a matter of form. There was little real thought of God, and no real approach to God. And even after I was converted, yes, even after I had entered the ministry, prayer was largely a matter of form.
>
> But the day came when I realized what real prayer meant, realized that prayer was having an audience with God, actually coming into the presence of God and asking and getting things from him. And the realization of that fact transformed my prayer life. Before that prayer had been a mere duty, and sometimes a very irksome duty, but from that time on prayer has been not merely a duty but a privilege, one of the most highly esteemed privileges of life. Before that the thought that I had was, "How much time must I spend in prayer?" The thought that now possesses me is, "How much time may I spend in prayer without neglecting the other privileges and duties of life?"[1]

A moment ago I wrote that true prayer is speaking to God and not merely going through some religious exercise. In verse 2 David refers to some of the forms of worship practiced at the temple in his day, specifically the use of incense and the offering of the evening sacrifice. He relates each of those practices to genuine prayer and the devotion of the worshiper.

Incense, which filled the Holy Place of the temple and rose heavenward in heavy fragrant clouds, is a common biblical symbol for prayer. We read in Revelation of the redeemed holding "golden bowls full of incense, which are the prayers of the saints" (Rev. 5:8). As for the sacrifices, in addition to pointing to the future atoning death of Jesus Christ for sin, the offering of animals also taught the need for a humble and contrite heart on the part of the one who was praying. The prophet Samuel told Saul, "To obey is better than sacrifice, and to heed is better than the fat of rams" (1 Sam. 15:22).

Verse 2 is a keen insight into the spiritual understanding of the most enlightened of the Old Testament saints, all of whom understood the spirit of the worshiper to be the essence of the sacrifice.

A Prayer for Purity

Verses 3–7 contain the substance of David's prayer, the things about which he was concerned and for which he was praying. Of these five verses, verses 3 and 4 are the clearest. In them David asks God to "set a guard" over his mouth, his heart, and his actions. Asking God to set a guard means asking God to keep him from sin and enable him to be upright or pure in these areas. David wanted purity most. Purity was a natural idea to follow the comparison of evening prayer to incense, since everyone in David's day understood that the temple incense had to be utterly pure and meticulously prepared.

1. *His mouth.* The first thing David asks God to guard is his mouth so he will not speak sinfully or in a way that might harm others. There is no biblical writer that seems so conscious of the harm that words can do as David. We find references to harmful words or speech in many of his psalms, sometimes about the words others have spoken in order to harm him and other times, as here, about his own propensity to speak wrongly. We have a saying that goes, "Sticks and stones may break my bones, but words can never hurt me," but words do hurt, and they have done far more harm in the long history of the human race than physical weapons.

Have you ever asked God to set a guard over your mouth so you might not say harmful things and might say only what is helpful? Xenocrates, the head of the famous Athenian Academy from 339–314 B.C., said on one occasion, "I have often repented of having spoken, but never of having been silent."[2]

2. *His heart.* Where do harmful words come from? They come from the heart, for, as Jesus said of the evil man, "Out of the overflow of his heart his mouth speaks" (Luke 6:45). If our heart is corrupt, our speech and actions will be corrupt too. If our heart is pure, our words will also be pure. How can that be the case, since our hearts are not pure but "deceitful above all things and beyond cure" (Jer. 17:9)? We need a transplant, and the only one who can give us one is God, the Great Physician, who has promised to do so. Ezekiel quotes God as saying, "I will give you a new heart and put a new spirit in you; I will remove from you your heart of stone and give you a heart of flesh" (Ezek. 36:26). Likewise, Jeremiah, the very prophet who described our hearts as being deceitful above all things, wrote,

> "This is the covenant I will make with the house of Israel
>   after that time," declares the LORD.
> "I will put my law in their minds
>   and write it on their hearts. . . .
> For I will forgive their wickedness
>   and will remember their sins no more" (Jer. 31:33–34).

The one who has received a new heart will begin to speak only wholesome words and begin to act in a wholesome manner too.

3. *His actions.* David makes his request for pure actions from the negative side, asking God to keep him from being "drawn to what is evil" or taking "part in wicked deeds." This is what we pray for when we say the Lord's Prayer, asking, "Lead us not into temptation" (Matt. 6:13).

David's prayer is not only that he might be kept from evil, however. It is also that he might be kept from the company of evildoers, so he will not be tempted to sit down with them and "eat of their delicacies" (v. 4). In the two preceding psalms David also asked God to keep him from the company and corruptions of the wicked. (This connection is one reason why we should think of these psalms as being written by the same man.) I repeat here what I said regarding the two earlier psalms. David is not too good for evil people; he is too much like them and therefore likely to be swept away by their wickedness if in their company.

David swept away by evil company? If that was a danger for David, how much more so for you and me? Shouldn't we also be praying, "Let not my heart be drawn to what is evil" and "Lead me not into temptation"? Derek Kidner comments rightly: "There is a Puritan vigor and single-mindedness about this psalm to put one in mind of Christian and Faithful at Vanity Fair, whose prayer was 'Turn away mine eyes from beholding vanity,' and whose reply to the challenge 'What will you buy?' was 'We buy the truth.'"[3]

Friendly Fire

Verses 5–7 may seem unrelated, but the New International Version probably does as good a job as any in showing their connection with the rest of the psalm and with each other. The link between verse 5 and verse 4 seems to be that in verse 5 the psalmist, having asked God to keep him from the allure of evil and evil persons, professes his preference for the friendship of the righteous, even if they reprove him for his sin. Proverbs 27:6 says, "Wounds from a friend can be trusted."

Franz Delitzsch takes the psalm's ascription to David seriously and gets a plausible meaning for this difficult middle section by relating it to the time David was driven from Jerusalem because of Absalom's rebellion. In those days David was cut off from the temple, was well aware of his failures as a king, welcomed reproof from friendly sources, and prayed for the overthrow of those who had wrongly usurped power. The New International Version takes verse 7 as being spoken of the wicked who are to be destroyed—*their* bones will be scattered—but Delitzsch thinks they are being spoken by David concerning himself and his followers.

> Assuming the very extreme, it is a look of hope into the future: should his bones and the bones of his followers be even scattered about the mouth of Sheol . . . it would nevertheless be only as when one in ploughing cleaves the earth; i.e. they do not lie there in order that they may continue lying, but that they may rise up anew, as the seed that is sown sprouts up out of the upturned earth. . . . We discern here the hope of a resurrection.[4]

It is tempting to accept Delitzsch's proposed setting for the psalm, especially his suggestion that it may contain an anticipation of a future resurrection of the righteous, but the extreme setting of Absalom's revolt is not necessary to explain David's preference for the company of righteous persons, even if they should rebuke him. We ought to welcome reproof from the righteous at all times. It is also probably best to take David's words about people being thrown from cliffs and bones being scattered as referring to the just end of those who would do so to others, especially since he has also been writing in the preceding psalms about those who practice evil (Pss. 138:7; 139:19; 140:9–11).

Walking by Faith

In the last stanza of this psalm (vv. 8–10) the prayer is finished or, we could say—making the link between prayer and worship—the time of worship ends. The service is now over. We hear the benediction and are about to go back out into the world. What should have happened to us as a result of the time spent with God? David suggests that, having been with God and having prayed to God, we should leave with our eyes still fixed on God. In the world there are dangers. Snares have been set by the wicked, traps by evildoers; but if our eyes are fixed on God, we will be able to walk safely through these many dangers and temptations.

There is another scene from *Pilgrim's Progress* by John Bunyan that has always struck me forcefully. Pilgrim is making his way up a steep path by night toward the Porter's Lodge. He comes to a place where two lions are chained by the path, one on his right and the other on his left. He does not know they are chained, and he is afraid and about to turn back when the porter calls to him, saying, "Fear not the Lions, for they are chained, and are placed there for trial of faith where it is, and for discovery of those that have none. Keep in the midst of the Path, and no hurt shall come unto thee." So Pilgrim presses forward, keeping on the straight path by fixing his eyes on the porter and refusing to look at the lions lunging at him from the sides of the path.[5] This is the image David paints. He is fixing his eyes on God as he makes his way through the dangers of life.

One day Jesus will have destroyed those dangers. Hebrews applies the words of Psalm 8 to him:

> You crowned him with glory and honor
> and put everything under his feet. . . .

"At present we do not see everything subject to him. But we see Jesus . . ." (Heb. 2:6–9). Therefore, "Let us fix our eyes on Jesus, the author and perfecter of our faith. . . . Consider him who endured such opposition from sinful men, so that you will not grow weary and lose heart" (Heb. 12:2–3). That is the secret of an effective godly life as well as the point at which all true worship should begin and end.

Psalm 142

Alone but for the Lord

I cry aloud to the LORD;
  I lift up my voice to the LORD for mercy.
I pour out my complaint before him;
  before him I tell my trouble.

When my spirit grows faint within me,
  it is you who know my way.
In the path where I walk
  men have hidden a snare for me.
Look to my right and see;
  no one is concerned for me.
I have no refuge;
  no one cares for my life.

I cry to you, O LORD;
  I say, "You are my refuge,
  my portion in the land of the living."
Listen to my cry,
  for I am in desperate need;
rescue me from those who pursue me,
  for they are too strong for me.
Set me free from my prison,
  that I may praise your name.

Then the righteous will gather about me
  because of your goodness to me.
                    verses 1–7

Few things in life are worse than to be in trouble and be entirely alone. Yet when things go wrong for us, when life turns sour, or when we are in serious trouble, we almost always have to go through it by ourselves. Alexander Maclaren wrote, "The soul that has to wade through deep waters has always to do it alone; for no human sym-

1228

pathy reaches to full knowledge of, or share in, even the best loved one's grief. We have companions in joy; sorrow we have to face by ourselves." Yet Maclaren adds, still speaking of the dark side of things but pointing upward to our hope, "Unless we have Jesus with us in the darkness, we have no one."[1]

Ella Wheeler Wilcox (1855–1919), an American poet, wrote,

> Laugh and the world laughs with you;
> Weep and you weep alone.

Cynical words, but true. Nevertheless, Christians find that although others may desert us in our troubles, we are never deserted by Jesus, who knows us thoroughly, understands all we are going through, and supports us in it.

This Lonely Prison

In Psalm 142 David is alone and in trouble. We know this not only because the psalm speaks of his being alone and in trouble, but also because it begins with a title line saying that it was written "when [or about the time when] he was in the cave." This is the only psalm in this final collection of Davidic psalms (Psalms 138–45) that provides the reader with a setting: "A *maskil* of David. When he was in the cave. A Prayer." The setting is helpful for our understanding of the psalm since we know something about David's situation at this time from 1 Samuel 22:1–2. Even more, it makes Psalm 142 a companion to Psalm 57, which likewise begins: "Of David. A *miktam*. When he had fled from Saul into the cave."

After killing Goliath, the Philistine hero, David entered the military service of King Saul, but his natural abilities and successes provoked Saul's jealousy, and after a short time David needed to escape from Saul's court into the wilderness. David had no provisions, no followers, and no place to turn. Ahimelech, the priest at Nob, gave him food and the sword that was once Goliath's; Saul later killed Ahimelech because of it. David then went to Gath, the Philistine city, but this proved to be both dangerous and unworkable, and David eventually escaped into the wilderness again and hid in the cave of Adullam.

It was about his early months in this cave, before his brothers and other distressed and discontented men began to gather around him and become the core of his future army, that Psalms 57 and 142 were written.

Psalm 142 probably came first, because it is the most desperate and in it David seems to be most isolated. Kidner finds the earlier psalm "bold and animated," and it is. David praises God for the deliverance he has given, crying, "Be exalted, O God, above the heavens" (Ps. 57:5, 11). Of Psalm 142 Kidner rightly says, "In [it] the strain of being hated and hunted is almost too much, and faith is at full stretch." Yes, but David is not defeated, and in the final words his faith "is at last joined by hope."[2] Kidner has a useful outline of this psalm, based on the stanzas of the New International Version and David's perspective: 1) my plea, 2) my plight, 3) my portion, and 4) my prospect.

My Plea

The first two verses set the tone for the psalm, because here David is pouring out his distress before God, seeking God's help in his trouble. He is praying urgently.

From time to time in these studies I have written of the psalms' use of parallelism as their most prominent poetic device. These two verses are a good example of such parallelism, since each of the lines says essentially the same thing. "I cry aloud to the LORD" is the same as "I lift up my voice to the LORD for mercy," except that the second line adds a plea for mercy as the subject matter of the cry. Likewise, "I pour out my complaint before him" is the same as "before him I tell my trouble," except that "trouble" begins to explain what the poet's complaint is about.

This fourfold repetition underscores the fervency of David's prayer, as do the words "cry aloud" (v. 1), which read literally, "With my voice I cry." The psalm actually begins, "With my voice I cry to God" and "With my voice I ask for mercy." David is not only praying in his heart—that is, silently and calmly—but also outwardly—verbally and loudly.

I wonder if many of our prayers are like that. We probably pray with some regularity if we are Christians: when we read the Bible, at church, probably even at scattered times throughout the day. But I suspect that not many of our prayers are fervent prayers and that none, except when we are taking part in a prayer meeting, are out loud. What does it take to lift our prayers from the wasteland of mere routine to the high ground of actually pleading with Jehovah?

One thing that seems to work well is trouble, the very thing we are considering in this study. In easy times our prayers are easy too, but they take on a new urgency when trouble comes. The same day I sat down to write this chapter, I received a letter from South Africa telling me that one of my friends, a leader in the church in Johannesburg, had collapsed at work and was diagnosed with a brain tumor. He had an operation, received a guarded prognosis, and at the moment I received the letter seemed to be doing fine. It had been a frightening occurrence. His testimony is that this was the most important spiritual experience of his life, since it threw him on God in new ways. When there are none to help but God, Christians do learn to trust him, and they find that he is attentive to their cries.

My Plight

It is possible that verse 3 should be placed at the end of stanza one, with verses 1 and 2, explaining why David is placing his troubles in God's hands. It is because he is fainting away, and only God knows what is before him and can help. Kidner sees verse 3 as "the first of three modest summits of the psalm," with the sense, "When I am ready to give up, it is you who know my way." That is, I don't, but you do.[3]

Still the New International Version is probably right to put verse 3 where it does, for it is here that David begins to describe what his trouble really is. In verses 3 and 4 he lays his difficulties before God. Notice the change of pronouns. In the first two verses David writes in the first person: "*I* cry aloud . . . *I* lift up my voice . . . *I* pour out my complaint . . . *I* tell my trouble"; in verses 3 and 4 he speaks to God himself, saying, "It is *you* who know my way" (italics added). Even verse 4 is spoken to God, as bold as it may seem: "Look to my right and see; no one is concerned for me."

The change in pronouns reminds me of Psalm 23, which is also by David. In the earlier part of Psalm 23, when David was describing the Lord's ample provision for him in good days, he used the pronoun "he."

> *He* makes me lie down in green pastures,
> *he* leads me beside quiet waters,
>   *he* restores my soul.
> *He* guides me in paths of righteousness
>   for his name's sake.

As soon as David speaks of walking through the valley of the shadow of death, the language changes. Now it is no longer "he" but "you" and "your."

> Even though I walk
>   through the valley of the shadow of death,
> I will fear no evil,
>   for *you* are with me;
> *your* rod and *your* staff,
>   they comfort me (Ps. 23:2–4, italics added).

Things are different when the fierce troubles of life, especially those that are a shadow of our imminent death, come. In times of trouble our prayers become fervent and we find ourselves running to God and throwing ourselves on God as our only adequate helper.

In verses 3 and 4 David's "complaint" (v. 2) comes to full expression. It has two parts: First, the path before me is a dangerous one, full of the snares of my enemies; I need help. Second, I have no friends here, I am alone; if you don't support me, I am lost. As it turned out, God did protect David from Saul's snares, and it was while he was at the cave of Adullam that his brothers and others came to join him, making about four hundred faithful fighting men.

David asks God to "look to [his] right" because it is on his right that he would normally have friends waiting to help him. Honored guests were seated to one's right. Friends and soldiers with high authority were given that position. David had enemies in front, behind, and on his left, but there was nobody on his right. Nobody? I wonder if when David penned these lines he remembered that he had also written in Psalm 16,

> I have set the LORD always before me.
> Because he is at my right hand
> I will not be shaken (Ps. 16:8).

I think David did remember, as the next stanza (vv. 5–7) will show. God did not need to look to David's right, but David did, and when he looked he found God there.

My Portion

Kidner calls verse 5 "the second summit of faith in the psalm" because it expresses confidence in God in spite of circumstances.[4] As far as David could see, he was deserted. He was in the cave alone. However, in solitude faith sees what is invisible to the physical senses, and David saw that God was four important things to him and for him, all of which are included in the idea of "portion," that God was all David needed.

1. *God is my refuge* (v. 5). In verse 4 David cried, "I have no refuge; no one cares for my life," but here he says, "You are my refuge, my portion in the land of the living." God was a refuge from David's enemies, from those who had "hidden a snare" for him and who "pursue" him (vv. 3, 6). Psalm 57, the companion psalm, describes David's enemies as "ravenous beasts" who "pursue" him, "spread a net" for his feet, and dig "a pit" in his path (vv. 4, 6); but then David says,

> . . . in you my soul takes refuge.
> I will take refuge in the shadow of your wings
> until the disaster has passed (Ps. 57:1).

God is our refuge from enemies too, but he is also our refuge from God. We are subject to the wrath of God as sinners, and the wrath of God is a far greater terror for us than any mere human beings can be, however great their power or their hatred. How are we to escape this greater danger? The only way is by hiding in God himself, who offers us refuge from his wrath in Jesus Christ. Charles Wesley wrote, "Other refuge have I none, hangs my helpless soul on thee." Augustus Toplady praised the same reality when he prayed:

> Rock of Ages, cleft for me,
> Let me hide myself in thee.

Have you found a refuge from the just wrath of God in God's Son, the Lord Jesus Christ? It is far more important for you to discover that refuge than to escape your earthly enemies.

2. *God is my portion* (v. 5). When Abraham was returning from battle against the kings of the east who had captured Sodom and carried off Lot, his nephew, he was met by Melchizedek, the king of Salem, who was a priest of the Most High God. Abraham gave Melchizedek a tenth of the spoils of the battle, then returned the people who had been captured as well as all the rest of the spoils to the king of Sodom, who had been defeated earlier. At this point Abraham was again alone. He had gained nothing from the battle. Even more, he was in danger of a possible retaliatory attack from the powerful kings he had defeated. God then appeared to him in a vision, saying,

> Do not be afraid, Abram.
> I am your shield,
> your very great reward (Gen. 15:1).

God was promising to be his shield against enemies and a far greater reward than the spoils of any battle.

Are you aware that the person who possesses God is richer than even the wealthiest of this world? If you are, why do you work so hard for things that will soon pass away? Remember how Jesus said, "Where your treasure is, there your heart will be also" (Matt. 6:21).

3. *God is my Savior* (v. 6). God saved David from those who were too strong for him and who were pursuing him. This confession is not expressed in direct speech as the two previous points were; it is expressed as a prayer, or plea, for help ("rescue me from those who pursue me, for they are too strong for me"). Still it is an expression of faith that God will indeed be his Savior.

So I ask you, Is God your Savior? You need a Savior from sin and its destruction; you need a Savior from Satan and his wiles; you need a Savior from the world and its enticements; you need a Savior from yourself. If God is not your Savior, you will be defeated by each and all of these mighty enemies, and you will perish in your sins. If you have God for your Savior, you will triumph over them.

4. *God is my liberator* (v. 7). David asks God, "Set me free from my prison, that I may praise your name" (v. 7). David needed to be rescued, but more than that he wanted to be free from the prison of his cave in order to serve God and praise him.

My Prospect

These last verses bring the psalm to a satisfying climax. David is in danger of being killed by King Saul, but he has found a refuge in God. He has been driven away from home, possessing nothing; but God is his portion. He is in danger of being overcome by people who are stronger than he is, but God is his Savior. He feels that he is shut up in the prison of his cave, but God is his liberator. David knows he is to be king of Israel, therefore, he anticipates a day when he will enjoy the fellowship of God's people.

The first "summit of faith" Derek Kidner sees in this psalm was in verse 3: "When my spirit grows faint within me, it is you who know my way," a confession that although David could not see into the future, he knew that God could and that God would order the future well. The second was in verse 5: "You are my refuge, my portion in the land of the living," a declaration that David was content with God even if he was lacking other things and other people for the moment. The third is in verse 7: "The righteous will gather about me because of your goodness to me," a prophecy of a day when David would no longer be alone, as when writing this psalm, but would be surrounded by "the righteous," who would gather around because of God's goodness to him. In the final analysis David knew he was not going to be alone, for he knew that not only God but also the righteous remnant of the people would be with him.

We return to where we started: There are parts to suffering that are entirely individual—no one can experience our trouble as we do—still the righteous are with us and will stand by us. The company of the redeemed are our friends and will be with us both here and in glory.

No one was ever more alone than Jesus in his hours on the cross. All forsook him, and, unlike ourselves, he was even abandoned by God: "My God, my God, why have you forsaken me?" he cried (Matt. 27:46). Yet he knew that God would return to him again and even, as Psalm 22 indicates, that one day he would be surrounded by many "brothers" (Ps. 22:22).

Remember Jesus! Remember Hebrews 4:14–16!

> Therefore, since we have a great high priest who has gone through the heavens, Jesus the Son of God, let us hold firmly to the faith we profess. For we do not have a high priest who is unable to sympathize with our weaknesses, but we have one who has been tempted in every way, just as we are—yet was without sin. Let us then approach the throne of grace with confidence, so that we may receive mercy and find grace to help us in our time of need.

Do you feel alone? Jesus was alone. Do you feel deserted by those who have been closest to you? So was Jesus. Remember that Jesus has not deserted you; moreover, he knows and understands what you are going through and will help you. Some of the righteous may even stand by you too!

Job went through great suffering, but he had this testimony: "He knows the way that I take; when he has tested me, I will come forth as gold" (Job 23:10).

Psalm 143

The Last of the Penitential Psalms

O LORD, hear my prayer,
  listen to my cry for mercy;
in your faithfulness and righteousness
  come to my relief.
Do not bring your servant into judgment,
  for no one living is righteous before you. . . .

Answer me quickly, O LORD;
  my spirit fails.
Do not hide your face from me
  or I will be like those who go down to the pit.
Let the morning bring me word of your unfailing love,
  for I have put my trust in you.
Show me the way I should go,
  for to you I lift up my soul.
Rescue me from my enemies, O LORD,
  for I hide myself in you.
Teach me to do your will,
  for you are my God;
may your good Spirit
  lead me on level ground.

For your name's sake, O LORD, preserve my life;
  in your righteousness, bring me out of trouble.
In your unfailing love, silence my enemies;
  destroy all my foes,
  for I am your servant.

verses 1–12

Psalm 143 is the last of the psalms that have been called penitential in the liturgical tradition of the church. The others are Psalms 6, 32, 38, 51, 102, and 130, making seven in all. It is easy to see why the other psalms are called penitential: In each of them the writer confesses his sin and asks God for mercy and forgiveness. At first glance it is hard to see why Psalm 143 belongs with the others. Some writers have suggested that Psalm 143 has been added to this "penitential" list only because church liturgy calls for series of sevens, matching either the seven days of the week or the seven weeks of Lent, but this is too superficial a reaction.

Is Psalm 143 Really Penitential?

It is true that only verse 2 acknowledges wrongdoing, and even then the confession of sin is not personal. It says only, "No one living is righteous before you." That is, "All have sinned" (Rom. 3:23). It is only verse 1 that asks for mercy. Aside from these beginning verses, the psalm is mostly about David's enemies (vv. 3–4), from whom David asks to be delivered (vv. 11–12).

Still it is not wrong to think of Psalm 143 as a penitential psalm. For one thing, although the opening verses are in the form of a general confession of sin rather than a personal one, they nevertheless hit on the chief problem for anyone who seeks mercy from God: God is righteous; we are not. God is the judge of all and must act justly. How can he show mercy to sinners like ourselves? How can God be just and justify the sinner at the same time? This is the question Paul raises in Romans 3:25–26. As Paul explains in Romans, the ultimate and only answer is the cross of Jesus Christ. Jesus suffered for our sin and has become our righteousness.

The development of thought is instructive for those who are truly penitent, because receiving mercy from God is not the whole of Christianity. It is the place to begin, as David does, with a plea for mercy in verses 1 and 2. But then he describes his dangerous condition, reminds himself of God's past work, seeks God's guidance, and at last asks for God's preserving grace so he might continue to live and serve him.

When Martin Luther wrote the Ninety-five Theses that he posted on the door of the Castle Church at Wittenberg, which launched the Reformation, the first of his theses read, "When our Lord and Master, Jesus Christ, said 'repent,' he meant that the entire life of believers should be one of repentance." Luther was opposing a distortion of the biblical idea of repentance that had grown up in the church of the Middle Ages. In the Latin Vulgate, which was the common Bible of those days, Matthew 4:17 ("Repent, for the kingdom of heaven is near") had been translated in part by the words *penitentiam agite,* which meant "do penance." This turned repentance into a sacrament that Christians should do from time to time. When Luther studied this and other such texts in the Greek New Testament recently published by the Renaissance scholar Erasmus, he discovered that doing penance was not the idea at all.

Luther discovered that Jesus demanded a radical change of mind resulting in an equally deep transformation of one's life. He later wrote to

Staupitz, his spiritual father and mentor, "I venture to say they are wrong who make more of the act in Latin than of the change of heart in Greek."[1]

This understanding of repentance as affecting all of life needs to be recovered by evangelical churches today, and a better understanding of Psalm 143 may be one way to begin. In April 1996, the Alliance of Confessing Evangelicals held a conference of key evangelical leaders in Cambridge, Massachusetts, out of which came "The Cambridge Declaration." One of the papers presented at this conference was by Sinclair B. Ferguson on the matter we are considering, the nature of repentance. Ferguson discussed the errors of the Middle Ages against which Luther was reacting, and he argued that at least five features of that old medieval Christianity are noticeable now in contemporary evangelicalism.

1. Repentance has increasingly been seen as a single act, severed from a lifelong restoration of godliness.

2. The canon for Christian living has increasingly been sought in a "Spirit-inspired" living voice within the church rather than in the Spirit's voice heard in Scripture.

3. The divine presence was brought to the church by individuals with sacred powers deposited within them and communicated by physical means.

4. The worship of God is increasingly presented as a spectator event of visual and sensory power, rather than a verbal event in which we engage in a deep soul dialogue with the Triune God.

5. The success of ministry is measured by crowds and cathedrals rather than by the preaching of the cross, by the quality of Christians' lives, and by faithfulness.[2]

If we put these insights into our reflections on Psalm 143, we can say that repentance needs to be present in each of the items mentioned in the psalm: David's dangerous condition, his remembrance of God's past works, his plea to God for guidance, and his desire for God's preserving grace to live and serve him. Repentance must be part of each of these matters for us too, because none of us do even the best of what we do without sin. Luther once said wisely, "I have learned that even my repentance needs to be repented of."

A Cry for Mercy

In the first stanza (vv. 1–2) verse 1 asks for mercy from God and verse 2 explains why. It is because the writer, like all men and women, is unrighteous; he sins constantly.

Some commentators regard this as a weak confession because it is neither personal nor specific. It does not say, "I have sinned," as the other penitential psalms do. Nor does it say what sins the writer has committed. True enough, but this opening stanza is profound in other ways. For one thing, it acknowledges the universality of sin, an awareness echoed in the New Testament. Romans 3:20 says, "No one will be declared righteous in his sight by observing the law; rather, through the law we become conscious of sin." Galatians 2:16 adds, "By observing the law no one will be justified."

It is vital to acknowledge that no human being, however moral or upright by our fallible human standards, will be justified by God on the basis of his or her own righteousness. We think we are righteous, but in God's sight "all our righteous acts are like filthy rags" (Isa. 64:6). So if we are to be saved by God, it must be on the basis of a righteousness that is not our own, an "alien righteousness," which is what Luther called it. It is made available to us by the life and death of Jesus Christ.

David's appeal for mercy is on the basis of God's "faithfulness and righteousness" (v. 1). How can we appeal to God for mercy on the basis of God's righteousness, when it is God's righteousness and our lack of it that is the problem? The answer is in the word "faithfulness," which throws us back on God's promise of salvation. We can appeal to mercy because God has promised to be merciful to those who repent and seek salvation. God can save us and still be righteous only because of Jesus Christ, who is the essence of the promise God made from the beginning of the Bible on to send a Savior. He sent Jesus, who died for us. Paul said, "God made him who had no sin to be sin for us, so that in him we might become the righteousness of God" (2 Cor. 5:21).

I do not know if David understood the promise of a savior when he wrote verse 1, but I know that what he wrote is exactly what the apostle John wrote in the opening chapter of his first letter. John declared, "If we confess our sins, he [God] is faithful and just and will forgive us our sins and purify us from all unrighteousness" (1 John 1:9). "Faithful and just" in 1 John are the same as "faithfulness and righteousness" in Psalm 143. Both of these verses teach that we are saved righteously on the basis of the death of Jesus Christ alone.

A Dangerous Condition

In verses 3 and 4 David unfolds the circumstances in which he is asking God for mercy. They should be familiar to us by now. David is beset by enemies, in this case a single enemy who "pursues" him, "crushes [him] to the ground," and "makes [him] dwell in darkness like those long dead." Since this account immediately follows David's confession of sin in verse 2, it must be a recognition that his problems are due in part at least to God's judgment on him for his sins.

David acknowledges in verse 4 that his enemy has succeeded in crushing him by relentless opposition: "My spirit grows faint within me; my heart within me is dismayed." This verse echoes Psalm 142:3 ("my spirit grows faint within me") and ties the psalms together. These are also like Jesus' words before his crucifixion: "My soul is overwhelmed with sorrow to the point of death" (Matt. 26:38), reminding us that Jesus experienced all that we experience and is therefore qualified to help us when we go through similarly tough times. Hebrews 4:15–16, which I cited at the end of the last chapter, encourages us therefore to "approach the throne of grace with confidence, so that we may receive mercy and find grace to help us in our time of need." It is what David does.

God's Mighty Acts

Yet it is not all he does. In the third stanza David puts himself under an important spiritual discipline: to remember God's acts for him and other godly people in past days. He uses three verbs to describe what he does: *remember, meditate,* and *consider.*

This stanza is a short statement of what in other psalms is often a long recital of God's power in creating the world and of his miraculous acts for the Jewish people. In Psalm 136, for example, the poet recalls God's power in creating the heavens and the earth, the sun, the moon, and the stars. He reflects on the exodus from Egypt and remembers how God brought Israel through the desert into her own land. Psalms 18, 68, 89, 104, and 105 are additional examples. Why does David do this? It is in order to work through his painful distress and fear of enemies. He *remembers* how God had been with him previously; he *meditates* on that deliverance; then he *considers,* or reasons, from that past experience to the present. If God helped him in the past, why should God fail to help him in the present? He is the same God.

H. C. Leupold explained verses 5 and 6 like this: "The sacred Scriptures list a vast array of mighty works that God did, works of power and deeds of deliverance. Upon these the psalmist 'meditated' and 'mused.' That is an effective way of getting one's bearings. God does not change." Therefore, Leupold says, "his works reveal . . . what an attitude he has toward his people."[3]

Verse 6, "I spread out my hands to you; my soul thirsts for you like a parched land," is like the beginning of Psalms 42 and 63, the second of which is also by David. This sentence shows that David was not merely looking for what God could do for him in his trouble, though he clearly needed help. More than that, he is thirsting for God himself, which is far better. Do you thirst for God himself? Shouldn't we all repent always for not thirsting after God as we should?

A Plea for Guidance

In the next section of the psalm David turns to God in direct appeal, asking God chiefly for guidance. He is in trouble; he is in danger. In what direction should he move?

Derek Kidner notes that in verses 8–10 David asks for guidance three times and each instance has its own special nuance.

> *The way I should go* (8b) gives slight prominence to the fact of individual destiny, *i.e.,* that each of us is uniquely placed and called (cf. Jn. 21:21f.). *Teach me to do thy will* (10a) settles the priorities, making the goal not self-fulfillment but pleasing God and finishing his work. The words *lead me* (10b) speak with humility of one who knows his need of shepherding, not merely of having the right way pointed out to him.[4]

The progression I see is like this. First, "Bring me word of your unfailing love"; David needs *revelation.* Second, "Show me the way I should go"; David needs *direction.* Third, "Teach me to do your will"; David needs *motivation.* In other words, it is not enough merely to know God's will; David knows it is also necessary to do it. Many Christians talk about seeking God's will—what job they should take, whom they should marry, what church they should join, and such things. They pray the prayer of verse 8: "Show me the way I should go," but do they also pray the prayer of verse 10: "Teach me to do your will, for you are my God"?

Here is another area in which we need to repent: our sad, lackluster following after God. We want God to give us pointers, as long as we have the final word as to whether we will take God's advice, but we do not ask for the ability actually to do what God commands.

God's Servant

In the final verses of the psalm David returns to the problem of his enemies, asking God to silence or destroy them so that he can continue to live and serve God. This sounds like another of those imprecatory passages that bother contemporary people so much, but it is not quite, for there are priorities here. The important matters, in order of importance, are for God to preserve David's life, bring him out of trouble, and silence his enemies. Then, if this is what is required for David to live and continue to be God's servant, he asks God to destroy all his foes.

These prayers are accompanied by three arguments urging God's favorable response. The first is "for your name's sake," meaning "for your honor." God has promised to stand by his people and defend them. Therefore, David asks God to preserve his life in order that all may know God as the utterly trustworthy God he is. We are on solid ground when we plead for God's honor rather than our own. The second argument is "in your righteousness," meaning "justly and in accord with your very nature." God is utterly righteousness. Therefore, David asks God to deliver him and overturn the malice of his foes that right might prevail and evil be judged. We are on solid ground when we ask for God's righteousness to prevail, but to do so we need to be pursuing righteousness ourselves. The third argument is "in your unfailing love." In the final analysis, our hope is in the love of God, which is undeserved but is the only true cause of the salvation and deliverance we need.

Then in the very last line, echoing verse 2 David says, "I am your servant." What an honor to be a servant of the Most High God! Yes, but a responsibility too. Sadly, we need to confess that even when we have done everything we are told to do, "we are [at best] unworthy servants" (Luke 17:10). So even at the end of the psalm we find ourselves repenting.

Martin Luther on Psalm 143

Among Martin Luther's sermons on the psalms are studies of the seven penitential psalms. In interpreting Psalm 143 Luther understood nearly every verse to refer to God's grace through Jesus Christ in the gospel. For example, Luther notes regarding verse 3, "The enemy persecutes my soul," that the wicked always "persecute the pious, who live only in the faith and righteousness of God." He saw "I remember the days of old" (v. 5) to be teaching that God "has never sustained anyone through his own works, abilities, knowledge or piety" but through the gospel. Concerning "For thy name's sake, O LORD, preserve my life" Luther wrote, "God's name is honored when men declare that he gives life and righteousness by grace without merit."[5]

As I read these notes it seemed to me that, however right his theology might be, Luther was reading into the text what was really not there, and I was about to put the book down when I came upon these final comments: "Now someone might say to me: 'Can't you ever do anything but speak only about the righteousness, wisdom and strength of God rather than of man, always expounding Scripture from the standpoint of God's righteousness and grace, always harping on the same string and singing the same old song?'" That caught my attention, because that was exactly what I had been thinking.

Luther went on. "To this I answer:

"Let each one look to himself. [But] as for me, I confess: Whenever I found less in the Scriptures than Christ, I was never satisfied; but whenever I found more than Christ, I never became poorer. Therefore it seems to me to be true that God the Holy Spirit does not know and does not want to know anything besides Jesus Christ. . . . [For] Christ is God's grace, mercy, righteousness, truth, wisdom, power, comfort, and salvation, given to us by God without any merit on our part." Then, in his final sentences, the great Reformer talked about our sins and the need to "weep over them, and then with humble awe to long earnestly for grace and mercy."[6]

Luther's may not be strict academic exposition, but it is the gospel, and it is what Luther meant when he said rightly that our entire lives should be marked by repentance.

Psalm 144

Blessings on God's People

Praise be to the LORD my Rock,
*   who trains my hands for war,*
*   my fingers for battle.*
He is my loving God and my fortress,
*   my stronghold and my deliverer,*
my shield, in whom I take refuge,
*   who subdues peoples under me. . . .*

Deliver me and rescue me
*   from the hands of foreigners*
whose mouths are full of lies,
*   whose right hands are deceitful.*

Then our sons in their youth
*   will be like well-nurtured plants,*
and our daughters will be like pillars
*   carved to adorn a palace.*
Our barns will be filled
*   with every kind of provision.*
Our sheep will increase by thousands,
*   by tens of thousands in our fields;*
*   our oxen will draw heavy loads.*
There will be no breaching of walls,
*   no going into captivity,*
*   no cry of distress in our streets.*

Blessed are the people of whom this is true;
blessed are the people whose God is the LORD.
verses 1–15

Martin Luther used to say that true religion is to be found in personal pronouns. He meant that it is only when we are able to speak of God as *our* God and call Jesus *our* Savior that Christianity becomes more than mere ideas and is truly real for us.

A biblical example of this right use of pronouns is Thomas, who fell at Christ's feet exclaiming, "*My* Lord and *my* God" (John 20:28, italics added), his doubts about Jesus' resurrection overcome by the presence of the Lord. No single work of ancient literature is more genuinely Christian than *The Confessions* of Saint Augustine, which from its very first line to its ending is addressed to God personally. Augustine begins, "Great are *thou,* O Lord, and greatly to be praised; great is *thy* power, and *thy* wisdom infinite" (italics added), a statement drawn from Psalms 145:3 and 147:5. Only a few lines into his work we read these well-known words, some of the best known of all literature (which I quoted in the chapter on the third part of Psalm 119): "*Thou* hast formed us for *thyself,* and our hearts are restless, till they rest in *thee*" (italics added).[1] That is true religion indeed.

"My Lord and My God"

In Psalm 144 David is extremely personal as he confesses who he had found God to be. He says "*my* Rock," "*my* loving God," "*my* fortress," "*my* stronghold," "*my* deliverer," and "*my* shield" (vv. 1–2, italics added). These verses set an exalted tone. Then, from this high beginning, the psalm turns into a prayer in which David (1) acknowledges human frailty, especially his own; (2) asks God for help in his trouble; (3) offers a "new song" of praise to God; and then (4) repeats his prayer for deliverance while looking forward to a day when the people of his kingdom will live in genuine peace and security and will be prospered. The psalm ends:

> Blessed are the people of whom this is true;
> blessed are the people whose God is the LORD (v. 15).

These last lines commend David's God to the people. They say, in effect: Happy are those who can make the same confession I do, who can say as I have been doing, "My Lord and my God."

Psalm 144 is a lot like Psalm 18, and any careful comparison, matching phrase for phrase, will suggest at once that they have been written by the same individual, though they are noticeably different in their tone.[2] In Psalm 18 David is explaining how he had been in desperate trouble at one time but

God had delivered him from it. The "cords of death" had entangled him (v. 4). The "cords of the grave" had coiled around him (v. 5). He was in "distress" (v. 6). But then, he says, the Lord "reached down from on high" and took hold of him, and drew him "out of deep waters" (v. 16); he pursued his enemies "and overtook them" (v. 37); he "crushed them so that they could not rise" (v. 38). In Psalm 144 David's enemies are a present threat. "Deliver me and rescue me from the hands of foreigners whose mouths are full of lies," he prays (v. 11), but the tone is nevertheless settled, calm, and trusting, for David knows that the Lord, who is his Rock, his fortress, his stronghold, his deliverer, and his shield, will give victory and the blessing of a safe and prospering kingdom: "no breaching of the walls, no going into captivity, no cry of distress in our streets" (v. 14).

Psalm 18 is identified as an early psalm of David, "which he sang to the LORD . . . when the LORD delivered him from the hand of all his enemies and from the hand of Saul" (title line). It is a victory song, a celebration. In Psalm 144 victory is needed; it is still to come. But the psalm breathes a mature assurance that results from a lifetime of experiencing God's unlimited power and grace.

Human Frailty: "What Is Man?"

What strikes David as he reflects on the majesty and power of God is the astonishing fact that this majestic God actually stoops to help as insignificant a person as himself.

> O LORD, what is man that you care for him,
>   the son of man that you think of him?
> Man is like a breath;
>   his days are like a fleeting shadow (vv. 3–4).

The first two of those lines are almost exactly like Psalm 8:4, except that parts of the two parallel sentences are exchanged. Psalm 8 reads, "What is man that you are mindful of him, the son of man that you care for him?" In Psalm 8 what follows is surprise at man's place in the cosmos, that God has "crowned him with glory and honor" and "made him ruler over the works of [God's] hands" (vv. 5–6), while in Psalm 144 the surprise is that God should be a help and stronghold for David, actually intervening in the affairs of his life to give him military victories. Once again we see how intensely personal the religion of this writer truly is. And how triumphant!

G. Campbell Morgan suggests that we will appreciate Psalm 144 better if we remember the psalms that precede it (Psalms 135–43), those following the Songs of Ascents. "Five of them elaborate the sufficiency of God. These are followed by four which declare the utter helplessness of man." Both truths are present here, but, says Morgan, "The divine sufficiency is seen encompassing the human helplessness until it is so lost sight of as hardly to be discoverable."[3] In other words, David is utterly aware of his weakness. He is not swept up into being arrogant just because he is a king. However, David is not trembling in fear either, because his faith is real and the God in whom he has faith is all-powerful.

Help in Trouble

With the exception of the two opening verses of Psalm 144, which pick up five of the seven images for God in Psalm 18:1–3 (only "strength" and "horn of my salvation" are neglected), the part of Psalm 144 that is most like Psalm 18 is the stanza to which we come now (vv. 5–8). It is a section in which David asks God to come down from heaven and rout his enemies.

> Part your heavens, O LORD, and come down;
>> touch the mountains, so that they smoke.
> Send forth lightning and scatter the enemies;
>> shoot your arrows and rout them.
> Reach down your hand from on high;
>> deliver me and rescue me
> from the mighty waters,
>> from the hands of foreigners
> whose mouths are full of lies,
>> whose right hands are deceitful.

Psalm 18 also describes God's parting the heavens to come down (v. 9), touching the mountains so they shake (v. 7), and scattering the people's enemies with lightning like arrows (vv. 12, 14); but the important thing about these similarities is not that Psalm 144 is like Psalm 18. The later psalm is not just copying the earlier one, as some commentators suggest. Instead, both are drawing on this common store of Old Testament imagery.

Verse 5 uses language associated with the descent of God to Sinai to give the law through Moses. This descent was accompanied by a shaking of the earth, dark clouds, and lightning. In the same way, Hebrews describes Sinai as "a mountain . . . burning with fire; . . . darkness, gloom and storm," so terrifying that even Moses said, "I am trembling with fear" (Heb. 12:18–21). David alludes to this event by asking God to "touch the mountains" so they [will] "smoke." He wants God to be as present in his day as he was when he revealed himself at Sinai. Verse 6 touches on God's intervention in the war against the Canaanites at the time of the Jewish conquest under Joshua as described in Joshua 10. God sent hailstones, probably accompanied by flashes of lightning, against the Jews' enemies. The reference to deliverance from "the mighty waters" in verse 7 may be to the parting of the Red Sea at the time of the exodus from Egypt or the parting of the waters of the Jordan River at the time of the crossing into Canaan, though the image is used a bit differently in the psalm.

In these verses David is reflecting on the manifestations of God's presence and power in the past and is asking for something of that same power to be demonstrated in God's deliverance of him from his present danger. It also means this: By alluding to these past proofs of God's presence, David is declaring that the God of Moses, Joshua, and the judges is his God too and that he is standing with them in the long succession of God's people within the covenant made at Sinai.

So do we, if we have been joined to God's covenant people through the work of Jesus Christ! The God of Moses, Joshua, and David is our God too, and he is the same today as he ever was. He is also our Rock and our deliverer.

A New Song

What should be our response to the fact that this is our God and to our deliverances, particularly our deliverance from sin's penalty and power? David's response was to sing "a new song," presumably the psalm we are studying. It is not the first time. The title to Psalm 18 says that David "*sang* to the LORD the words of this song when the LORD delivered him from the hand of all his enemies and from the hand of Saul," and toward the end of the psalm he himself said, "*I will sing* praises to your name" (v. 49, italics added). Psalm 40:3 declares,

> He put *a new song* in my mouth,
>   a hymn of praise to our God (italics added).[4]

In Psalm 18 the deliverance God gave was in the past, and the psalm is the "song" that thanks God for it. Here thanksgiving is petition. David is still waiting for God's intervention, but so confident is he of God's help that he is already singing about it.

If David were living in our time and were aware of our hymns, he might be singing,

> Our God, our help in ages past,
> Our hope for years to come,
> Our shelter from the stormy blast,
> And our eternal home.
>   from Psalm 90,
>   Isaac Watts, 1719

Since we are thinking here of our songs, let's not forget that "new song" in Revelation (Rev. 5:9). It is an antiphonal song, sung by the four-and-twenty elders, the angels, and the entire company of the redeemed in praise of Jesus Christ. The first who sing are the twenty-four elders:

> "You are worthy to take the scroll
>   and to open its seals,
> because you were slain,

> and with your blood you purchased men for God
> from every tribe and language and people and nation.
> You have made them to be a kingdom and priests to serve our God,
> and they will reign on the earth."

Then the angels perform their part:

> "Worthy is the Lamb, who was slain,
> to receive power and wealth and wisdom and strength
> and honor and glory and praise!"

At last "every creature in heaven and on earth and under the earth and on the sea" joins in, singing,

> "To him who sits on the throne and to the Lamb
> be praise and honor and glory and power,
>   for ever and ever!"

There is nothing to add to that triumphant song but "Amen," which is what the elders say, after which they fall down and worship (Rev. 5:9–14).

The Anticipated Blessing

The final section of Psalm 144 (vv. 11–15) anticipates the blessing the king expects God to give his kingdom after those who are threatening him are defeated. Alexander Maclaren called this section "an appended fragment" that has been attached to the earlier verses in an "embarrassing fashion,"[5] since it does not have echoes of other Davidic psalms, as the first verses do, and because he cannot see its connection to the rest of the psalm.

The flow of thought is obvious to me. When God delivers the nation from "the hands of foreigners, whose mouths are full of lies" and "whose right hands are deceitful" (v. 11), there will be no military threat ("no breaching of walls, no going into captivity, no cry of distress in our streets"), the young men will grow up like "well-nurtured plants," the young women will be like "pillars carved to adorn a palace," and the efforts of the people will be redirected from war to the fields and flocks so the country will flourish and become increasingly prosperous. These last verses are not added in "an embarrassing way," as Maclaren supposes. On the contrary, they are tied in beautifully; for the prayer for deliverance in verses 7 and 8 is repeated in verse 11 (with the omission of one line), implying that when the prayer is answered the days of prosperity have come.

The prayer for deliverance here is not a desperate plea, as in some of the other psalms, but rather a confident prayer leading to the vision of future blessing expressed in the last four verses. David is sure that when the deliverance is given, the blessing will be realized.

The blessing begins with the family as the foundation of any strong society (v. 12). It advances to the people's prosperity (v. 13), then to the security of the city (v. 14). Finally, the blessing is anchored in its only adequate source, God, which is why the psalm ends by saying that the greatest blessing of all is to have Jehovah as one's God (v. 15).

How different this blessing is from the world's way of thinking! Most people want the blessings of these last verses, but they suppose they can have them without God. People are not made to be alone. People need people, and most people dream of a loving, supportive family in which they can prosper and attain their potential, but without God the family has no strength and relationships are frequently destroyed. The collapse of the American family in our day is one proof of the effects of godlessness. People also want to prosper. Who does not? They want their work to go well and their bank accounts to grow, but even when this happens, they are still insecure and find that things alone do not satisfy them. Finally, people want to be safe, but when the culture is crumbling, as ours is, they know they are not secure and that violence and even death can strike them from nearly any source at any moment.

Having Jehovah as our God does not in itself immediately guarantee these blessings, for we live in a fallen world. Even David did not experience uninterrupted blessings. The families of believers also fail, as David's did; we do not always live utterly free from want; we are often in physical danger, as David was when he wrote this psalm. But we are blessed by God all the same. Besides, to know God is the greatest of all blessings, and knowing and serving God is the best and surest path to every other blessing.

The world says, "Blessed are those who put themselves first. Happy are those who look out for 'number one.'"

By contrast, the psalmist wrote at the beginning of the Psalter,

> Blessed is the man
>   who does not walk in the counsel of the wicked
> or stand in the way of sinners
>   or sit in the seat of mockers.
> But his delight is in the law of the LORD,
>   and on his law he meditates day and night.
> He is like a tree planted by streams of water,
>   which yields its fruit in season
> and whose leaf does not wither.
>   Whatever he does prospers (Ps. 1:1–3).

Psalm 145

The Last of the Acrostic Psalms

I will exalt you, my God the King;
  I will praise your name for ever and ever.
Every day I will praise you
  and extol your name for ever and ever.

Great is the LORD and most worthy of praise;
  his greatness no one can fathom.
One generation will commend your works to another;
  they will tell of your mighty acts.
They will speak of the glorious splendor of your majesty,
  and I will meditate on your wonderful works.
They will tell of the power of your awesome works,
  and I will proclaim your great deeds.
They will celebrate your abundant goodness
  and joyfully sing of your righteousness.

The LORD is gracious and compassionate,
  slow to anger and rich in love.
The LORD is good to all;
  he has compassion on all he has made. . . .

The LORD is faithful to all his promises
  and loving toward all he has made. . . .

The LORD is righteous in all his ways
  and loving toward all he has made. . . .

My mouth will speak in praise of the LORD.
  Let every creature praise his holy name
  for ever and ever.

                              verses 1–21

Psalm 145 is the last of David's psalms
as well as the last acrostic psalm in the Psalter.[1] An acrostic psalm is one in
which each verse (or a group of verses, as in Psalm 119) begins with one of
the twenty-two letters of the Hebrew alphabet in sequence: the first with
aleph, the second with *beth,* the third with *gimel,* and so on. In this case,
most Hebrew texts lack a verse for *nun,* which is why the psalm has only
twenty-one verses instead of twenty-two. One Masoretic text, the Dead Sea
Scrolls, and the ancient Syriac version supply the words, which appear as
the second half of verse 13 in the New International Version.

> The LORD is faithful to all his promises
> and loving toward all he has made.

What do you think should be the subject matter of David's last psalm? If
you know anything at all about David, you will expect this great Old
Testament figure to be praising God. Psalm 145 is indeed a monumental
praise psalm, a fit summary of all David had learned about God during a
long lifetime of following hard after the Almighty. It is also an appropriate
transition to the final "Hallelujah" psalms that close the Psalter.

An Opening Statement

David begins this psalm by an opening statement in which he salutes
Jehovah as his "God the King" (v. 1). This is a significant statement from the
mouth of Israel's king, for it acknowledges that although David may have
been king of the elect nation of Israel, God is nevertheless the King of kings
and therefore David's king too. And not only King of kings! He is the ultimate King of all creation and all persons. He is your King, because he made
you and rules over you, whether you acknowledge his rule or not.

What does this ultimate King deserve? What can we give him when we
come into his presence? It was usual to bring kings gifts, but there is no
mere thing that we can give God that God does not possess already.
Everything is already his. The only thing we can give is our praise, or worship. That is what David says he will do.

> I will praise your name for ever and ever.
> Every day I will praise you
> and extol your name for ever and ever (vv. 1–2).

These nearly parallel lines make three statements.

1. *"I will praise"* you. Praise is worship; it is acknowledging God to be what
he truly is: the sovereign, holy, just, righteous, merciful, awesome, and
majestic God we discover him to be in Scripture. Worship is not coming to

God to get things from him, though we are free to do that too. It is not even confessing our sins or pleading for grace, though these flow from worship naturally. It is acknowledging God to be God. Indeed, it is doing precisely what David does in the remainder of this composition.

2. *I will praise you "every day."* David is not going to praise God merely on the Sabbath, though the seventh day (or for us the first day of the week, Sunday) is explicitly set aside for that purpose. Rather, he is going to praise God "every day," Monday through Sunday (v. 2).

3. *I will praise you "for ever and ever."* "For ever and ever" means more than merely "to the end of my days, until I die." It means "forever," indicating David's belief he would be worshiping God in heaven even after his worship on earth was ended. You will be worshiping God forever also, along with the other redeemed saints from all other ages of world history. Therefore, why don't you practice worshiping God now? Let's practice. What should we praise God for? In this psalm David praises God for his greatness (vv. 5–7), his grace (vv. 8–13a), his faithfulness (vv. 13b–16), and his righteousness (vv. 17–20).

Great Is the Lord

Verse 3 starts by extolling God for being great.

> Great is the LORD and most worthy of praise;
> his greatness no one can fathom.

David is thinking here of the greatness of God displayed in his mighty works. The following verses make his intent clear: The word "works" occurs three times and the synonyms "acts" and "deeds" one additional time each.[2]

When we read of "mighty acts," "glorious splendor," "wonderful (or awesome) works," and "great deeds" it is natural to think of God's works in nature, which is not a bad place to start in our praise. If you can look at the surge of the ocean, the glory of the mountains, or the splendor of the sky on a cloudless night and not be moved to praise God, you are more to be pitied than a person who has lost his or her physical sight. As an evangelist said to some inmates in a federal prison on one occasion, "If that don't turn you on, you ain't got no switches."

Yet wonderful as God's works of creation are, a person who has come to know God's goodness in Jesus Christ can hardly stop there. The greatest of God's works are his salvation works. In the case of Israel, these were always understood to involve God's power in delivering Israel from slavery in Egypt and bringing them into their own land. For us above all else God's salvation works are his work of saving us from sin through Christ's atonement. Since David ends this stanza by writing of God's "abundant goodness" and "righteousness," it must be these particular, saving works of God that he is thinking about specifically.

Both goodness and righteousness were preserved and displayed in the death of Jesus. In Jesus' death God showed himself to be both good and righteous in saving sinners. Neither of these attributes of God is seen in nature.

In this stanza David also speaks of "one generation commending your works to another" (v. 4). This statement does not mean merely that the stories of God's past acts will be passed on by the redeemed community, though that is true, but that each generation of believers will add to that old story the account of what God also has done with them. God continues to act for us and in us. Our recognition of this truth and our confession of it are part of the praise we offer God.

The Lord Is Gracious

It was probably his reference to God's goodness in verse 7 that led the psalmist to deal with God's grace, compassion, patience, and rich love in stanza three (vv. 8–13a), the theme introduced by verse 8.

This verse is a nearly perfect echo of God's revelation of himself to Moses at Mount Sinai, recorded in Exodus 34:6. Exodus 34:6 is the verse most often quoted in the Old Testament, and with good reason, for it speaks of mercy, and mercy is the amazing, utterly surprising thing about God.[3] Certainly God is almighty and all-wise and all-knowing; God could not be God without being all those important things, and more. We can expect them, but not mercy! The unexpected thing is that God should be gracious to those who have spurned his rightful authority and even murdered his Son when he came to earth to save us from our sins.

In the Exodus account, as we have seen before, Moses had asked to see God's glory, meaning that he wanted to see him face-to-face in his splendor. God said that he would not be able to show Moses his face; no one can see God's face and live, but God would proclaim his name to Moses. The essence of this revelation is the meaning of God's name. His name is Jehovah, which means "I AM WHO I AM" (Exod. 3:14). If we go beyond the mere definition of God's name to ask, But what is "I Am" like? the answer is, "I am compassionate and gracious, slow to anger, abounding in love and faithfulness, maintaining love to thousands, and forgiving wickedness, rebellion and sin" (Exod. 34:6–7).

David celebrates God's mercy in verses 8–13. Just as the previous stanza of the psalm emphasized God's greatness by repeating words having to do with greatness (works, acts, and deeds), this stanza emphasizes mercy by using "gracious" (once), "compassion" (twice), "love" (once), and "goodness" (once). It picks up on verses 3–7 too, speaking of God's "mighty acts" again, in this case as evidence of his love.

In the latter half of this stanza there is also a strong emphasis on God's kingdom, which has led some writers to make this the theme of the stanza and even of the entire psalm, which began by calling God "King." Here "kingdom" occurs four times and "dominion" once. It is a reminder that one part of God's goodness is his rule over us. We cannot rule ourselves.

Moreover, it is a work of God's grace when we come to see the necessity of his rule, if we do. Nebuchadnezzar took the glory of God to himself when he looked out over the city of Babylon and declared in his pride, "Is not this the great Babylon I have built as the royal residence, by my mighty power and for the glory of my majesty?" (Dan. 4:30). God judged the king for his arrogance, depriving him of his sanity and causing him to be driven out to live with the beasts of the field and even behaving like them. He lived with the animals for seven years, but at last Nebuchadnezzar learned his lesson, and when he did he praised God in the words of this very psalm, quoting verse 13.

Then I praised the Most High; I honored and glorified him who lives forever.

His dominion is an eternal dominion;
    his kingdom endures from generation to generation (Dan. 4:34, Ps. 145:3).

When a person has learned that lesson he or she has learned much.
It is even more important to become a grateful subject of God's kingdom through faith in Jesus Christ. We read of this kingdom in Revelation.

You are worthy to take the scroll
    and to open its seals,
because you were slain,
    and with your blood you purchased men for God
    from every tribe and language and people and nation.
You have made them to be a kingdom and priests to serve our God,
    and they will reign on the earth (Rev. 5:9–10).

The Lord Is Faithful

The next section of Psalm 145 deals with God's faithfulness to his promises. Derek Kidner calls this section "God the Provider" (vv. 13b–20), noting four ways in which God provides for his creation: he helps the inadequate (v. 14); he gives food to all his creatures (vv. 15–16); he answers those who pray (vv. 18–19); and he protects those who are his (v. 20).[4] The New International Version probably follows the psalmist's intended stanza arrangement more closely when it links verses 13b–16 to God's faithfulness (v. 13) and verses 17–20 to God's righteous or upright way of acting: "The LORD is righteous in all his ways" (v. 17). This division is also suggested by the repetition of a line in verses 13b and 17. Verse 13b says, "The LORD is faithful to all his promises *and loving toward all he has made*," while verse 17 says, "The LORD is righteous in all his ways *and loving toward all he has made*" (italics added).[5]

How does God demonstrate his faithfulness? He does it by keeping his promises and by caring for his creation (v. 13). When we fall, he lifts us up (v. 14). When we are bowed down by distress, he restores us (v. 14). When we are hungry, he provides food (v. 15). When we look to him with our hands open, empty and held out, he satisfies us with good things (v. 16). God does this for human beings, of course, but what the psalmist seems to be thinking of here most is the faithfulness of God even to the animal kingdom, for he stresses: "to all he has made" (v. 13) and "every living thing" (v. 16). One promise referred to in verse 13 is probably God's promise to Noah following the flood: "Never again will I destroy all living creatures, as I have done. As long as the earth endures, seedtime and harvest, cold and heat, summer and winter, day and night, will never cease" (Gen. 8:21–22).

That is a great promise, but the promises of God to his redeemed people are much greater. What the animals need from God is food. Men and women need many things, but what we need most of all is God. Saint Augustine said in his *Confessions:* "Thou hast formed us for thyself, and our hearts are restless, till they rest in thee."[6] God promises to give us himself if we come to him through Christ. Then he also meets every other right desire we may have. God says, "Open wide your mouth and I will fill it" (Ps. 81:10). Paul testified, "My God will meet all your needs according to his glorious riches in Christ Jesus" (Phil. 4:19).

There is a wonderful universality in these last verses, through verse 20. It is seen in the word "all," which is repeated eleven times: "*all* his promises," "*all* he has made," "*all* those who fall," "*all* who are bowed down," "*all* look to you," "*all* his ways," "*all* he has made," "*all* who call on him" (twice), "*all* who love him," and "*all* the wicked" (italics added). Because God is good to all, all ought to praise him. Psalm 145 and the entire Psalter end on this note. Psalm 145 says, "Let every creature praise his holy name for ever and ever." The Psalter ends, "Let everything that has breath praise the LORD. Praise the LORD" (Ps. 150:6).

God Is Righteous

The last of these four praise stanzas refers to God being righteous: "The LORD is righteous in all his ways and loving toward all he has made" (v. 17). "Righteous" here does not mean morally upright, though God is that. He is the only true source of morality. It means rather that God is upright, or just, in responding to those who have needs and call on him, those who are in peril and seek salvation. When verse 18 says that God is "near to all who call on him," it means that he answers their prayers. Verse 19 says that he also "fulfills [their] desires . . . and saves them." Verse 20 adds, "The LORD watches over" them. In other words, throughout our entire lives God shows himself to be a good, caring, saving, and persevering God.

In verse 20, for the first time in this psalm, the wicked come into the picture.

> The LORD watches over all who love him,
>   but all the wicked he will destroy (v. 20).

Up to this point the psalm has been one unending chorus of praise, but this verse, much like Psalm 1:6, reminds us that our praise must still be offered in a sinful world. We are not in heaven yet, though we will be.

Franz Delitzsch makes an interesting observation on the reference to those who fear God in verse 19 and those who love him in verse 20. "Fear and love of God belong inseparably together. For fear without love is an unfree, servile disposition, and love without fear, bold-faced familiarity; the one dishonors the all-gracious One, and the other the all-exalted One."[7]

A Closing Invitation to Praise God

The last verse of Psalm 145 is the last word we have from David in the Bible. It is his last will and testament. If he had said nothing else in his long life, these words would be a fine legacy for future generations. In it he praises God and invites others to praise God also.

> My mouth will speak in praise of the LORD.
>   Let every creature praise his holy name
>   for ever and ever.

What will your legacy be? It will never be better than David's. Don't wait until you die. Praise God now, and get others to praise God with you.

Psalm 146

Praise the Lord, O My Soul

Praise the LORD.

Praise the LORD, O my soul.
   I will praise the LORD all my life;
   I will sing praise to my God as long as I live.

Do not put your trust in princes,
   in mortal men, who cannot save.
When their spirit departs, they return to the ground;
   on that very day their plans come to nothing.

Blessed is he whose help is the God of Jacob,
   whose hope is in the LORD his God,
the Maker of heaven and earth,
   the sea, and everything in them—
   the LORD, who remains faithful forever.
He upholds the cause of the oppressed
   and gives food to the hungry.
The LORD sets prisoners free,
   the LORD gives sight to the blind,

the LORD lifts up those who are bowed down,
the LORD loves the righteous.
The LORD watches over the alien
and sustains the fatherless and the widow,
but he frustrates the ways of the wicked.

The LORD reigns forever,
your God, O Zion, for all generations.

Praise the LORD.

verses 1–10

We come now to the very last psalms of the Psalter (Psalms 146–50), a group of five all beginning and ending with the word "hallelujah," translated "Praise the LORD" by most of our English versions. The Septuagint identifies them as psalms of Haggai and Zechariah, making them a second Hallel (like the Egyptian Hallel, Psalms 113–18), but this ascription adds nothing to our understanding of these psalms, and it is probably incorrect. What is important and correct is that the psalms as a whole, these glorious Hebrew worship hymns beginning with Psalm 1 and going all the way to Psalm 150, end on uninterrupted notes of praise to God as if to teach us that this is indeed the chief end of man: "to glorify God and to enjoy him forever."

In the earlier psalms, we have studied the writers' griefs, shames, sins, doubts, and fears. We have witnessed the people of God in their defeats and victories, their ups and downs in life. We have encountered rebellious words and struggling faith. All this is behind us now. In these final psalms every word is praise.

Praise is where all true religious contemplation should end. When all is said, the hearts of those who are truly God's people beat their last praising God. Do we understand all that God is doing in our lives or in the world? Of course not, but we understand enough about the nature of God to praise him in spite of the difficulties.

Particularly as our lives move toward their inevitable earthly ends, they should be full of praise. In *The Treasury of David* Charles Spurgeon reports that on his deathbed a man named John Janeway cried out:

Come, help me with praises. . . . Let every thing that hath being help me to praise God. Hallelujah! Hallelujah! Hallelujah! Praise is now my life work, and I shall be engaged in this sweet work now and for ever. Bring the Bible; turn to David's psalms, and let us sing a psalm of praise. Come, let us lift up our voices in the praises of the Most High. I will sing with you as long as my breath doth last, and when I have none, I shall do it better.[1]

Maclaren says that in these psalms "with constantly swelling diapason, all themes of praise are pealed forth, until the melodious thunder of the final psalm, which calls on everything that has breath to praise Jehovah."[2]

These last psalms have hymn versions that we frequently sing. Psalm 146 contributed this one.

> Hallelujah, praise Jehovah, O my soul, Jehovah praise;
> I will sing the glorious praises of my God through all my days.
> Put no confidence in princes, nor for help on man depend;
> He shall die, to dust returning, and his purposes shall end.
>
> Happy is the man that chooses Israel's God to be his aid;
> He is blessed whose hope of blessing on the Lord his God is stayed.
> Heav'n and earth the Lord created, seas and all that they contain;
> He delivers from oppression, righteousness he will maintain.

Hallelujah!

Roy Clements, the pastor of Eden Baptist Church, Cambridge, England, has a sermon on these last psalms in which he observes that there are three words that are understood in every language on earth: amen, hallelujah, and Coca Cola.[3] Amen we know, and Coca Cola we know. But what does hallelujah mean?

Our culture has trivialized this word, as it has so many other biblical terms. Not long ago I was given an add for Nicorette gum, which is supposed to help people stop smoking. It showed a package of the gum bursting through majestic clouds while the sun shown through like an end-time theophany. The copy read: "Nicorette gum is now available full strength without a prescription. Hallelujah!" Well, defeat of an entrenched habit like smoking may be a cause for rejoicing, but it is a trivialization of hallelujah to use it to celebrate the appearance of a gum.

Hallelujah is a compound word made up of two Hebrew words: *hallel* (an imperative verb meaning "praise") and *jah* (a contraction of the name for God, Jehovah). So hallelujah means "Praise the Lord (or Jehovah)." Hallelujah was often used as a liturgical response in Jewish worship, much as we might also use it. The leader would say something like, "The Lord is good; his love endures forever." The people would respond, "Hallelujah."

Yet, as Clements points out, the person who composed these last psalms of the Psalter

> is not content that the congregation of God's people should just repeat this great word of praise, Alleluia, as some trite jingle. Still less, does he use Alleluia as a mantra to be chanted like Hare Krishna in order to artificially work up some state of spiritual ecstasy. He sets these Alleluias as parentheses, enclosing songs which are very rich in theological content. In fact, you

could regard "Alleluia" in each case as a kind of liturgical alarm signal to the sluggish in the congregation. Alleluia, you've got to be alert, you've got to wake up, there's business in hand, praising the Lord.[4]

Clements's words imply a number of important things about worship.

1. *Worship is work.* A Lutheran woman named Marva J. Dawn has written a book about worship called *Reaching Out without Dumbing Down*, which I have found particularly helpful. As the title suggests, Dawn is concerned about the dumbing down of worship in the same way western culture is dumbing down just about everything. We live in an entertainment culture where everything is supposed to be fun and effortless, so Christians who come to church on Sunday expect the same environment. If it's worth doing at all, it must be easy, we suppose. Dawn says ours is a lazy Christianity and the church's problem is sloth.[5] We need to discover the truth that praising God is not something we can do in an apathetic passive state.

2. *Worship must engage our minds.* If worship is praising God for who he is, then we must know who he is, and that means understanding and thinking about God's attributes. This understanding is what John Stott writes about in *Your Mind Matters*.[6] He recalls how the psalms set the worship of God in the context of teaching about God and suggests that if we are not reflecting on what God is like and has done, we are not really worshiping.

3. *Worship is possible because of God's prior revelation.* To worship God we must know who God is, but we cannot know who God is unless God first chooses to reveal himself to us. God has done this in the Bible, which is why the Bible and the teaching of the Bible need to be central in our worship services. Clements writes,

> The only reason we can worship God is that we know something about him, ... something ... which excites our admiration, our gratitude, our faith, our joy. ... Worship is heartfelt, emotionally-charged expression; but it is also a rational and thoughtful expression. True worship is [thus] always a response to what we know of God, as a result of his revealing himself to us.[7]

4. *Worship is personal.* You must worship God yourself. No one else can do it in your place. The choir cannot worship for you, nor can the ministers. It is correct that worship is also corporate. We do it with others, and it is for the entire people of God, but each one must worship God personally, old and young, fathers and mothers, even children. If you are a Christian, worship is for you, whoever you may be.

Having called the congregation to worship in the first word of the psalm, the author of Psalm 146 immediately declares his determination to worship God himself, saying,

> I will praise the LORD all my life;
> I will sing praise to my God as long as I live (v. 2).

Spurgeon says, "It is a poor business if we solely exhort others, and do not stir up our own soul."[8]

Mortal after All

At first glance it seems strange that the psalmist's call to worship and his personal resolve to worship should be followed by the warning of verses 3 and 4 not to put our trust in princes.

> Do not put your trust in princes,
>   in mortal men, who cannot save.
> When their spirit departs, they return to the ground;
>   on that very day their plans come to nothing.

This warning does not seem to have anything to do with worship, even negatively, but it does in several ways.[9]

1. *We value others more than we value God.* Isn't the main reason we fail to worship God the fact that we value human beings more than we value God? Theoretically, we know that God is of supreme importance, but he is invisible to us and usually also remote from our thoughts. What we do see is other human beings, particularly those who seem important, so we focus on people and put our trust in them. We trust politicians, thinking that the president or congress or mayor or some other highly placed persons will be able to solve our problems, but they can't even solve their own. We trust science or education or anything else to be our ultimate savior. We do not actually trust God and worship him.

John King was a pastor who lived in the early seventeenth century. He explained in a funeral sermon based on this text why we should decline to put our trust in mere human beings: because they are *mere men,* no different from ourselves; because they are *weak men,* unable to give help; because they are *dying men;* because when they die they are *subject to dissolution*—they return to the earth; and because *their thoughts are as transitory as their bodies.*[10]

Verses 3 and 4 make these points by two plays on Hebrew words. In Hebrew *adam,* meaning "man," is the same word for "earth" or "ground." So dirt goes to dirt. Lest we should miss this point, verse 4 deliberately recalls God's words to Adam in Genesis 3:19: "For dust [earth] you are and to dust [earth] you will return." The second play on words has to do with "spirit" or "breath," which are the same word in Hebrew: *ruach.* Verse 4, like Isaiah 2:22, teaches that we are only one-breath beings. We live one breath at a time, and when that spirit (breath) departs we are gone.

2. *We value ourselves more than we value God.* We think we can handle our troubles by ourselves and surmount all emergencies by our wisdom. We do not think we need God and therefore do not take time to worship him. When Queen Elizabeth I was acting particularly dictatorial on one occasion, her wise spiritual counselor, Archbishop Grindal, rebuked her. "Remember,

Madam, you are a mortal creature," he said. Elizabeth did not like to be reminded of that fact, but it was true, despite her position.

William the Conqueror, the Norman who defeated King Harold at the Battle of Hastings in 1066 and thereby profoundly changed the course of English history, died in 1087 in circumstances that caused his biographer, Ordericus Vitalis, to moralize in the language of this psalm. King Philip of France had claimed lands on the border of Normandy that William believed were his. He crossed over to France and waged war on Philip. The war was progressing in his favor. In fact, he was on the verge of celebrating a complete triumph when the horse on which he was riding stumbled and William was thrown forward upon the iron pommel of his saddle, receiving a fatal injury. He was carried to the Abbey of St. Gervais near Rouen, where on the morning of September 9 he died. His nobles immediately mounted their horses and rode off to secure their own possessions. William's servants, after stripping the valuable clothes and jewelry off the dead king, made off too, leaving the naked body of the conqueror of England to lie on the abbey's bare floor.

The historian wrote, "Put not your trust in princes, which are nothing, O ye sons of men; but in the living and true God, who is the Maker of all. If riches increase, do not set your hearts on them. For all flesh is grass, and all the glory of it as the flower of grass. The grass withers, and the flowers fade away; but the word of the Lord endures forever."[11]

The only being in the universe that you can depend on unconditionally is God. So worship God! Verses 3 and 4 occur at the start of this final collection to direct our worship. Mere man cannot save, but "blessed is he whose help is the God of Jacob, whose hope is in the LORD his God" (v. 5).

The Greatest Blessing

The longest stanza of this psalm (vv. 5–9) begins with a beatitude. It is the last in the Psalter, and it promises blessing for those who have learned not to put their hopes in man but in God instead.[12] This stanza is all about God, here called "the LORD" (Jehovah). This covenant name for God occurs seven times in these verses, once each in four of them and three times in verse 8 alone. Each time it tells us something good about God.

1. *The Lord is our hope* (v. 5). God alone can save us, in contrast to the important people of this world, who cannot and would not even if they could. God saves us from our enemies—the psalms speak often of enemies—and ultimately from all human calamities and from sin through the work of Jesus Christ.

2. *The Lord remains faithful forever* (v. 6). Not only does God save us, but he also remains faithful to us after he has saved us. This faithfulness is what we usually call the perseverance of the saints. We persevere because God perseveres with us. Or, as we can also express it, the faithful remain faithful to God because God is faithful to them.

3. *The Lord sets prisoners free* (v. 7). Verses 7 and 8 take us to the New Testament, where Jesus announced the purpose of his mission in the synagogue at Nazareth (Luke 4:18–19), quoting from Isaiah 61:1–2.

> "The Spirit of the Lord is on me,
>   because he has anointed me
>   to preach good news to the poor.
> He has sent me to proclaim freedom for the prisoners
>   and recovery of sight for the blind,
> to release the oppressed,
>   to proclaim the year of the Lord's favor."

As far as we know from the Gospels, Jesus never literally freed anyone from prison. So that fact and the context here show that the deliverance in both places must be spiritual, a deliverance from sin.

4. *The Lord gives sight to the blind* (v. 8). Again, we are reminded of Jesus when the psalmist describes God as giving sight to the blind. The greatest blindness of all is blindness to the truth of God disclosed in Scripture. When Jehovah gives sight to the blind, the blind recognize the Bible to be true and place their faith in Jesus.

5. *The Lord lifts up those who are bowed down* (v. 8). Many things in life push us around or knock us down, but God cares for us and lifts us up again. The next psalm will say, "He heals the brokenhearted and binds up their wounds" (Ps. 147:3).

6. *The Lord loves the righteous* (v. 8). "Love" is an attitude rather than an action, as most of the previous items have been. It is mentioned here because it is the source of all the other actions. Why does God act in a trustworthy way toward us, uphold the oppressed, free prisoners, give sight to the blind, and lift up those who are bowed down? The answer is because he loves us. It is not because we have made ourselves righteous. God has made us righteous in Christ, and even that is because he loves us.

7. *The Lord watches over the alien* (v. 9). The three cases listed in this verse 9—the alien, the fatherless, and the widow—are often cited in the Old Testament as examples of those who are defenseless. God watches over them and protects them from the wicked. This verse is like Psalm 145:20.

Praise Forever

In the last verse of this psalm the writer says that the God he has been describing and praising will reign "for all generations." It follows that God also must be praised from generation to generation.

Will you put your hope in God and worship God as the only utterly trustworthy being in this universe? If you will not, your only alternative is despair and cynicism, for people will always let you down. The politicians will let you down. The intellectuals will let you down. The scientists will let you down. "Salvation comes from the LORD," said Jonah, and he was right (Jonah 2:9). God alone is utterly good, utterly powerful, and utterly trustworthy. Why settle for less? God is the only being about whom we can honestly and truly say, "Hallelujah."

Psalm 147

Praise the Lord for Everything

Praise the LORD.

How good it is to sing praises to our God,
how pleasant and how fitting to praise him!

The LORD builds up Jerusalem;
he gathers the exiles of Israel.
He heals the brokenhearted
and binds up their wounds.

He determines the number of the stars
and calls them each by name.
Great is our Lord and mighty in power;
his understanding has no limit.
The LORD sustains the humble
but casts the wicked to the ground. . . .

He has revealed his word to Jacob,
his laws and decrees to Israel.
He has done this for no other nation;
they do not know his laws.

Praise the LORD.

verses 1–20

In the last chapter I mentioned an excellent study of what it means to worship God called *Reaching Out without Dumbing Down* by Marva J. Dawn. One of the points it makes is that much of what we call worship today is not worship at all but rather a glorification of ourselves. This is particularly true of what we often call "praise" songs. Dawn gives this example.

> I will celebrate, sing unto the Lord.
> I will sing to God a new song. (repeat)
> I will praise God, I will sing to God a new song. (repeat)
> Hallelujah, hallelujah, hallelujah, hallelujah.
> I will sing to God a new song. (repeat)
> I will celebrate, sing unto the Lord.
> I will sing to God a new song. (repeat) (Repeat all)

I have never heard that particular song, but it is a fair example of what we hear in many so-called worship services. The chorus seems to be praising God—it claims to be praising him—but it does not. As Dawn points out, "The verbs say *I will*, but in this song I don't, because though God is mentioned as the recipient of my praise and singing, the song never says a single thing about or to God."[1]

What is the song about, then? If we look at it carefully, the answer is clear. With all the repeats, "I" is the subject twenty-eight times. Not God, but "I" myself. And not even myself along with other members of the covenant community, just "I." "With that kind of focus," says Dawn, "we might suppose that all the hallelujahs are praising how good I am . . . at celebrating and singing."[2] This is narcissism, a self-absorption characteristic of our contemporary secular culture. So if we are self-absorbed in worship, as we seem to be, it only means that we are worldly in our worship, and not spiritual, as we suppose. We are focused on ourselves.

The Psalter's Model Praise Songs

The praise songs of the Psalter do not fall into this trap, which is one reason why they are such good models for our worship and why they should be used in Christian worship more often than they are. Psalms 146–50 in particular develop aspects of what it means to praise God. Psalm 146 begins with the personal element of "I will praise the LORD all my life," (Ps. 146:2); then it invites all God's people to join in (Ps. 146:3, 5, 8). Psalm 148 explains where God must be praised: from the heavens above to the earth below (Ps. 148:1, 7). Psalm 149 tells how to praise God; it is with "a new song" (Ps. 149:1). Psalm 150 tells everyone to praise God: "Let everything that has breath praise the LORD" (Ps. 150:6). Psalm 147, the psalm we are going to be looking at now, tells us what we can praise God for.

Psalm 147 uses the pronoun "he," which refers to God, fourteen times and "LORD" eight times. In other words, the psalm is about God, not ourselves. "I" does not occur once, and "our" is used just twice. Isn't this how the worship of *God* should be done?

Many interpreters divide Psalm 147 into three parts, verses 1–6, 7–11, and 12–20, each part starting with a call to praise God, but the stanzas found in the New International Version handle the content well and give us *seven* distinct matters for which God should be praised.[3] Using this division, we can capture the thrust of the psalm's praise by considering (1) God's care for his people, (2) God's care of the least significant, (3) God's provision for his creation, (4) God's delight in the godly, (5) God's blessing on the nation, (6) God's rule over creation, and (7) God's revelation of himself to Israel. These considerations, like the psalm, focus on God entirely.

God's Care for His People

The first verse draws on Psalm 33:1, which says that it is "fitting" to praise God; Psalm 92:1, which declares that praising God is "good"; and Psalm 135:3, which says that praise is "pleasant." In Psalm 147:1 all three adjectives occur together:

> How good it is to sing praises to our God,
>> how pleasant and how fitting to praise him!

Why is praise of God good, pleasant, and fitting? Verses 2 and 3 answer that it is because of what God does or has done for his people: He builds up Jerusalem, gathers the exiles of Israel, heals the brokenhearted, and binds up their wounds.

Quite a few commentators suggest that Psalm 147 may have been written for the dedication of the reconstructed walls of Jerusalem in the time of Nehemiah, and they may be right. The twelfth chapter of Nehemiah tells how the Levites were brought to the city to lead a grand celebration "with songs of thanksgiving and with the music of cymbals, harps and lyres" (Neh. 12:27). The professional singers were collected, and when they were assembled two choirs led the people in worship, one choir proceeding in one direction along the top of the newly reconstructed walls and the other choir proceeding in the other direction. After the circuit they took their places in the temple along with the nation's leaders, singing under the direction of Jezrahiah, and the rejoicing was so loud that it could be heard far beyond the bounds of the city. We do not know if Psalm 147 was composed for that occasion or even if it was known by Nehemiah's choirs, but we can sense how good, pleasant, and fitting it would have been for them to have sung these words:

> The LORD builds up Jerusalem;
>> he gathers the exiles of Israel.
> He heals the brokenhearted
>> and binds up their wounds.

God had done exactly that in bringing the exiles back from remote Babylon and enabling them to rebuild their walls and repopulate Jerusalem.

As for us, we have no continuing city here, no earthly Jerusalem; but we are citizens of the heavenly Jerusalem, and we praise God for gathering us from this perishing, sinful world, binding up our hearts, healing our wounds, and building up our city, which is the Christian church. Surely it is good, pleasant, and fitting for us to sing the same kind of praises to God.

God's Care of the Least Significant

Reflections on how God brought the exiles back from distant Babylon and reestablished them in a rebuilt Jerusalem leads the psalmist to reflect on God's power, seen in his numbering and naming of the stars. Truly, "[God's] understanding has no limit," he writes (v. 5).

The major point of this stanza (vv. 4–6) is not that God cares for the stars—though he does—but that the one who is mighty enough to number and name the stars also concerns himself for us, who are insignificant and weak by comparison. We would expect God to have created the stars, but that God should sustain even the most humble of his creatures while saving them from the wicked, who would destroy them, and casting the wicked down—that is most remarkable and is worthy of the humble and godly person's praise.

Mary struck this note in the Magnificat, crying,

> He has brought down rulers from their thrones
>   but has lifted up the humble.
> He has filled the hungry with good things
>   but has sent the rich away empty (Luke 1:52–53).

God's Provision for His Creation

Many commentators begin a second section of the psalm here, as I said, since in verse 7 we find another invitation to praise God, in this case to "sing to [him] with thanksgiving," with a new reason to do so in verses 7–9.

In addition to praising God because of his care for his people (vv. 1–3), including those who seem to be least significant (vv. 4–6), we should praise God because he cares for the animal creation too. God covers the earth with clouds, the clouds give forth rain, the rain causes the grass to grow, the grass is food for the cattle; and, not only are the cattle provided with food but all other creatures too, including even baby ravens. These verses demonstrate a delicacy of thought and a sensitivity to nature on the part of the psalmist. He has spoken of Jerusalem and its people early in the psalm; he is one of those people. He will speak of the city again in verses 12–14, rejoicing in its security and peace. Here, before he does, he thinks of the animals and of God's care for them.

Most of us do not have this sensitivity to the rest of creation, unless we have a pet or belong to some "save the animals" organization, but we are the poorer for it. A few weeks before I first preached on this psalm, I was preaching on Psalm 145 and called attention to David's resolve to praise God "for ever and ever." I said that he was expecting to praise God in heaven since "for ever and ever" means more than simply "until I die." After the service was over a woman who is an artist asked me if that meant that there would also be animals in heaven since the last verse of the same song says, "Let every creature praise his holy name for ever and ever" (v. 21). When I hesitated she reminded me that in Revelation Jesus is described as coming out of heaven riding on a white horse. That was a new line of thought for me. I didn't know whether there will be horses or other animals in heaven, and I still don't. I think that most of the images in Revelation are figurative, and as far as I can determine, the animals do not have eternal souls, as we do; but I suppose God could create animals to bring variety to heaven, just as he has done here.

Yet that is not the point of my referring to this conversation. What interested me was this woman's sensitivity to animals and her interest in and concern for them. When I came to Psalm 147 and thought about this I realized that she is closer to the psalmist's frame of mind than I was. Both she and the psalmist would be thanking God for his care of the animal creation.

God's Delight in the Godly

At first glance verses 10 and 11 seem to be a digression in which the writer reflects on the value of godliness over physical strength. This is not really a digression at all. He is still thinking about God, saying that God is not like most of us, who are usually impressed with physical qualities—things we can see—and not with things we cannot see. Rather,

> the LORD delights in those who fear him,
>   who put their hope in his unfailing love (v. 11).

If we really believed that verse and wanted to please God, we would give more time to spiritual things than to worldly concerns. There is nothing wrong with physical strength or beauty; God made both. But physical things pass away, while the one who does the will of God lasts forever.

God's Blessing on the Nation

For some writers a final section of the psalm starts with the third of three calls to praise God: "Extol the LORD, O Jerusalem; praise your God, O Zion" (v. 12). Verses 12–14 actually stand apart from those that follow, since here the psalmist is thinking about Jerusalem again, just as he did at the psalm's beginning. After verses 12–14 he is going to write about God's care of the whole earth (again) and about God's giving his law to Israel. When he writes about Jerusalem he says that God strengthens its gates, blesses its people, grants peace to the nation, and satisfies its residents with good food.

Those are wonderful blessings for any people. If we have enjoyed the same things, as we surely have, we should be praising God for these mercies too. We need to remember what a blessing a nation's strength and safety are, because we tend to forget it when we have them. War is a terrible thing and a terrible waste both of lives and money. When a country is secure and at peace, as ours is, then the people who live there prosper and are able to enjoy what we call "the good life." They enjoy "the finest of wheat" and the finest of many other things too. If God gives peace, let's be sure to thank him for it. ·

God's Rule over Creation

Verses 15–18 return to the care of God for nature, in this case to his rule over its weather and the recurring seasons. It is part of a pattern in which the stanzas of the psalm alternate between God's care of Jerusalem and its people and his care for the earth and its creatures as a whole.

Verse 18 became of special interest to the English nation in the late sixteenth century after the defeat of the Spanish Armada. The Spanish were planning an invasion of England, and the Armada was launched in the summer of 1588 to defeat the English navy and then transport the Spanish army to England from the Netherlands. The Armada consisted of 130 ships containing 7,000 sailors and 17,000 soldiers. The English had 90 ships under the command of Francis Drake. The battle was fought for days, the English maintaining their distance and relentlessly bombarding the opposing fleet with alternating broadsides. They fought wisely and well, but the decisive factor in the battle was a strong wind that churned the waters of the English Channel and eventually drove the Spanish galleons up the channel into the North Sea, where many were destroyed. Attempting to return south by rounding Scotland and Ireland, even more of these impressive vessels were sunk, and in the end only half of the Armada returned to Spain or Portugal.

The English victory was complete. The Spanish defeat was total. The English celebrated their deliverance by minting a new issue of coins, which bore the Latin inscription *Affavit Deus* ("God blew"), taken from Psalm 147:18: "He stirs up his breezes, and the waters flow." In those days there was at least one nation that knew how to praise God for its safety.

God's Revelation of Himself to Israel

One reason why it is best to handle Psalm 147 according to the stanzas of the New International Version and not according to the three parts preferred by many commentators is that verses 19 and 20 stand by themselves as a climax. Of all the many blessings for which the people of God should be thankful, the greatest is that God has established a personal relationship with his people by means of a verbalized and written communication.

Paul wrote about the advantages possessed by Israel in the Book of Romans. He made exactly the same point as these last verses of the psalm. "What advantage, then, is there in being a Jew, or what value is there in circumcision? Much in every way! First of all, they have been entrusted with the very words of God" (Rom. 3:1–2).

None of us can experience anything in life of more personal advantage to our souls than possession of the Scriptures. Without them we are utterly confused. We are adrift on a sea of human speculation where all the big questions of life are concerned: Is there a God? If so, what is he like? How can we come to know him? Who are we? What are we here for? What is the solution to our sin? What way of life is best? Does what we do here matter? We can never find the answer to these questions by ourselves. It is only from the revelation of God in the Bible that we can have sure answers to any of these life-and-death questions.

John Wesley wrote:

> I am a creature of a day, passing through life as an arrow through the air. I am a spirit come from God and returning to God, just hovering over the great gulf 'till, a few moments hence, I am no more seen; I drop into an unchangeable eternity! I want to know one thing—the way to heaven, how to land safe on that happy shore. God himself has condescended to teach me the way. For this very end he came from heaven. He hath written it down in a book. O give me that book! At any price, give me the book of God! I have it: Here is knowledge enough for me. Let me be *homo unius libri* [a man of one book]. Here then I am, far from the busy ways of men. I sit down alone. Only God is here. In his presence I open, I read his book—for this end, to find the way to heaven. Is there a doubt concerning the meaning of what I read? Does anything appear dark or intricate? I lift up my heart to the Father of Lights: "Lord, is it not thy word, 'If any man lacks wisdom, let him ask of God'? Thou 'givest liberally, and upbraidest not.' Thou hast said, 'If any be willing to do thy will, he shall know.' I am willing to do, let me know thy will."[4]

John Wesley's words should be the cry of your heart if you truly value the Bible and want to thank God for it. Only the Spirit of God working through that Book will bring you to spiritual life and save your soul.

Psalm 148

Praise the Lord in Heaven and on Earth

Praise the LORD.

Praise the LORD from the heavens,
   praise him in the heights above.
Praise him, all his angels,
   praise him, all his heavenly hosts.
Praise him, sun and moon,
   praise him, all you shining stars.
Praise him, you highest heavens
   and you waters above the skies.
Let them praise the name of the LORD,
   for he commanded and they were created.
He set them in place for ever and ever;
   he gave a decree that will never pass away.

Praise the LORD from the earth,
   you great sea creatures and all ocean depths,
lightning and hail, snow and clouds,
   stormy winds that do his bidding,
you mountains and all hills,
   fruit trees and all cedars,
wild animals and all cattle,
   small creatures and flying birds,
kings of the earth and all nations,
   you princes and all rulers on earth,
young men and maidens,
   old men and children.

Let them praise the name of the LORD,
   for his name alone is exalted;

his splendor is above the earth and the heavens.
He has raised up for his people a horn,
 the praise of all his saints,
 of Israel, the people close to his heart.

Praise the LORD.

verses 1–14

We are asking a lot of questions about worship in our study of the last few psalms of the Psalter: what worship is, how we should worship, where we should worship, and so on. In Psalm 148 we find who should worship or praise God and where, the answer being everyone everywhere should praise God from the highest heavens to the lowest spots on earth. And not just human beings! Angels should worship God. So should the fish of the sea, wild animals, cattle, and birds. Even the inanimate creation should worship God: the sun, moon, and stars, lightning and hail, snow and clouds, mountains and hills, fruit trees and great cedars. Everyone and everything should praise God. Derek Kidner says of this psalm, "Starting with the angelic host, and descending through the skies to the varied forms and creatures of earth, then summoning the family of man and finally the chosen people, the call to praise unites the whole creation."[1]

Could any writer possibly be more comprehensive? It is hard to think so. Roy Clements, pastor of Eden Baptist Church in Cambridge, England, writes

The psalmist explores just about every area of human knowledge to catalogue the potential members of his cosmic congregation. He begins in the field of *cosmology:* angels, stars and waters above the skies. Then when he has satisfied himself that he has exhausted the celestial realm, he turns to the terrestrial. *Marine biology:* great sea creatures and all ocean depths. *Meteorology:* lightning and hail, snow and clouds, stormy winds that do his bidding. *Geo-morphology* and *dendrology:* mountains and hills, fruit trees and all cedars. *Zoology* and *ornithology:* wild animals, cattle, small creatures and flying birds. And to cap it all, *political geography, sociology* and *anthropology:* kings of the earth, all nations, princes and rulers, young men and maidens, old men and children. There really can't have been many unthumbed articles left in his encyclopedia.[2]

The preceding psalm told us we should praise God for his care of his people, his care of animals, his delight in the godly, his provision for Jerusalem, his rule over all creation, and the gift of his written Word. This psalm calls on the creation to acknowledge this care and worship God.

This psalm is so all-embracing in its call to worship God that not a few poets have labored to express its thoughts in English poetry. John Milton put words like these into the mouths of Adam and Eve in their morning

worship of God in Paradise before their fall *(Paradise Lost,* Book V, lines
153–209). William Cullen Bryant (1794–1878) wrote a poem that expanded
on verse 6. A lesser-known poet named Peter Pett wrote a poem similar to
Bryant's in the fifteenth century. The verse we probably know best is from
the *Bible Songs Hymnal* of 1927.

> Hallelujah, praise Jehovah, from the heavens praise his name;
> Praise Jehovah in the highest, all his angels, praise proclaim.
> All his hosts, together praise him, sun and moon and stars on high;
> Praise him, O you heav'ns of heavens, and you floods above the sky.
>
> Let them praises give Jehovah, they were made at his command;
> Them forever he established, his decree shall ever stand.
> From the earth, O praise Jehovah, all you seas, you monsters all,
> Fire and hail and snow and vapors, stormy winds that hear his call.
>
> All you fruitful trees and cedars, all you hills and mountains high,
> Creeping things and beasts and cattle, birds that in the heavens fly,
> Kings of earth, and all you people, princes great, earth's judges all;
> Praise his name, young men and maidens, aged men, and children small.
>
> Let them praises give Jehovah, for his name alone is high,
> And his glory is exalted far above the earth and sky.

Praise from Heaven Above

Looking upward first, the psalmist sees two entities he urges to praise
God. These are above man in the cosmic order, just as they are in Psalm 8,
in which David looks at "the moon and stars" and "the heavenly beings *[elo-
him]*" (Ps. 8:3–5).

1. *The angels.* There has always been a tendency of human beings to worship angels (either fallen or unfallen) rather than God. Pagan worship of the
gods and goddesses is one example, but an even better example is the worship of spirit "emanations" by the Gnostics. Gnosticism was a philosophy that
grew into a major religious movement and a serious challenge to Christianity
in the third century. It was called Gnosticism because it offered an imagined
superior knowledge *(gnosis)* that only the initiated were supposed to have.
One of the areas of this superior knowledge concerned the "emanations."
These were spirit beings who proceeded from God, each a little more distant
and thus a little less perfect than the former one until at last, at the end of
this long string of spirit beings, there came into being a creature, the demi-
urge, who made the universe. Since these spirits were all more or less divine,
they were all to be worshiped to varying degrees. How much and how they
should be worshiped was what the Gnostics taught.

Sadly we have a revival of a certain kind of Gnosticism in our day in such
New Age movements as EST; Scientology; witchcraft; channeling; the occult;

astrology; the worship of a female deity under such names as Sophia, the great Earth Mother, and Gaia; and the deification of self, popularized by Shirley MacLaine. Many buy into this outlook when they dismiss the Christian God as cruel, Christ as one of many lesser gods, man as fundamentally good, and the path to salvation as a discovery of one's true self.

In Psalm 148 the psalmist will have none of this paganism, for he looks to the angels not as gods to be worshiped but as beings who themselves must worship God. They are created beings ("he commanded and they were created," v. 5) and must, like man, thankfully acknowledge their creator.

2. *The heavenly bodies.* If fallen men and women do not worship the angels, they tend to worship the heavenly bodies next: the sun, moon, stars, and planets. This too is an aberration since the heavenly bodies are also created objects and, like the angels, worship God. We have a splendid statement of this idea in Psalm 19.

> The heavens declare the glory of God;
>   the skies proclaim the work of his hands.
> Day after day they pour forth speech;
>   night after night they display knowledge.
> There is no speech or language
>   where their voice is not heard.
> Their voice goes out into all the earth,
>   their words to the ends of the world (Ps. 19:1–4).

Psalm 19 helps us understand Psalm 148, for we are not to suppose that the writer imagines that the sun, moon, and stars literally speak words of praise to God. The way they glorify God is by their mere existence, and they are a model for our worship in two respects. First, their worship of God is always visible, not hidden or secret: "Their voice goes out into all the earth, their words to the ends of the world" (Ps. 19:4). Second, their worship of God is constant. It does not vary. "He set them in place for ever and ever," says the psalmist (Ps. 148:6).

Praise from Earth Beneath

Having looked upward to the heavens and having called on the angels and the many heavenly bodies to worship God, the psalmist now looks downward to earth and calls on things terrestrial to join the worship chorus. Worship on earth is to echo the worship in heaven. As in the preceding section, where the worship of heaven is sought from angels and the heavenly bodies, here worship is sought from two entities also.

1. *The animal creation.* The verses of this stanza (vv. 7–12) do not speak only of the animals but of the inanimate creation as well. The flow of thought seems to begin at the bottom and move up, just as the passage from the first stanza to the second is a motion from above to below. The psalmist

begins with creatures found in the ocean depths, moves up to speak about lightning and hail, snow, clouds, and stormy winds, then the mountains and hills, fruit trees and cedars, all the wild and domestic animals, and finally the smallest creatures and birds—before concluding with human beings of all ages and from every social position in this life. His point is that everything on earth as well as everything above the earth must praise God.

The mountains and hills, weather, trees, and animals of all kinds worship God. If we do not worship the angels or the heavenly bodies in our fallen state, we tend next to worship animals or even nature, as Paul said the pagans of his day did. He looked at the Greeks and Romans and said: "Although they claimed to be wise, they became fools and exchanged the glory of the immortal God for images made to look like mortal man and birds and animals and reptiles" (Rom. 1:22–23).

It is a sad thing that in our fallen state men and women make one of two mistakes regarding nature. Either we rape it ruthlessly for our own benefit, stripping the ground of its minerals and the surface for its wood, showing no regard for nature and its beauties at all, or else we worship it in place of God, attributing creative powers to nature and virtually deifying the dynamic within living things. In opposition to this sad pagan error, the psalmist reminds us that the animals themselves worship God.

2. *Human beings.* At last we come to human beings (vv. 11–12), the climax of God's creation, those who are made "in God's image" (Gen. 1:26–27) and who are therefore able to know and even converse with their Maker. Derek Kidner notes an important comparison between the worship of God by human beings here and the worship of God by the heavenly bodies in the previous stanza.

> In verse 5 the celestial bodies are called to praise God simply by the fact of their existence ("For he commanded and they were created"). But in 13, man may praise him consciously, since he has revealed himself ("For his name . . . is exalted"). Similarly, God's glory in the natural world is the reign of law (6), the regularity which invites us to "search out" his works (Ps. 111:2); but among his people his glory is redemptive love (14), in raising up *a horn* for them, *i.e.*, a strong deliverer (Lk. 1:69); above all, in bringing them *near to him.* That is the climax of the psalm, as it is of the gospel: "Behold the dwelling of God is with men. He will dwell with them, and they shall be his people" (Rev. 21:3).[3]

The problem is that in our fallen state we seek out substitutes for God. If we do not worship the angels, animals, or nature, we worship the only being left, which is ourselves.

In the final analysis, apart from God's grace in drawing us to faith in Jesus Christ, we all put ourselves in God's place. Adam and Eve did it in Eden. Nebuchadnezzar did it in his prideful boast over Babylon (see Dan. 4:30). We do it too, often subtly—we put our own interests before God's or other people's—but also blatantly sometimes. In our day the worship of man is most visible in the delusions of the New Age movements that I mentioned earlier.

An example is Shirley MacLaine, who did a television special based on her New Age book *Out on a Limb*. She is shown cavorting on the beach at Malibu, crying out gaily, "I am God." MacLaine has written, "A great awakening is taking place. Individuals across the world are tapping in to their internal power to understand who they are and using that knowledge to elevate their lives and their circumstances to a higher octave of happiness and productivity."[4] MacLaine's philosophy deifies man and his ability. Unfortunately, many deluded people actually believe this self-worship leads to the "higher octave of happiness and productivity" that MacLaine promises.

Another New Age writer, Carol Christ, wrote, "I found God in myself, and I loved her fiercely."[5]

Praise from God's People

Throughout the psalm the writer has been calling on the entire creation to worship God, which the angels, animals, and nature do; but the psalmist is no fool. Therefore he has called on the

> kings of the earth and all nations,
> . . . princes and all rulers on earth,
> young men and maidens,
> old men and children

to worship God (vv. 11–12). He knows that kings, princes, and people as a whole do not and will not worship God, though they should. Hence, in the last verses of the psalm he turns to those who have experienced God's salvation and holds them out as ones in whom the heathen may see God's saving acts and learn to worship God rightly.

"Horn" in verse 14 is a biblical way of talking about strength. The writer is probably thinking about the restoration of strength to Israel after the weakness they had known during the days of their exile. H. C. Leupold wrote, "The destiny of Israel is so important, and what God had recently done for his people in their restoration is of such vital importance to all nations and creatures that, if they grasped what it involved, they would be glad to add their praises to Israel's praises."[6]

Here is where we need to see ourselves in the picture, if we have come to know God in Jesus Christ. For this is the importance of Israel: Through this people, providentially preserved by God, the divine drama of redemption was unfolded. Through Israel the Messiah Savior came. Therefore, what was begun in the past and is referred to by the psalmist here was brought to fulfillment in the company of those who believe on that Savior. It is through the church and her message that God may be seen and worshiped now. Each of the orders of creation mentioned in the psalm share in the redemption of the church.

1. *The angels.* Paul writes about the church in Ephesians, saying of God, "His intent was that now, through the church, the manifold wisdom of God should be made known to the rulers and authorities in the heavenly realms, according to his eternal purpose which he accomplished in Christ Jesus our Lord" (Eph. 3:10–11). The angels are worshiping God at this moment. That is their chief function. They are doing it perfectly and without sin. But the angels will have more and more to worship God for as they see his wisdom worked out in the lives of Christian people.

2. *The natural creation.* In Romans 8 Paul describes the creation as being in bondage as a result of human sin and God's judgment on creation for man's transgression; but, he says, "The creation waits in eager expectation for the sons of God to be revealed. For the creation was subjected to frustration, not by its own choice, but by the will of the one who subjected it, in hope that the creation itself will be liberated from its bondage to decay and brought into the glorious freedom of the children of God" (vv. 19–21). He seems to be saying that, like human beings, the creation itself will one day experience something like a resurrection and will then join in the swelling chorus of God's praise. It will share in our redemption.

3. *The kings, princes, and people of this world.* At the present, this world's rulers and their subjects are taking their stand "against the LORD and against his Anointed One. 'Let us break their chains,' they say, 'and throw off their fetters'" (Ps. 2:2–3). God laughs at them, knowing that he has appointed a day when Jesus will rule even these rebellious kings "with an iron scepter" (v. 9), and that he has established a time when every knee will bow

> in heaven and on earth and under the earth,
> and every tongue confess that Jesus Christ is Lord,
> to the glory of God the Father (Phil. 2:10–11).

Are you among those who have confessed that "Jesus Christ is Lord to the glory of God the Father"? If not, this is the time to leave those who will not praise God and join the company of those who rejoice in Christ's death and resurrection and begin to serve him. These are the people who are "close to [God's] heart" (v. 14). They look forward to the day when "every creature in heaven and on earth and under the earth and on the sea, and all that is in them," will sing, "To him who sits on the throne and to the Lamb be praise and honor and glory and power, for ever and ever!" (Rev. 5:13).

Psalm 149

Praise the Lord with a New Song

Praise the LORD.

Sing to the LORD a new song,
his praise in the assembly of the saints.

Let Israel rejoice in their Maker;
let the people of Zion be glad in their King.
Let them praise his name with dancing
and make music to him with tambourine and harp.
For the LORD takes delight in his people;
he crowns the humble with salvation.
Let the saints rejoice in this honor
and sing for joy on their beds.

May the praise of God be in their mouths
and a double-edged sword in their hands,
to inflict vengeance on the nations
and punishment on the peoples,
to bind their kings with fetters,
their nobles with shackles of iron,
to carry out the sentence written against them.
This is the glory of all his saints.

Praise the LORD.

verses 1–9

W e need to begin this chapter by thinking about singing, not performing before an audience, but the kind of singing that takes place because a person is happy and singing seems a

1278

natural way to express delight. This happens when a person sings alone, like singing in the shower. It also happens when a person sings with other people, as Christians do in church.

The sad thing is that not many people sing today, which is probably a reflection of the unhappy times in which we live. People used to sing in their homes as they gathered around the piano, or they sang together in clubs. That doesn't happen much anymore. Someone has pointed out the possibility of tracing the changing mood of our century by remembering that the soldiers of the First World War sang as they marched to battle. The singing soldier was a heroic figure. The GI of the Second World War was not a heroic figure but a wise-cracking joker. He had nicknames for his officers and poked fun at them. By the time the Vietnam War came around, the typical fighting man neither sang nor joked. He took drugs instead.

Some of the best memories of my youth were singing fun songs with my friends at camp in Canada in the summer or with my sisters as my family drove places together on vacations. Today the young do not sing, though they listen to music. About the only place people today do sing is in church. Christians sing psalms, hymns, and spiritual songs, and it is good we do. We are preserving something precious.

God's Singing Saints

Psalm 149 encourages us to think about singing and what it means for the people of God. "Sing" is the psalm's first word after "Hallelujah."

Psalm 149 might be thought of as a response to Psalm 148:14. That verse notes God's special grace to Israel and urges the nation to "praise the LORD." In Psalm 149 they do. In Psalm 148 the whole creation, from heaven above to the earth beneath, has been praising God, but now it is time to hear specifically from God's saints. The word "saint" is found in each of the psalm's three stanzas (in vv. 1, 5, and 9).

How are the saints to praise God? The answer is what is special about this praise composition. It is by singing "a new song" (v. 1). To sing a new song is not a new idea. We have already come across these words in Psalms 33:3; 40:3; 96:1; 98:1; and 144:9. (They appear again in Revelation 5:9 and 14:3.) But they are unique to this final set of psalms (Psalms 146–50), and we ought to ask why a command to sing "a new song" is found here, in this next-to-last psalm in the Psalter. Probably it is to call attention to the importance of singing in our worship.

I have been emphasizing in these final studies of Psalms that worship is a serious mental activity. It involves hard thinking, and it is possible only because of God's prior revelation in the Bible, which means that we must begin our worship efforts by studying that Book. In order to praise God we must know who God is, and the only way we can know who he is and what he has done is by God's own disclosure of himself in Scripture. Still the things about God that we come to know by studying the Bible are not bare facts, things that are true but have no significance for us. On the contrary, they are truths that call for passionate response. They teach that God is a loving God who has given himself to us in Jesus Christ, who died for us, and that God continues to give himself to us by the presence of the Holy Spirit in our lives. God loves us, cares for us, preserves us, guides us, and lifts us up when we are down, and he will never stop doing these things. Such truth calls for our response.

Singing provides for this response. It provides a unique joining of biblical content and emotional assent. Music alone does not do this joining, though it can prepare us for worship by quieting our hearts to hear the voice of God in Scripture. Words alone, while we can and do respond to them personally and emotionally, become far more a part of us and far more joyful when we sing them. They become even more joyful when we sing them with others who believe as we do! When we sing together we confess that the things we have heard are true—we say "Amen" or "Hallelujah" to them. We confess that they are a delight and joy for us, and we join with others who make the same confession.

The reason God's people are called to sing is expressed in verse 4: "The LORD takes delight in his people; he crowns the humble with salvation." Our singing is a response to that truth. We express delight in God because he first took delight in us and saved us from sin.

Delight in God

The truths about God in which the writer of this song takes delight and for which he wishes to praise God have already been considered in studies of other psalms. Yet it is worth reviewing them here, because they are matters for which the people of God must perpetually be thankful. After the opening invocation, the first stanza (vv. 2–5) refers to three of them.

1. *God is our Creator.* This stanza refers to Israel as God's people (vv. 2, 4) and God's saints (v. 5). So when Israel is told to praise God as her Maker (v. 2) the idea is probably that God brought Israel into being as an elect spiritual nation. On the other hand, "Maker" means "Creator," and God has been praised as the Creator of everything in heaven and on earth in the immediately preceding psalm. However we take it, God has created us and we are indebted to him for everything we are or can ever hope to be.

I have been impressed recently with the fact that the Bible begins by introducing God as the Creator, even before going on to such other matters as the fall and God's plan of redemption. The later matters are of vast importance, but the starting point for us creatures must be our acknowledgment of the Creator, since it is only when we have begun to know God as our Creator that we can appreciate what we owe him and understand how we have failed to praise and thank him properly. Paul in his unfolding of the gospel and the historical plan of God in Romans 1 begins with God as the Creator and with the fact that God has made himself known as Creator to all persons. The problem with those who are unregenerate is that "although they knew God, they neither glorified him as God nor gave thanks to him" (Rom. 1:21), as a result of which the wrath of God has been displayed and is being displayed against them.

This is where we need to begin in most of our evangelism today since people know so little about the Bible. We can't assume that they know anything. We have to begin at the beginning.

2. *God is our King.* God is King of the entire universe, including all nations and all peoples. It is a cause for their just judgment that the rulers of the earth will not recognize God as King but "gather together against the LORD and against his Anointed One" (Ps. 2:2).

> "Let us break their chains," they say,
> "and throw off their fetters" (Ps. 2:3).

The peoples of this world are hostile to God's rule. They need to be taught that God is King in spite of their rejection of him, since it is only in this way that people can begin to understand sin to be rebellion against God and begin to realize how serious sin is. The people who must teach them are those who have accepted God's rule and praise him as King, which is what the writer of Psalm 149 does.

3. *God is our Savior.* In addition to being our Creator and King, against whom all human beings have rebelled, God is also our Savior, who saves us from our rebellion. He punishes our sin in Christ and draws us to holy fellowship with himself by the power of his Spirit. The psalmist says,

> . . . the LORD takes delight in his people;
> he crowns the humble with salvation (v. 4).

It would be possible to write an entire theology around these three truths about God. To know just these three things about God is the beginning of spiritual wisdom, and knowing them is clearly a cause for God's people to sing. We might even organize our hymnbooks along these lines.

Victory Songs

Victory songs also play a part in the worship of God by God's people, going all the way back to the song of Moses and Miriam after the Jews' exodus from Egypt and their crossing of the Red Sea. Led by this impressive worship team, the Israelites declared:

> I will sing to the LORD,
> for he is highly exalted.
> The horse and its rider
> he has hurled into the sea.

> The LORD is my strength and my song;
> he has become my salvation (Exod. 15:1–2).

Strictly speaking, the last stanza of Psalm 149 is not so much a victory song as it is an anticipation and prayer for victory. But its anticipation is so strong and its prayer so certain of being answered that we can almost visualize and hear the warriors as they march to battle with a song of praise "in their mouths and a double-edged sword in their hands" (v. 6).

This has been a problematic stanza for some people, especially those who are opposed to war and who cannot imagine a pious Jew or a pious anyone else engaging in it. Yet war is sometimes necessary in a fallen world, and being a soldier is not an unworthy calling for a follower of God. Leupold defends this view, saying, "It is quite possible that one may have the high praises of God upon his mouth . . . and a two-edged sword in one's hand."[1] That is a way of saying, "Praise the Lord, and pass the ammunition!"

I need to offer some qualifications, or what I have just said can be badly misunderstood. Christians are not to advance the work of God by killing enemies. A Christian can serve in the armed forces, but he does so as a citizen serving his country and its interests, not as a Christian battling for Christianity. He can contend for the faith, but when he does he must do it in a very different way.

According to Franz Delitzsch, one of the best older commentators, Thomas Muenzer used Psalm 149 to incite the German farmers to military action in the Peasants' War at the height of the Reformation.[2] It was a sad abuse of Christianity. The war began near Schaffhausen in 1524, seven years after Luther had nailed his Ninety-five Theses to the door of the Castle Church at Wittenberg, and it lasted until 1526. By the end of the first year there were some 30,000 farmers in arms, refusing to pay taxes, church tithes, or feudal dues. In March of 1525 they circulated a document called the "Twelve Articles" in which they claimed the right to choose their own pastors, pay only just tithes, be considered as free men rather than serfs, enjoy fair rents, and other such reasonable demands. They were also favorable to the Reformation and opposed to the Roman Catholic Church.

The peasants expected Luther to support their cause, and Luther's first response was sympathetic. He acknowledged the injustices done to the farmers and blamed the rulers of both state and church for their responsibility. However, Luther didn't endorse the rebellion, even though many of its goals coincided with his own.

Why did he react this way, when nearly everyone, the peasants above all, expected him to side with them? Luther feared anarchy, for one thing. He also believed that God has established the authority of princes and to rebel against the powers that exist is to rebel against God. Luther also knew that the power of the sword has not been given either to the church or to individual Christians, and he was aware that our weapons are not the world's weapons and that arguments alone have divine power "to demolish strongholds" (2 Cor. 10:4).

According to Luther, the Reformation would proceed *non vi, sed verbo*—not by force but by the power of God's Word. And it did!

The Peasants' War was a tragic episode in the Reformation period. More lives were lost in that war in Germany than in any tumult prior to the Thirty Years' War. Some 130,000 farmers died in battle or afterward as a result of retaliatory punishments. Germany was impoverished. The Reformation itself nearly floundered. It did not, because it was advancing by the power of the Word of God, by persuasion, and by prayer, as God blessed the teaching of the Reformers. Can we use the Bible's military language? Yes. We can sing "Onward Christian Soldiers." We can advance Christ's banner. But as we do, we must not forget the verse of that other battle-imaged song:

> For not with swords loud clashing, nor roll of stirring drums,
>   but deeds of love and mercy, the heav'nly kingdom comes.

Our equivalent of Psalm 149 is the spiritual warfare of the Christian life, and "our struggle is not against flesh and blood, but against the rulers, against the authorities, against the powers of this dark world and against the spiritual forces of evil in the heavenly realms" (Eph. 6:12). We will conquer, but we will do it, Revelation says, "by the blood of the Lamb and by the word of [our] testimony" (Rev. 12:11).

To Sing a New Song

We love old songs, just as we love old doctrines (Jer. 6:16), but each generation has fresh lessons of God's grace, and new experiences of God's grace call for new songs. Israel had experienced God's goodness in bringing the people back to their homeland and (probably) giving them a military victory. So they composed this psalm.

When Jesus was born, knowledge of salvation in Christ called for new songs too, beginning with the song of the angels over Bethlehem: "Glory to God in the highest, and on earth peace to men on whom his favor rests" (Luke 2:14). Another one is Philippians 2:6–11, the song beginning, "Who being in very nature God, did not consider equality with God something to be grasped . . ."

Later believers who fought the critical Trinitarian and Christological battles left us hymns celebrating the Trinity and the deity of Christ. The Gloria Patri comes from the second century: "Glory be to the Father, and to the Son, and to the Holy Ghost." A fourth-century hymn begins, "All glory be to thee, Most High, to thee all adoration; in grace and truth thou drawest nigh to offer us salvation." In the same century Ambrose of Milan (340–397) wrote, "O Splendor of God's glory bright, from light eternal bringing light, O Light of light, light's living Spring, true Day, all days illumining."

The recovery of the gospel at the Reformation led to powerful new songs by the Reformers, especially from Martin Luther (1483–1546), who wrote: "A mighty fortress is our God, a bulwark never failing"; "All praise to thee, eternal Lord, clothed in a garb of flesh and blood"; and "Great God, what do I see and hear! The end of things created! . . . prepare, my soul, to meet him."

A few centuries later John and Charles Wesley wrote hundreds of hymns, especially Charles (1707–1788), who has left us "O for a thousand tongues to sing," "Ye servants of God, your Master proclaim," "Hark! the herald angels sing," "Jesus Christ is risen today," "Arise, my soul, arise, shake off thy guilty fears," "And can it be that I should gain an interest in the Savior's blood?" and many more. About the same time Count Nikolas von Zinzendorf (1700–1760) composed "Jesus, thy blood and righteousness my beauty are, my glorious dress." These hymns capture something of the spirit of the revival movements in those days.

What of our time? Have experiences of God's grace led to the writing of good new songs today? I think so! Not all are great songs; some are poorly written and others badly man-centered. Those will fade in time. But there are many good hymns and many good hymnwriters. Michael Baughen, a contemporary English pastor, wrote a beautiful setting of Psalm 1. Margaret Clarkson, an English woman now living in Canada, wrote "We come, O Christ, to you, true Son of God and man" and "Our God is mighty, worthy of all praising." Daniel Iverson, who died in 1977, wrote "Spirit of the living God, fall fresh on me." There are David Clowney, who wrote "God, all nature sings thy glory, and thy works proclaim thy might" and his father, Edmund P. Clowney, who has given us "Vast the immensity, mirror of majesty, galaxies spread in a curtain of light."

Do you have a new song to God's glory? Most of us do not have the ability to write new songs. Don't be sad, if that is the case. One day you will sing a glorious new song in heaven, one composed especially for the saints:

> You are worthy to take the scroll
>   and to open its seals,
> because you were slain,
>   and with your blood you purchased men for God
>   from every tribe and language and people and nation.
> You have made them to be a kingdom and priests to serve our God,
>   and they will reign on the earth (Rev. 5:9–10).

I do not think we will ever get tired of singing that.

Psalm 150

Everybody, Praise the Lord

Praise the LORD.

Praise God in his sanctuary;
praise him in his mighty heavens.
Praise him for his acts of power;
praise him for his surpassing greatness.
Praise him with the sounding of the trumpet,
praise him with the harp and lyre,
praise him with tambourine and dancing,
praise him with the strings and flute,
praise him with the clash of cymbals,
praise him with resounding cymbals.

Let everything that has breath praise the LORD.

Praise the LORD.
                              verses 1–6

It is time to make noise, praise-noise for God. Not all worship should be noisy, of course. There are psalms of lament that call for heart-rending sorrow by God's people. Other psalms call for quiet reflection on the acts of God in history, acts that are sometimes puzzling and even incomprehensible to us. But there are times for celebration too. When David brought the ark to Jerusalem, to the place he had prepared for it, the arrival of the ark was announced by trumpets and David danced with abandon before God (2 Sam. 6:14–15). When the people praised God for the completion of the building of the walls of Jerusalem in Nehemiah's day, the sound of trumpets, cymbals, harps, lyres, and singing was so loud that "the sound of rejoicing in Jerusalem could be heard far away" (Neh. 12:43; see Neh. 12:27–44).

C. S. Lewis refers to the exuberant quality of Jewish worship as an "appetite for God," rejecting a phrase like "the love of God" as being almost too restrictive. In a paragraph from which I quoted earlier in these volumes Lewis said of this exuberant worship,

> It has all the cheerful spontaneity of a natural, even a physical, desire. It is gay and jocund. They are glad and rejoice (9, 2). Their fingers itch for the harp (43, 4), for the lute and the harp—wake up, lute and harp!—(57, 9); let's have a song, bring the tambourine, bring the "merry harp with the lute," we're going to sing merrily and make a cheerful noise (81, 2). Noise, you may well say. Mere music is not enough. Let everyone, even the benighted gentiles, clap their hands (47, 1). Let us have clashing cymbals, not only well tuned, but *loud*, and dances too (150, 6).[1]

Let's be done with worship that is *always* weak and unexciting. If you cannot sing loudly and make loud music to praise the God who has redeemed you in Jesus Christ and is preparing you for heaven, perhaps it is because you do not really know God or the gospel at all. If you do know him, hallelujah.

The Psalter's Last Psalm

Psalm 150 is the last of the psalms, and it is the obvious climax of the collection as well as of the final group of five praise songs. In Psalm 146 an individual Israelite praises God for his grace, power, and faithfulness to the needy. In Psalm 147 the inhabitants of Jerusalem are urged to praise God for their regathering, blessing, and security in the years following their exile. In Psalm 148 all creatures in heaven and on earth are told to praise God as their Creator and as the Redeemer of his people Israel. In Psalm 149 the saints are invited to praise God since they have been saved from their enemies and look forward to the blessings of the final judgment. In Psalm 150 every creature that has breath is exhorted to praise God everywhere and with every means available.

And loudly! A number of years ago when my middle daughter, Heather, was just a teenager, she asked me one day if I thought her music was loud and repetitive. I sensed that I was being set up, but I replied that, Yes, I did think most of it was loud and repetitive, to which she responded, "Please explain the 'Hallelujah Chorus.'"

After I had told that story once, one of our musicians explained to me that the "Hallelujah Chorus" is not really repetitious. It advances musically toward its climax. But it is loud! It has to be. And there are certainly repeating elements. That is what Psalm 150 is like. It is no mere repetition of an idea—it tells us where to praise God, why to praise God, how to praise God, and who should praise God—but it does repeat the praise idea. The Psalm says "Praise the LORD" three times, "Praise God" once, and "Praise him" nine times. These numbers are even more striking in Hebrew. The greatest number of words occurring between two of the thirteen *hallelujahs* is four, and that only once. In most cases only two words occur between *hallelujahs*. H. C. Leupold says of these last songs, "The note of praise swells out more and more strongly toward the close of the book, finally to break out in this crescendo which is full-toned and jubilant."[2]

There is more significance to the psalm than its volume. Alexander Maclaren wrote rightly,

> The psalm is more than an artistic close of the Psalter; it is a prophecy of the last result of the devout life, and, in its unclouded sunniness, as well as in its universality, it proclaims the certain end of the weary years for the individual and for the world. "Everything that hath breath" shall yet praise Jehovah.[3]

Where to Praise God

Where should "everything that has breath" praise God? The first verse gives us a comprehensive answer. It is "in his sanctuary" and "in his mighty heavens."

"His sanctuary" has been understood by some writers to mean the heavenly sanctuary or throne room, in which case the two lines of verse 1 ("Praise God in his sanctuary" and "Praise him in his mighty heavens") would be precise parallels.[4] But the list of musical instruments in verses 3–5 contains some that we know were used in the Jewish temple, suggesting "sanctuary" refers to the earthly temple there. In other words, it is best to see verse 1 calling for the praise of God on earth ("in his sanctuary") and in heaven (the words say literally "in his mighty firmament"). We are being told to praise God everywhere.

Today we do not have an earthly sanctuary, though we worship and praise God in our churches, but we do have bodies that are "temples of the living God" (2 Cor. 6:16; see 1 Cor. 3:16; 6:19), and we are told to praise God in and with our bodies, which means everywhere we go. The angels of God praise God everywhere they go; they praise God constantly. We should imitate them. Frances Havergal touched on this idea (1865):

> Lord, thou needest not, I know,
> Service such as I can bring;
> Yet I long to prove and show

> Full allegiance to my King.
> Thou an honor art to me:
> Let me be a praise to thee.

Why to Praise God

Just as "in his sanctuary" and "in his mighty heavens" mean that God is to be praised everywhere, so do the phrases of verse 2 embrace everything for which God should be praised. God's "acts of power" refer primarily to his works in creation and salvation history, what some writers list as creation, providence, and redemption. God's "surpassing greatness" refers to God's attributes, including qualities like sovereignty, holiness, omniscience, immutability, love, grace, goodness, compassion, justice, truth, and wisdom. God is to be praised both for who he is and for what he has done.

These psalms have been encouraging us to get to know God so we really can praise him. Do you know God? Are you able to praise him for who he is and for what he has done? The only way you will ever come to do it is by studying the Bible.

How to Praise God

After telling us where to praise God (v. 1) and reminding us why we should praise him (v. 2), the next three verses, exactly one half of the psalm, tell us how God should be praised (vv. 3–5). The answer: with everything you've got. If you have a trumpet, use that. If you have a lyre, tambourine, stringed instrument, flute, or cymbals, use them. If all you have is a harmonica, play that! The list of instruments is not meant to be comprehensive, though it may be. We do not know what instruments the ancient Jews had. The point is actually that everything you have can be used to worship God.

What about these instruments? The trumpet is actually the shophar, or ram's horn. It makes a tremendous noise, and the noise carries a long way. Tambourines are linked to dancing in verse 4, because they were normally used by women when they danced. Verse 5 mentions two kinds of cymbals; the words are not mere repetition. The first is a small instrument, perhaps like our castanets. The second was larger, hence a "resounding" cymbal. We would probably say "crashing." These instruments embrace all branches of musical instruments: wind, string, and percussion.

Trumpets were blown by priests; harps and lyres (psalteries) were played by the Levites; tambourines were played by women and other people. So the call to praise God is addressed to priests, Levites, and people; that is, to everyone. Everyone is to praise and worship God.

There are two extreme camps of opinion regarding instruments in worship.
1. *Those who forbid the use of instruments in worship.* People who exclude the use of any instruments in worship do so on the grounds that the Bible does

not authorize them and that we must stick strictly to what the Bible prescribes. The idea that nothing should be done in worship that isn't authorized in Scripture is called "the regulative principle," and it is worthwhile in itself. It means that God sets the terms and means by which he must be worshiped and that it is not our prerogative to do anything we want. Some parts of the church understand the regulative principle to mean that only psalms may be sung. Hymns and choruses are considered to be human compositions only, which means they should therefore be rigorously excluded. In other parts of the church, often overlapping with the first, instruments are excluded from worship services for the same reasons. It is pointed out that instruments were not used in the early church; Christians simply sang psalms together.

This is a matter that ought not to divide Christians from one another. It should be treated as Paul treats questions of not eating meat and observing holy days in Romans 14. "Each one should be fully convinced in his own mind," he says (Rom. 14:5), adding, "Let us therefore make every effort to do what leads to peace and to mutual edification" (Rom. 14:19).

However, we must also have reasons for thinking as we do. Respecting others for their diverse convictions about worship does not mean mindless acceptance of just anything another Christian might do. We need to be as biblical as we know how to be. So we should ask, Why do most Christians use instruments in worship? And why do most sing compositions in addition to the psalms?

As far as exclusive psalmody is concerned, I have already suggested a defense of additional compositions by what I wrote about singing "a new song" in the study of Psalm 149. I argued that it is always appropriate to sing new songs when these are based on new experiences of God's grace. I am not saying that any music is worship music. A secular song is not worship. But if we have learned something about the character and grace of God, it is not wrong to sing about it even in new words and new music, and the music can be in contemporary style. I pointed out that the elders sing "a new song" in Revelation (Rev. 5:9; see Rev. 14:3). We should also remember Paul's words to the Ephesians: "Speak to one another with psalms, hymns and spiritual songs. Sing and make music in your heart to the Lord, always giving thanks to God the Father for everything, in the name of our Lord Jesus Christ" (Eph. 5:19–20).

What about instruments? Surely Psalm 150 alone should have definitive bearing on this question. The arguments against them say that in the temple worship in Israel musical instruments were used only when the sacrifices were being offered. Today, since the sacrifices of Israel have been abolished by the completed sacrifice of Jesus on the cross, the music that was associated with the ancient sacrifices should be abolished too. That is certainly special and (I would say) unpersuasive pleading. Were instruments really used only when sacrifices were offered? How could we possibly know? What about this psalm? It tells us to praise God with a variety of instruments and says nothing about sacrifices. What about the worship of God in heaven according to Revelation? There are harps in heaven (Rev. 5:8) and trumpets (Rev. 8:6–8, 10, 12; 9:1, 13). There is singing, all of it in words not found explicitly in Psalms. How can we deny that Psalm 150 endorses the use of new songs and instruments in worship?

2. *Those who would employ everything in worship.* Yet we must look at the other side of the controversy too, because there are Christians who would use the arguments I have just used to justify putting anything and everything into a worship service, and not everything should be used in this way. Here caution is needed. First, there are pragmatic matters. Not all music promotes worship for most people. "Bump and grind" music would hardly be appropriate; it suggests a burlesque show rather than worship. Hard rock suggests a nightclub or disco setting for most people and ought to be rejected for that reason. On the other side of the musical spectrum, orchestral instruments are intrinsically secular for other people since they conjure up images of a concert hall or an opera house. They will not work as worship instruments for these people.

The other important matter is how the instruments are used and for what purpose. Are they effective in directing thoughts to God, or do they focus our thoughts on the one who is playing them instead? One measure of whether they contribute to worship or direct our praise to the performer is if the congregation applauds when the music is finished. If people applaud, chances are they are praising the performer and not thinking about God at all. This is one reason why the use of instruments in worship is best linked to singing. Instruments improve our singing and move us by enhancing the thoughts we are expressing. It is hard to conceive of a congregation applauding itself for a well-sung hymn.

Roy Clements, the English Baptist pastor whom I have frequently quoted, endorses variety in worship. He knows there are times when worship should be enthusiastic, but he also knows that if worship is to be true worship, it must be God-centered and must engage the mind. "It simply won't do to come and do my own musical thing in church and call that praise," Clements says.

He offers these thoughtful cautions.

> All too often the pop-singer, the beat guitarist and the jazz drummer of today are idols. And Christian groups can be infected with the same kind of worldly pride. The applause and admiration of others can quickly become an intoxicating drug that mars those who want to stand up and sing for Jesus. Worship in music has to begin and end with Alleluia, Praise the Lord. And for that reason, it is not the professionalism of the performance that counts, though it is right to do our best; it is not the genius of the composition or the profundity of the words that matter, because if that was the case the tambourine player would be a bit limited, wouldn't he? No, it is the

intended audience that counts. It is the One whom we are intending to see glorified in what we are doing that determines whether the music is real music in praise of God or not.[5]

Who Should Praise God

The final answer that Psalm 150 gives to the questions you or I might have about worship is to tell us who should praise God. The answer is as comprehensive as those given to each of the other questions. First question: Where should we praise God? Answer: Everywhere, in heaven and on earth. Second question: Why should we praise God? Answer: Because of everything God is and for all he has done. Third question: How should we praise God? Answer: With everything we've got.

Now at last, question four: Who should praise God? Answer: Everything and everybody. "Everything that has breath," says the Psalmist.

This is exactly what will happen, according to the Bible. At the moment, we see God insulted, blasphemed, denied, and ignored. We see Christ rejected. But one day "every knee [will] bow," whether willingly or not (Phil. 2:10). As far as the saints are concerned, the apostle John wrote in Revelation, "Then I heard every creature in heaven and on earth and under the earth and on the sea, and all that is in them, singing:

> "To him who sits on the throne and to the Lamb
> be praise and honor and glory and power,
>   for ever and ever!" (Rev. 5:13).

What a great choir! What a great song! What a great privilege. It will be ours if we have placed our faith in Jesus Christ, the Lamb of God who has indeed taken away the sin of those who trust him.

The End and a Beginning

At Tenth Presbyterian Church, where I preached through the psalms on Sunday mornings for the better part of six years, it is our custom to read through the psalms consecutively. When we get to the end we just go back and start again. There is a sense in which we should be doing that now. If we have actually come to the place where we have echoed the praise of that great heavenly choir that sings "to him who sits on the throne and to the Lamb" and if we are repeating the final words of the Psalter that cry, "Let everything that has breath praise the LORD," we will want to go back to where we started and seek ever more intently the blessing that comes from meditating on and delighting in God's Word.

> Blessed is the man
>   who does not walk in the counsel of the wicked
> or stand in the way of sinners
>   or sit in the seat of mockers.

> But his delight is in the law of the LORD,
>   and on his law he meditates day and night (Psalm 1:1–2).

We cannot praise God without meditating on his Word, for we will only praise God as we come to know him, and the only way we will come to know him is through his self-disclosure of himself in the Bible and by our meditating on it.

It works the other way too, for we cannot miss seeing that the book we have been studying begins with Bible study and ends with endless praise. Clements suggests that our hymnbooks probably have it all wrong. Most of them begin with hymns that praise God but end with songs about marriage, the home, national holidays, and patriotic tunes. The Psalter doesn't even end with a doxology, though it could. It does not end with an amen. It ends with a call to praise God, which is itself our great doxology to which we add our own sincere and loud "Amen."

"Let everything that has breath praise the LORD. Praise the LORD."

Notes

Psalm 107: *The Pilgrims' Psalm: Part 1*

1. William Bradford, *Of Plymouth Plantation 1620–1647* (New York: The Modern Library, 1952), 63.
2. C. H. Spurgeon, *The Treasury of David*, vol. 2b, *Psalms 88–110* (Grand Rapids: Zondervan, 1968), 398.
3. Bradford, *Of Plymouth Plantation*, 10.
4. Ibid., 14.
5. See Rowland E. Prothero, *The Psalms in Human Life* (New York: E. P. Dutton, 1904), 246.
6. Bradford, *Of Plymouth Plantation*, 77, n. 5.

Psalm 107: *The Pilgrims' Psalm: Part 2*

1. Bradford, *Of Plymouth Plantation*, 90, n. 8.
2. H. C. Leupold, *Exposition of the Psalms* (Grand Rapids: Baker, 1969), 760–61.
3. See Prothero, *The Psalms in Human Life*, 344–45.

Psalm 108: *A Warrior's Morning Song*

1. Alexander Maclaren, *The Psalms*, vol. 3, *Psalms 90–150* (New York: A. C. Armstrong and Son, 1894), 170.
2. For a study of these places and their significance see Leupold, *Exposition of the Psalms*, 450–51, and J. J. Stewart Perowne, *Commentary on the Psalms*, 2 vols. in 1 (Grand Rapids: Kregel, 1989), 1:472–73. Original edition 1878–1879. The page numbers refer to their study of these verses in Psalm 60.
3. See James Montgomery Boice, *Psalms*, vol. 2, *Psalms 42–106* (Grand Rapids: Baker, 1996), 498–99.

Psalm 109: *An Evil End for Evil Men*

1. The other imprecatory psalms are 7, 35, and 69, though individual imprecations are found throughout the Psalter. James E. Adams lists one hundred four imprecatory verses beginning with Psalm 5:10 and ending with Psalm 143:12. See James E. Adams, *War Psalms of the Prince of Peace: Lessons from the Imprecatory Psalms* (Phillipsburg, N.J.: Presbyterian and Reformed, 1991), 116.
2. C. S. Lewis, *Reflections on the Psalms* (New York: Harcourt, Brace & World, 1958), 20.
3. Perowne, *Commentary on the Psalms*, 2:285–86.

4. Particularly in my study of Psalm 35. See James Montgomery Boice, *Psalms*, vol. 1, *Psalms 1–41* (Grand Rapids: Baker, 1994), 299–306.

5. Martin Luther, *First Lectures on the Psalms II, Psalms 76–126*, vol. 11, in *Luther's Works*, ed. Hilton C. Oswald (St. Louis: Concordia, 1976), 353.

6. Leslie C. Allen, *Word Biblical Commentary*, vol. 21, *Psalms 101–150* (Waco: Word, 1983), 70–71.

7. G. Campbell Morgan, *Notes on the Psalms* (Westwood, N.J.: Revell, 1947), 212.

8. Christopher Marlowe, *The Tragical History of Dr. Faustus*, in *The Harvard Classics: Johann Wolfgang von Goethe, Faust, Part 1, Egmont, Hermann and Dorothea, and Christopher Marlowe, Doctor Faustus* (Norwalk, Conn.: The Easton Press, 1993), 241.

9. Maclaren, *The Psalms*, 179.

Psalm 110: *The Psalm Most Quoted in the New Testament: Part 1*

1. Quoted at length by Spurgeon, *The Treasury of David*, vol. 2b, 664–65.

2. Ibid., 460.

3. Walter J. Chantry, *Praises for the King of Kings* (Carlisle, Pa.: The Banner of Truth Trust, 1991), 48–82.

4. For example, Leslie C. Allen largely ignores its claims to have been written by David, even though so much is at stake (see *Word Biblical Commentary*, 83–87). For a sound answer to attempts to weaken the psalm by reassigning its authorship, see Leupold, *Exposition of the Psalms*, 770–75.

5. Derek Kidner, *Psalms 73–150: A Commentary on Books III–V of the Psalms* (Downers Grove, Ill.: InterVarsity, 1975), 391–92.

6. J. J. Stewart Perowne lists examples of this understanding from Arab and Greek sources. See his *Commentary on the Psalms*, 2:304.

7. Chantry, *Praises for the King of Kings*, 59.

8. Ibid., 59–60.

9. Martin Luther, *Selected Psalms II*, vol. 13 of *Luther's Works*, ed. Jaroslav Pelikan (St. Louis: Concordia, 1956), 279. The entire discussion of this verse is on pp. 264–84, that of the entire psalm on pp. 228–348.

10. Chantry, *Praises for the King of Kings*, 67–68.

Psalm 110: *The Psalm Most Quoted in the New Testament: Part 2*

1. John Calvin, *Commentaries on the First Book of Moses Called Genesis*, vol. 1, trans. John King (Grand Rapids: Eerdmans, 1948), 388.

2. Maclaren, *The Psalms*, 192.

Psalm 111: *An Acrostic Poem about God*

1. There are two sets of these: Psalms 103 and 104, each of which begins and ends with the words "Praise the LORD, O my soul," and Psalms 105 and 106, each of which seems to begin and end with a shorter "Praise the LORD." In our present Hebrew text the "Praise the LORD" that should begin Psalm 105 is actually at the end of Psalm 104, but this is probably a wrong division of the material.

2. The acrostic psalms are Psalms 9–10 (together), 25, 34, 37, 111, 112, 119, and 145. Not all of these are perfect alphabetical poems, however. In some, letters are missing; in others the order of the letters is not exact. Psalms 111 and 112 follow the Hebrew alphabet perfectly. Proverbs 31:10–31 also follows an acrostic pattern as do the first four chapters of Lamentations.

3. Arno C. Gaebelein, *The Book of Psalms: A Devotional and Prophetic Commentary* (Neptune, N.J.: Loizeaux Brothers, 1939), 416.

4. Leupold, *Exposition of the Psalms*, 781.

5. Derek Kidner, *Psalms 73–150*, 398.

6. Martin Luther, *What Luther Says: An Anthology*, vol. 3, compiled by Ewald M. Plass (St. Louis: Concordia, 1959), 1453.

7. C. H. Spurgeon, "The Immutability of God" (Malachi 3:6), in *The New Park Street Pulpit* (Pasadena, Tex.: Pilgrim Publications, 1975), 1. Original edition 1855.

Psalm 112: *An Acrostic Poem about Godliness*

1. Perowne, *Commentary on the Psalms*, 2:315.

2. Three truths were also taught in the corresponding verse in Psalm 111, dealing with the praise of God: we must praise God ourselves; we must praise God with all our hearts, not halfheartedly; and our praise of God should be open, visible, or public.

3. John Piper, *Desiring God* (Portland: Multnomah, 1986), and *The Pleasures of God* (Portland: Multnomah, 1991).

4. Kidner, *Psalms 73–150*, 399.

5. Exodus 34:6 is another verse referred to many times in the Old Testament, like Psalm 110:1 and 4. See Nehemiah 9:17; Psalm 86:15; 103:8; 145:8; Joel 2:13; and Jonah 4:2.

6. Franz Delitzsch, *Biblical Commentary on the Psalms*, vol. 3, trans. Francis Bolton (Grand Rapids: Eerdmans, n.d.), 200. Delitzsch also sees the adjectives of the second part of the verse as referring to God, just as they did in Psalm 111 (they are singular in both places). But the pattern already fixed of applying the characteristics of God to the godly person indicates that they probably refer to one who in this as in other respects is being remade in God's image.

7. Kidner, *Psalms 73–150*, 400.

Psalm 113: *Who Is Like God?*

1. Ibid., 401.

2. A. W. Tozer, *The Knowledge of the Holy* (New York: Harper and Row, 1961), 34.

3. Leupold, *Exposition of the Psalms*, 791.

4. C. H. Spurgeon, *The Treasury of David*, vol. 3a, *Psalms 88–119* (Grand Rapids: Zondervan, 1966), 31.

Psalm 114: *Make Way before God*

1. Ibid., 41.

2. Kidner, *Psalms 73–150*, 403.

3. C. H. Spurgeon, *The Treasury of David*, vol. 3a, 44.

Psalm 115: *The Victors' Psalm at Agincourt*

1. Will Durant, *The Reformation: A History of European Civilization from Wyclif to Calvin: 1300–1564*, vol. 6 in *The Story of Civilization* (Norwalk, Conn.: The Easton Press, 1992), 106.

2. Ibid., 70.

3. Historians recount that the psalm was used in a similar way on several other momentous occasions. When John Sobieski, the king of Poland, turned back the Turks from Vienna on September 12, 1683, thus ending the Muslems' final attempt to conquer Europe, the jubilant army sang the opening lines of the psalm, including verses 2 and 3: "Why do the nations say, 'Where is their God?' Our God is in heaven; he does whatever pleases him." Likewise, in 1510, when Cardinal Ximenes led Spanish troops against the Moors at Oran, the town was captured and the victorious cardinal rode through the streets declaiming, "Not unto us, O Lord, not unto us, but to your name be the praise." See Prothero, *The Psalms in Human Life*, 80–83, 182; and Herbert Lockyer Sr., *Psalms: A Devotional Commentary* (Grand Rapids: Kregel, 1993), 491.

4. A similar but somewhat shorter version of this polemic occurs in Psalm 135:15–18. It is so close that it may be copied from Psalm 115.

5. Saint Augustine, *Expositions on the Book of Psalms*, in *A Select Library of the Nicene and Post-Nicene Fathers of the Christian Church*, vol. 8, ed. Philip Schaff (Grand Rapids: Eerdmans, 1974), 552. I have modified some of the language from old to contemporary English usage.

6. See Lockyer, *Psalms: A Devotional Commentary*, 499; and Prothero, *The Psalms in Human Life*, 171.

7. Spurgeon, *The Treasury of David*, vol. 3a, 57.

Psalm 116: *Help of the Helpless*

1. Some Hebrew manuscripts make a similar break after verse 11.

2. Alexander Maclaren, *Expositions of Holy Scripture*, vol. 3, *The Psalms, Isaiah 1–48* (Grand Rapids: Eerdmans, 1959), part 2, 267.

3. Roy Clements, *Songs of Experience: Midnight and Dawn through the Eyes of the Psalmists* (Fearn, Scotland: Christian Focus Publications, 1993), 154.

4. Leupold, *Exposition of the Psalms*, 806.

5. Perowne, *Commentary on the Psalms*, 2:334.

6. Clements, *Songs of Experience*, 155. This interpretation also comes closest to the use Paul makes of this verse in 2 Corinthians 4:13. He quotes it from the Septuagint, which reads, "I believed; therefore I have spoken."

7. Spurgeon, *The Treasury of David*, vol. 3a, 70.

Psalm 117: *The Shortest Psalm of All*

1. Kidner, *Psalms 73–150*, 411.

2. Spurgeon, *The Treasury of David*, vol. 3a, 98. The doctrines are from a writer named Mollerus.

3. Martin Luther, *Selected Psalms III*, vol. 14 in *Luther's Works*, ed. Jaroslav Pelikan and Daniel E. Poellot (St. Louis: Concordia, 1958), 4–39.

4. Kidner, *Psalms 73–150*, 412.

5. Ibid., 411.

6. Luther, *Selected Psalms III*, 27.

Psalm 118: *Thanks to Our Good God: Part 1*

1. Frederick W. Evans Jr., *Christ in the Psalms* (Indianapolis: Bethany, 1991), 43–48.

2. Ibid., 46.

Psalm 118: *Thanks to Our Good God: Part 2*

1. Luther, *Selected Psalms III*, 45.

2. Prothero gives the French versification (*The Psalms in Human Life*, 225):

> La voici l'heureuse journée
> Qui respond a notre desir;
> Louons Dieu, qui nous l'a donnée;
> Faisons en tout notre plaisir.

3. See Prothero, *The Psalms in Human Life*, 226.

4. Ibid., 228. Rochette's story is on pages 226–28.

5. Spurgeon, *The Treasury of David*, vol. 3a, 104.

6. Luther, *Selected Psalms III*, 67.

7. See Prothero, *The Psalms in Human Life*, 320.

8. Luther, *Selected Psalms III*, 87.

9. Spurgeon, *The Treasury of David*, vol. 3a, 120–21.

Psalm 119: *Delight in God's Decrees: Part 1*

1. Delitzsch, *Biblical Commentary on the Psalms*, 243.

2. Kidner, *Psalms 73–150*, 416.

3. This George Wishart is not to be confused with the Scottish Reformer and martyr by the same name who lived a century earlier and was executed at Saint Andrews in 1546.

4. Spurgeon, *The Treasury of David*, vol. 3a, 133.

5. See Psalm 111, n. 2.

6. See Prothero, *The Psalms in Human Life*, 327; and Spurgeon, *The Treasury of David*, vol. 3a, 132.

7. See Prothero, *The Psalms in Human Life*, 307; and Spurgeon, *The Treasury of David*, vol. 3a, 133.

8. Leupold, *Exposition of the Psalms*, 824.

9. J. I. Packer, *Keep in Step with the Spirit* (Old Tappan, N. J.: Revell, 1984), 258–61.

Psalm 119: *Delight in God's Decrees: Part 2*

1. Lockyer, *Psalms: A Devotional Commentary*, 542. It would be far-fetched to argue that each letter gives a theme to its particular stanza. However, *aleph*, the theme letter of verses 1–8, means "ox" in Hebrew, a useful beast of burden and hence a blessing to those who possess one, and blessing is the theme of that stanza: "Blessed are they whose ways are blameless" (v. 1).

2. This is not the only place in the psalm where the young are mentioned. The psalmist speaks as a young man again in verses 99–100, though without the use of the word "young." Franz Delitzsch argued that the psalmist was a young man, but this is not demanded by the language of the psalm. There is a good discussion of the psalmist's age in J. J. Stewart Perowne, who thinks the writer was neither young nor old but rather in midlife. See Perowne, *Commentary on the Psalms*, 2:349–50; and Delitzsch, *Biblical Commentary on the Psalms*, 3:243.

3. James Montgomery Boice, *Daniel: An Expositional Commentary* (Grand Rapids: Zondervan, 1989), 23–24.

4. Charles Bridges, *Psalm 119: An Exposition* (Carlisle, Pa.: The Banner of Truth Trust, 1977), 19. Original edition 1827.

5. Maclaren, *Expositions of Holy Scripture*, 286.

6. Spurgeon, *The Treasury of David*, vol. 3a, 159. Herbert Lockyer has a similar outline:

> The Best Possession—"Thy Word"
> The Best Plan—"Have I hid"
> The Best Place—"In my heart"
> The Best Purpose—"That I might not sin against thee."

Lockyer, *Psalms: A Devotional Commentary*, 544.

7. Martin Luther, *First Lectures on the Psalms, II*, 420.

Psalm 119: *Delight in God's Decrees: Part 3*

1. E. M. Blaiklock, *The Bible & I* (Minneapolis: Bethany House, 1983).

2. Ibid., 91.

3. Saint Augustine, *The Confessions of St. Augustine*, in *A Select Library of the Nicene and Post-Nicene Fathers of the Christian Church*, vol. 1, ed. Philip Schaff (Grand Rapids: Eerdmans, 1974), 45.

4. Maclaren, *The Psalms*, 251.

5. Spurgeon, *The Treasury of David*, vol. 3a, 177–78.

Psalm 119: *Delight in God's Decrees: Part 4*

1. Allen, *Word Biblical Commentary*, 142.

2. Charles Bridges, *Psalm 119*, 84.

3. John R. W. Stott, *Your Mind Matters: The Place of the Mind in the Christian Life* (Downers Grove, Ill: InterVarsity, 1972).

4. See James Montgomery Boice, *Romans*, vol. 2, *The Reign of Grace: Romans 5–8* (Grand Rapids: Baker, 1992), 649–56.

5. Stott, *Your Mind Matters*, 26.

6. Thomas Manton, *Psalm 119* (Carlisle, Pa.: The Banner of Truth Trust, 1990), 1:334. Original edition 1680.

7. Lockyer, *Psalms: A Devotional Commentary*, 549.

8. John Bunyan, *Pilgrim's Progress*, vol. 15, *The Harvard Classics* (Norwalk, Conn.: The Easton Press, 1993), 95.

9. This four-part outline for verses 34–37 is in Spurgeon (from Marchant, one of the tutors at the Pastors' College), but I have handled it somewhat differently, basing it on verses 34–37 rather than verses 33–36 as Marchant did. This changes the order of the points. See Spurgeon, *The Treasury of David*, vol. 3a, 213.

10. Delitzsch, *Biblical Commentary on the Psalms*, 249.

11. Maclaren, *The Psalms*, 256.

12. Leupold, *Exposition of the Psalms*, 831.

13. Manton, *Psalm 119*, 1:380–81. He works this out at length on pages 380–92.

Psalm 119: *Delight in God's Decrees: Part 5*

1. Bruce Waltke, *Finding the Will of God: A Pagan Notion?* (Gresham, Ore.: Vision House, 1995), 89.

2. From J. H. Merle D'Aubigné, *The Life and Times of Martin Luther*, trans. H. White (Chicago: Moody, 1958), 423–34.

3. Psalm 119:46 also appears at the head of the Augsburg Confession, in Latin from the Vulgate version: *Et loquebar de testimoniis tuis in conspectu regum et non confundebar.* Its choice as a theme verse for this confession of the German-speaking church reflects the Reformation experience.

4. This was an easy stanza for the psalmist to write because it is the *waw* stanza and *waw* means "and." Not many Hebrew words begin with *waw*, so the author has solved the problem by beginning each verse with "and." It reminds us of how "and" is sometimes used in English poetry to give a soft first syllable to lines, as in Wesley's hymn, beginning "And can it be that I should gain . . ." Alexander Maclaren gives a translation of this stanza in which he was able to make each verse begin with "and":

> And let thy loving kindnesses come to me, Jehovah . . .
> And I shall have a word to answer him that reproaches me . . .
> And pluck not the word of truth out of my mouth . . .

and so on. See Maclaren, *The Psalms*, 256.

5. Spurgeon, *The Treasury of David*, vol. 3a, 254.

6. The account of the distribution of the priestly cities to Levi is in Joshua 21.

7. See Lockyer, *Psalms: A Devotional Commentary*, 558.

8. Leupold, *Exposition of the Psalms*, 836.

Psalm 119: *Delight in God's Decrees: Part 6*

1. This is the way C. S. Lewis states the critic's objection at the start of his study of human suffering in *The Problem of Pain* (New York: Macmillan, 1962), 26. It is also the problem raised by the Boston rabbi Harold S. Kushner in *When Bad Things Happen to Good People* (New York: Avon, 1981), though Kushner, being a rabbi, does not deny God's existence. He solves the problem by denying God's omnipotence. He advises us to love God and "forgive him despite his limitations" (p. 148).

2. Quoted by Bridges, *Psalm 119*, 181–82.

3. Lockyer, *Psalms*, 565.

4. Spurgeon, *The Treasury of David*, vol. 3a, 304.

5. See Spurgeon, *The Treasury of David*, vol. 3a, 308; and Lockyer, *Psalms: A Devotional Commentary*, 569.

Psalm 119: *Delight in God's Decrees: Part 7*

1. Quoted by Joel R. Beeke and Ray B. Lanning, "The Transforming Power of Scripture," in *Sola Scriptura: The Protestant Position on the Bible,* ed. Don Kistler (Morgan, Pa.: Soli Deo Gloria Publications, 1995), 331–32.

2. Verse 90 is the second verse (following v. 84) that does not seem to mention the Scriptures specifically, but "faithfulness" probably refers to God's Word. The best argument for this interpretation is the parallel structure of verses 89–91, in which "your word," "your faithfulness," and "your laws" seem to be used as synonyms.

3. Psalm 119:92 meant a great deal to Martin Luther. The words of this verse are written in his own hand in his own Bible, preserved in the Brandenburg Mark Museum, Berlin.

4. Spurgeon, *The Treasury of David,* vol. 3a, 317.

5. Kidner, *Psalms 73–150,* 426–27.

Psalm 119: *Delight in God's Decrees: Part 8*

1. Lewis, *Reflections on the Psalms,* 59–60. The whole discussion is on pages 54–65.

2. Kidner, *Psalms 73–150,* 427.

Psalm 119: *Delight in God's Decrees: Part 9*

1. Exodus 40 is not the only chapter to mention this unique phenomenon. It is also described in Exodus 13:21–22; Numbers 9:15–23; 10:34–36; and other passages.

2. Maclaren, *The Psalms,* 273.

Psalm 119: *Delight in God's Decrees: Part 10*

1. Ibid., 275.

2. See Prothero, *The Psalms in Human Life,* 59.

3. David F. Wells, *No Place for Truth: Or Whatever Happened to Evangelical Theology?* (Grand Rapids: Eerdmans, 1993).

4. William Hazlitt, "On Persons One Would Wish to Have Seen," in *The Harvard Classics, English Essays from Sir Philip Sidney to Macaulay* (Norwalk, Conn.: The Easton Press, 1994), 295. In the original form of this essay the speech is given to Leigh Hunt.

5. For example in Psalm 38 (vv. 17, 21, 22) and Psalm 70 (vv. 1–5).

Psalm 119: *Delight in God's Decrees: Part 11*

1. Neil Postman, *The Disappearance of Childhood* (New York: Vintage Books, 1994). Original edition 1982.

2. Spurgeon, *The Treasury of David,* vol. 3a, 378.

3. Ibid.

4. Luther, *First Lectures on the Psalms, II,* 500.

5. James Patterson and Peter Kin, *The Day America Told the Truth: What People Really Believe about Everything That Really Matters* (New York: Prentice Hall Press, 1991), 201.

Psalm 119: *Delight in God's Decrees: Part 12*

1. Notably in verses 23, 51, 61, 69, 70, 78, 84–87, 95, 98, 110, 115, 121, 122, 134, and 139.

2. Kidner, *Psalms 73–150,* 428.

3. Spurgeon suggested an eight-part outline for this section, one point for each of its eight verses: (1) How David prayed (v. 145); (2) What he prayed for (v. 146); (3) When he prayed (v. 147); (4) How long he prayed (v. 148); (5) What he pleaded (v. 149); (6) What happened (v. 150); (7) How he was rescued (v. 151); and (8) What was his witness to the whole matter (v. 152). See Spurgeon, *The Treasury of David,* vol. 3a, 401.

4. Ronald A. Jenson, *Biblical Meditation: A Transforming Discipline* (Oakland, Calif.: ICBI Press, 1982), 11.

5. Ibid., 41.

6. H. A. Ironside, *In the Heavenlies: Practical Expository Addresses on the Epistle to the Ephesians* (Neptune, N.J.: Loizeaux Brothers, 1937), 86–87.

7. Spurgeon, *The Treasury of David*, vol. 3a, 404.

Psalm 119: *Delight in God's Decrees: Part 13*

1. Kidner, *Psalms 73–150*, 428.

2. John Charles Ryle, *Expository Thoughts on the Gospels: St. Luke*, vol. 1 (Cambridge: James Clark & Co., 1976), 195.

3. Spurgeon, *The Treasury of David*, vol. 3a, 425–26.

4. "Peace" is linked to "salvation" even here, since verse 166 ("I wait for your salvation, O LORD") follows immediately on verse 165 ("Great peace have they who love your law, and nothing can make them stumble").

5. Maclaren, *Expositions of Holy Scripture*, 329–35.

6. Saint Augustine, *The City of God*, book 22, chapter 22, in *A Select Library of the Nicene and Post-Nicene Fathers of the Christian Church*, vol. 2, ed. Philip Schaff (Grand Rapids: Eerdmans, 1977), 500.

7. The monks used this verse as the basis for their observance of the seven hours for their prayer times. Chapter 16 of the Rule of St. Benedict reads, "This hallowed number of seven is fulfilled by us in this way: We perform the duties of our service at Matins, Prime, Terce, Sext, Nones, Vespers and Compline, because it was about these daily hours that he said, 'Seven times a day I have given praise to thee'" (footnote in Luther, *First Lectures on the Psalms, II*, 525). Luther himself believed that the psalmist prophesied the canonical hours.

Psalm 119: *Delight in God's Decrees: Part 14*

1. Kidner, *Psalms 73–150*, 429.

2. Perowne, *Commentary on the Psalms*, 367. Perowne concludes, "The figure, therefore, seems in this place to denote the helpless condition of the psalmist, without protectors, exposed to enemies, in the midst of whom he wanders, not knowing where to find rest and shelter." Leupold says the same thing. "He indicates nothing more than that his present situation is perilous like that of a sheep that has gotten beyond the shepherd's care" (Leupold, *Exposition of the Psalms*, 861).

3. Luther, *First Lectures on the Psalms, II*, 534.

4. C. A. Davis, quoted by Spurgeon, *The Treasury of David*, vol. 3a, 479.

5. See Boice, *Psalms*, vol. 1, 206–12.

6. Bridges, *Psalm 119*, 470.

7. Ibid., 480.

8. Quoted by Spurgeon, *The Treasury of David*, vol. 3a, 440.

Psalm 120: *Marching to Zion*

1. Eugene H. Peterson, *A Long Obedience in the Same Direction: Discipleship in an Instant Society* (Downers Grove, Ill.: InterVarsity, 1980), 13. The quotation is from Friedrich Nietzsche, *Beyond Good and Evil*, trans. Helen Zimmern (London, 1907), section 188, 106–9.

2. This is a title given to them by Spurgeon, *The Treasury of David*, vol. 3b, *Psalms 120–150* (Grand Rapids: Zondervan, 1966), 2; and by Maclaren, *The Psalms*, vol. 3, 290.

3. Peterson, *A Long Obedience*, 12.

4. See Delitzsch, *Biblical Commentary on the Psalms*, 264–68.

5. Leupold, *Exposition of the Psalms*, 862.

6. In my opinion the best discussion of these options is in Leupold, *Exposition of the Psalms*, 862–63. I have already referred to the very thoughtful discussion in Delitzsch (see footnote 4).

7. Leupold, *Exposition of the Psalms*, 863.

8. Kidner, *Psalms 73–150*, 430.

9. Peterson, *A Long Obedience in the Same Direction*, 22.

10. Ibid., 23.

11. Ibid.

12. *Encyclopedia Britannica*, 1959, s.v. "war."

13. Herodotus, *Histories*, III:94; VII:78. Meshech is also found in Genesis 10:2, 23; 1 Chronicles 1:5, 17; and Ezekiel 27:13; 32:26; 38:2–3; 39:1.

14. Kedar is also mentioned in 1 Chronicles 1:29; Song of Songs 1:5; Isaiah 42:11; Jeremiah 2:10; and Ezekiel 27:21.

15. Kidner, *Psalms 73–150*, 430–31.

Psalm 121: *Unto the Hills*

1. These and other such stories are in Lockyer, *Psalms: A Devotional Commentary*, 622–23.

2. Spurgeon, *The Treasury of David*, vol. 3b, 14.

3. Leslie C. Allen offers the most complete summary of these views in *Word Biblical Commentary*, 152–53.

4. Kidner, *Psalms 73–150*, 431.

5. Spurgeon, *The Treasury of David*, vol. 3b, 14.

6. Peterson, *A Long Obedience in the Same Direction*, 38.

7. Ibid., 40–41.

Psalm 122: *Pray for the Peace of Jerusalem*

1. Psalms 124 and 133 in this collection also bear the title "Of David."

2. Kidner, *Psalms 73–150*, 434.

3. Murdoch Campbell, *From Grace to Glory: Meditations on the Book of Psalms* (Carlisle, Pa.: The Banner of Truth Trust, 1970), 177.

Psalm 123: *Looking Up*

1. Maclaren, *The Psalms*, 308.

2. Spurgeon, *The Treasury of David*, vol. 3b, 39–40.

3. Ibid., 40.

4. Derek Kidner, *Ezra & Nehemiah: An Introduction and Commentary* (Downers Grove, Ill.: InterVarsity, 1979), 90.

5. Some of this material is borrowed from James Montgomery Boice, *Nehemiah: Learning to Lead* (Old Tappan, N.J.: Revell, 1990), 77–80.

6. Arthur W. Pink, *The Attributes of God* (Grand Rapids: Baker, n.d.), 83–84.

7. Peterson, *A Long Obedience in the Same Direction*, 60.

Psalm 124: *"If"*

1. Leupold, *Exposition of the Psalms*, 881.

2. Perowne, *Commentary on the Psalms*, 2:384.

3. Maclaren, *The Psalms*, 310.

4. Kidner, *Psalms 73–150*, 436.

5. See Prothero, *The Psalms in Human Life*, 183. This seal is also mentioned in Lockyer, *Psalms: A Devotional Commentary*, 639.

6. See Spurgeon, *The Treasury of David*, vol. 3b, 56.

7. Ibid., 57.

Psalm 125: *Like Mount Zion*

1. This comparison is developed carefully by Charles Colson with Ellen Santilli Vaughn in *Against the Night: Living in the New Dark Ages* (Ann Arbor, Mich.: Servant Publications, 1989).

2. Thomas Cahill, *How the Irish Saved Civilization: The Untold Story of Ireland's Heroic Role from the Fall of Rome to the Rise of Medieval Europe* (New York: Doubleday, 1995), 29–30.

3. Eugene Peterson says, "People of faith have the same needs for protection and security as anyone else. We are no better than others in that regard. What is different is that we find that we don't have to build our own: 'God is our refuge and strength, a very present help in trouble'" (Peterson, *A Long Obedience in the Same Direction*, 81).

4. Leupold, *Exposition of the Psalms*, 884; and Perowne, *Commentary on the Psalms*, 2:388.

5. See Spurgeon, *The Treasury of David*, vol. 3b, 63; and also Lockyer, *Psalms: A Devotional Commentary*, 643.

6. Cahill, *How the Irish Saved Civilization*, 124.

7. Ibid., 117–19.

Psalm 126: *Those Were the Days*

1. Quoted by Peterson, *A Long Obedience in the Same Direction*, 92.

2. Ibid., 97–98.

Psalm 127: *God's Blessing on the City*

1. Quoted by Prothero, *The Psalms in Human Life*, 231–32.

2. Peterson, *A Long Obedience in the Same Direction*, 104.

Psalm 128: *God's Blessing on the Home*

1. Kidner, *Psalms 73–150*, 443.

2. Ronald J. Sider, "The State of Evangelical Social Concern, 1978," *Evangelical Newsletter* 5, no. 13 (30 June 1978).

Psalm 129: *Struck Down, but Not Destroyed*

1. Kidner, *Psalms 73–150*, 444.

2. Spurgeon, *The Treasury of David*, vol. 3b, 110.

3. Kidner, *Psalms 73–150*, 445.

Psalm 130: *Luther's "Pauline Psalm"*

1. John Owen alone has a 323-page study, nearly three-fourths of which deals with verse 4: "But with you there is forgiveness; therefore you are feared." Owen explains his special interest in this psalm as resulting from a time early in his public life when he became sick and nearly died. "My soul," he said, "was oppressed with horror and darkness; but God graciously relieved my spirit by a powerful application of Psalm 130:4, 'But there is forgiveness with thee, that thou mayest be feared' [KJV], from whence I received special instruction, peace and comfort in drawing near to God through the Mediator, and preached thereupon immediately after my recovery" (John Owen, "Prefatory Note" to "A Practical Exposition upon Psalm 130," in *The Works of John Owen*, vol. 6, ed. William H. Gold [Carlisle, Pa.: The Banner of Truth Trust, 1974], 324). The exposition we have is probably the preaching to which he refers.

2. See Prothero, *The Psalms in Human Life*, 304; and Lockyer, *Psalms: A Devotional Commentary*, 667.

3. Psalms 6, 32, 38, 51, 102, 130, and 143.

4. Kidner, *Psalms 73–150*, 446.

5. Peterson, *A Long Obedience in the Same Direction*, 131–41. He calls this chapter "Hope."

6. Owen, *The Works of John Owen*, 6:331.

7. William Ernest Henley, "To R. T. H. B.," in *The Harvard Classics, English Poetry*, vol. 3, *From Tennyson to Whitman* (Norwalk, Conn.: The Easton Press, reprint 1994), 1258.

8. C. H. Spurgeon, "There Is Forgiveness," in *C. H. Spurgeon's Sermons on the Psalms*, selected and edited by Chas. T. Cook (London and Edinburgh: Marshall, Morgan & Scott, 1960), 206. I drew from this sermon in developing the preceding four points.

Psalm 131: *Like a Satisfied Child*

1. Spurgeon, *The Treasury of David*, vol. 3b, 136.

2. Perowne, *Commentary on the Psalms*, 2:407.

3. Peterson, *A Long Obedience in the Same Direction*, 146, 148.

4. Ibid., 148–49.

5. Quoted by Spurgeon, *The Treasury of David*, vol. 3b, 140; and Lockyer, *Psalms: A Devotional Commentary*, 677.

Psalm 132: *The Ascent of God's Ark to Zion*

1. Leupold, *Exposition of the Psalms*, 910.

2. The title "Mighty One of Jacob" occurs first in Genesis 49:24 in the mouth of dying Jacob himself. Besides that it occurs only three other times, all in Isaiah: Isaiah 1:24 ("Mighty one of Israel"); 49:26; 60:16.

3. Spurgeon, *The Treasury of David*, vol. 3b, 145.

4. The first part of verse 6 is notoriously difficult, though it does not affect the meaning of the verse. Ephrathah usually refers to Bethlehem. In Micah 5:2 the names are joined together. The difficulties are these: (1) There is no record of the ark ever having been in Bethlehem, though the Hebrew seems to indicate that the people "heard" that it was in Bethlehem and that they "came upon it" there, and (2) Keriath-jearim is not Bethlehem. One explanation is to regard Ephrathah as a larger area embracing Bethlehem and Jearim, as well as other villages. The reasoning behind this is explained in the major commentaries. Yet the New International Version is probably right in suggesting, as a better explanation, that the search parties heard where the ark was located when they were in Bethlehem, the home city of David, and that, when they followed up on the report, they found the ark at Jaar. For one valuable discussion of this problem and the various solutions see Perowne, *Commentary on the Psalms*, 2:412–14.

5. Maclaren, *The Psalms*, 352.

6. An example is the servant texts of Isaiah, which Jewish scholars at one time understood to refer to the Messiah but now generally regard as referring to the Jewish people as a whole.

7. W. H. Rogers, *The End from the Beginning* (New York: Arno C. Gaebelein, 1938), 262–63.

Psalm 133: *Unity and Community*

1. Perowne, *Commentary on the Psalms*, 2:417.

2. References to Aaron's anointing are in Exodus 29:7; 30:22–33; Leviticus 8:12; and 21:10.

3. Perowne, *Commentary on the Psalms*, 2:420.

4. Daniel Yankelovich, *New Rules: Searching for Self-Fulfillment in a World Turned Upside Down* (New York: Random House, 1981), 10–11.

5. Ibid., 5.

6. Tom Wolfe, "The 'Me-Decade' and the Third Great Awakening," *New York Magazine*, 23 August 1976, 26–40.

7. Margaret Halsey, "What's Wrong with Me, Me, Me?" *Newsweek*, 17 April 1978, 25.

8. Charles Reich, *The Greening of America: The Coming of a New Consciousness and the Rebirth of a Future* (New York: Bantam Books, 1971), 7.

9. Michael Scott Horton, *Made in America: The Shaping of Modern American Evangelicalism* (Grand Rapids: Baker, 1991), 169.

Psalm 134: *Praising God in Zion*

1. John R. W. Stott, *Christ the Controversialist: A Study in Some Essentials of Evangelical Religion* (London: Tyndale, 1970), 160.

2. Kidner, *Psalms 73–150*, 453.

3. Peterson, *A Long Obedience in the Same Direction*, 184.

4. Spurgeon, *The Treasury of David*, vol. 2b, 177.

5. James Montgomery Boice, *Mind Renewal in a Mindless Age* (Grand Rapids: Baker, 1993).

6. A. W. Tozer, *The Pursuit of God* (Harrisburg, Pa.: Christian Publications, 1948), 9.

7. R. Kent Hughes, *Disciplines of a Godly Man* (Wheaton: Crossway, 1991), 106.

8. David F. Wells, *No Place for Truth*.

Psalm 135: *Praise the Lord*

1. Judy Raphael, "God and Country," *Los Angeles Times Magazine,* 6 November 1994, 14, quoted by John F. MacArthur Jr., "How Shall We Then Worship?" in *The Coming Evangelical Crisis,* ed. John H. Armstrong (Chicago: Moody, 1996), 175.

2. E. Gustav Niebuhr, "Mighty Fortress Megachurches Strive to Be All Things to All Parishioners," *The Wall Street Journal,* 13 May 1991, sec. A, 6, quoted by MacArthur, "How Shall We Then Worship?" 176.

3. Kidner, *Psalms 73–150,* 455. Kidner gives many examples in his running commentary. Leslie C. Allen provides a list of parallels (*Word Biblical Commentary,* 224–25), and so does Leupold (*Exposition of the Psalms,* 923).

4. William Temple, *The Hope of a New World,* 30, quoted by Donald P. Hustad, *Jubilate! Church Music in the Evangelical Tradition* (Carol Stream, Ill.: Hope Publishing, 1981), 78.

5. Kidner, *Psalms 73–150,* 145.

6. Spurgeon, *The Treasury of David,* vol. 3b, 200.

7. MacArthur, "How Shall We Then Worship?" in ed. Armstrong, *The Coming Evangelical Crisis,* 177.

Psalm 136: *His Love Endures Forever*

1. "O give thanks unto the Lord" (KJV).

2. Kidner, *Psalms 73–150,* 457.

3. Spurgeon, *The Treasury of David,* vol. 3b, 204.

4. John Milton, *The Complete Poems of John Milton,* in *The Harvard Classics,* ed. Charles W. Eliot (Norwalk, Conn.: The Easton Press, 1993), 16–18. Only a selection of these stanzas appear in most hymnals.

5. The story is told at length in Prothero, *The Psalms in Human Life,* 29–30; and in Gaebelein, *The Book of Psalms,* 472.

Psalm 137: *By the Rivers of Babylon*

1. Saint Augustine, *The City of God,* 282–83.

2. Kidner, *Psalms 73–150,* 459.

3. Spurgeon, *The Treasury of David,* vol. 3b, 226–27.

4. See Prothero, *The Psalms in Human Life,* 205–6; and Lockyer, *Psalms: A Devotional Commentary,* 703–4.

5. Other examples of such strongly imprecatory psalms are Psalms 7, 35, 69, and 109. They seem to grow in vehemence as we progress through the Psalter.

6. Spurgeon, *The Treasury of David,* vol. 3b, 226.

7. Kidner, *Psalms 73–150,* 459–60.

Psalm 138: *A Bold Man's Praise*

1. Psalms 3–9, 11–32, 34–41, 51–65, 68–70, 86, 101, 103, 108–110, 122, 124, 131, 133, 138–145. There are seventy-three Davidic psalms in all.

2. Leupold, *Exposition of the Psalms,* 938. There is also an echo of verse 6 in Psalm 113:5–9, though Psalm 113 is not by David.

3. Kidner, *Psalms 73–150,* 461.

4. Maclaren, *The Psalms,* 376–77.

5. Leupold, *Exposition of the Psalms,* 938.

6. Delitzsch, *Biblical Commentary on the Psalms,* 3:339.

7. Perowne, *Commentary on the Psalms*, 2:435; Leupold, *Exposition of the Psalms*, 939; Maclaren, *The Psalms*, 3:378.

8. Kidner, *Psalms 73–150*, 462.

9. Of the commentators writing on this verse the most helpful is probably Charles Spurgeon, who collects a variety of views all based on the wording of the text as it stands (*The Treasury of David*, vol. 3b, 249–52). For example: "There are higher and clearer manifestations of himself, of his being, of his perfection, of his purposes in the volume of revelation, than in any which his works have disclosed or can disclose" (Albert Barnes); "In fulfilling thy word thou hast magnified thy name above all things" (James Nalton); "He cares not much what becomes of the world and all in it, so that he keeps his word and saves his truth" (William Gurnall); "This may refer to the Incarnate Word, the Son of God, who was called 'the Word'" (Joseph C. Philpot); "God has a greater regard unto the words of his mouth, than to the works of his hand" (Ebenezer Erskine); and "His word or promise shall have, as it were, and exercise a kind of sovereignty over all his prerogatives and attributes, wisdom, justice, power, etc. So that men need not fear that any of them shall at any time, or in any case whatsoever, move in the least contrariety thereunto" (John Goodwin).

10. Lockyer, *Psalms: A Devotional Commentary*, 716.

11. Ibid.

12. Quoted by Spurgeon, *The Treasury of David*, vol. 3b, 255.

Psalm 139: *A Hymn to the All-Knowing God: Part 1*

1. Leupold, *Exposition of the Psalms*, 942.

2. Allen, *Word Biblical Commentary*, 263.

3. Maclaren, *The Psalms*, 383.

4. Arthur W. Pink, *Gleanings in the Godhead* (Chicago: Moody, 1975), 19.

5. A. W. Tozer, *The Knowledge of the Holy: The Attributes of God, Their Meaning in the Christian Life* (New York: Harper & Row, 1961), 61–62.

6. Pink, *The Attributes of God*, 13.

7. Tozer, *The Knowledge of the Holy*, 63.

8. Clements, *Songs of Experience*, 170–71.

9. Leupold, *Exposition of the Psalms*, 945.

10. Milton imagines Satan constructing a "paradise" in hell, a new seat of his power called Pandemonium. He has Satan cry defiantly,

> Hail horrors, hail
> Infernal world, and thou profoundest Hell
> Receive thy new Possessor: One who brings
> A mind not to be chang'd by Place or Time.
> The mind is its own place, and in itself
> Can make a Heav'n of Hell, a Hell of Heav'n.
> (*Paradise Lost*, Book 1)

Dante is closer to the truth when he imagines Satan being imprisoned forever in the tenth and very lowest ring of hell.

11. Leupold, *Exposition of the Psalms*, 945.

Psalm 139: *A Hymn to the All-Knowing God: Part 2*

1. John R. W. Stott, *Favorite Psalms* (Chicago: Moody, 1988), 120.

2. Kidner, *Psalms 73–150*, 465.

3. Leupold, *Exposition of the Psalms*, 946.

4. Pink, *The Attributes of God*, 28.

5. Gaebelein, *The Book of Psalms*, 484–85.

Psalm 140: *Evil for Evil's Sake*

1. Perowne, *Commentary on the Psalms*, 446.
2. Maclaren, *The Psalms*, 394.
3. Lockyer, *Psalms*, 726.
4. M. Scott Peck, *People of the Lie: The Hope for Healing Human Evil* (New York: Simon & Schuster, 1983). Peck also wrote *The Road Less Traveled*, an earlier best-seller.
5. Ibid., 174.
6. Ibid., 168.
7. Ibid., 176.
8. In Romans 3:10–18 Paul quotes Psalm 14:3 (par. 58:1–3); 5:9; 140:3; 10:7; Isaiah 59:7–8; and Psalm 36:1.
9. Spurgeon, *The Treasury of David*, vol. 3b, 294.
10. C. H. Spurgeon, "David's Five-Stringed Harp," in *Sermons on the Psalms*, ed. Chas. T. Cook (Edinburgh: Marshall, Morgan & Scott, 1960), 221–31.

Psalm 141: *A Prayer before Retiring*

1. Reuben A. Torrey, *The Power of Prayer and the Prayer of Power* (Grand Rapids: Zondervan, 1955), 75–77.
2. Quoted by Lockyer, *Psalms*, 731.
3. Kidner, *Psalms 73–150*, 470.
4. Delitzsch, *Biblical Commentary on the Psalms*, 3:366.
5. *Pilgrim's Progress by John Bunyan and the Lives of John Donne and George Herbert by Izaak Walton*, in *The Harvard Classics*, ed. Charles W. Eliot (Norwalk, Conn.: The Easton Press, 1933), 49–50.

Psalm 142: *Alone but for the Lord*

1. Maclaren, *The Psalms*, 408.
2. Kidner, *Psalms 73–150*, 473.
3. Ibid.
4. Ibid.

Psalm 143: *The Last of the Penitential Psalms*

1. Quoted by Ronald Bainton, *Here I Stand* (Nashville: Abingdon, 1978), 67.
2. Sinclair B. Ferguson, "Repentance, Recovery, and Confession," in *Here We Stand: A Call from Confessing Evangelicals*, ed. James Montgomery Boice and Benjamin E. Sasse (Grand Rapids: Baker, 1996), 137–45.
3. Leupold, *Exposition of the Psalms*, 965.
4. Kidner, *Psalms 73–150*, 476.
5. Luther, *Selected Psalms III*, 197–99, 203.
6. Ibid., 204–5.

Psalm 144: *Blessings on God's People*

1. Augustine, *The Confessions of St. Augustine*, 1:45.
2. It is common among commentators to explain these similarities as a later writer's borrowing from Psalm 18 or other earlier Davidic psalms. Even the normally conservative Alexander Maclaren regards the first half of the psalm (vv. 1–11) as merely "a *rechauffe* of known psalms" (Maclaren, *The Psalms*, 419–20). The phrases that reappear in Psalm 144 are not mere borrowing; the psalm is an original composition. A similarity of lines can be an argument for Davidic authorship, as well as against it. "Its language is of David, if ever language can belong to any man" (Spurgeon, *The Treasury of David*, vol. 3b, 354).
3. Morgan, *Notes on the Psalms*, 279.
4. References to "a new song" are also found in Psalms 33:3; 96:1; 98:1; and 149:1; though these are not said to be by David.

5. Maclaren, *The Psalms*, 3:420. Charles Spurgeon was exercising sound literary judgment when he wrote, "To us the whole psalm appears to be perfect as it stands, and to exhibit such unity throughout that it would be a literary vandalism, as well as a spiritual crime, to rend away one part from the other" (*The Treasury of David*, vol. 3b, 354).

Psalm 145: *The Last of the Acrostic Psalms*

1. There are eight acrostic psalms in all (Psalms 9–10, 25, 34, 37, 111, 112, 119, and 145), five of them ascribed to David.

2. Verse 3 is the verse with which Saint Augustine began his famous spiritual autobiography, *The Confessions*. He took the first half of Psalm 145:3, "Great is the LORD and most worthy of praise," and added to it the second half of Psalm 147:5, "His understanding has no limit."

3. Exodus 34:6 is quoted in Numbers 14:18; Nehemiah 9:17; Psalms 86:15; 103:8; 111:4; 145:8; Joel 2:13; and Jonah 4:2.

4. Kidner, *Psalms 73–150*, 482.

5. It should be noted, however, that verse 13b is the verse added to provide the missing *nun* for the acrostic. In the Hebrew text the only difference between verses 13b and 17 is the initial word. In verse 17 it is *tsadek* ("righteous"). In verse 13b it is *ne-amen* ("and true"), the *n* being the missing letter. Possibly a scribe, noticing the missing letter, supplied it by using verse 17 at this point with the new word added. Less likely, but also possible, 13b could have been left out inadvertently because of the near repetition.

6. Augustine, *The Confessions of St. Augustine*, 1:45.

7. Delitzsch, *Biblical Commentary on the Psalms*, 3:392.

Psalm 146: *Praise the Lord, O My Soul*

1. Spurgeon, *The Treasury of David*, vol. 3b, 404.

2. Maclaren, *The Psalms*, 434.

3. Clements, *Songs of Experience*, 186.

4. Ibid.

5. Marva J. Dawn, *Reaching Out without Dumbing Down: A Theology of Worship for the Turn-of-the-Century Culture* (Grand Rapids: Eerdmans, 1995), 12.

6. Stott, *Your Mind Matters*, 29–33.

7. Clements, *Songs of Experience*, 187.

8. Spurgeon, *The Treasury of David*, vol. 3, 400–401.

9. Other Scriptures give nearly identical counsel. See, for example, Psalm 118:8–9; Isaiah 2:22; and Jeremiah 17:5–6.

10. See Spurgeon, *The Treasury of David*, vol. 3b, 406.

11. Quoted by Prothero, *The Psalms in Human Life*, 93–94.

12. There are twenty-four beatitudes in all in the Psalter, beginning with the very first word: Psalms 1:1; 2:12; 32:1–2; 33:12; 34:8; 40:4; 41:1; 65:4; 84:4–5, 12; 89:15; 94:12; 106:3; 112:1; 118:26; 119:1–2; 127:5; 128:1; 144:15 (two times); and 146:5. "Blessed" occurs in other verses too, but they are not beatitudes.

Psalm 147: *Praise the Lord for Everything*

1. Dawn, *Reaching Out without Dumbing Down*, 108.

2. Ibid.

3. The Septuagint divides Psalm 147 into two psalms, the second starting with verse 12, but combines Psalms 9 and 10. So the numbering of the psalms, which diverged from the established Hebrew text through most of the Psalter, gets back into agreement here, making the total number of psalms 150.

4. John Wesley, *The Works*, vol. 5 (Grand Rapids: Zondervan, n.d.), 3. From the authorized edition of 1872.

Psalm 148: *Praise the Lord in Heaven and on Earth*

1. Kidner, *Psalms 73–150*, 487.
2. Clements, *Songs of Experience*, 197–98.
3. Kidner, *Psalms 73–150*, 488.
4. Shirley MacLaine, *Going Within: A Guide for Inner Transformation* (New York: Bantam Books, 1989), 56–57.
5. Carol Christ, "Why Women Need the Goddess," in Carol Christ and Plaskow, *Womanspirit Rising: A Feminist Reader in Religion* (New York: Harper and Row, 1979), 277.
6. Leupold, *Exposition of the Psalms*, 1000.

Psalm 149: *Praise the Lord with a New Song*

1. Ibid., 1004.
2. Delitzsch, *Biblical Commentary on the Psalms*, 3:411.

Psalm 150: *Everybody, Praise the Lord*

1. Lewis, *Reflections on the Psalms*, 51–52.
2. Leupold, *Exposition of the Psalms*, 1005.
3. Maclaren, *The Psalms*, 458.
4. For example, Leupold, *Exposition of the Psalms*, 1006.
5. Clements, *Songs of Experience*, 204–5.

Subject Index

Scripture Index

Genesis

1:1—1195
1:3—1205
1:4–9—1181
1:4, 10, 12, 18, 21, 25, 31—1175
1:26–27—1275
1:28—1118
2—1164
2:2—1119
2:7—1007
2:18—1162
3:1—1029
3:8—1021
3:15—1134
3:19—1127, 1260
4—1126
5:21–24—1126
7:18—953
8:21–22—1254
11—900
11:4–7—925
12:3—949
14:18—1082
14:18–20—899
15:1—1233
17:5—1121
17:8—1218
22:17—1121
25:13—1072
33:17–18—880

Exodus

3:14—922, 1252
15:1–2—1282
15:2—957
17:11—952
18:11—1176
19:6—929
19:18–19—930
20:2—1218f

20:4–6, 8—937
20:5–6—888
30:22–24, 33—1160
33:6–7—1008
33:20—1043
34:6—917, 951, 956, 1252
34:6–7—1043, 1055, 1093, 1140f, 1252
40:36–38—1025

Leviticus

10:1–2—1064

Numbers

6:24–26—1043
10:35–36—1154
14:18—1056
16:1–35—1064
21:21–35—1177
22:31—986
28—946
28:7—946

Deuteronomy

1:31—1149
2:24–3:11—1177
4:28—936
5:9–10—1056
8:3—986, 994
10:8—1167
10:17—1181
13:6—975
28:36—936
29:29—1149
32:36—904
32:43—950

Joshua

1:7–8—1050

10—1245
13:33—1001
18:1—1154

Judges

9:13—946, 1128
20:27—1154
21:5—1154

Ruth

2:4—1134
4:1–12—1085

1 Samuel

1:3—1070
2:8—925
7:2—1154
15:22—1224
17—964
17:28—1146
21:11–12—964
22:1–2—1229
24–26—885
24:10—885

2 Samuel

5:1—1159
5:6–12—1082
5:17–25—1097
6—1083, 1153f
6:14–15—1286
6:16–23—1145
7—1194
7, 9—1195
7:4–17—1155
7:20–21—1196
8:1–14—881
12:25—1117

1 Kings

12:25–33—1083
18:44—1048

2 Kings

6:16–17—1105
18–19—1132
23:29–30—1132

1 Chronicles

9:26–33—1167
12:38–40—1159
13–16—1153f
13:3—1154
15–16—1083
15:12—1154
16:23–33—878
16:34—951
18:1–13—881
23:28–29—1171
23:28–32—1167
25—1171
25:1, 6—1167

2 Chronicles

6:41–42—1152
26:16–21—1064
26:16–23—901

Ezra

3:10–11—956f
7:9—1069

Nehemiah

4:2–3—1090
4:4—1091
4:4–6—1092
8:3, 8—1170
9:17—1056
12:27—1266
12:27–44—1286

Job

1:6—1195
1:21–22—918

1319